S0-AAD-253

FINANCIAL ENGINEERING
Tools and Techniques to
Manage Financial Risk

FINANCIAL ENGINEERING

Tools and Techniques to Manage Financial Risk

Dr. Lawrence C. Galitz

IRWIN

Professional Publishing

Burr Ridge, Illinois
New York, New York

To Valerie

Originally published by Pitman Publishing, a division of Longman U.K. Ltd., copyright 1994.

This edition of *Financial Engineering: Tools and Techniques to Manage Financial Risk* is published by arrangement with Pitman Publishing Company, London.

© LAWRENCE GALITZ, 1995

All rights reserved. No part of this publication may be reproduced, stored in a retrieval system, or transmitted, in any form or by any means, electronic, mechanical, photocopying, recording, or otherwise, without the prior written permission of the publisher.

This publication is designed to provide accurate and authoritative information in regard to the subject matter covered. It is sold with the understanding that neither the author or the publisher is engaged in rendering legal, accounting, or other professional service. If legal advice or other expert assistance is required, the services of a competent professional person should be sought.

From a Declaration of Principles jointly adopted by a Committee of the American Bar Association and a Committee of Publishers.

Senior sponsoring editor: Amy Hollands Gaber
Project editor: Karen M. Smith
Production supervisor: Pat Frederickson
Designer: Larry J. Cope
Art coordinator: Kim Meriwether
Compositor: PanTek Arts
Typeface: 10/12 Times Roman
Printer: Buxton Skinner Printing Company

Library of Congress Cataloging-in-Publication Data

Galitz, Lawrence.
   Financial engineering : tools and techniques to manage financial risk
/Lawrence Galitz.
      p. cm.
   "Originally published by Pitman Publishing . . . 1994. "--CIP's pub.
info.
   Includes index.
   ISBN 0–7863–0362–X (alk. paper)
   1. Financial engineering. I. Title.
HG176.7.G35 1995
   658. 15—dc20   94–37806

Printed in the United States of America
1 2 3 4 5 6 7 8 9 0 BUX 2 1 0 9 8 7 6 5

Preface

There are many books that concentrate on specific financial products such as options or swaps, but there are very few that deal with the entire range of products. Again, there are a number of books that examine particular applications such as the management of interest rate risk, but few books deal with all manner of financial risks.

This book attempts to fill this gap by providing a comprehensive and integrated treatment of a wide spectrum of financial engineering products and applications.

The first part of the book explains each of the important financial engineering tools: FRAs, SAFEs, futures, swaps, and options. The second part shows how the various tools can be used, either singly or in combination, to manage and structure interest rate risk, currency risk, equity risk, and commodity risk.

The topics covered are important for a wide readership, and I have therefore tried to write this book so that there is something for everyone.

Beginners will find that each new topic starts with a gradual introduction – defining each financial product and explaining the terminology involved. The coverage then develops so that advanced users will be able to enhance their understanding of the finer nuances of each tool and learn about some of the latest ideas and techniques. Theoreticians will discover that virtually every formula and relationship is explained and justified, sometimes in a novel way. Practitioners, on the other hand, can skip the detailed mathematics and look at a wide variety of real-life applications, complete with numerous worked examples.

In a subject like financial engineering, it is difficult to avoid some mathematics and formulae. For those who take fright when they see an equation, please don't be discouraged! It is not strictly necessary for everyone to understand the minutiae of derivatives pricing, just as it is not necessary to understand the detailed workings of the internal combustion engine in order to drive a car. The detailed sections on swap pricing (Sections 9.7 to 9.11) and on option pricing (Sections 10.6 to 10.8) can be omitted by those readers who just want to get on with using the products. However, these sections are included in the main body of the text, rather than relegated to an appendix, so that the interested reader can follow the conceptual flow without interruption.

Practitioners mainly interested in applications can concentrate on Part Two, where a myriad of examples and comparisons demonstrate how the financial tools available can successfully be used to manage risk. Each practical use is fully illustrated with a worked example, so that readers can see exactly how to apply the techniques for themselves.

Acknowledgements

I am greatly indebted to Nicholas Warren of Chase Manhattan Bank for first bringing to my attention a good many of the products discussed in this book and for providing challenging opportunities to present these concepts and techniques to professional audiences from within Chase. Nick also took upon himself the thankless task of reading an earlier draft of the book, and I am most grateful for the many helpful comments and suggestions that he has made.

I am also indebted to professor John Welch. He read the very first draft of the book and made innumerable helpful suggestions on improving the clarity of the text, the style, and the grammar. While I have never been one to happily split infinitives, or to leave participles dangling, I know my writing has improved as a result of this guidance.

Finally, I must thank Amy Gaber and her team at Irwin Professional Publishing, and also David Crosby and his team at Pitman Publishing (who produced the original UK edition of the book), for their tremendous efforts in turning the concept of the book into reality.

Lawrence Galitz

Contents

TOOLS

Chapter One

Introduction

1.1 A QUARTER-CENTURY OF EVOLUTION

As we look around us, it is easy to think that the world has always been just as we see it today.

We take for granted pocket calculators, laptop PCs, satellite TV, and instant global communications. We don't marvel that we can sit in an office in London, dial a number in San Francisco, and hear a ringing tone the moment we tap in the last digit. Need to send an urgent document to Tokyo? We simply use a fax machine, knowing that our document will arrive just seconds after we send it.

The media bombard us daily with world news, economic figures, and analysis, and we know that the financial markets will respond without delay. Stock markets will rally or collapse, interest rates tighten or ease, and new exchange rates will alter the relative value of currencies and even the prestige and wealth of whole countries.

It wasn't always like this.

In 1970, a four-function pocket calculator was an expensive novelty, and financial calculators were unknown. Computers really did sit in big air-conditioned rooms and were the preserve of scientists and mathematicians or were used for the routine bulk processing of commercial accounts.

In 1970, exchange rates were fixed. The dollar would be worth four Deutschmarks today, four Deutschmarks tomorrow, and four deutsch marks next month. Interest rates were stable, and the price of a barrel of oil rarely changed.

The last 25 years have seen enormous changes in both the financial and technological environments, but the revolution in finance would not have been possible without parallel advances in technology. Today's markets rely on the global dissemination of price-sensitive information, traders' ability to communicate instantly, and the availability of powerful PCs and sophisticated analytical software at dealers' fingertips.

Some of the financial changes would have taken place anyway. For example, the switch from fixed to floating exchange rates in the early 1970s was precipitated by irreconcilable differences in growth rates between different economies, principally those of Germany and the United States. We would have had floating exchange rates even if satellites had not been available to carry the news. However, many would argue that the volatility of financial markets is a product of the speed with which new information reaches traders and the swiftness with which traders can respond.

In other cases, one can argue that financial innovation was made possible only through technology. For example, the seminal paper that made modern option pricing viable was published in 1973 by Professors Black and Scholes. Although trading in individual stock options started in the same year with the opening of the Chicago Board Options Exchange, it was at least 10 years before currency options and interest rate products such as caps and floors became readily available. Could it be that these products had to await the arrival of desktop PCs before dealers were able to price and hedge them effectively?

Regardless of how today's environment came about, two things are certain. First, the volatility of market rates has created an ever-increasing demand for clever financial products to manage financial risk. Second, current technology has made it possible for financial institutions to create, price, and hedge products specifically designed to neutralise these financial risks. From these foundations, financial engineering was born.

1.2 WHAT IS FINANCIAL ENGINEERING?

The term *engineering* has many connotations. It may suggest the honing of precision components that form part of a complex system, working with special tools or instruments, or tinkering with adjustments to achieve mechanical perfection. Financial engineering has many associations with its mechanical cousin.

The tools used by financial engineers comprise the new financial instruments created over the past two decades: forwards, futures, options, and swaps, to name but a few. These instruments are both the tools of the trade and the components used to build more complex systems. Like mechanical components, these financial instruments can be used in standard form, "off-the-shelf," or may be individually tailored to meet a particular requirement. Like mechanical components, they can also be combined in many different ways. For example, currency options can be combined in one way to create a *forward-band contract* or in another way to create a *participating forward*. If one configuration is not quite right, financial instruments can be tinkered with or adjusted to behave in exactly the way desired.

Mechanical perfection for the financial engineer is the achievement of a particular financial goal. For the investor, it may be the superior expected returns available from a foreign stock market, but without the currency risk. For a financier, it may be the funding of a large construction project at rates below the current market norm, coupled with a guarantee that rates will never be more than x%. For the company treasurer, perfection may be the elimination of currency exposure on a project that has reached only the tendering stage. There are limitless examples, but there is a unifying theme that provides a useful definition of the concept of *financial engineering*:

> **Financial engineering is the use of financial instruments to restructure an existing financial profile into one having more desirable properties.**

Of course, what is desirable for one party may be undesirable for another, but that should not cause any problems. After all, an investor choosing to buy a share costing $10 may think it desirable to buy at that price, while the dealer selling it may think it undesirable to hold at that price. Both may be happy to execute the deal despite having differences of opinion.

Financial engineering can help achieve excellence, but not the impossible. The cleverest financier will not be able consistently to raise funds at a negative interest rate, and it is unthinkable that someone nowadays could steadily sell the pound sterling at £1=DEM 12 (the rate prevailing in the early 1960s). These are the same kind of limitations that prevent the mechanical engineer from building a car capable of 100 miles per gallon and 200 miles per hour.[1] Financial engineering is nevertheless capable of achieving striking and valuable results, as the remainder of this book will illustrate.

1.3 THE NATURE OF RISK

Even if there were no uncertainty, financial engineering would provide users with valuable alternatives. For example, the treasurer borrowing for five years at a floating rate may prefer to use an interest rate swap to create a level cost of funds in order to simplify budgeting decisions. However, in the presence of risk, financial engineering techniques come into their own.

But what is risk? Intuitively, we all have a feel for what risk is, and we normally associate risk with the unexpected and the undesirable. However, we really need a more reliable definition, both qualitatively and quantitatively:

> **Risk is ANY variation in an outcome.**

This definition is useful because it includes both undesirable and desirable outcomes. This may seem strange in the everyday world—we would not

---

[1] About 3 litres per 100 km and 300 km/h.

FIGURE 1.1
$/DEM Exchange Rate, January 1963–1992

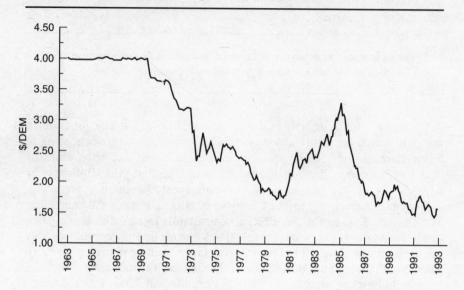

FIGURE 1.2
Dollar 3-Month Interest Rates, January 1963–1992

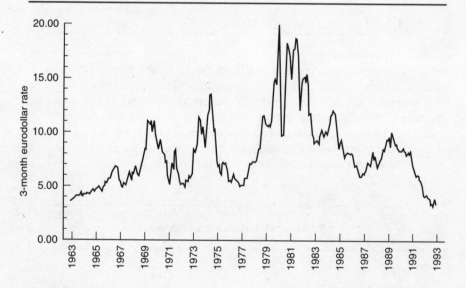

normally think of winning the jackpot at Las Vegas as a risk—but it makes sense in the financial world where there are always two easily identified parties to every deal, and these parties have diametrically opposed viewpoints.

Consider, for example, a bank lending floating-rate funds to a company. A sudden rise in interest rates would be undesirable for the borrower, but an attractive outcome for the lender. Similarly, a fall in interest rates would be an adverse risk to the lender, but a beneficial risk to the borrower. In either case, the risk exposure to both these parties arises from the same event—a change in interest rates. It therefore makes sense to think of *any* change in interest rates, up or down, beneficial or adverse, as being a risk.

The above definition gives us a good qualitative definition of risk. If the outcome of a situation or event is absolutely fixed and determined, there is no risk; if some variation in outcomes is possible, the situation involves risk. In using the term *variation*, the definition also provides a clue as to how we can calculate risk quantitatively. If we can find a precise mathematical way to measure the degree of variation, then we have a numerical indicator for the degree of risk. Fortunately, such a method has existed since the eighteenth century, and statisticians have been using the *standard deviation* as a precise way to measure variation. Chapter Ten (Section 10.9) will demonstrate how the standard deviation can be calculated, and how this has important implications for options pricing.

Even without a quantitative measure of risk, one can see just by looking at Figures 1.1 and 1.2 that the financial world has become a much more risky place over the past 20 or so years.

With the collapse of fixed parities in the early 1970s, exchange rates were free to fluctuate according to the supply and demand for different currencies. Some of the currency flows were long term and strategic, giving rise to secular movements and trends in rates. Other flows arose from the short-term decisions of currency speculators, and led to brief bouts of extreme volatility. Both combined to create far greater instability than had previously been known.

Once exchange rates were free to float, interest rates became one of the weapons of exchange rate policy—and a victim of the same forces. An extreme example in recent times was the decision by the Swedish authorities that the krona should shadow the deutsch mark. Amidst the extraordinary uncertainty prevailing in September 1992 it was necessary for Swedish money market rates to rise from 20% to 75%, and eventually to 500%. No less dramatic, even though the numbers are smaller, was the excursion of sterling's key interest rates from 10% to 12% to 15%, and back down to 10%, all in 24 hours.

1.4 FINANCIAL ENGINEERING AND RISK

In the face of risk, financial engineering can offer two broad alternatives. In the first instance, risk can be replaced with certainty. The second alternative is to replace only the adverse risk, leaving the beneficial risk alone. We shall examine each alternative in turn.

Forwards, FRAs, futures, and swaps are all examples of financial engineering tools that can offer the comfort of certainty to anyone exposed to

FIGURE 1.3
Hedging Currency Risk Using a Forward Deal

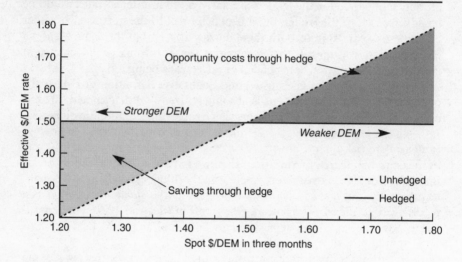

financial risk. For example a U.S. company with a deutsch mark payable in three months can buy D-marks today for delivery three months in the future, *at a fixed price*. This forward deal completely eliminates the currency risk. No matter what the exchange rate turns out to be in three months' time, the company has purchased its D-marks at a known and fixed price, and will not be affected by the then-prevailing rate.

Figure 1.3 contrasts the risk profile for the company by plotting the effective $/DEM exchange rate against the spot rate prevailing in three months. The diagonal dashed line shows the position before the company hedges by buying D-marks forward. The company must pay whatever spot prevails at the time, which might be $1 to buy as much as DEM 1.80 if the D-mark weakens, or $1 to buy only DEM 1.20 if the D-mark strengthens. The horizontal solid line shows the position if the company buys its D-marks forward at the fixed rate of $1=DEM 1.50. In that case it does not matter what spot exchange rate prevails at the time; the company will pay exactly $1 to buy DEM 1.50 regardless.

In this example, if the D-mark strengthens during the three-month exposure period the company is certainly delighted that it chose to hedge, because it still buys its D-marks at the original fixed price of $1=DEM 1.50; The shaded area on the lower left of the diagram shows the savings provided by the hedge. But what if the D-mark were to weaken? The company must originally have been prepared to buy its D-marks at $1=DEM 1.50 otherwise, it would not have entered into the forward deal in the first place. So even if the D-mark turns out to be weaker in three months, the company should still be happy!

FIGURE 1.4
The Perfect Hedge

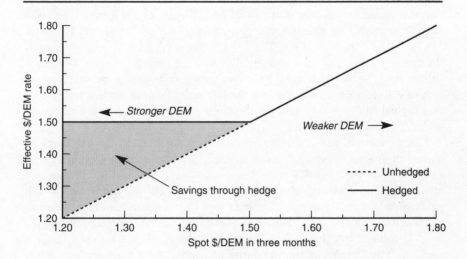

Of course, everyone understands the discomfort that the company treasurer may feel, thinking that the company would have been better off had it not hedged but simply bought its D-marks at the prevailing rate when they were needed. The shaded area on the top right of Figure 1.3 shows the opportunity costs incurred by the existence of the hedge. While understandable, it would be quite wrong for the treasurer to think in this way. His original decision was based on the desire to avoid risk and create certainty; his later regret was based on hindsight, once he knew which way rates eventually turned out.

The first alternative offered by financial engineering replaces risk with certainty, but in eliminating the adverse risks, it also eliminates the beneficial risks. Chapter Twelve discusses risk assessment, attitudes to risk, and setting hedging objectives (see Sections 12.2 to 12.4). In many cases, eradicating all risk is just what is wanted, but it is easy to imagine the desire to eliminate only the adverse risk, leaving the beneficial risks in place. Fortunately, financial engineering can also offer something approaching this as a second alternative.

Figure 1.4 illustrates a perfect hedge, providing all the benefits of the forward deal if the D-mark eventually becomes stronger than $1=DEM 1.50 and all the benefits of no hedge if the D-mark were to weaken.

Unfortunately, such a hedge is impossible to achieve in practice, because no bank would be willing to take the opposing position, where it could only lose and never gain! Nevertheless, while the perfect hedge is unachievable, financial engineering allows something very close.

Instead of buying D-marks forward at $1=DEM 1.50, the treasurer could instead buy a currency option granting the right to buy D-marks in three months at $1=DEM 1.50, *but not the obligation to do so*. Such an option might cost 5 pfennigs per dollar. If the D-mark were stronger than $1=DEM 1.50 in three months, the treasurer would exercise his right under the option and buy D-marks at $1=DEM 1.50, just as if a forward deal had been executed. On the other hand, if the D-mark were weaker than $1=DEM 1.50, he would buy D-marks in the market, taking advantage of the cheaper prevailing rate, and simply allow the option to expire worthless. In this way, the treasurer would obtain the best of both worlds—the protection of a fixed rate if required, but the flexibility of an open commitment if that turned out to be the best choice. Figure 1.5 shows the new risk profile under this second alternative.

Later chapters will illustrate how the treasurer could choose from an almost unlimited number of permutations. The degree of protection against an adverse move in market rates, the level of gains realised for a beneficial move, the range over which protection was granted, the range over which gains were possible, the cost of protection—all of these could be varied to suit the hedger's objectives. Want to obtain protection, but pay nothing for it? No problem, but the bank will want to share some of your profit opportunities. The beauty of financial engineering is that it offers an almost unlimited range of possibilities, allowing deals and hedges to be tailored precisely to match individual requirements.

Financial engineering thus offers the user two broad alternatives. One choice is for risk to be eliminated completely, while the other approach gives those affected by financial risk the means to adjust their exposure profiles according to their preferences.

FIGURE 1.5
Hedging Currency Risk Using a Currency Option

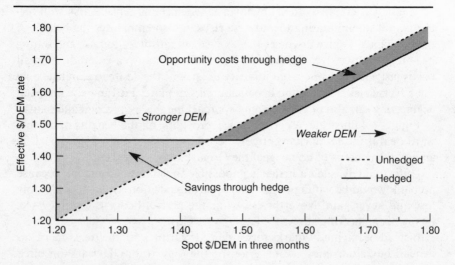

1.5 LAYOUT OF THIS BOOK

This book is divided into two main sections. Part One covers the *tools* of financial engineering, dealing with:

- FRAs.
- SAFEs.
- Financial futures.
- Currency and interest-rate swaps.
- Currency options.

- Interest-rate options and IRGs.
- Caps, floors, and collars.
- Swaptions.
- 'Exotic' options (e.g., AVROs, captions, lookbacks, and knockouts).

Various chapters define each instrument carefully, describe the markets on which they are traded, and explain in considerable detail how each product is priced and hedged.

Part Two then goes on to consider the *applications* in which financial engineering techniques may be applied. Here we are concerned with the practical use of financial instruments in handling interest rate, currency, and commodity risk. Questions addressed will include

- Should we buy a cap, buy a collar, or pay the fixed rate on an interest-rate swap?
- Are futures better than FRAs?
- Is 11.5¢ a fair price for this currency option, or are we paying over the odds?
- How do we "tail" a futures hedge to account for timing differences and margin flows?

To discover more about the tools of financial engineering and exactly how they are used in practice, read on.

Chapter Two

The Cash Markets

This chapter provides a brief description of the *cash markets*, describing traditional financial markets like the foreign exchange and money markets. This will prepare the necessary foundation for studying the derivatives markets, the important markets within which the instruments of financial engineering are created and traded.

2.1 OVERVIEW OF FINANCIAL MARKETS

With the developments in finance over the past quarter-century, there may seem to be a bewildering array of financial products. To bring order to this confusion, we can organise markets under a number of clear headings:

- The foreign exchange market.
- The money markets.
- The bond markets.
- The equities market.

while instruments can be categorised under:

- Cash instruments.
- Derivatives.

Later sections in this chapter will introduce these markets in a little more detail and explain the key differences between cash instruments and derivatives. First, however, we should consider why these markets exist in the first place and what purposes they serve.

The money, bond, and equities markets are often grouped together under the term *capital markets*.[1] Their principal purpose, as the generic heading suggests, is for the raising of capital by companies, financial institutions, and even whole countries. These markets bring together those who wish to raise funds and who are willing to pay for the use of those funds, investors who seek a return on the capital they have available to invest, and financial institutions who intermediate between the two.

In a world increasingly dominated by international trade, the foreign exchange, FX, market provides the means by which exporters in one country can receive payment in their domestic currency, while importers in another country can make payment in their currency. The FX market is therefore instrumental in facilitating international commercial trade and for centuries has fulfilled this role. More recently, the FX market has become an important adjunct to the international capital markets, allowing borrowers to meet their financing requirements in whichever currency is most conducive to their needs. This is especially relevant to multinational corporations, which buy materials, manufacture and sell their goods in a number of different countries, and which therefore have complex FX exposure in a range of currencies.

We have so far seen that two of the reasons why these markets exist are to enable financing and investing and to facilitate commercial trade. A third important reason is to allow hedging and speculation. It may seem strange to group both these activities together, but the deals executed by hedgers and speculators may be identical, even though their motivations may be different. A hedger may buy deutsch marks because they are needed for the purchase of goods from Germany. A speculator may buy deutsch marks because he thinks that the D-mark will strengthen against other currencies.

Now that we have a better idea of why the financial markets exist, we can take a very brief look at each one. At the very end of this chapter there are suggestions for further reading for the reader who wishes to study particular markets in greater depth.

2.2 THE FOREIGN EXCHANGE MARKET

The foreign exchange market is the international forum for the exchange of currencies. Until the early 1970s, major currencies such as the D-mark and pound sterling were linked to the U.S. dollar through a system of fixed parities.

---

[1] Some use the term *capital markets* to take in virtually all the financial markets, including FX and all derivatives. I prefer to restrict the term to those markets directly involved in the raising of capital. Others limit the definition even further and only include markets dealing in instruments having an original maturity greater than one year.

This system was established by the Bretton Woods agreement in 1944 and, despite occasional adjustments to the scheme, worked well for a quarter of a century. By the 1960s, however, differences in economic growth among countries became more prominent, and there was a series of currency realignments. These became more and more frequent. Eventually the system of fixed exchange rate parities broke down completely in the early 1970s, and a system of floating exchange rates took its place.

This change revolutionised the foreign exchange market. Instead of steady exchange rates, punctuated by the occasional parity change, FX rates were free to fluctuate continuously and without bounds. Governments would intervene from time to time, usually to support their currencies, but for the most part exchange rates were free to follow supply and demand.

This new environment of floating exchange rates created a need for banks and their clients to manage their currency exposure on an active and continual basis. At the same time, it provided an opportunity for speculators to gamble on which major currencies would strengthen, and which would weaken. Coincidentally, developments in computers and telecommunications made possible the instant global dissemination of news and comment and the instant dealing facilities that characterise the foreign exchange market as we know it today.

FIGURE 2.1
Daily FX Dealing Volumes

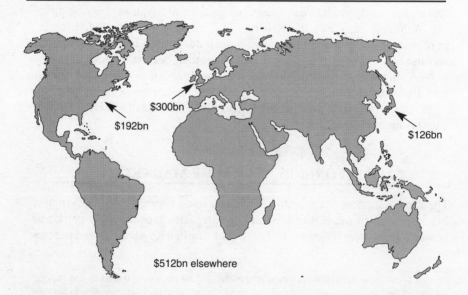

Source: Bank for International Settlements, *Central Bank Survey of Foreign Exchange Market Activity in April 1992* (March 1993).

Unlike traditional stock exchanges, the FX market is not to be found in any one place, but is spread throughout the world in dealing rooms linked to each other through a web of telephone communications and computer networks. As Figure 2.1 illustrates, although dealing takes place in each of the world's financial capitals, three centres are dominant: London, New York, and Tokyo. The figures show the estimated daily volume of transactions in dollar equivalents but are only approximate, for in the absence of any central clearing agency, no one knows for sure the actual amounts traded.

The generally accepted figure for the daily volume of transactions worldwide is around $1 trillion, but this is more than just a "telephone number" magnitude. To try to comprehend a number on this scale, imagine that you were charged with the task of counting out this sum of money in cash, and you were able to count out two notes every second, and could work nonstop without taking a break. To be reasonable, suppose that the $1 billion was paid, not in dollar bills, but in $100 bills. You could therefore count as much as $12,000 per minute, $720,000 per hour, and $17,280,000 per day. Yet, it would still take you around 160 years to complete the task! (Remember, this was the trading volume arising from just *one day*.)

It is difficult to know exactly what proportion of this trading volume arises from commercial transactions, but estimates range from just 5% to 20%. This does not mean that the remaining 80% to 95% are speculative. Many of these latter deals are interbank transactions as one bank lays off its position with another. A single commercial transaction may set off a dozen interbank trades as the component currencies are broken up and spread among banks operating around the globe.

Around one half the volume of FX deals is for *spot* delivery. This is normally two working days after the dealing date to allow for settlement instructions to be processed in different time zones. The remainder of deals are *forward* deals, which might be up to one year after the spot date. Forward deals are either *outright forwards*, where there is a single exchange of currencies on some future date, or *swaps*, where there is an exchange of currencies on one date and a re-exchange in the opposite direction on another date. The concept of quoting forward exchange rates will be discussed in Section 3.1 of Chapter Three.

2.3 THE MONEY MARKETS

The money market is an electronic marketplace for the trading of short-term debt. Maturities range from as short as overnight (i.e., literally from one day to the next) to as long as one year, and the size of a typical deal can range from the equivalent of $250,000 up to $50 million.

Some of this debt is based on negotiable paper and instruments traded include:

- Treasury bills.
- Trade bills.
- Bankers' acceptances.
- Bank certificates of deposit (CDs).
- Commercial paper (CP).
- Eurocommercial paper (ECP).
- Euronotes (issued through NIFs, RUFs, or MOFs).

For most of these negotiable instruments, secondary markets exist that allow buyers and sellers to trade debt prior to maturity. This means that an investor who buys a negotiable six-month CD, and who then needs access to his funds after just one month, can sell the CD to another investor for cash. The price at which an instrument is issued or traded depends upon a number of factors, including its time to maturity, credit quality, prevailing rates of interest, and any interest accrued. Some instruments, such as CDs, carry a specific rate of interest and are issued at a price near or at par. Other instruments, such as bills and CP, pay no interest at all and are always issued at a discount relative to their face value. The investor's return on these *discount instruments* is based on the difference between the price originally paid and the face value at maturity.

In contrast to paper-based debt, a substantial section of the money markets revolves around nonnegotiable debt, including:

- Interbank deposits.
- Federal funds (in the U.S.).
- Repos and reverses.
- Local authority and finance house deposits (in the UK).

Although an active primary market exists in all these instruments, there is no secondary market upon which a depositor or investor can trade these assets. Once Bank A has lent Bank B DEM 10 million for three months, there is no recognised way in which Bank A can gain access to these funds before the deposit is repaid. Much of this market is therefore very short term, like the U.S. federal funds market, which is predominantly a market in overnight funds. Yields for nonnegotiable instruments tend to be a little higher than yields for the corresponding paper-based instruments. For example, a bank bidding for three-month interbank deposits may typically have to offer $^1/16\%$ or $^1/8\%$ higher interest than for its three-month CDs.

Interest rates for most discount instruments are normally quoted on a *discount yield* basis, which is the discount expressed as a percentage of the face value and then converted to an annual basis. For example, a T-bill priced at 98 and redeemed at par in three months might be quoted as a discount yield of 8%. Other money market instruments are normally quoted on a *money market yield* basis, which expresses the interest as a percentage of the current price rather than the face value. To complicate things further, both these bases can be quoted using either a 360-day or a 365-day year. This means that yield comparisons among different money market instruments must be undertaken with the utmost care.

2.4 THE BOND MARKETS

The segregation between money markets and bond markets is mainly on the basis of maturity. While most money market instruments have an original maturity of one year or less, notes and bonds are issued with a maturity greater than one year. The majority of these instruments have original maturities in the range from two to ten years, but maturities up to 30 years are not uncommon, and a number of bonds are perpetual, having no fixed maturity date.

The biggest issuers of notes and bonds in most countries are central government and local government agencies, while most of the remainder are issued by large corporations. This leads to the following convenient classification:

- Government bonds.
- Corporate bonds.
- Floating-rate notes (FRNs).
- Eurobonds.
- Medium-term notes (MTNs) and Euro-MTNs.

Most bonds pay a regular interest payment called the coupon, although there are some zero-coupon bonds that are, to all intents and purposes, long-term bills. The coupon for most bonds is fixed in advanced, giving rise to the term *fixed-income securities*, but a number of issues have coupons that are reset on a regular basis and therefore float, hence the term *floating-rate note* (FRN). With the growth in international finance, prime borrowers can issue securities in a range of currencies or countries. A bond issued outside the country and currency of the borrower is a *eurobond*. Finally, the range of debt instruments open to large corporate borrowers has expanded to encompass bills and commercial paper at the short end of the maturity spectrum, corporate and eurobonds at the longer end, and *medium-term notes* (MTNs) in between.

The yield, and hence the price, at which bonds trade depends upon the level of interest rates generally prevailing in a particular currency. Yields will usually differ for different maturities, giving rise to the *yield curve*, which defines the current yield for each possible maturity. It is usually the case that yields increase for longer maturities, rewarding the investor for the additional risk involved in holding bonds with longer maturities. One component of this risk is the chance that the bond issuer will default. Bonds issued by major governments normally are considered riskless and set the base level for bond yields in a particular currency. On the other hand, bonds issued by other borrowers are considered to have a finite risk of default. The level of this default risk is assessed by bond rating agencies, which assign ratings to issuers and particular instruments. The lower the rating for a particular bond, the higher will be its yield in comparison to government bonds of the same maturity.

The largest bond markets are those denominated in dollars and yen, which together account for about two-thirds of the world market in bonds. The huge size of these markets reflects the large amount of government debt issued in these countries. The bond markets in D-marks, Italian lire, sterling, and the French franc come next in size and are also driven largely by the size of government debt.

2.5 THE EQUITIES MARKETS

The money markets and bond markets both involve debt instruments. With a debt instrument, there is a great deal of certainty regarding the cash flows that an investor will receive. Either the value at maturity will be defined, as with all discount instruments, or the stream of regular coupons will be known in advance, as with all fixed-income securities, or both.

Equities are quite different. An equity, or common share, is a participation in the ownership of a company. Although a share certificate may have some face value, this is purely nominal, as there is no promise to repay that face value at any time. Nor is there any certainty as to the stream of dividends that will be paid. A company issuing shares has sole discretion each year as to the size of the dividend paid or even whether a dividend will be paid at all. In the event that the company goes into liquidation, the shareholders are the last to receive any benefit from the sale of assets, as all other liabilities must be discharged first.

Equities are therefore much more risky, both in the expectation of future income and in the event of the company going bankrupt. In the light of their seemingly unattractive position, the reason why any investor should wish to hold shares is the hope of better returns than those available from debt instruments. Over the long term, equities normally outperform debt securities, although this will not necessarily happen every year or over the shorter term. This additional return is necessary to compensate investors for the additional risk they face with equities, and an important theory in finance, the Capital Asset Pricing Model (CAPM), seeks to relate the risk and return available from different investments.

The two largest equity markets in the world are both in the United States, with the New York Stock Exchange (NYSE) and the National Association of Securities Dealers Automated Quotation stock exchange (NASDAQ) both being based in New York. Next in size come the London Stock Exchange and the Tokyo Stock Exchange.

Although we have drawn a sharp distinction between debt and equity markets, there are some financial instruments that straddle the divide. Preferred shares are like bonds in that their dividends are a prespecified percentage of their face value, but unlike bonds in that failure to pay a dividend does not constitute a default. Likewise, in the event of the issuer entering into liquidation, preferred shares usually rank between bonds and equity in terms of any claim to the issuer's assets. A convertible bond is another hybrid instrument that starts life as a bond but gives the holder the right to convert the bond into a certain number of shares of the issuing company at certain times or periods. A third hybrid is the perpetual floating-rate note (PFRN), with debtlike characteristics of coupons that behave like those of an FRN, but the distinctly equity-like characteristic of having no maturity date (and therefore a purely nominal face value).

2.6 CASH INSTRUMENTS VERSUS DERIVATIVES

In the case of all the markets discussed so far, deals executed within these markets result in flows of cash—or flows of principal, to be more precise—at some time or other. For example, if IBM Corporation issues a $10 million bond paying an 8% coupon, it will receive $100 million (less fees) when the bond is actually issued, pay out around $8 million a year in coupons, and eventually repay $100 million when the bond matures. If the Ford Motor Corporation buys $100 million spot against D-marks at $1=DEM 1.50, it will receive $100 million and pay out DEM 150 million in cash in two working days' time.

For this reason, the foreign exchange, money, bond, and equities markets are all considered *cash* markets. However, one of the consequences of there being actual cash flows is that parties are exposed to considerable risk if something goes wrong. It is probably unthinkable, but what if IBM were unable or unwilling to repay its borrowing of $100 million when the bond matured? What if Ford had paid away its DEM 150 million in Frankfurt, and then found that the dollars it expected to receive in New York later that day were not there? In both cases, there is a potential loss to one party of $100 million.

In many cases, the flow of cash is essential to the deal. For example, if a borrower requires finance, nothing but cash will do. However, when it comes to hedging or speculation, the actual flow of cash is often not only unnecessary but even undesirable. This is not to say that cash markets are not used for these purposes. On the contrary, a good deal of the trading volume within the cash markets arises from hedging and speculation.

Since the 1970s, however, the evolution of derivative markets and instruments has provided a far more efficient way of managing risk. Derivatives are linked to underlying instruments in the cash markets. For example, a currency option is linked to particular currency pairs in the FX market, a bond future to certain bonds in the bond market, and stock-index futures to the performance of a specified stock market. Derivatives provide holders with exposure similar to currency fluctuations, interest rates, or stock market swings, like their parallels in the cash markets, *but without the exposure to loss of principal*.

For example, if you held an option to buy $1 billion against sterling, you would be exposed to similar profits or losses to those experienced by someone who actually had bought $1 billion spot against a sale of sterling.[2] However, if the bank that sold you the option collapsed, the most you could lose would be the value of the option today, which would be just a few percent of the $1 billion underlying value. Someone who executed the spot deal in the cash market could conceivably lose the full $1 billion.

---

[2] The precise exposure from holding an option will actually depend on the option's delta, a concept explored in Section 10.11 of Chapter Ten.

Since the risk from derivatives is smaller than that of the underlying instruments, commercial banks are required to set aside less capital for their use, as we shall now see in the next section.

2.7 CAPITAL ADEQUACY REQUIREMENTS

Commercial banks have, over the decades, been subject to various regulations and controls. One of the most important demands within the system of supervision is the requirement for banks to have sufficient capital. Although banks, like other corporate entities, use capital to support their infrastructure and general operations, banks need capital as a cushion against the risks they face in their everyday operations.

In the late 1980s, central banks meeting under the auspices of the Bank for International Settlements (BIS) agreed on a relatively uniform system for defining exactly how much capital a bank required.[3] The new rules, which finally came into force at the end of 1992, set a minimum ratio of capital to *weighted risk assets* of 8%. Each asset on the bank's balance sheet is assigned a weighting, which can be from 0% for assets considered riskless to 100% for the most risky assets. As examples, most interbank deposits are given a 20% weighting, while most bank lending receives the full 100% weighting. A £100 million corporate loan would therefore consume £8 million of the bank's capital, and even a £100 million interbank deposit would require a £1.6 million allocation of bank capital.

Capital for banks is a scarce and expensive commodity, and some fairly simple calculations can demonstrate that the cost of the capital required to support an asset with a 100% risk weighting can be 60 basis points. This means that a bank borrowing funds at LIBOR − 10 basis points and lending to a prime corporate customer at LIBOR + 50 basis points is just breaking even when the cost of capital is taken into account, and banks face a host of other costs as well.

The capital requirements for derivative products are far less, because the principal is rarely at risk. Certain interest-rate derivatives with a residual maturity less than one year have no capital requirement at all. Even long-term currency swaps, which are considered one of the more risky derivatives, only require capital of between 0.08% and 0.20% of the nominal principal. A £100 million five-year currency swap with another bank as the counterparty would tie up just £80,000 of the bank's capital. Compare this to the £1.6 million required for an interbank loan of the same size, and £8 million of capital for the equivalent corporate loan.

That the capital requirements are but a fraction of those for any equivalent on-balance-sheet product is one reason why derivatives are such attractive

---

[3] See the Basle Commitee on Banking Regulations and Supervisory Practice, *International Convergence of Capital Measurement and Capital Standards* (July 1988).

tools for banks to use in the management of their own risk and that of their clients. Another reason is their flexibility and versatility. It is therefore no surprise to find that derivative products have become the essential tools of financial engineering, and the remaining chapters in this book are devoted to explaining how derivatives work and how they are used in practice to create efficient and effective risk management solutions.

Further Reading

Foreign Exchange

Anthony, Steven, *Foreign Exchange in Practice* (IFR Publishing, 1989).

Bishop, Paul, and Don Dixon, *Foreign Exchange Handbook* (McGraw-Hill, 1992).

Money Markets

Andersen, Juul Torben, *Euromarket Instruments* (New York Institute of Finance, 1990).

Sarver, Eugene, *The Eurocurrency Market Handbook* (New York Institute of Finance, 1990).

Stigum, Marcia, *The Money Market*, 3rd edition (Irwin, 1990).

Bond Markets

Fabozzi, Frank J., and Irving M. Pollack, *The Handbook of Fixed Income Securities,* 3rd edition (Dow Jones-Irwin, 1991).

Fabozzi, Frank J., *Fixed Income Mathematics* (Probus Publishing, 1988).

General

Grabbe, J. Orlin, *International Financial Markets*, 2nd edition (Elsevier 1991).

Walmsley, Julian, *The Foreign Exchange and Money Markets Guide* (Wiley, 1992).

Chapter Three

Forward Rates

Before looking at financial engineering products like FRAs and futures, it is necessary to introduce the important concept of the *forward rate*. The forward rate is the price the market sets for an instrument traded today, but where the resulting transaction is executed on some date in the future, sometimes the far distant future. The most common forward rates are those quoted for forward FX deals and forward interest rates, and these are now discussed in turn.

3.1 FORWARD EXCHANGE RATES

At first sight, it may seem highly risky for a bank to quote the rate for a foreign exchange deal set in the future, when it is difficult enough to estimate where the exchange rate will be in just a few hours' time. Fortunately, it is not necessary for bank dealers to look into a crystal ball to predict the future. Instead, they can price a forward FX deal using the principal of *risk-free arbitrage*.

The concept of risk-free arbitrage is an important one and is used for pricing a wide range of derivative products as well as forward foreign exchange. To price an instrument using this technique, a dealer will consider how to hedge the resulting position using other transactions whose price is known.

Consider a forward foreign exchange dealer working for a UK bank who is asked by a U.S. client to quote a rate for D-marks against the dollar for delivery one year after spot. The customer wants to buy exactly 1,980,000 D-marks from the bank in order to settle an account that will be payable at that time, and so the bank will be selling 1,980,000 D-marks and receiving dollars. The questions to be resolved are:

1. How many dollars should the bank receive in exchange for the D-marks?
2. What is the fair exchange rate for $/DEM one year forward?

Of course, the answer to the first question implies the answer to the second.

Suppose that our dealer knows that the spot rate is $1=DEM 1.8000, that one-year dollar interest rates are 6%, and one-year D-mark interest rates are 10%. Figure 3.1 shows the sequence of transactions that would allow the dealer to hedge the forward $/DEM transaction with other deals, all at known rates.

FIGURE 3.1
Pricing Forward Foreign Exchange

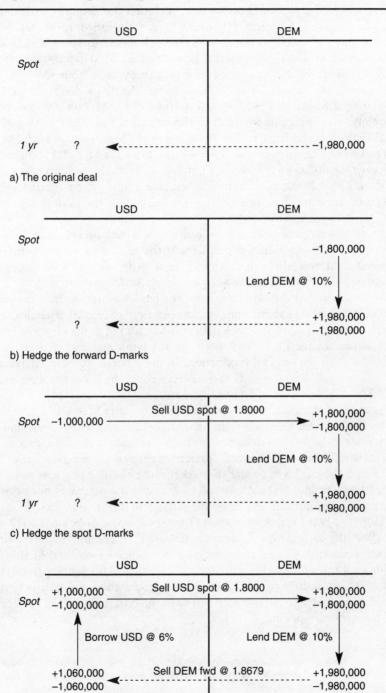

a) The original deal

b) Hedge the forward D-marks

c) Hedge the spot D-marks

d) Forward transaction completely hedged

Figure 3.1a shows the bank's exposure after agreeing to sell DEM 1,980,000 to its client in one year. In order to have this sum of D-marks, the bank could lend a sum of D-marks now, such that the D-marks repayable in one year together with interest would be exactly DEM 1,980,000. With German one-year interest rates at 10%, the bank should therefore lend exactly DEM 1,800,000. The interest on this sum would be DEM 180,000, giving the total of DEM1, 980,000 repayable in one year, just what is required.

Figure 3.1b shows the cash flows after the bank lends the DEM 1,800,000, showing that the forward outflow of DEM 1,980,000 has been completely hedged. But where does the bank get the DEM 1,800,000 to lend? How does the bank hedge its exposure to D-marks, as it is still short of D-marks? The answer: the bank simply buys DEM 1,800,000 spot in exchange for dollars, as shown in Figure 3.1c. With the spot exchange rate at $1=DEM 1.8000, the bank sells exactly $1million to receive DEM 1,800,000 spot and has now completely hedged all the cash flows in D-marks, both spot and forward.

Unfortunately, this still leaves an outflow of $1million spot, but this can easily be financed by borrowing dollars. If the bank borrows the $1million required right now, this will eliminate the spot deficit, but will require the repayment of $1,060,000 in one year, including the 6% interest.

We have now come almost full circle. The bank has transformed the original DEM 1,980,000 liability one year forward into a $1,060,000 liability, also in one year. However, if the bank demands this sum of dollars from its client in exchange for the D-marks being sold, the bank will have hedged every cash flow from the original transaction. In the process, we have determined the amount of dollars the bank should receive and the correct exchange rate of 1,980,000 ÷ 1,060,000 = 1.8679.

Figure 3.1d shows the bank's position after quoting $1 = DEM 1.8679 as the forward rate for the client transaction.[1] By executing a spot deal, lending D-marks and borrowing dollars, the dealer has hedged the complete exposure arising from the forward foreign exchange transaction, and has eliminated the bank's exposure to market rate risk. The dealer is not concerned how the spot $/DEM rate will evolve over the next year, nor does he worry what the spot rate will be on the settlement date in one year. Whether the exchange rate for dollars against D-marks is above or below 1.8679 will not affect the cash flows arising from the original lending and borrowing, and it is these cash flows that are hedging the client's forward transaction.

Since all rates for the hedging deals are known in the market today, the dealer has successfully priced a forward FX deal, without necessarily having any opinion on where the spot rate will be in the future. This is the essence of risk-free arbitrage pricing.

---

[1] In fact, the dealer would have to quote a rate slightly lower than 1.8679 so that the bank receives slightly more than the $1,060,000 indicated by the above deals. Otherwise there would be no profit for the bank in executing the forward deal with the client.

From the above relationships, we can derive a simple formula to price a forward exchange rate:[2]

$$F = S \times \left[\frac{1 + \left(i_q \times \dfrac{DAYS}{BASIS_q}\right)}{1 + \left(i_b \times \dfrac{DAYS}{BASISb}\right)} \right] \tag{3.1}$$

where

F	is the outright forward exchange rate
S	is the current spot exchange rate
i_q	is the interest rate in the quoted currency (e.g., D-marks)
i_b	is the interest rate in the base currency (e.g., dollars)
$DAYS$	is the number of days from spot to the forward date
$BASIS_q$	is the day count convention in the quoted currency (360 for D-marks)
$BASIS_b$	is the day count convention in the base currency (also 360 for dollars)

and all interest rates are quoted as decimal fractions (e.g., 6% would be 0.06).

In practice, the foreign exchange market does not quote forward exchange rates as an absolute figure—the outright forward rate—but rather as the difference between the spot and forward rate—the forward margin or *swap points*. This is because the outright forward rate is extremely sensitive to movements in the spot rate and moves almost exactly one-for-one with the spot rate. The forward FX dealer would have to adjust his quote with every slight movement in the spot rate. The swap points, on the other hand, are hardly affected by the spot rate and quotations are therefore much more stable. Equation 3.2 shows the formula for swap points:

$$W = S \times \left[\frac{1 + \left(i_q \times \dfrac{DAYS}{BASIS_q}\right)}{1 + \left(i_b \times \dfrac{DAYS}{BASISb}\right)} - 1 \right] = F - S \tag{3.2}$$

where

W is the forward margin or *swap points*

and all the other symbols are as before.

As an example, if the spot rate in the previous example were to move 100 points from 1.8000 to 1.7900, the outright rate would decrease from 1.8679

---

[2] This formula applies to forward rates up to one year in the future. For long-term FX (LTFX) transactions, the formula must be modified to include compound interest.

to 1.8575—a fall of almost 100 points, but the swap rate would only move from 679 points to 675 points—just a 4-point move. The change in swap points for a forward deal of shorter maturity would be even less.[3]

3.2 FORWARD INTEREST RATES

As finance developed in the 1960s and 1970s, banks were able to offer their customers an increasing range of borrowing facilities. In particular, the medium-term loan became a popular financing vehicle, allowing customers to borrow for up to seven or ten years, instead of having to rely on the frequent renewal of short-term facilities. Banks, however, were compelled to finance themselves short term from retail or money market deposits. This was no great problem, for one of the roles traditionally ascribed to banks is to borrow short and lend long, the so-called *maturity transformation* function.

Banks were not terribly worried about their ability to roll over their funding requirements as, short of a full-blown banking crisis,[4] they had confidence in their ability to raise funds from the market if necessary. Banks may have had to bid an additional ⅛% to obtain the funds they needed, but raise the funds they did.

What banks were unable to do was to fix in advance the interest rate for the funds thus raised. Banks were forced to pay the going rate at the time and then had to pass on that rate to their borrowers. Medium-term loans could therefore guarantee the availability of funds for a company, but not the rate at which those funds were provided.

As interest rates became more volatile in the 1970s and early 1980s, corporate treasurers sought from their banks a means to protect their exposure to higher borrowing costs. To an extent, banks were able to offer a limited solution in the form of the *forward-forward* loan, so-called because both the draw-down and repayment dates were in the future.

Let's say that a bank is asked to quote a fixed rate for a six-month loan of £1million, to start six months from now. The bank wishes to take no risks, and therefore needs to fix its own financing costs for the six-month period starting in six months. Unfortunately, nobody in the 1970s was really willing to quote a fixed rate for a period in the future. The bank might find that six-month cash rates were 9½%, while 12-month cash rates were 9⅞%, but these were rates for funds drawn down right now, not in six months from now.

---

[3] Using calculus it is easy to show that $\frac{\partial F}{\partial S} \approx 1$, but $\frac{\partial W}{\partial S} \approx 0$.

[4] Occasionally crises do occur. In the UK 1973–1974 fringe banking crisis, the Bank of England had to organise a "lifeboat" whereby strong banks recirculated funds to weaker banks. Similarly, in 1982 the U.S. Federal Reserve had to step in to support Continental Illinois when the market for its CDs collapsed.

Once again, however, the principle of risk-free arbitrage can be applied to determine the fair rate to be quoted. To fix the costs for the six-month period starting in six months, the bank borrows now for 12 months at 9⅞%. Unfortunately, this not only covers the forward period but also the first six months, when finance is not required. To cope with these unwanted funds, the bank lends them for the first six months at 9½%. The proceeds of this 6-month loan are then available to the client in 6 months' time, and the repayment from the client 12 months from now should, if our arithmetic is correct, be just enough to repay the bank's original 12-month borrowing.

Figure 3.2 demonstrates the cash flows arising from these transactions.

The bank borrows £954,654 for 12 months at 9⅞%, and immediately

FIGURE 3.2
Forward-Forward Loan

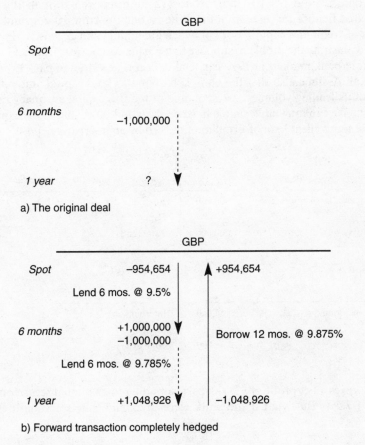

a) The original deal

b) Forward transaction completely hedged

lends it for 6 months at 9½%. The maturing proceeds from the six-month loan come to exactly £1million with interest and provide the funds to lend to its client. If the bank quotes at least 9.785% for this forward-forward loan, the proceeds will be enough to repay the principal and interest on the original 12-month borrowing, namely, £1,048,926.

By borrowing long term and lending short term, the bank has created a *synthetic* forward borrowing, which enables it to quote a rate for forward-forward lending and then to finance such lending without suffering interest rate risk. As we saw in the previous chapter with forward exchange deals, the bank need not be concerned with the level of interest rates which eventually prevail; the combination of 12-month borrowing at 9⅞% and 6-month lending at 9½% guarantees a source of finance at 9.785% regardless of market rates at the time.

Forward-forward loans were in demand in the late 1970s, but were not popular from the banks' viewpoint. What made these loans unattractive was the need for banks to borrow money the entire time from the dealing date until the final maturity of the forward-forward loan. In the above example, the bank would need to borrow for 12 months even though the client required finance for just 6 months. When a bank borrows, it consumes both lines of credit and capital, both of which are limited and expensive resources.

To illustrate the problem, suppose that a bank can borrow from and lend to the interbank markets at 10%, can lend to clients at 11%, and pays 15% for its capital. Assume also that the bank is required to hold capital amounting to 8% of its lending volume, corresponding to the BIS capital adequacy requirements. We can draw up a simple balance sheet and profit and loss account for a six-month client loan of £1million financed by an interbank deposit.

Balance Sheet

Assets		*Liabilities and Capital*	
Customer loan (6 months)	1,000,000	Interbank deposit (6 months)	920,000
		Capital	80,000
Total assets	1,000,000	Total funds	1,000,000

Profit and Loss Account (six months)

Income		*Expense*	
Customer loan	55,000	Interbank deposit	46,000
		Capital	6,000
Total income	55,000	Total expense	52,000

This leaves a net profit of £3,000, corresponding to an annual return on capital of 7.5%. But what if the bank were to extend the same facilities as a six-month forward-forward loan? During the first six months, the balance sheet would look like this:

Balance Sheet (first six months)

Assets		Liabilities and Capital	
Interbank loan (6 months)	1,000,000	Interbank deposit (12 months)	920,000
		Capital	80,000
Total assets	1,000,000	Total funds	1,000,000

and for the last six months:

Balance Sheet (last six months)

Assets		Liabilities and Capital	
Customer loan (6 months)	1,000,000	Interbank deposit (12 months)	920,000
		Capital	80,000
Total income	1,000,000	Total expense	1,000,000

The resulting profit and loss account would therefore show a much reduced profit:

Profit and Loss Account (twelve months)

Income		Expense	
Interbank loan	50,000	Interbank deposit	92,000
Customer loan	55,000	Capital	12,000
Total income	105,000	Total expense	104,000

The profit is now only £1,000 for a full year, corresponding to a paltry 1.25% return on capital, one-sixth the return on the previous lending example. It is no wonder that banks disliked forward-forward lending!

The greatest damage to the bank's profits in this example arises from the bank's need for capital to support the balance sheet for the extended period involved. There is a sound reason why central banks insist on this capital requirement: it is to protect banks in the event of a default on their loans. With an 8% capital requirement, it is theoretically possible for 8% of the bank's loans to go bad without prejudicing the bank's depositors. If a way could be found to remove forward-forward loans from the balance sheet, this would eliminate the need for capital and restore profitability to the banks. As we will see in the next chapter, this is where the FRA comes in.

3.3 DO FORWARD RATES PREDICT FUTURE
SPOT RATES?

Expectations are *subjective* estimates of where prices will be in the future. In contrast, this chapter has thus far presented forward prices as being *objectively* derived from current market rates using risk-free arbitrage calculations. Inasmuch as these forward prices are mathematically derived from prevailing market rates, there is no need to refer to subjective expectations in order to derive objective forward prices.

Nevertheless, we can prove that objective forward prices must necessarily match subjective expectations. If they did not, market forces would drive current prices so as to achieve equality. This is an important point.

For example, suppose that the spot dollar D-mark exchange rate was $1=DEM 1.8000, and using current market interest rates, the three-month outright forward rate was calculated objectively to be $1=DEM 1.8180. One can therefore say that market expectations for the spot rate in three months' time must also be $1=DEM 1.8180. Why?

Imagine for one moment that the market really expected the spot rate in three months' time to be higher, say $1=DEM 1.8400. In that case, traders would execute deals today to buy dollars outright for delivery three months later at the current three-month forward rate of $1=DEM 1.8180, and then just wait for three months. Two days before the value date for these deals, they would sell the dollars at the then-prevailing spot rate. If they had been right in their original expectations, that spot rate would be $1=DEM 1.8400, realising a 220-point profit, equivalent to DEM 22,000 per $1million traded. A $100million position would realise over DEM 2million profit.

With such an incentive, everyone would buy dollars forward to profit from their expectations. Of course, the demand for forward dollars would force the price up, but traders would still keep buying and buying. They would only stop buying when the forward price equalled the expectation of $1=DEM 1.8400. A similar argument in the opposite direction would apply if traders had thought that the forward price were overvalued.

In other words, market forces will always drive forward rates (and spot rates with them) until forward rates equal market expectations for the spot rate on that date. Therefore the forward rate one actually observes in the market must be equal to market expectations for the spot rate on that date.

Although this argument has been developed in the context of exchange rates, the same applies to interest rates. The forward interest rate is not only determined objectively by manipulating cash market rates for different maturities, it is also the subjective forecast of where the cash market rate will be in the future. For example, if 6-month rates are 9½% and 12-month rates are 9⅞%, we calculated earlier that the rate for a forward-forward loan of six months starting in six months was 9.785%. This also implies that the current market expectation for six-month interest rates is that they will rise from their present level of 9½%, and will reach 9.785% six months from now.

3.4 SPOT AND FORWARD RATES IN PRACTICE

Many studies have been undertaken to answer the question, Do spot rates in practice eventually match up to prior expectations? The answer is, No, they do not. The solid line in Figure 3.3 shows the spot exchange rate for dollars against D-marks from January 1986 to December 1988. The dotted line starting in July 1986 shows the six-month forward rate six months previously. The two are almost never the same.

Figure 3.4 shows even more clearly the gap between the spot rate and the forward rate six months earlier.

But this seemingly disappointing answer has no bearing on the conclusion established in the previous section, that forward rates must match the market's expectations of future spot rates.

At any given time, the market absorbs all available information and establishes spot and forward prices. At that moment, a six-month forward rate forecasts the spot rate in six months. However, during the six-month period many things can happen. There will be economic and political developments, and dramatic events could occur. All of these alter market expectations, and prices will adjust accordingly.

FIGURE 3.3
Spot Rates Compared with Forward Rates Six Months Earlier

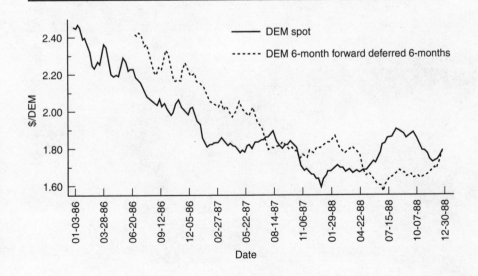

FIGURE 3.4
Gap between Spot Rates and Forward Rates Six Months Earlier

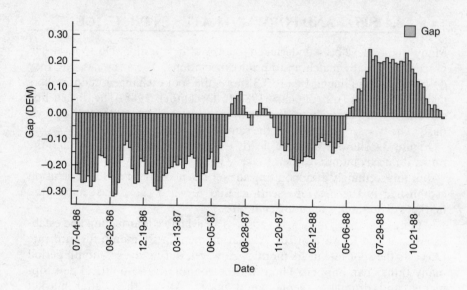

So when studies compare the spot rate with the six-month forward rate quoted six months earlier, they are trying to compare rates based on two sets of price-sensitive information. No wonder the rates turn out to be different *ex post facto*. This does not negate the fact that forward rates and expectations of future spot rates were once the same.

Chapter Four

FRAs

The previous chapter introduced and explained the concept of forward rates. This chapter and the next look in turn at two financial engineering instruments, the FRA and the SAFE. The FRA, originating from the money markets, is by far the more widespread of the two and offers a flexible tool for hedging against or speculating on the movements of a specific interest rate. The SAFE was developed more recently from the foreign exchange markets and provides a means of working with the *differentials* between two specific interest rates.

4.1 WHAT IS AN FRA?

The initials FRA stand for *Forward Rate Agreement*.[1] In essence, an FRA is a forward-forward loan granted at a fixed interest rate, but *without the actual lending commitment*. Removing the flows of principal from the FRA takes the instrument off the balance sheet and removes the onerous capital requirements that made forward-forward loans so unattractive. While there is still a requirement for banks to allocate some capital to cover their FRA books, the amount is around one-hundredth of the requirement demanded for forward-forward loans.

But what exactly is an FRA? One way to answer that question is to look at FRAs from the user's viewpoint:

> An FRA is an agreement between two parties motivated by the wish either to hedge against or to speculate on a movement in future interest rates.

The hedger already has interest rate exposure but wants to obtain protection against rate movements. After taking a position in FRAs, the hedger's

---

[1] Some take FRA to stand for *Future Rate Agreement*. Although the words *future* and *forward* are similar, I prefer to avoid the word *future* in the context of FRAs because of the possible confusion with financial futures, which are a different product.

net risk will be reduced or eliminated. The speculator, on the other hand, starts with no exposure but wants to profit from an anticipated movement in interest rates. Taking a position in FRAs creates for the speculator precisely the exposure desired. Since their inception in the early 1980s, FRAs have provided an invaluable tool in the management of interest rate risk.

FRAs are an *over-the-counter* (OTC) product offered by banks. Like the foreign exchange market, the market for FRAs is a global market offered by banks operating from their dealing rooms, linked together by telephone, information feeds, and computer networks. The two parties to an FRA are usually a customer and a bank or two banks. As with their other activities in the financial markets, banks intermediate between those who are exposed to risk. Alternatively, banks can absorb customers' risks within the totality of their trading books across all the financial markets.

The FRA market really started to grow in 1984, and the daily turnover in London alone now regularly exceeds $5 billion. For dollar FRAs, banks post prices for all combinations of standard 3-, 6-, 9-, and 12-month periods with final maturity dates up to two years into the future; for the other major currencies there is good liquidity up to one year. Banks also stand ready to quote prices for odd dates and nonstandard periods. Figure 4.1 illustrates a typical broker's screen carrying FRA rates. The meaning of each of the numbers will become clearer once all the terminology has been defined in the next two sections.

4.2 DEFINITIONS

We know so far that an FRA is an agreement between two parties wishing to modify their exposure to interest rates. Let us take a closer look at the features of that agreement.

FIGURE 4.1
Example of FRA Rates

1321	BABCOCK FULTON PREBON NEW YORK – 212–952–2676		–	EURODOLLAR FRA STRIPS LOS ANGELES – 213 622–1141		FPRF	
1×4	4.75-80	1×7	4.66-71	1×10	4.70-75	1×13	4.80-87
2×5	4.53-58	2×8	4.59-64	2×11	4.71-76	2×14	4.85-92
3×6	4.52-57	3×9	4.59-64	3×12	4.71-76	3×15	4.90-97
4×7	4.54-59	4×10	4.64-69	4×13	4.80-85	4×16	5.00-07
5×8	4.57-62	5×11	4.70-75	5×14	4.90-95	5×17	5.09-16
6×9	4.61-66	6×12	4.75-80	6×15	4.99-04	6×18	5.18-25
9×12	4.85-90	9×15	5.13-18	9×18	5.34-39	9×21	5.54-61
12×15	5.45-50	12×18	5.53-58	12×21	5.73-78	12×24	5.93-00
15×18	5.54-59	15×21	5.82-87	15×24	6.07-12		
CALL FOR FIRM PRICES			* ALL STRIP RATES ARE SPOT *				

Source: *Reuters Monitor.*

One party to an FRA is defined to be the *buyer* of the FRA, the other party is the *seller*. The seller of an FRA agrees notionally to lend a particular sum of money to the buyer. The terms "buyer" and "seller" therefore have nothing to do with who is providing a service, they refer to which party is the notional borrower and which the notional lender. Banks can be buyers and sellers, as can customers.

The notional loan is of a specified size in a specified currency, will be drawn down on a particular date in the future, and will last for a specified duration. Most important of all, the notional loan will be made at a fixed rate of interest, this rate being agreed when the FRA deal is struck.

Let's recap these important concepts:

Under an FRA:

- the BUYER agrees notionally to BORROW

- the SELLER agrees notionally to LEND

- a specified notional principal amount

- denominated in a specified currency

- at a FIXED rate of interest

- for a specified period

- to commence on an agreed date in the

- future.

The *buyer* of an FRA is therefore a notional borrower and is protected against a rise in interest rates, though he must pay if rates fall. The buyer may have a real borrowing requirement and be using the FRA as a hedge. Alternatively, the buyer may have no underlying interest-rate exposure, but may be using the FRA simply to speculate on a rise in interest rates.

The *seller* of an FRA is a notional lender and fixes the rate for lending or investing. The FRA seller is therefore protected against a fall in interest rates, but must pay if rates rise. A seller may be an investor who would really suffer if rates fell but could also be someone with no underlying position who just wanted to profit from a fall in rates.

We have repeatedly emphasised the word *notional*. It is important to remember that no lending or borrowing actually takes place under the FRA itself. Although one or both parties may have borrowing or investment commitments, separate arrangements to handle these requirements must be made. What the FRA does provide is protection against a movement in interest rates. This protection manifests itself in the form of a cash payment—the *settlement sum*—which compensates each party for any difference between the rate of interest originally agreed and that prevailing when the

FRA eventually matures. An example should serve to make this clearer.

Consider a company that anticipates the need to borrow $1million in three months' time for a six-month period. For simplicity, we will assume that the borrower is able to raise funds at The London Interbank Offered Rate (LIBOR) flat. Suppose that interest rates are around 6% right now, but the borrower fears rates may rise over the next three months. If the borrower does nothing, he could face a much higher interest rate when the loan is drawn down in three months time.

To protect against this interest rate risk, the borrower could today buy an FRA to cover the six-month period starting three months from now. This would be known in the market as a "3-against-9 month" FRA, or simply a 3×9 FRA. A bank might quote a rate of 6.25% for such an FRA, and this would enable the borrower to lock into a borrowing rate of 6.25%. There is no "insurance premium" payable when buying or selling FRAs, although banks would normally charge their clients a commission on the deal.

Now suppose that the borrower's fears were realised, and interest rates did indeed rise over the initial three-month period to 7%. Despite the FRA, the borrower is still forced to borrow in the market and pay the going rate, namely 7%. Over a six-month period, the borrower would therefore have to pay an extra $3,750 interest on the $1million borrowed. This is where the FRA comes in. Under the FRA, the company would receive approximately $3,750 to compensate for the extra 0.75% interest payable on the $1million loan over the six-month period, the settlement sum effectively offsetting the higher borrowing costs.[2] While the FRA has not guaranteed the interest rate on the specific financing facility used by the company, the borrower has nonetheless managed to secure its finance at the rate fixed by the FRA, which operates to bring the effective cost of the loan down to the level originally agreed.

4.3 TERMINOLOGY

Nearly all FRAs dealt in practice fall under standard market documentation drawn up in 1985 by the British Bankers' Association, the so-called "FRABBA terms." In addition to establishing the proper legal arrangements, the documentation defines a number of important terms:

- *Contract amount:* The principal sum notionally lent or borrowed.
- *Contract currency:* The currency in which the contract amount is denominated.
- *Dealing date:* The date when the FRA deal is struck.
- *Settlement date:* The date when the notional loan or deposit commences.

---

[2] As we will see shortly, the exact sum depends upon the exact number of days in the period covered and is discounted to adjust for the timing of the payment.

- *Fixing date:* The date when the reference rate is determined.
- *Maturity date:* The date when the notional loan or deposit matures.
- *Contract period:* The number of days between settlement and maturity dates.
- *Contract rate:* The fixed interest rate agreed under the FRA.
- *Reference rate:* The market-based rate used on the fixing date to determine the settlement sum.
- *Settlement sum:* The amount paid by one party to the other on the settlement date, based on the difference between the contract and reference rates.

Figure 4.2 illustrates many of these key concepts and may make the terms more readily understood.

We start on the dealing date, when the two parties to the FRA agree to all the terms. Let's suppose that the *dealing date* is Monday, April 12, 1993, and the two parties agree to trade a 1×4 FRA in $1million at 6.25%. The *contract currency* is therefore the U.S. dollar, the *contract amount* is $1million, and the *contract rate* is 6.25%.

The "1×4" refers to a one-month period between the normal spot date and the settlement date and a four-month period between the spot date and the final maturity date of the notional loan. Spot date is normally two days after the dealing date, making it Wednesday, April 14, in this case. This means that the notional loan or deposit would start on Friday, May 14, 1993, exactly one month after spot, and would mature on Monday, August 16, 1993, just over three months later.[3] The *settlement date* is therefore May 14, the *maturity date* August 16, and the *contract period* 94 days.

For a regular eurocurrency loan or deposit, the rate is fixed on the dealing *date*, but the principal does not change hands until the value date, normally

FIGURE 4.2
Timing Diagram for FRAs

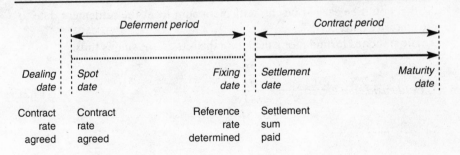

---

[3] As August 14, 1993 is a Saturday, the three-month period rolls forward to the following business day.

two working days later. This pattern is repeated with FRAs. The notional loan or deposit would theoretically be drawn down on the settlement date, Friday, May 14, in the above example, but the rate would be determined two days earlier on the *fixing date*, Wednesday, May 12, here.

Under most FRAs, the *reference rate* is the LIBOR fixing on the fixing date. LIBOR in its turn is determined by seeking quotes from a number of designated banks at the appointed time, ranking the quotes in order from lowest to highest, striking out the lowest and highest figures, taking the average of the remaining figures, and then rounding this average up to the nearest $1/16\%$. Let's suppose that the reference rate on the fixing date, May 12, turns out to be 7.00%.

The final step is to calculate the *settlement sum*. We have all the information we need to do this, and the next section explains exactly how to do it.

4.4 THE SETTLEMENT PROCESS

In the above example, the buyer of the FRA has theoretically locked into a borrowing rate of 6.25%, but now faces a market rate of 7.00% on the fixing date. The extra interest payable on a $1million facility for 94 days can easily be calculated:

$$Extra\ interest = \frac{(7.00\text{-}6.25)}{100} \times \$1,000,000 \times \frac{94}{360} = \$1,958.33 \qquad (4.1)$$

This extra interest cost would be suffered when the interest payment for the borrowing was made, which is on the final maturity date of the underlying loan. If the settlement sum under the FRA were paid on the same date, then it should also be $1,958.33 so as to compensate exactly for the higher interest rate on the borrowing.

In practice, however, FRAs usually pay the settlement sum on the settlement date, which is at the *beginning* of the underlying loan or deposit. As this sum is paid earlier than it is needed, it could be invested to earn interest. To adjust for this timing, the settlement sum is reduced by exactly the interest that could be earned on the settlement sum from the settlement date to the maturity date.

The standard formula for calculating the settlement sum is thus:

$$Settlement\ sum = \frac{(i_r\text{-}i_c) \times A \times \dfrac{DAYS}{BASIS}}{1 + \left(i_r \times \dfrac{DAYS}{BASIS}\right)} \qquad (4.2)$$

where

i_r \qquad is the reference interest rate
i_c \qquad is the contract interest rate

A is the contract amount
$DAYS$ is the number of days in the contract period
$BASIS$ is the day count convention (e.g., 360 for dollars, 365 for sterling)

and all interest rates are quoted as decimal fractions (e.g., 6.25% would be 0.0625).

Showing the formula in this way shows directly how it is derived. The numerator is simply the extra interest cost caused by the change in interest rates from the original rate agreed i_c to the rate eventually prevailing i_r. In the example of equation 4.1, this would be $1,958.33. The denominator then discounts this to allow for the fact that the settlement sum is paid at the beginning rather than at the end of the contract period. If we insert the values of the previous example, we will get a settlement sum of $1,923.18 due to the FRA buyer on the settlement date.

It is important to remember that FRAs are a class of financial engineering instrument which replaces risk with certainty. In this example, as rates have turned out higher than the contract rate of 6.25%, the buyer of the FRA receives the settlement sum from the seller to compensate for higher borrowing costs. If rates had turned out to be lower, however, the buyer would have to pay the seller to compensate the notional lender for lower than expected investment rates. In either case, both buyer and seller end up with an effective LIBOR of 6.25%, whatever LIBOR actually turns out to be.

Equation 4.2 is defined in such a way that a positive settlement sum implies a payment from seller to buyer, while a negative settlement sum implies a payment from buyer to seller. Another way to think of this is to consider the settlement sum as being the value of the FRA to the buyer, the party who is "long" the FRA. If $i_r > i_c$, the settlement sum will be positive. The buyer has purchased an FRA when rates were lower, rates have subsequently risen, and a positive value will be realised. This is nothing other than a trader's "buy low sell high" mentality. If $i_r < i_c$, the settlement sum will be negative, and it will now be the seller, who is "short" the FRA, who will realise a gain.

It is possible to rearrange equation 4.2 in order to get a slightly simpler formulation:

$$Settlement\ sum = \frac{(i_r - i_c) \times A}{\dfrac{BASIS}{DAYS} + i_r} = 1,923.18 \tag{4.3}$$

4.5 HEDGING WITH FRAs

In the previous example, the FRA buyer would receive $1,923.18 as the settlement sum but would pay a higher interest rate at the maturity of the three-month loan. Let's check to make sure that the arithmetic of the FRA really works.

On the fixing date, Wednesday, May 12, the settlement sum will be known, and the borrower should make arrangements to invest it for exactly three months. The settlement sum received on Friday, May 14, the settlement date, is thus invested to earn 7.00%, the prevailing LIBOR. After 94 days, the interest earned will be $35.15, bringing the value of the settlement sum with interest up to $1,958.33.

Wednesday, May, 12, will also be the date when the rate for the three-month borrowing facility will be fixed at 7.00%. The funds would be drawn down on Friday, May, 14, and repaid on Monday, August 16, together with interest of $18,277.78. The invested settlement sum will, however, reduce the effective interest cost to $16,319.45. What interest rate does this sum represent?

$$\textit{Effective interest cost} = \frac{16,319.46}{1,000,000} \times \frac{360}{94} = 6.25\% \qquad (4.4)$$

In this example, the FRA has indeed lowered the borrower's effective cost to the contract rate agreed when the FRA was bought.

In practice, there are two minor departures from this simple illustration.

First, most borrowers are compelled to pay some margin above LIBOR, say 1.00%. This means that the effective borrowing will be effected at the same margin above the contract rate. For example, a borrower used to paying 1.00% above LIBOR who buys an FRA at 6.25% will be locking his borrowing cost at 7.25%, regardless of the eventual outcome for LIBOR.

Second, the discounting implicit in determining the settlement sum assumes that parties to the FRA can invest or borrow the settlement sum at LIBOR. In practice, only banks would be able to do this; commercial customers would normally only achieve a margin below LIBOR.

Let's rework the above example assuming that the borrower must pay LIBOR plus 1.00% for his funds, but can only earn LIBOR minus 1.00% on funds invested. The borrower buys an FRA at 6.25%, and the reference rate turns out to be 7.00%, leading to the same settlement sum being paid as before.

Settlement sum	$ 1,923.18
Interest earned on settlement sum invested for 94 days at 6.00%	30.13
Total proceeds from FRA	1,953.31
Interest payable on $1million borrowed for 94 days at 8.00%	20,888.89
Net borrowing costs after deduction of FRA proceeds	$18,935.58

The effective interest rate implied by net borrowing costs of $18,935.58 is 7.25%, still 1.00% above the contract rate originally agreed. The lower interest earned on the settlement sum only costs the borrower $5.02, equivalent to just 0.002% on borrowings of $1 million for 94 days, a negligible amount.

FIGURE 4.3
FRA Pricing: "Filling the Gap"

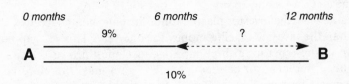

4.6 PRICING FRAs

The simplest way to think about FRA pricing is to think about an FRA as "filling the gap" between different maturities in the cash market.

Consider someone with funds available right now to invest for one year. Suppose that 6-month rates are at 9%, but 12-month rates are at 10%. The investor has many choices, including these two alternatives:

1. Invest for one year and earn 10%.
2. Invest for six months and earn 9%. At the same time, sell a 6 × 12 FRA to lock in a guaranteed return for the second six-month period.

These two possibilities are pictured in Figure 4.3. In the diagram, there are two ways of getting from A to B, as is often the case in financial markets. When this happens, the efficiency of the financial markets will ensure that whichever path is chosen the end result should be the same. In this example, the investor placing his money for a year under alternative (1) will earn an additional 1% for the first six months when compared with alternative (2). For both these alternatives eventually to come out the same, the return over the second six months must gain 1% for the investor who chooses alternative (2). To a first approximation, the 6 × 12 FRA must be priced at 11%, as pictured in Figure 4.4.

FIGURE 4.4
Determining the Rate for a 6 × 12 FRA

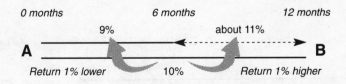

This technique gives us an intuitive insight into the pricing of FRAs and provides a "quick and dirty" way of estimating the price for any given FRA, if we know the appropriate rates in the cash markets. Figure 4.5 extends the technique and shows how to price 6×9 and 9×12 FRAs.

In Figure 4.5c, the investor placing funds for nine months receives 1% less return than the investor placing money for one year. This 1% gap must be made up in the remaining three months, just one-third of the time over which this difference can be recouped. The gain must therefore be three times as great, implying that the 9×12 FRA must be 3% higher than the 12-month rate, or around 14%.

In all these cases, this quick and dirty technique has been able to give only a rough estimate for the FRA rate. This is because an investor choosing the shorter-term investment followed by another short-term investment protected by an FRA has the opportunity to earn interest-on-interest. Not only can the principal be reinvested over the second term, but the interest on that principal can be reinvested as well. This means that in all these examples, the actual FRA rate would be somewhat lower than the rough estimates. In the

FIGURE 4.5
Further Examples of FRA Pricing

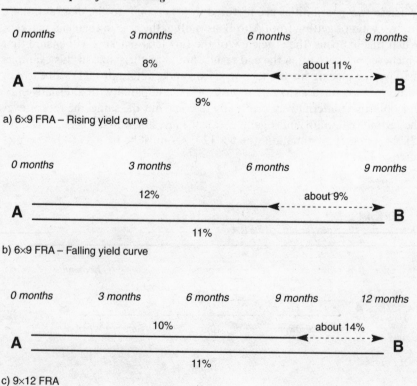

a) 6×9 FRA – Rising yield curve

b) 6×9 FRA – Falling yield curve

c) 9×12 FRA

case of the 6×12 FRA, the true FRA rate should be 10.53%, not the 11% previously estimated.

While thinking about FRAs as "filling this gap" provides a useful introduction to the concept of FRA pricing, there is a need for a more accurate formula for use in practice. Figure 4.6 generalises the risk-free arbitrage process using algebraic symbols and derives the desired formula, including consideration of the interest-on-interest.

If we equate the returns through both investment paths in the diagram, we obtain this equality for periods of time up to one year:

$$(1 + i_S t_S)(1 + i_F t_F) = (1 + i_L t_L) \qquad (4.5)$$

where

i_S	is the cash market interest rate to the settlement date
i_L	is the cash market interest rate to the maturity date
i_F	is the FRA rate
t_S	is the time from spot date to the settlement date
t_L	is the time from spot date to the maturity date
t_F	is the length of the contract period

and all interest rates are quoted as decimal fractions and all times as fractions of a year.

Substituting day counts instead of time fractions, equation 4.5 can be rearranged to solve for i_F:

$$i_F = \frac{i_L D_L - i_S D_S}{D_F \left(1 + i_S \dfrac{D_S}{B}\right)} \qquad (4.6)$$

where

D_S	is the number of days from spot date to the settlement date
D_L	is the number of days from spot date to the maturity date
D_F	is the number of days in the contract period
B	is the day count convention (e.g., 360 for dollars, 365 for sterling)

and the other symbols are as in equation 4.5.

FIGURE 4.6
Algebraic Terms Used for FRA Pricing

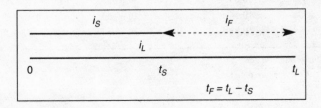

For example, if we take the dates given earlier in this chapter for the 1×4 FRA, we get $D_S = 30$, $D_L = 124$, and $D_F = 94$. If $i_S = 6\frac{1}{8}\%$ and $i_L = 6\frac{1}{4}\%$, we can solve for i_F as follows:

$$i_F = \frac{0.0625 \times 124 - 0.06125 \times 30}{94 \times \left(1 + 0.06125 \times \dfrac{30}{360}\right)} = 0.062580 \approx 6.26\% \tag{4.7}$$

Let's have a look at some actual cash market rates and FRA quotations to see how they compare in practice with the formula above. On Monday, February 18, 1991, sterling and dollar LIBOR for different maturities were as shown in Table 4.1.

From these rates, we can first construct the sterling yield curve, which is pictured in Figure 4.7. The actual values from the above table are plotted on the graph as square markers, and a computer has been used to fit a smooth curve through these points.

TABLE 4.1
Sterling and Dollar LIBOR Rates on February 18, 1991

Maturity	£ LIBOR	$ LIBOR
1 month	13.6875%	6.6500%
2 months	13.4375%	6.5625%
3 months	13.1250%	6.6250%
6 months	12.6250%	6.6250%
9 months	12.2500%	6.6875%
12 months	12.0625%	6.8125%

TABLE 4.2
Comparison of Actual and Theoretical Sterling FRA Rates

FRA Period	Calculated Rate	Market Rates	Difference (bp)
1×4	12.60[a]	12.68/73	−10
	12.52[b]		−18
3×6	11.76	11.79/84	−5
6×9	10.83	10.83/88	−2
9×12	10.54	10.50/55	+2
6×12	10.83	10.79/84	+2

[a]Calculated by linear interpolation.
[b]Calculated by cubic spline interpolation.

FIGURE 4.7
Sterling Yield Curve on February 18, 1991

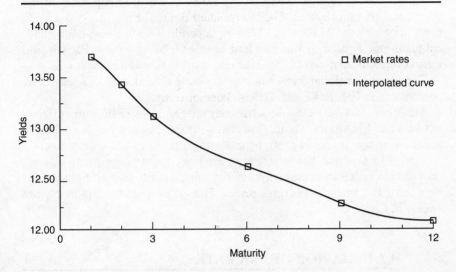

We can use these figures in conjunction with equation 4.6 to calculate the theoretical FRA rates for sterling. Table 4.2 compares these with the actual FRA rates quoted that day.

Apart from the 1 × 4 FRA, the calculated rates are within a few basis points[4] of the actual FRA rates quoted in the market. In the case of the 1 × 4 FRA, the difference is probably due to difficulties in the interpolation

TABLE 4.3
Comparison of Actual and Theoretical Dollar FRA Rates

FRA Period	Calculated Rate	Market Rates	Difference (bp)
1×4	6.63[a]	6.67/72	−6
	6.66[b]		−3
3×6	6.52	6.50/55	0
6×9	6.59	6.66/71	−9
9×12	6.84	6.90/95	−8
6×12	6.77	6.83/88	−8

[a]Calculated by linear interpolation
[b]Calculated by cubic spline interpolation.

---

[4] One basis point (bp) is 0.01%.

of the four-month cash market rate, which has a great influence on the calculated 1×4 FRA rate. There was an unusually steeply inverted yield curve at the time, with very high one-month rates, and a 50bp gap between the three- and six-month rates. The interpolated figure for the four-month rate comes out between 12.89% and 12.96%, depending upon which mathematical technique is used. If this rate had been 13.03%, the 1×4 FRA would have come out exactly at 12.70%, the mid-market rate actually quoted.

The results for dollar FRA rates on the same date also show a very close correlation, as Figure 4.8 and Table 4.3 demonstrate.

That there is a very close link between interest rates in the eurocurrency markets and FRA rates is hardly surprising. If there were significant discrepancies, arbitrageurs could profit by executing a set of risk-free deals to close any gaps. In practice, however, FRAs are priced and hedged with interest rate futures rather than eurocurrency deposits, leading to even tighter links between FRA rates and futures prices. These links will be explored more closely in Chapter Seven.

4.7 BEHAVIOR OF FRA RATES

We have so far determined what FRA rates should be in absolute terms. This is an important consideration for anyone buying or selling FRAs in order to hedge existing interest rate exposures or using FRAs to speculate. A bank trading FRAs, however, will also be very concerned about the sensitivity of FRA rates to *changes* in interest rates.

FIGURE 4.8
Dollar Yield Curve on February 18, 1991

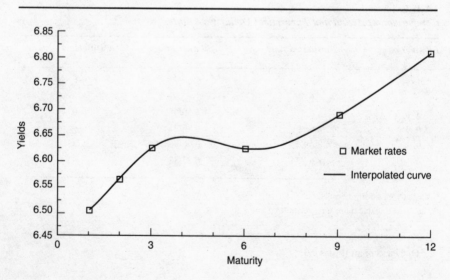

To see how FRA rates move, let's go back to the 6×9 FRA shown in Figure 4.5a. The diagram showed that if six-month rates were 8% and nine-month rates were 9%, the 6×9 FRA would be priced at about 11%. Now consider what would happen if these component rates were to change. Figure 4.9 analyses the effects of a 1% rise in just the six-month rate, a 1% rise in just the nine-month rate, and then a rise in both rates together.

Remember that the principle of risk-free arbitrage requires that the total return be the same, whichever way the investor gets from A to B. If the rate for the first period increases as in Figure 4.9a, the FRA rate must decrease. How much the FRA rate falls depends on the ratio of the deferment period

FIGURE 4.9
Sensitivity of FRA Rates to Changes in Interest Rates

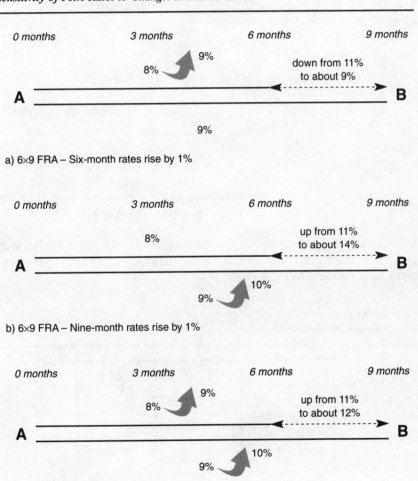

a) 6×9 FRA – Six-month rates rise by 1%

b) 6×9 FRA – Nine-month rates rise by 1%

c) 6×9 FRA – Both six- and nine-month rates rise by 1%

to the contract period. In this example, the deferment period of six months is twice as long as the contract period of three months. For a 1% rise in the six-month rate, the FRA rate therefore should fall by about 2%.

Similarly, if the rate for the total period increases, the FRA rate must increase, this time depending on the ratio of the total period to the contract period. For a 6×9 FRA, we would therefore expect the FRA rate to increase by 3% for a 1% rise in the nine-month rate. This is illustrated in Figure 4.9b.

Finally, common sense tells us that FRA rates should follow interest rates generally. For a general rise in interest rates of 1%, as pictured in Figure 4.9c, we would expect FRA rates also to increase by about 1%, and this is what we find. If the two previous scenarios are combined, the same result follows. A 1% rise in both the six- and nine-month rates should drop the FRA rate by 2% and then immediately raise it by 3%, a net increase of 1%.

We could obtain the same result mathematically by applying calculus to equation 4.6. If we take the partial derivatives of i_F with respect to i_S and to i_L, we obtain to a first approximation:

$$\frac{\partial i_F}{\partial i_S} \approx -\frac{D_S}{D_F} \tag{4.8}$$

$$\frac{\partial i_F}{\partial i_L} \approx \frac{D_L}{D_F} \tag{4.9}$$

$$\frac{\partial i_F}{\partial i_{ALL}} \approx 1 \tag{4.10}$$

Equation 4.10, showing the sensitivity of FRA rates to a general movement in interest rates, follows from equations 4.8 and 4.9 because $D_F = D_L - D_S$.

A useful way to summarise these findings is to construct a "behaviour profile" for some of the standard FRAs. Figure 4.10 demonstrates how many basis points each FRA moves if:

FIGURE 4.10
FRA Behavior Profiles

	$i_S \nearrow$ 1bp	$i_L \nearrow$ 1bp	i_S & $i_L \nearrow$ 1bp
3–6 month FRA	−1	+2	+1
6–9 month FRA	−2	+3	+1
9–12 month FRA	−3	+4	+1
6–12 month FRA	−1	+2	+1

1. The short-term interest rate i_S increases by one basis point.
2. The long-term interest rate i_L increases by one basis point.
3. Both rates increase by one basis point.

We now have a good idea of what FRAs are, how FRA rates are derived, and how these prices change when interest rates move. This chapter has also provided some basic examples illustrating the use of FRAs in practice. Chapter 14 provides a deeper appraisal of FRA applications and compares FRAs with other interest-rate risk management tools.

Chapter Five

SAFEs

FRAs were a logical development from the money markets, creating an off-balance-sheet alternative to the forward-forward deposit. This chapter reviews a more recent instrument, the SAFE, which has many parallels with the FRA.

5.1 WHAT IS A SAFE?

To understand a SAFE, it is first necessary to understand a forward-forward FX swap. Earlier chapters have introduced the concept of the traditional FX swap transaction,[1] in which a pair of currencies is exchanged on the spot value date and reexchanged on some forward date at a rate that differs from the spot rate by the number of swap points. A typical FX swap transaction is illustrated in Figure 5.1.

Remember that FX swap transactions and FX swap rates are mainly susceptible to differences in interest rates between the two currencies, as equation 3.2 demonstrated.

FIGURE 5.1
Example of One-year FX Swap

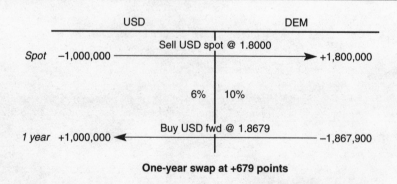

One-year swap at +679 points

---

[1] The traditional FX swap transaction described here should not be confused with the more recent development of *currency swaps*, discussed along with interest rate swaps in Chapter Nine.

In the current example, D-mark interest rates at 10% compared with dollar interest rates at 6% give the investor in D-marks an apparent edge. A U.S. investor could use a spot FX deal to switch out of dollars into D-marks and invest the proceeds for a year to pick up the additional return. Such a transaction would, however, be very much subject to currency risk if the investor did nothing until the end of the year and then executed a spot deal at the prevailing rate. Given the volatility of currency rates over a year, a weakening of the D-mark could easily wipe out the additional 4% return. To avoid the currency exposure, the investor could execute a forward deal at the outset to fix the forward exchange rate. Unfortunately for the investor, the forward exchange rate of $1=DEM 1.8679 makes the forward value of the D-mark around 4% weaker than its current spot value, completely eliminating the additional return.

Of course, it is the difference in the interest rates that gives rise to the difference between the spot and forward rate in the first place. It is therefore no surprise that the forward premium on the dollar wipes out the interest differential on the D-mark; they are two sides of the same coin.

Now suppose that a more sophisticated investor wanted to profit from a view that D-mark interest rates would soon go even higher than their present level, while dollar interest rates would decrease. The investor executing the FX swap pictured in Figure 5.1 would successfully exploit such a divergence in interest rates. Why? As dollar rates subsequently fell and D-mark rates rose, the gap between the rates would widen. As a consequence, the FX swap points would increase, taking the forward dollar to an even greater premium. The forward dollars that were purchased at a 679-point premium could then be sold at a higher premium, and hence at a higher price, thereby reaping a profit from the position.

Unfortunately, there is one awkward feature of using a plain FX swap such as the one illustrated. It may take weeks or even a few months before the expected movement in interest rates occurs. Yet two working days after executing the swap, settlement of the spot component of the transaction will occur, creating a shortfall of dollars to be financed and an inflow of D-marks to invest. These cash flows are a nuisance and are an unnecessary feature of the strategy.

One way around this problem is for the investor to execute a second FX swap at the same time, but for a shorter duration and in the opposite direction. The sole purpose of this short-term swap is to absorb the spot cash flows created by the first swap. Although this shorter swap would lose some value if the desired movement in interest rates occurred, the loss would not only be minimal but totally outweighed by the profits on the original long-term swap.

Figure 5.2 illustrates the resulting cash flows if a one-month swap were executed. Note that the cash flows at the spot date net out, and the earliest time the investor needs to take action is one month hence. By that time the expected interest rate movement may have occurred, and the investor would simply execute an 11-month swap to close out the position and take profits.

FIGURE 5.2
Pair of Back-to-Back Swaps

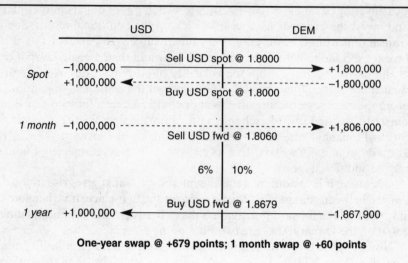

One-year swap @ +679 points; 1 month swap @ +60 points

FIGURE 5.3
Forward-Forward Swap

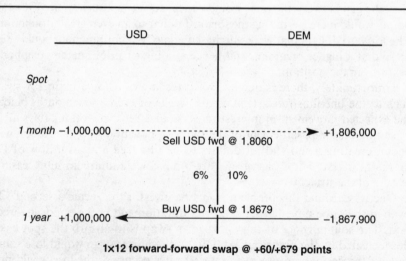

1×12 forward-forward swap @ +60/+679 points

This structure is sufficiently common for the FX market to package the pair of back-to-back swaps as a single deal, the forward-forward swap illustrated in Figure 5.3.

This has the identical forward cash flows as the separate swaps, but avoids the need for settlement of any transactions on the spot date. With the pair of back-to-back swaps, settlement of the spot components of both swaps would still need to be handled, even though the cash flows net out.

If interest rate differentials did widen after one month by 1%, the 11-month swap would increase to around 785 points. If the investor closed out the position at that time, a profit of around DEM 16,600 (equivalent to about $9,200) would be realised.

Notice the parallels with the forward-forward deposit. While a forward-forward deposit in its time was normally used for real hedging purposes, it could have been used to exploit a view of interest rates. Unfortunately, a forward-forward deposit involves real cash flows and the capital adequacy requirements that go along with these. The same is true of the forward-forward FX swap, which can be used to exploit a view of interest rate differentials, but which also involves real cash flows and the need for capital. This is where the SAFE comes in.

The acronym SAFE stands for *synthetic agreement for forward exchange*. If an FRA is an off-balance-sheet forward-forward deposit, a SAFE is an off-balance-sheet forward-forward FX swap. This similarity in structure means that there are many parallels between FRAs and SAFEs, just as there are between forward-forward deposits and forward-forward FX swaps.

The first resemblance can be seen from the definition of a SAFE:

A SAFE is an agreement between two parties motivated by the wish either to hedge against or to speculate on a movement in future

- **interest rate differentials or**
- **FX swap spreads**

This is very similar to the definition of an FRA, except that SAFEs operate on interest rate *differentials* rather than on the absolute level of interest rates.

SAFEs were developed toward the end of the 1980s and, like FRAs, are traded as an OTC product. All the major currency pairs are available in standard maturities from 1 to 12 months; odd or broken dates are also obtainable on request. Being somewhat more specialised than FRAs, however, SAFEs are not offered by as wide a range of banks, and liquidity is therefore rather more restricted.

5.2 DEFINITIONS

The two parties to a SAFE agree to execute a notional forward-forward FX swap between a pair of currencies. One currency is defined as the *primary currency*, while the other is the *secondary currency*. These currencies will notionally first be exchanged on one date in the future, the *settlement date*, and notionally reexchanged back on the *maturity date*. Most SAFEs are structured so that the amounts of primary currency notionally exchanged on both dates is the same, although it is possible to work with two different notional principals.

The *buyer* of a SAFE is the one who notionally purchases the primary currency on the settlement date and sells it on the maturity date. The *seller* of the SAFE takes the opposite position. As with FRAs, the terms "buyer" and "seller" refer only to the direction of notional cash flows, not to which party initiates the deal.

The term "notional" features heavily in the above description because, as with FRAs, no exchanges of principal actually occur. When the two parties first agree to execute the SAFE, they agree to the exchange rates at which the notional deals will be executed. On the settlement date, one party pays the other a settlement sum calculated on the difference between the rates originally contracted and the rates eventually prevailing.

To recap:

Under a SAFE:

- **the parties agree to execute a notional forward-forward swap**
- **between the PRIMARY and SECONDARY currencies**
- **for specific principal amounts**
- **at particular spot and swap exchange rates**
- **for a particular pair of dates in the future**
- **the BUYER agrees initially to buy the primary currency**
- **the SELLER agrees initially to sell the primary currency**

5.3 TERMINOLOGY

The terms governing SAFEs are formally defined in the SAFEBBA document published by the British Bankers' Association, and it is not surprising to find many similarities between this and the FRABBA terms previously referred to. However, SAFEs are more complex than FRAs because there are two notional cash flows and two rates that have to be agreed, rather than the FRA's single notional cash flow and rate. Figure 5.4 depicts the important terms and will aid comprehension of the terminology involved.

The key terms are:[2]

---

[2] Here we use the same terms and symbols as in the SAFEBBA document. Later in this chapter we will develop a more consistent notation.

FIGURE 5.4
SAFE Terminology

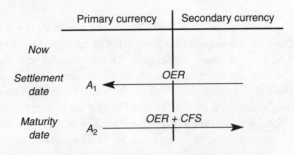

a) On the dealing date

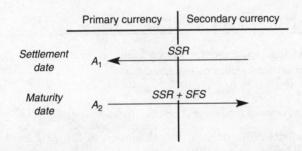

b) On the fixing date

A_1	the first contract amount
A_2	the second contract amount
OER	the outright exchange rate
CFS	the contract forward spread
SSR	the spot settlement rate
SFS	the settlement forward spread

The settlement and maturity dates follow the same conventions as with FRAs. For example, a 1×4 SAFE would have the settlement date one month after spot, the maturity date four months after spot, and the spot date two working days after the dealing date. Like FRAs, the eventual outcome of the SAFE would be determined on the fixing date, normally two days before the settlement date. Figure 4.2 in the previous chapter pictured the relationships of these dates.

On the dealing date, the parties would agree to the notional amounts of primary currency, A_1 and A_2, to be exchanged on the settlement and maturity dates respectively. Usually these amounts would be the same. They would also agree to the OER and the CFS. Together, these fix the outright exchange rates for the settlement and maturity dates and allow the notional amounts of the secondary currency to be calculated.

On the fixing date, the SSR and SFS are determined in the same way as LIBOR, by obtaining quotes selected from a list of reference banks and taking the average of all but the smallest and greatest figures. The SSR and SFS are published on the Reuters monitor[3] and are available for anyone to inspect.

The settlement sum under the SAFE is then calculated by comparing the exchange rates established at the outset for the settlement and maturity dates, namely, the OER and the CFS, with the rates eventually prevailing for the same dates, namely, the SSR and the SFS. The next section discusses exactly how the settlement sum is determined.

5.4 THE SETTLEMENT PROCESS

The term SAFE actually encompasses a family of synthetic FX agreements, of which the two most common are the

- ERA or *Exchange Rate Agreement.*
- FXA or *Forward Exchange Agreement.*

These products differ only in the calculation of the settlement sum, but this alters subtly the nature of the protection afforded.

The ERA covers only the difference between the swap points originally contracted (the CFS) and the swap points ultimately prevailing (the SFS). The settlement sum therefore depends on the evolution of only one variable, the swap points between settlement and maturity dates. As such, the ERA is closer to an FRA, whose value also depends on one variable, the interest rate between settlement and maturity dates.

The FXA, on the other hand, not only covers the swap points over the contract period but also any change in the absolute level of exchange rates. In other words, it not only covers any gap between the CFS and SFS but also any difference between the OER and the SSR.

As with FRAs, the settlement sum in each case compensates each party for the difference between the contract rate(s) originally agreed and the market rate(s) ultimately prevailing on the fixing date.

Which contract to use will depend upon the applications involved. Someone wishing to hedge a book of traditional FX swaps would prefer to use an FXA, because the payoff most accurately reflects the underlying exposure. Someone else exposed solely to the movement in interest rate differentials would prefer the ERA, which removes most of the influence of fluctuating exchange rates. Examples later in this chapter will illustrate the differences.

---

[3] Pages SAF1 to SAF5.

The SAFEBBA document defines the settlement sum calculations using the symbols used so far in this book. Here, we prefer to use a different and more consistent notation that will help to make clearer the distinction between ERAs and FXAs. Let's redefine the following terms:

A_S is the notional amount of primary currency exchanged on the settlement date

A_M is the notional amount of primary currency exchanged on the maturity date

F_{SC} is the outright forward rate for value on the settlement date as originally contracted

F_{SR} is the outright forward rate for value on the settlement date as determined on the fixing date

F_{MC} is the outright forward rate for value on the maturity date as originally contracted

F_{MR} is the outright forward rate for value on the maturity date as determined on the fixing date

W_C is the swap points over the contract period as originally contracted

W_R is the swap points over the contract period as determined on the fixing date

i is the interest rate in the secondary currency

D is the days in the contract period

B is the day-count convention prevailing in the secondary currency (360 or 365)

All the F terms are outright exchange rates. The first subscript denotes whether the rate applies to the settlement date (S) or the maturity date (M). The second subscript denotes whether the rate was originally contracted (C) on the dealing date or was the reference rate (R) determined on the fixing date. They are all true forward rates except for F_{SR}, which is actually the spot rate on the fixing date, though an outright rate nonetheless. The W terms refer to the swap points between the settlement date and the fixing date rather than to outright rates. Consequently, they only have one subscript, C or R, referring again to whether they are rates originally contracted or reference rates.

The settlement sum for an ERA is then

$$\text{Settlement sum }_{ERA} = A_M \times \left[\frac{W_C - W_R}{1 + \left(i \times \frac{D}{B} \right)} \right] \tag{5.1}$$

Note the similarities between this equation and equation 4.2 in the previous chapter, which defined the settlement sum for an FRA. In both cases, the difference between the contract and reference rates is multiplied by the notional principal involved and then discounted by a term adjusting for the fact that the settlement sum is paid on the settlement, rather than the maturity, date. In the case of the ERA, there is no need to multiply by the length of

the contract period, because the swap points already incorporate this factor.
For an FXA, the settlement sum is

$$\text{Settlement sum }_{FX} = A_M \times \left[\frac{F_{MC} - F_{MR}}{1 + \left(i \times \dfrac{D}{B} \right)} \right] - A_S \times [F_{SC} - F_{SR}] \qquad (5.2)$$

The distinguishing characteristic of the FXA is that it refers explicitly to
the outright exchange rates. The first term therefore replaces the difference
in swap points of equation 5.1 with the difference in outright exchange rates
at the maturity date, while the second term allows for the difference in
exchange rates on the settlement date. There is no need to discount the
second term, because it already refers to the settlement date.

For both ERAs and FXAs, although the notional amounts are defined in
terms of the primary currency, the settlement sums are defined in terms of
the secondary currency. This follows the normal convention in the spot
market. For example, a trader buying and selling equal amounts of dollars
against D-marks will be trading dollars (the primary currency) but realise
the profit or loss in D-marks (the secondary currency).

As with FRAs, the settlement sum formulae are defined to indicate the
value of the SAFE to the buyer, who is said to be "long" the SAFE. A positive outcome therefore implies a payment from seller to buyer, while a
negative outcome would imply payment by buyer to seller.

For those who prefer the SAFEBBA terms, the principal equivalents are

$$
\begin{array}{ll}
W_C = CFS & W_R = SFS \\
F_{SC} = OER & F_{SR} = SSR \\
F_{MC} = OER + CFS & F_{MR} = SSR + SFS
\end{array}
$$

5.5 PRICING SAFEs

This section explains how SAFEs are priced and demonstrates the relationships between SAFE prices, swap points, and the spot exchange rate.
Readers who wish to avoid the algebra can turn to Sections 5.6 and 5.7,
which discuss market conventions and provide a fully worked example of
SAFEs in action.

The easiest way to think about pricing a SAFE is to reason that the fair
price should be set so that the settlement sum is expected to be zero. Any
price different from this will give a positive or negative expected value,
thereby giving an unfair advantage to one side or the other in the deal.

Let's start with the ERA first. The settlement sum defined in equation 5.1
depends principally upon the difference between the swap points originally
contracted (W_C) and the swap points prevailing on the fixing date (W_R).
Pricing an ERA implies setting W_C on the dealing date such that the settlement sum is expected to be zero. We can represent this condition thus:

$$E(\text{settlement sum}) = 0 \implies W_C = E(W_R) \qquad (5.3)$$

where

$E(.)$ is the expectation operator.

This means that the ERA price on the dealing date should be equal to the *expected swap points* on the fixing date. We know from equation 3.2 that swap points are determined by three variables: the spot rate (S), the interest rate in the quoted currency (i_q), and the interest rate in the base currency (i_b). To obtain the expected swap points on a future date, we must substitute expectations for these three key variables. These expectations are nothing other than the forward rates, as we established in Chapter 3.

Rewriting equation 3.2, we get

$$ERA = F_S \times \left[\frac{1 + \left(i_{F2} \times \dfrac{DAYS}{BASIS_2}\right)}{1 + \left(i_{F1} \times \dfrac{DAYS}{BASIS_1}\right)} - 1 \right] \tag{5.4}$$

where

ERA is the fair price for the ERA
F_S is the forward rate for value on the settlement date
i_{F1} is the primary currency FRA rate for the ERA period
i_{F2} is the secondary currency FRA rate for the ERA period
$DAYS$ is the number of days in the contract period
$BASIS_1$ is the day-count convention for the primary currency (360 or 365)
$BASIS_2$ is the day-count convention for the secondary currency (360 or 365)

and all interest rates are quoted as decimal fractions.

We can use a number of the relationships determined earlier to simplify this expression. First, we can rearrange equation 4.5 in the previous chapter to obtain expressions for the fair FRA rates:

$$i_{F1} = \frac{1}{t_F}\left[\frac{1 + i_{L1}t_L}{1 + i_{S1}t_S} - 1\right] \quad and \quad i_{F2} = \frac{1}{t_F}\left[\frac{1 + i_{L2}t_L}{1 + i_{S2}t_S} - 1\right] \tag{5.5}$$

where

i_{S1}, i_{S2} are the cash market interest rates to the settlement date for primary and secondary currencies
i_{L1}, i_{L2} are the cash market interest rates to the maturity date for primary and secondary currencies
t_S is the time from spot date to the settlement date
t_L is the time from spot date to the maturity date
t_F is the length of the contract period

The t terms are calculated by dividing the number of days in the relevant period by the appropriate day-count convention (360 or 365).

Next, we can rewrite equation 3.1 to obtain a fair expression for the forward rate at the settlement date F_S:

$$F_S = S \left[\frac{1 + i_{S2}t_S}{1 + i_{S1}t_S} \right] \tag{5.6}$$

where

S is the current spot rate.

By combining equations 5.4, 5.5, and 5.6, we obtain

$$ERA = S \left[\frac{1 + i_{L2}t_L}{1 + i_{L1}t_L} - \frac{1 + i_{S2}t_S}{1 + i_{S1}t_S} \right] \tag{5.7}$$

Now we can use equation 3.2 to obtain fair expressions for the cash market swap points for the settlement and maturity dates:

$$W_L = S \left[\frac{1 + i_{L2}t_L}{1 + i_{L1}t_L} - 1 \right] \text{ and } W_S = S \left[\frac{1 + i_{S2}t_S}{1 + i_{S1}t_S} - 1 \right] \tag{5.8}$$

where

W_S is the swap points to the settlement date
W_L is the swap points to the maturity date

and hence

$$(W_L - W_S) = S \left[\frac{1 + i_{L2}t_L}{1 + i_{L1}t_L} - \frac{1 + i_{S2}t_S}{1 + i_{S1}t_S} \right] \tag{5.9}$$

and therefore

$$ERA = W_L - W_S \tag{5.10}$$

Thus the ERA price should simply be the difference between the swap points for the settlement and maturity dates. This should not come altogether as a surprise, since the SAFE was originally defined as an off-balance-sheet forward-forward swap.

Equations 5.4 and 5.10 should normally yield identical answers in an efficient market, and this is normally the case. If there were any discrepancies, SAFEs would normally be priced more reliably from FRA rates using equation 5.4 rather than from the swap rates themselves. When a range of related derivatives is available, it is more efficient to hedge one derivative with another derivative, and therefore it is sensible to price the derivatives accordingly.

We have yet to derive an expression for the price of FXAs, but fortunately nearly all the work has now been done. Equation 5.2 defined the settlement sum for an FXA, and a fair price for the FXA will only be obtained if the expected value of the settlement sum is zero, just as with the ERA. This implies that

$$F_{MC} = E(F_{MR}) \text{ and } F_{SC} = E(F_{SR}) \tag{5.11}$$

The expected spot rate for the settlement date $E(F_{SR})$ is simply the current spot rate plus the forward points to the settlement date. Similarly, the expected forward rate for the maturity date is the current spot rate plus the forward points to the maturity date. An FXA is therefore priced fairly when:

$$F_{SC} = S + W_S \text{ and } F_{MC} = S + W_L \tag{5.12}$$

The OER would therefore be $S + W_S$ and the CFS would be $(W_L - W_S)$. An FXA involves fixing two prices, much in the same way as pricing a traditional FX swap involves fixing both the swap points and the spot rate. However, the more important of these two prices—the contract forward spread— is simply the difference between the swap points at the settlement and maturity dates, just like the ERA.

Now that we have seen how SAFEs are priced, we can move on to discuss some of the practical issues arising out of their use.

5.6 MARKET CONVENTIONS IN QUOTING SAFEs

SAFEs are quoted in a way similar to quotes for other financial products, and market makers will normally indicate both a bid and an offer price when asked to quote. A typical response to a request to quote the 1 × 4 month $/DEM ERA might be "158/162." What is important to note about this quotation is that the figures go *offer/bid*, not the other way round. The market maker in this illustration is offering to sell a 1 × 4 ERA at 158 points, or to buy it at 162 points. It may seem that the normal "buy low, sell high" convention is reversed, and that is indeed the case.

The explanation for this can be found in the definition of the SAFE itself and in the formulae for calculating the settlement sum. In each of the formulae there is a key term of the form $(X_C - X_R)$, where the Xs may be swap points or outright rates, depending upon whether we are using an ERA or an FXA. The settlement sum is defined so that a positive figure implies a profit for the buyer. The first term is the contracted rate, which is fixed on the dealing date. Someone buying a SAFE at a particular price X_C then hopes that SAFE rates will *fall*, so that $X_R < X_C$, and the settlement sum will then be positive. In other words, to profit from a SAFE one must follow a "buy high, sell low" strategy.

Contrast all this with the definition of an FRA for which the settlement sum involves a term $(i_R - i_C)$. In this case, an FRA buyer fixing the price at i_C subsequently wants rates to rise so that $i_R > i_C$. This is the usual "buy low, sell high" rule.

Had SAFEs been defined the other way around, namely, that buying a SAFE involved buying the primary currency at the maturity date and not the settlement date, the settlement sum formulae could be reversed, and SAFEs would follow more intuitive lines. However, we must accept the world as it is.

The following section provides an example of ERAs and FXAs in use, which may help to clarify this apparent anomaly. As we will see, an investor anticipating swap points increasing would *sell* a SAFE and would realise a profit if the swap points were eventually higher than at the outset.

5.7 EXAMPLE OF USING A SAFE

SAFEs are closely related to forward-forward FX swaps, so our example here will use such a swap as a comparison. FXAs and ERAs are themselves very closely related—the swap points component of their prices being identical—but they differ in the calculation of their settlement sums when the *spot* exchange rate moves. We will therefore compare the different instruments under two alternative scenarios, one where spot rates remain static, the other where the spot rate moves substantially.

First, we set out the initial market rates:

	Spot	1 Month	4 Months	1×4 Months
$/DEM FX rates	1.8000	53/56	212/215	158/162
U.S. interest rates		6%	6¼%	6.30%
DEM interest rates		9⅝%	9⅞%	9.88%

and then the rates prevailing one month later under each scenario:

	Scenario A		Scenario B	
	Spot	3 Months	Spot	3 Months
$/DEM FX rates	1.8000	176/179	1.7000	166/169
U.S. interest rates		6%		6%
DEM interest rates		10%		10%

Interest rates in Scenario B are identical to those in Scenario A; only the spot exchange rate differs.

Let's suppose that an investor observes that the gap between 1×4 month dollar and D-mark forward interest rates is currently 3.58% but anticipates correctly that this gap will widen. The investor is therefore considering the following three strategies:

1. Sell and buy dollars against D-marks in the 1×4 month forward-for ward swap.
2. Sell the 1×4 month FXA.
3. Sell the 1×4 month ERA.

In selling and buying the 1×4 swap, the investor has bought forward dollars at a net premium of 162 points, which is the difference between the 53 points bid for the one-month component and the 215 points offered for the four-month component. If the interest rates widen, so will the premium on the forward dollar, and the investor would then be able to sell these forward dollars at a higher premium and hence a higher price.

In both scenarios, the interest rate gap does indeed widen after one month. The three-month swap points bid become 176 points under scenario A (a gain of 14 points) and 166 points under scenario B (a gain of 4 points). An assessment of the profits based simply on the change in points over the month therefore suggests profits of DEM 1,400 and DEM 400, respectively.

Figure 5.5 shows the cash flows, deals, and profits accruing for the forward-forward swap under each scenario.

This diagram also calculates the true profits using present value methods, which account properly for the time value of money. Under Scenario A, the final profits are DEM 1,495 (compared to DEM 1,400) and are DEM 2,959 under Scenario B (compared with just DEM 400).

The big difference under the second scenario arises directly from the change in the spot FX rate. The spot/three-month swap used to close out the original forward-forward deal after one month involves a commitment to buy dollars spot and sell them three months forward. As the dollar has fallen substantially, the D-marks received in three months will be considerably fewer than those sold under the original forward-forward deal. Figure 5.5 shows the shortfall of DEM 104,900 almost wiping out the surplus on the spot account of DEM 105,300 and leaving an apparent profit of just DEM 400. However, the impact of the DEM 104,900 shortfall is reduced because it occurs in the future and can be discounted. Alternatively, one could consider investing the DEM 105,300 surplus to earn interest over the three-month period before it is needed to offset the DEM 104,900 shortfall. Either way, the true profit increases to DEM 2,959 when this timing gap is taken into account.

FIGURE 5–5
Evaluation of Forward-Forward Swap

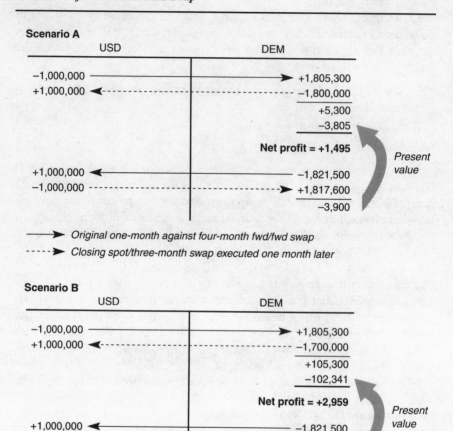

Scenario A

Original one-month against four-month fwd/fwd swap
Closing spot/three-month swap executed one month later

Scenario B

Original one-month against four-month fwd/fwd swap
Closing spot/three-month swap executed one month later

Using the nomenclature of equations 5.1 and 5.2, we can extract the following data from the market rates supplied at the outset:

A_s	=	1,000,000	A_m	=	1,000,000
F_{sc}	=	1.8053 (the OER)			
F_{mc}	=	1.8215	D	=	90
W_c	=	0.0162 (the CFS)	B	=	360

Then, the rates prevailing under each scenario are

	Scenario A			Scenario B	
F_{sr}	=	1.8000 (the SSR)	F_{sr}	=	1.7000 (the SSR)
F_{mr}	=	1.8176	F_{mr}	=	1.7166
W_r	=	0.0176 (the SFS)	W_r	=	0.0166 (the SFS)
i	=	0.10	i	=	0.10

By inserting these values into the formulae given by equations 5.1 and 5.2, we obtain the following results for the settlement sums (all in D-marks):

	Scenario A		Scenario B	
FXA	−1,495.12	FXA	−2,958.54
ERA	−1,365.85	ERA	−390.24

In all cases here, the negative settlement sums imply a payment from buyer to seller. As the investor had sold the SAFE, these figures actually represent profits.

The FXA results under both scenarios are precisely the same as those earned by the conventional cash market forward-forward swap, which it is designed to replicate exactly. The profits not only take into account the movement in swap points caused by the change in interest rates, they also adjust for the movement in the spot exchange rate and the resultant effect on the settlement and maturity date cash flows. When the dollar weakens in Scenario B, the profits for the forward-forward and the FXA both double as a result of the residual currency exposure inherent in these instruments.

The ERA profits are those arising from the change in swap points, pure and simple. Movements in the spot rate have a much smaller effect on the results because of the minor influence of the spot rate on swap points. In the above example, a 5.6% decrease in the spot $/DEM rate from 1.8000 to 1.7000 under Scenario B has a proportional effect on the swap points, which also decrease by 5.6% from 176 to 166. The ERA results are therefore the same as the DEM 1400 and DEM 400 profits calculated earlier from the straightforward change in swap points but are discounted by the 10% D-mark interest rates over the three-month contract period.

To summarise these results: FXAs and ERAs give similar results when there is no change in the spot exchange rate, but if spot rates do move, the FXA will take the spot FX exposure into account, replicating as it does the conventional cash market forward-forward FX swap.

5.8 HEDGING SAFEs AGAINST MOVEMENTS IN SPOT RATES

In some applications, the sensitivity of a SAFE to movements in spot rates may be just what is required. This would be true, for example, if a bank were using FXAs to hedge its book of FX swaps. In other applications, the effect of fluctuations in spot rates may be undesirable. In these latter circumstances, there is a way to hedge the spot rate exposure.

Consider a traditional FX swap deal where an amount (A) of the primary currency is sold spot and bought forward against the secondary currency. By discounting the future leg of the swap back to the spot date and using the formula for swap points derived in equation 3.2, it is easy to show that the net present value of the primary currency side of the swap is

$$NPV_1 = -\frac{Ai_1t}{1 + i_1t} \tag{5.13}$$

and that of the secondary currency is

$$NPV_2 = S\left[\frac{Ai_1t}{1 + i_1t}\right] \tag{5.14}$$

where

S is the spot FX rate
A is the amount of primary currency sold and bought
i_1 is the interest rate in the primary currency
t is the time to maturity

and all interest rates are quoted as decimal fractions and all times as fractions of a year.

To hedge a traditional FX swap against all movements in the spot rate, it is therefore only necessary to execute a spot FX deal in the amount NPV1 of the primary currency, in the direction *opposite* to the spot leg of the swap. Thus

$$H_{SWAP} = \frac{Ai_1t}{1 + i_1t} \tag{5.15}$$

where

H_{SWAP} is the size of the spot deal for hedging a swap.

Extending this example, a forward-forward swap, and therefore an FXA, can also be hedged by using a single spot deal:

$$H_{FWD-FWD} = H_{FXA} = A\left[\frac{i_{L1}t_L}{1 + i_{L1}t_L} - \frac{i_{S1}t_S}{1 + i_{S1}t_S}\right] = \frac{Ai_{F1}t_F}{1 + i_{L1}t_L} \tag{5.16}$$

where

$H_{FWD-FWD}$ is the size of the spot deal for hedging a forward-forward swap
H_{FXA} is the size of the spot deal for hedging an FXA

and the remaining symbols are as defined earlier.

Equation 5.16 gives the size of the spot deal, which must be executed in the opposite direction to that of the FXA.

In the case of the previous example, the size of the spot hedge would therefore have involved buying $15,433 against DEM 27,779. If the dollar subsequently fell from 1.8000 to 1.7000, the spot hedge would lose DEM 1,543. This would bring the net profit of the FXA under Scenario B down to DEM 1,415—extremely close to the profit of DEM 1,495 earned under Scenario A, when there was no change in the spot rate.[4]

As there is no exact parallel in the cash market for an ERA, we must use a different technique in order to obtain the size of the spot hedge. The perfect hedge will be one that counteracts the sensitivity of the settlement sum to movements in the spot rate. We therefore need an expression for

$$\frac{\partial settlement\ sum\ _{ERA}}{\partial S}$$

If we take equation 5.1, which defines the ERA settlement sum, substitute the normal formula for swap points as defined in equation 3.2, and take the partial derivative with respect to the spot rate, we obtain

$$H_{ERA} = A\left[\frac{1 + i_{S2}t_S}{1 + i_{S1}t_S}\right]\left[\frac{1}{1 + i_{F2}t_F} - \frac{1}{1 + i_{F1}t_F}\right] \qquad (5.17)$$

where

H_{ERA} is the size of the spot deal for hedging an ERA

and the remaining symbols are as defined earlier.

Equation 5.17 also defines the size of the hedge with the direction *opposite* in sign to that of the ERA. Unlike equation 5.16, however, it is possible for H_{ERA} to be negative if $i_{F1} < i_{F2}$; when this occurs, the spot hedge will be in the *same* direction as that of the ERA.

When we apply the figures from the example of the previous section, we find that H_{ERA} is –$8,618, a negative quantity. This means that the spot hedge for the ERA would require the *sale* of $8,618 against a purchase of DEM 15,513. Note that this hedge is in the opposite direction to the spot hedge for the FXA. This time, the movement in spot from 1.8000 to 1.7000 in Scenario B would result in the hedge gaining DEM 862,

---

[4] The small discrepancy arises because the actual three-month interest rate in dollars turned out to be 6%, not the 6.30% implied by the 1 × 4 FRA and used in calculating the size of the hedge.

boosting the result to DEM 1,252, just a little short of the profit under Scenario A of DEM 1,366.[5]

5.9 CAPITAL ADEQUACY REQUIREMENTS FOR FRAs AND SAFEs

The BIS capital adequacy rules class both FRAs and SAFEs as interest-rate products rather than as currency products.[6] The capital adequacy requirements for derivative products in general, and for interest rate products in particular, are far smaller than their counterparts in the cash markets.

Capital adequacy requirements in general stipulate that a bank's capital base should exceed 8% of *weighted risk assets* (WRA). WRA includes all assets on a bank's balance sheet, each asset group being given a weighting according to the level of perceived risk. For example, T-bills are given a 10% weighting, while commercial loans are weighted in full with 100%. Products off the balance sheet, such as derivatives, are assigned a *credit equivalent* amount so that they can be included with the other balance sheet items, and credit equivalents are given either a 20% or a 50% weighting, depending on the counterparty. Equation 5.18 summarises these rules symbolically:

$$CAPREQ = 8\% \times WRA$$
$$WRA = 20\% \times CREDEQ \quad (for\ most\ banks) \qquad (5.18)$$
$$WRA = 50\% \times CREDEQ \quad (for\ other\ counterparties)$$

where

$CAPREQ$	is the actual amount of capital required against a position in FRAs and SAFEs
WRA	is the weighted risk assets
$CREDEQ$	is the credit equivalent of the derivatives position

Credit equivalents are designed to measure the possible adverse impact of a default on a derivatives position. As derivatives do not involve flows of principal, the sole source of credit risk is nonpayment of the settlement sum. A bank due to receive payment of the settlement sum could perhaps discover that the counterparty has become insolvent and can no longer honour his obligations, but the worst that can ever happen is loss of the potential settlement sum. The principal is never at risk.

---

[5] Again, the discrepancy arises from the fact that three-month rates turned out to be 6% and 10%, respectively, rather than the 6.30% and 9.88% implied by the FRA prices. Had the hedge been calculated knowing what interest rates would actually have prevailed, the spot deal would have been $9,641, and the hedge would have brought the Scenario B profits to within $10 of the Scenario A result.

[6] This classification for SAFEs applies to all ERAs and to FXAs where the notional principals A_S and A_M are within 10% of each other.

Let's see if we can quantify the size of the potential loss and hence determine an appropriate measure for the credit equivalent.

If a default is discovered on the settlement date itself, there is no problem in quantifying the potential loss; it is simply the settlement sum. Prior to the settlement date, the potential loss can be quantified by a process called *marking-to-market*. This process involves valuing the deal at current market rates. In the case of FRAs and SAFEs, the settlement sum formulae are used to obtain a valuation, but the relevant forward rates for the settlement date are inserted instead of the reference rates, and the settlement sum thus calculated must be discounted back from the settlement date to give today's valuation. There are two broad outcomes to this marking-to-market process. The valuation can either turn out positive or negative.

If the mark-to-market valuation is positive, the profits forgone in the event of a default would represent a loss to the bank. This loss would be both the manifestation and quantification of the credit risk. The credit equivalent should therefore be equal to this valuation.

If, on the other hand, the derivative had been losing money, the default could potentially be beneficial to the bank. In this case, it would be imprudent for the bank simply to cancel the deal and recoup the losses, as the counterparty's successors might still insist that the deal be honoured. However, having already marked the position to market and accounted for the potential loss on the deal, there is no further loss potential to the bank.

We can therefore define one component of the credit equivalent, the *replacement cost*:

$$REPCOST = \max(0, MARKMKT) \tag{5.19}$$

where

REPCOST	is the replacement cost of the position
MARKMKT	is the mark-to-market valuation of the derivative.

The replacement cost measures the potential loss today, right now, but what about tomorrow? In forming the capital adequacy rules, the BIS decided to add a second component to reflect the additional riskiness of longer-dated interest rate derivatives. For FRAs and SAFEs with more than one year to maturity, the *add-on* is

$$ADDON = 0.5\% \times A \tag{5.20}$$

where

ADDON	is the additional loss potential
A	is the notional principal.

The credit equivalent then is the sum of the replacement cost and the add-on:

$$CREDEQ = REPCOST + ADDON \tag{5.21}$$

To illustrate these relationships, Table 5.1 gives some examples of FRAs and SAFEs and the resultant capital requirements that would be imposed on a non-bank counterparty in each case:

TABLE 5–1
Capital Requirements for FRAs and SAFEs

Type	Tenor	Notional Principal	Mark-to-Market Profits / Losses	Replacement Cost	Add-On	Credit Equivalent	Capital Requirement
FRA	1 × 4	$ 1m	$ 500	$ 500	0	$ 500	$ 20
SAFE	3 × 6	10m	–2,000	0	0	0	0
FRA	12 × 18	5m	1,000	1,000	25,000	26,000	1,040

Note that, apart from the longer-dated FRA, the capital requirements are minuscule. Even with the $25,000 add-on for the last FRA, the total capital requirement is one four-hundredth the amount that would have been required for a cash deposit of $5 million.

Although these calculations satisfy the regulatory requirements, many banks perform additional "what if . . . ?" analyses to determine what the worst-case credit exposure might be under a range of different rate scenarios.

5.10 BENEFITS THROUGH FRAs AND SAFEs

For anyone requiring an instrument that affords protection against movements in interest rates, the FRA provides an effective answer. For someone who wants or needs an instrument that responds to interest rate differentials rather than to the absolute level of interest rates, the SAFE is an efficient tool. As derivative products, FRAs and SAFEs have vastly reduced credit risk and consequently impose less demanding capital adequacy requirements. Lower credit risk benefits all users directly. More lenient capital requirements affect only banks directly, but as these lessen the costs incurred by banks in running portfolios of FRAs and SAFEs, the savings can be passed on to banks' clients, thereby benefitting everyone.

Consider the forward-forward FX swap in the cash market, which involves an exchange of principals on two separate dates and the attendant settlement risks that these flows of principal entail. In addition, the exposure on a forward-forward lasts all the way until the final maturity date.

Contrast these problems with the advantages of SAFEs. With a SAFE there are, of course, no exchanges of principal. This means that credit risk is limited only to the settlement sum, rather than to the notional principal, and is therefore marginal. Moreover, all outstanding obligations under SAFEs are eliminated on the settlement rather than the maturity date, reducing the period over which the risk exposure runs. With only one payment transaction to settle, administrative costs are also reduced.

Of course, these considerations apply equally to FRAs. Moreover, as both FRAs and SAFEs are OTC products, every feature of the instrument can be negotiated to suit a client's particular needs. It is usually possible to obtain a quotation for odd dates, odd amounts, odd periods, and even for currencies where liquidity is more restricted. This is in marked contrast to futures contracts, introduced in the next chapter, where every aspect of the deal is standardised, and where there is no room for negotiation. Despite this apparent lack of flexibility, futures contracts create an important foundation on which other financial engineering instruments can be built and are therefore vitally important for the functioning of the financial markets, as we shall now see.

Chapter Six

Financial Futures

Futures contracts and futures exchanges have been in operation since the middle of the nineteenth century, when the Chicago Board of Trade first started to offer "to arrive" and "time" contracts on agricultural products. Surprisingly, more than 100 years were to pass before *financial futures* contracts were conceived in the early 1970s. Since then, financial futures have become a vital mainstay for the other financial markets.

Financial futures contracts are used directly by those exposed to risk and, more significantly, by financial institutions needing to hedge their books of OTC products. Trading in financial futures has become so significant that in a number of important markets the volume of futures traded exceeds that in the original market upon which the contract was based. For example, the value of the shares represented by trading in the S&P stock-index futures each day normally exceeds that of the actual shares traded on the New York Stock Exchange.

This chapter introduces financial futures and explains some of the terminology and procedures unique to the futures markets. Chapters Seven and Eight then go on to explore specific types of futures contract in more detail.

6.1 A BRIEF HISTORY OF FUTURES MARKETS

It was the collapse of the fixed-exchange-rate regime in the early 1970s that provided the initial impetus for financial futures. Figure 1.1 showed the $/DEM exchange rate in the period 1963 to 1992 and demonstrated the dramatic change once the D-mark finally floated in 1971. Figure 6.1 illustrates this sharp increase in risk by showing annual volatility over the same period.[1]

Annual volatility averaged only 0.4% over the five-year period from 1963 to 1967 but increased sevenfold to 2.8% over the next five years, 1968 to 1972. Then, in every subsequent five-year period, annual volatility averaged around 9%, a further increase of between three and four times.

Officials at the Chicago Mercantile Exchange (CME)—then and now one of the largest futures exchanges in the world—correctly anticipated that demand for an efficient way to hedge financial risk would grow. Research

---

[1] The concept of volatility is explained in Section 10.9 of Chapter Ten.

FIGURE 6.1
Annual Volatility of $/DEM Exchange Rate 1963–1992

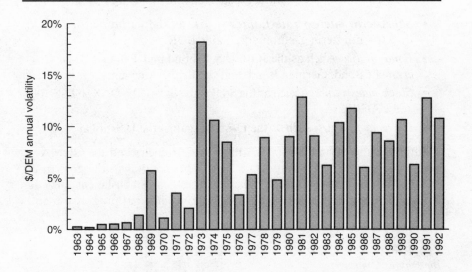

was undertaken to determine the viability of trading contracts based on financial instruments rather than on physical commodities. This project culminated with the establishment of the International Monetary Market (IMM) of the CME and the launch in 1972 of futures contracts based on foreign currencies.

The new regime of floating exchange rates was to lead to increased volatility in interest rates, both short-term and long-term. In 1975, the first interest-rate futures contract—based on the U.S. Government National Mortgage Association (GNMA) securities—was launched by the 'other' Chicago futures exchange, the Chicago Board of Trade (CBOT).

The 1980s saw the expansion of futures trading to other countries. The London International Financial Futures Exchange (LIFFE) opened its doors in 1982 with a range of contracts, some based on the dollar, some on the pound sterling. LIFFE has since grown to be the world's third-largest futures exchange, ranking behind the CME and the CBOT. Although September 16, 1992—when the United Kingdom withdrew from the Exchange Rate Mechanism (ERM)—was dubbed "Black Wednesday" by some observers, it was the day when the volume of futures contracts traded on LIFFE exceeded that at either of the two Chicago exchanges.

The Marché A Terme des Instruments Financiers (MATIF) started futures trading in Paris in 1986, and almost every year since has witnessed the opening of new exchanges: SOFFEX in Switzerland (1988), the IFOX in Dublin (1989), the DTB in Germany (1990), the ÖTB in Austria (1991), and the MIF in Italy (1992).

Table 6.1 lists those futures contracts in which the heaviest trading currently takes place and provides some indication of the relative trading volumes in U.S. dollar equivalents. The contracts listed fall into four categories:

- *Short-term interest rate futures*—such as the eurodollar, euroyen, three-month sterling, euromark, and PIBOR.
- *Bond futures*—such as the JGB, U.S. T-bond and T-note, French Government Bond, German Bund, and the British long gilt.
- *Stock-index futures*—such as the S&P 500, Nikkei 225, DAX, FTSE 100, and CAC 40.
- *Currency futures*—such as the D-mark against the U.S. dollar.

Although the earliest contracts—those on currencies and the GNMA— have since diminished in importance or been withdrawn, the growth in financial futures has continued unabated since their establishment some 20 years ago. Competition between exchanges has ensured progression and

TABLE 6.1
Top Futures Contracts

Contract	Exchange	Open Interest[1]	Monthly Volume[2] (contracts)	Monthly Volume[3] ($billion equivalent)
Eurodollar	CME	1,325,487	5,044,256	5,044
Euroyen	TIFFE	439,263	1,247,314	1,122
10-yr. JGB	TSE	132,153	989,011	890
3-mo. sterling	LIFFE	211,626	941,361	724
Euromark	LIFFE	369,878	1,014,453	628
30-yr. U.S. T-bond	CBOT	304,740	5,833,658	583
PIBOR	MATIF	145,884	535,898	492
10yr. Notionnel	MATIF	231,188	2,583,570	237
S&P 500	CME	157,251	1,034,513	232
German Bund	LIFFE	139,443	1,133,710	176
Nikkei 225	Osaka	148,976	949,622	172
10-yr U.S. T-note	CBOT	176,644	934,828	93
D-mark	CME	132,558	966,098	75
Long gilt	LIFFE	53,752	733,720	56
DAX	DTB	51,088	272,588	29
FTSE 100	LIFFE	43,988	218,219	24
CAC 40	MATIF	41,101	300,123	22

[1]At end of December 1992.
[2]Average of monthly figures January–December 1992.
[3]Based on market rates April 19, 1993.
Source: Adapted from data in *Futures and Options World* (February 1993).

innovation, both in the variety of contracts offered and in the systems used for futures trading. One of the latest developments, screen trading, promises to challenge the traditional way in which futures contracts are traded and is discussed in Section 6.5.

6.2 WHAT IS A FINANCIAL FUTURE?

The standard textbook definition goes something like this:

A futures contract is:

- a legally binding agreement
- to take or make delivery
- of a given quantity and quality of a commodity
- at an agreed price
- on a specific date or dates in the future.

However, there is a much simpler way to define the essence of a futures contract:

A futures contract fixes the price and

conditions

NOW

for a transaction that will take place in the

FUTURE

Before the advent of financial futures, the commodities that were the subjects of futures contracts included agricultural products, such as sugar, soybeans, and live cattle, and physical commodities, such as crude oil, aluminium, and gold. A financial future is just like any other futures contract, except that the "commodity" is a financial instrument. In some cases the instrument is tangible, like a treasury bond or foreign currency. In other cases, the instrument is intangible, like a stock index or an interest rate. Section 6.8 explains what happens on the expiry date of a futures contract when the underlying instrument is intangible and cannot actually be delivered.

In the jargon of the futures trading, the markets in which the underlying commodities are traded are called the *cash markets*, because cash normally changes hands when the commodities are bought and sold. In the wider context, the term "cash markets" includes all the markets other than the derivatives markets.

6.3 TRADING FEATURES

The film *Trading Places* has probably done much to create the image of futures markets in the popular mind. While life on the floor of a futures exchange may not always be as frenzied as Eddie Murphy and Dan Aykroyd would have us believe, the film does focus attention on the *futures pit* where all the action takes place.

Unlike the OTC market, where trading takes place in hundreds of bank dealing rooms around the world, the futures pit concentrates trading in a single crowded location. Orders to buy and sell futures contracts may originate from anywhere in the world, but they all converge on one spot, the pit itself, where all such trades actually take place.

Someone who wishes to buy (or sell) a futures contract would contact his broker, perhaps a bank, who acts as his agent. If the bank is a member of the relevant futures exchange, the order will be transmitted directly to their desk or booth situated just outside the trading pits. If the bank is not a member, the order will be transmitted to the desk of an organisation that is a member. From the member's desk, a messenger or "runner" takes the order to a *floor broker* operating within the futures pit itself. This process is illustrated in Figure 6.2.

Only members of futures exchanges are allowed to execute orders within the trading pits. In many cases, these members are acting merely as brokers, executing orders on behalf of others. Some members, however, act as principals and trade on their own behalf. These latter members, often called *locals*, provide liquidity to the market and provide depth when trading would otherwise be quiet.

Locals make their money by attempting to buy low and sell high but are sometimes given different names, depending upon their time horizon. *Scalpers* run a position for just a few seconds or minutes and operate with small profit margins but on high volumes. *Day traders* close out their positions at the end of each day, while *position traders* may maintain a position for days or even weeks. In these latter cases, the emphasis on generating profits is switched from volume to margins; day and position traders aim to close out their position with a substantial difference between buying and selling price but operate with a lower turnover than the scalper.

The floor broker carrying the original customer order attempts to execute the transaction in the pit. This might be done with another floor broker representing a customer who wishes to trade in the opposite direction. Alternatively, one of the locals might be willing to take the opposite side. Once the trade is executed, the details are noted by both parties and, in the case of orders originating from outside the exchange, transmitted back to the customer who initiated the order.

FIGURE 6.2
Order Execution Process

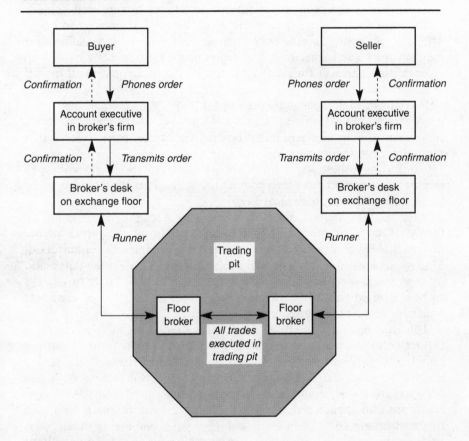

Some may think this whole process is convoluted and time-consuming. Orders received in the bank's dealing room must be transmitted to their desk near the pit and then via a runner to the floor broker, who finally executes the trade. Then the trade confirmation must follow the reverse route. In practice, however, the whole process normally takes place in less than a minute.

What gives the futures pit a unique edge is the *transparency* achieved through the openness of the procedures followed in the trading pit. Everything is done in full public view and is subject to careful scrutiny by the exchange authorities. Traders must call out or signal by hand the prices at which they are prepared to deal. Only the highest bid and lowest offer are then allowed to prevail; traders with other prices must remain silent. All trades must be executed within the pit,[2] in public, out loud. The market

---

[2] There is an important exception to this rule involving *Exchange for Physicals* (EFP) transactions in which two parties agree on nonstandard terms for the physical delivery of the underlying commodity in exchange for liquidating two opposing futures positions. EFP trades can be executed outside the trading pit.

forces of supply and demand—the relative volume of buyers and sellers—are there for all to see.

These procedures, unique to futures exchanges, ensure that spreads between bid and offer are remarkably small, usually just one or two *ticks*.[3] They also guarantee that the price obtained is the very best available at the moment the trade is executed. The requirement for openness, backed up through surveillance by the exchange authorities, helps to prevent off-market or insider deals.

In contrast, while a customer executing a trade with a bank normally will get a very good deal, there is no way of knowing whether another bank somewhere else in the world might be offering a better price. Information services such as the Reuters Monitor help to disseminate price information very quickly, but these screen prices are indicative only. Someone wishing to execute a transaction must then contact the bank to get the latest quote, by which time prices may have moved on.

What the OTC market can offer is flexibility. Almost every aspect of an OTC deal can be negotiated, and the terms varied to suit the parties' particular needs. By contrast, futures contracts are completely standardised. Matters such as the underlying financial instrument, delivery dates, and other technical specifications are all predefined. This leaves only two details to be settled when a futures trade takes place: the number of contracts bought or sold and the price.

This standardisation within the futures market means that users of futures contracts may have to accept a compromise: the futures contract they buy or sell may not match their precise needs. However, funneling trades from a broad cross-section of users down to a small number of futures contracts creates tremendous liquidity. For example, more than 300,000 contracts are traded each day in the CBOT T-bond future, the most liquid financial futures contract in the world. Moreover, simplifying the negotiations to the fixing just of size and price makes for speed. The resultant volume of trading and frequency of execution are fundamental to the success of futures markets.

6.4 BUYING AND SELLING

In the cash markets, there is sometimes a procedural distinction between the act of buying and the act of selling. This is particularly true when the commodity is a security, such as a bond or a share, and market rules impose restrictions on selling short, i.e., selling something that one does not currently own.

In the futures markets there is no such distinction. Buying and selling contracts are completely symmetrical transactions, and the conditions imposed on holders of long and short positions are identical. This is entirely

---

[3] A tick is the smallest difference between two adjacent prices.

appropriate, because a futures contract binds the parties to a transaction that will take place on a future date, not now. It is true that the party who is short futures is obligated to deliver the underlying commodity on the maturity date of the contract. However, while the short may not be in possession of the underlying asset right now, there is nothing preventing him from purchasing the commodity in the meantime, nor from reversing the futures contract before maturity.

6.5 PITS VERSUS SCREENS

Few deny the success of futures exchanges based on pit trading in a physical marketplace. Nonetheless, technology provides the financial markets with a modern alternative—screen trading—which can take one of two forms. The first alternative is where prices are broadcast using a service such as the Reuters Monitor, but where deals are actually executed by telephone and confirmed by telex. The more recent alternative is where price dissemination and the execution of trades both take place through the screen. Reuters Dealing 2000 and Quotron's FX Trader provide good examples.

Some markets, like the foreign exchange market, are completely dominated by screen trading, and have known nothing else for some 20 years. Other markets, like the stock markets, fall into both camps and feature physical trading floors—like the New York Stock Exchange—and screen-based systems like NASDAQ in the United States and SEAQ in the United Kingdom.

Until the mid-1980s, all futures exchanges were designed exclusively around physical trading floors and pit-based trading procedures. Even relatively new exchanges such as LIFFE and the MATIF followed the traditional model. However, most of the exchanges established more recently have decided to abandon the concept of the trading floor and have opted instead for a system based completely around the computer screen. SOFFEX and the DTB are two such examples, but there are now many more. The institutional problems of establishing a physical futures market with sufficient liquidity have biased the trend recently towards the screen-based infrastructure, particularly for smaller futures markets.

Some of the screen-based systems are computerised order-matching systems. Those willing to trade enter details of the numbers of contracts and the price at which they wish to deal. The computer constantly searches to see whether orders to buy can be matched against orders to sell and combines trades which pair up. Other systems attempt to mimic the trading pit as closely as possible and feature graphic representations of the trading pit and the traders within.

Although the world's largest futures markets—the CBOT, CME, LIFFE, and MATIF—have emphasised the value of retaining their trading pits, all are hedging their bets by adopting screen-based systems to extend their trading hours. The most prominent among these is GLOBEX, pioneered jointly by Reuters and the CME and adopted by the CBOT, MATIF, and a number of other exchanges. At the time of writing, LIFFE is using its own screen-based system, called APT. In each case, these are strictly for use outside normal trading hours and seek to extend market liquidity through longer trading hours. It will remain to be seen whether, in the fullness of time, the computer screen will supplant the trading floor.

6.6 THE CLEARING MECHANISM

Whether trading takes place in the pit or on the screen, all futures exchanges share an important advantage over the OTC markets: the clearing mechanism.

For any trade to take place, there must first be a buyer and a seller who come together in order to consummate the deal. Their relationship is but a fleeting one, however, because the clearing mechanism interposes a third party—the *clearing house*—between buyer and seller. Figure 6.3 illustrates how the clearing house fits in. As we will see, this intervention provides a number of significant benefits.

The clearing house is the organisation responsible for all the settlement procedures arising from futures trading at a particular exchange. It may be

FIGURE 6.3
The Clearing Mechanism

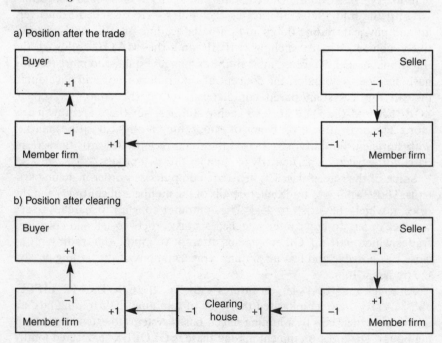

owned by the futures exchange itself, as at the Chicago Mercantile Exchange Clearinghouse, or may be independent, as at the International Commodities Clearing House (ICCH) in London.

After every trade is executed, details of the trade itself and of the members of the exchange responsible for executing the trade are given to the clearing house. The clearing house ensures that the precise details of every transaction are correct by matching up the dealing slips from both sides of the trade. Occasionally mistakes or misunderstandings can occur, especially under the hectic conditions that sometimes prevail within the trading pit, and the clearing house attempts to reconcile these *out trades*.

However, the clearing house is responsible for more than just this operational role. By coming between buyer and seller, the clearing house removes counterparty risk. This is most important. Although the clearing house never initiates any transaction, after every trade it becomes the buyer to every seller and the seller to every buyer.

In the OTC market, customers and banks are justifiably concerned about the integrity of the counterparties with whom they are dealing, and it is not uncommon for potential deals to be called off if the counterparty risk is considered too high.

By contrast, there is little need to fear counterparty risk when dealing in the futures markets. The identity of the counterparty when a deal is struck is of no concern at all; whoever one buys from or sells to will immediately be replaced by the clearing house. Of course, this is not a complete elimination of risk, but a transfer of risk from the multitude of potential counterparties to one specific one, the clearing house itself. However, futures exchanges ensure that their clearing house is well capitalised and, as much as is possible, beyond reproach. Even in the aftermath of the 1987 "crash," when a number of financial and non-financial organisations failed, no clearing house has ever defaulted, although the Hong Kong Futures Exchange came close.

Removing specific counterparty risk means that trading can proceed swiftly, without pausing to check on individual credit limits. Once again, there are only two variables that need to be agreed when trading in futures: size and price.

The clearing mechanism has a further important advantage. No matter how many times one enters the market to buy or sell and no matter when the deals are struck, there will always be one ultimate counterparty, the clearing house. If a customer buys 10 contracts one day and sells these contracts one week later, the customer will end up with no position. This is not the same as having two offsetting positions that remain on the books. Once the original position is closed out, all profits or losses to date are realised, and nothing whatsoever remains on the customer's books.

This feature enhances liquidity and makes it very easy to reverse any position in futures.

This is in sharp contrast to the OTC market. If a customer buys an FRA from one bank and then sells an FRA to another bank, there are two FRAs on the customer's books. This will utilise two credit lines and result in two settlement sums, even if the FRAs cover the same period. Of course, most banks stand ready to quote a price to a customer for canceling an FRA or other OTC derivative, but the customer must accept this price and cannot easily "shop around."

6.7 FUTURES MARGINS

An important benefit of the clearing mechanism is the transfer of counter-party risk from members of the futures exchange to the clearing house. However, the potential for loss is enormous when one considers the volume of futures contracts traded and the underlying positions these represent. The clearing house could not contemplate taking on such a risk without some means of protecting its own financial position in the event of default by a member. The protection necessary is provided through the *margining system*.

The specification of every futures contract defines the level of margin that must be deposited by members with the clearing house. For example, at the time of writing the margin required for positions in the eurodollar future traded on the CME is $500 per contract. If a member were long 100 contracts, he would have to deposit cash or securities with the clearing house in the value of $50,000. The margin requirement would be the same if the position were short 100 contracts.

The margin is in no way a "down-payment" for the underlying commodity. As we will see in the next section, futures contracts seldom result in physical delivery of the underlying, so it would be inappropriate to levy such a requirement. Futures margins are therefore quite unlike buying shares or bonds on margin, where the margin does act like a deposit. Instead, futures margins act as a "performance bond." They provide the clearing house with a financial guarantee against default by a member. When the member eventually closes out a position, the margin is refunded.

How large should the margin requirement be? The simple answer is that the margin per contract should exceed the maximum amount that could potentially be lost while running a position. Unfortunately, some contracts have maturity dates stretching years into the future. If the margin were deposited just once, when the position was initially established, and then refunded when the position was finally liquidated, the potential losses could be sizeable over a long holding period. Such a simple margining system would not function effectively.

To make the system work, an integral part of the margining process is a daily marking-to-market. At the close of trading, the futures exchange publishes the *settlement price*, the official closing price that day. Every outstanding position is then marked to this closing price. Any losses incurred since the previous settlement price or the dealing price for new positions established that day are debited to the member's margin account and must be made good the following morning. Any profits are credited to the account and may be withdrawn the next day. This creates a distinction between the *initial margin* paid in when a position is first established and the *variation margin*, which may be positive or negative, arising from the regular marking-to-market process.

With this daily procedure, the margin accounts are replenished every working day. The potential loss is then limited to the maximum amount the market price can move in a single day, rather than to price movement over the entire life of the contract.

An illustration of the daily workings of the margining system may help to clarify the process. Let us suppose a member is long one contract in the FTSE-100 stock-index future on LIFFE. The value per full point is defined as £25 and the initial margin, at the time of writing, is £2,500 per contract. Let us further suppose that the contract was purchased on Monday at a price of 2575, the daily settlement prices from Monday to Thursday were 2580, 2560, 2550, and 2555, and that the position was liquidated on Friday at a price of 2565. The resulting margin flows are illustrated in Table 6.2.

The member need only pay £2,375 into the margin account on Monday, because the £125 profit earned will be credited to the margin account, bringing the total balance to the £2,500 required. Losses on Tuesday and Wednesday lead to margin calls of £500 and £250 respectively, which must be paid in the following mornings. On Thursday a profit of £125 is earned,

TABLE 6.2
Illustration of Margin Flows

Day	Closing Price (£)	Change in Price	Margin Account (£)	Margin Flow (£)*	Explanation
Monday	2,580	+5	2,500	–2,375	initial margin of £2500 less profit of £125
Tuesday	2,560	–20	2,500	–500	margin call of £500
Wednesday	2,550	–10	2,500	–250	margin call of £250
Thursday	2,555	+5	2,625	0	member opts to leave £125 profit in margin account
Friday	n/a	+10	0	+2,875	margin account of £2625 returned plus further profit of £250

* These flows all take place the following morning.

which could be withdrawn in cash on Friday morning. Instead, the member elects to have the balance credited to the margin account, bringing the balance to £2,625. With the margin account at this level, the member could afford to suffer a subsequent loss of up to £125 before receiving a margin call. Friday's profit of 10 points—the difference between Thursday's settlement price and the selling price of 2565—is also credited to the margin account, which can finally be liquidated on Monday.

Adding up the total margin flows, the member pays in £3,125 and is refunded £2,875. The net loss of £250 represents the 10-point difference between the original purchase price of 2575 and the final selling price of 2565.

Margin payments are normally made by funds transfer between members and the clearing house. However, most futures exchanges will also accept certain securities instead of cash when the initial margin is established. By depositing securities, members can effectively earn interest on their margin accounts. Variation margin, on the other hand, can normally only be paid by funds transfer. Remember that the clearing house always has a net position of zero in every futures contract. Therefore, the profits made by one member must be equal to the losses made by another member. Since the margining system allows members making mark-to-market profits to realise the proceeds in cash, the clearing house normally must insist on variation margin calls also being settled in cash.

The operation of the margining system leads to a useful side effect. All profits and losses are realised on a daily basis *in cash*. This differs from the so-called cash markets where mark-to-market losses, while real enough, are only on paper. A losing position in the cash markets can accumulate paper losses, but these may not be heeded until the position is closed out, by which time it is too late. By contrast, a losing position in the futures markets results in a steady stream of margin calls, and the resulting cash drain enforces a financial discipline on everyone using futures.

Variation margins are calculated at the end of the trading day by using the settlement price that evening and are normally due for payment by a specified time the following morning. In the unusual event that a member defaults by failing to pay in sufficient variation margin, the exchange has the right to liquidate the futures position, take any losses out of the margin account, and eventually refund anything remaining. The clearing house would suffer a loss only if the price movement that day exceeded the margin account; in such a case the loss would be met from a general fund maintained by all members of the exchange.

There are some variations on margining systems adopted by different futures exchanges around the world.

Most exchanges recognise that a member who is long a futures contract for one delivery date and short *the same contract* for another delivery date is exposed to far less risk than an outright position in either date. Rather than exacting a separate margin for each contract, exchanges usually specify a reduced margin for the combined position. This reduced margin is called a *spread margin* or *straddle margin*. For example, at the time of writing the FTSE-100 contract introduced earlier has a normal margin of £2,500 but a straddle margin of only £100 for the pair of offsetting contracts. Intracommodity spread margin—applying to offsetting positions in different dates for the same contract—are quite common. Some exchanges also allow intercommodity spreads, offering a reduced margin requirement for offsetting positions in related contracts: for example, T-bills against three-month eurodollars.

On the other hand, some exchanges increase margin requirements in the delivery month, recognising that price volatility usually increases as futures approach maturity and as price movements in the futures markets approach those in the cash markets. This requirement is known, not surprisingly, as the *delivery-month margin*.

A number of exchanges, particularly those in the United States, adopt a two-tier margining system. This introduces a second margin level, called the *maintenance margin*, usually set at three-quarters of the initial margin level. When a position is first established, the member must deposit the initial margin in the usual way. However, margin calls then occur only when the margin account falls below the maintenance level; only then is the member required to restore the balance to the level of the initial margin. Rather than insisting that the margin account always be maintained at the level of the initial margin, the futures exchange therefore tolerates the balance in the margin account lying between the levels defined by the initial and maintenance levels. This can reduce drastically the number of margin payments that members need to make, particularly when the futures price is fluctuating up and down, and therefore reduces the cost and administrative burden associated with running a futures account.

This is illustrated in Figure 6.4, which contrasts the margin payments under a scheme having just one margin level with a scheme having a mainte-

FIGURE 6.4
Comparison of Margining Systems

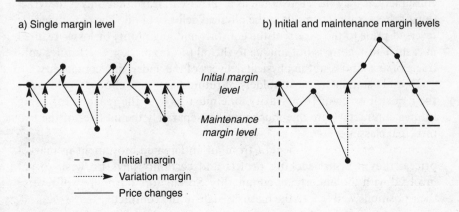

a) Single margin level

b) Initial and maintenance margin levels

Initial margin level

Maintenance margin level

– – – ➤ Initial margin
·············➤ Variation margin
———— Price changes

nance margin level as well. In this example, the maintenance level is set at five ticks below the initial margin level, and the settlement price movements in both cases follow the sequence: –3, +2, –3, –5, +2, +3, –2, –4, –3.

Figure 6.4a shows that nine separate flows of variation margin occur, one following every change in the settlement price. Compare this with Figure 6.4b, where there is only one margin call after the fourth day, when the balance in the margin account fell below the maintenance margin level.

Finally, in this chapter we have discussed margin requirements only for members of the futures exchange. Nonmembers—many banks, and most corporate customers and private individuals—are also subject to margin requirements, but these are set at the discretion of the member firm through which they are dealing. The largest corporate customers, ones who can offer adequate security and have access to same-day payments systems, may be offered the same terms as the member firm itself. Other customers would be expected to lodge additional security and maintain margin levels at some multiple of those set by the exchange. Even so, the tremendous leverage and opportunities offered through futures markets still make them a highly attractive tool in financial engineering applications. Remember also that the amount of margin deposited is not a cost but a temporary transfer of assets. It is only any interest forgone on the margin that constitutes a cost. If interest-bearing securities are lodged, the initial margin is effectively costless.

6.8 PHYSICAL DELIVERY VERSUS CASH SETTLEMENT

The definitions of futures contracts have traditionally been based upon the physical delivery of some underlying commodity. For example, the crude oil contract traded on the New York Mercantile Exchange calls for the delivery of 1,000 barrels (42,000 U.S. gallons) of West Texas intermediate crude oil. Although speculators undoubtedly form a significant proportion of the oil futures market, many of those using this contract will be oil producers or consumers. It may therefore come as a surprise to learn that only a tiny fraction of these contracts result in the physical delivery of oil. The remainder are reversed prior to the expiry of the contract and any profits or losses realised in cash. This feature is not unique to the oil futures market; few futures contracts of any kind result in physical delivery of the underlying commodity.

To understand why most holders of futures contracts choose to close out their positions prior to maturity, one must look at the reasons for using futures contracts. Here one must consider separately the motives of the two principal classes of users.

Speculators intend to benefit from an anticipated movement in market prices; they are just seeking profits and certainly have no wish to get involved with the underlying commodity. Speculators normally will reverse their positions well before the maturity date of the contract.

Hedgers seek protection against adverse price movements in the underlying commodity, and futures provide an efficient means to manage this price risk. In this light, futures should be considered as a means to reduce price risk rather than as a source of supply for the underlying commodity. Those whose business involves handling the commodity will have long-standing arrangements for buying and selling the commodity and well-established links with suppliers, shippers, and agents. Therefore, even when hedgers may need to execute the underlying transaction, they will normally find it more convenient to use their existing channels to execute the physical transaction and use futures as the means to reduce the price risk arising from these transactions. So hedgers will normally also close out their positions before the futures contracts mature.

Given that physical delivery of the underlying commodity seldom occurs, it became apparent that having to design futures contracts to include the provision for physical delivery imposed unnecessary restrictions and complexities. This paved the way for the concept of futures contracts based on intangible commodities like the level of a stock index or the rate of interest.

A good example of such a contract is the S&P 500 contract, which is traded on the CME. In this contract, the index is given a financial value of $500 per full point. If the index were at 450.00, it would be deemed to be "worth" $225,000. If the index rose to 460.00, it would then be "worth" $230,000. Someone who bought an S&P 500 contract at 450.00 and sold it at 460.00 would make $5,000 profit. This profit would be realised in cash through the margining process. Even if the position were held until maturity, the value of the contract would be determined in just the same way and *cash settled*. With these contracts, physical delivery is never a consideration; all positions will be rewarded or penalised by a cash payment from one party to the other.

Although many financial futures contracts allow for physical delivery, the most notable examples being contracts on government bonds, the newest contracts usually specify cash settlement and preclude physical delivery. This simplifies the management of a futures book and avoids a particular problem faced by those holding long futures positions. This problem arises when someone holding a short position in futures notifies the exchange of his intention to make physical delivery. The futures exchange nominates someone who is long the futures and calls on that person to receive the physical commodity. The nominee suddenly finds that, not only is his position closed out unexpectedly, he must also go to the trouble of receiving the underlying, which may be inconvenient or costly.

Although the concept of cash settlement allows a much wider scope for the design of new futures contracts, it must still be possible for someone physically to create a matching position from other instruments if he or she wants to replicate the new futures contract. Were this not the case, it would be impossible to determine a fair price for the future, and it would leave the new contract open to price manipulation. As the next two chapters will show, the design of interest-rate and stock-index contracts—two of the most heavily traded contracts involving cash settlement—allows these contracts to be syn-

TABLE 6.3
Futures Markets and Cash Markets Compared

Futures Market	Cash Market
• Contracts specifications are standardised.	• Every aspect of deal is negotiable.
• Clearing house guarantees against default of any specific counterparty.	• Counterparty risk present.
• Positions easily reversed with anyone at any time.	• Positions can only be offset at discretion of deal counterparty.
• Requirement to meet daily margin requirements.	• No mandatory requirement for margin.
• Profits and losses realised in cash daily.	• Mark-to-market profits realisable only on paper.
• Most contracts are reversed or cash-settled; delivery of underlying is rare.	• Physical delivery is usual (except for certain derivatives).

thesised from instruments readily traded in the cash markets. This guarantees that the cash and futures markets move closely in line with each other.

6.9 FUTURES AND CASH MARKETS COMPARED

We have examined the operation of futures markets and, where appropriate, contrasted futures with the cash and OTC markets. Table 6.3 summarises these differences.

6.10 THE ADVANTAGES OF FUTURES

We can summarise the advantages of the futures markets under a number of headings:

- **Liquidity** The standardisation of contracts and the efficiency of trading serve to encourage tremendous liquidity. In a number of cases, liquidity in the futures market exceeds that in the underlying cash market.
- **Clearing** The clearing mechanism removes individual counterparty risk and allows for the easy reversal of existing futures positions.
- **Margining** The margining system offers holders of futures contracts the ability to control large positions in the underlying financial commodity with the minimum of capital. Hedgers can reduce their risk exposure cheaply and without the physical purchase or sale of underlying instruments. Speculators can exploit their views of market movements without committing vast cash resources or tying up credit lines.

- **Transaction costs** Futures exchanges aim to keep trading costs as low as possible. Normally, the cost of executing a futures contract is a fraction of the equivalent transaction in the OTC market.

These advantages must also be set against some of the limitations of futures markets:

- **Inflexibility** Futures markets require that the specification of each futures contract be rigidly standardised. OTC markets allow every aspect of a transaction to be individually negotiated.

- **Liquidity** While liquidity may be very high for the futures contract with the nearest delivery date, there may be limited liquidity in the "back contracts" for certain futures.

- **Margining** Some find that managing the margin account and the resultant daily cash flows is a considerable administrative burden.

These advantages and limitations must be weighed against each other before deciding which is more suitable for a given need: a futures contract, or the corresponding OTC product. Chapter Fourteen provides a number of examples illustrating where and when futures can be used to achieve a particular hedging objective.

Further Reading

This chapter has introduced futures markets and outlined the way in which they work. For a fuller description of the exact procedures that take place, a description of the different types of order, and details of the accounting for futures, see: Duffie, J. Darrell, *Futures Markets* (Prentice Hall, 1989).

Chapter Seven

Short-Term Interest Rate Futures

The previous chapter introduced financial futures and explained the terminology and procedures common to all contracts. In this chapter we will explore in detail one of the most heavily traded contracts—the short-term interest rate future. Nearly all major exchanges offering financial futures contracts provide a market in these instruments, sometimes in a wide range of currencies. LIFFE, for example, lists three-month contracts in sterling, dollars, deutsch marks, Swiss francs, lire, and ECUs. Sections in this chapter will explain how they are priced, how they respond to shifts in market rates, their basic use in hedging, the link between these interest-rate contracts and OTC products such as FRAs, and the concept of spread positions. First, however, we need to define exactly what a short-term interest rate future is.

7.1 DEFINITIONS

Chapter Six provided a simple but clear definition of any futures contract: a futures contract fixes the *price* and conditions now for a *transaction* that will take place in the future. In the case of a short-term interest rate future, the transaction is a notional fixed-term deposit, and the "price" is the fixed rate of interest that will apply during the term of that deposit, which covers a particular period in the future. Buying a futures contract is equivalent to making a deposit, while selling a futures contract is equivalent to taking a deposit, or borrowing.

The three-month sterling contract on LIFFE provides a typical example; this contract is defined in Table 7.1.

There are many similarities with the definition of an FRA, as the two products have much in common. Nonetheless, there are some important differences, as will be evident when we study each of the above terms in more detail.

Each contract covers a sterling deposit having a fixed size of £500,000, and this defines the *unit of trading*. It is possible to buy or sell any whole number of contracts, but this restricts the size of deals to a multiple of £500,000, as contracts are not divisible. An FRA, by contrast, can be negotiated in any marketable amount up to around £50 million.

TABLE 7.1
Definition of Short Sterling on LIFFE (December 1992)

Unit of trading	£500,000
Delivery months	March, June, September, December
Delivery date	First business day after the last trading day
Last trading day	11:00 AM Third Wednesday of delivery month
Quotation	100.00 minus rate of interest
Minimum price movement	0.01%
Tick value	£12.50
Trading hours	08:05 – 16:02 (trading pit) 16:27 – 17:57 (APT screen trading)

Futures contracts originally involved the physical delivery of the underlying asset but, as we saw in Chapter Six, cash settlement is normally the rule with financial futures contracts. Nonetheless, the term "delivery" is still used to denote the date and time when contracts expire. All futures contracts follow a rigid calendar with predefined delivery dates, usually four per year, and nearly all financial futures are designed to have these dates falling in March, June, September, and December. The *delivery months*, *delivery date*, and *last trading day* together define exactly when these delivery dates occur. For example, the March 1996 contract will cease trading at 11 AM on Wednesday, March 20, and final cash settlement will take place the following day. The last trading day for futures is analogous to the fixing date for an FRA, and the delivery date for futures is equivalent to the FRA's settlement date.

A futures contract is defined as a fixed-rate *deposit*. Someone who wanted to speculate using futures would wish to borrow funds (sell futures) at a low interest rate and deposit funds (buy futures) at a high interest rate. Unfortunately, this implies a buy high, sell low strategy, which is unnatural. Especially in the fast-moving futures pit, where many traders operate on instinct, mistakes could be made all too easily. For this reason, the original designers of interest rate futures decided that these contracts would be traded on an indexed "price" rather than the interest rate itself, where the price is defined as

$$P = 100 - i \qquad (7.1)$$

where

P is the price index
i is the future interest rate in percent

This system of *quotation* simply reverses the behaviour of futures prices when interest rates change. If interest rates rise, then the price falls; when rates fall, the price rises. Now traders can follow a buy low, sell high strategy with success, so long as they follow the quoted price rather than the rate.

As an example, suppose that futures were trading at exactly 92.00, corresponding to an interest rate of 8.00%. A trader anticipates that rates will fall and the price will rise. He buys 10 contracts and waits. Within a few minutes, interest rates have edged down to 7.95%, so that the price rises to 92.05. The trader closes out his position and makes five ticks' profit, having bought at 92.00 and sold at 92.05.

It is important to note that the futures price for these short-term contracts is not a price in the usual sense. A price of 92.00 does not mean £92, $92, or any other monetary amount. Rather, the futures price is just an alternative representation for the interest rate at which the underlying notional deposit or loan could be executed; it is a token for the general level of interest rates. The futures price is therefore similar to a stock index, which indicates the general level of the stock market rather than the actual price of any particular share or group of shares.

Note that there is no need for these contortions when working with FRAs, because they were defined so that the buyer of an FRA is the notional borrower, not the depositor. If short-term interest futures had originally been defined in the same way, they could be traded by quoting the interest rate directly, just like FRAs.

All contracts specify the *minimum price movement* or *tick*, the smallest difference between two consecutive price quotations. This, along with the other definitions, enables the *tick value* to be calculated. With a minimum price movement of 0.01%, a trading unit of £500,000, and a three-month contract period, the tick value is

$$0.01\% \times £500,000 \times \frac{3}{12} = £12.50 \tag{7.2}$$

Equation 7.2 is similar to equation 4.2, which defined the settlement sum for an FRA, but there are two notable differences. First, the futures contract is for a three-month deposit, and it therefore seems natural to use 3/12 as the appropriate fraction of a year. However, nearly every other market uses a day-count fraction divided by 360 or 365. For example, a three-month contract in the normal deposit and FRA markets would involve three calendar months, which could vary between 87 and 94 days.[1] If the tick value were calculated using the number of days in such a period and a divisor of 365, it could lie between £11.92 and £12.88. Furthermore, although the period between futures contracts is normally 91 days, it can sometimes be 84 or 98 days. If the tick value were calculated using these day counts, it could fall between £11.51 and £13.42, a considerable range.

---

[1] Taking into account adjustment for weekends, holidays, and the so-called end-month rule.

Second, the final cash settlement for a future takes place on the expiry date of the contract, which is at the *beginning* of the period covered by the underlying deposit.[2] Yet interest in the normal deposit markets is paid at the *end* of this period. FRAs allow for this by discounting the settlement sum, as explained in Chapter Four (Section 4.4). If the tick value for futures allowed for this, it could be as low as £11.25 for an 84-day period if interest rates were at 10%.

Yet despite all this, the tick value for these particular futures contracts is always defined to be £12.50. While this simplicity makes trading and settlement that much more straightforward, it can create extra work for those wishing to hedge the interest rate risk on an underlying exposure for which the interest is calculated using actual day counts. Adjustments can be made to account for the tick value always being £12.50, and these are explained in Chapter Fourteen (Section 14.3).

The short-term interest rate contracts in other currencies are all defined in exactly the same manner, differing only in the unit of trading and in technical details such as trading hours. For example, for the three-month PIBOR[3] contract traded at the MATIF, the unit of trading is FRF 5m, the tick size is FRF 125, and the last trading date is two business days before the third Wednesday of the delivery month.

7.2 ARBITRAGE PRICING

Interest rate futures are invariably cash-settled, and the transaction that takes place on the delivery date is therefore only a notional deposit or loan, not an actual one. Nonetheless, futures prices are still closely related to rates in the cash markets, just as FRA rates are.

What guarantees this relationship is the procedure on the last trading date, where the final settlement price for contracts is determined, not by prices in the trading pit, but rather by reference to the prevailing rates in the cash market itself. For example, the Exchange Delivery Settlement Price (EDSP) for the short sterling contract on LIFFE is defined as 100 minus the British Bankers' Association Interest Settlement Rate (BBAISR) for three-month sterling deposits at 11 AM that day. That for the PIBOR contract on the MATIF is 100 minus the average PIBOR quoted at 9:30 AM, 11 AM, and 12:30 PM.

> **When a short-term interest rate futures contract expires, the futures price will be exactly equal to 100 minus the cash market interest rate, by definition.**

---

[2] In fact, the flows of variation margin mean that the settlement sum is actually paid or received *continuously* while the contract is being held.

[3] Paris InterBank Offered Rate.

In algebraic terms, we can say

$$P_{EDSP} = 100 - i_{REF} \qquad (7.3)$$

where

P_{EDSP} is the exchange delivery settlement price
i_{REF} is the reference market interest rate in percent

This definition ensures that, no matter what occurs during the life of a futures contract, the very final price will always match those in the cash markets.

Knowing this gives us the insight necessary to understand how futures prices will behave during the lifetime of the contract. The three-month cash market rate will act like a magnet, drawing the futures price ever closer. Prior to maturity, however, the futures price will not depend on where the cash market rate is right now, but on where that rate is expected to be when the contract expires, i.e., the forward rate.

Chapter Four (Section 4.6) developed a formula for calculating the forward rate and hence for pricing FRAs. Equation 4.6 can be used almost as it stands, except that we must first define some additional terms.

Let

T_0 be the dealing date when the future is originally bought or sold
T_D be the last trading (or expiry) date for the futures contract
T_{SPOT} be the normal value date for cash market deposits traded on T_0
T_S be the normal value date for cash market deposits traded on T_D
T_L be the maturity date for a three-month cash market deposit traded on T_D

Equation 4.6 can then be modified to obtain P, the futures price prior to expiry:

$$P = 100 - \left[\frac{i_L D_L - i_S D_S}{D_F \left(1 + i_S \dfrac{D_S}{B}\right)} \right] \qquad (7.4)$$

where

P is the futures price
i_S is the cash market interest rate to T_S
i_L is the cash market interest rate to T_L
D_S is the number of days from T_{SPOT} to T_S
D_L is the number of days from T_{SPOT} to T_L
D_F is the number of days from T_S to T_L
B is the day-count convention (e.g., 360 for most currencies, 365 for sterling)

Suppose that today is Tuesday, February 8, 1994, so that T_{SPOT} will be Thursday, February 10. The expiry date of the March 1994 contract will fall on Wednesday, March 16, making T_S Friday, March 18, and T_L Monday, June 20 (because June 18, 1994, falls on a Saturday). This makes $D_S = 36$ days, $D_L = 130$ days, and $D_F = 94$ days. Suppose also that cash market rates are 7½%, 7¹¹/₁₆%, 7¾%, and 7⅞% for one-, two-, three-, and six-month LIBOR, respectively. From these figures, we can interpolate the 36-day rate to be 7.55%, and the 130-day rate as 7.81%. Inserting these values in equation 7.4 gives the three-month forward rate on March 16 to be 7.85%, so the fair futures price should be 92.15.

Let's compare some actual cash market rates with futures prices to see how they relate in practice. Chapter Four (Section 4.6) provided a set of cash market rates for sterling and the dollar on Monday, February 18, 1991. These can be used to calculate fair values for the March, June, September, and December contract prices. Table 7.2 compares the calculated values with the actual futures prices that day.

With only a couple of exceptions, the calculated figures are within ¹/₁₆% of the actual figures. Where there are discrepancies, they probably arise when interpolating the cash market rates and when calculating from LIBOR rates, which themselves are quoted only to the nearest ¹/₁₆%.

Interestingly enough, if one compares the March sterling futures price of 87.29 with the quote of 12.68/73 for the 1×4 FRA (see Table 4.2 in Chapter Four), the dates and prices match exactly. The same is true for the dollar contract, where the price of 93.31 corresponds exactly to the quoted 1×4 FRA price of 6.67/72 (see Table 4.3). Banks make extensive use of futures contracts in order to hedge their FRA books, so the prices of the two instruments track each other very closely, even more closely than either of them tracks the cash market prior to expiry.

Finally, note that the sterling three-month rate on February 18, 1991, of 13⅛% corresponds to a futures price of 86.88, but this bears no resemblance to any of the futures prices quoted that day. Once again, this is because the figure of 13⅛% is the interest rate for three-month deposits made right now, but these futures contracts quote the interest rate for three-month deposits made in the future. We should therefore not be surprised to find that the prices for cash and futures differ.

TABLE 7.2
Comparison of Actual with Calculated Futures Prices

	Sterling Futures			Dollar Futures		
Contract	Calculated Price	Actual Price	Difference (bp)	Calculated Price	Actual Price	Difference (bp)
MAR	87.40	87.29	+11	93.37	93.31	+6
JUN	88.57	88.59	−2	93.47	93.41	+6
SEP	89.30	89.38	−8	93.34	93.27	+7
DEC	89.65	89.58	+7	93.12	92.95	+17

7.3 BASIS AND CONVERGENCE

Prior to expiry, futures prices match the implied forward rate, but there will normally be a gap between this forward rate and the cash market rate right now. The gap between cash prices and prices in the futures market is given a special name in futures terminology—the *basis*. Basis is formally defined as

$$BASIS = CASH\ PRICE - FUTURES\ PRICE \qquad (7.5)$$

To get a better understanding of basis, we need to return to the idea introduced in Chapter Four (Section 4.6), where the FRA was said to "fill the gap" between different maturities in the cash market. The same idea, of course, applies equally well to interest rate futures.

Consider the two situations depicted in Figure 7.1.

In Figure 7.1a, three-month rates are 9% while six-month rates are 10%. This is a steeply positive, or upward-sloping, yield curve. Under these circumstances, the 3×6 forward interest rate of around 11% lies well above the cash market rate of 9%. In Figure 7.1b, the opposite is true. Three-month rates of 11% and six-month rates of 10% create a negative yield curve sloping steeply downwards. The 3×6 forward interest rate of around 9% in this case lies well below the cash market rate of 11%.

This example illustrates a general rule:[4]

FIGURE 7.1
Rising and Falling Yield Curves

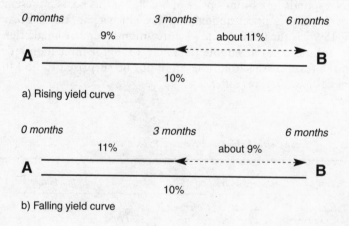

a) Rising yield curve

b) Falling yield curve

---

[4]Strictly speaking, $i_F > i_S$ only when $i_L > i_S\left(1 + i_S \dfrac{t_S t_F}{t_L}\right)$. This means that forward rates will also be lower than cash rates when the yield curve is flat (i.e., when $i_S = i_L$).

> **Positive yield curve: Forward rates are higher than cash rates.**
> **Negative yield curve: Forward rates are lower than cash rates.**

If we convert this rule into futures terminology by transforming rates into prices, we obtain

> **Positive yield curve: Cash prices are higher than futures prices.**
> **Negative yield curve: Cash prices are lower than futures prices.**

Applying the definition of basis given in equation 7.5, we can see that basis and the yield curve are closely related. A positive basis arises when the yield curve is positive; a negative basis arises when the yield curve has a negative slope.

As an illustration, contrast the sterling and dollar yield curves for February 18, 1991, which are illustrated in Figure 7.2.

The sterling yield curve is negative, sloping steeply downward, and points to lower interest rates in the future. With a negative yield curve, we should

FIGURE 7.2
Sterling and Dollar Yield Curves on February 18, 1991

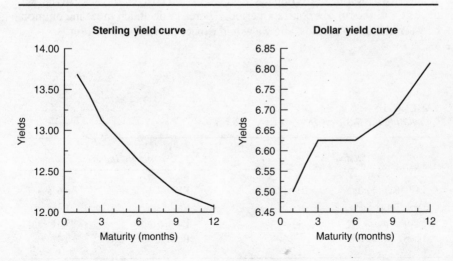

expect that the basis will also be negative. The dollar yield curve, on the other hand, is slightly upward sloping, implying a small positive basis. Table 7.3 sets out the calculations for determining the basis in each case, and confirms these expectations.

Some hedgers believe that futures contracts provide a way of locking into today's cash market rates for a future transaction. Such a possibility would often be very useful, but that is not what futures provide. Futures allow a user to lock into a rate for a future transaction, but that rate is the forward rate. The basis is the gap between today's cash market rate and the forward rate on a particular date in the future.

As the last trading date of a futures contract approaches, cash and futures prices move closer together. This process is known as *convergence*, and it can best be understood by comparing the periods covered by a three-month cash deposit and a three-month futures contract. Figure 7.3 illustrates this using the March 1996 contract as an example.

The last trading date for the March 1996 contract will be Wednesday, March 20, 1996, and the three-month period covered by the underlying deposit starts on March 22 and finishes on June 24 (June 22, 1996, is a Saturday). This period is fixed and never changes.

Figure 7.3a starts by examining the period covered by a three-month deposit traded on December 20, 1995, which would have a value date of December 22 and mature on March 22. As is evident, there is no overlap whatsoever between the period covered by the cash market deposit and the period covered by the futures contract. As they relate to two different periods of time, cash and futures rates might be quite different.

Just over four weeks later, cash market rates on January 18, 1996 relate to the period from January 22 to April 22. Now there are 31 days of overlap between the period covered by the cash market and the period covered by the future, as Figure 7.3b illustrates. On February 20, one month later on, there are now two months of overlap between the period covered by the cash market deposit and the futures contract period. There is now much more in common between these two periods, and we would expect the rates to be closer.

TABLE 7.3
Calculating the Basis for Interest Rate Futures

Sterling		Dollar	
LIBOR 3-month	13.125%	LIBOR 3-month	6.625%
Cash "price"	86.88	Cash "price"	93.38
Futures price	87.29	Futures price	93.31
Basis	−0.41	Basis	+0.07

FIGURE 7.3
Comparison of Periods Covered by Cash and Futures

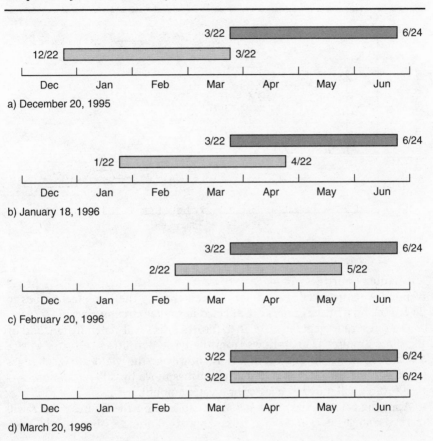

a) December 20, 1995

b) January 18, 1996

c) February 20, 1996

d) March 20, 1996

Finally, on the last trading date of the futures contract, the period covered by cash and futures are one and the same, as Figure 7.3d demonstrates. On this day, cash and futures prices must also be the same, and convergence is complete.

Figure 7.4 provides a practical illustration of convergence, showing how the basis gradually narrows and finally becomes zero on the last trading date of the contract, when convergence is complete.

7.4 BEHAVIOR OF FUTURES PRICES

Equation 7.4 defines the basic relationship between futures prices and rates in the cash markets, and this equation is almost identical to equation 4.6, which was used to price FRAs from cash market rates. These formulae tell us how to calculate what the futures or FRA prices should be, if we know the interest rates for the relevant maturities.

FIGURE 7.4
Illustration of Convergence

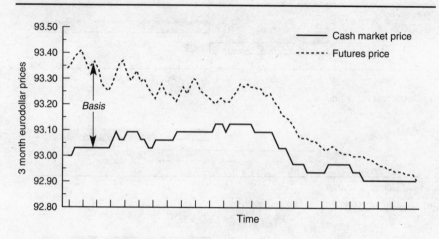

Chapter Four (Section 4.7) then went on to examine how FRA prices respond when market rates move. We can employ the same techniques to determine how futures prices are affected in similar circumstances.

If interest rates generally rise, then futures prices will generally fall, and by the same amount. This follows from the basic definition of futures price quotations given in equation 7.1. If, however, the yield curve changes shape—if interest rates of different maturities move by different amounts—then futures will move by a lesser or greater amount.

Applying calculus to equation 7.4, we can see how the futures price P will react to changes in i_S and i_L. To a first approximation, we obtain

$$\frac{\partial P}{\partial i_S} \approx \frac{D_S}{D_F} \tag{7.6}$$

$$\frac{\partial P}{\partial i_L} \approx -\frac{D_L}{D_F} \tag{7.7}$$

$$\frac{\partial P}{\partial i_{ALL}} \approx -1 \tag{7.8}$$

Equation 7.8 confirms the inverse relationship between interest rates and futures prices, while equation 7.7 demonstrates a similar effect if just long-term rates move. Equation 7.6, however, implies that rises in short-term rates will be accompanied by a *rise* in futures prices, if long-term rates do not move. This can be understood if we return to the analogy of futures contracts "filling the gap" between short-term and long-term rates.

Let's suppose that there is a futures contract that matures in exactly three months' time. By buying such a contract, an investor can effectively lock into a fixed rate for the three-month period starting in three months. The futures price will fix the rate such that the two strategies

1. Invest for six months, or
2. Invest for three months and buy a future to lock in the rate for the second three months,

will achieve the same end result. If three-month interest rates then rose, while six-month interest rates stayed the same, the return from the first strategy would be unchanged. In order for the return under the second strategy also to remain the same, the interest guaranteed by the futures contract would have to fall, meaning that futures prices would have to rise.

Figure 7.5 summarises the way in which different futures contracts would react if short-term rates i_S increase by one basis point, long-term rates i_L increase by one basis point, and interest rates generally rise by one basis point. This is very similar to the FRA "behaviour profile" described in Chapter Four (Section 4.7).

This is the theory. As an example of what happens in practice, we can study what happened between February 25 and 27, 1991, when sterling bank base rates were lowered by 0.5%. Figure 7.6 shows the cash market yield curve and the interest rates implied by the futures prices, both before and after the change in rates.

In the cash markets, rates at the short end dropped by a full half-point, overnight rates by a fraction more. One-month and three-month rates fell by between $3/16$% and $1/8$%, while six-month rates dropped just $1/16$%, and 12-month rates were left unchanged.

The effect on the series of short sterling futures varied from contract to contract. As interest rates fell for all maturities, futures prices rose. The contract maturing on March 20, 1991, just three weeks away, rose by 28bp, and the June contract rose by 21bp, while the September and December contracts rose just 6bp and 4bp, respectively.

FIGURE 7.5
Behavior Profile for Interest Rate Futures

Contract maturing in...	i_S / 1bp	i_L / 1bp	i_S & i_L / 1bp
1 month	+0.33	−1.33	−1
3 months	+1	−2	−1
6 months	+2	−3	−1
9 months	+3	−4	−1

FIGURE 7.6
Sterling Interest Rates on February 25 and 27, 1991

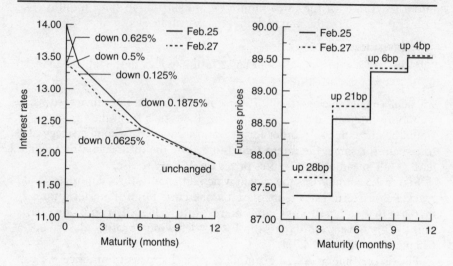

We can calculate what effect the change in interest rates should have on the March future by using equations 7.6 and 7.7. The behaviour profile for this contract, maturing in exactly three weeks, should be (+0.25 −1.25). Three-month rates fell around 19bp which, by itself, should have lifted the future by 24bp. The fall in one-month rates of ¹/₈% should, however, have dropped the future price by 3bp. Together, this gives an expected net rise of 21bp in the futures price, compared with the 28bp rise that actually occurred. This is quite close, given the relative coarseness of cash market rates, which are quoted to the nearest ¹/₁₆%.

In contrast, the June future in theory should have *fallen* by around 6bp because of the sharp fall in three-month rates compared with virtually no change in the six-month rates. Yet the June contract *rose* by 21bp. The reason: a change in the relative expectations of cash and futures markets. On February 25, the three-month implied forward rate for June was 11.30% compared with a futures implied rate of 11.44%. The cash market was therefore discounting a bigger fall in rates than the futures market. By February 27, following a 50bp fall in short-term cash market rates, the cash markets were implying an 11.37% rate for June—slightly higher than before—while the futures market continued to discount a further fall in rates to 11.23%. The basis therefore changed from +14bp to −14bp, which is entirely feasible, but this led to the unexpected discrepancy in our prediction. Changes in the basis can also upset carefully contrived futures hedges. Fortunately Chapter Fourteen (Section 14.6) explains some of the advanced methods available to minimise this problem. In the meantime, the next section demonstrates basic futures hedging techniques.

7.5 BASIC HEDGING EXAMPLE

Consider an investment manager who makes continual use of the euromarkets for placing short-term funds in dollars and sterling until strategic long-term investment opportunities are identified. It is Monday, February 18, 1991, and the manager believes that interest rates in both countries will decline by the end of the year. He wishes to hedge against this anticipated decline and expects to have £25 million and $50 million to invest before the end of the year. Rates quoted in the cash and futures markets are summarised in Table 7.4.

Dealing first with the dollar, he notes that December eurodollar futures contracts are trading at 92.95, implying a three-month rate in December of 7.05%. This compares with the cash market rate of 6⁵/₈% for three-month deposits and a gently rising yield curve. Although the market is anticipating a small rise in rates, the investment manager nonetheless adheres to his view that dollar rates will fall. He buys 50 December eurodollar contracts (each contract having a notional principal of $1 million), effectively securing a rate of return of 7.05% on notional deposits of $50 million.

Turning now to the pound sterling, the manager finds that December eurosterling contracts are trading at 89.58, implying a three-month rate of 10.42% in December. This appears very low when compared with the three-month rate prevailing in February of 13¹/₈% and gives rise to a large negative basis of 270bp. Unfortunately for the investment manager, it appears that the market this time shares his view that sterling rates will also decline, and the futures prices reflect the view that sterling rates will be around 10¹/₂% by the end of the year. Nonetheless, the manager also buys 50 December eurosterling contracts (each contract having a notional principal of £500,000) in case market rates fall even lower. In doing so, he has effectively secured a rate of 10.42% on £25 million of notional deposits.

On Wednesday, October 23, the manager arranges to lend $50 million for three months and therefore decides to lift the hedge. Cash market rates have indeed fallen to those summarised in Table 7.5, and three-month money is bid at 5¹/₂%. This is all that can be earned on the cash deposit. The December contracts, however, are now trading at 94.45, implying a forward rate of 5.55%, quite close to the prevailing cash market rate. In liquidating these contracts, the

TABLE 7.4
Market Rates on February 18, 1991

	Sterling		Dollar	
LIBOR 3-month	13.125%		LIBOR 3-month	6.625%
DEC futures	89.58		DEC futures	92.95
Basis	–2.70		Basis	+0.43

TABLE 7.5
Market Rates on October 23, 1991

Sterling		Dollar	
LIBOR 3-month	10.25%	LIBOR 3-month	5.625%
LIBID 3-month	10.125%	LIBID 3-month	5.5%
DEC futures	89.83	DEC futures	94.45
Basis	–0.08	Basis	–0.07

manager makes 150bp profit, the difference between the 92.95 purchase price and the 94.45 selling price. This futures profit increases the effective return on the deposit from $5\frac{1}{2}$% to 7%, within 5bp of the 7.05% originally secured.[5]

In the case of the dollar, the hedge has worked very well indeed. The investment manager has achieved a return of 7%, far higher than the prevailing $5\frac{1}{2}$% three-month rate.

In addition to the dollars just placed, the manager also has £25 million available to lend on October 23. Sterling base rates have dropped from $13\frac{1}{2}$% in February down to $10\frac{1}{2}$% in October, bringing down other market rates, and the manager can only lend at $10\frac{1}{8}$%, the three-month bid rate for sterling. Futures have risen only slightly to 89.83 when the manager liquidates them to realise 25bp profit. As sterling interest rates have already dropped below the level originally anticipated in February and there is still some time before the contracts expire, the futures market is allowing for a further easing of rates before December. The 25bp futures profit boosts the manager's effective return on the sterling deposit from $10\frac{1}{8}$% to $10\frac{3}{8}$%.

In the case of sterling, the hedge has achieved an effective lending rate of $10\frac{3}{8}$%, again within four or five basis points of the 10.42% rate implied by the original futures price of 89.58. This hedge has also been highly successful, because the rate obtained is very close to the rate anticipated. While this rate is much lower than the $13\frac{1}{8}$% cash rates prevailing when the hedge was established, it is important to remember that futures allow hedgers to secure the *forward* rate for the future period, not the cash rate.

Finally, although both hedges achieved results very close to the rate anticipated when the hedge was initiated, they were not exact. There are two principal reasons for this. The most obvious one is that futures prices are determined by LIBOR, while the investment manager was placing funds at LIBID, which is usually $\frac{1}{8}$% lower. Less obvious is the fact that only on the last trading date do futures prices and cash rates match exactly. Prior to that date, futures prices are converging to the cash rate, but there is a gap between the two, the basis. If, as in the above examples, futures contracts are liqui-

---

[5] Chapter 14 provides full details of the calculations involved in evaluating hedge profits.

dated prior to the last trading date, convergence will not be complete, and there is a risk that the nature of the basis may have changed. This *basis risk* is normally quite small and is invariably much smaller than interest-rate risk itself. There are methods of handling basis risk, and Chapter Fourteen (Sections 14.4 to 14.8) provides some examples.

7.6 SHORT-TERM FUTURES CONTRACTS COMPARED

The three-month interest rate future illustrated so far in this chapter is by far the most heavily used contract for hedging short-term interest-rate risk and is available in a range of major currencies including: the U.S. dollar, pound sterling, deutsch mark, French franc, Swiss franc, Italian lira, Irish punt, and the ECU. Some contracts are offered by a number of futures exchanges around the globe, giving users access to particular contracts 24 hours a day. In certain cases, exchanges have linked their margining and clearing procedures so that contracts opened on the floor of one exchange may be closed in the trading pit of another. An example of this is the link between SIMEX in Singapore and the CME in Chicago.

In addition to the three-month future, there are a number of other short-term contracts available. These fall into two groups:

1. Contracts based on a notional eurocurrency deposit, but for a different maturity.

2. Contracts based on other short-term securities.

The only two contracts in the first group currently traded are the 30-day interest rate contract on the CBOT and the one-month LIBOR contract on the CME. Trading in the CME contract dominates, owing to the tremendous liquidity generated by the three-month contracts traded in the same pit and to reduced margin requirements for offsetting positions between the one-month and three-month contracts.

The contract specification for the one-month LIBOR contract is identical to that for the three-month contract, including the same tick value of $25 per contract. This is accomplished by increasing the size of the notional underlying deposit from $1 million for the three-month contract to $3 million for the one-month contract:

$1,000,000 \times 0.01\% \times \{^3/_{12}\} = \$25$

$3,000,000 \times 0.01\% \times \{^1/_{12}\} = \$25$

Tables 7.6 and 7.7 illustrate some trading statistics for these two contracts. The columns show:

1. The opening, highest, lowest, and closing (settlement) futures prices during the day.

2. The change in settlement price between yesterday and today.
3. The yield implied by the futures price (i.e., 100 less the futures price).
4. The change in yield between yesterday and today.
5. The open interest—the total number of long (or short) contracts outstanding at the end of the day (i.e., the aggregate number of positions carried
   forward from day to day rather than being closed out during the day).

From these two tables, there are a number of interesting features to note:

- Trading volume in the three-month contract is 100 times that of the
  one-month contract, while open interest is some 40 times larger.

TABLE 7.6
Three-month Eurodollar Contract (Trading Statistics for October 27, 1992)

EURODOLLAR (IMM) – $1,000,000; points of 100%

	Open	High	Low	Settle	Change	Yield Settle	Yield Change	Open Interest
Dec	96.36	96.43	96.32	96.41	+.04	3.59	−.04	329,208
Mar 93	96.33	96.42	96.26	96.38	+.06	3.62	−.06	309,045
Jun	95.82	95.94	95.75	95.91	+.09	4.09	−.09	213,231
Sep	95.32	95.48	95.26	95.45	+.12	4.55	−.12	143,458
Dec	94.67	94.84	94.60	94.81	+.13	5.19	−.13	97,524
Mar 94	94.40	94.57	94.36	94.56	+.14	5.44	−.14	80,364
Jun	94.02	94.21	93.98	94.19	+.15	5.81	−.15	63,318
Sep	93.73	93.92	93.70	93.90	+.15	6.10	−.15	49,881
Dec	93.32	93.50	93.31	93.49	+.15	6.51	−.15	44,292
Mar 95	93.23	93.40	93.22	93.40	+.15	6.60	−.15	43,665
Jun	93.00	93.17	92.99	93.17	+.15	6.83	−.15	31,594
Sep	92.84	93.01	92.83	93.01	+.15	6.99	−.15	25,724
Dec	92.58	92.74	92.58	92.74	+.15	7.26	−.15	25,169
Mar 96	92.55	92.72	92.55	92.72	+.15	7.28	−.15	23,410
Jun	92.38	92.54	92.37	92.54	+.15	7.46	−.15	13,651
Sep	92.25	92.41	92.24	92.41	+.15	7.59	−.15	9,043
Dec	92.12	92.19	92.06	92.20	+.14	7.80	−.14	6,335
Mar 97	92.15	92.22	92.09	92.23	+.14	7.77	−.14	6,078
Jun	92.02	92.09	91.98	92.10	+.14	7.90	−.14	7,991
Sep	91.86	91.99	91.86	92.00	+.14	8.00	−.14	3,777

Est. vol. 312,539; vol. Mon 201,435; open int 1,526,758, −4,705

TABLE 7.7
LIBOR One-Month Contract (Trading Statistics for October 27, 1992)

LIBOR–IM (IMM) – $3,000,000; points of 100%

						Yield		
	Open	*High*	*Low*	*Settle*	*Change*	*Settle*	*Change*	*Open Interest*
Nov	96.69	96.75	96.69	96.74	+.02	3.26	–.02	22,243
Dec	96.14	96.18	96.12	96.17	+.03	3.83	–.03	9,934
Jan 93	96.60	96.67	96.60	96.67	+.03	3.33	–.02	6,518
Feb	96.55	96.58	96.54	96.58	+.02	3.42	–.02	1,317
Mar				96.47	+.06	3.53	–.06	523

Est. vol. 3,530; vol. Mon 2,031; open int 40,575, –87

- Liquidity in the three-month contract extends to contracts maturing in five years' time, while liquidity in the one-month contract tails off rapidly after the *front contract*.[6] For example, open interest in the March 1996 three-month contract is greater than in the November 1992 one-month contract.
- Both contracts clearly show market expectations. For example, the three-month contract demonstrates the market's view that three-month dollar rates will rise from around 3½% at end-1992 to around 8% by mid-1997.

Despite the much-attenuated liquidity of the one-month contract, it may prove more suitable when trying to hedge an exposure whose interest-rate risk is linked to one-month rather than to three-month rates. For example, a company issuing 30-day commercial paper may find that the one-month futures contract provides a more accurate hedge than the three-month contract.

The second group of short-term futures contracts are based on securities like treasury bills or bankers acceptances (BAs). In fact, the first short-term interest rate contract ever traded was the 13-week T-bill contract at the CME.

There are many similarities between security-based contracts and the eurodollar contracts. In particular, most use the same indexed price system of quotation introduced in equation 7.1, in which the futures price is defined as

$$P = 100 - i \tag{7.9}$$

---

[6] The front contract is the one with the nearest delivery date.

where

P is the price index
i is the future security yield (in percent)

Of course, while the yield on 13-week T-bills and three-month eurodollar deposits will be similar, they will differ in two respects. First, the enhanced credit quality of T-bills will ensure that these instruments trade at lower yields than bank-based deposits. Second, it is customary for T-bills to be quoted on a discount basis, while eurodollars are quoted on an add-on yield basis. Discount yields are always lower than the equivalent add-on yield, further widening the gap between quoted T-bill and eurodollar yields.

Table 7.8 provides an example of T-bill futures prices and trading statistics for the same date as used for compiling the figures for eurodollar futures.

Trading volume and open interest in the T-bill contract is of the same order of magnitude as for the one-month LIBOR contract. Although it was the first interest rate contract to be introduced, it has diminished in importance following the ascendancy of the ubiquitous three-month contract.

There is one significant difference between security-based futures and eurodollar contracts. In the case of T-bill contracts and the like, the possibility exists for physical delivery of specific treasury bills. This means that a different system of arbitrage pricing is used. Instead of relating futures prices to forward interest rates, security-based futures are priced using *cash-and-carry* arbitrage. This method is explained in detail in the next chapter.

7.7 COMPARISON OF FUTURES AND FRAs

Table 6.3 in Chapter Six summarised the principal institutional and operational differences between the futures and cash markets. Here we discuss some additional technical distinctions between eurocurrency futures and FRAs.

TABLE 7.8
13-week T-Bill Contract (Trading Statistics for October 27, 1992)

TREASURY BILLS (IMM) – $1,000,000; points of 100%

	Open	High	Low	Settle	Change	Yield Settle	Yield Change	Open Interest
Dec	96.90	96.94	96.86	96.93	+.03	3.07	–.03	18,874
Mar 93	96.77	96.83	96.73	96.81	+.04	3.19	–.04	12,964
Jun	96.33	96.45	96.33	96.43	+.08	3.57	–.08	1,250

Est. vol. 5,151; vol. Mon 3,792; open int 33,244, +890

The definition of the futures contract implies that someone who buys one futures contract and holds it until maturity will receive a payoff defined by

$$PAYOFF = (P_{EDSP} - P_0) \times 100 \times TV = (i_0 - i_{EDSP}) \times 100 \times TV \qquad (7.10)$$

where

P_{EDSP} is the exchange delivery settlement price
P_0 is the original purchase price
i_{EDSP} is the reference interest rate used to determine P_{EDSP} (in percent)
i_0 is the original interest rate implied by the futures contract $(100 - P_0)$
TV is the tick value of the contract

Equation 7.10 is very similar to equation 4.2, which defined the settlement sum for an FRA. The reference rate i_{EDSP} in equation 7.10 corresponds to i_r in equation 4.2, while the original rate i_0 in equation 7.10 matches i_c in equation 4.2. There are two differences, however:

1. Equation 7.10 features $(i_0 - i_{EDSP})$, while equation 4.2 uses $(i_r - i_c)$. The order of the corresponding terms is reversed, because buying futures is defined as making a deposit, while buying FRAs is equivalent to taking a loan.

2. Equation 7.10 uses a constant tick value, while equation 4.2 calculates the tick value according to the period of time covered by the FRA and then discounts this to allow for the settlement sum being paid at the beginning rather than at the end of the FRA contract period.

Depending upon the day count and the level of interest, the payoff from a futures contract and an FRA maturing on the same day could differ by up to 10% in extreme cases. For banks hedging large FRA books with futures, this can be accommodated by adjusting the number of futures contracts purchased, as explained in Chapter Fourteen (Section 14.3).

A further distinction arises through the operation of the margin account. As Chapter Six (Section 6.7) explained, the flows of variation margin compel holders of futures to realise their profits and losses on a daily basis, in cash. Holders of positions in FRAs may also mark their positions to market on a daily basis, but there is only one occasion when the profit or loss is paid in cash, and that is on the settlement date. This makes a difference when one accounts for the interest earned or forgone through the flows of variation margin.

As an example, consider a bank that anticipates a fall in forward interest rates over the next three months and simultaneously buys futures and sells FRAs, both maturing on the same date.[7] If the bank is correct, as time passes profits will be earned both on the long futures position and on the short FRA position. The futures profit, however, will be credited to the margin account, as variation margin can be drawn off as cash and can be invested to earn interest. The FRA profits are only mark-to-market profits, and these can only be realised in cash when the position is closed out or the FRA matures.

---

[7] This is possible because banks make an active market in FRAs whose dates match those of the futures contracts, the so-called IMM dates.

The effect of interest on variation margin flows can be taken into account when designing more advanced hedging strategies. The method is explained in Chapter Fourteen (Section 14.3).

Finally, the vast majority of FRAs are quoted with fixed periods. A 3×6 FRA, for example, covers a moving three-month period always commencing three months after the spot value date. The period covered by a 3×6 FRA traded today will therefore be different from the period covered by a 3×6 FRA traded tomorrow. Futures are based on fixed dates rather than fixed periods. As the last trading date approaches, the price of a specific futures contract and three-month cash rates will move ever closer together. No such convergence between 3×6 FRA prices and cash rates takes place.

7.8 SPREAD POSITIONS

The concept of a spread of futures contracts was first introduced in the previous chapter in the context of spread margins. It was explained that offsetting positions for different dates in the same contract, an intracommodity spread, attracted a substantially smaller margin than was normally levied for the positions separately. At the time of writing, the short sterling contract on LIFFE attracts a normal full margin of £750, corresponding to a 60bp move in interest rates, but the spread margin is just £200 for the pair of contracts.

It is clear that someone who is long futures for one date and short the same number of contracts for another date has an offsetting position that is much less exposed to movements in interest rates. This raises the question: What exactly is the residual exposure?

To understand the exposure of a spread position to changes in interest rates, we need to refer back to the futures behaviour profile illustrated in Figure 7.5. This quantified how any futures contract would respond to movements in i_S and i_L. For a contract maturing in three months' time, the profile $(+1\ -2)$ means that the future will rise one tick for a 1bp rise in the three-month rate and will fall two ticks for a 1bp rise in the six-month rate. For another futures contract maturing in six months' time, the profile $(+2\ -3)$ means that this future will rise two ticks for a 1bp rise in the six-month rate and will fall 3bp for a rise of 1bp in the nine-month rate.

Now consider a spread position of long one contract that matures in three months' time and short one contract that matures in six months' time.

Being long the near-dated contract and short the far-dated contract is known as being *long the spread*.

The combined profile will now comprise three numbers, showing the separate exposure to three-, six-, and nine-month rates. It can be obtained by combining the $(+1\ -2)$ profile for the long contract and minus $(+2\ -3)$ for the short contract:

$$
\begin{array}{cccc}
(\ +1 & -2 &) & \\
(\ & -2 & +3 &) \\
\hline
(\ +1 & -4 & +3 &)
\end{array}
$$

The resulting profile (+1 -4 +3) means that the spread position will:

1. Increase in value by one tick for a 1bp rise in three-month rates.
2. Decrease in value by four ticks for a 1bp rise in six-month rates.
3. Increase in value by three ticks for a 1bp rise in nine-month rates.

This composite behaviour profile gives us a very powerful way of quickly evaluating the effect on a spread position of any possible movement in the yield curve. Of course, there are an infinite number of ways in which interest rates could change, but it is interesting to consider three specific types of movement:

1. A parallel shift in the yield curve, where rates for all maturities move up or down by the same amount.
2. A nonparallel shift in the yield curve, where the slope of the yield curve becomes more positive.
3. A nonparallel shift in the yield curve, where the slope of the yield curve becomes more negative.

The case of the parallel shift is easy to evaluate. Let's suppose that all rates go up by exactly 1bp. The effect on the spread will then be

$$(+1 \times +1) + (-4 \times +1) + (+3 \times +1) = 0$$

In other words, the spread is *totally unaffected* by a parallel shift in the yield curve. Under such circumstances, the long and the short positions offset each other perfectly.

Now consider the general situation where the slope of the yield curve becomes more positive. For this to happen, the six-month rate must increase by more than the three-month rate, and the nine-month rate must increase by more again. If d_3, d_6, and d_9 are defined as the respective increases in these three rates, we can say that

$$d_9 > d_6 > d_3$$

and that

$$(d_9 - d_6) \geq (d_6 - d_3)$$

From the spread behaviour profile, the change in value of the spread position will be

$$d_3 - 4d_6 + 3d_9 = 3(d_9 - d_6) - (d_6 - d_3)$$
$$> 0$$

since $(d_9 - d_6) \geq (d_6 - d_3)$. This means that someone who is long the spread will always profit if the yield curve becomes more positive, regardless of what happens to the general level of rates. The above proof will also hold true if all the d's are negative, i.e., if rates generally decline, so long as the slope of the yield curve becomes more positive.

In the last situation, where the slope of the yield curve becomes more negative, we can reverse the inequalities in the preceding proof to demonstrate that someone who is long the spread will always lose money, no matter what happens to the general level of interest rates.

Table 7.9 summarises the effect of movements in interest rates on outright and spread positions.

As an illustration of the effect of changing interest rates on a spread position, consider the family of yield curves illustrated in Figure 7.7.

The initial yield curve in all cases has three-, six-, and nine-month yields at 9%, 9½%, and 9¾%, respectively. In the two scenarios illustrated in the first graph, the yield curve first rises by ½% ("up" scenario), and then falls by ½% ("down" scenario), both movements being parallel shifts. In the three scenarios illustrated in the second graph, the slope of the yield curve always becomes ½% more positive, but rates either rise ¾% ("up" scenario), fall ¾% ("down" scenario), or remain at the same general level ("pivot" scenario).

TABLE 7.9
Effect of Yield Curve on Futures Position

	Long Futures	Short Futures	Long Spread	Short Spread
Interest rates higher	–	+	0	0
Interest rates lower	+	–	0	0
Yield curve slope more +ve	depends	depends	+	–
Yield curve slope more -ve	depends	depends	–	+

FIGURE 7.7
Parallel and Nonparallel Yield Curve Shift Scenarios

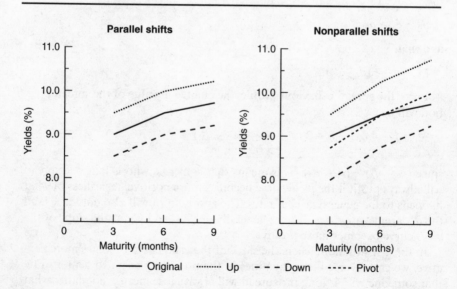

—— Original   ·········· Up   - - - Down   ----- Pivot

TABLE 7.10
Evaluation of Rate Scenarios on Future Spread

		Fair Prices		Profits (bp)		
		Jun	Sep	Jun	Sep	Net
	Original	90.22	90.21			
Parallel	Up	89.74	89.76	-48	+45	-3
shift	Down	90.70	90.67	+48	-46	+2
Non-	Pivot	89.97	89.50	-25	+71	+46
parallel	Up	89.26	88.82	-96	+139	+43
shift	Down	90.69	90.18	+47	+3	+50

We can now analyse the effect of these various scenarios on the June/September spread, purchased immediately after the expiry of the March contract. The set of fair futures prices for the June and September contracts can be calculated using equation 7.4. These prices, along with the resultant profits and losses, are presented in Table 7.10.

As expected from the preceding analysis, the spread is virtually unaffected by a parallel shift in the yield curve but produces an almost consistent 50bp of profit when the slope of the yield curve increases by 50bp. Although not evaluated here, the spread would consistently lose 50bp if the slope of the yield curve were to decrease by 50bp.

Chapter Fourteen will demonstrate how interest rate futures, FRAs, and interest rate swaps may be used to manage interest rate risk in both simple and more complex situations. In the meantime, the next chapter reviews the other major types of futures contracts: bond futures and stock-index futures.

Chapter Eight

Bond and Stock Index Futures

While short-term interest rate futures are the largest contracts when measured in terms of trading volume in the underlying asset, bond futures—and specifically the U.S. T-bond contract on the CBOT—are the most heavily traded financial futures contracts when measured in sheer numbers of contracts per day. Most major futures exchanges offer at least one such contract. Some—like the CBOT—offer contracts along the whole length of the yield-curve spectrum. Others—like LIFFE—provide a market in contracts on bonds denominated in a range of major currencies.

Closely related to bond futures are stock index futures, both being contracts on capital market instruments. Although bond futures are based on a tangible asset while stock index contracts are based on an abstract number, there are great similarities in the way they are priced.

This chapter starts by explaining exactly what bond futures are and then moves on to deal with pricing, the delivery mechanism, and simple hedging applications. Later sections discuss the pricing and application of stock index futures.

8.1 DEFINITION OF BOND FUTURES CONTRACTS

It is easier to understand the concept of a bond future than it is to understand the short-term interest rate contracts discussed in the previous chapter. This is because bond futures, like most commodity futures, are based on the delivery of a tangible asset—a particular bond—at some date in the future. As an example, the CBOT T-bond contract, the most active of all financial futures contracts, is defined in Table 8.1.

The definition of this contract calls for the delivery of a U.S. Treasury bond with a minimum effective maturity of 15 years, and an 8% coupon. We could envisage the holder of a long position in T-bond futures paying the futures price in dollars on the delivery date and receiving such a bond.

However, there would be problems if the definition of deliverable bonds were restricted solely to those with a coupon of exactly 8%. Sometimes there simply may be no bonds having this precise coupon. Even if there were one or two such bonds, the size of the futures market in relation to the size of the

TABLE 8.1
Definition of T-Bond Contract on CBOT (December 1992)

Unit of trading	U.S. T-bond having a face value of $100,000, and a coupon of 8%
Deliverable grades	U.S. T-bonds with minimum time to maturity or first call of 15 years from first day of delivery month
Delivery months	March, June, September, December
Delivery date	Any business day during delivery month
Last trading day	12:00 noon Seventh business day before last business day of delivery month
Quotation	Percent of par, expressed as points and $1/32$nds of a point, e.g., 80-16 means 80 $16/32$ or 80.50%
Minimum price movement	$1/32$nd of 1 percent
Tick value	$31.25
Daily price limit	Three full points (96 ticks)
Trading hours	07:20 – 14:00 (trading pit) 17:20 – 20:05 22:30 – 06:00 (Globex screen trading)

bond issue could expose the bond futures market to price manipulation. It would not be difficult for a group of investors to buy T-bond futures contracts *and* a major portion of the underlying bonds. When the delivery month came, those who were short the futures contracts would either have to close out their positions or buy up the underlying bonds. Futures prices and bond prices would both be driven up while this *short squeeze* was on, resulting in a handsome profit for the original investors.

To avoid this, futures exchanges design contracts in such a way as to prevent anyone cornering the market. In the case of the T-bond and most similar contracts, this is achieved by allowing delivery of *any* bond with a sufficient maturity. Of course, the holder of a long position in futures would prefer to receive a high-coupon bond with significant accrued interest, while those who were short futures would favour delivering a cheaper low-coupon bond shortly after the coupon date. This apparent conflict of interests is resolved by adjusting the *invoicing amount*—the amount paid in exchange for the bond—to account for coupon rate and timing of the bond actually delivered. Equation 8.1 defines the invoice amount:

$$INVAMT = FP \times CF + ACC \qquad (8.1)$$

where

INVAMT	is the invoice amount
FP	is the futures price

CF   is the conversion factor

ACC   is the accrued interest

Every bond deliverable under a particular futures contract will have its own conversion factor, which is intended to compensate for the coupon and timing differences of deliverable bonds. The futures exchange publishes tables of conversion factors well in advance of each delivery date. These numbers will be smaller than 1.0 for bonds having coupons less than 8% and greater than 1.0 otherwise. As an example, Table 8.2 lists the set of conversion factors calculated by the CBOT for all bonds deliverable under the March 1993 T-bond futures contract.

A particular bond deliverable on several dates will have similar, but not identical, conversion factors. For example, the $11\frac{1}{4}\%$ bond maturing on February 15, 2015, has conversion factors of 1.3310, 1.3293, and 1.3280, for the contracts maturing in June, September, and December 1993, respectively.

In the bond market, bonds with a high coupon trade at a higher price than those with a low coupon. An investor choosing between two bonds with similar maturities but different coupons would have to weigh up the advantage of receiving a higher coupon against the disadvantage of paying a higher price. In a perfect market, the prices would adjust so that the effective return to the investor was identical for both bonds.

To take a simple example, consider two bonds with just one year to mature. One pays an annual 5% coupon, while the other pays an annual 15% coupon. If the price of the low-coupon bond were 95.45 and the price of the

TABLE 8.2
Conversion Factors for T-Bond Futures Deliverable under March 1993 Contract

Coupon (%)	Maturity	Amount ($billion)	Conversion Factor	Coupon (%)	Maturity	Amount ($billion)	Conversion Factor
$7\frac{1}{4}$	May 15, 2016	18.82	0.9217	$8\frac{3}{4}$	Aug 15, 2020	21.01	1.0825
$7\frac{1}{4}$	Aug 15, 2022	10.01	0.9155	$8\frac{7}{8}$	Aug 15, 2017	14.02	1.0928
$7\frac{1}{2}$	Nov 15, 2016	18.86	0.9474	$8\frac{7}{8}$	Feb 15, 2019	19.25	1.0946
$7\frac{5}{8}$	Nov 15, 2022	10.30	0.9578	9	Feb 15, 2018	9.03	1.1081
$7\frac{5}{8}$	Feb 15, 2021	11.01	0.9860	$9\frac{1}{8}$	May 15, 2018	8.71	1.1208
8	Nov 15, 2021	32.33	1.0000	$9\frac{1}{4}$	Feb 15, 2016	7.27	1.1298
$8\frac{1}{8}$	May 15, 2021	11.75	1.0139	$9\frac{7}{8}$	Nov 15, 2015	6.90	1.1943
$8\frac{1}{8}$	Aug 15, 2021	12.01	1.0137	$10\frac{5}{8}$	Aug 15, 2015	7.15	1.2706
$8\frac{1}{8}$	Aug 15, 2019	20.01	1.0134	$11\frac{1}{4}$	Feb 15, 2015	12.67	1.3322
$8\frac{1}{2}$	Feb 15, 2020	10.06	1.0546	$11\frac{3}{4}$	Nov 15, 2009-14	6.01	1.3403
$8\frac{3}{4}$	May 15, 2017	18.19	1.0795	12	Aug 15, 2008-13	14.76	1.3485
$8\frac{3}{4}$	May 15, 2020	10.01	1.0825	$12\frac{1}{2}$	Aug 15, 2009-14	5.13	1.4050

high-coupon bond were 104.54, the investor should be indifferent between the two, as both would offer a return of 10% on the money invested.

In the first case, the investor would invest 95.45 and would receive the face value of 100 at maturity plus the coupon payment of 5, a total of 105. The effective annual return is then 10%:

$$\frac{105 - 95.45}{95.45} = 10\%$$

In the case of the high-coupon bond, the investor would receive at maturity the face value of 100 plus a coupon of 15, or 115 in total, for an original investment of 104.54. The effective annual return here is also 10%:

$$\frac{115 - 104.54}{104.54} = 10\%$$

In other words, by adjusting the price, the market can provide investors with the same return from two bonds with vastly different coupon rates.

Exactly the same principle is used to calculate the conversion factors for different bonds. The conversion factor for each bond is simply the price per $1 (or per £1, DEM1, FRF1, etc.) such that every bond would provide an investor with the same yield if purchased. The yield selected for the calculations is the same as the coupon rate in the definition of the futures contract, 8% in the case of the T-bond futures contract on the CBOT.

Other things being equal, bonds with a higher coupon will have larger conversion factors than those with lower coupons. As an example, compare the 7¼% of May 2016, whose conversion factor is 0.9217, with the 9¼% of February 2016, which has a conversion factor of 1.1298. Both bonds mature at almost the same time, but the bond carrying the 9¼% coupon has the higher conversion factor. This follows directly from the simple example given above, which demonstrated that bonds bearing a higher coupon trade at higher prices.

For bonds with the same coupon, maturity has an influence, though this is slightly less obvious. For bonds with coupons below the nominal coupon rate defined in the contract specification, the conversion factor is smaller for bonds with a longer maturity. Compare the conversion factor of 0.9217 for the 7¼% of May 2016 with 0.9155 for the 7¼% of Aug 2022. The opposite is true for bonds carrying coupons in excess of the nominal coupon rate, for which the conversion factor will be larger the longer the maturity. This can be demonstrated by comparing the 1.0795 factor for the 8¾% of May 2017 with 1.0825 for the 8¾% of May 2020.

This latter effect stems from the mathematics of fixed-interest securities. Bonds whose coupon lies below current market yields will trade at a discount. This discount is larger the longer the maturity, because it is a disadvantage to hold a bond paying a coupon lower than current market rates, and this disadvantage is greater the longer the period until the bond matures. Conversely, bonds with coupons above current market yields trade at a premium, which will be greater the longer the maturity.

Most futures exchanges calculate conversion factors effective on the exact delivery date if a single date is defined or on the first day of the delivery month if delivery can take place at any time during that month. The CBOT, however, rounds the maturity of the bond down to the nearest quarter of a year before performing the calculation. For example, on March 1, 1993, the 12½% bond has a maturity of just under 16½ years until its first call on August 15, 2009; the CBOT would therefore use an effective maturity of 16¼ years. With a bond calculator, it is possible to verify that the price at which the above bond would yield 8% with 16¼ years to mature is indeed 1.4050.[1]

This chapter has so far concentrated on the T-bond contract traded at the CBOT, the most liquid of all bond futures contracts. Table 8.3 summarises some of the other major bond futures contracts traded.

As the table demonstrates, the different futures contracts differ only in some of the finer details. The principles underlying their pricing, behaviour, and applications are all identical.

8.2 THE CHEAPEST-TO-DELIVER BOND

The system of conversion factors provides a good, but not a perfect, system for making all deliverable bonds perfect substitutes for one another.

For a start, we have already seen how the CBOT rounds the bond maturity to the next lowest quarter before calculating the conversion factor. Even if it did not, bonds can be delivered any day during the delivery month against the CBOT contract, while the conversion factor remains constant throughout. Many other exchanges avoid this particular problem by defining a single day as the delivery date and calculating the conversion factor as of that date.

Nonetheless, there is still a fundamental flaw. Conversion factors are calculated to equalise returns at a single uniform yield, the coupon rate specified in the contract definition. In practice, however, different bonds trade at different yields, giving rise to the concept of a yield curve first discussed in Chapter Two (Section 2.4). Even if all bonds traded at the same yield, it is unlikely that this would be exactly the same as the coupon rate specified in the definition of the bond futures contract.

This means that, despite using conversion factors, not all bonds are equal when it comes to delivery. Some bonds will be relatively more expensive, some will be cheaper, and one in particular will be the *cheapest-to-deliver bond*—an important concept when it comes to the pricing of bond futures contracts.

To determine which bond is the cheapest-to-deliver, consider someone who executes the following strategy during the delivery month:

1. Buy $100,000 face value of a deliverable bond.
2. Sell one futures contract.
3. Immediately initiate the delivery process.

---

[1] If the exact maturity were used, the conversion factor would work out at 1.4078.

TABLE 8.3 *Definitions of Major Bond Futures Contracts (December 1992)*

Contract	2-yr. U.S. T-Note	5-yr. U.S T-Note	10-yr. U.S T-Note	Long Gilt	Bund	BTP	Notional
Exchange	CBOT	CBOT	CBOT	LIFFE	LIFFE	LIFFE	MATIF
Unit of trading	US Treasury Note	US Treasury Note	US Treasury Note	UK Government Bond (Gilt)	German Government Bond	Italian Government Bond	French Government Bond
Face value	$200,000	$100,000	$100,000	£50,000	DEM 250,000	ITL 200m	FRF 500,000
Notional coupon	8%	8%	8%	9%	6%	12%	10%
Deliverable grades	U.S. T-notes with $1\frac{3}{4}$-2 yrs to mature	U.S. T-notes with $4\frac{1}{4}$-5 yrs to mature	U.S. T-notes with $6\frac{1}{2}$-10 yrs to mature	UK Gilts with 10-15 yrs to mature	Bundesanleihe $8\frac{1}{2}$-10 yrs to mature	BTPs with 8-$10\frac{1}{2}$ yrs to mature	French Gov't Bonds with 7-10 yrs to mature
Delivery months	Mar, Jun, Sep, Dec	Mar, Jun, Sep, Dec	Mar, Jun, Sep, Dec	Mar, Jun, Sep, Dec	Mar, Jun, Sep, Dec	Mar, Jun, Sep, Dec	Mar, Jun, Sep, Dec
Delivery dates	Any business day during delivery month	Any business day during delivery month	Any business day during delivery month	Any business day during delivery month	10th calendar day of delivery month	10th calendar day of delivery month	Any business day during delivery month
Last trading day	12:00 noon Seven business days before last business day of delivery month	12:00 noon Seven business days before last business day of delivery month	12:00 noon Seven business days before last business day of delivery month	11:00 Two business days before last business day of the delivery month	11:00 (Frankfurt) Three Frankfurt business days before delivery date	12:30 (Milan) Four business days before delivery date	Four business days before last business day of delivery month
Quotation	Points and one quarter of a $\frac{1}{32}$nd of a point, e.g., 80-162 means $80\,^{16.25}/_{32}$	Points and one half of a $\frac{1}{32}$nd of a point, e.g., 80-165 means $80\,^{16.5}/_{32}$	Points and $\frac{1}{32}$nds of a point, e.g., 80-16 means $80\,^{16}/_{32}$	Points and $\frac{1}{32}$nds of a point, e.g., 80-16 means $^{16}/_{32}$	Points and 0.01 of a point, e.g., 80.50	Points and 0.01 of a point, e.g., 80.50	Points and 0.02 of a point, e.g., 80.50
Tick value	$15.625	$15.625	$31.25	£15.625	DEM 25	ITL 20,000	FRF 100
Daily price limit	One full point (128 ticks)	Three full points (192 ticks)	Three full points (96 ticks)	-	-	-	250 ticks
Pit trading hours	07:20 - 14:00 17:20 - 20:05	07:20 - 14:00 17:20 - 20:05	07:20 - 14:00 17:20 - 20:05	08:30 - 16:15	07:30 - 16:15	08:00 - 16:10	09:00 - 16:30
Screen trading hours	22:38 - 06:00	22:36 - 06:00	20:34 - 06:00	16:30 - 18:00	16:20 - 17:55	16:21 - 17:58	

The amount paid out for the bond will simply be the prevailing market price plus any accrued interest:

$$BNDAMT = P + ACC \tag{8.2}$$

where

$BNDAMT$	is the amount paid to purchase the bond
P	is the prevailing market price of the bond
ACC	is the accrued interest.

The invoice amount $INVAMT$ received when delivering the bond against the short futures position has already been defined in equation 8.1. The resultant profit from the complete strategy is then

$$\begin{aligned} PROFIT &= INVAMT - BNDAMT \\ &= (FP \times CF + ACC) - (P + ACC) \\ &= (FP \times CF - P). \end{aligned} \tag{8.3}$$

The bond for which this expression is maximised will be the cheapest-to-deliver bond during the delivery month. A slightly more complex formula taking into account carrying costs can be derived to determine which bond is the cheapest-to-deliver prior to the delivery month.

As an example, on March 3, 1993, the bonds deliverable under the March 1993 T-bond contract were available at the prices summarised in Table 8.4. On the same date, the March contract was trading in the range 111-26 to 112-26 and settled at 112-21. Table 8.4 demonstrates for each deliverable

TABLE 8.4
Determining the Cheapest-to-Deliver T-Bond in March 1993

Coupon (%)	*Maturity*	*Bond Price*	*Conversion Factor*	*FP×CF −P*	*Coupon (%)*	*Maturity*	*Bond Price*	*Conversion Factor*	*FP×CF −P*
7¼	May 15, 2016	104–16	0.9217	−0.66	8¾	Aug 15, 2020	122–26	1.0825	−0.86
7¼	Aug 15, 2022	105-00	0.9155	−1.86	8⅞	Aug 15, 2017	123-18	1.0928	−0.45
7½	Nov 15, 2016	107-11	0.9474	−0.61	8⅞	Feb 15, 2019	123-29	1.0946	−0.59
7⅝	Nov 15, 2022	109-28	0.9578	−1.97	9	Feb 15, 2018	125-15	1.1081	−0.63
7⅝	Feb 15, 2021	112-02	0.9860	−0.98	9⅛	May 15, 2018	126-27	1.1208	−0.58
8	Nov 15, 2021	113-28	1.0000	−1.22	**9¼**	**Feb 15, 2016**	**127-19**	**1.1298**	**−0.31**
8⅛	May 15, 2021	115-10	1.0139	−1.09	9⅞	Nov 15, 2015	134-31	1.1943	−0.42
8⅛	Aug 15, 2021	115-09	1.0137	−1.08	10⅝	Aug 15, 2015	143-17	1.2706	−0.39
8⅛	Aug 15, 2019	114-26	1.0134	−0.65	11¼	Feb 15, 2015	150-15	1.3322	−0.39
8½	Feb 15, 2020	119-16	1.0546	−0.69	11¾	Nov 15, 09-14	151-26	1.3403	−0.82
8¾	May 15, 2017	122-02	1.0795	−0.45	12	Aug 15, 08-13	152-30	1.3485	−1.02
8¾	May 15, 2020	122-24	1.0825	−0.80	12½	Aug 15, 09-14	159-08	1.4050	−0.97

bond the profit that would be available from buying the bond, selling the futures contract at 112-21, and then immediately delivering the bond against receipt of the invoice amount.

As the table illustrates, the results span the range from –0.31 down to –1.97, these figures representing the dollar losses per $100 of bonds traded. The best (or least bad) result arises from using the 9¼% of February 2016, which is therefore the cheapest-to-deliver bond in this example. The figure of –0.31 therefore implies a loss of $310 if the strategy were executed for $100,000 face value of bonds.

Although the 9¼% of February 2016 is the cheapest-to-deliver, several other bonds have very similar values for the expression $FP \times CF - P$. If the 9¼% of February 2016 were trading at ³⁄₃₂nd higher, the 10⅝% of August 2015 and the 11¼% of February 2015—both being bonds with very similar characteristics—would then become the cheapest-to-deliver

It is interesting to note that all the bonds produce a small negative result for the strategy of buying the bond, selling the futures, and initiating the delivery process. This might suggest that the opposite strategy, buying the futures and selling the bond short (known as a reverse cash-and-carry), would lead to a profit. However, the party who is short futures always initiates the delivery process and can, among other things, choose which bond to deliver. Anyone tempted to execute a reverse cash-and-carry by shorting the 7⅝% of 2022, in a bid to secure a 1.97% riskless profit should, therefore, note that the seller would be most unlikely to deliver that particular bond. In addition to choosing which bond to deliver, the futures seller can also exploit a number of features inherent in the delivery process to gain a slight advantage over the party who is long futures. These features, which will be explained in Section 8.5, are called *seller's options* and have a positive value to the holder of a short futures position, offsetting the small losses revealed in Table 8.4.

8.3 CASH-AND-CARRY PRICING FOR BOND FUTURES

The previous section discussed the strategy of buying a deliverable bond and selling the futures contract and demonstrated how this can provide a method for determining which bond is the cheapest-to-deliver during the delivery month. Among all the deliverable bonds, the one that maximises the expression in equation 8.3 is the cheapest-to-deliver. Table 8.4 demonstrated that the result from executing this strategy was almost zero and would be zero if the value of the seller's options are taken into account.

This near-zero result is to be expected, of course. If the strategy created a significant profit for any bond, arbitrageurs would intervene immediately to exploit the opportunity. Their action would drive up the price of the cheapest-to-deliver bond and drive down futures prices, thereby eliminating the profit potential.

So far, the strategy of buying a bond and selling the futures contract has been applied only to the delivery month and only as a means of determining which bond is the cheapest-to-deliver against a short position in the futures. However, the idea can be extended to yield two very important benefits. First and foremost, the strategy can be exploited in order to determine the fair price at which bond futures contracts should trade. Second, this technique can be applied not only in the delivery month but at any time prior to the contract's maturity.

Consider the following strategy executed by an arbitrageur some time before the delivery month:

1. Buy $100,000 face value of a deliverable bond.
2. Finance the bond through a repo (sale and repurchase agreement, a form of secured borrowing).
3. Sell one futures contract.
4. Hold the bond until the last day of the delivery month.[2]
5. Deliver the bond against the short futures position.

As this involves buying a bond for cash and carrying it for a period of time, the strategy is known as a *cash-and-carry*. It is easier to understand the underlying principles if the transactions are summarised pictorially, as in Figure 8.1.

FIGURE 8.1
Pictorial Representation of Cash-and-Carry

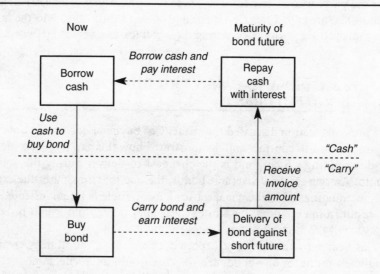

---

[2] Or until the delivery date, in the case of contracts that define a single day on which delivery can take place.

Figure 8.1 starts at the top left with the arbitrageur borrowing a sum of money. The top leg of the diagram represents the *cash* part of the cash-and-carry operation. This money is used to finance the purchase of a deliverable bond, which is held or carried until the end of the delivery month. The bottom leg illustrates the *carry* part of the cash-and-carry operation. Finally, on the last day of the delivery month, the bond is delivered to extinguish the short futures position, and the proceeds are used to repay the original borrowing.

Suppose that on March 3, 1993, an arbitrageur decides to undertake a cash-and-carry using the 9¼% of February 15, 2016, the bond that turned out to be cheapest to deliver against the March contract in the delivery month. To allow sufficient time for the cash-and-carry to earn a possible profit, the arbitrageur decides to sell the June contract, with the intention to deliver the bond at the end of June. The rates prevailing for the various transactions would be as follows:

Dealing date	March 3, 1993
Value date	March 4, 1993
Bond	9¼% maturing February 15, 2016
Bond price	127-19
Conversion factor	1.1295
Repo rate	2.82%
Future	June 1993 T-bond future
Futures price	111-11
Holding period	118 days
Final delivery date	June 30, 1993

Figure 8.2 shows the detailed cash flows arising from these transactions.[3] At the inception of the strategy, the bond is purchased for a total consideration of $128,028.14. This comprises the $127,593.75 quoted price of the bond plus 17 days accrued interest of $434.39. The bond is immediately repo'd out in order to obtain the funds required to finance the purchase of the bond in the first place.

The strategy terminates at the end of the delivery month, when the bond is delivered against the short futures position. The invoice amount is known at the outset, being determined solely by the futures price, the conversion factor, and the accrued interest on the delivery date. This sum can be calculated by inserting the appropriate values into equation 8.1:

$$INVAMT = \frac{111.34375 \times 1.1295 + 3.44959}{100} \times \$100,000 = \$129,212.36$$

---

[3] For simplicity, the margin flows arising from the futures position are ignored.

FIGURE 8.2
Detailed Cash Flows for a T-Bond Futures Cash-and-Carry Strategy

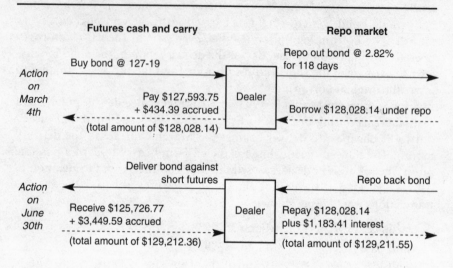

The amount repaid under the repurchase agreement is the principal of $128,028.14 plus interest at 2.82% for 118 days:

$$REPAMT = 128,028.14 \times (1 + 0.0282 \times \frac{118}{360}) = \$129,211.55$$

These two sums are virtually identical, being within 0.0007% of each other. If the repo rate had been 2.822% instead of 2.82%, the figures would have matched precisely.

With these rates, an arbitrageur executing a cash-and-carry operation would obtain neither a profit nor a loss. The same would be true, of course, if the opposite strategy—a reverse cash-and-carry—had been executed. This implies that the futures price of 111-11 must have been fair. If the price had been any different, the arbitrageur would have been able to exploit the opportunity and profit as a result.

An important feature of this cash-and-carry strategy is that all rates are known in advance. The purchase price of the bond, the conversion factor, the repo rate, and the selling price of the future are all fixed at the inception of the strategy. Nothing remains to be negotiated or determined thereafter. The profit or loss through entering into the cash-and-carry can therefore be determined in advance and has three components.

First, the invoice amount from equation 8.1 is

$$INVAMT = FP \times CF + ACC_D \tag{8.4}$$

where

INVAMT	is the invoice amount
FP	is the futures price

CF is the conversion factor

ACC_D is the accrued interest when the bond is delivered

Second, the amount repaid under the repurchase agreement is

$$REPAMT = (P + ACC_0) \times (1 + rt) \tag{8.5}$$

where

$REPAMT$ is the amount repaid to repurchase the bond

P is the quoted (clean) price of the bond

ACC_0 is the accrued interest when the bond is purchased

r is the repo rate (expressed as a decimal fraction)

t is the fraction of a year over which the bond is repo'd

Finally, we must take into account any coupons paid while the bond is being carried, which belong to the owner of the bond even though it has been repo'd out. We can assume that the coupons can also earn the repo rate, so that the total value of coupons plus interest earned is

$$CPNINT = \sum_{i=1}^{N} CPN_i (1 + rt_{i,D}) \tag{8.6}$$

where

$CPNINT$ is the value of coupons received plus interest earned thereon

N is the total number of coupons received during the carrying period

CPN_i is the ith coupon

r is the repo rate (expressed as a decimal fraction)

$t_{i,D}$ is the fraction of a year from receipt of the ith coupon until the delivery date

The net profit from the cash-and-carry strategy is therefore

$$
\begin{aligned}
PROFIT &= INVAMT + CPNINT - REPAMT \\
&= FP \times CF + ACC_D + \sum_{i=1}^{N} CPN_i (1 + rt_{i,D}) - (P + ACC_0) \times (1 + rt)
\end{aligned}
\tag{8.7}
$$

If we set the net profit to be zero, so that arbitrageurs cannot gain from either the forward or reverse cash-and-carry strategy, we can rearrange equation 8.7 to obtain an expression for the fair futures price:

$$FP = \frac{(P + ACC_0) \times (1 + rt) - \sum_{i=1}^{N} CPN_i (1 + rt_{i,D}) - ACC_D}{CF} \tag{8.8}$$

If we insert the values used in the previous illustration, we obtain

$$FP = \frac{(127.59375 + 0.43439) \times (1 + 0.0282 \times \frac{118}{360}) - 0 - 3.44959}{1.1295} = 111.34303 = 111\text{--}11$$

which is the futures price actually observed.

With the exception of the repo rate, all the prices used in this illustration were actual market rates at the close of business on February 15, 1993. In practice, the repo rate would probably have been somewhat higher than the 2.82% used here, at a little over 3%. If we use 3% instead of 2.82%, we obtain a loss from the cash-and-carry strategy of $74.72, equivalent to 0.0584% or 18bp on an annualised basis. This represents the value of the seller's options previously referred to and discussed more fully in a later section. This discrepancy can also be considered the difference between the actual futures price of 111-11 and the theoretical futures price of 111-13 obtained by using a repo rate of 3% in equation 8.8. The fact that these contracts trade at two ticks below their theoretical price is another way of measuring the value of the seller's options.

Let's summarise the key points behind cash-and-carry pricing:

- A cash-and-carry strategy comprises borrowing money, buying a deliverable bond, and selling the future.
- The prices, rates, and final outcome are all known at the outset, when the cash-and-carry is executed.
- The cash-and-carry strategy is riskless if the bond is delivered against the short futures position.
- The net profit must be zero when seller's options are taken into account, given that:
  - All prices are known at the outset.
  - The strategy is a riskless one.
- The fair price for a futures contract can therefore be derived by applying the zero profit constraint to the cash-and-carry strategy.

There is therefore no need to forecast future bond prices in order to price a bond futures contract. Just as with short-term interest rate contracts, it is possible to construct a set of deals at known rates to hedge completely a bond futures position. With short-term futures contracts, the hedge comprised borrowing at one maturity and lending at another maturity to create a synthetic forward-forward position. With bond futures contracts, the hedge comprises borrowing money and buying the cheapest-to-deliver bond.

Running a cash-and-carry position involves paying out interest at the repo rate and earning interest at the coupon rate on the cheapest-to-deliver bond. When repo rates are higher than the coupon rate, it will cost money to carry the bond. This is called *negative carry*, and bond futures prices will be higher the longer the carry period. On the other hand, if repo rates are lower than the coupon rate, someone running the cash-and-carry will benefit. In this *positive carry* environment, futures prices will be lower for later delivery months. This compensates the party who is long futures, who must wait longer for delivery and therefore forgoes the opportunity to earn the attractive coupon interest while waiting.

TABLE 8.5
Closing Prices on March 3, 1993, for CBOT T-Bond Futures

Contract	Closing Price
March 93	112-21
June	111-11
September	110-02
December	108-28
March 94	107-23
June	106-20
September	105-19

As an example, consider the set of T-bond futures prices at the close of business on March 3, 1993, shown in Table 8.5.

The futures prices decline by about one full point between successive delivery months, reflecting the positive carry caused by repo rates of about 3% and a coupon rate of $9\frac{1}{4}\%$. The gap between March 1994 and June 1994 contracts of 34 ticks is less than that between March 1993 and June 1993 contracts of 42 ticks, reflecting market expectations that repo rates will rise in the future.[4]

8.4 THE IMPLIED REPO RATE

In the example discussed in the previous section, the $9\frac{1}{4}\%$ of February 2016 was used to illustrate cash-and-carry pricing; why choose this particular bond? For anyone contemplating executing a cash-and-carry strategy, the correct bond to choose is the one that maximises the net profit when delivered against the short futures position, in other words, the cheapest-to-deliver bond. During the delivery month, this is the one that maximises equation 8.3. Before the delivery month, the cheapest-to-deliver bond is the one that maximises the net profit defined in equation 8.7.[5] We can write this latter condition as follows:

$$\max (PROFIT) \Rightarrow \max \left(FP \times CF + ACC_D + \sum_i^N CPN_i (1 + rt_{i,D}) - (P + ACC_0) \times (1 + rt) \right) \tag{8.9}$$

---

[4] It is possible to show that, as a rough approximation, the difference in futures prices from one contract to the next is one-quarter of the difference between the repo rate and the *nominal* coupon rate defined in the contract specification.

[5] Equation 8.3 is actually a simplified version of equation 8.7 and can be obtained by assuming that purchase and delivery are actioned at the same time, so that $ACC_0 = ACC_D$, $N=0$ and $t=0$.

There are a number of ways of solving this problem, all of which are equivalent and will lead to the same choice of cheapest-to-deliver bond. The most obvious method is simply to calculate the net profit for each deliverable bond and find which bond gives the largest profit. Alternatively, we could use the device of setting the net profit to zero and rearrange the equation to solve for the bond giving the lowest fair futures price, as in equation 8.8. As a final alternative, we could once again set the net profit to zero and search for the bond giving the highest repo rate. The last method has the attraction that the futures price is more readily observable and therefore easier to insert into an equation than the repo rate.

By setting the net profit to zero and rearranging equation 8.9, we can obtain an expression for the *implied repo rate*:

$$ r = \frac{(FP \times CF + ACC_D) - (P + ACC_0) + \sum_{i}^{N} CPN_i}{t(P + ACC_0) - \sum_{i}^{N} (CPN_i \, t_{i,D})} \tag{8.10} $$

where

  r is the implied repo rate.

The implied repo rate is the repo rate at which a cash-and-carry strategy would produce a zero profit. If the cash-and-carry could be executed at a repo rate lower than the implied repo rate, the strategy would result in a profit. If the actual repo rate were higher than the implied repo rate, the cash-and-carry would result in a loss. The implied repo rate is therefore a break-even interest rate—the higher the rate, the better.

An alternative way to look at the implied repo rate is to liken the cash-and-carry strategy to an ordinary investment. The cash-and-carry involves a cash outflow at the beginning, arising from buying the bond at the outset. When the bond is eventually delivered against the short futures position, there is a cash inflow. With an ordinary investment, there is a cash outflow at the outset when the investment is made and a cash inflow at the end when the investment is liquidated. In both cases, the rate of return can be measured by comparing the cash inflow at the end with the cash outflow at the beginning. Looked at this way, the implied repo rate is simply the rate of return earned by investing in a bond and selling it at the price originally fixed by the futures contract.

Table 8.6 shows the implied repo rates on March 3, 1993 (value date March 4) for the set of bonds deliverable into the June 1993 T-bond futures contract, assuming that delivery would take place on June 30. In each case, the implied repo rate is calculated according to equation 8.10. For example, using the 9¼% of February 2016 as the deliverable bond gives an implied repo rate of 2.82%.

TABLE 8–6
Implied Repo Rates for T-Bond Futures Deliverable under June 1993 Contract

Coupon (%)	Maturity	Implied Repo Rate (%)	Coupon (%)	Maturity	Implied Repo Rate (%)
7¼	May 15, 2016	1.39	8¾	Aug 15, 2020	1.41
7¼	Aug 15, 2022	–1.90	8⅞	Aug 15, 2017	2.45
7½	Nov 15, 2016	1.59	8⅞	Feb 15, 2019	2.12
7⅝	Nov 15, 2022	–2.10	9	Feb 15, 2018	1.81
7⅝	Feb 15, 2021	0.85	9⅛	May 15, 2018	1.98
8	Nov 15, 2021	0.10	**9¼**	**Feb 15, 2016**	**2.82**
8⅛	May 15, 2021	0.49	9⅞	Nov 15, 2015	2.40
8⅛	Aug 15, 2021	0.68	10⅝	Aug 15, 2015	2.76
8⅛	Aug 15, 2019	1.84	11¼	Feb 15, 2015	2.82
8½	Feb 15, 2020	1.79	11¾	Nov 15, 2009–2014	1.78
8¾	May 15, 2017	2.23	12	Aug 15, 2008–2013	1.63
8¾	May 15, 2020	1.36	12½	Aug 15, 2009–2014	1.81

As the figures in Table 8.6 demonstrate, the implied repo rate varies from –2.10% to +2.82%, being highest for the 9¼% of February 2016. Using the criterion of highest implied repo rate, this bond is therefore the cheapest-to-deliver, which explains why this particular bond was chosen to illustrate all the examples in this section.

$$r = \frac{(111.34375 \times 1.1295 + 3.44959) - (127.59375 + 0.43439) + 0}{\dfrac{118}{360} \times (127.59375 + 0.43439) - 0} = 2.82\%$$

8.5 THE DELIVERY MECHANISM

The vast majority of futures positions are closed out, reversed, or liquidated prior to maturity. As a clear example of this, consider the statistics illustrated in Figures 8.3 and 8.4. These show, respectively, the open interest and trading volume figures for the March 1993 and June 1993 CBOT T-bond contracts during February and March 1993.

From an average of just under 400,000 contracts traded each day during the last four working days in February, trading volume in the March contract drops immediately to 90,895 contracts on the first day in March and down to around 32,235 by March 4, one-tenth the volume of the previous week. At the same time, volume in the June contract increases tenfold, from around 50,000 contracts per day at the end of February to 262,853 contracts on March 1, alone, and over 503,566 contracts on March 4.

FIGURE 8.3
Open Interest for CBOT T-Bond Futures February–March 1993

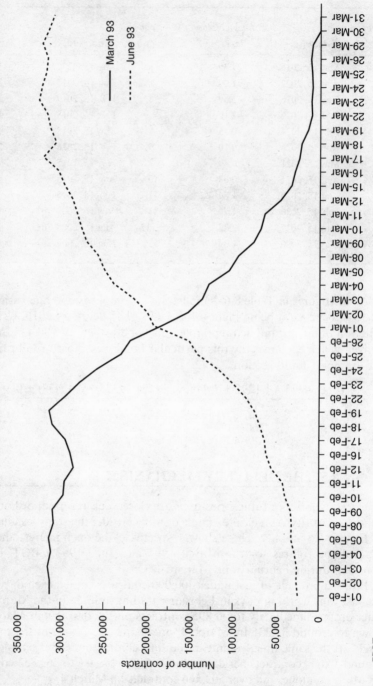

Source: CBOT.

FIGURE 8.4
Trading Volume for CBOT T-Bond Futures February–March 1993

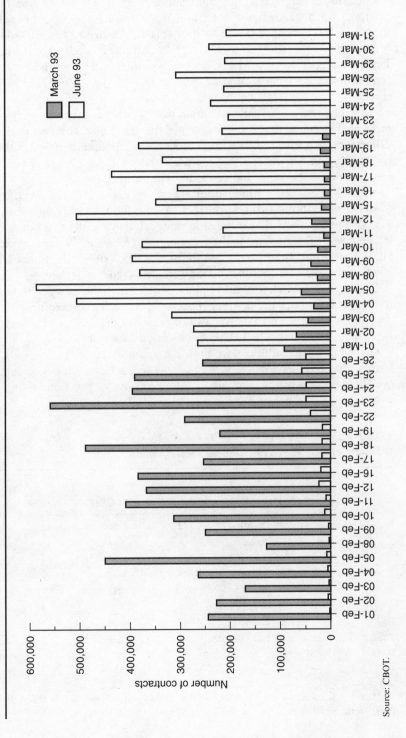

Source: CBOT.

Open interest in the March contract declines in a similarly spectacular fashion, from a steady figure of around 315,000 contracts throughout almost the whole of February down to half this figure in the first few days of March, finally petering out to just 11,094 contracts by the end of the month. The declining interest in March contracts is mirrored by an increase in the June contract, up from around 27,000 contracts at the start of February to a steady 318,000 contracts by the end of March.

Although these figures demonstrate that positions in the vast majority of expiring T-bond contracts are rolled into the next liquid contract during the delivery month, the 11,094 March 1993 contracts remaining after the last trading day on March 23, 1993 represent the small percentage of contracts, less than 4% in this case, that do result in physical delivery.[6]

Table 8.7 analyses which bonds were actually delivered against the March 1993 T-bond futures contract. As the figures clearly show, in over 95% of the contracts that resulted in physical delivery, the two bonds ranking highest in Table 8.4 using the criterion $\max(FP \times CF - P)$ were selected. In all, the top four bonds accounted for over 99.95% of the deliveries, leaving just five contracts where other bonds were delivered.

When physical delivery takes place, it is always the party who is short futures who initiates the delivery process. Most exchanges require shorts to declare their intention to deliver two days before the required delivery date. If the delivery date is called D, the notification date is then D–2.

On the day after notification, D–1, the exchange assigns someone who is long futures to receive delivery. Some exchanges select a long systematically: the oldest long position, the largest long position, or pro rata amongst the

TABLE 8.7
Deliveries Against March 1993 T-Bond Futures Contract

Coupon (%)	Maturity	Contracts delivered	FP x CF - P	Ranking
7¼	May 15, 2016	2	–0.66	12
7¼	Aug 15, 2022	1	–1.86	13
7½	Nov 15, 2016	2	–0.61	9
9¼	Feb 15, 2016	5,686	–0.31	1
9⅞	Nov 15, 2015	312	–0.42	4
10⅝	Aug 15, 2015	150	–0.39	3
11¼	Feb 15, 2015	4,941	–0.39	2

Source: Chicago Board of Trade

---

[6] In fact, there were an additional nine contracts that resulted in delivery on March 25, 1993. All the remaining 11,094 were delivered on March 31.

largest long positions. Other exchanges may simply select a long at random. Also on D–1, the short names the particular bond that is to be delivered.

Finally, on D itself, the short delivers the bond, and the long makes payment for value that day. The invoice amount actually paid is calculated according to equation 8.1.

Although this scheme may seem perfectly straightforward, the delivery sequence operating in conjunction with the definition of the bond futures contract gives rise to a number of advantages for the holder of a short position in futures. These advantages, collectively called the *seller's options*, have already been alluded to at the end of Section 8.2, and are explained here in more depth.

The timing option. Some exchanges specify a range of dates when delivery may take place, often allowing delivery on any date in the delivery month. This gives the short the right to choose when during the delivery month to effect delivery. If repo rates are lower than the nominal coupon rate, the short would usually choose to defer delivery until late in the month and earn the difference.

The wildcard option. On some exchanges, the futures settlement price for invoicing purposes, normally the closing futures price, may be fixed before the last possible time when a short may notify his intention to deliver. If bond prices decline after the futures settlement price is established, the short may elect to deliver and make an extra profit.

The quality option. The short advises the exchange of his intention to deliver on D–2, but has until D–1 to choose which bond will actually be delivered. If bond prices move during this period, a more attractive bond may become available.

The end-of-month option. Once again, for exchanges that allow delivery to take place at any time during the delivery month, trading in the futures contracts ceases several days beforehand. Bond prices may therefore move after the futures settlement price is determined, but before the final delivery date.

In each case, these features operate in favour of the short, who can act on favourable movements in bond prices but can wait out unfavourable ones. For this reason, bond futures will normally trade a few points below the theoretical futures price given by equation 8.8. In the example given in Section 8.3, the June 1993 future should trade at 111–13 if repo rates were 3%; the actual price observed was 111–11, valuing the seller's options at $\frac{2}{32}$nds of a point.[7]

---

[7] For a formal analysis of the valuation of the seller's options, see Gay, G., and Manaster, S., "Implicit Delivery Options and Optimal Exercise Strategies for Financial Futures Contracts," *Journal of Financial Economics* 16 (1986) pp. 41–72, or Arak, M., and Goodman, L., "Treasury Bond Futures: Valuing the Delivery Options," *Journal of Futures Markets* 7 (1987), pp. 269–86.

8.6 BASIC HEDGING WITH BOND FUTURES

One of the principal uses for bond futures is to hedge existing bond portfolios. A full discussion of the technique appears in Chapter Fourteen (Section 14.12), but we can illustrate here an example of hedging a simple portfolio, one containing just the cheapest-to-deliver bond.

At first sight, it would seem sensible to hold futures contracts so that the notional value of the contracts matched that of the bonds held. For a $10 million bond portfolio, 100 T-bond contracts, each with a notional underlying amount of $100,000, would seem to be the right number. However, this does not take into account the difference between the notional bond underlying the futures contract and the actual bonds held in the portfolio.

From equation 8.8, which provides an expression for the fair futures price, we can derive an equation that shows how the futures price will move for small changes in the price of the cheapest-to-deliver bond:

$$\frac{\partial FP}{\partial P} = \frac{1+rt}{CF} \tag{8.11}$$

therefore

$$\Delta FP \simeq \frac{\Delta P}{CF} \tag{8.12}$$

where

FP is the futures price
P is the bond price
CF is the conversion factor

Equation 8.12 means that, for small changes in the bond price ΔP, the futures price will move a small amount: $\Delta P/CF$. The futures price follows price movements of the cheapest-to-deliver bond, not one-for-one, but divided by the conversion factor. If the conversion factor were 1.3333, for example, a four-point movement in the bond price would be followed by just a three-point movement in the futures price.[8]

Thus, in order to hedge the cheapest-to-deliver bond, it is necessary to hold futures contracts equivalent to CF times the value of the bonds held. If the conversion factor of the cheapest-to-deliver bond were greater than one, more futures contracts would need to be held to adjust for the fact that movements in the futures price would be less than movements in the bond price, as illustrated in the previous paragraph. The opposite would be true if the conversion factor were less than one.

---

[8] Like the proverbial chicken and egg, it is difficult nowadays to say which comes first, movements in the bond price or movements in the futures price. Suffice it to say that they will move in tandem.

Suppose that an investor holding $10 million face value of the 9¼% of February 2016 on February 12, 1993, seeing that yields had fallen some 50bp over the previous six months, was now concerned to protect the value of the portfolio against an anticipated rise in yields. The investor could sell T-bond futures to hedge the portfolio against any further movements in bond prices.

On February 12, the relevant details were

Dealing date	February 12, 1993
Bond	9¼% maturing February 15, 2016
Bond price	122-26
Face value held	$10 million
Conversion factor	1.1298
Future	March 1993 T-bond future
Futures price	107-26
Underlying amount	$100,000 per contract

With the conversion factor in this case being 1.1298, the investor would need to sell 113 contracts in order to hedge the $10 million bond portfolio.

As the days passed, the investor saw that yields continued to fall, and by March 15, he was convinced that the trend in yields would continue downward. He therefore decided to lift the hedge and issued an instruction to his futures broker to buy back the 113 contracts at the opening of the market on March 16. That morning, prices were

Dealing date	March 16, 1993
Bond price	125-30
Opening futures price	110-18

We can now evaluate the effectiveness of this hedge. Over the 32-day period, the bond price rose 3-04, resulting in an increase in the value of the portfolio of exactly $312,500. Over the same period, the futures hedge lost 88 ticks because the investor sold initially at 107-26 and had to buy back at 110-18. Recalling that the tick value for T-bond contracts is $31.25, the magnitude of this loss on the 133 contracts can be calculated as

$$88 \times \$31.25 \times 113 = \$310,750$$

While the futures position lost money, the amount lost matches the profit on the underlying bond portfolio almost exactly. The total result for the investor is that the value of the portfolio has indeed been protected against any developments in bond prices after February 12, when the hedge was established. In this case it so happens that the portfolio has been insulated against a beneficial rise in bond prices, but this is the nature of futures hedges, which protect indiscriminately against both adverse and beneficial price developments.

To measure the success of the hedge, it is not enough simply to see whether the futures position made or lost money. Instead, it is necessary to compare the futures result with that of the underlying position and to see to what extent the futures and underlying positions mirrored each other. Equation 8.13 provides a simple measure of hedge efficiency:

$$\text{Hedge efficiency} = -\left[\frac{\text{Futures Result}}{\text{Bond Result}}\right] = -\left[\frac{-310,750}{312,500}\right] = 99.44\% \quad (8.13)$$

This is an impressive result. However, it would have depended very much on timing. Had our investor closed out the position at the end of the day on March 16, the futures price would have been 111-01, 15 ticks higher. The loss would have been $363,718.75, leading to an overall loss on the exercise of $51,218, compared to a profit of $1,750. In practice, therefore, hedging requires more than the execution of mechanical decisions; Part 2 of this book will explore practical hedging mechanisms in more detail.

8.7 STOCK INDICES AND STOCK INDEX FUTURES

Short-term interest rate futures and bond futures are the most heavily traded futures contracts by far, the top two contracts accounting for trading volume in excess of 130 million contracts during 1992. Nonetheless, there is also a highly active market in futures based on stock market indices, in which the two most active stock index futures accounted for trading volume of almost 24 million contracts during the same period.

Most people are familiar with the basic concept of a stock index as being a mathematically derived number representing the relative level of the stock market at any moment in time. The best known indices are probably the Dow-Jones Industrial Average (DJIA), the Nikkei, and the FTSE 100.

From the entire population of companies quoted on the particular stock exchange, a subset is selected that attempts to reflect the market as a whole. This subset usually comprises the largest companies, or the most representative companies, from each of the major industry classifications.

In the most basic case, an index can be calculated by adding the prices of the companies and taking a simple average. The DJIA is the best example of such a *price-weighted* index. This technique benefits from simplicity but unfortunately gives undue weight to those companies with relatively few high-priced shares while diminishing the importance of those with a larger number of low-priced shares. If this scheme were applied to the London stock market, for example, it would attribute equal significance to a 10-pence rise in the shares of Micro Focus, a moderately sized computer software company, as to a 10-pence rise in the mighty BT (British Telecom), a company more than 80 times as big.[9] Not only is this equal

---

[9] Price quotations on April 16, 1993: Micro Focus £22.55 (market capitalisation £313m); BT £4.11 (market capitalisation £25,416m)

treatment illogical when comparing companies of such different sizes, it is also unreasonable when compared with the share prices themselves. The 10-pence rise represents just an 0.4% rise in the value of Micro Focus, but a 2.4% rise in that of BT.

A better scheme is one adopted by most other indices, which sum, not the share prices themselves, but the market capitalisations of each company in the subset. If share prices rise, then the market capitalisations will also rise. However, the index will respond in proportion both to the percentage rise in the share prices and to the relative size of companies. Such a construction leads to a *market-weighted* index.

Although the DJIA average is the best known U.S. stock index, the major U.S. stock index futures are based on the S&P 500 index. The S&P possesses the twin advantages of being a market-weighted index and being based on a broader set of 500 quoted companies accounting for about 80% of the capitalisation of NYSE stocks. This is much broader and more reliable than the limited set of 30 companies whose prices constitute the DJIA. In a similar fashion the FTSE 100 index, representing approximately 70% of London's stock market capitalisation, has taken over from the older FT Ordinary Share index, which was also based on just 30 shares. In addition to being as broadly based as possible, an index suitable as the basis for a stock index future must also be calculated continuously and be available in real time.

8.8 DEFINITION OF STOCK INDEX FUTURES CONTRACTS

Although stock indices are mathematically derived from the share prices and capitalisations of quoted companies, they only convey information about relative movements in share prices over time and say nothing about the absolute level of the market. This is because the initial value for the index is an arbitrary number chosen when the index is first established or rebased.

For example, the S&P 500 is quoted relative to the average price of shares in the years 1941–1943, which were arbitrarily assigned the index value 10. If the S&P 500 index has a value of 448.94 on April 19, 1993, one can say that the shares within the index on that date are worth 44.894 times their value in 1941–1943. One could not, however, compare the S&P 500 index with the value of the FTSE 100, which was 2830.0 on that date, and say that UK stocks are worth six times those of U.S. stocks! The reason why the FTSE 100 index is so much larger is simply because the total market capitalisation of the component shares were assigned the arbitrary value of 1000 when the FTSE 100 was established.

Although the absolute level of a stock index is therefore arbitrary, it can be turned into something more meaningful by assigning a monetary value for each level of the index. For example, each full point of the FTSE 100 could be arbitrarily assigned £25 in value, so that an index level of 2830 would be "worth" £70,750. It may seem that we are getting further and further from reality by assigning an arbitrary monetary value to an index whose absolute level is also arbitrary. However, this device makes it possible to equate the "value" of a stock index with that of a specific basket of shares having the following specifications:

- The total value of the shares must match the monetary value of the index.
- The shares selected must correspond to the set of shares used to create the index.
- The amount of each holding must be in proportion to the market capitalisation of each of the companies.

If the FTSE 100 stood at 2830, the specific basket could be created by buying a portfolio of shares worth £70,750. The shares selected would be those of the 100 companies comprising the FTSE 100 index, and the relative value of each individual holding would correspond to the relative market capitalisations of each company within the index.

The behavior of this basket would then replicate the index exactly.[10] If the index went from 2830 to 2850, the arbitrary value of the index would increase from £70,750 to £71,250, and the value of the basket of shares would also increase to £71,250.

The definition of stock index futures takes advantage of this feature. A stock index future is a contract to buy or sell the face value of the underlying stock index, where the face value is defined as being the value of the index multiplied by a specified monetary amount. Table 8.8 illustrates the face values of the major stock index futures contracts on April 19, 1993.

As the figures demonstrate, there is a wide disparity between the index numbers and the multipliers, with the largest numbers being some 40 times

TABLE 8.8
Stock Index Face Values on April 19, 1993.

Index	Value	Multiplier	Face Value	Dollar Equivalent
S&P 500	448.94	$ 500	$ 224,470	$ 224,470
Nikkei 225	20,112.34	¥ 1,000	¥ 20,112,340	$ 180,948
FTSE 100	2,830.00	£ 25	£ 70,750	$ 108,778
CAC 40	1,968.91	FRF 200	FRF 393,782	$ 72,267
DAX	1,693.30	DEM 100	DEM 169,330	$ 104,855

---

[10] This is true so long as the stock index is calculated as the weighted arithmetic average of the market capitalisations of the component companies..

as big as the smallest ones. Nevertheless, the contracts have been designed so that the face values fall within a fairly narrow range, mostly between $100,000 and $200,000 equivalent.

Table 8.9 provides a fuller specification of one typical contract, the FTSE 100 stock index future.

8.9 ADVANTAGES OF USING STOCK INDEX FUTURES

Created in 1982, stock index futures provide investors and portfolio managers with an important new tool having a number of significant advantages:

1. Stock index futures permit investment in the stock market without the trouble and expense involved in buying the shares themselves. Section 8.10 provides an example of such a transaction.
2. Operating under a margining system like all other futures, stock index contracts allow full participation in market moves without significant commitment of capital. Margin levels allow leverage of between 10 and 40 times.
3. Transaction costs are typically many times lower than those for share transactions. The fees for a "round trip"—the creation and subsequent liquidation of a futures position—are around £25 or $25 per contract, often less. The costs involved in buying or selling an equivalent volume of shares are typically several hundred pounds.
4. It is much easier to take a short position. When selling securities short, it is often necessary to enter into a share borrowing arrangement so that the shares sold can be delivered. In addition, some stock markets

TABLE 8.9
Definition of FTSE 100 Contract on LIFFE (December 1992)

Unit of trading	£25 per index point of FTSE 100 index
Delivery	Cash settlement based on exchange delivery settlement price
Delivery months	March, June, September, December
Delivery date	First business day after the last trading day
Last trading day	10:30AM, third Friday in delivery month
Quotation	Index points, expressed as points and halves of a point, e.g., 2830.5
Exchange Delivery Settlement Price (EDSP)	Average level of FTSE 100 index between 10:10 and 10:30 on the last trading day
Minimum price movement	0.5 point
Tick value	£12.50
Trading hours	08:35 -16:10 (trading pit); 16:32 - 17:30 (APT screen trading)

impose an "up-tick" rule permitting short sales only after the market has moved up. No such hindrances operate in the futures market.

5. Portfolio managers responsible for large share portfolios can hedge the value of their investment against bear moves without having to sell the shares themselves. This is also illustrated in Section 8.10.

These advantages provide valuable new opportunities for investment managers and speculators alike.

8.10 CASH-AND-CARRY PRICING FOR STOCK INDEX FUTURES

Although bond futures specifically permit physical delivery of a bond, whereas stock index contracts are invariably cash-settled, there are many parallels between the two contracts. Both are capital markets instruments: the bond future works in conjunction with treasury and other bonds, while the stock index future works with equities. Furthermore, despite the fact that there is no deliverable instrument in the case of a stock index future, the contracts can be priced using the same cash-and-carry principles as were used to determine a fair price for bond futures.

Consider the following strategy executed before the delivery day:

1. Buy a portfolio of shares that replicate the stock index (with proportions matching construction of index and total value equal to face value of index).
2. Finance the portfolio by secured borrowing.
3. Sell one stock index futures contract.
4. Hold the portfolio until the last trading day, collecting and investing any dividends received.
5. Liquidate the shares immediately when trading in the future ceases.
6. Cash-settle the futures contract.
7. Use the proceeds of the share sale and futures settlement to repay the borrowing.

As with the bond future arbitrage, this is also a cash-and-carry operation, because the portfolio of shares is bought with cash and carried until the maturity of the futures contract. Figure 8.5 pictures this sequence of transactions, which is similar to Figure 8.1, but with some subtle differences.

The middle and lower parts of Figure 8.5 represent the cash-and-carry: borrowing money to buy the portfolio of shares and repaying the loan with the proceeds of the portfolio liquidation. The top part of the diagram shows the parallel transactions in the futures market, which hedge the portfolio against movements in the market. For example, if the stock market dropped while the cash-and-carry was in progress, the proceeds from selling the shares may not be enough to repay the borrowing. However, the futures contracts would make a profit under these circumstances.

FIGURE 8.5
Cash-and-Carry for Stock Index Futures

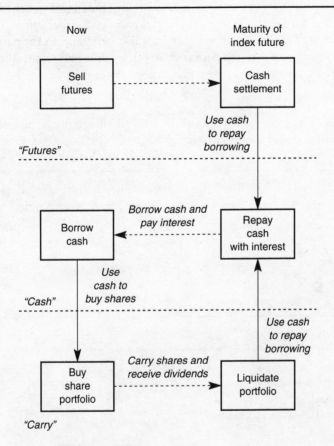

If the selection and amounts of the share deals are chosen carefully, the cash-and-carry operation, together with the futures contracts, form a riskless combination and can be used to determine a fair price for the futures contracts themselves.

Suppose that on October 27, 1992 market rates were

FTSE 100 index	2669.8
Face value of index	£66,745
Dividend yield	3.5%
Future	March 1993 FTSE 100 future
Futures price	2696.0
Last trading day	Friday March 19
Holding period	143 days
Interest rate	6%

Suppose also that the FTSE 100 rose during the five-month period and finally averaged exactly 2900 during the 20-minute closing period on March 19. This represents a rise of 8.62%. If the shares purchased matched exactly those in the FTSE 100 index, they would rise by a similar amount and be worth exactly £72,500 at the end of the holding period. With the parallel rise in the futures price over the period of 204 full points (408 ticks), the futures position would lose

$$408 \times £12.50 = £5,100$$

Summarizing the resulting cash flows at the beginning and end of the cash-and-carry operation:[11]

October 27, 1992

Purchase of shares to match index	-66,745.00
Borrowing	+66,745.00
Sale of future	0.00
Net cash flow	0.00

March 19, 1993

Sale of shares	+72,500.00
Dividends received during period	+915.23
Loss on futures	-5,100.00
Repayment of borrowing plus interest	-68,313.96
Net cash flow	+1.27

Apart from the small residual of £1.27 due to rounding, the end result of the cash-and-carry is effectively zero, showing that the future was correctly and fairly priced on October 27, 1992 at 2696. Had the price been any higher or lower, an arbitrageur would have been able to make a riskless profit through executing the cash-and-carry or the reverse cash-and-carry.

In principle, therefore, the concept of the riskless cash-and-carry can be applied to price stock index futures in exactly the same way as for bond

---

[11] The simple example here ignores the small amount of interest that could be earned on reinvesting dividends and the nontrivial costs of executing the share transactions.

futures. Equation 8.8 can be adapted to provide a formula for pricing these contracts:

$$FP = I_0 (1 + rt) - \sum_{i=1}^{N} DIV_i(1 + rt_{i,D}) \tag{8.14}$$

where

- FP is the fair stock index futures price
- I_0 is the stock index when the cash-and-carry is established
- r is the borrowing rate (expressed as a decimal fraction)
- t is the fraction of a year over which the cash-and-carry operation is executed
- N is the total number of shares in the index
- DIV_i is the dividend paid on the ith share during the cash-and-carry period
- $t_{i,D}$ is the fraction of a year between receipt of the ith dividend and the delivery date

Equation 8.14 allows for the receipt of discrete dividends during the cash-and-carry period and must be used if there are relatively few shares in the index, as with the CAC 40 index, for example. This is because the stream of dividends will be "lumpy" rather than a smooth flow. For a very broad-based index like the S&P 500, where dividends are more evenly spread throughout the year, it is sometimes possible to approximate the flow of discrete dividends with a dividend yield instead. This leads to a simple formulation for the fair futures price:

$$FP = I_0 [1 + t(r - d)] \tag{8.15}$$

where

d is the dividend yield.

Substituting the figures in the previous example into equation 8.15 gives

$$FP = 2669.8 \left[1 + \frac{143}{365} \times (0.06 - 0.035)\right] = 2695.95 \approx 2696$$

This approximation works well in this example. However, there are some practical difficulties in hedging stock index futures with shares. These problems sometimes lead to discrepancies between the calculated futures price and the actual price observed and are discussed in the next section.

8.11 PROBLEMS OF HEDGING STOCK INDEX FUTURES

While stock index futures provide a valuable tool for investors and portfolio managers, they are not as simple as bond futures for market makers to hedge. A number of features all contribute to the difficulties in ensuring that the fair price calculated from equations 8.14 and 8.15 is close to the actual futures price encountered in practice.

Constructing the index portfolio. Most stock indices used as the basis for index futures comprise several hundred separate shares. This is in sharp contrast to the bond future, where only a single bond needs to be held. This complexity creates numerous difficulties in constructing a share portfolio designed to mimic the index.

Transactions costs. These will be many orders of magnitude greater than for bond futures, reflecting the number of separate transactions involved. Transactions costs will also be doubled, because the share portfolio must be bought initially and then liquidated at the end of the cash-and-carry operation. With a bond future, it is possible to deliver the bond and therefore avoid the final transaction cost of liquidating the hedge.

Tracking error. In practice, many market makers hedge stock index futures by using a smaller subset of the companies within the index. The aim is to capture a significant proportion of the composition of the index with relatively few transactions. While this can reduce transactions costs, it introduces a tracking error, in that the value of the share portfolio may not correlate perfectly with movements in the index.

Lag between index price and share prices. In markets where share transactions are executed manually, it may be difficult or impossible to execute all the necessary transactions at the same time. If the market is moving while the cash-and-carry is being established, this may introduce a price risk. Even if it were possible to execute all the transactions simultaneously at one moment in time, the index price is normally based on *last sale price* of the component shares, whereas the cost of buying the shares is based on the *current offer price*. In a fast-moving market, there could be a considerable gap between these two prices.

Changes in index composition. The index composition may change during the cash-and-carry period. This may arise from stock splits, capital restructurings, the shrinkage or disappearance of some companies, or the growth of others. If this happens, new transactions must be executed to bring the shares held in line with the new formulation of the index. (This is somewhat analogous to the situation when the cheapest-to-deliver bond changes.)

Short sales. Some stock markets impose certain restrictions on short sales of shares, and this could impair the efficiency of a reverse cash-and-carry operation, which involves selling shares and buying futures.

Dividends. With a bond, the coupon is constant, known in advance, and is paid on set dates. Dividends on shares can only be estimated in advance and are paid at various times during the year. Even for broad-based indices like the S&P 500, there is a strong bunching of dividends in January–February, April–May, July–August, and in October–November. The effective carrying cost can therefore vary substantially throughout the year, especially before the payment of a large dividend on a narrow-based stock index. This means that hedging a stock index future can at best only be an approximate, rather than an exact, science.

The result of all these practical difficulties is to create a band of fair prices, rather than a single price. This band will be wider when there are high transactions costs, more uncertainty regarding dividends, more volatility, and less market efficiency. It must be remembered that the force that keeps actual market prices in line with theoretical ones is the possibility for arbitrageurs to make a risk-free profit. If this possibility is reduced or eliminated through excessive transactions costs or market inefficiency, market prices can drift away from theoretical prices.

Despite being one of the broadest based of stock indices, the S&P 500 actually exhibits the closest relationship in practice between actual and theoretical futures prices. This is aided by the existence of computerised order execution systems such as the Designated Order Turnaround (DOT) system at the New York Stock Exchange and others. These reduce transactions costs and make it much easier to execute the hundreds of transactions necessary in performing cash-and-carry arbitrage deals. The S&P 500 index future normally trades within ±0.5% of its theoretical price.

8.12 TURNING CASH INTO SHARE PORTFOLIOS AND SHARE PORTFOLIOS INTO CASH

Stock index futures mimic the behavior of the stock market as a whole, and they are easy to trade. They therefore provide the portfolio manager with a flexible and effective tool for restructuring an investment portfolio. Combining a long position in cash (i.e., an interest-bearing deposit) with the requisite number of stock index futures will effectively convert cash into shares. Alternatively, combining a long position in shares with a short position in futures will effectively turn the share portfolio into cash. Both these possibilities are illustrated with brief examples in the following paragraphs.

Cash into shares. Suppose that in the aftermath of sterling's departure from the ERM an investment manager decided to place £1 million of funds on deposit to earn interest fixed at 6.00%. The decision was made amidst the turmoil of the market on September 16, 1992; the funds were placed on September 18 for six months and will be repaid on March 18, 1993. There is no provision for early withdrawal of these funds.

By the end of October, the investment manager expects a significant rise in UK share prices to take place and wishes to benefit from this view. Unfortunately, the funds have already been committed and are no longer available to invest in shares, at least for the time being.

The investment manager therefore decides to buy FTSE 100 futures in order to profit from any rise in the market. On October 27, 1992, the FTSE 100 stands at 2669.8, and March contracts are quoted at 2696.0. The face value of the FTSE 100 is therefore

£25 × 2669.8 = £66,745

The manager therefore needs to buy

£1,000,000 / 66,745 = 15 contracts

On March 18, 1993, the FTSE 100 closed 7.862% higher, at 2879.7, while the March contract closed at 2880.0. We can now compare the performance of the cash plus futures strategy with the performance of the stock market itself, had the portfolio manager been able to switch into shares on October 27.

Cash plus futures

£1 million plus 6% interest for 142 days	1,023,342.47
Profit on futures: 368 ticks x £12.50 × 15 contracts	69,000.00
Total	1,092,342.27

Shares

£1 million index portfolio plus 7.862% capital appreciation	1,078,620.00
Dividends received at annual yield of 3.5%	13,616.44
Total	1,092,236.44

These two results are within 0.01% of each other, demonstrating that the combination of an interest-earning deposit plus the appropriate number of futures contracts effectively replicates the performance of an index portfolio.

Shares into cash. Let us suppose that on October 27, 1992, another investment manager needed to lock in the value of a modest share portfolio at the prices then prevailing. Perhaps the portfolio had attained a certain critical value that day, and guaranteeing that value was more important than the opportunity to profit from any subsequent rises in the UK stock market. Table 8.10 shows the composition and valuation of the portfolio on October 27, 1992.

All of these shares are included in the FTSE 100 index and in total represent approximately 13% of the weighting of the index. The investment

TABLE 8.10
Share Portfolio on October 27, 1992

	No. of Shares	Share Price (p)	Value of Holding
BTR	25,202	496	£125,001.92
Cadbury Schweppes	27,174	460	125,000.40
Forte	72,674	172	124,999.28
GEC	51,229	244	124,998.76
Hanson	53,648	233	124,999.84
Marks & Spencer	36,443	343	124,999.49
J Sainsbury	25,303	494	124,996.82
Thorn EMI	15,263	819	125,003.97
Total			£1,000,000.48

TABLE 8.11
Share Portfolio on March 19, 1993

	No. of Shares	Dividends Paid (p)	Share Price (p)	Value of Holding	% Change	Price Increase	Dividend Yield
BTR	25,202	9.00	599	153,228.16	22.58%	20.77%	1.81%
Cadbury Schweppes	27,174	6.60	479	131,956.94	5.57%	4.13%	1.43%
Forte	72,674	4.96	202	150,402.48	20.32%	17.44%	2.88%
GEC	51,229	4.80	305	158,707.44	26.97%	25.00%	1.97%
Hanson	53,648	5.70	238	130,740.18	4.59%	2.15%	2.45%
Marks & Spencer	36,443	3.55	359	132,124.10	5.70%	4.66%	1.03%
J Sainsbury	25,303	4.38	525	133,947.76	7.16%	6.28%	0.89%
Thorn EMI	15,263	15.05	872	135,390.44	8.31%	6.47%	1.84%
Total				1,126,497.49	12.65%	10.86%	1.79%

manager decides that the portfolio is sufficiently representative of the market that using FTSE 100 futures will provide an adequate hedge. With the FTSE 100 index at 2669.8, the face value of the index at £66,745, and a portfolio worth £1 million to hedge, it is once again necessary to work with

£1,000,000 / 66,745 = 15 contracts

This time, however, the investment manager must sell futures in order to hedge a long position in shares. He therefore sells 15 contracts at the market price of 2696.

When the futures contracts eventually expires on March 19, 1993, the investment manager decides to lift the hedge rather than extend it. Table 8.11 summarises the performance of the share portfolio over the 143-day period.

The share portfolio has shown an overall rise in value of 12.65%, comprising an average rise in price of the shares held of 10.86%, and dividends received equivalent to 1.79% of the portfolio's original value.[12] In particular, the holdings of BTR, Forte, and GEC have proved to be star performers, each producing a return in excess of 20% over the holding period.

However, with the general rise in share prices, the futures lost money over the period. The FTSE 100 March 1993 contract eventually settled at exactly 2900, resulting in a loss of

$$408 \text{ ticks} \times £12.50 \times 15 \text{ contracts} = £76,500$$

The total result was therefore £1,126,497.49 (the value of the share portfolio plus dividends received), less the £76,500 futures loss, a net value of £1,049,997.49, corresponding to a gain of 5.00%.

If the investment manager had instead decided to liquidate the shares and invest short-term at 6% for 143 days, the fund, including interest, would stand at 1,023,507.34. This would be a gain of 2.35% over the period.

In this particular example, combining the short futures position with a long position in shares did produce a return closer to that obtained with a pure cash position, but the results did not coincide exactly. This is because the eight shares actually held outperformed the market, both in price and in dividend yield. The market as a whole rose 8.62%, while the particular shares rose 10.86%, an extra gain of 2.24%. At an annual dividend yield of 3.5%, the dividends should have been 1.37% over the period, but they actually amounted to 1.79%, a further surplus of 0.42%. Combining these two gives a bonus return of 2.66%. This explains why the hedged shares produced a return of 5.00%, 2.65% over the expected return of 2.35% from a pure cash investment.

If the shares held had been more representative of the index portfolio, the combination of shares and short futures would have generated a return closer to the 2.35% cash return over the period, and the futures would have been more effective at turning shares into cash. Of course, a perfect result would have arisen had the investment manager held the index portfolio, just as in the previous example.

Chapter Sixteen will illustrate more sophisticated hedging and trading strategies, especially those involving options. These allow investment managers to protect their portfolios against detrimental market movements, while still allowing them to gain from beneficial developments.

---

[12] For simplicity we assume here that the dividends received are not invested to earn interest.

Chapter Nine

Swaps

Swaps are one of the outstanding success stories of the 1980s and are a vivid illustration of the benefits brought about through financial innovation. From virtually nothing in 1980, the swap market had grown to exceed $2,000billion a year by the end of the decade. This chapter first recounts the development of the swap market and then goes on to explain the two principal types of swap product: interest rate and cross-currency swaps. The remainder of the chapter is devoted to a thorough explanation of swap pricing and valuation based on zero-coupon concepts. Some of the many and varied applications for swaps are dealt with in Chapters Fourteen and Eighteen.

9.1 DEFINITION OF INTEREST RATE AND CROSS-CURRENCY SWAPS

In order to understand how the swap market developed, we need to start with a basic definition of interest rate and cross-currency swaps. Later sections in this chapter provide more details and much more rigid and detailed definitions of the two major type of swap products.

An interest rate swap is:

* an agreement between two parties

* to exchange a stream of cash flows

* denominated in the same currency

* but calculated on different bases

The most common type of interest rate swap is where one stream of cash flows is the fixed-rate coupons on a notional principal sum, while the other stream is floating-rate coupons. For example, one party may agree to pay fixed annual coupons of 10% on a notional principal sum of £1million, in return for receiving the prevailing sterling LIBOR rate on the same principal.

The fixed-rate payer would benefit if LIBOR were higher than 10% in a given period but would lose if LIBOR were lower than 10%. An interest rate swap is therefore similar to an FRA but operates over multiple periods.

A cross-currency swap is:

- **an agreement between two parties**
- **to exchange a stream of cash flows**
- **denominated in different currencies**
- **calculated on similar or different bases**

The distinguishing feature of a cross-currency swap is that the two streams of cash flows are denominated in different currencies. For example, one party could agree to pay quarterly coupons fixed at 9% per annum on a notional principal of DEM 10 million while receiving quarterly floating-rate coupons determined by three-month dollar LIBOR on a notional principal of $6.25 million. In practice, both coupons can be fixed-rate, both floating-rate, or one fixed and the other floating.

9.2 DEVELOPMENT OF THE SWAP MARKET

Swaps originated in the parallel and back-to-back loans that evolved during the 1970s. At the time, exchange controls operating in most countries limited the opportunities for companies to obtain cross-border finance or for investors to lend overseas.

Consider two companies, one based in the United Kingdom and the other based in the United States. Each company has a foreign subsidiary operating in the other country that requires finance. The most direct way would be for each parent company to finance its subsidiary through a loan, as illustrated in Figure 9.1.

The existence of exchange controls may have made this difficult, expensive, or even impossible. The alternative developed in the 1970s was the structure depicted in Figure 9.2.

Each parent company lends to the subsidiary of the other company operating in its own country. The U.S. parent company lends to the U.S. subsidiary of the UK company and similarly for the other parent and subsidiary operating in the United Kingdom. Parallel and back-to-back loans have similar structures and cash flows; the difference between them arose in the event of a default. A back-to-back loan provided each party with the right of offset in the event of a default, whereas the parallel loan offered no such right, nor was there any cross-collateralisation between the loans.

FIGURE 9.1
Direct Financing of Subsidiaries by Parents

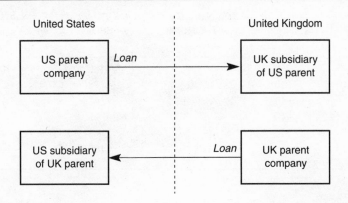

FIGURE 9.2
Parallel or Back-to-Back Loan

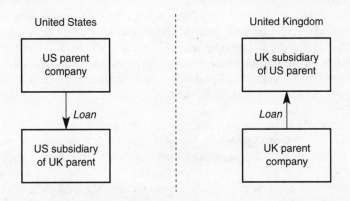

As an example, suppose market rates are £1=$2, sterling interest rates are 8%, and dollar rates 5%. Consider a UK subsidiary requiring finance of £100 million and a U.S. subsidiary wishing to borrow $200 million, both for a five-year period. Table 9.1 shows the cash flows for each party under a parallel or back-to-back loan.

The key advantage of these structures is that the restrictions imposed by exchange controls could be avoided, as there was no transfer of funds across borders. Of course, for the arrangement to work, there had to be a pair of companies with a pair of subsidiaries both needing similar amounts of finance and both willing to accept the credit risk involved.

The last factor, that of credit risk, was a significant one. One of the key benefits that financial institutions provide is that of intermediation—coming

TABLE 9.1
Cash Flows for Parallel or Back-to-Back Loan

Year	US Parent $ million	US Subsidiary of UK Parent $ million	UK Parent £ million	UK Subsidiary of US Parent £ million
0	−200	+200	−100	+100
1	+10	−10	+8	−8
2	+10	−10	+8	−8
3	+10	−10	+8	−8
4	+10	−10	+8	−8
5	+210	−210	+108	−108

between two parties. In the case of normal bank deposit-taking and lending, it is the bank that absorbs the credit risk if a borrower defaults, not the depositors who provided the finance. Yet with a parallel loan, the companies fund each other directly and must suffer the consequences in the event of a default.

Fortunately, as governments and central banks came to terms with the new environment of floating exchange rates, exchange controls were relaxed and eventually removed altogether in the case of the major currencies. This meant that multinational companies could more easily lend to their overseas subsidiaries. It did not, however, remove the exchange rate risk. A UK company lending dollars to its U.S. subsidiary would receive a stream of interest payments and the eventual repayment of principal, all of which would be denominated in dollars.

The solution to the latter problem, evolved in the early 1980s, was the cross-currency swap. The easiest way to depict this is by example, and Figure 9.3 shows how the parallel or back-to-back loan just discussed could be replaced by a pair of cross-currency swaps.

Starting with the UK parent and its subsidiary, the first cash flow is the payment of £100 million by the parent into the swap, which pays the subsidiary $200 million (at £1=$2 as before). Thereafter, the subsidiary pays into the swap the fixed dollar rate of $10 million per year, while the parent receives from the swap the fixed sterling rate of £8 million per year. There is a final reexchange of principals at the maturity of the swap. As far as the UK parent is concerned, the cash flows arising from the swap are exactly equivalent to lending £100 million fixed at 8% per annum, with no currency risk whatsoever. From the UK subsidiary's viewpoint, the cash flows are identical to borrowing $200 million dollars fixed at 5%.

An analogous situation obtains for the U.S. parent company and its subsidiary operating in the UK. The swap transaction is identical, except that all the cash flows are reversed. For all parties concerned, the cash flows associated with the pair of swaps are exactly the same as for the parallel or back-to-back loan enumerated in Table 9.1 and therefore need not be repeated again here.

FIGURE 9.3
Illustration of Simple Cross-Currency Swap

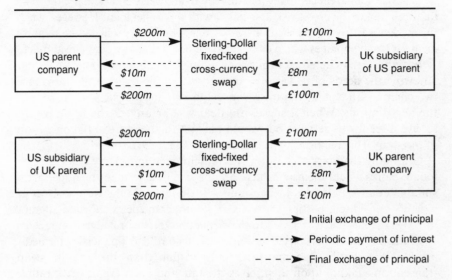

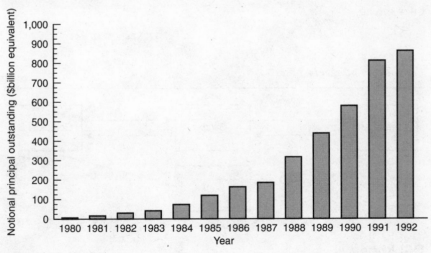

FIGURE 9.4
Growth of Cross-Currency Swap Transactions

Adjusted for double-counting.
Source: ISDA.

The evolution of currency swaps eliminated the need for parallel and back-to-back loans, and the market grew rapidly, as Figure 9.4 demonstrates.

Not only do cross-currency swaps eliminate the currency exposure that would arise if a parent company lent directly to an overseas subsidiary, they virtually eliminate the credit risk associated with a parallel loan. However, when the market was first established, there was one remaining problem: the requirement for two companies with a coincidence of needs that mirrored one another.

Initially, banks acted as brokers, bringing two counterparties together. Knowing the needs of its various counterparties, the bank would introduce two clients with similar but mirroring requirements, advise, and assist with the negotiations. When a successful deal was arranged, the bank would receive a fee for its services but would play no further part in the operation of the swap. This relationship is illustrated in Figure 9.5.

Gradually the market evolved. If a matching counterparty could not be found, banks would themselves take on one side of a swap in the hope that a suitable counterparty could be found a little later. Banks would also put together two counterparties whose needs did not coincide exactly and attempt to hedge the mismatch. This led to the dealer market illustrated in Figure 9.6.

In this mode, banks started to fulfil their true role as financial intermediaries. They would become principals rather than brokers in swap transactions, taking upon themselves the rate and counterparty risk rather than expecting their clients to absorb these risks. The concept of a *swap warehouse* was introduced, whereby banks would "warehouse" nonmatching swaps until a corresponding counterparty could be found. Instead of levying a fee on the counterparties to a swap, banks would instead obtain their remuneration from the margin between rates quoted to each side—the bid-offer spread.

FIGURE 9.5
Early Broker Market in Swaps

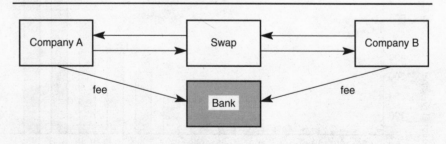

FIGURE 9.6
Swap Intermediation by Banks

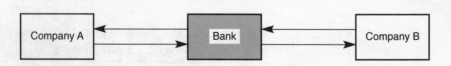

These developments increased liquidity tremendously, as it was no longer necessary to wait until matching counterparties could be found, and this has led to the tremendous explosion in swap volumes since the mid-1980s.

Although cross-currency swaps were the first type of swap instrument to be developed, the interest rate swap followed shortly afterwards. Just as with cross-currency swaps, where it can be said that market imperfections in the form of exchange controls led to the development of the market, so it was with interest rate swaps.

At the time, it was possible for large companies to borrow either at a fixed rate or a floating rate. However, the risk premiums in these two markets often differed. For example, a triple-A company might be quoted LIBOR + 10bp to borrow floating for five years or 11% to borrow fixed for the same period, whereas a triple-B company might be quoted LIBOR + 50bp and 12%, respectively, for floating and fixed borrowings. Note that the BBB company must pay a risk premium of 40bp for borrowing at a floating rate, but 100bp for borrowing fixed.

Suppose that AAA prefers to borrow floating, while BBB prefers to borrow fixed. By themselves, AAA would manage to borrow at LIBOR + 10bp, while BBB would pay 12% fixed. However, consider what happens if AAA borrows fixed at 11%, BBB borrows floating at LIBOR + 50bp, and they enter into an interest rate swap in which AAA agrees to pay to BBB periodic payments based on LIBOR in return for receiving periodic payments fixed at 11.20%. For this to work, both borrowings and the interest rate swap must all be for the same principal amount. Figure 9.7 depicts the periodic cash flows that result from this arrangement.

For AAA, the net result of borrowing fixed at 11%, receiving fixed payments at 11.20%, and paying LIBOR is to borrow at LIBOR—20bp. Similarly, BBB ends up borrowing at a fixed rate of 11.70%. Both borrowers have managed to borrow using their preferred method of funding, but each at a cost of 30bp lower than they could otherwise have achieved. By joining together and using an interest rate swap, AAA and BBB have managed to exploit the inefficiency in the credit market which charged BBB a different risk premium depending upon whether it borrowed fixed or floating. The swap has arbitraged the 60bp gap in risk premiums, and the gain in this example has been shared equally between both borrowers.

For simplicity, Figure 9.7 shows the two counterparties dealing with each other, as took place in the very early stages of the swap market. However, it was not long before banks intermediated between the two parties to a swap, as pictured in Figure 9.6. In the above example, the bank might pay AAA 11.15% fixed while receiving 11.25% fixed from BBB, thereby making a spread of 10bp.

Imperfections in the market provided the impetus for the interest rate swap market, but just as with cross-currency swaps, once the tool had been created, a myriad of opportunities and applications opened up. This has led to an even more dramatic growth than for cross-currency swaps, as Figure 9.8 clearly shows.

FIGURE 9.7
Illustration of Simple Interest Rate Swap

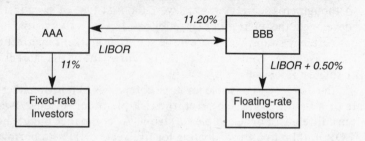

FIGURE 9.8
Growth of Interest Rate Swap Market

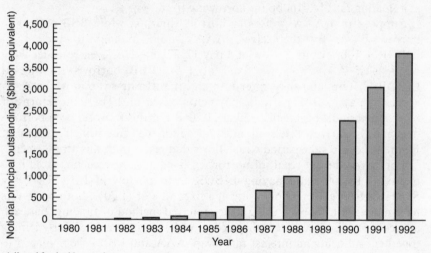

Adjusted for double-counting.
Source: ISDA.

Swaps have now established themselves as one of the principal tools of financial engineering. The continuing uncertainty and volatility over exchange and interest rates have created a growing demand for effective risk management techniques. Deregulation and globalisation of financial markets have removed the restrictions that had stifled progress. Finally, growing sophistication among both banks and their customers has led to a greater acceptance of swaps and to increased demand for these and other derivative products.

Innovative product design and advanced hedging techniques now make it possible for banks to tailor swaps in order to match the precise needs of borrowers and investors. Attractive new products like the diff swap have been created by combining swaps with other derivative products, and this has led to the final stage in swap development depicted in Figure 9.9.

FIGURE 9.9
Integrating Swaps with Other Derivative Products

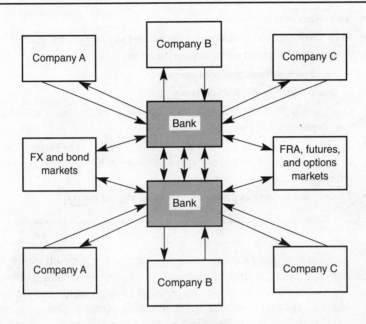

The first swaps were arranged by banks acting as brokers. Later, the swap warehouse technique evolved, in which banks would intermediate directly between counterparties. Banks specialising in swaps now integrate their currency and risk management across all derivative products. Swaps are no longer hedged by matching two identical but opposing swaps. Instead, swaps are hedged by combining positions in spot, forward and long-term FX, bonds, FRAs, short-term interest rate futures, bond futures, option-based products such as caps and floors, and other swaps, of course. In this way, banks can offer comprehensive risk management without the cost involved in hedging individual deals. The swap market has come a long way since 1980.

9.3 INTEREST RATE SWAPS

A basic definition of interest rate swaps was provided at the beginning of this chapter; it is now appropriate to refine the definition and provide more detail.

The cash flows resulting from a typical interest rate swap are illustrated in Figure 9.10 using the normal convention in which cash inflows are shown as an arrow pointing up, while cash outflows are shown as an arrow pointing down.

The diagram also demonstrates some of the key dates during the lifetime of a swap. The *trade date*—shown as t_0 in the diagram—is the date on which the two parties to the swap agree to their contractual commitments.

> **A standard interest rate swap is:**
>
> * An agreement between two parties.
> * Each party contracts to make periodic interest payments to the other.
>   - On a predetermined set of dates in the future
>   - Based on a notional principal amount
>   - Denominated in the same currency.
> * One party is the FIXED RATE PAYER—the fixed rate being agreed at the inception of the swap.
> * The other party is the FLOATING RATE PAYER—the floating rate being determined during the lifetime of the swap by reference to a specific market rate.
> * There is no exchange of principal—only exchange of interest.

Given the volume of swaps trading that takes place, nearly all swaps conform to standard documentation prepared by the International Swaps and Derivatives Association (ISDA), and the legal arrangements are therefore usually a formality. Although the form of the contract is standard, there are a number of important items that must be agreed at the inception of the swap. The most important of these are

* The fixed rate at which the fixed interest payments will be calculated.
* The frequency and basis for both the fixed-rate and floating-rate payments—payments are usually annual, semi-annual, or quarterly, but various day-count conventions can apply (these are discussed shortly).

The trade date is usually also the first *setting date*—shown as t_{s1} in the diagram—when the floating rate for the next period is determined. Most swaps use LIBOR as the market rate for the floating leg and, just as is conventional with eurocurrency deposits and FRAs, the rate is normally set two business days before the period commences. The second setting date t_{s2} will occur just before the beginning of the second swap period; again this is normally two business days beforehand. Subsequent setting dates follow the same pattern until the last setting date, just prior to the last swap period.

The *effective date*—shown as t_e in Figure 9.10—is the date when interest starts to accrue on both the fixed and floating legs of a swap, and this is usually two business days after the trade date. The time lag is designed to correspond to the similar gap between dealing date and value date in the eurocurrency markets. Since the floating rate for each period is always determined in advance of that period, both parties know the rates at which they should be accruing interest and the size of both the fixed and floating payments at the end of that period.

FIGURE 9.10
Cash Flows for Typical Interest Rate Swap

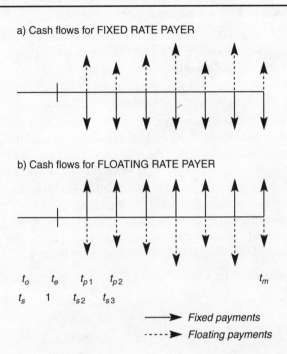

a) Cash flows for FIXED RATE PAYER

b) Cash flows for FLOATING RATE PAYER

t_o t_e t_{p1} t_{p2} t_m
t_s 1 t_{s2} t_{s3}

——▶ *Fixed payments*
- - - -▶ *Floating payments*

The first *payment date*, t_{p1}, comes at the end of the first swap period, when one party will be a net creditor and the other will be a net debtor. Rather than each party paying the entire interest payment to the other, the net debtor simply pays over the difference to the creditor. Most swaps involve each party being a net creditor for part of the time and a net debtor for the remainder.

This cycle then repeats itself until the final net payment is made on the *maturity date* of the swap, t_m.

The interest payments themselves are calculated using the standard formula

$$INT = P \times r \times t \tag{9.1}$$

where

INT is the interest payment
P is the nominal principal
r is the annual interest rate for the period (expressed as a fraction)
t is the day-count fraction

Although the principal is never exchanged in an interest rate swap, the parties to the swap must nonetheless agree to a nominal principal amount in the agreed currency in order for the interest payments to be calculated. The day-count fraction is the proportion of the year covered by the particular swap period and can be calculated in a number of ways:

- Actual/365 (fixed): This uses the actual number of days in the particular swap period divided by 365, even in a leap year. This convention is common among sterling interest rate swaps.

- Actual/360: This also uses the actual number of days in the swap period but divides by 360; this is common for dollar-denominated swaps.

- 30/360: This convention assumes that each month has exactly 30 days and uses the nominal number of days in the swap period divided by 360. For example, if the period covered July 15 to October 15, the numerator would be 90 days, even though there are actually 92 days in that period.

- Actual/Actual: The numerator is the number of days in the period. The denominator is made equal to the numerator for annual interest payments, twice the numerator for semi-annual payments, and four times the numerator for quarterly payments. This makes the day count respectively 1.00, 0.50, or 0.25, depending upon the payment frequency.

As an example, consider a swap having the following characteristics:

Principal	$10,000,000
Fixed rate	8.64%
Floating rate	LIBOR flat
First floating-rate setting	8.50%
Day-count convention (fixed)	Actual/360
Day-count convention (floating)	Actual/360
Trade date	February 3, 1993
Effective date	February 5, 1993
Maturity date	February 5, 1998
Payment frequency (fixed)	Annual (every February 5 or modified following business day)
Payment frequency (floating)	Annual (every February 5 or modified following business day)

Let's assume that LIBOR eventually turned out to be 8.25%, 9.25%, 9.375%, and 9.75% on the four remaining setting dates. Table 9.2 illustrates the cash flows that would result on each payment date, from the viewpoint of the fixed-rate payer.

Note that, apart from 1995 and 1996, the fixed payments are all different, even though the fixed rate is the same throughout. This arises because this swap uses the actual/360 day-count convention, and the days elapsed in four

TABLE 9.2
Example of cash flows from interest rate swap

Date	Days Elapsed	Floating Rate	Floating Receipt	Fixed Payment	Net Payment
05-Feb-93					
07-Feb-94	367	8.5000%	866,527.78	880,800.00	(14,272)
06-Feb-95	364	8.2500%	834,166.67	873,600.00	(39,433)
05-Feb-96	364	9.2500%	935,277.78	873,600.00	61,678
05-Feb-97	366	9.3750%	953,125.00	878,400.00	74,725
05-Feb-98	365	9.7500%	988,541.67	876,000.00	112,542

of the five swap periods are different. It is also interesting to note that the fixed-rate payer is the net payer in the first two periods but a net receiver later on. This is quite typical; it would be odd for anyone to enter into a swap transaction expecting to be a net payer throughout the swap's life.

The swap illustrated in Table 9.2 is an example of a *generic* or "plain vanilla" swap, which are the most common swaps encountered in practice. Generic swaps have the following fundamental characteristics:

- One leg of the swap is fixed while the other leg is floating.
- The fixed rate remains constant throughout the life of the swap.
- The floating rate is set in advance of each period and paid in arrears.
- Both legs have the same payment frequency with regular payments.
- The original swap maturity is 1, 2, 3, 4, 5, 7, or 10 years.
- The notional principal remains constant throughout the life of the swap.

However, interest rate swaps can now be created with many variations, and the resultant flexibility of swap contracts is one of the factors that has led to their success. The next section explains some of the more common permutations.

9.4 NONSTANDARD INTEREST RATE SWAPS

Virtually any of the characteristics of a swap contract can be modified to give a *nonstandard* swap contract that can be tailored more closely to meet the needs of one or both the swap counterparties.

Accreting, amortising, and roller-coaster swaps. Instead of remaining constant, the notional principal can vary through the life of the swap according to a predetermined pattern. An *accreting* or *step-up* swap is one in which the principal starts off small and increases over time. The converse, where the principal reduces in successive periods, is called an *amortising* swap. If the principal increases in some periods and reduces in others, the swap is described as a *roller-coaster* swap. Figure 9.11 depicts these three alternatives.

The accreting swap would be attractive in, for example, construction finance, where the amount being borrowed gradually increases during the lifetime of the project. The amortising swap, on the other hand, might be ideal for a borrower hedging a bond issue that featured sinking fund payments. For project finance, where the amount borrowed may increase initially and then decline as stage payments are made to the contractor, a roller-coaster swap can be designed to match the outstanding principal in

FIGURE 9.11
Accreting, Amortising, and Roller-Coaster Swaps

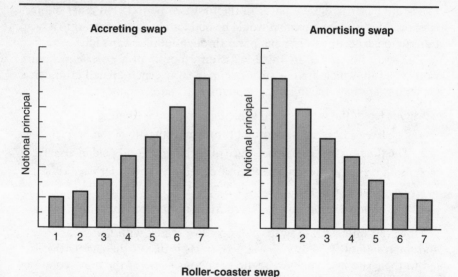

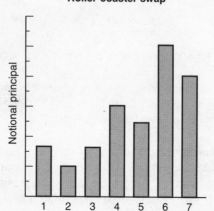

every period. In each case, it is not necessary for the underlying principal to follow a regular pattern; the only requirement is that the notional principal for each swap period be defined at the inception of the swap.

Basis swaps. In a generic swap, one leg is fixed, while the other is floating. In a *basis* swap, both legs are floating but linked to different bases. One floating leg is normally linked to LIBOR of a particular period, while the other may be linked to a different market-determined rate, e.g., commercial paper, CD, or federal funds rates. A company might, for example, have assets yielding LIBOR financed by a rolling commercial paper programme; a basis swap would eliminate the basis risk between income and expense streams. Alternatively, a company issuing commercial paper might wish to fix its cost of funds and combine a basis swap with a generic swap, thereby switching a floating CP rate first into a floating LIBOR rate and then into a fixed rate.

A variant of the basis swap links both floating rates to the same type of market rate, but for different tenors, e.g., one-month LIBOR against six-month LIBOR. In such cases, not only is the basis different, but the payment frequencies also differ. The party receiving six-month LIBOR and paying one-month LIBOR would make five successive monthly interest payments before receiving the net of the six-month rate, less the final one-month rate. Counterparty risk in such swaps is a little higher than for swaps where the payment frequencies coincide.

Margin swaps. Another variant of the floating side includes a margin above or below LIBOR instead of using LIBOR flat. Not surprisingly, such swaps are called *margin* swaps. A borrower raising finance at LIBOR+50bp may prefer to enter into a swap receiving LIBOR+50bp rather than LIBOR flat, so that the floating cash flows match exactly. However, the net result is little different from adding the margin to the fixed rate on a generic swap. For example, if the rate for a generic swap were 7.00% fixed against LIBOR flat, the quote for a similar margin swap might simply be 7.50% against LIBOR+50bp. A difference would only arise if the day-count conventions or payment frequencies on each side of the swap were to differ, e.g., actual/365 fixed against 30/360 floating.

Forward-start swaps. A *forward-start* swap defers the effective date not just one or two days after the trade date, but weeks, months, or even longer. A swap counterparty may wish to fix the effective cost of borrowing for floating-rate financing to be arranged some time in the future. For example, a company may have just won a project mandate and now be committed to raise finance that will be drawn down on some future date. If the company were to wait until later before arranging the swap, it would run the risk that interest rates might rise.

Off-market swaps. Most swaps are priced so that there is no advantage to either side at the outset, and so there is no need for any payment from one counterparty to the other at the outset. With an *off-market* swap, however, the fixed rate differs from the standard market rate, and one party must therefore compensate the other accordingly. One application for such a swap is when a company issues a floating-rate bond and wishes to use a swap not only to convert its floating obligations into a fixed-interest stream but also to pay the up-front costs of issuing the bond. An off-market swap can be designed so that the issuer receives an initial sum and periodic floating-rate interest payments against paying a fixed rate slightly higher than the market rate for a generic swap. The extra fixed-rate margin effectively amortises the up-front issuing costs over the lifetime of the swap.

Zero-coupon and back-set swaps. There are a number of other variations. A *zero-coupon* swap replaces the stream of fixed payments with a single payment, either at the beginning or, more usually, when the swap matures. In a *back-set* swap the setting date is just before the end of the accrual period, not just before the beginning. The floating rate is therefore set in arrears rather than in advance, which is why this kind of swap is also known as a LIBOR-in-arrears swap. Such swaps would be attractive to a counterparty who thought that interest rates would evolve differently from market expectations. For example, in a rising yield curve environment, forward rates will be higher than current market rates, and this will be reflected in pricing the fixed rate of a swap. A back-set swap would be priced higher still. If the fixed-rate receiver believed that interest rates would rise more slowly than the forward rates suggested, a back-set swap would be more advantageous than a conventional swap.

Diff swaps. The *diff swap* is a kind of basis swap whereby two floating-rate cash flows are exchanged. One stream comprises the floating-rate coupons in one currency. The other stream comprises coupons based on the floating-rate index in another currency, plus or minus a margin, but denominated in the first currency. For example, a diff swap may involve one party paying six-month dollar LIBOR in dollars on a notional principal of $10 million, and receiving six-month D-mark LIBOR less 1.90%, also in dollars on the same notional principal. Diff swaps became popular in the early 1990s when dollar interest rates were very low, but with a steep positive yield curve, while D-mark interest rates were quite high, with a steep downward yield curve. The party paying dollar LIBOR and receiving D-mark LIBOR less 1.90%, but paid in dollars, would therefore initially receive net payments under the swap. If interest rates followed the implied forward yields, these net receipts would turn to net payments later on. However, many investors believed that dollar rates would remain lower than the implied forwards while D-mark rates would remain higher, thereby benefiting under the swap for a much longer period, even throughout. Diff swaps are somewhat difficult to categorise, because they involve the interest rates in two different currencies, like a cross-currency swap, but payments in a single currency, like an interest-rate swap. Moreover, when a bank hedges a diff swap, the problem involves pricing a complex instrument called a quanto option.

9.5 CROSS-CURRENCY SWAPS

Now that we have defined interest rate swaps more precisely, it is easier to discuss cross-currency swaps in greater depth. One way of defining a cross-currency swap is to liken it to a special kind of interest rate swap.

A standard cross-currency swap is like an interest rate swap, except:

- The currencies of the two legs are different.

- There is always an exchange of principal at maturity.

- There is optionally an exchange of principal on the effective date.

- The legs may be:
  – Both fixed-rate.
  – Both floating-rate.
  – One fixed and one floating.

Alternatively, one could think of an interest rate swap as being a special kind of cross-currency swap for which both currencies were the same. In that analogy the exchange of principals is irrelevant; being in the same currency they would always net to zero.

Figure 9.12 provides two examples of the cash flow streams arising from a cross-currency swap. In the first example, the swap exchanges fixed-rate sterling for floating-rate dollars, but with no initial exchange of principals. The second example illustrates the cash flows when there is an initial exchange of principals followed by the exchange of fixed-rate dollars for fixed-rate ECUs.

In both cases illustrated by Figure 9.12, there is the mandatory final exchange of principals that is always a feature of standard cross-currency swaps. At first sight, this may appear to create a currency risk. Paradoxically, however, it is the final exchange of principals that removes the currency risk that otherwise would be present. This point will be proved later in this chapter.

In practice, it matters little whether there is an initial exchange of principals. A spot exchange deal can always be executed at the inception of the swap to create a desired initial exchange of principals if this is absent from the swap. Similarly, a spot deal can reverse the effect of an unwanted initial exchange of principals.

FIGURE 9.12
Examples of Cash Flows from Cross-Currency Swaps

Example 1: Floating dollars for fixed sterling; no initial principal exchanges

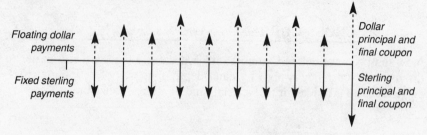

Example 2: Fixed ECU for fixed dollars; exchange of principals

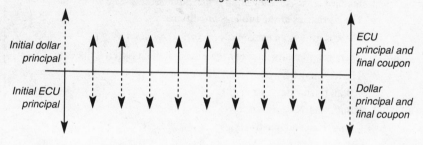

9.6 BASIC APPLICATIONS FOR SWAPS

Interest rate and cross-currency swaps have opened up innumerable opportunities in a wide number of applications. Chapters Fourteen and Eighteen will explore these in greater depth, but the following examples illustrate the major areas in which swaps have made an impact.

Fixing financing costs. A company currently borrowing at six-month LIBOR+100bp fears that interest rates may rise in the three remaining years of its loan. It enters into a three-year, semi-annual generic interest rate swap as the fixed-rate payer at 8.75% against receiving six-month LIBOR. This fixes the company's borrowing costs at 9.75% (9.99% effective annual rate) for the next three years, as Figure 9.13 illustrates.

Asset-linked swap. A U.S.-based insurance company is seeking to improve the yield on its portfolio of dollar-denominated securities. Ten-year U.S. T-bonds are currently yielding 8.14%, while German Bunds are offering a return of 8.45% for bonds of a similar tenor. Banks are quoting 10-year

FIGURE 9.13
Fixing Financing Costs with Interest Rate Swap

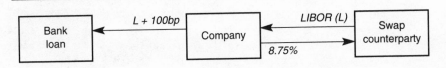

FIGURE 9.14
Asset-Linked Cross-Currency Swap

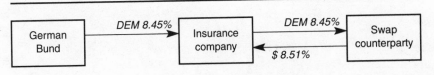

fixed-fixed dollar-mark cross-currency swaps whereby the insurance company could pay D-marks fixed at 8.45% against receiving dollars fixed at 8.51%. If the company were to buy Bunds and enter into the swap, it would receive a dollar income stream yielding 8.51%, some 37bp higher than investing directly in U.S. treasuries. This is pictured in Figure 9.14.

Liability-linked swap. A British company, having already made extensive use of the domestic capital market, is now seeking to raise additional finance. However, the quotes of 10.50% fixed or LIBOR+90bp floating reflect the reluctance of the sterling market to provide further funds at this time. The company therefore decides to turn to the burgeoning ECU bond market, where it can raise fixed-rate funds at 8.75%. The company does not, however, wish to be exposed to the risk that sterling could weaken against the ECU and therefore enters into a fixed-floating sterling-ECU cross-currency swap in which it pays sterling LIBOR+50bp against receiving ECU fixed at 8.75%. The net result shown in Figure 9.15 is to secure synthetic sterling financing at LIBOR+50bp, which is 40bp cheaper than the rate available by borrowing sterling directly.

9.7 ZERO-COUPON SWAP PRICING

When swaps were first introduced, the rates for generic swaps were determined by adding a suitable spread above treasury bond yields. This convention still survives today and can be seen in some swap quotations, as Table 9.3 illustrates.

In this example, the rates for each of the standard swap maturities is obtained by adding the swap spread to the yield on a benchmark T-bond of

FIGURE 9.15
Asset-Linked Cross-Currency Swap

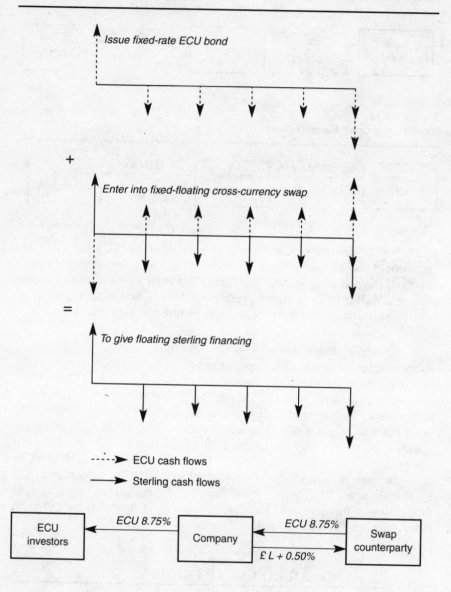

the appropriate maturity.[1] If the swap rate is quoted on a different basis than the bond, for example 30/360 as against actual/365, a straightforward interest conversion can be done. The swap spread itself depends largely on

---

[1] In this example, the rate for the four-year bond was interpolated from the three- and five-year bond yields, even though there were several suitable four-year bonds available at the time.

TABLE 9.3
Swap Quotations on November 18, 1992

Tenor	Treasury	Spread	Bond Yield	Swap Rate
2 yrs	9½% October 1994	30-34	4.61	4.91-4.95
3 yrs	9½% November 1995	38-42	5.15	5.53-5.57
4 yrs	(interpolated)	40-44	5.60	6.00-6.04
5 yrs	8¾% October 1997	35-40	6.05	6.40-6.45
7 yrs	6% October 1999	36-41	6.46	6.82-6.87
10 yrs	6⅜% August 2002	38-43	6.84	7.22-7.27

Source: Intercapital Brokers

prevailing credit conditions, and since the mid-1980s has usually varied over the range 30-100bp.

This system is quite convenient, because banks dealing in swaps use treasury bonds as one of the main tools to hedge their swap books. In addition, while bond yields may fluctuate from moment to moment during the day, swap spreads tend to remain more stable, so the banks quoting in terms of the swap spread do not have to keep revising their quotations.

As the swap market developed, banks started to offer nonstandard swaps of increasing complexity. These were priced by finding the most similar generic swap—called the *comparison swap*—and then calculating whatever adjustments were found necessary. The comparison swap method can also be applied to valuing swaps already on the bank's books, for example, when a counterparty wishes to cancel an existing swap and the appropriate cancellation fee needs to be calculated.

Unfortunately, calculating adjustments to the comparison swap can be a tedious process and must be done separately for every swap that needs pricing or valuation. What was needed was a standard method to price and value *any* kind of swap in a consistent and straightforward manner. The answer came with the *zero-coupon* method of swap pricing.

The term "zero-coupon" originates from the bond market, and describes a bond that has no coupons. An investor buying the bond will only receive the face value on the bond's maturity date and no interim payments whatsoever. At first sight, such an investment may seem unattractive, because there can be a long period between investing in the bond and receiving a return. A bond paying a regular coupon, on the other hand, provides periodic payments every 6 or 12 months. Paradoxically, however, these interim coupon payments can prove a headache. The investor must administer the reinvestment of coupons received, and the overall return depends on the interest rates prevailing when each coupon is reinvested.

The common measure of bond return—the yield to maturity—makes the assumption that coupons can be reinvested at that same yield. If interest rates turn out to be different, so does the eventual return. For example, if a five-year bond carrying a 10% coupon paid semi-annually is bought to yield 10%, but interest rates drop to 8% immediately afterwards, the effective yield would drop to 9.67%. For a 30-year bond under the same circumstances, the yield would fall to 8.73%.

A zero-coupon bond avoids these problems. As there are no coupons, there is no reinvestment involved and no interim cash flows vulnerable to the rates prevailing during the lifetime of the bond. If a zero-coupon bond is purchased at a given yield to maturity and then held to maturity, the effective yield earned will be exactly the same as the original yield to maturity, no matter what happens to interest rates in the meantime.

Zero-coupon swap pricing relies on a number of important assumptions:

- A set of zero-coupon rates exists for every major currency.
- These zero-coupon rates can be used to value any future cash flow.
- All swaps, no matter how complex, are simply a series of cash flows.
- To value and price a swap, present-value each of the cash flows using the zero-coupon rates and sum the results.

Let's examine each of these assumptions in turn. In a number of instances we will need to refer forward to formulae and proofs supplied in later sections. Nonetheless, it is worthwhile to show how each of these assumptions can be justified before proceeding any further.

A set of zero-coupon rates exists for every major currency. If zero-coupon bonds are quoted and traded, then the yield on a zero-coupon bond of a particular maturity is, by definition, the zero-coupon rate for that maturity. However, it is not necessary to have zero-coupon bonds in order to deduce zero-coupon rates. As we will demonstrate, it is possible to calculate zero-coupon rates from a wide range of market rates and prices, including coupon bonds, interest-rate futures, FRAs, and eurocurrency deposits. The calculations can adjust for the different credit risks involved: for example, the spread between LIBOR rates and T-bill yields.

These zero-coupon rates can be used to value any future cash flow. The price of a zero-coupon bond of a particular maturity defines directly the value today of a cash flow due on the bond's redemption date and indirectly the zero-coupon rate for that maturity. For example, if a five-year zero-coupon bond is priced at 60, the present value of any other cash flow due on the same date is also 60% of its future value. A cash flow of 30 due in five years would therefore be worth $30 \times 0.60 = 18$ today. By using equation 9.4 the corresponding zero-coupon rate can also be calculated as 10.76%. For cash flows occurring on intermediate dates, it is possible to interpolate using the technique explained in Section 9.8.

All swaps, no matter how complex, are simply a series of cash flows. Ultimately, even the most nonstandard swap can be systematically broken down into a stream of cash inflows and outflows.

To value and price a swap, present-value each of the cash flows using the zero-coupon rates and sum the results. The fixed-rate payments are known in advance and can be present-valued directly. The present value of the floating-rate payments can be estimated in two steps. First, the implied forward rates can be calculated using equation 9.14, presented later in this chapter, and these rates imply the size of the floating-rate payments. Second, once the size of floating-rate payments have been estimated, they can be valued by again applying the zero-coupon rates. The total value of the fixed leg is just the sum of the values of all the fixed payments, as for the floating leg. Finally, the net present value of the swap is simply the difference between the total values of the fixed and floating legs.

9.8 DISCOUNT FACTORS AND THE DISCOUNT FUNCTION

The first step in zero-coupon swap pricing is to determine a set of *discount factors* from market rates. A discount factor is simply a number in the range zero to one that can be used to obtain the present value of some future cash flow.

$$PV_k = v_k \times FV_k \tag{9.2}$$

where

PV_k is the present value of the future cash flow occurring at time k
FV_k is the future cash flow occurring at time k
v_k is the discount factor for cash flows occurring at time k

Discount factors can be calculated most easily from zero-coupon rates, although the next section will show how discount factors can be obtained from a blend of different sources. Short-term eurocurrency deposits and longer-term zero-coupon bonds are both sources of zero-coupon rates, but they are quoted a little differently, depending upon the period concerned. Zero-coupon rates for periods less than or equal to one year are normally quoted assuming simple interest, with no compounding, and equation 9.3 applies. Zero-coupon rates for longer periods assume internal compounding, and equation 9.4 should then be used.

$$v_k = \frac{1}{(1 + z_k t_k)} \tag{9.3}$$

$$v_k = \frac{1}{(1 + z_k)^{t_k}}$$

(9.4)

where

v_k is the discount factor for cash flows occurring at time k
z_k is the zero-coupon rate for the period to time k
t_k is the time from the value date to time k, expressed in years and fractions of a year

As an example, Table 9.4 illustrates the discount factors calculated from a set of zero-coupon rates covering periods from three months to five years,[2] while Figure 9.16 depicts the zero-coupon yield curve and the resulting discount factors graphically.

The individual zero-coupon rates allow discount factors to be calculated at specific points along the maturity spectrum. However, cash flows may occur at any time in the future, and not necessarily at convenient times such as three months or one year from now. The second step in zero-coupon swap pricing is to calculate discount factors for every possible date in the future; the complete set of discount factors is called the *discount function*.

The usual technique for finding intermediate values is called *interpolation*, and in this case there are two possibilities. We could interpolate between known zero-coupon rates to obtain the zero-coupon rate for an in-between date and then calculate the resulting discount factor. Alternatively, we could interpolate directly between known discount factors to obtain the factor for an intermediate date.

The problem with the first method is that we must make an assumption about the shape of the yield curve between adjacent points. Unfortunately,

TABLE 9.4
Discount Factors Calculated from Zero-Coupon Rates

Period	Zero-Coupon Rate	Discount Factor
3 months	9.50%	0.976801
6 months	9.75%	0.953516
1 year	10.00%	0.909091
2 years	10.25%	0.822702
3 years	10.50%	0.741162
4 years	10.75%	0.664699
5 years	11.00%	0.593451

---

[2] The discount factors are calculated assuming the actual/actual day-count convention

FIGURE 9.16
Zero-Coupon Yield Curve and Discount Factors

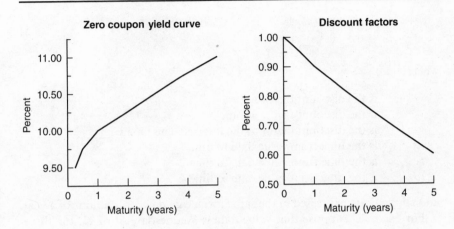

the yield curve can have many shapes: upward-sloping, downward-sloping, flat, convex, concave, humped, or dished. Simply assuming that it follows a straight-line path between adjacent points and applying linear interpolation would be potentially dangerous.

The discount function, however, must always follow an exponential curve of the form e^{-kt}, as this is the shape of the expressions given in equations 9.3 and 9.4.[3] It is therefore not necessary to make any assumptions about the nature of this curve; it will be an exponential no matter what the shape of the underlying yield curve. The exponential will decay more quickly the higher the level of interest rates, but it will remain an exponential function.

---

[3] This can be demonstrated by using the Taylor's expansion of equations 9.3, 9.4, and the expression e^{-rt}, all of which give similar results.

$$\frac{1}{(1 + zt)} \approx 1 - zt + (zt)^2 - (zt)^3 + (zt)^4 - \ldots$$

$$\approx 1 - \log(1+zt) + \frac{(\log(1+zt))^2}{2!} - \frac{(\log(1+zt))^3}{3!} + \frac{(\log(1+zt))^4}{4!} - \ldots$$

$$\frac{1}{(1 + z)^t} \approx 1 - t\log(1+z) + \frac{(t\log(1+z))^2}{2!} - \frac{(t\log(1+z))^3}{3!} + \frac{(t\log(1+z))^4}{4!} - \ldots$$

$$e^{-rt} \approx 1 - rt + \frac{(rt)^2}{2!} - \frac{(rt)^3}{3!} + \frac{(rt)^4}{4!} - \ldots$$

In fact, by substituting $r = \log(1+z)$ into the penultimate expression and $r = [\log(1+zt)]/t$ into the first expression, thereby substituting the continuously compounded rate r instead of the periodic rate z, all three expressions become identical.

The appropriate technique to use is therefore one called *exponential interpolation*. Given any two known points v_1 and v_2 on the discount function, an intermediate point v_t can be interpolated using equation 9.5:

$$v_k = v_1^{\left[\frac{t_k}{t_1}\left(\frac{t_2-t_k}{t_2-t_1}\right)\right]} \, v_2^{\left[\frac{t_k}{t_2}\left(\frac{t_k-t_1}{t_2-t_1}\right)\right]} \tag{9.5}$$

where

v_1	is the discount factor at time 1
v_2	is the discount factor at time 2
v_k	is the discount factor at the intermediate time k
t_1	is the time from value date to time 1
t_2	is the time from value date to time 2
t_k	is the time from value date to time k

and all the ts are expressed in the same form, e.g., days or fractions of a year.

For example, suppose that value date is Wednesday, April 21, the three-month date is Wednesday, July 21 (91 days later), and the six-month date is Thursday, October 21 (183 days later). If three-month rates are 9.50%, six-month rates are 9.75%, and the day-count convention is actual/360, the respective discount factors for these dates will be 0.976549 and 0.952778.[4] To find the discount factor for the four-month date on Monday, August 23 (124 days later) the vs and ts can be inserted into equation 9.5 to give[5]

$$v_k = 0.976549^{\left[\frac{124}{91}\left(\frac{183-124}{183-91}\right)\right]} \, 0.952778^{\left[\frac{124}{183}\left(\frac{124-91}{183-91}\right)\right]} = 0.968028$$

When interpolating before the first known discount factor or beyond the last discount factor, an alternative form of equation 9.5 must be used, and this is given in equation 9.6:

$$v_k = v_n^{\left[\frac{t_k}{t_n}\right]} \tag{9.6}$$

where

v_n	is the first (or last) known discount factor at date d_n
v_k	is the discount factor at the required date d_k before (after) d_n
t_n	is the time from value date to d_n
t_k	is the time from value date to d_k

---

[4] These factors differ slightly from those in Table 9.4 because of the different day-count convention adopted here.

[5] In this particular example, the answer obtained from linear interpolation of the yield curve is 0.968025, which happens to be very close to the correct answer of 0.968028. If the yield curve were less smooth or the periods longer, the results could have differed more.

Given a set of zero-coupon rates, equations 9.3 to 9.6 make it possible to construct the complete discount function for all future dates.

9.9 RELATIONSHIP BETWEEN ZERO, PAR, SWAP, AND FORWARD RATES

The third step in zero-coupon pricing is to determine the rate for a generic swap. To gain an insight into how this is done, it is first necessary to demonstrate the link between swap rates and the yield on a par bond with the same credit risk.

As the name suggests, a par bond is one that trades at par, and this implies that the yield to maturity is the same as the coupon rate. Let the yield and coupon rate be denoted as i. Consider buying 100 nominal of such a par bond. The resulting cash flows are pictured in Figure 9.17.

Now consider financing the purchase of the par bond by borrowing at LIBOR. The cash flows from this financing are shown in Figure 9.18.

Combining these two sets of cash flows gives the net flows illustrated in Figure 9.19.

FIGURE 9.17
Cash Flows Resulting from Purchase of Par Bond

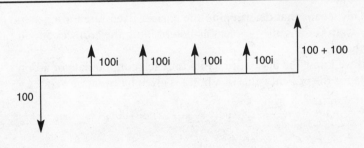

FIGURE 9.18
Cash Flows Resulting from LIBOR Financing

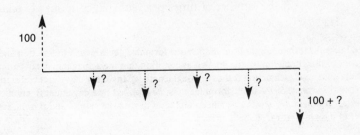

FIGURE 9.19
Net Cash Flows from Par Bond and LIBOR Financing

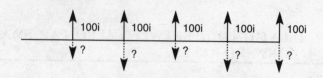

The cash flows from principals cancel out, leaving just the fixed coupons on the par bond and the floating interest payments from the LIBOR financing. Interestingly enough, these are exactly the same cash flows as those of Figure 9.10b for a generic interest-rate swap! This finding leads to an important conclusion:

**FIXED RATE ON A GENERIC
INTEREST RATE SWAP**

is the same as

YIELD AND COUPON ON A PAR BOND

This means that determining the correct fixed rate for a generic interest-rate swap is the same problem as determining the correct coupon rate for a par bond.

If we know the discount factors for each coupon date of a bond, the formula for the present value of a bond is given by equation 9.7:

$$P = \frac{100i_k}{F} \, v_1 + \frac{100i_k}{F} \, v_2 + \ldots + \frac{100i_k}{F} \, v_k + 100v_k \tag{9.7}$$

where

k	is the total number of coupons
$v_1, v_2, \ldots$	are the discount factors on the first, second, etc., coupon dates
F	is the number of times per year that coupons are paid[6]

---

[6] To make the terminology a little simpler, the formulae developed in this section and in the remainder of this chapter make the implicit assumption that the actual/actual day-count convention is used, and each period is thus of equal length. If any other day-count convention is used, each occurrence of $1/F$ in the formulae must be replaced by a day-count fraction of the form $d_{k,k+1}/B$, where $d_{k,k+1}$ is the assumed number of days in the period, and B is the assumed number of days in a year (360, 365, or 366).

i_k is the coupon rate for a k-period bond (expressed as a decimal fraction)

P is the present value of the bond

For a par bond, however, the present value P must be 100. Substituting $P=100$ into equation 9.7, and rearranging to solve for i_k gives

$$i_k = \frac{1 - v_k}{\dfrac{v_1}{F} + \dfrac{v_2}{F} + \ldots + \dfrac{v_k}{F}} = \frac{1 - v_k}{\displaystyle\sum_{j=1}^{k} \frac{v_j}{F}} \tag{9.8}$$

Equation 9.8 is important and provides an equation for determining the par yield and hence the swap rate i_k for a k-period swap. As an example, using the discount factors from Table 9.4 enables us to calculate the three-year annual swap rate as follows:

$$i_3 = \frac{1 - 0.741162}{0.909091 + 0.822702 + 0.741162} = 10.47\%$$

The calculated three-year swap rate is just a little less than the three-year zero-coupon rate of 10.50%.

By rearranging equation 9.8, it is possible to determine the kth discount factor, knowing the k-period swap rate:

$$v_k = \frac{1 - i_k \displaystyle\sum_{j=1}^{k-1} \frac{v_j}{F}}{1 + \dfrac{i_k}{F}} \tag{9.9}$$

Note that the summation in this case stops at k-1. This means that, for example, the discount factor for year five can be calculated using the discount factors from year one to year four and the five-year swap rate. Once the five-year discount factor has been determined, it can be inserted into equation 9.9 with the six-year swap rate to obtain the six-year discount factor and so on. Determining discount factors from swap rates in this way is an iterative process colloquially known as "bootstrapping."

Equation 9.4 already provided a formula for calculating the discount factor from a zero-coupon rate longer than one year. Inverting this formula gives a means of calculating the zero-coupon rate from a discount factor:

$$z_k = \sqrt[t_k]{\frac{1}{v_k}} - 1 \tag{9.10}$$

Equations 9.8, 9.9, 9.10, and 9.4 give us a means of calculating swap rates from discount factors, discount factors from swap rates, zero-coupon rates from discount factors, and discount factors from zero-coupon rates. Together, they provide a mathematical link between swap rates and zero-coupon rates. This link will shortly be illustrated graphically, but there is one further type of rate to consider—forward rates.

Equation 9.3 provided a means of calculating a discount factor from a zero-coupon rate. Suppose that the length of time t_k was a fraction of a year given by $1/F$, in other words, that there were F periods during the year of equal length t_k. Equation 9.3 could then be rewritten to give the discount factor v_1 at the end of the first period:

$$v_1 = \frac{1}{\left(1 + \frac{z_1}{F}\right)} \tag{9.11}$$

Equation 9.11 tells us that the present value of 1 after the first period is 1 discounted by the zero-coupon rate using the expression in the denominator of equation 9.11. Once this first discount factor is known, the second discount factor can be obtained by discounting by a similar expression, but this time using the *forward rate*:

$$v_2 = \frac{v_1}{\left(1 + \frac{f_1}{F}\right)} \tag{9.12}$$

where

f_1 is the first forward rate

This formula can be generalised to find the discount factor at any point in time from the previous discount factor and the forward rate:

$$v_{k+1} = \frac{v_k}{\left(1 + \frac{f_k}{F}\right)} \tag{9.13}$$

where

f_k is the forward rate from time k to time $k+1$

Equation 9.13 can easily be rearranged to solve for the intervening forward rate, given the discount factors either side:

$$f_k = \left(\frac{v_k}{v_{k+1}} - 1\right) F \tag{9.14}$$

As an example, using once again the discount factors from Table 9.4 enables us to calculate the 6-month against 12-month forward rate as follows:

$$f_{6 \times 12} = \left(\frac{v_{6m}}{v_{12m}} - 1\right) \times 2 = \left(\frac{0.953516}{0.909091} - 1\right) \times 2 = 9.77\%$$

With a little more effort, equation 9.13 can be manipulated to solve for the discount factor at time k from all the previous forward rates:

$$v_k = \frac{1}{\left(1 + \frac{f_{k-1}}{F}\right)} \times \frac{1}{\left(1 + \frac{f_{k-2}}{F}\right)} \times \ldots \times \frac{1}{\left(1 + \frac{f_0}{F}\right)} = \prod_{j=0}^{k-1} \left[\frac{1}{1 + \frac{f_j}{F}}\right] \tag{9.15}$$

The equations thus developed now give us a versatile means to convert readily between discount factors, swap rates, zero-coupon rates, and forward rates. Figure 9.20 provides a "route-map" through the maze and highlights exactly which equation is needed to convert between one set of rates and another.

Note that discount factors are drawn at the centre of the diagram. This is the appropriate place, because discount factors provide the foundation for zero-coupon pricing. Discount factors can be calculated from a number of different market rates. Once the discount factors are known, it is then possible to calculate any other market rate or to price a wide range of financial engineering products.

As an example, consider the market interest rates for D-marks on March 18, 1993 shown in Table 9.5.

TABLE 9.5
Market Rates and Discount Factors for D-Marks on March 18, 1993

	Maturity	Market Rate	Discount Factors
Eurocurrency rates	1 month	8.1875	0.99322332
	2 months	7.8125	0.98714653
	3 months	7.6875	0.98114365
	6 months	7.2500	0.96501809
	9 months	6.8750	0.95096582
	12 months	6.6250	0.93786635
Annual swap rates	2 years	6.2500	0.88600786
	3 years	6.1900	0.83539145
	4 years	6.2900	0.78345300
	5 years	6.3800	0.73355382

FIGURE 9.20
"Route-Map" of Links between Rates and Discount Factors

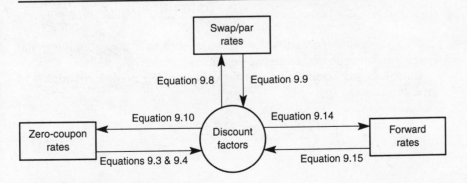

The eurocurrency interest rates up to one year are effectively zero-coupon rates, and equation 9.3 can therefore be used to calculate the discount factors up to one year. Given the one-year discount factor and the two-year swap rate, equation 9.9 can be used to calculate the two-year discount factor. Equation 9.9 can then be used repeatedly to calculate the discount factors up to five years, each discount factor providing the information necessary to calculate the next factor. The complete set of discount factors is also shown in Table 9.5.

In practice, market rates would be culled from a number of sources, including:

- Eurocurrency rates (up to one year).
- FRA rates (up to two years).
- Interest-rate futures prices (up to four years).
- Swap rates (two years to 10 years).
- Bond yields (two years to 30 years).

These would be combined or *blended* to produce a single discount function spanning the entire range of maturities. When several different rates for the same part of the maturity spectrum are available, these can be weighted, usually giving heavier weight to the most liquid market with the narrowest spread. With the speed and volume of trading that is characteristic of the derivatives market, FRA rates, futures prices, and swap rates are normally preferred to eurocurrency rates and bond yields.

Once the discount factors are known, any zero-coupon rate, forward rate, or swap rate can be calculated. For example, the five-year zero-coupon rate can be calculated using equation 9.10:

$$z_5 = \sqrt[5]{\frac{1}{0.73355382}} - 1 = 6.39\%$$

The two-year semi-annual swap rate can be calculated using equation 9.8:

$$i_{2y \text{ semi-annual}} = \frac{1 - v_{2y}}{\dfrac{v_{6m}}{2} + \dfrac{v_{1y}}{2} + \dfrac{v_{18m}}{2} + \dfrac{v_{2y}}{2}}$$

$$= \frac{1 - 0.88600786}{\dfrac{0.96501809}{2} + \dfrac{0.93786635}{2} + \dfrac{0.91074083}{2} + \dfrac{0.88600786}{2}} = 6.16\%$$

(The 18-month discount factor was calculated by exponential interpolation between the one-year and two-year rates.)

If the four-year against five-year forward rate were needed, equation 9.14 gives the answer:

$$f_{4y \times 5y} = \left(\frac{v_4}{v_5} - 1\right) = \left(\frac{0.78345300}{0.73355382} - 1\right) = 6.80\%$$

The foregoing equations and the routemap of Figure 9.20 provide a symbolic prescription for the relationship between zero-coupon, swap, and forward rates. With a little more effort, it is possible to obtain two further equations that enable us to obtain a better feel for the way in which these rates are linked.

By combining and manipulating equations 9.8 and 9.14, the following relationships can be proved:

$$i_k = \frac{\sum_{j=1}^{k} \frac{f_{j-1} v_j}{F}}{\sum_{j=1}^{k} \frac{v_j}{F}} \tag{9.16}$$

$$1 + z_k = \sqrt[t_k]{\prod_{j=0}^{k-1}\left(1 + \frac{f_j}{F}\right)} \tag{9.17}$$

The interpretation of these apparently complex equations is actually quite simple.

Equation 9.16 says

**The SWAP RATE is
the WEIGHTED ARITHMETIC AVERAGE
of the FORWARD RATES**

This should come as no surprise and provides an insight into the similarities between an interest rate swap and a strip of FRAs. Buying an FRA provides a settlement sum to compensate for the difference between the fixed rate originally agreed and the market rate that eventually transpires. If interest rates float higher than the fixed rate agreed, the FRA buyer receives the net payment; if interest rates float lower, the FRA buyer pays. This is directly analogous to the fixed-rate payer under a swap. If the floating rate in any swap period is higher than the fixed rate, the fixed-rate payer receives the net interest payment, while the opposite is true if the floating rate turns out to be lower.

Buying a strip of FRAs to cover multiple periods in the future is virtually the same as entering into a swap agreement for the same period. There are two significant differences:

1. Each FRA within the strip would normally be executed at a different contract rate, each rate corresponding to the forward rate for that contract period. An interest rate swap is normally executed with a constant fixed rate.

2. Under an FRA, the settlement sums are normally discounted and paid at the beginning of the contract period. With an interest rate swap, the net interest payments are normally undiscounted and paid at the end of each period during the life of the swap.

If a single rate could be found to replace the set of individual FRA rates, that single rate would be the swap rate. Common sense would suggest that some kind of average is appropriate, and the mathematics of equation 9.16 shows that it should be a weighted average, the weights being the set of discount factors for each period.

Equation 9.17 says

ONE plus the ZERO-COUPON RATE is the GEOMETRIC AVERAGE of ONE plus the FORWARD RATES

Each of the individual forward rates provides a link between the discount factor at the beginning of a period and the discount factor at the end. To obtain the discount factor at the end of multiple periods, all the individual discount factors must be combined by multiplying them together. By definition, this must give the same result as using the single zero-coupon rate for the entire period.

Swap rates and zero-coupon rates are both therefore averages of the forward rates, and so will be very similar. The swap rate is the weighted arithmetic average of the forward rates, while (one plus) the zero-coupon rate is the geometric average of (one plus) the forward rates.[7] Although the geometric average of a set of numbers must always be less than or equal to the simple arithmetic average, this does not necessarily follow for a weighted arithmetic average. In fact, it can be proved mathematically that the difference between the swap rate and zero rate depends upon the shape of the

---

[7] It is also possible to relate zero-coupon rates and forward-rates through another kind of average. By transforming the zero-coupon rate z_k and the forward rates f_j into their continuously compounded equivalents

$$z'_k = ln\,(1 + z_k) \text{ and } f'_j = ln\,(1 + f_j)$$

Equation 9.17 becomes a simple arithmetic average:

$$z'_k = \frac{1}{t_k}\sum_{j=0}^{k-1}\frac{f'_j}{F}$$

This says that the continuously compounded zero-coupon rate is the simple average of the continuously compounded forward rates.

yield curve. When the yield curve is positive, zero-coupon rates will actually lie slightly above the swap rates, and when the yield curve is negatively sloped, zero-coupon rates will be lower than swap rates.

Table 9.6 illustrates two yield curve scenarios, one with swap rates rising from 7% to 8% for maturities from one to five years, the other with swap rates falling from 8% down to 7%. The table shows the zero rates, forward rates, and discount factors for each year.

To visualise this information more clearly, Figure 9.21 shows the various interest rates under both scenarios. In each case the swap and zero rates are

TABLE 9.6
Illustration of Swap Rates, Zero Rates, Forward Rates, nd Discount Factors

Tenor (yrs)	Positive Yield Curve				Negative Yield Curve			
	Swap Rates	Zero Rates	Forward Rates	Discount Rates	Swap Rates	Zero Rates	Forward Rates	Discount Rates
1	7.0000%	7.0000%	7.0000%	0.93457944	8.0000%	8.0000%	8.0000%	0.92592593
2	7.2500%	7.2591%	7.5188%	0.86922423	7.7500%	7.7403%	7.4813%	0.86147633
3	7.5000%	7.5256%	8.0606%	0.80438579	7.5000%	7.4747%	6.9453%	0.80553008
4	7.7500%	7.8008%	8.6306%	0.74047825	7.2500%	7.2034%	6.3938%	0.75712112
5	8.0000%	8.0861%	9.2350%	0.67787647	7.0000%	6.9272%	5.8293%	0.71541706

FIGURE 9.21
Graphic Illustration of Swap, Zero-Coupon, and Forward Rates

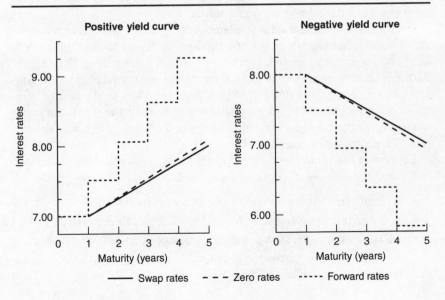

the cumulative averages of the forward rates. This means that in the positive yield curve environment, for example, the swap and zero rates rise more slowly than the forward rate. Alternatively, one could consider the forward rates rising ever more rapidly than the swap and zero rates. Take the four-year and five-year rates for instance. The four-year swap rate of 7.75% is the weighted average of the four preceding forward rates. If the five-year swap rate is 25bp higher at 8.00%, the four-year against five-year forward rate must be very much higher in order for the addition of one extra forward rate to boost the average that much. If it were a simple average of five figures, the 4yr × 5yr forward rate would need to be five times 25bp, or 125bp, higher than 7.75% to increase the five-year swap rate to 8.00%. This would make the forward rate 9.00%. In fact, with the discount factor weightings, the forward rate turns out to be 149bp higher at 9.24%.

Similar arguments apply to the negative yield curve environment, where all rates fall, but where the forward rates fall much faster than either the swap or zero rates. Note that in this scenario, the zero-coupon rates are a fraction smaller than the swap rates, but that this relationship is reversed when the yield curve is positive.

9.10 VALUATION AND PRICING OF INTEREST-RATE SWAPS

The last three sections have explained how zero-coupon rates can be derived, and equations 9.2, 9.3, and 9.4 in particular define how these rates can be used to value any future cash flow. We can now build on this foundation to demonstrate how interest-rate swaps of arbitrary complexity can be priced and valued using the zero-coupon technique.

In fact, the technique used is fundamentally the same whether one is pricing or valuing a swap. Pricing normally implies trying to find the correct fixed rate for a new swap such that the net present value is zero. Valuing, on the other hand, normally involves finding the net present value of an existing swap for which the fixed rate has already been set. Thus, in the case of pricing, the net present value is known (to be zero), while the fixed rate is the unknown. In the case of swap valuation, it is the fixed rate that is known, while the net present value has to be determined.

Let's recap the principles underlying zero-coupon swap pricing as set out in Section 9.7:

- A set of zero-coupon rates exists for every major currency.
- These zero-coupon rates can be used to value any future cash flow.
- All swaps, no matter how complex, are simply a series of cash flows.
- To value and price a swap, present-value each of the cash flows using the zero-coupon rates and sum the results.

The last two principles tell us that once we have the zero-coupon rates, swap valuation proceeds in two steps: identify the cash flows, then use the discount factors to obtain the present values of these cash flows.

To illustrate the technique, let's start with a $10 million generic five-year interest rate swap using the actual/actual day-count convention and use the set of market rates illustrated in Table 9.6 under the positive yield curve environment. What is the net present value of this swap if it is booked at the prevailing market rate for swaps of this maturity?

If the five-year swap rate is 8.00%, the cash flows under the fixed leg are simply $800,000 each year. The first floating leg payment will be 7.00%, because this is the prevailing one-year rate on the trade date, and the trade date is also the first setting date. However, there is a problem: the remaining floating leg payments are unknown at this stage and will only be determined on the future setting dates. Nevertheless, for valuation purposes we can *estimate* what these floating payments will be by using the set of forward rates as the best guess of where the cash market rates will eventually be.[8]

Even if one does not accept this view, a bank could nevertheless use FRAs or futures to create a riskless hedge for a stream of floating payments priced using the implied forward rates.

Table 9.7 reproduces the market rates and discount factors from Table 9.6 and then sets out the resulting fixed and floating payments together with the present values of these cash flows.

The figures show that at the inception of the swap the present values of both legs are equal, and the net present value is therefore zero. This demonstrates that the swap is correctly valued at 8.00%. The example also illustrates why there is no need for any up-front payment from one counterparty to the other under a generic swap.

TABLE 9.7
Valuation of Generic Five-Year Swap with Five-Year Swap Market Rates at 8.00%

Years	Swap Rates	Zero Rates	Forward Rates	Discount Factors	Fixed Payments	Floating Payments	PV of Fixed Payments	PV of Floating Payments
1	7.0000%	7.0000%	7.0000%	0.93457944	800,000.00	700,000.00	747,663.55	654,205.61
2	7.2500%	7.2591%	7.5188%	0.86922423	800,000.00	751,879.70	695,379.39	653,552.06
3	7.5000%	7.5256%	8.0606%	0.80438579	800,000.00	806,061.52	643,508.63	648,384.43
4	7.7500%	7.8008%	8.6306%	0.74047825	800,000.00	863,057.60	592,382.60	639,075.38
5	8.0000%	8.0861%	9.2350%	0.67787647	800,000.00	923,498.45	542,301.17	626,017.87
TOTAL							3,221,235.34	3,221,235.34

---

[8] Refer back to Chapter Three (Section 3.3) for a discussion on this point.

Of course, it is no real surprise that the swap is found to be fairly priced at 8.00%, because this was the swap rate used to derive the discount factors, which in turn were used to value the swap! Nonetheless, the figures at least prove that the system is self-consistent.

Suppose the swap were executed at 8.00%, and moments later the five-year swap rate moved up to 8.01%. What is the value of the swap to the fixed-rate payer now? Table 9.8 values the swap under the new market rates.

The value of the fixed leg has declined by just $298.23, caused by the higher swap rate reducing the five-year discount factor by a small amount. The biggest change, perhaps surprisingly, occurs to the floating leg, which *increases* in value by $3,727.94 despite the weaker discount factor. The explanation follows from the nature of swap rates, which are an average of the component forward rates, as proved in the previous section. The five-year swap rate is the weighted average of the strip of five one-year forward rates. If the one-year to four-year swap rates do not change, then the first four forward rates must also remain unchanged. The 1bp increase in the five-year swap rate must therefore go hand-in-hand with a much larger rise in the last forward rate, which increases by 6bp.

The combined effect is for the net present value for the fixed-rate payer to move from zero to $4,026.17. The figures were relatively easy to calculate in this case, because we assumed that the swap rate moved immediately after the swap was executed. However, exactly the same method can be used to value a swap at any other time. The only complicating feature is the need to interpolate the discount factors from available market rates to give the discount factors on the dates when the swap cash flows occur.

The real power of zero-coupon pricing emerges when it comes to pricing nonstandard swaps. Consider the following specification:

Description	3year accreting margin swap, deferred 1year
Principal	$4,000,000 (1st period)

TABLE 9–8
Valuation of Generic Five-Year Swap with Five-Year Swap Market Rates at 8.01%

Years	Swap Rates	Zero Rates	Forward Rates	Discount Factors	Fixed Payments	Floating Payments	PV of Fixed Payments	PV of Floating Payments
1	7.0000%	7.0000%	7.0000%	0.93457944	800,000.00	700,000.00	747,663.55	654,205.61
2	7.2500%	7.2591%	7.5188%	0.86922423	800,000.00	751,879.70	695,379.39	653,552.06
3	7.5000%	7.5256%	8.0606%	0.80438579	800,000.00	806,061.52	643,508.63	648,384.43
4	7.7500%	7.8008%	8.6306%	0.74047825	800,000.00	863,057.60	592,382.60	639,075.38
5	8.0100%	8.0980%	9.2951%	0.67750367	800,000.00	929,509.06	542,002.94	629,745.80
TOTAL							3,220,937.11	3,224,963.28

	$7,000,000 (2nd period)
	$10,000,000 (3rd period)
Floating rate	LIBOR+50bp
Day-count convention (fixed)	Actual/360
Day-count convention (floating)	Actual/360
Trade date	February 3, 1993
Effective date	February 7, 1994
Maturity date	February 7, 1997
Payment frequency (fixed)	Annual (every February 7 or modified following business day)
Payment frequency (floating)	Annual (every Feb 7 or modified following business day)

Three features distinguish this particular instrument from a generic swap. First, there is the deferred start. If the trade date was on February 3, 1993, the effective date for a generic swap would be February 5, 1993. However, deferring this by one year should push the start of the swap to February 5, 1994, but as this is a Saturday the effective date becomes February 7, 1994, and the maturity date three years later falls on February 7, 1997. Second, instead of a constant notional principal of $10,000,000, this accreting swap has a notional principal of $4,000,000 for the first swap period, increasing by $3,000,000 each year for the next two years. Finally, the floating margin is not LIBOR flat, but LIBOR+50bp.

To price the fixed rate for this nonstandard swap, we use the discount factors to value the floating leg and then find the fixed rate, which makes the present value of the fixed leg equal to that of the floating leg.

Table 9.9 summarises the valuation and pricing of the swap and shows that with the floating margin of LIBOR+50bp and a fixed rate of 8.7041%, the present values of the fixed and floating legs are indeed identical. The correct price for this particular nonstandard swap must therefore be 8.7041%.

TABLE 9.9
Valuation of Accreting, Margin, Deferred-Start, Three-Year Swap

Date	Swap Rates	Zero Rates	Forward Rates	Discount Factors	Not'l Prn (m)	Fixed Payments	Floating Payments	PV of Fixed Payments	PV of Floating Payments
07-Feb-94	7.00%	7.0000%	7.0000%	0.93339210	0	0.00	0.00	0.00	0.00
07-Feb-95	7.25%	7.2550%	7.5205%	0.86726337	4	352,999.60	325,277.33	306,143.62	282,101.11
07-Feb-96	7.50%	7.5217%	8.0631%	0.80172197	7	617,749.29	607,741.60	495,263.18	487,239.79
07-Feb-97	7.75%	7.7969%	8.6320%	0.73704008	10	884,916.80	928,423.11	652,219.15	684,285.05
TOTAL								1,453,625.95	1,453,625.95

Note that, despite the quoted swap rates being the same as those in Table 9.7, the calculated zero-coupon rates, forward rates, and discount factors are all a little different. For example, the four-year zero-coupon rate was 7.8008% in Table 9.7 but 7.7969% here. This is because the day-count convention is actual/360 in this example rather than the simpler actual/actual used in the previous example.

The correct swap rate of 8.7041% could have been found by trial and error, but there is a more systematic method. Once again, we start by valuing the floating leg.

In general, the present value of the floating leg of a k-period swap is

$$PV_{float} = \sum_{j=1}^{k} f_{j-1} \, P_j \frac{d_j}{B} v_j \tag{9.18}$$

where

PV_{float} is the present value of the floating leg
f_j is the floating rate from time $j\text{-}1$ to time j
P_j is the notional principal from time $j\text{-}1$ to time j
d_j is the number of days from time $j\text{-}1$ to time j
v_j is the discount factor at time j
B is the day-count convention divisor (normally 360 or 365)

In this example, the present value of the floating payment at the end of period 2 is

$$(7.52053679\% + 0.5000\%) \times 4{,}000{,}000 \times \frac{365}{360} \times 0.86726337 = 282{,}101.11$$

as shown in the last column of Table 9.9, which also reveals the values for the remaining two periods. The total present value of the floating leg is $1,453,625.95.

A similar equation provides the present value of the fixed leg:

$$PV_{fixed} = i_k \sum_{j=1}^{k} P_j \frac{d_j}{B} v_j \tag{9.19}$$

where

PV_{fixed} is the present value of the fixed leg
i_k is the fixed rate for the entire duration of the swap

and the other symbols are as defined for equation 9.18.

Using equation 9.19, PV_{fixed} for this nonstandard swap is

$$PV_{fixed} = i_k \times \left(4,000,000 \times \frac{365}{360} \times 0.86726337 + 7,000,000 \times \frac{365}{360} \times 0.80172197 + \right.$$
$$\left. 10,000,000 \times \frac{366}{360} \times 0.73704008 \right) = i_k \times 16,700,474.60$$

The fixed rate is then obtained by equating the value of fixed and floating legs. Setting Pv_{fixed} to 1,453,625.95 gives

$$1,453,625.95 = i_k \times 16,700,474.60 \therefore i_k = \frac{1,453,625.95}{16,700,474.60} = 8.7041\%$$

The zero-coupon method thus provides a powerful and flexible technique for valuing and pricing swaps of any type and at any stage in their lives. Once the swap is reduced to its component cash flows, discount factors obtained from market rates can be used to value an existing swap or to price a new one.

Before extending the technique to currency swaps, there is an interesting shortcut available. The technique as explained so far necessitates two steps in valuing the floating leg of a swap:

1. Forward rates must be calculated in order to determine the size of each floating payment.
2. Each floating payment must then be valued using the appropriate discount factor for that date.

This can be quite a lengthy calculation.

Figure 9.22 recaps what the floating leg cash flows look like to the counterparty receiving the floating-rate payments on a five-year generic swap with annual payments. Of course, the size of each payment is unknown until the setting date is reached, and therefore the total present value is also unknown at the outset.

Suppose that the counterparty were offered an alternative. Rather than receiving the five floating interest receipts on a notional principal of $1 million, the counterparty would receive instead the principal itself, $1 million

FIGURE 9.22
Cash Flows from Floating Leg of Swap

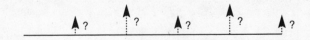

up-front, but would have to repay the same $1 million in five years time. The cash flows from this alternative are illustrated in Figure 9.23.

Clearly, the nature of these two alternatives is quite different. The stream of cash flows in Figure 9.22 is regular but uncertain. Those of Figure 9.23 are irregular, but known. Which should the counterparty prefer if he has a choice?

If the counterparty chose the second alternative, he could invest the initial inflow of $1 million for successive periods of one year. At the start of each investment period, the interest rate would be set according to prevailing market rates, and the resulting interest payment would be received at the end of each period. At the end of the last period, the $1 million investment would be returned and would be available to meet the final obligation to repay the $1 million. Figure 9.24 summarises the effect of these cash flows.

As should now be apparent from the diagram, the two $1 million payments at the beginning cancel each other out, and so do the two at the end. The net cash flows that are left are exactly the same as those in Figure 9.22. If the investor were to choose the second alternative and were to invest the principal received at the prevailing market rates, the end result would be to create exactly the same cash flows as those receivable under the first alternative. In other words, despite the apparent differences, the two alternatives are actually equivalent!

FIGURE 9.23
Replacing Floating Leg Cash Flows with Exchange of Principals

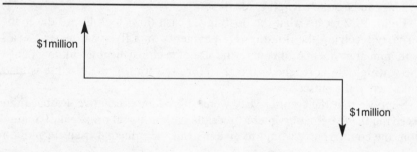

FIGURE 9.24
Investing the Principals

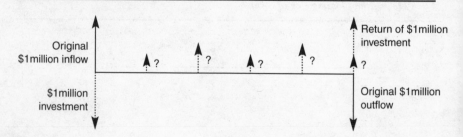

This leads to an important finding:

A stream of floating cash flows can be replaced, for valuation purposes only, with an exchange of principals.

A stream of floating-rate receipts can therefore be replaced, for valuation purposes, with

- An *inflow* of the notional principal at the start of the first accrual period.
- An *outflow* of the notional principal at the end of the final accrual period.

This substitution is much easier to value, as there are only two cash flows and no need to calculate the complete set of forward rates. If the stream of floating-rate payments starts accruing immediately, the valuation becomes easier still, because the present value of a sum paid immediately is the sum itself.

As an example, refer back to Table 9.7, which valued the generic five-year swap. The present value of the floating leg was found to be $3,221,235.34 after summing the present values of each of the floating payments. This result could have been obtained in a single step just by knowing the five-year discount factor, which is 0.677876466:

$$PV_{float} = 10,000,000 \times 1 - 10,000,000 \times 0.677876466 = 3,221,235.34$$

Replacing a stream of floating payments with an exchange of principals is therefore a useful time-saving technique. However, it is important to emphasise that this replacement is purely a device for calculation and valuation purposes; there is never an actual exchange of principals under an interest rate swap.

9.11 VALUATION AND PRICING OF CURRENCY SWAPS

The principles of zero-coupon swap valuation can now be extended, enabling cross-currency swaps to be valued and priced. Although the foreign exchange element intrinsic to cross-currency swaps may at first sight appear to complicate matters, and the exchange of principals likewise, these design features actually combine to eliminate currency risk and to simplify the resulting structure.

Consider first a generic interest-rate swap in one currency, as pictured in Figure 9.25. The swap rate i_1 is such that the swap is fairly priced and thus has a net present value of zero.

Now replace the stream of floating-rate payments with an actual exchange of principals, as explained at the end of the previous section. The resulting cash flows are depicted in Figure 9.26.

FIGURE 9.25
Generic Interest Rate Swap in One Currency

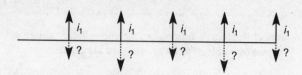

FIGURE 9.26
Interest Rate Swap with Floating Leg Replaced by Exchange of Principals

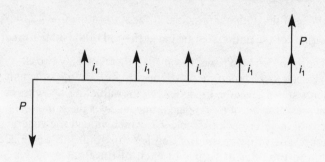

FIGURE 9.27
Fixed-Fixed Currency Swap

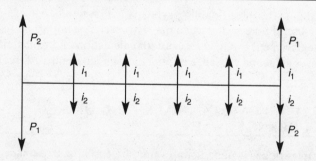

Finally, couple this structure with an equal and opposite structure in a second currency to produce the streams of cash flows depicted in Figure 9.27. The sizes of the two swaps are made equivalent by ensuring that the principals are in the same ratio as the prevailing spot exchange rate. The swap rate in the second currency i_2 is also the fair market rate for swaps of that maturity, so that the entire structure still has a zero net present value.

The result is identical to the fixed-fixed cross-currency swap illustrated earlier in this chapter in Figure 9.12. We have therefore built a generic cross-currency swap priced fairly with zero net present value measured in either currency. It follows that the two swap rates in a fixed-fixed cross-currency swap should be the same as those for interest rate swaps in the respective currencies.

For example, suppose that five-year U.S. interest rate swap rates were 7% for the fixed-rate payer, and five-year D-mark interest rate swaps were priced at 6% for the fixed-rate receiver. A $/DEM cross-currency swap would be fairly priced if the counterparty paid dollars fixed at 7% against receiving D-marks fixed at 6%.

If there were no initial exchange of principals, the swap would still have a zero net present value. Consider the stream of interest payments and final principal pictured in Figure 9.26, but without the initial outflow of principal.

Remembering that the swap rate is the same as the coupon rate on a par bond and that the par bond by definition is priced at par, the present value of the stream of payments is simply P_1. Similarly, the entire stream of outflows in the second currency shown in Figure 9.27, once again omitting the initial inflow of principal, is $-P_2$. If the exchange rate between the currencies is S, such that one unit of the first currency is equivalent to S units of the second, then $P_2/P_1 = S$ so that the ratio of principals is the same as the prevailing exchange rate. The net present value of the swap in terms of the first currency is then $P_1 - (P_2/S) = 0$.

Remember that while the initial exchange of principal is optional, the final exchange is mandatory for a standard currency swap.

A floating-floating cross-currency swap can be constructed in the same way. Figure 9.28 shows one leg of such a swap, including both the initial and final exchange of principals.

FIGURE 9.28
One Leg of a Floating Cross-Currency Swap

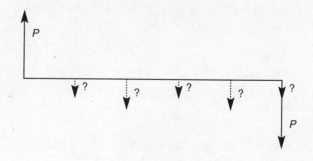

To value this structure, we can once again use the ploy of replacing the stream of floating payments with an exchange of principals to produce the structure illustrated in Figure 9.29.

It is obvious from Figure 9.29 that the present value of this structure is zero, because the principals cancel out, leaving nothing. Each leg of a floating-floating cross-currency swap has zero value initially and, in theory, both legs should therefore be quoted as LIBOR flat.[9] In practice, banks dealing in cross-currency swaps must quote a two-way price with a spread between bid and offer rates. Table 9.10 provides an illustration of market quotes on November 18, 1992. In every case, the quotation is for the nondollar currency against dollar LIBOR flat. As an example, the bank quoting sterling is willing

FIGURE 9.29
Floating Payments Replaced by Exchange of Principals

TABLE 9.10
Cross-Currency Swap Quotes on November 18, 1992

Currency	Pay	Receive	Mid-Rate
GBP	0	+5	+2.5
DEM	−1	+4	+1.5
ECU	−5	0	−2.5
CHF	0	+6	+3.0
JPY	−6	0	−3.0
LIT	−12	−3	−7.5
FFR	+3	+9	+6.0
Average			0.0

Source: Intercapital Brokers, London.

---

[9] A similar conclusion could be reached by building a floating-floating cross-currency swap from a fixed-fixed swap and two fixed-floating interest-rate swaps.

to pay sterling LIBOR flat against receiving dollar LIBOR flat and is also willing to receive sterling LIBOR+5bp against paying dollar LIBOR flat.

Some of the currencies, such as the Swiss and French francs, are here quoted at LIBOR plus a margin; others, such as the Japanese yen and the Italian lire, are quoted beneath LIBOR. These biases are due to forces of supply and demand and to views or preferences held by banks from time to time. As it happens, taking the simple average of all the quotes gives a mid-market rate of LIBOR flat exactly, as we should expect from the preceding analysis.

The last permutation, a fixed-floating cross-currency swap, presents no new challenges. From the foregoing discussion, we would expect the fixed rate to be identical to the rate for interest-rate swaps of the same maturity, while the floating rate should be quoted as LIBOR flat in that currency. If the floating-floating swap rate is not quoted at par, any difference would be added or subtracted from the fixed rate.

For example, suppose sterling interest-rate swaps were quoted as 7.43%-7.48% against sterling LIBOR flat and floating-floating dollar-sterling swaps were quoted as 0/+5 against dollar LIBOR flat. A bank would then be willing to pay sterling fixed at 7.43% against receiving dollar LIBOR flat or would expect to receive sterling LIBOR fixed at 7.53% against paying dollar LIBOR flat.

For nonstandard cross-currency swaps, pricing and valuation use the same zero-coupon method that was applied to interest rate swaps.

To price a nonstandard swap, the cash flows in each currency are valued using the set of discount factors derived from market rates in that currency. This gives two net present values, one in each currency. The surplus or deficit in one currency is then transferred into the other currency at the prevailing spot rate. Finally, the swap rate in the latter currency is adjusted to arrive at a zero net present value overall.

Valuing cross-currency swaps follows the same steps but stops when the balance in one currency is converted to the other; the net present value in the latter currency is the valuation of the swap.

Chapter Ten

Options—from Basics to Greek

Each of the financial engineering tools discussed so far in this book has, in its own way, made an important contribution to the successful management of financial risk. FRAs and interest rate futures allow a borrower to secure a guaranteed rate of interest for months or years into the future. Swaps extend the scope of this guarantee for up to 10 years. A forward currency deal provides a company with foreign currency at an exchange rate fixed, once again, months or even years into the future. All these tools provide certainty, an immunity from future movements in market rates, peace of mind. What more could anyone want?

The trouble is, certainty may not always be the best thing, especially when looking back. With hindsight, a borrower may prefer to have secured certainty if interest rates turned out higher than were expected. On the other hand, the same borrower would naturally prefer to have retained the original exposure to risk if interest rates eventually turned out lower. Achieving certainty with tools such as FRAs, futures, forwards, and swaps is sometimes a mixed blessing.

Recall the definition of risk presented in Chapter One: risk is *any* variation in an outcome. Risk therefore encompasses both adverse and beneficial developments in market rates. Avoiding risk implies avoiding not only the bad outcomes but also the good ones.

Options are unique among all the tools of financial engineering, for they give the buyer the ability to avoid just the bad outcomes and to retain the benefit of the good ones. As such, options—and all the products derived from them—seem to provide the best of all worlds. Regrettably for the user, options do not come free. There is a price that must be paid to acquire something that can never be bad. Nonetheless, options frequently provide the ideal solution for controlling risk, for managing risk rather than avoiding it completely.

Although options in one form or another have been used for several centuries, financial options only really became established in the early 1970s, and their use did not become widespread until the 1980s. Nowadays, options are among the most versatile and exciting of all financial engineering tools. Their flexibility has created a huge range of opportunities, and options are often embedded or hidden within other financial engineering tools.

This chapter introduces the concept of options, explains how they are priced, and describes their behaviour under different circumstances. Options are a big subject, so this chapter is a correspondingly long one. Readers who already know the basic terminology can proceed straightaway to Section 10.4, which discusses the value and profit profiles for options at maturity. Those who wish to skip the more mathematical sections on the behaviour of financial prices and on the Black-Scholes (B-S) and binomial models can avoid Sections 10.6 through 10.8. We begin, however, by explaining why options are unique.

10.1 WHY OPTIONS ARE DIFFERENT

All the tools of financial engineering reviewed so far have one thing in common, a "straight-line" characteristic. As an example, suppose a treasurer buys a 3 × 6 month FRA on a notional amount of $1 million at a price of exactly 5%. The eventual payoff will depend upon the reference rate determined on the fixing date. If the reference rate turns out to be higher than 5%, the treasurer would receive payment under the agreement. On the other hand, if the reference rate is lower, the treasurer will be compelled to pay out. Figure 10.1 graphs the exact relationship between settlement sum and reference rate.

As the diagram shows, the characteristic is just a straight line:[1] the higher interest rates rise, the larger will be the benefit to the FRA buyer.

FIGURE 10.1
Payoff under a Forward Rate Agreement

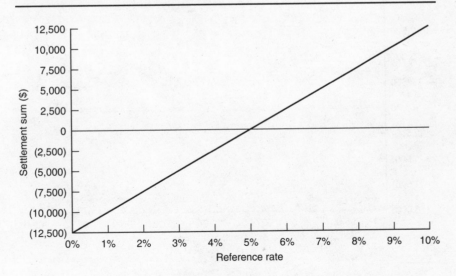

---

[1] The payoff for FRAs is, in fact, very slightly curved due to discounting, in this case deviating from the truly linear by about 2½% when the reference rate is 500 basis points higher than the contract rate. Nonetheless, FRA payoffs are, to all intents and purposes, linear.

Conversely, the lower interest rates fall, the larger will be the disadvantage to the FRA buyer.

The same applies to futures, forward FX, SAFEs, and swaps. Figure 10.2 shows the same kind of characteristic for the bund futures contract on LIFFE. This time, however, the diagram shows the payoff for both the buyer and seller of one contract at a market price of exactly 98. Recall from Table 8.3 that the tick size of the bund contract is 0.01, and the tick value is DEM 25.

Not only is the linear characteristic evident from this diagram, but also the symmetry of payoffs for buyer and seller. The buyer thinks, on balance, that the market price will rise and he will therefore profit. The seller takes the opposite view. If the market price of a bond future is 98, then it follows that the buyer's expected gain from a rise in the market price above that level must be equal to the seller's expected gain from a fall in the market price below that level.

To see that this is true, consider for one moment what would happen if the majority of people, say 60%, thought that potential gains exceeded potential losses. Buyers would then outweigh sellers, and the law of supply and demand would gradually drive the price higher. As the price rose, more and more people would revise their subjective probability[2] estimates. Eventually, the price would rise to the level where a consensus was reached whereby the

FIGURE 10.2
Payoff for Parties under a Bond Futures Contract

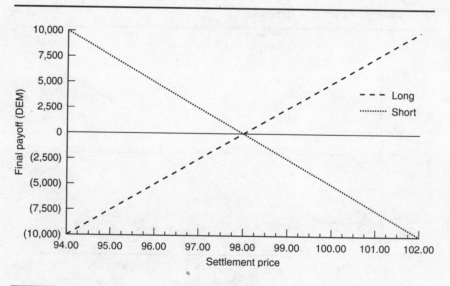

---

[2] Subjective probability is the human perception of likelihood; objective probability is the statistical measurement of likelihood. The objective probability of a fatal airline crash is infinitesimal, but for the passenger with a fear of flying it is the subjective probability that counts. Although one can analyse past market data, it is only subjective probability that matters when considering the future development of market prices.

expected gains of buyers now equalled the expected gains of sellers. At this point, the number of buyers would equal the number of sellers, and the price would stabilise. In an efficient market, the market price at any time will therefore always adjust to this level.

Under these circumstances, both the buyer and seller of a futures contract have an equal chance of gaining and losing, and the expected value of the deal is zero. That is the reason why there is no need for any up-front payment at the outset between buyer and seller. The buyer of an FRA, or a future, or a swap, simply enters into a binding agreement with the seller; they notionally shake hands on the deal but no entry fee need be involved. The market price is the fair price for both parties to the contract.

Options are quite different. As they allow the buyer to benefit from market movements in one direction but not to lose from movements in the other direction, there is no longer a symmetry between buyer and seller.

Consider an option that gives the holder the right, but not the obligation, to purchase one bond futures contract at 98 on the expiry date of the future. If the price of the bond future turns out higher than 98, the holder will exercise the option and will benefit from the same payoff as in the top-right quadrant of Figure 10.2. On the other hand, if the price turns out lower than 98, the holder will simply elect not to exercise the option. The resultant payoff for the holder of such an option is illustrated in Figure 10.3, along with the payoff from the counterparty who is short the option.

It is important not to confuse the symmetry between the top and bottom of this diagram with the lack of symmetry between left and right. The top

FIGURE 10.3
Payoff for Parties under Option Contract

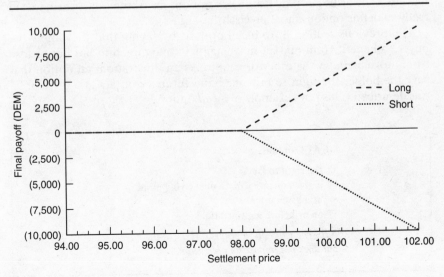

and bottom halves must inevitably be mirror images of each other, because the buyer's profit must always be the seller's loss. No such symmetry exists between the left and right halves of the diagram, unlike that present in Figure 10.2.

This means that the holders of long and short positions in this option do not have an equal chance of gaining and losing. The holder of the long position will gain if the market price of the underlying future rises but will not lose if the price falls. Conversely, the holder of the short position can only lose and can never gain, even if the market price of the future falls below 98. The expected value of this deal is therefore not zero.

The holder of a long position in options therefore gains an advantage without suffering a disadvantage, a right without an obligation. The option buyer cannot expect to obtain this position without paying something for it. It would be equally senseless for someone to sell an option without receiving compensation for entering into a contract in which he can only lose or break even.

With options there is thus an up-front payment from buyer to seller. This rewards the seller for taking on obligations without compensating rights and is a fair payment for the buyer to make when acquiring rights without offsetting obligations. This is in direct contrast to FRAs, futures, and swaps, where the rights acquired by each side are offset by matching obligations, and where an up-front payment is therefore inappropriate.

Thus what makes options different from all the other financial instruments is the asymmetry of the payoff profile and the consequent need for an up-front payment between buyer and seller.

10.2 DEFINITIONS

Now that the distinguishing features of options have been established, we are ready to define options more precisely.

The previous section introduced options by saying that they allow the buyer to benefit from market movements in one direction but not to lose from movements in the other direction. As an illustration, an option that gave the holder the right to buy one bond futures contract at a price of 98 was described. This is an example of a *call* option.

A CALL option is:

- **the right to BUY**
- **a given quantity of an underlying asset**
- **at a given price**
- **on or before a given date.**

NB: The call option grants a right to the buyer but does not impose an obligation.

Such an option allows the holder to benefit from a rise in the market price of the underlying. In the case of the bond future option, the holder would elect to exercise the option only if the price rose above 98.

Suppose, however, that someone in the market wants to benefit if bond futures prices fall. Perhaps an investment manager holding a portfolio of bonds wants to construct a hedge against a fall in bond prices. Selling a call option would not provide the protection sought. While the holder of a short position in call options would not lose if the market fell, this is not the same as gaining.

The fundamental asymmetry of options, which respond differently depending upon the direction of the market, means that there needs to be another kind of option, the put option, which is the mirror image of the call option defined above.

A PUT option is:

- **the right to SELL**
- **a given quantity of an underlying asset**
- **at a given price**
- **on or before a given date.**

NB: The put option grants a right to the buyer but does not impose an obligation.

Put options sometimes can seem confusing at first. The notion of buying a call option is easy to grasp—it confers the right to buy the underlying asset at some future time. If call options can be bought, they can also be sold. If the market price is sufficiently high, the call option will be exercised, and the call buyer will receive the underlying from the call seller at an advantageous price or settle in cash instead.

Put options are just the mirror image of calls. They too can be bought or sold. The buyer of a put gains a right, just as the buyer of a call does. In the case of a put, that right is the right to sell the underlying asset. If the market price falls sufficiently, the put option will be exercised, and the put buyer will sell the underlying to the put seller at an advantageous price or elect to settle in cash.

These definitions of call and put options are very similar to the definition of a futures contract given in Chapter Six (Section 6.2). Indeed, there are many similarities between these two types of derivative instruments, but the key difference is that a futures position always confers both rights and obligations to perform under the contract, whereas an option separates rights from obligations. The holder of a long position in options, whether a call or a put, has only rights, no obligations. Conversely, someone who is short options has contingent obligations without any rights. Figures 10.4 and 10.5 illustrate this separation of rights and obligations.

FIGURE 10.4
Futures: Rights and Obligations Together

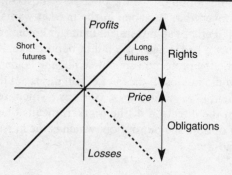

FIGURE 10.5
Options: Separation of Rights and Obligations

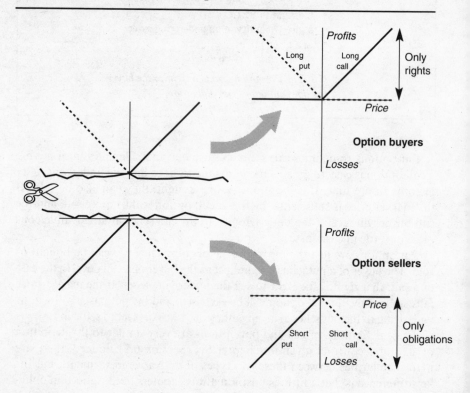

Options are available on a very wide range of underlying instruments, including

- Shares • Foreign currencies
- Bonds • Commodities
- Bills

They can also be created with other derivatives as the underlying instrument, giving rise to options on

- FRAs
- Futures
- Stock indices
- Swaps
- Commodities

The last instance, an option on an option, may seem quite esoteric, but there are examples illustrated in Chapter Thirteen (Section 13.12) and Chapter Fifteen (Section 15.4) where such an instrument may turn out to be the optimal choice.

10.3 OPTIONS TERMINOLOGY

Being different from other instruments, options introduce a new set of jargon. Table 10.1 provides a concise summary of the nomenclature involved before we define each of the key terms in greater detail.

Call, put, buy, sell. The four combinations—buy a call, sell a call, buy a put, sell a put—can perhaps best be appreciated using a diagrammatic representation. Figure 10.6 depicts the four possible payoff profiles, following the same conventions as Figure 10.3.

Strike or exercise price. As an example, consider a call option to buy 100 shares in ABC plc at a strike price of £5.60. If the holder of the call decides to exercise the option, he must pay £5.60 over to the seller for every share purchased. Someone exercising a put option conferring the right to sell XYZ Inc. shares at a strike price of $23 would deliver the shares and expect to receive $23 for each one.

American or European style. The terms *American* and *European* arose from the conventions once adopted by the options exchanges either side of the Atlantic. Nowadays, geographic location is irrelevant, but the names have stuck. Although a European option cannot be exercised prior to maturity, it can usually be traded. Even for OTC options, it is usually possible to obtain a closing-out price from the original bank or to find another bank that will agree to a price for an offsetting trade.

Premium. We have already established that the asymmetry of option contracts means that the buyer of an option must pay the seller in order to acquire the rights granted under the option. The sum paid is called the premium. The option premium has two components: intrinsic value and time value (sometimes called extrinsic value).

Intrinsic value. The intrinsic value is the easiest component to understand, for it represents the net positive amount that an option would realise if

FIGURE 10.6
Basic Option Payoff Profiles

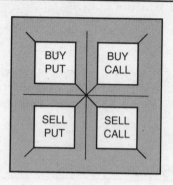

TABLE 10.1
Option Terminology

CALL	The right to buy the underlying instrument.
PUT	The right to sell the underlying instrument.
Option BUYER	The party with the right to exercise the option.
Option SELLER	The party with the obligation to perform if the option is exercised.
STRIKE or EXERCISE price	The price at which the option can be exercised, normally fixed at the outset.
EXPIRY or MATURITY date	The last date on which the option can be exercised.
AMERICAN style	An option that can be exercised at any time until maturity.
EUROPEAN style	An option that can only be exercised on the maturity date and not before.
PREMIUM	The amount paid by buyer to seller to acquire the option.
INTRINSIC VALUE	The net positive value if an option were to be exercised immediately.
TIME VALUE	The amount by which the option premium exceeds the intrinsic value.
IN-THE-MONEY	An option which has intrinsic value.
OUT-OF-THE-MONEY	An option with no intrinsic value.
AT-THE-MONEY	An option for which the strike price is equal to the underlying price.

it were exercised immediately. For example, consider a call option struck at 95 on an underlying asset that currently trades at 100. The intrinsic value of this option is simply 5, because the holder of the call could exercise the option and acquire the underlying asset by paying 95, and then immediately sell the asset in the open market to realise 100, a net profit of 5. In contrast with the call, a put option struck at 95 would have no intrinsic value, because there would be no benefit in exercising it if the underlying asset were priced at 100.

There are two features to note about intrinsic value. First, it is not necessary to know anything about the option premium in order to determine an option's intrinsic value; all one needs to know is the strike price, the underlying price, and whether the option is a call or a put. Second, the concept of intrinsic value applies equally to European and American options, even though it is not possible to exercise them prior to maturity. The intrinsic value is defined in the same way.

However, where a well-developed forward market exists, as in the case of currency options, a little caution must be exercised. In such cases, the intrinsic value of a European option is always calculated relative to the forward rate, whereas that of an American option is calculated relative to either the spot or forward rate, whichever gives the largest result. For example, if the spot rate for sterling against the dollar is £1= $1.5000, and the three-month forward rate is £1= $1.4900, the intrinsic value of an American call on sterling struck at $1.4500 would be 5¢ (using the spot rate), while that of an American sterling put struck at $1.5500 would be 6¢ (using the forward rate).

Time value. In virtually all cases, the option seller will demand a premium over and above the intrinsic value. The reasons for this will be discussed in detail later in this chapter but revolve around the risk that the seller takes on. Although the option may have a particular intrinsic value today, the intrinsic value may be different tomorrow, and the asymmetry of options means that the option seller has more to lose than to gain. This excess is called the time value, because time to maturity is one of the major factors determining the size of the time value.

To clarify the concepts of total premium, intrinsic value, and time value, Figure 10.7 illustrates these amounts for three call options with different strike prices. In each case, the price of underlying asset is 100.

In the case of the options struck at 90 and 95, a portion of the premium is intrinsic value, while the remainder is time value. The last option has no intrinsic value, as the strike price and underlying price are the same, and so the entire premium comprises time value alone.

In-, at-, and out-of-the-money. Once intrinsic value has been defined, defining in-the-money and out-of-the-money options is straightforward. An option with intrinsic value is said to be in-the-money, while an out-of-the-money option is one without intrinsic value. For a call, an in-the-money option is one in which the underlying price exceeds the strike price, while for a put the opposite is true. The term *at-the-money* is normally used when an option contract is first written and refers to an option in which the strike price is set to the prevailing price of the underlying asset. Figure 10.8 illustrates these terms.

FIGURE 10.7
Premium, Intrinsic Value, and Time Value

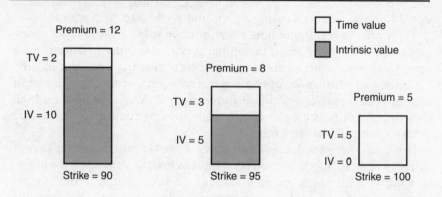

FIGURE 10.8
In-, At-, and Out-of-the-Money Options

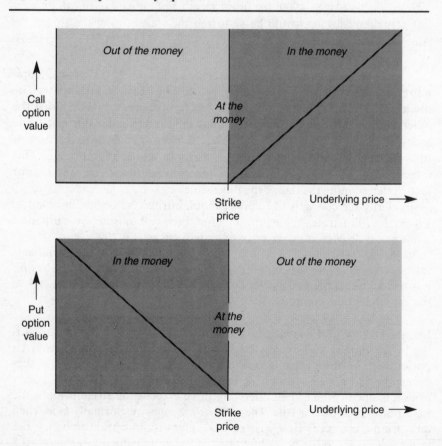

10.4 VALUE AND PROFIT PROFILES AT MATURITY

With the definitions and terminology in place, we are now ready to explore the price and value characteristics of options. This is an important step in understanding how options can be used in practice.

To start with, consider the value of an option at expiry. As an example, we will take a currency option that gives the holder the right to buy one dollar (against deutsch marks) at a strike price of $1=DEM1.7000. Such an option could be considered either as a call on dollars (against D-marks), or as a put on D-marks (against dollars), but we shall refer to it simply as a dollar call. Figure 10.9 graphs the value of this option on its expiry date, for values of $/DEM from 1.4000 to 2.0000.

While the shape of this diagram should by now be familiar, this time we can see exactly how much the option value changes when the underlying price of $/DEM moves. If the $/DEM ends up below the strike price of DEM 1.7000 on the expiry date, this option would expire worthless. Above 1.7000, the value of the option increases 1pfg for every 1pfg rise in the $/DEM. If $/DEM were at 1.7500 on the expiry date, for example, the option would be worth exactly DEM 0.0500.

This one-for-one relationship is the same for all options that expire in-the-money and should not be surprising. When a call option expires in-the-money, it will always be exercised, either to receive the underlying or for cash settlement. Either way, the option is replaced by the underlying itself or its cash equivalent, so the value of an in-the-money option at expiry must rise in lock-step with rises in the value of the underlying.

While Figure 10.9 illustrates the *value* of the option on expiry, it does not show the *profit* from holding the contract. For this we need to know how much the option cost when it was purchased. The profit is then the difference between the value of the option at expiry and the premium originally paid.

Suppose that this currency option was originally purchased as an at-the-money option with six months to expire, and the premium paid was exactly 6pfg. Figure 10.10 takes this into account to show the profit profile at expiry.

Now we can see clearly that buying a call option does not lead to a guaranteed gain, once the premium is taken into account. If the option expires out-of-the-money and is therefore worthless, the buyer has sacrificed the premium for no gain. The loss is therefore equal to the premium paid. Even if the option expires in-the-money, this does not necessarily secure a profit if the terminal value of the option is less than the premium paid. In fact, in order to break even the option must expire as much in-the-money as the original premium paid. In this example, this does not occur until the $/DEM rises above 1.7600.

Some people studying this profit diagram for the first time confuse profit and loss with the decision whether to exercise the option or not. Seeing that

FIGURE 10.9
Value Profile for Call Option on U.S. Dollars against D-marks

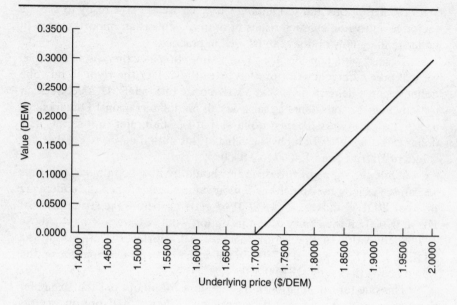

FIGURE 10.10
Profit Profile for Call Option on U.S. Dollar against D-marks

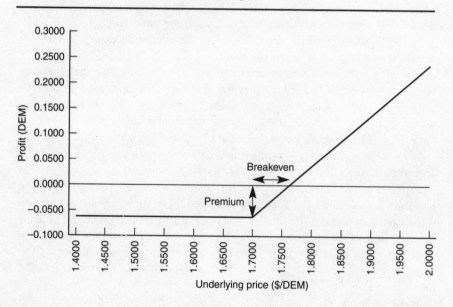

the option loses money if $/DEM is in the range 1.7000 to 1.7600, they mistakenly think that the option should not be exercised. Even though the net result is still a loss, that loss would be greater if the option were not exercised. So long as the option has some value at expiry, it should be exercised to release that value. For example, if $/DEM is at 1.7200 when the option expired, exercising the option yields 2pfg, reducing the 6pfg loss to 4pfg, as shown on the graph. At expiry, there are only two factors influencing the decision whether to exercise: the underlying price and the strike price. The premium paid originally is irrelevant.

Figure 10.10 shows the profit profile for just one option. It is useful to compare profit profiles for options with different strike prices. Perhaps one option will be prove to be better than others. Table 10.2 summarises the premiums paid for five $/DEM currency options with different strike prices ranging from 1.5000 to 1.9000. In each case, the premiums are typical market prices for six-month options at a time when the $/DEM was trading at $1=DEM1.7000.

Figure 10.11 now shows the profit profiles for each of these options. The shape of each graph is the same in each case: a horizontal section, then a kink, then a diagonal section with a slope of 1:1. As one moves from the most in-the-money option (the 1.5000 dollar call) to the most out of-the-money option (the 1.9000 call), the position of the kink is higher and further to the right. The vertical position of the kink is governed solely by the option premium: the more expensive the premium, the deeper each line starts. The horizontal position is determined only by the strike price: the bigger the strike price, the further to the right is the kink.

As these are profit profiles, the best option is the one that lies highest in the diagram. This implies one that has a small premium but also a low strike price. Unfortunately, as the diagram and table reveal, these two requirements conflict with one another. The smaller the premium, the higher the strike price, and this means accepting some kind of compromise.

Further examination of Figure 10.11 shows that there is no clear choice of one option over another. Take the 1.5000 and 1.6000 strike options as examples. Although the 1.6000 option is 9pfg cheaper, the strike price is 10pfg higher. For the 1.6000 option, the kink is 9pfg higher, which is better, but 10pfg to the right, which is worse. The two graphs therefore cross over,

TABLE 10.2
Option Premiums for Different Strikes

	Strike	Premium
In-the-money	1.5000	0.2200
	1.6000	0.1300
At-the-money	1.7000	0.0600
Out-of-the-money	1.8000	0.0200
	1.9000	0.0100

FIGURE 10.11
Profit Profiles for Five Call Options on U.S. Dollar against D-marks

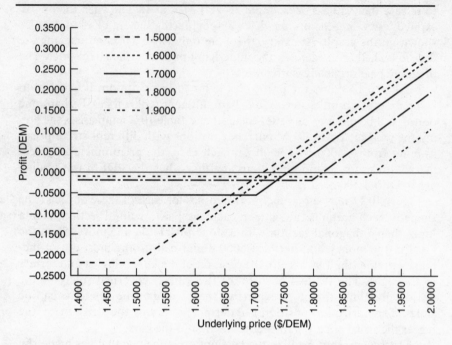

meaning that neither option is universally better than the other. If the $/DEM finishes below 1.5900, the option struck at 1.6000 is better. On the other hand, if the underlying ends above 1.5900, the 1.5000 strike provides a superior financial result, albeit by just 1pfg.

This outcome holds true in every case. All the lines in Figure 10.11 exhibit this crisscrossing characteristic, ensuring that no one option totally dominates any other.

If the $/DEM finishes low, so that all call options on the dollar expire worthless, the best one (or the least bad) is the 1.9000 strike. This is because the premium on all these options is thrown away if they expire worthless, and the 1.9000 strike option was the cheapest, being the most out-of-the-money.

On the other hand, if the $/DEM rallies so that all call options expire in-the-money, it is now the 1.5000 strike that provides the best result. Despite having the most expensive premium at the outset, the advantage of the 1.5000 strike is that it starts already in-the-money. For every 1pfg increase in the underlying price of the dollar at expiry, this option is worth 1pfg more. Although the other options eventually exhibit this behaviour as the dollar rises through 1.8000 and eventually through 1.9000, the options that are already in-the-money at 1.7000 have a head start. Compare, for example, the options struck at 1.7000 and 1.8000. Although the higher strike option is 4pfg cheaper at the outset, the $/DEM has to rise 10pfg from the original level of 1.7000 before the 1.8000 option finishes in-the-money. In the meantime, the 1.7000 option has been increasing in value all the time. This is why the 1.7000 option produces 6pfg more profit for any level of $/DEM above 1.8000.

The conclusion from this is an important one. If fairly priced, no single option can dominate any other option for all possible future outcomes. There will always be some range of outcomes in which one option proves better and another range in which it fares worse. With the benefit of hindsight it is of course possible to say that one option did outperform another, but with hindsight it is possible to improve on almost every decision in life. In prospect, however, all options offer a reasonable choice. How to make that choice will be discussed in Part Two of this book.

For completeness, Figure 10.12 demonstrates that the profit profiles for put options demonstrate the same kind of trade-offs as those of call options. The graphs depict the profit characteristics for a set of currency options with the same original maturity and set of strikes as in the previous example, except that these are put options on the dollar conferring the right to sell dollars against D-marks at the strike prices indicated.

FIGURE 10.12
Profit Profiles for Five Put Options on U.S. Dollars against D-marks

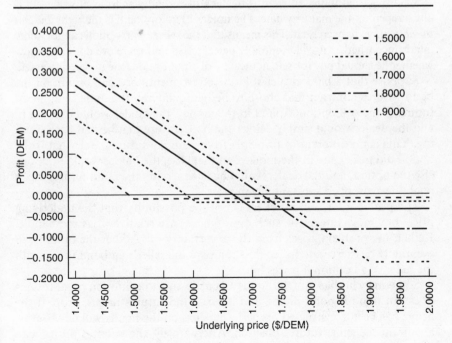

10.5 PRICING OPTIONS

Profit profiles at maturity are very useful in comparing strategies involving different options, but they rely on one important piece of information: the price of the option when it was originally purchased. While value profiles at maturity are easy to construct and depend solely on the underlying and strike prices, it is impossible to construct the profit profile—even on the maturity date—without knowing the original premium paid.

For all the derivative products reviewed until now, it has been possible to determine the fair price by constructing some kind of riskless hedging strategy. For example, someone selling a bond futures contract can hedge by buying a deliverable bond and financing it under repo. This cash-and-carry process was explained in Chapter Eight (Section 8.3). Riskless strategies such as these work because on the maturity date of the derivative there is

1. A rigid relationship between the price of the derivative and rates in the underlying markets.
2. A definite procedure that takes place upon maturity.

For options there is also a rigid relationship at maturity between the value of an option and the underlying price, as illustrated by the examples in Figures 10.3 and 10.9. In the case of the call option on the bond futures contract struck at 98, the option was worth nothing if the bond future expired below 98 and DEM 25 for every basis point the futures price exceeded 98. This is a rigid relationship.

What makes options different is the lack of certainty as to what will eventually happen on the maturity date. The holder of an option has the right, *but not the obligation*, to exercise it. This means that the seller of an option cannot know in advance whether it will eventually be exercised and therefore does not know whether he should buy (or sell, in the case of a put option) the underlying asset.

Suppose that a bank dealer sold the above-mentioned call option on the bond futures contract and chose to hedge by buying the underlying bond future. If the call option expired in-the-money, the holder would exercise it, and the dealer would simply deliver the bond future that he had been holding. This is no different in principle from hedging futures. But what if the option did not expire in-the-money? In that case, the holder would not exercise the option, and the dealer would be left carrying the bond future, which might have dropped substantially in price.

The problem for option sellers is not the possibility that the underlying price may move adversely; such eventualities are relatively easy to handle. Rather, the problem arises from the uncertainty of whether the option will eventually be exercised. To see this, compare the seller of a bond future with the seller of an option if prices fall.

Someone who has bought bonds against a short position in bond futures does not mind if bond prices, and hence bond futures prices, drop. If the hedge has been constructed properly, any loss on the bonds will be offset by a gain on the short futures position. Alternatively, the seller of futures can simply elect to deliver the loss-making bonds against the short futures position. The counterparty who is long futures, and who therefore loses money when bond prices fall, has no choice but to accept these losses, because futures contracts are binding.

On the other hand, someone who has bought the underlying asset against a short position in call options may well mind if prices fall. If an option expires out-of-the-money and is therefore not exercised, the option seller can no longer off-load his losses by delivering the underlying asset. Once the call option moves out-of-the-money, mounting losses from holding the underlying asset are no longer compensated by gains on the options position. Unlike the buyer of a futures contract, the counterparty who is long call options does have a choice and is not compelled to exercise these options if prices have fallen below the strike price.

This uncertainty—whether the option will ultimately be exercised—makes options much more difficult to hedge and therefore much more difficult to price. There are two principal ways to deal with this uncertainty and thereby to find the fair price for an option.

One method makes an assumption about the way in which the underlying price behaves over time. From this the expected value of the option at maturity can be estimated. This method can lead to the well-known Black-Scholes model of option pricing. Another method relies upon the possibility of constructing a riskless hedge when an option is first sold and then adjusting this hedge continually until the option expires. This can lead to the so-called binomial model. Despite the apparent differences in approach, both models eventually lead to the same answer to the question: What is the fair price for an option?

Professors Fischer Black and Myron Scholes published their seminal paper on option pricing in 1973, and this established for the first time a firm foundation for the pricing of options. Unfortunately, though it is relatively easy to implement, a complete derivation of the Black-Scholes model involves some fearsome mathematics, which, to the relief of many readers, we shall avoid restating here. Instead, this chapter will present a more intuitive explanation of the B-S model and what the various terms mean. Those readers not concerned with how the price is derived can skip straight to Section 10.10, which discusses value profiles prior to maturity. On the other hand, those interested in pursuing the mathematics even further are directed to the books cited at the end of this chapter, which present a number of alternative derivations of the B-S model.

Before coming to the B-S model itself, we first need to study the behaviour of financial prices.

10.6 THE BEHAVIOR OF FINANCIAL PRICES

One of the key assumptions underlying the B-S model is that asset prices follow a lognormal distribution. What does this mean? Most people are already familiar with the normal distribution pictured in Figure 10.13.

FIGURE 10.13
The Normal Distribution

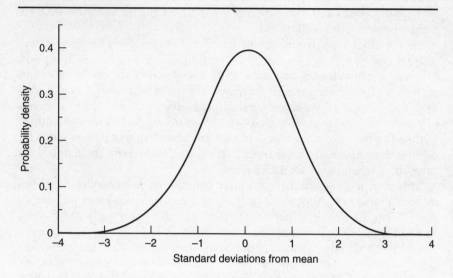

The normal distribution occurs frequently in nature. For example, if one were to take 1,000 men drawn at random and construct a histogram illustrating how their heights were distributed, the result would be a normal distribution. The distribution would peak at the mean (average) height of the group, but there would be a spread around this mean. The statistical measure for the degree of spread is called the *standard deviation*, and a property of the normal distribution is that 68.3% of the distribution lies within ±1 standard deviation of the mean, while 95.4% lies within ±2 standard deviations. In our height illustration, we might find that the mean height was 1.72m, and the standard deviation was 0.09m. This would imply that 95.4% of the men in our sample had heights between 1.54m and 1.90m and we could infer that 95.4% of men in the wider population from which our random sample was drawn also have heights within this range

With the normal distribution being so common in nature, it would be tempting to assume that financial prices also followed a normal distribution. Such an assumption would create several problems, however, not least of which is the possibility for a variable that is normally distributed to take on negative values, something that most financial prices can never do.

It turns out that, while prices themselves are not normally distributed, returns mostly are. An investor buying a share at 100 is just as likely to see a return of +10% as a return of –10%. However, we need to be extremely careful what is meant by "return."

At first sight, one would think that an investor should not be upset if his investment first went up by 10%, and then down by 10%; he would simply be back where he started. Or would he? A 10% increase takes the value of his shares from 100 up to 110, but the subsequent 10% decrease brings it from 110 down to 99.

The reason the investor ends up with less than he started arises from the way in which return has been measured here. The rise from 100 to 110 is an increase of 10 on a starting price of 100, or +10%. The fall from 110 to 99 is a decrease of 11 on a starting price of 110, or –10%. The size of the price change differs, despite the fact that the percentage price change itself is the same in both cases, because the basis for measuring the percentage has altered.

The problem with using straight percentages in this way is that one is tempted to add successive percentage changes to obtain the overall result. This leads to the wrong result, as the above example illustrates, because 10% – 10% = 0%, but the end result was patently a loss of 1%. The correct result is obtained, not by adding percentage changes, but by multiplying *price relatives*. A price relative is simply the ratio of successive prices. In the above example, the two price relatives are 110/100 = 1.10, and 99/110 = 0.90. The product of the price relatives is 1.10 × 0.90 = 0.99, which gives the correct result, namely, that the final price is 0.99 times the original price.

Fortunately, there is a mathematical device that enables us once again to use addition rather than multiplication. Adding the logarithms of two numbers gives the logarithm of the product of those numbers.[3] Applying this technique here gives the following result:

$$\ln(110/100) = \qquad 0.0953 \quad \text{or} \quad +\ 9.53\%$$
$$\ln(99/110) = \quad -\ 0.1054 \quad \text{or} \quad -10.54\%$$
$$\ln((110/100) \times (99/100)) = \quad -\ 0.0101 \quad \text{or} \quad -\ 1.01\%$$

The decrease from 110 to 99 is shown for what it is, a greater effective reduction than the original increase from 100 to 110. That is why the end result is negative, implying an overall price decrease. To find out exactly what the final price implied by the –1.01% figure is, we need to use the opposite of logarithms, exponents. As logarithms to the base e have been used, we must take $e^{-0.0101}$ to obtain 0.99 or 99%. The calculation therefore implies that the final price should be 99, which we know is the correct answer.

Summarising the argument so far, we have demonstrated that taking the logarithm of price relatives gives a more consistent method for calculating returns than taking the price relatives themselves. In other words, defining return as

$$return = \ln\left(\frac{S_{t+1}}{S_t}\right) \tag{10.1}$$

is more consistent than using the more traditional definition

$$traditional\ return = \left(\frac{S_{t+1}}{S_t} - 1\right) \tag{10.2}$$

---

[3] Logarithms to any base could be used, but in finance it is most useful to use natural logarithms (logarithms to the base e).

where S_t is the market price at time t, and S_{t+1} is the price one period later.

Using this method, what happens to the price if the return in the first period is +10%, and in the next period –10%? Starting at a price of $S_0 = 100$, we obtain:

$$S_1 = 100 \times e^{+0.10} = 110.52$$
$$S_2 = 110.52 \times e^{-0.10} = 100.00$$

This time the price does return to its original level following a 10% increase and then a 100% decrease, just as common sense would dictate.[4]

Consider the effect on price if the return was +10% every year for seven years. Starting at 100, the price would increase as follows:

100, 110.52, 122.14, 134.99, 149.18, 164.87, 182.21, 201.38

In absolute terms, the price doubles over seven years, with every successive price change being greater than the previous one. Now consider the effect of seven years of price decreases, also starting at 100:

100, 90.48, 81.87, 74.08, 67.03, 60.65, 54.88, 49.66

In this case, the price halves over the seven-year period, with every successive price change being smaller than before. If we plotted these two series on a horizontal scale showing how the prices progressed over time, we would obtain a diagram like that of Figure 10.14. This shows very clearly the ever-expanding series of prices on the right side of the diagram, and the compression of prices on the left.

We can now return to the concept of financial returns being normally distributed. If the returns follow a symmetric normal distribution, the

FIGURE 10.14
Successive Price Movements over Time

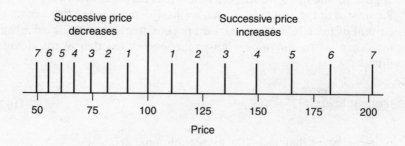

---

[4] Seeing a 10% increase leading to what seems like a 10.52% increase in price should not appear too strange. Exactly the same result would arise if a bank paid interest at 10% per annum, but paid interest continuously rather than at discrete intervals. Paid just twice a year, 10% per annum would compound to an effective return of 10.25%, to 10.47% paid monthly, to 10.5156% daily, and finally to 10.5171% if paid continuously.

distribution of prices will follow a distorted normal distribution, distorted in the same way as Figure 10.14, with the left side being compressed and the right side being stretched. This is clear from a comparison of Figure 10.15, which depicts normally distributed returns having a mean of 10% and a standard deviation of 20% in absolute terms, with Figure 10.16, which depicts the resulting distribution of prices.

The distribution of prices illustrated in Figure 10.16 is called a *lognormal distribution*, because the logarithm of the variable—prices in this case—is normally distributed. To better understand the relationship between returns and prices, let us start with the distribution of returns.

Returns are defined as the logarithm of the price relatives and are assumed to follow the normal distribution such that

$$\ln\left(\frac{S_t}{S_0}\right) \sim N(\mu t,\ \sigma\sqrt{t}) \tag{10.3}$$

where

S_0 is the price at time 0
S_t is the price at time t
$N(m,s)$ is a random normal distribution with mean m and standard deviation s
μ is the annual rate of return
σ is the annualised standard deviation of returns

and the symbol "~" has the meaning "is distributed according to . . ."

FIGURE 10.15
Normal Distribution of Returns

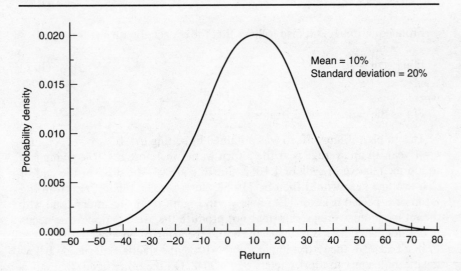

Mean = 10%
Standard deviation = 20%

FIGURE 10.16
Lognormal Distribution of Prices

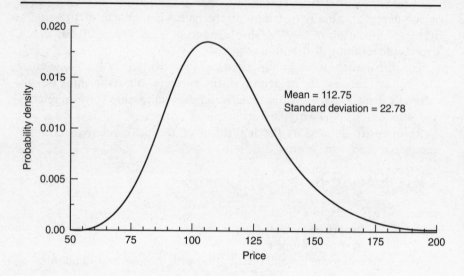

It follows directly from equation 10.3 that the logarithm of the prices is normally distributed, because

$$\ln(S_t) \sim \ln(S_0) + N(\mu t, \sigma \sqrt{t}) \tag{10.4}$$

and S_0 is a constant. Prices are therefore lognormally distributed and follow the relationship

$$\frac{S_t}{S_0} \sim e^{N(\mu t, \sigma \sqrt{t})} \tag{10.5}$$

From equation 10.3 it also follows that the expected return is simply μt

$$E\left[\ln\left(\frac{S_t}{S_0}\right)\right] = \mu t \tag{10.6}$$

where

E[.] is the expectation operator

The graph in Figure 10.15 was obtained by setting $\mu = 10\%$, $\sigma = 20\%$, and $t = 1$ year. In an average year the return would therefore be 10%, giving rise to a price relative of $e^{0.10}$ or 1.1052. Starting at 100, the price at the end of that average year would then be 110.52. Surprisingly, this differs from the mean or expected price of 112.75 shown in Figure 10.16. To understand why the return in an average year does not produce the average price, one needs to consider what happens across the entire spectrum of possible returns.

In a bad year, the return might fall to −10%, one standard deviation below the mean, leading to a price relative of 0.9048. On the other hand, the return might rise to +30% in a good year, one standard deviation above the mean, and this would result in a price relative of 1.3499. As returns are normally distributed with a mean of +10%, there is an equal chance of finding returns of –10% and +30%, and therefore of finding price relatives of 0.9048 and 1.3499.

If we take the geometric average of 0.9048 and 1.3499, we obtain $(0.9048 \times 1.3499)^{0.5} = 1.1052$. In other words, if a bad year was followed by a good year, the price would end up the same as if two average years had followed one another. This is a direct consequence of the way we have defined returns and is perfectly consistent.

However, if we wish to obtain an estimate of the expected price after one year, we must take an arithmetic average of all the possible price relatives, not the geometric average. The arithmetic average of a typical bad year and a typical good year is now $(0.9048 + 1.3499)/2 = 1.1273$, which is somewhat larger than the value of 1.1052 obtained before (and very close to the price relative of 1.1275 implied by Figure 10.16). In fact, it is a well-known property that the arithmetic mean of a set of numbers is always greater than or equal to the geometric mean.

The expected price relative is therefore going to be more than $e^{\mu t}$, and it is possible to prove[5] that the expected price relative is, in fact

$$\mathrm{E}\left[\frac{S_t}{S_0}\right] = e^{\left(\mu t + \frac{\sigma^2 t}{2}\right)} \qquad (10.7)$$

In the above example, the expected price relative is therefore $e^{0.10 + 0.04/2} = 1.1275$. If the original price were 100, the expected price is then 112.75, which is the mean of the price distribution shown in Figure 10.16.

The average price is therefore greater than the price obtained from average return. Though paradoxical, the reason lies once again in the asymmetry of the lognormal distribution. For returns below the mean, the price distribution is compressed, while for above-average returns the price distribution is stretched. While good and bad returns are symmetrical and cancel out, the prices resulting from these returns are not symmetrical and do not cancel out. In general, if the return in a good year is $\mu + \delta$, and the return in the corresponding bad year is $\mu - \delta$, the average price relative from these two years is

$$\frac{e^{\mu+\delta} + e^{\mu-\delta}}{2} = e^{\mu}\left(\frac{e^{\delta} + e^{-\delta}}{2}\right) = e^{\mu} \, cosh(\delta) \geq e^{\mu}$$

because $cosh(\delta)$ is always greater than 1 for all δ. This means that the expected price relative will always exceed e^{μ}. In the arithmetic example given previously, μ was 10% and δ was 20%, giving an average price relative of 1.1273, very close to the correct expected price relative of 1.1275. Equation 10.7 tells us that the bigger the variance σ^2, the bigger will be the asymmetry of the price distribution, and the bigger the expected price relative will be.

---

[5] Equation 10.7 follows from the relationship between the logarithm of an expectation and the expectation of a logarithm. If x is a random variable, then: $\ln(\mathrm{E}[x]) = \mathrm{E}[\ln(x)] + 0.5 \times \mathrm{var}[\ln(x)]$.

We have thus seen that:

- Returns should be measured by taking the natural logarithm of price relatives (equation 10.1).
- Returns follow a normal distribution (equation 10.3).
- Prices follow a lognormal distribution (equation 10.5).
- The expected price relative is greater than the price relative from the expected return (equation 10.7).

Before seeing how these findings lead to the B-S model, let us return to an assertion made at the beginning of this section and repeated here: Returns follow a random normal distribution. Much empirical research has been undertaken within each of the major financial markets, and there seems little doubt that most rates and prices most of the time follow a random walk according to equation 10.5. Note that this does not preclude trends or patterns from emerging. The existence of a trend is recognised explicitly by the drift term μt, while patterns may appear in the same way as people identify objects from a Rorschach ink blot.

As an example, consider the four lines depicted in Figure 10.17. One of the lines shows the evolution of the £/$ exchange rate between 1986 and 1988. The other three lines start with the same initial value and have similar

FIGURE 10.17
Random Walk Nature of Financial Prices

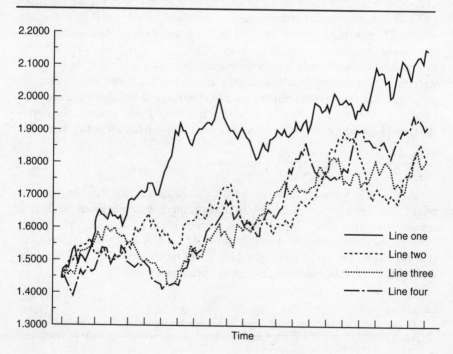

means and variances, but are streams of prices generated completely at random using equation 10.5. It is difficult, if not impossible, to determine just by looking which line represents the real data. This is by no means proof of the random walk nature of financial prices, but it demonstrates visually that random data looks real and real-life data looks random. Which line was the real data? The answer lies at the foot of this page.[6]

The lognormal behaviour of financial prices is an important assumption upon which the B-S model rests. The next section explains how this assumption can be used to determine a fair price for options.

10.7 OPTION PRICING—THE BLACK-SCHOLES MODEL

The fair price for any financial asset is its expected value. For example, if a share had a 30% chance of achieving a price of 40, and a 70% chance of achieving a price of 50, the fair value at that time would be:

$$(0.30 \times 40) + (0.70 \times 50) = 47$$

The same principle applies to options. The fair value of an option at expiry is the sum of every possible value it could achieve multiplied by the probability of that value occurring. In the simple example given above, there were just two discrete outcomes. Options, however, can take on almost any value, so it is necessary to use continuous rather than discrete probability distributions. Figure 10.18 illustrates three discrete and one continuous distribution. With a discrete distribution, the probability of a particular outcome can be measured directly from the height of the bar. For continuous distributions, the probability of a particular range of outcomes is measured by taking the area beneath that section of the curve.

From the definition of a call option, the expected value of the option at maturity is

$$E[C_T] = E[\max (S_T - X, 0)] \qquad (10.8)$$

where
$E[C_T]$ is the expected value of the call option at maturity
S_T is the price of the underlying asset at maturity
X is the strike price of the option.

There are two possible situations that can arise at maturity. If $S_T > X$, the call option expires in-the-money, and $\max(S_T - X, 0) = S_T - X$. If $S_T < X$, the option expires out-of-the-money, and $\max(S_T - X, 0) = 0$. If p is defined as the probability that $S_T > X$, equation 10.8 can be rewritten

---

[6] Line four depicts the real data.

FIGURE 10.18 *Discrete and Continuous Distributions*

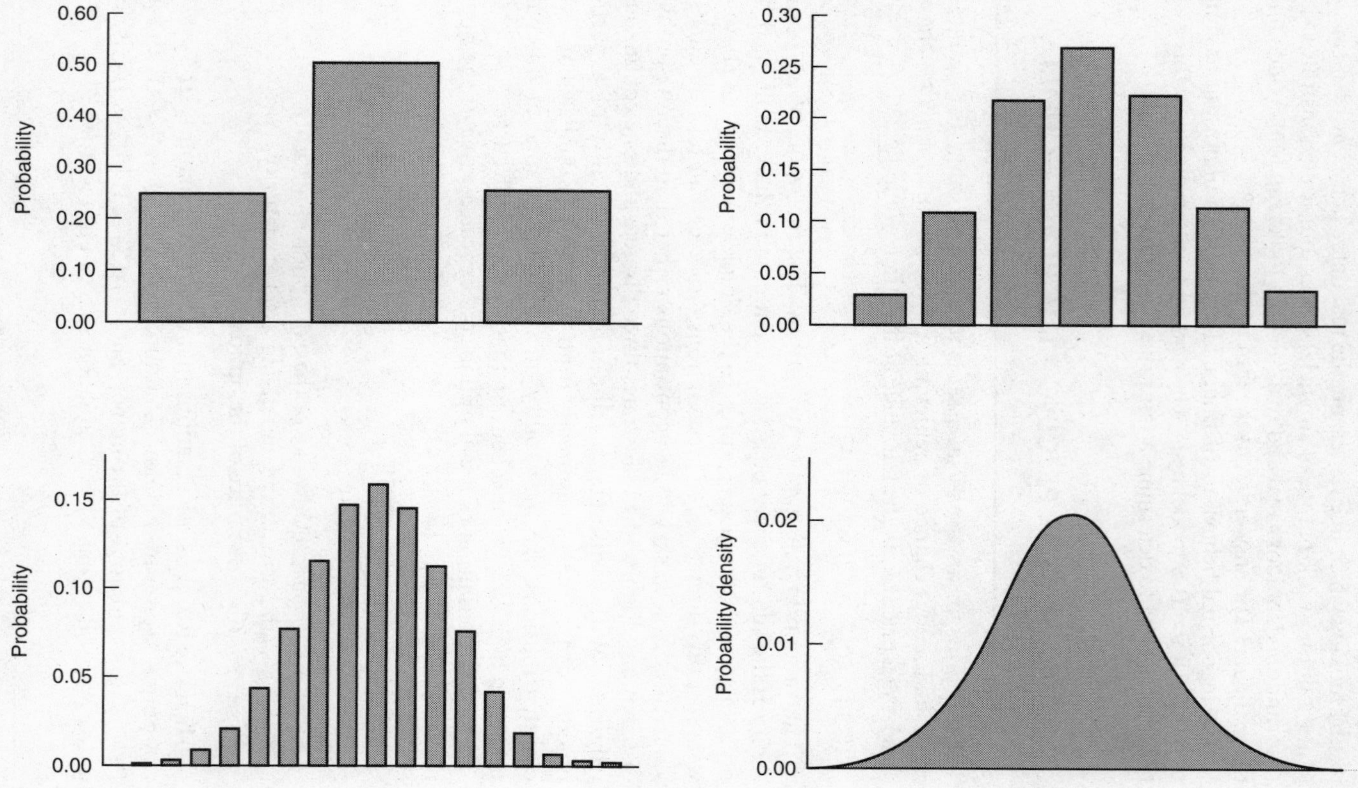

$$E[C_T] = p \times (E[S_T|S_T > X] - X) + (1 - p) \times 0 \qquad (10.9)$$
$$= p \times (E[S_T|S_T > X] - X)$$

where

p is the probability that $S_T > X$

$E[S_T|S_T > X]$ is the expected value of S_T, given that $S_T > X$.

Equation 10.9 gives us an expression for the expected value of the call at maturity. To obtain the fair price at the inception of the contract, the expression must be discounted back to its present value to obtain the following:

$$C = p \times e^{-rt} \times (E[S_T|S_T > X] - X) \qquad (10.10)$$

where

C is the fair price for the option at inception

r is the continuously compounded riskless rate of interest

t is the length of time until maturity.

The problem of pricing an option has been reduced to two slightly simpler problems:

1. Determine p, the probability that the option ends in-the-money such that $S_T > X$.
2. Determine $E[S_T|S_T > X]$, the expected value of the underlying asset given that the option ends in-the-money.

The solution for both of these problems can be found in the lognormal distribution of financial prices. Figure 10.19 shows the same lognormal price distribution as that of Figure 10.16, but highlights the part of the distribution for which the price exceeds 120. This will be of interest if we wish to price an option whose strike price was set at 120.

The area of the shaded part is 34% of the area under the graph as a whole, so the probability that the final price will exceed 120 is 0.34. The expected value of the shaded part[7] is 137.894. If continuously compounded interest rates are 12%, the fair price for the option struck at 120 is

$$C = 0.34 \times e^{-0.12} \times (137.894 - 120) = 5.40$$

This is, in fact, exactly the value of the option as suggested by the B-S model.

How were the values of 0.34 and 137.894 calculated? It is relatively straightforward to derive an expression for the probability p, but rather more difficult to do so for the expectation expression $E[S_T|S_T > X]$. We therefore will show here how the probability can be calculated, but not how the expectation can be derived; for the latter we will merely state the end result. Combining the two expressions will give us the formula for the B-S model itself.

Finding the probability p that the underlying price at maturity S_T will exceed some critical price X is the same as finding the probability that the

---

[7] If you were to take a piece of cardboard in the shape of the shaded part, it would balance at exactly the point corresponding to 137.894.

FIGURE 10.19
Lognormal Distribution for In-the-Money Outcomes

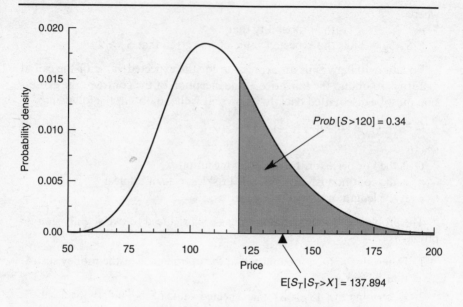

return over the period will exceed some critical value r_X. This is an easier problem to solve, because returns follow a normal distribution, and normal distributions are easier to work with than lognormal distributions. Remembering that returns are defined according to equation 10.1 as the logarithm of the price relatives means that we must find the probability p such that

$$p = Prob\ [S_T > X] = Prob\left[return > \ln\left(\frac{X}{S_0}\right)\right] \tag{10.11}$$

where S_0 is the underlying price at the outset.

In general, the probability that a normally distributed variable x will exceed some critical value x_{crit} is given by

$$Prob\ [x > x_{crit}] = 1 - N\left(\frac{x_{crit} - \mu^*}{\sigma^*}\right) \tag{10.12}$$

where

μ^* is the mean of x
σ^* is the standard deviation of x
$N(.)$ is the cumulative normal distribution.

In the context of equation 10.11, we need to find expressions for μ^* and σ^*, the mean and standard deviation of returns. Equation 10.7 provided an expression for the expected value of the price relative S_T/S_0. If we define r such that

$$r = \mu + \frac{\sigma^2}{2} \tag{10.13}$$

we can then rewrite equation 10.7 in a simpler way:

$$\mathrm{E}\left[\frac{S_t}{S_0}\right] = e^{rt} \tag{10.14}$$

The new variable r is not only a convenient shorthand for the expression $\mu + \sigma^2/2$, it is actually the continuously compounded riskless rate of interest. It may seem surprising that this is the relevant interest rate to use when valuing risky investments like options, but the answer to this conundrum lies in the risk neutrality argument.

The basis for the risk neutrality argument is the possibility of constructing a riskless portfolio combining an option with some proportion of the underlying asset. In fact, this approach is the foundation of the binomial method for option valuation discussed in the following section. A riskless portfolio is one that has the same financial outcome regardless of events, and therefore future cash flows should be discounted at the riskless interest rate. With such a portfolio, investors' risk preferences are irrelevant, and the portfolio should be worth the same whether being valued risk-averse or risk-neutral investors. Since it is easier to value the portfolio at the riskless rate used by risk-neutral investors, we may as well choose the riskless rate.

Note that the risk neutrality argument does not imply that all financial assets actually do grow at the riskless rate implied by equation 10.14. What the argument says is that the same answer for the price of an option will be obtained whether we choose the riskless rate or some higher interest rate. If a higher rate were selected, the underlying asset would grow at a faster rate, but the payoffs from an option on this asset would also have to be discounted back at a higher rate, and the two effects cancel out.

Another way to consider this is to remember that the option price is determined in proportion to the price of the underlying asset; double both the underlying asset price and the strike price, and the option price will also double. If the underlying asset price happens to be depressed because risk-averse investors are discounting future cash flows at a particularly high rate, the price of the option will also be depressed since it is calculated in proportion, but this is just as it should be. To be consistent, the same investors should discount future cash flows from the option at the same high rate.

Equation 10.6 now becomes

$$\mathrm{E}\left[\ln\left(\frac{S_t}{S_0}\right)\right] = \mu t = \left(r - \frac{\sigma^2}{2}\right)t = \mu^* \tag{10.15}$$

which gives an expression for μ^*, the mean return. Equation 10.3 already defined the standard deviation of returns as $\sigma\sqrt{t}$. Combining equations 10.11 and 10.12, we now have

$$Prob[S_T > X] = Prob\left[return > \ln\left(\frac{X}{S_0}\right)\right] = 1 - N\left(\frac{\ln\left(\frac{X}{S_0}\right) - \left(r - \frac{\sigma^2}{2}\right)t}{\sigma\sqrt{t}}\right)$$

$$\tag{10.16}$$

The symmetry of the normal distribution means that $1 - N(d) = N(-d)$, so

$$p = Prob[S_T > X] = N\left(\frac{\ln\left(\frac{S_0}{X}\right) + \left(r - \frac{\sigma^2}{2}\right)t}{\sigma\sqrt{t}}\right) \tag{10.17}$$

Substituting the values in the previous example, we have

$$Prob[S_T > X] = N\left(\frac{\ln\left(\frac{100}{120}\right) + \left(0.12 - \frac{0.20^2}{2}\right) \times 1}{0.20\sqrt{1}}\right) = N(-0.4116) = 0.34$$

and this is the value for the probability p obtained before.

Finding a formula for the expression $E[S_T|S_T > X]$ involves integrating the normal distribution curve over the range X to ∞. When this is done,[8] the result is

$$E[S_T|S_T > X] = S_0 e^{rt} \frac{N(d_1)}{N(d_2)} \tag{10.18}$$

where

$$d_1 = \frac{\ln\left(\frac{S_0}{X}\right) + \left(r + \frac{\sigma^2}{2}\right)t}{\sigma\sqrt{t}} \quad \text{and} \quad d_2 = \frac{\ln\left(\frac{S_0}{X}\right) + \left(r - \frac{\sigma^2}{2}\right)t}{\sigma\sqrt{t}} = d_1 - \sigma\sqrt{t} \tag{10.19}$$

Now we have expressions for p (equation 10.17) and $E[S_T|S_T > X]$ (equation 10.18) and can insert these into equation 10.10 to obtain the complete formula for a call option:

$$C = N(d_2) \times e^{-rt} \times \left(S_0 e^{rt} \frac{N(d_1)}{N(d_2)} - X\right)$$

$$\therefore C = S_0 N(d_1) - X e^{-rt} N(d_2) \tag{10.20}$$

This is the famous Black-Scholes model. It provides a single formula that enables the fair price for a call option to be calculated. As the foregoing derivation has demonstrated, the formula can be interpreted as measuring the expected present value of the option based on the key assumption that prices follow a lognormal distribution.

As an illustration of this, Figures 10.20 and 10.21 show the results of a Monte Carlo simulation. The behaviour of a financial asset was simulated by a computer over 10,000 trials. In each trial, the return was sampled at random from a normal distribution with mean $\mu = 10\%$ and standard deviation $\sigma = 20\%$. If the return in a given trial turned out to be p, the price S_t after a period of time t would be given by $S_t = S_0 e^{pt}$, and the present value of

---

[8] See Jarrow and Rudd, page 94, cited in the bibliography at the end of the chapter.

the option would be $(S_t-X)e^{-rt}$ if $S_t>X$, and 0 otherwise.

Starting always with an initial price of 100, this experiment gave rise to the distribution of prices after one year illustrated in Figure 10.20. This has a mean of 112.75 and a standard deviation of 22.77, almost exactly that predicted by equation 10.7 and illustrated in the theoretical distribution of Figure 10.16. The probability of the underlying price being below 120 was 0.66, the same as the theoretical figure of 0.66 (1.00-0.34) predicted by equation 10.17.

The corresponding distribution of option prices is illustrated in Figure 10.21. The option expired out-of-the-money in 66% of the trials, while in the remainder of cases it expired in-the-money with values ranging from just above zero to as high as 110. The mean of this wide distribution was 5.40, exactly the price calculated using the B-S model in equation 10.20.

Thus, starting only with an assumption of returns that are normally distributed and using nothing other than very simple arithmetic, the Monte Carlo simulation arrives at the same answer for the expected value of the option as the B-S model.

Although the existence of normally distributed returns is one of the principal assumptions underlying the B-S model, there are a number of other assumptions that it relies on:

- The underlying asset can be bought and sold freely, even in fractional units.
- The underlying asset can be sold short, and the proceeds are available to the short seller.

FIGURE 10.20
Distribution of Underlying Asset Prices

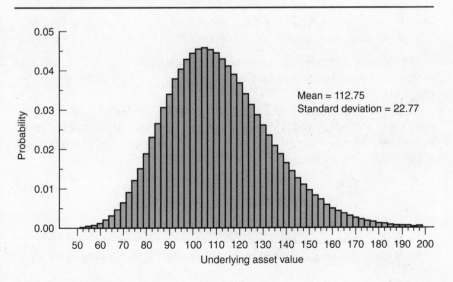

Mean = 112.75
Standard deviation = 22.77

FIGURE 10.21
Distribution of Option Values

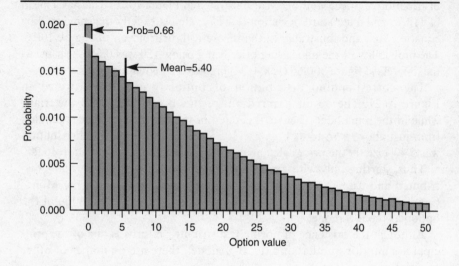

- The underlying asset pays no dividends or other distributions before maturity.
- Lending and borrowing is possible at the same riskless interest rate, which accrues continuously in time.
- The option is European style and cannot therefore be exercised prior to maturity.
- There are no taxes, transaction costs, or margin requirements.
- The underlying price is continuous in time, with no jumps or discontinuities.
- Variability of underlying asset prices and interest rates remains constant throughout the life of the option.

While many of these conditions are not strictly true in practice, the basic model can be adjusted—in many cases quite simply—to handle departures from these assumptions.

Take, for example, a currency option, where the underlying asset—a foreign currency—does pay a distribution, namely, the interest that can be earned on a currency deposit. To price such an option, the standard B-S formula of equation 10.20 can be modified thus:

$$C = Se^{-r_b t} N(d'_1) - Xe^{-r_p t} N(d'_2) \tag{10.21}$$

where

S is the spot exchange rate

r_b is the continuously compounded interest rate in the base currency

r_p is the continuously compounded interest rate in the pricing currency and

$$d'_1 = \frac{\ln\left(\frac{S}{X}\right) + \left(r_p - r_b + \frac{\sigma^2}{2}\right)t}{\sigma\sqrt{t}} \text{ and } d'_2 = d'_1 - \sigma\sqrt{t}$$

to arrive at the so-called Garman-Kohlhagen model for currency options.

The great virtue of the B-S model is that it is relatively easy to calculate, and it produces reasonable and consistent pricing. For this reason it has been adapted to cope with many different types of options, and in the majority of cases practitioners prefer to use the B-S formula or its derivatives rather than more complex models.

For example, it now appears that the distribution of prices in practice is not exactly lognormal but follows a distribution with fatter tails. This happens because market prices do occasionally jump, and therefore the real-life probability of a price move of, say, three standard deviations away from the mean is slightly greater than that predicted by the lognormal distribution. How do market makers responsible for option pricing cope with this? Rather than work with a model that explicitly takes the fat-tailed price distribution into account, they still use the B-S model but insert inflated volatility numbers when pricing in-the-money and out-of-the-money options. This has the effect of increasing the prices of these options relative to those of at-the-money options, which is just what is required to reflect the increased chance of significant price moves affecting these options.

We have concentrated on pricing call options and so far ignored the problem of pricing puts. Fortunately, there is no need to develop a separate model, because the price of a call option and the price of a put option are inextricably linked through a relationship called the *put-call parity theorem*.

To illustrate put-call parity, consider executing the following transactions:

1. Sell one call option with time to maturity t and strike price X.
2. Buy one put option with the same maturity date and strike price.
3. Buy the underlying asset.
4. Borrow a sum of money Xe^{-rt}, where r is the continuously compounded riskless interest rate.

If S_0 is the original price of the underlying asset, C the price of the call, and P the price of the put, the total cash flow generated through carrying out these transactions is

$$C - P - S_0 + Xe^{-rt}$$

At maturity, whatever the price of the underlying asset, the borrowing will need to be repaid, and this will lead to an outflow of X. What happens next depends upon the underlying asset price.

Consider first what happens at maturity if $S_t > X$. The call option expires in-the-money and is exercised against the seller, who therefore delivers the underlying asset and receives the strike price X. This provides exactly the cash required to repay the original borrowing. The put expires worthless. The net cash flow is therefore exactly zero.

Now consider the situation at maturity if $S_t < X$. This time the call option expires worthless, but the put can now be exercised. This gives the buyer the right to sell the underlying asset and receive the strike price X, which is exactly the cash flow required to repay the borrowing. Once again the net cash flow is zero.

In the unlikely event that $S_t = X$ at maturity, both options expire worthless. This time the underlying asset can be sold in the market at its prevailing price to receive X and the proceeds used to repay the borrowing. The net result: a zero cash flow once more.

In other words, this set of transactions will produce a zero net cash flow whatever happens. If the final value of the portfolio must always be zero, then the initial value must always be zero. If it were less than zero, an opportunity for riskless profit would arise. If it were greater than zero, the reverse set of transactions could be executed to secure a riskless profit. This means that

$$C - P - S_0 + Xe^{-rt} = 0$$

Therefore:

$$P = C - S_0 + Xe^{-rt} \qquad (10.22)$$

This provides a formula for pricing a put option from a call, and there is therefore no need for a separate pricing model for put options.

The model developed by Professors Black and Scholes established a milestone in finance. For the first time it provided a reliable means for pricing options on stocks, and variations developed since have extended the formula to cover a wide range of option types and underlying assets. There are, however, some options that the B-S model cannot price successfully. For these, an alternative method must be used, the binomial model.

10.8 OPTION PRICING—THE BINOMIAL APPROACH

In introducing option pricing, Section 10.5 referred to a method that relies upon the possibility of constructing a riskless hedge when an option is first sold and then adjusting this hedge continually until the option expires. If such a riskless hedge can be found, then pricing options becomes similar to pricing other financial derivatives such as futures. The only difference is that, as we shall see, the options hedge will need constant revision, whereas hedges like the cash-and-carry futures hedge can be set up and then left alone.

To see how this hedging process works, we must first suspend belief for a little while and suppose that at any given moment in time a financial asset can only move up or down by a prespecified proportion. If the asset price is S at time t, it can move either up to uS or down to dS at time $t + \Delta t$. Suppose there is a call option on this asset with a price C at time t. If the underlying asset moves up to uS, the option will also move up to C_{up}, but if the underlying asset moves down to dS, the option will also move down to C_{down}. Figure 10.22 illustrates these parallel movements. As the financial asset can only achieve two possible prices, the sequence is appropriately called a binomial process. The scenario described thus far is completely general, as we have not yet specified values for any of the variables.

For the sake of illustration, suppose that $S = 100$, $u = 1.20$, and $d = 0.90$, and that the call option is struck at 100 and has one period to mature. Under these circumstances we now know that if the underlying asset moves up to 120, the option will be worth 20 at maturity, but if the asset goes down to 90, the option will expire worthless. Figure 10.23 depicts this specific scenario.

The only unknown in Figure 10.23 is C, the value of the call option one period prior to maturity. We will demonstrate that a suitable value for C can be determined by forming a riskless hedge between the option and the underlying asset.

Consider a portfolio comprising of:

1. Selling three call options at price C each.
2. Buying two of the underlying assets at 100 each.
3. Borrowing 163.64 at 10% over the period.

The net cash flow at the outset thus will be $3C - 200 + 163.64 = 3C - 36.36$. At maturity, there are two possible outcomes, and the financial impact of each situation is summarised in Table 10.3.

FIGURE 10.22
One-Period Binomial Process—General Case

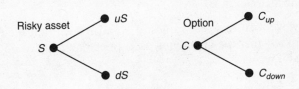

FIGURE 10.23
One-Period Binomial Process—Specific Case

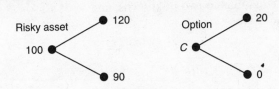

TABLE 10.3
Outcome from Portfolio of Options and Underlying Assets

	Up	Down
Proceeds from selling asset	$2 \times 120 = 240$	$2 \times 90 = 180$
Payout on short call position	$3 \times (-20) = -60$	$3 \times (0) = 0$
Repay borrowing	-180	-180
Net cash flow	0	0

The amazing result is that this particular combination of underlying asset, borrowing, and options has the same financial outcome whether the underlying asset goes up or down in price. This is a riskless hedge. If the outcome of this particular portfolio is always zero, then the fair price for acquiring the portfolio at the outset must also be zero. This means that $3C - 36.36 = 0$, so $C = 12.12$.

We have therefore determined a fair price for an option on a risky underlying asset one period before maturity. The only information required are the extent to which the underlying asset could move up or down and the riskless rate of interest. Knowing the probability of an up-move or a down-move is, surprisingly enough, not necessary.

The concept of the riskless options hedge has been illustrated by means of a specific example, but the technique is universal. In the general case, consider the portfolio comprising of:

1. Selling one call option.
2. Buying h units of the underlying asset.
3. Borrowing an amount B.

At maturity, we wish to select values of h and B such that the financial outcome is zero whether the underlying asset price moves up or down. This can be achieved if we set

$$huS - C_{up} - BR = 0$$

$$hdS - C_{down} - BR = 0 \tag{10.23}$$

where R is e^{it}, and i is the continuously compounded riskless interest rate. This is a pair of equations in two unknowns, and with a little algebra the solutions for h and B are

$$h = \frac{C_{up} - C_{down}}{S(u-d)} \text{ and } B = \frac{dC_{up} - uC_{down}}{R(u-d)} \tag{10.24}$$

Setting the initial cash flow to zero gives the condition

$$C - hS + B = 0 \tag{10.25}$$

Substituting the values for h and B from equation 10.24, we obtain

$$C = \frac{(R-d)C_{up} + (u-R)C_{down}}{R(u-d)} \tag{10.26}$$

Finally, making the substitution

$$p = \frac{R-d}{u-d} \tag{10.27}$$

gives a slightly more manageable expression for the value of a one-period option:

$$C = \frac{pC_{up} + (1-p)C_{down}}{R} \tag{10.28}$$

The terms p and $(1-p)$ look like probabilities, because they always fall in the range zero to one, and they provide a ready interpretation of equation 10.28: The option value at each step is simply the present value of the expected outcomes, each outcome being weighted by the probability of its occurrence.

To illustrate how these equations work, we can insert the values from the previous example to obtain

$$h = \frac{20-0}{100(1.20-0.90)} = 0.6667 \text{ and } B = \frac{0.90 \times 20 - 1.20 \times 0}{1.10 \times (1.20-0.90)} = 54.55$$

and therefore

$$C = hS - B = 0.6667 \times 100 - 54.55 = 12.12$$

This technique for valuing a one-period option can readily be extended in order to value options with a longer time to maturity. To illustrate this, we can examine the case of a two-period option. Figure 10.24 extends the example

FIGURE 10.24
Two-Period Binomial Option Pricing

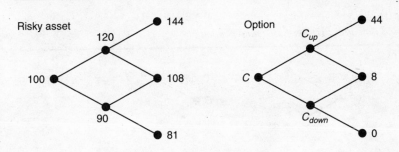

illustrated in Figure 10.23 for an additional period. The initial price is still 100, $u = 1.20$, and $d = 0.90$, just as before. If the price rises two periods in a row, the final price will be $100 \times 1.20 \times 1.20 = 144$. Similarly, if the asset price falls both periods, it will finish at 81. Finally, if the asset rises and then falls or falls and then rises, the price will eventually turn out to be 108.

The way to value the two-period option is to break the big problem into a series of little problems, a "divide and conquer" approach. We can start with the top right of Figure 10.24, which is reproduced separately in Figure 10.25.

This is exactly the same problem as valuing a one-period option. We can apply equations 10.24 and 10.28 to find the hedge ratio and C_{up}, which turn out to be 1 and 29.09, respectively. The bottom-right branch of Figure 10.24 can be evaluated in a similar way to calculate the hedge ratio as 0.30 and C_{down} as 4.85. We now have the values of the option one period before maturity. If these figures are inserted into Figure 10.24, the final step is to value the left-hand branch, which is now illustrated separately in Figure 10.26.

This is once again just like valuing a one-period option, so the previous formulae can be applied once more to find that the hedge ratio for this branch is 0.81, and the option price is 19.10. Figure 10.27 illustrates the complete two-period model with all the values inserted.

In the two-period model, there are three nodes in the lattice where the price may move up or down. Each node can be valued by using equation 10.24 to form a riskless hedge between the option and the underlying asset. The hedge ratio will differ from node to node, but this is an essential feature of the binomial model and reflects the reality that practitioners hedging a book of options constantly have to rebalance their hedges to restore risk neutrality. In the two-period example of Figure 10.27, the option could

FIGURE 10.25
Two-Period Binomial Pricing, Top-Right Branch

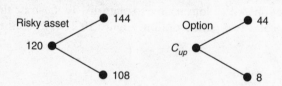

FIGURE 10.26
Two-Period Binomial Pricing, Left-Hand Branch

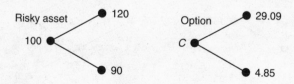

be hedged with 0.81 of the underlying asset. If the asset price then moved down, 0.51, would need to be sold to bring the hedge ratio down to 0.30. On the other hand, if the asset price moved up, another 0.19 would be purchased to increase the hedge ratio to 1.

If the one-period model can be extended to two periods, it can be extended to any number of periods to obtain the full lattice structure pictured in Figure 10.28. Each point in the lattice represents the underlying asset price at one moment in time. At every step, the price may move up or down. Starting with the current market price at the left, the lattice gradually expands to cover every possible price that the underlying asset may achieve as time passes. The longer the time to maturity and the more volatile the underlying asset, the wider the lattice will be.

As an illustration of the binomial technique, Tables 10.4 and 10.5 provide the full set of asset prices and option values using a 10-step binomial model to price the option discussed in the previous section .

FIGURE 10.27
Two-Period Option Pricing, Complete Tree

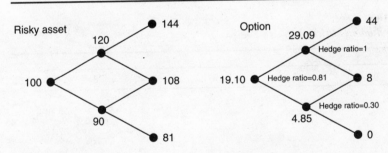

FIGURE 10.28
The Binomial Lattice

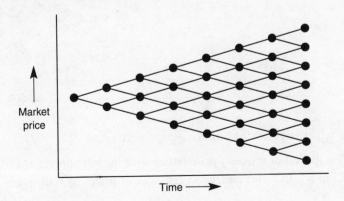

TABLE 10.4
Ten-Step Binomial Pricing, Asset Prices

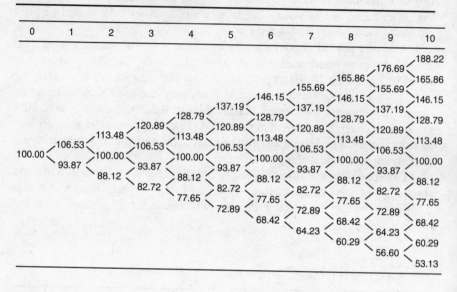

0	1	2	3	4	5	6	7	8	9	10
										188.22
									176.69	165.86
								165.86	155.69	146.15
							155.69	146.15	137.19	128.79
						146.15	137.19	128.79	120.89	113.48
					137.19	128.79	120.89	113.48	106.53	100.00
				128.79	120.89	113.48	106.53	100.00	93.87	88.12
			120.89	113.48	106.53	100.00	93.87	88.12	82.72	77.65
		113.48	106.53	100.00	93.87	88.12	82.72	77.65	72.89	68.42
	106.53	100.00	93.87	88.12	82.72	77.65	72.89	68.42	64.23	60.29
100.00	93.87	88.12	82.72	77.65	72.89	68.42	64.23	60.29	56.60	53.13

TABLE 10.5
Ten-Step Binomial Pricing, Option Values

0	1	2	3	4	5	6	7	8	9	10
										68.22
									58.12	45.86
								48.70	37.12	26.15
							39.94	29.00	18.63	8.79
						31.97	21.90	12.76	5.03	0.00
					24.99	16.08	8.50	2.88	0.00	0.00
				19.09	11.51	5.55	1.65	0.00	0.00	0.00
			14.29	8.08	3.57	0.94	0.00	0.00	0.00	0.00
		10.50	5.57	2.27	0.54	0.00	0.00	0.00	0.00	0.00
	7.58	3.78	1.43	0.31	0.00	0.00	0.00	0.00	0.00	0.00
5.40	2.54	0.89	0.18	0.00	0.00	0.00	0.00	0.00	0.00	0.00

To obtain these figures, the following steps were taken:

1. Start at the left of the asset price lattice with the initial price of 100.
2. Working left to right, insert successive asset prices by multiplying the

previous price either by u or d. In this example $u = 1.065288$ and $d = 0.938713$, (Why these figures were used will be explained shortly.) The highest price achieved after 10 successive moves up is therefore $100 \times 1.065288^{10} = 188.22$.

3. For each of the terminal asset prices, evaluate the value of the option at expiry. With a strike price of 120 the top-right option value will be $188.22 - 120 = 68.22$.

4. Now work right to left through the option value lattice applying equation 10.28, the one-period option pricing model, each time. R in this example was 1.012072, and, again, this value will be justified shortly. This choice of values makes $p = 0.579570$ and $(1-p) = 0.420430$.

5. The option value at the start of the lattice is the fair price for the option at the outset.

In this example, the 10-step binomial model produces an answer of 5.40 as the fair price for the option, exactly the same as the B-S value. The binomial model therefore seems to be consistent. In practice, however, it is usual to use a larger number of steps than 10, otherwise the answers produced by the binomial model can prove to be unreliable. Figure 10.29 illustrates the answers obtained by using binomial models with steps ranging from as few as 1 up to 100. Many commercial pricing models use around 50 steps as a reasonable compromise between reliability and calculation speed.

FIGURE 10.29
Reliability of Binomial Model

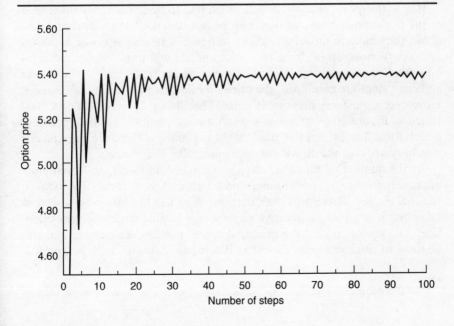

The binomial model is flexible enough to work with underlying assets whose prices follow any distribution of returns. By inserting the appropriate values for u and d, which could be altered at different parts of the lattice if desired, any progression of prices may be simulated. The most common choices in practice for u and d are those that enable the binomial model to approximate the lognormal distribution of prices found in practice. With a little algebra[9] it is possible to show that

$$u = e^{\sigma\sqrt{t/N}}$$
$$d = e^{-\sigma\sqrt{t/N}}$$
$$R = e^{i(t/N)}$$

$$(10.29)$$

where

σ is the annualised standard deviation of returns
t is the time to maturity (expressed as a fraction of a year)
i is the continuously compounded riskless interest rate
N is the number of binomial steps used.

Inserting $\sigma = 20\%$, $t = 1$ year, $i = 12\%$, and $N = 10$ steps gives $u = 1.065288$, $d = 0.938713$, and $R = 1.012072$, the figures cited earlier to create the 10-step model illustrated in Tables 10.4 and 10.5. Note that the greater the volatility of the underlying asset, the larger σ will be. This will make u bigger and d smaller, and the resulting binomial lattice will exhibit a wider spread of prices, just as one would expect.

Figure 10.30 illustrates how the binomial model eventually approaches the lognormal distribution when this choice for u, d, and r are made. Even when as few as 10 steps are used, the skewed lognormal shape appears, and this becomes very obvious by the time a 50-step process is used.

It is at this point that our belief, which had to be temporarily suspended at the beginning of this section, can be reinstated. The whole discussion about the binomial model started by our assuming that prices at each step could only move up or down by predetermined amounts. While this seems an unrealistic assumption at first, if the steps are made small enough and sufficient steps are combined, the price over an extended period of time can move over almost any reasonable range. The 50-step binomial process illustrated in Figure 10.30 provides a result almost identical to the lognormal distribution. The assumption made at the beginning is therefore a reasonable one, provided that the individual steps are small.

As the number of binomial steps gets larger and larger, and eventually approaches infinity, the binomial model ultimately becomes identical to the B-S model. This poses the question: Why use the binomial model at all, when it involves an iterative process that is time-consuming to calculate? The answer is that the binomial model has few restrictions and can be used to price options where the B-S model cannot easily be applied.

---

[9] See Cox and Rubinstein, pages 196–200, cited in the bibliography at the end of this chapter.

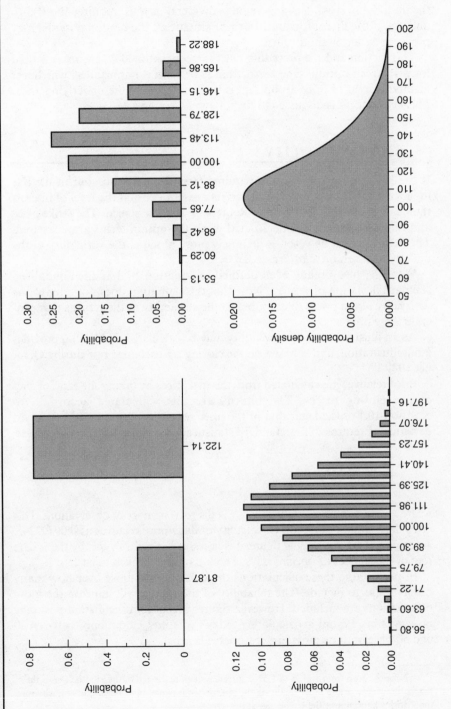

FIGURE 10.30 *1-Step, 10-Step, and 50-Step Binomial, and Lognormal Models*

For example, pricing American-style options or stock options for which the underlying stock has an irregular dividend payout, requires the B-S to undergo difficult contortions. In these situations, the binomial model may prove an easier method to use.

This section and the preceding one have concentrated on the models used for pricing an option. One factor that is of central importance, whichever method is used to price an option, is the variability of the underlying asset. This key concept is discussed in the following section.

10.9 VOLATILITY

If one looks at the information required to price an option, four of the five inputs are easy to obtain. The underlying asset price and the level of interest rates can be read directly from a Reuters or Telerate screen. The strike price and time to maturity are negotiated when the option terms are discussed. The fifth variable, however, is definitely more obscure: the variability of the underlying asset, or *volatility*.

Volatility has already been defined in equation 10.3 as the annualised standard deviation of returns. Note that this definition does not refer to the variability of the prices directly, but to the variability of the returns that generate these prices.

As an illustration of how volatility may be calculated, Table 10.6 provides a full illustration, and is based on the closing £/$ exchange rate during October 1989.[10]

Price relatives are calculated from the raw prices by taking the ratio of successive closing prices. The returns are then calculated according to equation 10.1 as the logarithm of the price relatives. The mean and standard deviation of returns follow standard statistical procedures using the formulae

$$\mu = \sum_{i=1}^{N} \frac{x_i}{N} \text{ and } \sigma = \sqrt{\sum_{i=1}^{N} \frac{(x-\mu)^2}{N-1}}$$

where x_i is the ith price relative, and N is the total number of observations. This gives the standard deviation or volatility of daily price relatives as 0.00793245. To convert this to an annual figure, it is necessary to multiply this by the square root of the number of working days in a year, normally taken to be 250.

In performing these calculations there is a compromise over how many observations to include. The reliability of the answer will improve the more observations are included. However, figures taken from the distant past may no longer be relevant in calculating today's volatility. Commonly, between 20 and 50 observations provide a reasonable balance.

---

[10] Note the drop from 1.6125 to 1.5765 three days before the end of the month. This is the biggest daily change and arose following the unexpected resignation of Nigel Lawson, who was the British Chancellor of the Exchequer at the time.

TABLE 10.6
Calculating historic volatility

£/$	Price Relatives	Log Price Relatives	Deviations	Squared Deviations
1.6180				
1.6055	0.992274	−0.007756	−0.006564	0.00004308
1.6045	0.999377	−0.000623	0.000569	0.00000032
1.6100	1.003428	0.003422	0.004614	0.00002129
1.6025	0.995342	−0.004669	−0.003477	0.00001209
1.5790	0.985335	−0.014773	−0.013581	0.00018445
1.5580	0.986700	−0.013389	−0.012197	0.00014876
1.5445	0.991335	−0.008703	−0.007511	0.00005641
1.5510	1.004208	0.004200	0.005392	0.00002907
1.5640	1.008382	0.008347	0.009539	0.00009099
1.5750	1.007033	0.007009	0.008201	0.00006725
1.5825	1.004762	0.004751	0.005943	0.00003531
1.5885	1.003791	0.003784	0.004976	0.00002476
1.5940	1.003462	0.003456	0.004648	0.00002161
1.5885	0.996550	−0.003456	−0.002264	0.00000513
1.5950	1.004092	0.004084	0.005276	0.00002783
1.6065	1.007210	0.007184	0.008376	0.00007016
1.6095	1.001867	0.001866	0.003058	0.00000935
1.6125	1.001864	0.001862	0.003054	0.00000933
1.5765	0.977674	−0.022579	−0.021387	0.00045738
1.5785	1.001269	0.001268	0.002460	0.00000605
1.5780	0.999683	−0.000317	0.000875	0.00000077
Means		−0.001192		0.00006292

Standard deviation = $\sqrt{0.00006292}$ = 0.00793245
Annual volatility = 0.00793245 × $\sqrt{250}$ = 12.5%

There are a number of adjustments that can be made to this method. One is to weight recent price relatives more heavily. Another is to use an alternative formula that includes the day's range as well as successive closing prices. However, no matter how sophisticated the method used, all the calculations produce a figure for *historic volatility*. What is required, though, is a figure for *future volatility*. After all, it is the future variability of returns that is relevant for pricing an option expiring in the future, not the past variability.

If the past provides a reasonable prediction of the future, then historic volatility may give a reasonable guide to future volatility. This is not always the case, however. For example, following the 1987 stock market crash, 20-

day volatility in the S&P 500 stock index soared to 150% from its usual level of around 12%. If market makers relied solely on historic volatility, in the month following the crash they would be pricing options as if another similar crash (or a mirror-image boom) was about to happen.

The problem is that future volatility can never be measured directly, because it is purely subjective. The variations in returns that are needed for the calculation have yet to happen. Although future volatility cannot be measured directly, it can be observed indirectly. Market makers must use some figure for volatility in order to price an option. If option prices can be determined from volatility, then volatility can also be determined from option prices. The idea is to use an option pricing model "backwards," as depicted in Figure 10.31.

Normally, an option pricing model calculates the option price from volatility and other information. Used in the opposite sense, the model can calculate the volatility implied by the option price. Not surprisingly, volatility measured in this way is called *implied volatility*. Since quotations for option prices are readily available, and most participants in the market use similar or identical pricing models, evaluating implied volatility is straightforward and is generally more appropriate than using historic volatility.

As an illustration of the contrast between historic and implied volatility, Figure 10.32 shows how these figures progressed in the period October to December 1989 for the £/$ exchange rate. Note that the implied volatility remained remarkably steady during the entire period in contrast to historical volatility, which ranged from 16% down to just 6%. Despite the jumps in the exchange rate during the period, market makers treated them as "one-off" events unlikely to recur in the future.

FIGURE 10.31
Calculating Implied Volatility Using an Option Pricing Model

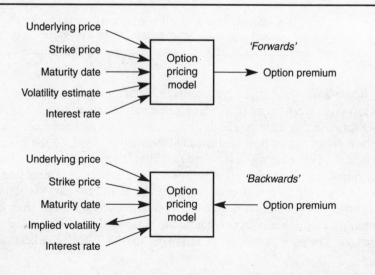

FIGURE 10.32
Comparison of Historic and Implied Volatility

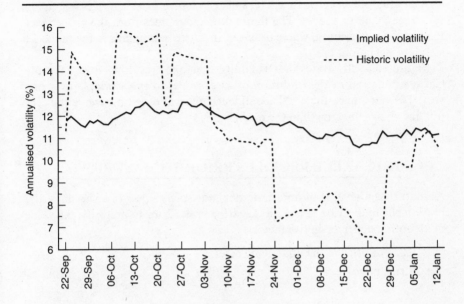

While volatility refers directly to the variability of returns, it is possible to use volatility to make inferences about the distribution of prices. If annual returns are normally distributed with mean μ and standard deviation (or volatility) σ, we can make the following statements:

1. The mean price at time t is $S_0 e^{(\mu + \sigma^2/2)t}$.
2. The median price at time t is $S_0 e^{\mu t}$.
3. There is a 68.3% chance that prices will fall in the range $S_0 e^{\mu t - \sigma\sqrt{t}}$ and $S_0 e^{\mu t + \sigma\sqrt{t}}$.
4. There is a 95.4% chance that prices will fall in the range $S_0 e^{\mu t - 2\sigma\sqrt{t}}$ and $S_0 e^{\mu t + 2\sigma\sqrt{t}}$.

To illustrate this, consider once again the example where $\mu = 10\%$, $s = 20\%$, and $S_0 = 100$.

After one year, the mean price will be 112.75 as determined before, while the median price will be 110.52. Some people get confused between means and medians, as they are both averages of a sort. Consider taking 1,000 different shares, all starting at a price of 100, and all having returns normally distributed with μ and σ as above. The arithmetic average of the 1,000 share prices at the end of the year would be 112.75; this is the mean price. However, half the shares would have a price below 110.52, while half would have a price above 110.52; this is the median price. If prices were distributed normally, the mean and the median would be the same, but as they follow an asymmetric lognormal distribution, the mean and the median will be different.[11]

Also after one year, there will be a 68.3% chance that the prices will fall in the range 90.48 to 134.99. The figure of 68.3% comes from the property of the normal distribution, where 68.3% of the distribution falls in the range ±1 standard deviation.

Figure 10.33 illustrates the "volatility envelope" resulting from a Monte Carlo simulation of the evolution of asset prices in this example over one year. The bars mark the 68.3% confidence interval over time, while the central line shows the growth in the median price.

10.10 VALUE PROFILES PRIOR TO MATURITY

At maturity, the value of an option depends solely upon two variables: the price of the underlying asset and the strike price. Prior to maturity, the value of an option depends on five factors:

- Current price of the underlying asset.
- Strike price.

FIGURE 10.33
Volatility Envelope

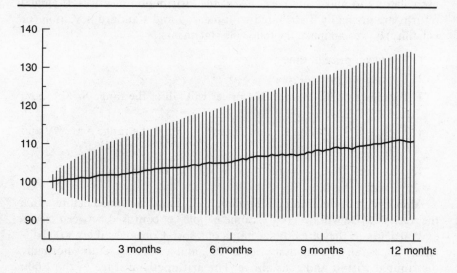

---

[11] As another example, consider a bag containing six green balls, four blue balls, and one red ball. You are allowed to pick a ball unseen and will receive 1 if you pick a green ball, 2 if you pick a blue one, and 19 if you pick the red one. The median payoff is 1 and the mean (or average) payoff is 3, but there is less than a 10% chance of receiving the average payoff or more.

- Time to maturity.
- Volatility.
- Interest rates.

Note that there is no need to make any assumption about the future expectations for the underlying asset. In an efficient market, these expectations will already have been taken into account and will be reflected in the current price of the underlying asset. To consider them again would be double counting.

Using either the B-S model explained in Section 10.7 or the binomial model analysed in Section 10.8, it is possible to derive a satisfactory and fair price for an option prior to maturity. Figure 10.34 illustrates the typical price characteristic using the example of a European style $/DEM currency option struck at-the-money at a time when the exchange rate between this pair of currencies was $1=DEM 1.7000. The graph illustrates the value of a call on the U.S. dollar denominated in D-marks on four distinct dates as the underlying exchange rate changes. Although this and the remaining sections in this chapter illustrate the pricing and behaviour of options using currency options as the example, the findings are quite general and can be applied to options on almost any underlying asset.

The pair of straight lines that was typical for the profile of an option at maturity is now replaced with a curve. Figure 10.34 shows the value of four options, all with the same strike price and other characteristics but differing

FIGURE 10.34
Value of an Option prior to Maturity

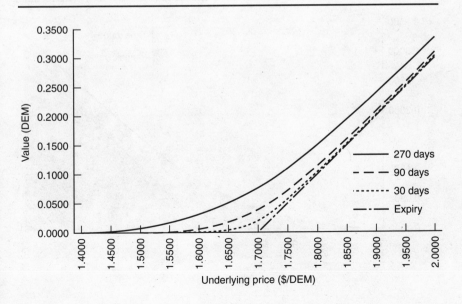

in their maturity. The option with 270 days to mature features quite a smooth curve, but as time passes the smooth curve gradually approaches the straight line profile characteristic of an option at maturity. Not surprisingly, longer-dated options are more expensive than shorter-dated ones.

The total premium of an option can be split into two components, intrinsic value and time value, and Figure 10.35 portrays the value of the 270-day option in a different way to emphasise these two components.

Now it is clear that the art and science of pricing an option prior to maturity is really a question of pricing the time value. For a given strike and underlying price, an option's intrinsic value is the same both at and prior to maturity.

A study of Figure 10.35 makes it clear that option pricing models imbue time value with at least two interesting properties:

- Time value is greatest for at-the-money options.
- Time value is greater for the illustrated in-the-money option than for the corresponding out-of-the-money option.

To see if this is reasonable, consider what a market maker would need to do when writing: (1) an out-of-the-money call option, (2) an in-the-money call option, (3) an at-the-money call option. In each case we will identify a suitable hedging strategy and the implications of this strategy for the time value of the option. In this simplified exposition it will be assumed that hedging by buying the underlying asset is an all-or-nothing affair. Later on we will demonstrate what happens if a more sophisticated hedging strategy is used.

FIGURE 10.35
Instrinsic Value and Time Value for Call Option

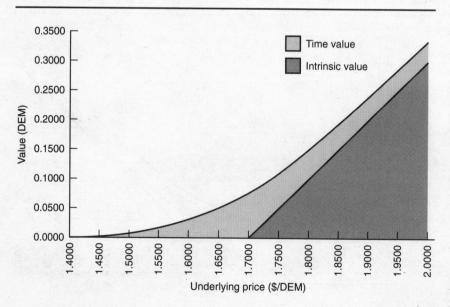

Writing an out-of-the-money call option. As the likelihood of exercise is low, the market maker might elect not to hedge the call. The only risk with this strategy is that the price of the underlying asset may rally sufficiently for the option to expire in-the-money. In that eventuality the market maker would be forced to buy the underlying asset in the market at a price much higher than at the outset, thereby losing money. However, the more out-of-the-money the option was at the outset, the less likely is this risk. The lower the risk, the lower the time value should be.

Writing an in-the-money call option. In this case it is more than likely that the option will expire in-the-money, and the market maker should therefore hedge by buying the underlying asset. There is a risk with this strategy: The price of the underlying asset may fall sufficiently for the option to expire out-of-the-money. If this occurred, the market maker would no longer be able to deliver the underlying asset, as the option would no longer be exercised; instead, the asset would be disposed of at a loss. However, the more in-the-money the option was at the outset, the less likely is this risk to occur, and this is reflected in a time value that becomes progressively smaller as one moves more and more in-the-money. Note that there is an additional factor in this case: the cost of financing the purchase of the underlying asset.

Writing an at-the-money call option. This creates the biggest problem for the market maker, because the chance of the option expiring in-the-money is about 50–50. Does the market maker hedge by buying the underlying asset or not? If the asset is bought and the option expires out-of-the-money, it must be sold at a loss. If the asset is not bought and the option expires in-the-money, the asset must be purchased also at a loss. There is no easy answer. Writing at-the-money options poses the biggest problems for the market maker and creates the greatest uncertainty. The time value is correspondingly at its greatest reflecting this.

In the same way that the total option premium has two parts, time value and intrinsic value, time value itself is split into two components.

The first component is unique to options, and is:

> **The value to the holder in being able to defer
> the decision whether or not to exercise.**

Recall from Section 10.5, which introduced the concepts of option pricing, that it is the lack of certainty as to what will eventually happen on the maturity date that makes options special.

From the viewpoint of the holder of an option, this component of time value invariably has a positive value. It is always advantageous to be able to delay until the last moment the decision whether or not to exercise, because it provides the opportunity for the holder to change his mind if he so wishes. There is not so much benefit in the case of options that are deep in-the-money or deep out-of-the-money, because it is already fairly clear which way the decision will go. In contrast, the ability to defer the decision is of greatest benefit to the holder of an at-the-money option, because the ultimate decision could easily go either way.

From the viewpoint of the market maker wishing to hedge options, at-the-money options create the greatest problems, but as one moves further and further away from the strike price, hedging options becomes simpler and less risky.

All this goes to explain why time value is greatest for at-the-money options and less for out-of-the-money and in-the-money options.

The second component is common to a number of derivative instruments, and is:

> **The value to the holder in being able to defer the cash flows arising from the sale or purchase of the underlying asset.**

This is effectively the cost-of-carry, and there is a difference here between out-of-the-money and in-the-money call options, between calls and puts, and between options on cash instruments and options on derivatives.

When the market maker writes an in-the-money call option, there is a more than likely chance that the option will be exercised, and the market maker therefore needs to buy the underlying asset as a hedge. For most options this incurs a financing cost. In contrast, when writing out-of-the-money options it is not necessary to buy the underlying asset, and the financing cost therefore is not a factor. This explains why in-the-money call options usually have a greater time value than the corresponding out-of-the-money options.

With this component of time value, however, there is a difference between European-style calls and puts. When a call is exercised, the holder pays over a sum of money equal to the strike price and receives the underlying asset. The holder therefore gains an advantage in deferring this cash flow, because the money can be invested to earn interest in the meantime. This advantage to the holder (and disadvantage to the writer) is reflected in a larger time value for in-the-money calls. In contrast, when a put is exercised, the holder delivers the underlying asset and receives a sum of money equal to the strike price. Delaying exercise is a disadvantage for the holder of a put option, because it is now the writer of the option who can earn interest on the strike price.

This second component of time value is therefore *positive* for in-the-money calls on cash instruments and *negative* for in-the-money puts. This difference can be seen by comparing Figure 10.35, which showed time value for a call option, with Figure 10.36, which illustrates time value for the corresponding put option.

It is interesting to note that at values of $/DEM below about 1.6210, this put option has negative time value. The put option gives the holder the right to sell dollars and receive D-marks at 1.7000. As the dollar weakens progressively below the strike price, it becomes more and more likely that the put will be exercised. The magnitude of the first component of time value therefore becomes progressively smaller and smaller. As this option was priced in an environment where dollar interest rates were about 3% and D-mark interest rates were around 6%, it becomes an increasing disadvantage for the holder to have to wait before being able to exchange dollars for D-marks and earn an extra 3% interest. The second component of time value is therefore negative in this case and becomes progressively larger as the dollar falls. At $1=DEM 1.6210 the two components cancel out, while below this point the negative second component dominates the positive first component, and the net time value is negative.

The second component of time value, the cost-of-carry, is predominantly a feature for options on cash instruments, for which there is an explicit interest cost involved in holding the underlying asset. With options on derivative instruments, such as options on futures or options on swaps, there is little or no such

FIGURE 10.36
Instrinsic Value and Time Value for Put Option

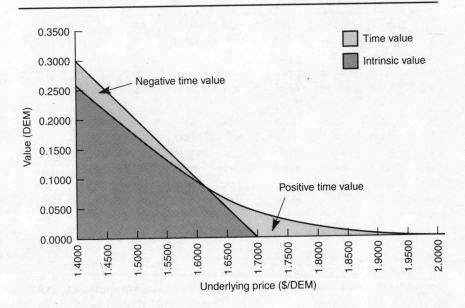

cost. For these options, only the first component of time value is significant, and there will be an almost perfect symmetry between out-of-the-money and in-the-money options,[12] and also between calls and puts.

In introducing the concepts underlying time value, we assumed that the writer of a call option could hedge by buying the underlying asset, but that this was an all-or-nothing affair. In reality, of course, an option can normally be hedged by buying whatever proportion of the underlying asset was appropriate. Both the B-S and binomial models can suggest what the appropriate hedge ratio is. In the B-S model the hedge ratio is $N(d_1)$ as defined in equation 10.20, while in the binomial model it is defined as h in equation 10.24. Table 10.7 provides an illustration of the cash flows involved in dynamically managing an options hedge over 10 periods until maturity. In this example, the underlying asset price starts at 100, and the option is struck at 120.

At inception, with a hedge ratio of 0.4309, this proportion of the underlying asset is purchased, resulting in an initial cash outlay of 43.09. Next period, the underlying asset price has risen to 111.74, and the hedge ratio to 0.6269. This means that a further 0.1961 of the underlying asset must be bought at the higher price, generating a further outlay of 21.91. When the asset price drops substantially in period 6, the hedge ratio drops in sympathy, and some of the asset is sold to realise a cash inflow of 32.73. Finally, as

TABLE 10.7
Dynamically Managing a Hedge against a Short Call Option

Step	Under-lying	Hedge Ratio	Asset Traded	Value of Asset Held	Hedging Cash Flow	Option Cash Flow	Total Cash Flow	PV of Cash Flow
0	100.00	0.4309	0.4309	43.09	−43.09	0.00	−43.09	−43.09
1	111.74	0.6269	0.1961	70.06	−21.91		−21.91	−21.65
2	120.95	0.7592	0.1323	91.83	−16.00		−16.00	−15.62
3	118.07	0.6985	−0.0607	82.47	7.17		7.17	6.92
4	116.08	0.6395	−0.0590	74.24	6.85		6.85	6.53
5	116.73	0.6279	−0.0116	73.29	1.36		1.36	1.28
6	106.66	0.3210	−0.3069	34.24	32.73		32.73	30.46
7	108.86	0.3135	−0.0075	34.13	0.81		0.81	0.75
8	115.29	0.4531	0.1396	52.24	−16.09		−16.09	−14.62
9	124.79	0.8029	0.3498	100.19	−43.65		−43.65	−39.18
10	137.91	1.0000	0.1971	137.91	−27.18		−27.18	−24.11
Maturity			−1.0000	0.00	137.91	−17.91	120.00	106.43
NPV								−5.90

---

[12] For deep in-the-money European-style options on futures, time value will eventually become negative. See the discussion on American options at the end of this section for a fuller explanation.

the call option in this example was struck at 120, it finishes in-the-money, and sufficient of the underlying asset is bought at the end of the final period to bring the holding up to 100%. At maturity, the underlying asset is then sold to realise 137.91, but settling the call option involves an outlay of 17.91. The NPV of all these cash flows is –5.90, implying that managing this hedge has cost the writer 5.90 in this example.

The figures in Table 10.7 provide an example of the cash flows that would arise if that particular sequence of underlying prices were to occur. Of course, the price of the underlying asset could follow many different paths in practice. Some paths would lead to higher hedging costs, while other paths might lead to lower costs. To illustrate what the market maker would experience in the long run, a Monte Carlo simulation was carried out in which returns on the underlying asset were assumed to follow a normal distribution with a mean of 10% and volatility of 20%. In each run, the same hedging strategy was applied and the net cash flow recorded. Figure 10.37 illustrates the distribution of hedging costs that arose.

The average cost is 5.40, implying that the fair price for the option should be an up-front premium of 5.40. Interestingly enough, this is exactly the same price as determined by both the B-S and binomial models in the examples given in Sections 10.7 and 10.8 for the same option. Another way of determining the fair price of an option is therefore to evaluate what the cost of hedging will be, just as was done with other derivatives. There is one key difference, however. The cost of hedging instruments like FRAs and futures is deterministic, while the cost of hedging options is stochastic.

FIGURE 10.37
Distribution of Hedging Costs

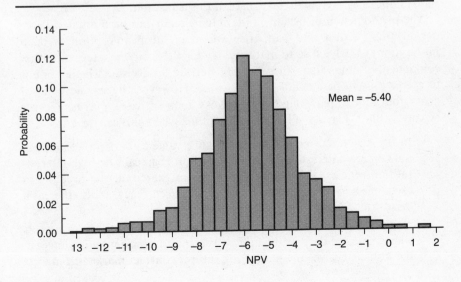

Before leaving the topic of value profiles, we should pause to consider American-style options. Until now, this chapter has concentrated solely on the pricing of European-style options. At first sight, it would seem that an American option should be worth more than its European counterpart, because it gives the holder the right to exercise the option at any time, including the maturity date, whereas exercising a European option can only be done on the maturity date itself. Since an American option gives the holder everything a European option offers, plus more, the American option should be worth more. Whether this is actually the case will turn upon the answer to the question: Is it ever rational for the holder of an option to exercise it prior to maturity?

The simple answer is no. When an option is exercised, the holder receives only the intrinsic value. If, on the other hand, the option is *sold*, the holder receives the full value of the option, including the time value. In almost all circumstances, since the holder of an option will receive more if the option is sold rather than exercised, it is not rational to exercise an American option prior to maturity. This is captured in the aphorism that an option is worth more alive than dead. The one quality that distinguishes an American from a European option is the ability to exercise it prior to maturity, but if it is not rational to do so, there is then no reason why an American option should be worth more than its European counterpart after all.

In most circumstances, an American option is worth just the same as a European option with the same characteristics. Models like the B-S model, which were designed to price only European options, can usually be used to value and price American options as well.

There are exceptions, however, and one situation arises whenever an option, if it were European, would have a negative time value. In those circumstances, the option is worth more dead than alive, and it does become rational for early exercise to take place, if this is possible.

The phenomenon of negative time value already has been discussed earlier in this section and can arise when a European option is deep in-the-money fairly close to maturity. Under these circumstances the first component of time value—the value of deferring the decision whether or not to exercise—will be a small positive value. However, the second component—the value of deferring the cash flows upon exercise—may be a larger negative value. There are a number of examples where this can occur:

- In the case of currency options, negative value can arise for European puts on low-interest-rate currencies or European calls on high-interest-rate currencies. When these options are exercised, the holder can exchange a low-rate currency for a high-rate currency, and so there is a disadvantage in deferring exercise.

- Negative time value can also arise for European options on futures when these are deep in-the-money. When a futures option is exercised, the holder receives the underlying futures contract marked-to-market at the prevailing price. Any profit on the future is then realised in cash, which can be invested to earn interest. There is therefore a disadvantage for holders of both calls and puts in deferring the exercise of a deep-in-the-money futures option, because the opportunity to earn interest on the variation margin is lost.

When valuing American options under these circumstances, the possibility for early exercise needs to be taken into account. Figure 10.38 illustrates the similarity between European and American calls on the dollar and the divergence between the pricing of European and American puts. In all cases, the counter-currency is the D-mark, which is assumed to be the higher-rate currency in this illustration, and the options are struck at 1.7000 and have 270 days to mature.

To price the American options, a 101-step modified binomial model was used. At each node, the value of the option is the greater of (1) the option's value if retained and (2) its value if exercised immediately. As the graphs show, the possibility of early exercise places a higher value on the American put for all values of the dollar below about DEM 1.8000. Below DEM 1.5600, the American put is priced purely at its intrinsic value, but above this price the American put does have some time value. It should be emphasised here that American options can never have negative time value, only European options can.

Since the possibility for early exercise is taken into account when valuing an American option, the prospect for negative time value consequently dis-

FIGURE 10.38
Contrast between Prices of American and European Options

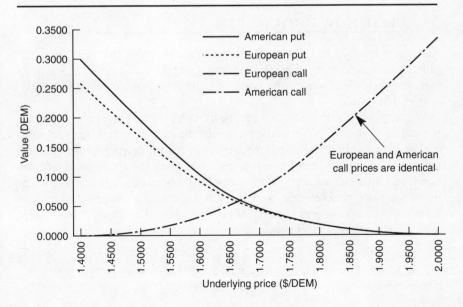

appears. Furthermore, there will be a range of prices when such an option has positive time value and is still in-the-money. This raises the question: If an American option has a positive time value, should it actually be exercised in practice?

Again the simple answer is no, because it will always be better to sell the option than to exercise it. However, if selling the option is not feasible for any reason, early exercise may be advisable if the time value is smaller than the expected loss of intrinsic value. When an American option is exercised before maturity, any time value is lost, but the present intrinsic value is captured. If instead the holder exercises the option at maturity, the intrinsic value at that time is realised. If it is expected that the intrinsic value may fall, and this decline is greater than the time value sacrificed, early exercise may be warranted. Consider the case of the previous example with an American put on the dollar against the D-mark. With U.S. interest rates below those in Germany, the forward dollar will be priced above spot, and the spot dollar is likely to appreciate.[13] If it does, then the intrinsic value of a put on the dollar is likely to decline, and the put option may become a candidate for early exercise. A reasonable rule of thumb under these circumstances is to consider early exercise if the time value is less than the forward points.

Other situations in which American options may be valued higher than their European counterparts occur when the underlying asset makes a cash distribution. A good example of this is when a share pays a dividend. Holders of the share itself will receive the benefit, but holders of the option do not and suffer moreover from the drop in share price when the share goes ex-dividend. Exercising an American option may be advantageous just prior to a dividend payment if the time value sacrificed is less than the dividend paid.

10.11 HOW OPTIONS BEHAVE

As readers must by now appreciate, options are probably the most complex of financial instruments to price. Compare the problems faced by a treasurer managing a book of swaps or a book of bond futures with one managing a portfolio of options.

While pricing a swap is not easy, any swap on the treasurer's books responds mainly to just one market variable, the swap rate, and that response is almost perfectly linear. Similarly, equation 8.8 for pricing a bond future requires many inputs, but bond futures prices track the cheapest-to-deliver bond, and little else matters. In other words, the treasurer only needs to keep his eye on one market rate, and there is generally a linear relationship between that variable and the derivative instrument. This linear relationship means, for example, that if swap rates' increasing by one basis point causes a

---

[13] See Chapter Three for a justification that the forward rate is the best predictor of the future spot rate.

particular swap to appreciate by $450, then an increase of 10 basis points should cause the swap to appreciate by 10 times as much.

Options are not so simple, for two reasons. First, options respond not only to the price of the underlying asset changing, but also to volatility, the passage of time, and changes in interest rates. Second, this response is not always linear. At first sight it may seem a superhuman task to follow the behaviour of just one option in a changing market, let alone a whole portfolio of options. Fortunately there is a solution to this seemingly intractable problem.

Rather than trying to understand how an option will behave when everything changes at once, we will examine how the price and value of an option behaves when one thing changes at a time. These separate effects can eventually be put together.

Recall from the previous section that the price of an option depends upon just five variables:

- Current price of the underlying asset.
- Strike price.
- Time to maturity.
- Volatility.
- Interest rates.

One of these, the strike price, is normally fixed in advance and therefore does not change. That leaves the remaining four variables. We can now define four quantities, each of which measures how the price of an option will change when one of the input variables changes while all the others remain the same. The definitions are as follows:

- *Delta* is the change in premium for a unit change in the underlying asset price.
- *Theta* is the change in premium for a unit change in the time to maturity (usually the passage of one day).
- *Vega* is the change in premium for a unit change in volatility (usually 1%).
- *Rho* is the change in premium for a unit change in interest rates (usually 1%).

These are some of the Greek letters that users of options often refer to.[14] In fact, there are several others as well, of which the two most common are

- *Lambda* is the percentage change in premium for a percentage change in the underlying asset price.
- *Gamma* is the change in delta for a unit change in the underlying asset price.

---

[14] Actually, the term *vega* is an imposter because there is no Greek letter of that name. The sensitivity of an option's price to changes in volatility is sometimes called *kappa*, which really is a Greek letter, but most options experts prefer the alliteration of vega/volatility to the classical perfection of sticking consistently to the Greek alphabet.

We shall now examine each of these in turn.

Delta. This is undoubtedly the most important measure of option price sensitivity, for it defines exactly how much the option price will move when the underlying asset price changes, and it is this sensitivity that most concerns all users of options. If the underlying asset price moves up by 100, an option with a delta of 0.40 will move up by 40, while an option having a delta of -0.70 would move down 70 points. Figure 10.39 shows the value profiles again for two call options struck at $1=DEM 1.7000, but this time the graphs are annotated with the values for delta at a number of key points.

For both the 30-day and 270-day options, the delta starts at zero, when the options are well out-of-the-money. By the time the options are at-the-money, the deltas have reached values of around 0.5. Finally, when they are deep in-the-money, the delta reaches 1.0. In the case of the 270-day option, this transition is very smooth, which is in sharp contrast to the 30-day option, where delta only moves away from zero at around $1=DEM 1.6000 and all but reaches unity at $1=DEM 1.8000.

There are two important interpretations of delta. One that follows directly from its definition is that delta is the slope of the premium/underlying asset price curve. This is readily visible from the graph in Figure 10.39. A second interpretation is that delta is the hedge ratio that should be used when hedging an option with the underlying asset.

FIGURE 10.39
Value Profile Showing Deltas

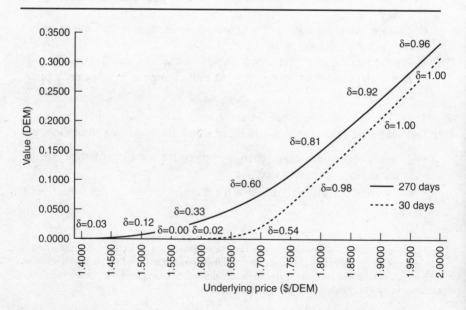

Put another way, the delta describes numerically how similar the option behaves to the underlying asset. When delta is close to zero, the option will hardly respond to movements in the underlying asset price; in other words, the option behaves nothing like the underlying asset. On the other hand, when delta approaches unity, the option moves almost one-for-one with the underlying asset and therefore behaves very much like it. Given this interpretation of delta, it is not surprising why this measure is considered so important.

Theta. This term expresses how the option behaves over time. Long-dated options have more time value than short-dated ones. Therefore, as an option ages and approaches maturity, the time value will gradually erode. Theta defines exactly how much time value is lost from day to day and is a precise measure of *time decay*. To illustrate this concept, Figure 10.40 graphs the time value of three $/DEM currency options as they approach maturity. All of them start with 270 days to mature and were written at a time when $1=DEM 1.7000. One option is struck at the money, while others have strikes of DEM 1.5000 and DEM 1.9000.

In-the-money and out-of-the-money options have little time value to start with, so it is not surprising that the decay of this time value is small. In the illustration, theta starts at –0.0001 for the options struck at DEM 1.5000 and DEM 1.9000, which means that the options lose about DEM 0.0001 each day, and there is an almost linear decay of time value as they approach maturity.

The at-the-money option starts with a much larger time value and a higher value for theta of -0.0002. Perhaps surprisingly, time decay stays

FIGURE 10.40
Time Decay and Theta

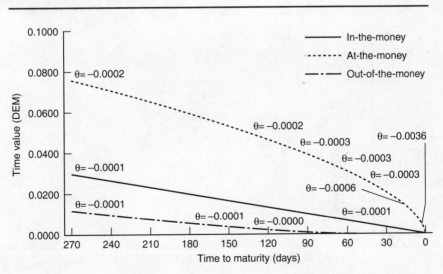

almost constant for almost two-thirds of the option's life, when it very gradually begins to pick up. Even so, theta is only –0.0004 just 30 days prior to maturity, increasing to –0.0007 a week prior and growing still further each day until the option expires. This phenomenon gives rise to a parabolic shape for the decay of time value. About 70% through the life of an option it still retains around half its original time value, but this disappears quite quickly thereafter.

Time decay is therefore principally a feature of at-the-money options close to maturity. For other options at other times, time decay is less of an issue. The nature of theta has significant implications for buyers of options, who stand to lose time value fastest in the last few weeks of the option's life.

Vega. This term defines the response of an option to volatility. Since higher volatility means more uncertainty, and uncertainty manifests itself as the first component of time value, options become progressively more expensive with higher volatility. This is evident from Figure 10.41, which graphs value against volatility for two at-the-money options, one with 270 days to expire and the other with 30 days.

Vega is essentially a property of longer-dated options, in contrast to theta, and is also quite linear. Across almost the entire spectrum of volatility levels pictured in Figure 10.41, for every rise in volatility of 1% the 270-day option increases in value by 56 points, while the 30-day option increases likewise by 19 points.

FIGURE 10.41
Sensitivity to Volatility—Vega

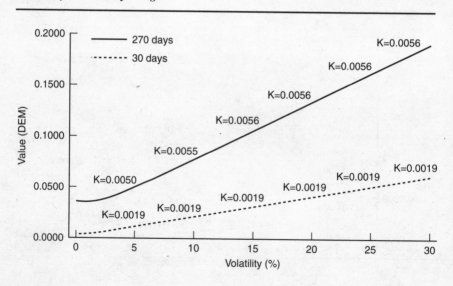

Rho. This is probably the least used measure of sensitivity, perhaps because interest rates are relatively stable, and there is therefore less need to monitor how the option premium will move when interest rates change. For completeness, Figure 10.42 shows the option premium for different levels of interest rates, together with values of rho at three key points. Like vega, rho is more prominent for longer-dated options.

All of the sensitivity measures so far have had one thing in common: they all express how much an option's premium will change for a unit change in one of the pricing variables. Since they measure changes in premium, delta, theta, vega, and rho will all be expressed in the same units as the option premium. In the case of the currency option used in all the examples in this section, a call option on the dollar priced in D-marks, the units will therefore all be fractions of a D-mark.

Lambda. This is similar to delta in measuring how the option premium changes when the underlying price changes. However, instead of expressing this in absolute terms, lambda measures the percentage change in the premium for a percentage change in the underlying asset price and can be calculated by multiplying delta by the ratio of the underlying asset price over the option premium. Lambda is thus an expression of the gearing or leverage of an option, and it is an easy matter to demonstrate that lambda must always be greater than one. Figure 10.43 shows the same set of option prices as those in Figure 10.39, but annotated this time with values for lambda.

FIGURE 10.42
Sensitivity to Interest Rates—Rho

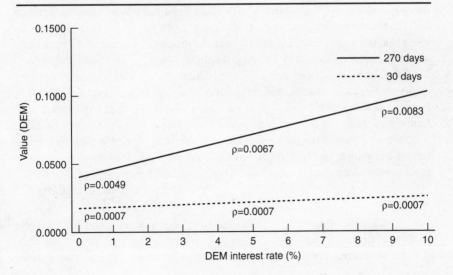

FIGURE 10.43
Option Gearing—Lambda

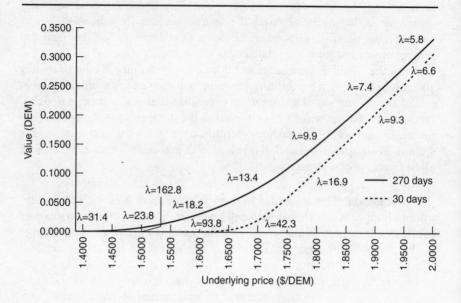

   As the numbers show, even the most in-the-money options illustrated have a gearing of at least five times. This means that if the dollar were to rise, an investor could obtain five times the benefit if he were to invest, say, DEM 100,000 in options rather than in dollars directly. Of course, gearing works both ways. The same investor could lose five times more with options than with the underlying asset if the dollar fell.

   Some of the gearing numbers are positively astronomical for out-of-the-money options, but these can be misleading for a number of reasons. First, a market maker pricing such out-of-the-money options is likely in practice to use a much higher implied volatility, but the graphs in Figure 10.43 were constructed assuming volatility stayed constant throughout. If the at-the-money 1.7000 options are priced using 10% volatility, the out-of-the-money options may well be priced at 15% volatility. For a 30-day option this makes a big difference: instead of the theoretical premium of 0.0004, which gives rise to a lambda of 93.8, the market price would be 0.0141 giving a lambda of 25.0. Second, an investor would be unwise to commit his entire wealth to buying out-of-the-money options in the hope of making a quick fortune. Even if the market were deep enough, the most likely outcome for any out-of-the-money option is that it will expire worthless, and the investor will lose everything.

   Gamma. This is the "odd one out," because it is the only Greek letter that does not measure the sensitivity of the option's premium. Instead, gamma measures how the option's delta changes when the underlying asset price moves. As delta is the single most important measure of an option's sensitivity, it makes sense to track how delta is affected by movements in the underlying asset price. Figure 10.44 once again repeats the option prices illustrated in Figure 10.39, but shows the values for gamma. In practice, gamma can be expressed in a number of different ways depending upon the conventions in different markets, but the figures in Figure 10.44 show the absolute change in delta for a 100-point movement in the underlying price.

The simplest interpretation for gamma is that it measures the *curvature* of the option premium when graphed against the underlying price. The graph of the 270-day option illustrated in Figure 10.44 is mostly quite a smooth and shallow curve, so gamma for this option is relatively small and does not change much over quite a wide range of underlying prices. In contrast, the premium curve for the 30-day option has three distinct sections: a straight part below DEM 1.6000, a very curved part between 1.6000 and 1.8000, and then another straight part above 1.8000. The gamma reflects this, being zero for values of the dollar below 1.6000 and above 1.8000 but being large in between, especially when the option is at-the-money.

Recalling that the delta of an option is the hedge ratio, the gamma therefore expresses how much the hedge ratio changes when the underlying asset price moves. Options with a small gamma are therefore easy to hedge, because the hedge ratio will not change much when the underlying asset price fluctuates. Those with a high gamma cause problems, however, because the market maker will constantly have to readjust the hedge in order to avoid

FIGURE 10.44
Sensitivity of Delta—Gamma

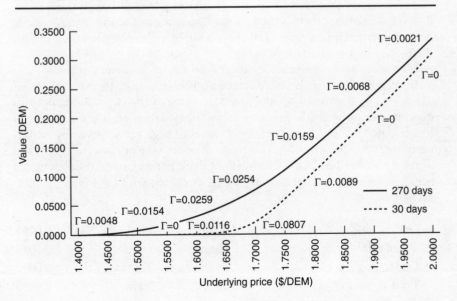

Underlying price ($/DEM)

risk. This is costly, as the figures of Table 10.7 demonstrated, and is further justification for at-the-money options, which have the highest gamma, being the most expensive.

We have so far reviewed each of the Greek letters separately. Figure 10.45 illustrates four of the key measures—delta, gamma, theta, and vega—all together, so that comparisons can easily be drawn. Each graph shows one of the measures plotted against the underlying asset price but for an option at four moments in its life: 270 days to maturity, 90 days, 30 days, and finally one day before expiry.

The graphs of delta show quite clearly how the smooth nature of a longer-dated option gradually grows more acute as it approaches maturity, until delta becomes virtually a zero-one variable when the option has just one day to mature. This reflects the gradual resolution of the key issue affecting any option, whether it will be exercised. With many months to mature, the issue is largely unresolved even when the underlying price is away from the strike price. The hedge ratio does not stray far from 0.50 as the option "hedges its bets," so to speak. As maturity approaches, there is less and less time for any significant move in the underlying price, so it becomes more and more apparent whether the option will expire in-the-money or out-of-the-money.

The behaviour of gamma follows directly from that of delta. Not only does gamma measure the curvature for the premium/underlying price curve, it is the slope of the delta/underlying price graph. Far from maturity, delta does not change much, and gamma remains small even for at-the-money options. As maturity approaches, delta becomes unstable at-the-money, with correspondingly large values of gamma. Away from the strike price, though, delta approaches either zero or one with a stable and flat characteristic, so gamma once again takes on small values.

The shape of theta is very similar to that of gamma, though it is upside-down. Like gamma, theta is predominantly a feature of at-the-money options near maturity. Unlike gamma, there is a slight asymmetry between out-of-the-money and in-the-money options. This reflects the cost-of-carry, which only becomes an issue when hedging and pricing in-the-money options.

In these graphs vega is the odd one out. With the other three Greek letters illustrated in Figure 10.45, the characteristics of the short-dated options dominate the picture. Sensitivity to volatility, however, is the preserve of longer-dated options, and the largest values of vega are achieved by longer-dated options across quite a wide range of underlying prices.

As a simple illustration of how the Greek letters can be used, consider someone holding an at-the-money currency option with the following characteristics:

Option type	Call on $/put on DEM	Premium	0.0763
Strike price	1.7000	Delta	0.6014
Underlying price	1.7000	Theta	−0.0002
Time to maturity	270 days	Vega	0.0055

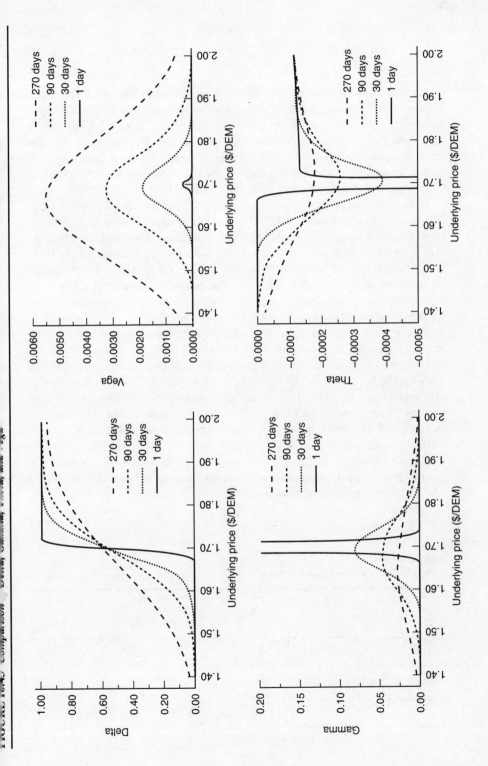

Interest rate (DEM)	6%	Rho	0.0071
Interest rate ($)	3%	Lambda	13.40
Volatility	10%	Gamma	0.0254

Suppose after one week the underlying price were to rise to 1.7500, DEM interest rates were to fall 1%, and volatility were to rise 2%. What effect would this combination have on the price of the option? This can be answered by using the Greek letters to assess the effect of each separate influence and combining the result. Table 10.8 analyses the separate impacts and shows that the combined effect is for the premium to rise by 0.0326. This implies that the premium would be 0.0763 + 0.0326 = 0.1089.

In fact, if the option is repriced properly, the premium comes out to 0.1106, an actual increase of 0.0343. The true answer is just a little different because of the magnitude of the changes that have taken place. Some of the Greek letters, particularly delta, are only accurate over a limited range. In fact, the gamma of this at-the-money option implies that delta should increase by about 0.13 by the time the underlying price reaches 1.75. Nonetheless, in this example, using the Greek letters makes it possible to perform a quick calculation and obtain an answer within 2% of the true result.

Where the Greek letters really come into their own is in evaluating the impact of market fluctuations on an entire portfolio of options. By taking the weighted sum of the deltas, thetas, vegas, and gammas of the individual options, the behaviour of the entire options portfolio can be summarised in just four numbers. Then, instead of having to reprice perhaps a thousand options when market rates change, a calculation similar to the one presented in Table 10.8 will reveal quite accurately what the combined effect is.

It is possible to extend this idea. To make an entire options portfolio immune to changes in the underlying asset price, it is only necessary to ensure that the portfolio delta sums to zero, making the portfolio *delta-neutral*. This is the essence of delta-hedging.

TABLE 10.8
Using the Greek Letters

Influence	Greek Letter	Change × Sensitivity	Effect
Change in underlying price	delta	0.0500 × 0.6014	+0.0301
Passage of time	theta	7 × (-0.0002)	-0.0014
Change in volatility	vega	2 × 0.0055	+0.0110
Change in interest rate	rho	-1 × 0.0071	-0.0071
Total			+0.0326

Further Reading

There are many books devoted entirely to options. Those readers wishing to delve deeper would do well to start with the original 1973 article by Professors Black and Scholes. While there is a certain amount of common ground, each of the remaining books offers a different perspective on this fascinating subject.

Black, Fischer and Myron Scholes, "The Pricing of Options and Corporate Liabilities," *Journal of Political Economy* 81 (1973).

Cox, John C., and Mark Rubinstein, *Options Markets*, Englewood Cliffs, NJ: Prentice Hall, 1985, (pp. 637–659).

Figlewski, Stephen, William L. Silber, and Marti G. Subrahmanyam, *Financial Options—From Theory to Practice*, Salomon Brothers Center for the Study of Financial Institutions, 1990.

Gemmill, Gordon, *Options Pricing—An International Perspective*, New York: McGraw-Hill, 1993.

Hull, John C., *Options, Futures, and other Derivative Securities*, 2nd ed. Englewood Cliffs, NJ: Prentice Hall, 1993.

Jarrow, Robert and Andrew Rudd, *Option Pricing*, Burr Ridge, IL: Richard D. Irwin, 1983.

Chapter Eleven

Options—from Building Blocks to Exotics

One of the main reasons options have enjoyed such extraordinary growth since the 1980s is their tremendous versatility. First and foremost, options can be assembled in a myriad of combinations and permutations. As such, they can be thought of as elemental building blocks that can be put together to form a wide range of financial structures. Second, their specifications can be altered to create exotic new variations. For example, the payoff on expiry could depend on the average of the underlying prices throughout the option's life, not just the price on the expiry date itself. The strike price could be averaged in the same way. Exercise could be allowed on specific dates throughout the life of the option, so that the option is somewhere between American-style and European-style. The possibilities are almost endless. Third, options can be embedded either overtly or covertly within other products. For example, consider a retail investment that offers a geared return equal to 133% of the performance of the FTSE 100 index over five years or the investor's money back in full if the index falls. This investment contains an embedded option.

Contrast the versatility provided by options with the limited possibilities offered by other derivative products. The FRA, for example, is a straightforward interest rate risk management product with few frills. Its scope and specification have changed little, if at all, and there has been no real innovation since its introduction in the early 1980s. By comparison, option-based products now include interest rate guarantees, caps, floors, zero-cost collars, participating caps, swaptions, and captions, to name but a few, and the list continues to grow.

This chapter covers an extensive range of topics. It starts by demonstrating how options can form the basic building blocks for a number of different financial structures and reviewing some of the most common option combinations. It moves on to show how strips of options can be combined to create multiperiod products such as caps, floors, and collars. Options are available on a wide range of underlying financial instruments, including other derivatives, and the chapter goes on to review options on swaps and options on options. The next section examines the definitions and characteristics of "second generation" or exotic options, which have become prominent in the early 1990s. Finally, the chapter reviews some of the ways in which options can be found embedded within other financial products.

11.1 THE BUILDING BLOCK APPROACH

Consider an investor who simultaneously buys some asset and an at-the-money put option on the same asset. If the asset price subsequently falls so that the option expires in-the-money, the investor will exercise the option, deliver the asset, and receive the exercise price. As the option was originally struck at-the-money, receiving the exercise price exactly offsets the price paid to acquire the asset originally. This sequence will occur for any asset price below the strike price of the put, fixing the net loss for the investor at the original premium paid for the put. On the other hand, if the asset price finishes at any level above the strike price, the put option will expire out-of-the money and will not be exercised. The investor can then sell the asset on the open market to receive the prevailing price, yielding net proceeds of the gain in the market price less the original premium paid. Summarising the outcomes: the net proceeds at maturity are a constant loss if the asset price finishes below the strike price of the put option and rise one-for-one if the underlying asset price finishes above the strike.

Compare this with the outcome if the investor did not buy the asset itself, but bought an at-the-money call option on the asset instead. If the underlying asset price finished below the strike, the call would not be exercised, and the net loss would be the premium paid for the call. If the asset price rose, however, the option would expire in-the-money, producing a net profit equal to the gain in the underlying asset price, less the premium paid. Again, the net proceeds at maturity are a constant loss if the asset price finishes below the strike and rise one-for-one otherwise.

Qualitatively, the payoffs from these two strategies are the same. In fact, if the options are fairly priced, by applying the principle of put-call parity introduced in the previous chapter, one can show that the payoffs are *exactly* the same. In other words, combining an asset with a put option gives exactly the same effect as a call option at the same strike price. Figure 11.1 shows the corresponding profit profiles, illustrating this "option arithmetic" pictorially.

For outcomes below the strike, the diagonal profile of the long asset position is exactly cancelled by the diagonal profile of the put option, leaving a

FIGURE 11.1
Option Arithmetic

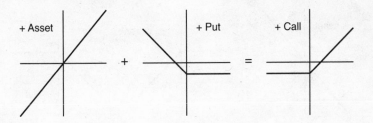

level result identical to that of the call option. Above the strike, the flat profile of the put does not affect the diagonal profile of the long asset position, and the result is an unchanged diagonal profile again mirroring that of the call.

We can express this kind of arithmetic symbolically as well. Let an outcome with a negative slope be denoted as {−1}, one with a positive slope as {+1}, and one with a level result as {0}. Where payoffs are different under different circumstances, they can be listed sequentially separated by commas. The result from buying a call option would then be symbolised as {0, +1}, indicating the level outcome {0} if the option expires out-of-the-money and a positive slope {+1} otherwise.

Using this nomenclature, the relationship depicted in Figure 11.1 becomes

Buying an asset	{+1, +1}
Buying a put option	{−1, 0}
Net result	{ 0, +1}

which is equivalent to the payoff from a call option.

What would the result be if an investor bought an asset and sold a call option on the same asset? Using this system we obtain

Buying an asset	{+1, +1}
Selling a call option	{ 0, −1}
Net result	{+1, 0}

which is the same as selling a put. Figure 11.2 illustrates this combination.

There are two other basic combinations, both of which involve selling the underlying asset:

FIGURE 11.2
More Option Arithmetic

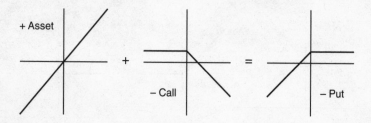

Selling an asset	{–1,	–1}	
Buying a call option	{ 0,	+1}	
Net result	{–1,	0}	(equivalent to buying a put)

and

Selling an asset	{–1,	–1}	
Selling a put option	{+1,	0}	
Net result	{ 0,	–1}	(equivalent to selling a call)

These simple examples show that it is possible to combine the underlying asset with an option of one type and obtain the exact equivalent of another type of option. So far, however, nothing new has been created, but then we have hardly begun to explore the possibilities. By putting the elementary building blocks together in different ways, entirely novel structures can be created.

In all, there are just six basic building blocks, and these are illustrated in Figure 11.3. In just the same way that a child with a Lego® set can build an enormous range of structures and objects, it is possible to create an almost

FIGURE 11.3
Basic Building Blocks

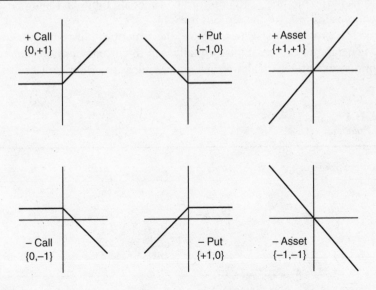

unlimited number of financial instruments simply by combining long or short positions in call options, put options, and the underlying asset. Just as with Lego®, the possibilities are limited solely by the imagination of the user.

The next four sections describe some of the more common structures found in practice. For convenience, these have been organised under the following headings:

- *Spreads*—comprising the purchase of one option and the sale of another option of the same type, but with a different strike price and/or time to maturity.
- *Volatility structures*—usually designed to take advantage of an anticipated shift in volatility.
- *Arbitrage structures*—which seek to profit from a temporary mispricing.
- *Structures comprising strips of options*—to create products which operate over an extended period of time.

Some of these combinations are awarded their own names, acknowledging that the resultant products are important enough to warrant treatment as instruments in their own right. A good example is the interest rate cap, which is simply a strip of options, but which is invariably packaged as a product in its own right. The selection presented in this chapter is by no means exhaustive, and Part 2 of this book will provide illustrations of other option-based structures, often packaged with a proprietary name.

To provide a concrete example here, the spread, volatility, and arbitrage structures are all illustrated using European-style options on a particular equity that is currently trading at a price of exactly 100. Expiry takes place in 270 days, volatility over this period is expected to be 20%, the nine-month interest rate is 10% per annum, and the stock is not expected to pay any dividends during the lifetime of the options considered. Table 11.1 summarises the premiums for most of the options used.

While this provides a specific example, the structures illustrated are completely general and can be applied equally well to currency options, interest rate options, or options on almost any underlying asset or derivative.

TABLE 11.1
Option Premiums

Strike	Calls	Puts
80	25.79	0.27
90	17.47	1.27
100	10.67	3.77
110	5.84	8.26
120	2.89	14.61

Although the basic building blocks are easiest to understand by thinking of the straight-line shapes shown in Figure 11.3 or of the equivalent nomenclature {−1, 0, +1} introduced earlier, this simplicity can often be misleading, for it represents the characteristic of the option only on its maturity date. While this may be good enough for structures intended to be held until that date, many structures are designed to be bought and sold prior to maturity. For this reason, all the ensuing diagrams show the characteristics of these structures as they change over time, not just on the maturity date. In addition, to illustrate the behaviour of volatility structures properly, they are pictured, not just over time, but over a range of volatility levels.

11.2 OPTION SPREADS—HORIZONTAL, VERTICAL, AND DIAGONAL

A *spread* position in options is defined as a long position in one type of option and a matching short position in the same type of option, but with a different strike price and/or a different maturity date. If both options are calls, the result is a call spread. If both option positions involve puts, the combination is, not surprisingly, a put spread.

Many published tables of option prices are organized with different maturity dates as the column headings and different strike prices as the row headings. If a dealer's position is recorded in such a table, it can show at a glance where he is long options and where he is short. Spread positions can be identified by adjacent cells having opposite positions, as illustrated in Figure 11.4.

It is now clear from this illustration how horizontal, vertical, and diagonal spreads got their names:

FIGURE 11.4
Horizontal, Vertical, and Diagonal Spreads

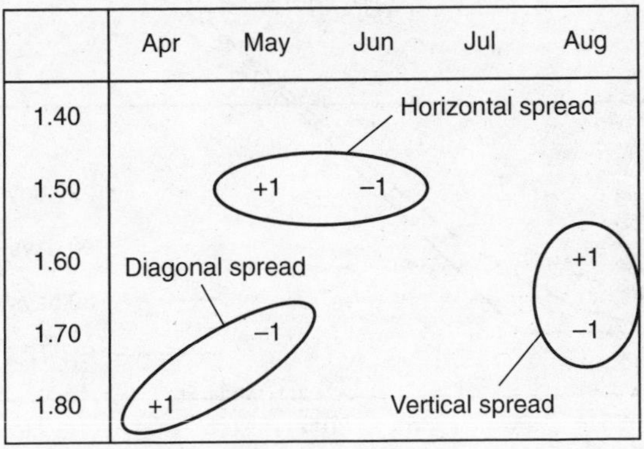

- A *vertical spread* is the purchase of one option and the sale of a similar option with a different strike price.
- A *horizontal spread* is the purchase of one option and the sale of a similar option with a different maturity date.
- A *diagonal spread* is the purchase of one option and the sale of a similar option with a different strike price and maturity date.

We shall now examine each type of spread in turn.

Vertical spreads. If the option purchased has a lower strike price than the option sold, the result is a *bull spread*. If, on the other hand, the option purchased is the one with the higher strike price, the resulting structure is called a *bear spread*. Figure 11.5 shows the profit profile resulting from buying the 90 call and selling the 110 call.

The zigzag shape of the profit profile at maturity is characteristic of any bull spread and can easily be explained by combining the contribution from each of the options:

Buying a call with lower strike	{0,	+1,	+1}
Selling a call with higher strike	{0,	0,	−1}
Net result	{0,	+1,	0}

FIGURE 11.5
Profit Profile for Bull Call Spread

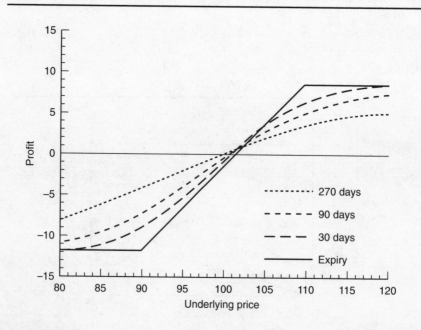

The {0, +1, 0} profile implies a characteristic starting flat, then rising with a positive slope, and then becoming flat again, just as illustrated in Figure 11.5.

The bull spread is a strategy often favoured by those who believe that the underlying asset price will rise and who wish to obtain a geared return through using options, but who do not wish to incur the full expense of buying an at-the-money option. Selling the call option with a higher strike price brings in premium income, thus reducing the net premiums paid. In the example of the 90/110 spread featured in Figure 11.5, contrast the premium of 17.47 for the 90 call with a net cost of 11.63 for the bull call spread, a reduction of 33%. This net cost is similar to the premium of 10.67 for the at-the-money 100 call, but the result for the spread dominates that of the simple option strategy over a wide range of underlying asset prices at maturity. As Figure 11.6 shows, the profit from the spread is greater if the underlying asset finishes anywhere between 91 and 119.

The main sacrifice in buying a bull spread is the profit potential forgone if the underlying asset rises higher than the second strike. At that point, increasing profits on the long call with the lower strike are exactly offset by losses on the short call with the higher strike. This means that the profits with a bull spread are limited, in fact, to the difference between the strike prices less the original net premium paid, 8.37 in this example (20.00 – 11.63). This contrasts with the potentially unlimited profits available from buying a call.

Against this slight drawback, the bull spread has one distinct benefit—its time decay characteristic. A close study of Figure 11.5 reveals that the lines

FIGURE 11.6
Comparison of Bull Call Spread with Simple Option Strategy

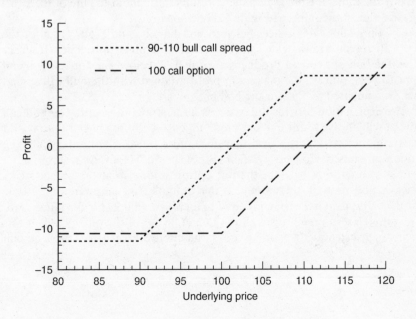

tracing out the profit profile tend to cluster together near the midpoint between the strike prices. Moreover, above a certain underlying price, around 102 in this illustration, time decay appears to benefit the holder. As one moves from the dotted lines towards the solid line showing the profit at maturity, the profit actually rises. The explanation for this is in two parts. First, the time decay of the option sold works in favour of the holder of the bull spread, counteracting the negative time decay of the in-the-money option. Second, this effect becomes more prominent as the underlying asset approaches the higher strike price of the option sold.

A clearer picture of this beneficial time decay is evident if we plot theta for the entire portfolio, and Figure 11.7 does this both for the 90-110 bull call spread and for the simple 100 call option strategy. Compare the theta of around –0.03 for the simple call, implying a loss of one full point every 30 days or so, with the almost negligible theta for the bull spread. The switch to positive theta at around 102 for the spread is also plain to see.

The bull spread can also be constructed with put options in just the same way. A straightforward analysis of the portfolio gives an identical result to that for the bull call spread:

Buying a put with lower strike	{–1, 0, 0}
Selling a put with higher strike	{+1, +1, 0}
Net result	{ 0, +1, 0}

In fact, it matters little to the final result whether a bull spread is built with calls or with puts. Not only is the broad characteristic of {0, +1, 0} exactly the same, the precise financial results throughout the life of the strategy are almost the same, as Figure 11.8 demonstrates.

The only minor differences between this diagram and Figure 11.5 for the bull call spread are the exact profit figures as expiry approaches. In every case, the bull put spread produces a result 1.38 below that for the bull call spread. For example, the maximum profit attained with the bull call spread is 8.37, compared to 6.99 for the bull put spread.

The explanation for this difference is quite straightforward. The bull call spread will always result in a net premium cost, because the call option sold is at a higher strike price and therefore more out-of-the-money than the option purchased. Conversely, the bull put spread will always result in a net inflow of premium, because the put option sold, also at the higher strike price, is now more in-the-money. In this example, the net premium outflow for the call spread is 11.63, compared to an inflow of 6.99 for the put spread. The difference in premiums is thus 18.62 in favour of the put spread. If this saving is invested at 10% for 270 days, the interest earned[1] is 1.38. The bull

---

[1] As options involve continuous interest rates, the interest factor must be calculated as $((1 + 0.10)^{270/360} - 1)$.

put spread must therefore underperform by exactly this amount when compared to the bull call spread.

FIGURE 11.7
Theta for Bull Call Spread Compared to Simple Call Strategy

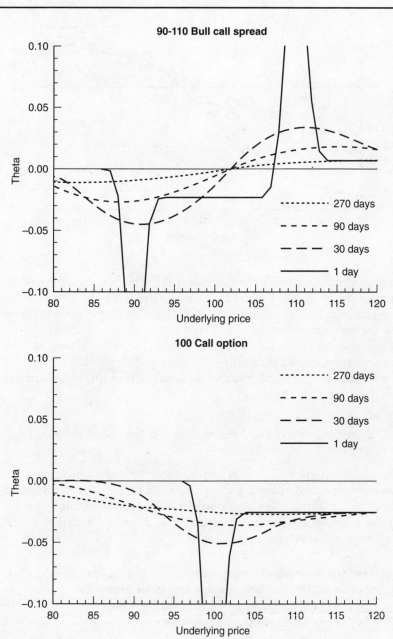

FIGURE 11.8
Profit Profile for Bull Put Spread

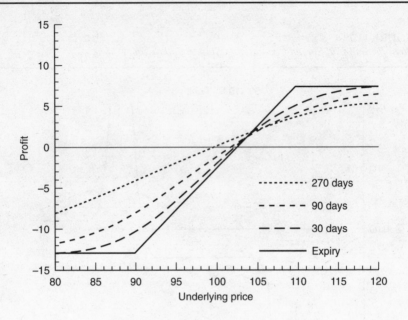

Bear spreads can be constructed in just the same way as bull spreads, except that the option sold must now be the one with the lower strike price. Figure 11.9 shows the resulting profit profile from a bull put spread. This is simply the mirror image of the bull call spread illustrated in Figure 11.5 with similar time decay characteristics working in favour of the holder, but this time when the underlying price falls.

In selecting the options to create either a bull or bear spread, an investor or speculator must weigh:

- The net premium cost.
- The likely strength of any directional move in the underlying asset price.
- Timing.

If a significant price move is expected, a speculator may prefer options with widely separated strike prices to produce a profile with an extended diagonal middle section. Any benefit will be offset to some extent by a more expensive premium and higher adverse time decay until the market moves. All option strategies involve a compromise.

Horizontal spreads. These spreads involve buying and selling options with the same exercise price but with different times to maturity. This means that it is impossible to hold such a spread until the final maturity of both options, because one of the options will have matured earlier. This means

FIGURE 11.9
Bear Put Spread

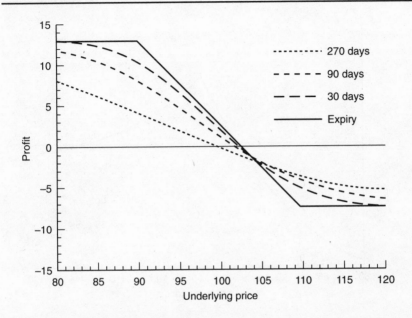

that any analysis based on maturity profiles, such as the {0, +1} nomencla-ture introduced earlier, is inappropriate here. Instead, it is necessary to analyse the characteristics of the component options prior to maturity.

Consider a horizontal spread that comprises the purchase of a long-dated option and the sale of a short-dated option, both at-the-money. If there is little movement in the underlying asset price, both options will exhibit time decay. The long position in the long-dated option will therefore lose value for the spread holder, and the short position in the short-dated option will gain value. However, as time decay will be greater for the short-dated option, and this decay works in favour of the holder, the spread as a whole will make money as time passes. Figure 11.10 illustrates the characteristics of this spread, using 270-day and 90-day options.

The dotted lines in Figure 11.10 show the profit profile 90 days and 30 days prior to the expiry of the short-dated option, while the solid line shows the result upon expiry. Unlike with previous profit profiles, the solid line is curved, not straight, because the long-dated option still has 180 days to mature and therefore exhibits a curved characteristic.

The scale of Figure 11.10 shows that there is not much to be gained or lost from a horizontal spread, largely because rather similar options have been bought and sold. The strategy will make money in a relatively static market through the beneficial effect of time decay and will remain profitable even if the underlying price drops to 96 or rises to 113, a relatively wide range.

FIGURE 11.10
Horizontal Spread

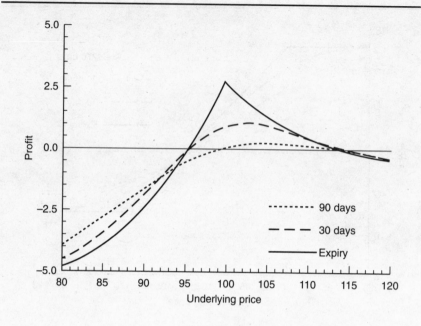

Of course, it is possible to create a horizontal spread with the opposite profile, by buying the short-dated option and selling the long-dated one. The profit profile would be the same as Figure 11.10, only upside down. Such a strategy would lose through the action of time decay, but would gain if there was a shift in the market, and also from the possibility to earn interest on the net premiums received.

Diagonal spreads. A vertical spread has a definite direction but little time decay. A horizontal spread has little directional bias but exploits time decay. As one might imagine, a diagonal spread is a mixture of the two, and features both a directional bias and time decay. Figure 11.11 illustrates two different diagonal spreads. The first involves selling a short-dated 100 call and buying a long-dated 90 call at a net premium cost of 12.25. The second spread involves switching the strikes: selling a short-dated 90 call and buying a long-dated 100 call for a net premium inflow of 1.88.

The first diagonal spread is relatively expensive to establish, because the option bought is long-dated and in-the-money, while the option sold is short-dated and at-the-money. In return, the spread is profitable if the short-date option expires while the underlying asset is anywhere above 97. This reflects the bullish directional slant arising from buying the option with the lower strike, just as in a vertical spread. Maximum profits are achieved if the asset finishes at exactly 100, reflecting the beneficial action of time decay at the strike price of the short-dated option, just as in a horizontal spread. The flavours of both vertical and horizontal spreads come clearly through.

FIGURE 11.11
Diagonal Spreads

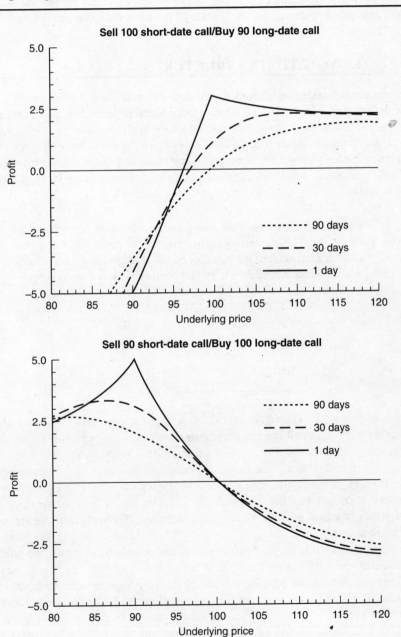

The second diagonal spread actually brings in premium income, because the premium income of 12.55 from the in-the-money option, despite its short time to maturity, just exceeds the premium expense of 10.67 from the at-the-money longer-dated option. Selling the option with the lower strike gives this diagonal spread its distinctly bearish tendency, as is evident from the diagram. Profits now emerge if the underlying asset finishes anywhere below 100, and maximum profits occur at the strike price of the short-dated option, 90.

11.3 VOLATILITY STRUCTURES

Certain combinations of options are designed to react to a shift in volatility, but the concept of a "shift in volatility" can mean different things to different people. Some view it as a significant move in the market price of some asset, for example, a jump in interest rates or the sudden devaluation of a currency. Others view this concept as meaning a change in the implied volatility of options. We will examine both viewpoints initially by reference to the most common volatility structure, the straddle.

Straddles. A *long straddle* is the purchase of a put option and a call option with identical characteristics: the same strike price, the same time to maturity, and the same underlying asset, of course. We can obtain an idea of the resulting profile by combining the individual characteristics of the two options:

Buying a put option	$\{-1, \quad 0\}$
Buying a call option	$\{\ 0, \quad +1\}$
Net result	$\{-1, \quad +1\}$

which implies a "V" shape. At first sight, it might appear that buying an at-the-money put and call creates a combination that cannot possibly lose. If the underlying asset drops in price, the put expires in-the-money, while if the asset rises in price, the call expires in-the-money. Unless the underlying asset price is exactly equal to the strike price at maturity, an unlikely outcome, one or other of the options must provide the straddle holder with a payoff, one that grows in size the further away the asset price deviates from the strike price at maturity.

Unfortunately, this simple vision ignores the premiums that must be paid to acquire the options in the first place. Furthermore, if at-the-money options are chosen, the premiums will be relatively large because time value is greatest for options struck at-the-money. Figure 11.12 provides a more complete illustration, showing not only the V-shaped characteristic at maturity, but also the behaviour of the straddle over time.

FIGURE 11.12
Long Straddle

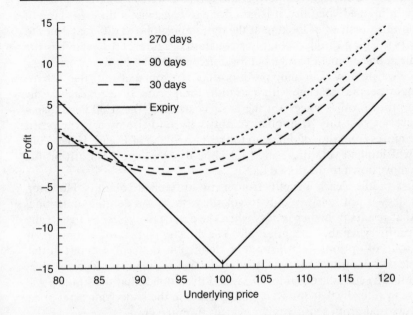

In this illustration, with both options struck at 100 the total premium amounts to 14.44. This means that the underlying asset price must move up or down by at least this amount if the straddle is to prove profitable at maturity. The break-even asset prices are therefore at 85.56 and 114.44, where the solid line crosses the zero profit axis in the diagram. If the underlying asset price finishes between these points at maturity, the straddle will end up losing money for the holder.

A straddle therefore requires a significant shift in the market price of the underlying asset in order to prove profitable, one that is statistically less than likely to occur. In fact, by applying equation 10.17 from the previous chapter, it is possible to calculate that in this case there is only a 43.5% chance of the straddle earning money. When interest on the premiums is taken into account, the break-even prices move even further away and lower the chance of profit to just 40.3% here.

Another feature evident from Figure 11.12 is the vicious time decay close to maturity. The curved profiles tracing out the profit profiles before maturity are clustered quite close together. Even after 240 days have elapsed, almost 90% through the life of the straddle, the worst possible loss is 3.71 in this example, around 25% of the premium paid. Only in the last few weeks of the straddle's life does time decay really become significant. This provides one saving grace for the speculator buying a straddle to take advantage of an anticipated shift in the market. If the shift does not occur, the options can be sold a month before expiry at comparatively little loss.

This first view of a shift in volatility as being equivalent to a significant move in market prices does not place the straddle in such a flattering light. To examine the alternative interpretation, that a shift in volatility means a change in implied volatility, it is necessary to construct a different kind of profit profile. Instead of looking at the option portfolio at different times to maturity keeping implied volatility constant, Figure 11.13 examines the straddle at one moment in time but for different levels of implied volatility.

Since we are now examining profit profiles far from maturity, the V-shape that many people associate with a straddle disappears. Instead, each of the curved profit profiles traces out the profits earned by the straddle at a specific level of volatility. If implied volatility were to rise by 5%, the profit profile moves from the solid line up to the dashed line of Figure 11.13. Conversely, if implied volatility were to decline by 5%, then the profit profile would move down to the dotted line.

This straddle clearly benefits from a rise in implied volatility. However, the strategy is not sensitive only to volatility; there is a definite directional slant that results in higher profits when the asset price rises, and generally lower profits when the asset price falls. The directional bias for an option, or a portfolio of options, is measured by delta. The delta for the put in this example is -0.31, while that for the call is +0.69. Adding these together gives a delta for the straddle equal to +0.38, and this implies that the straddle will increase in value by 0.38 for every unit increase in the underlying asset price. This slope and profit sensitivity are evident from the graph.

FIGURE 11.13
Volatility Profit Profile for Straddle

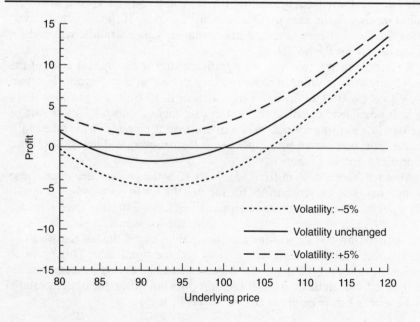

There are two principal ways in which the directional bias could be removed: by ratioing the amount of calls and puts or by selling a quantity of the underlying asset. In this case, we will adjust the straddle by buying more puts than calls in the ratio 1.38 puts to 0.62 calls. This will ensure that the delta of the entire portfolio is zero at the prevailing market prices, resulting in the more symmetrical profit profile of Figure 11.14. The alternative would have been to sell 0.38 of the underlying asset, which would have achieved an almost identical result.

The solid line in Figure 11.14 now sits squarely on the zero axis. For small movements in the asset price, either up or down, the ratioed straddle makes neither a profit nor a loss. This is exactly how a delta-neutral portfolio should be. However, if implied volatility rises by 5%, there will be an almost constant profit of between 2.5 and 3.2 no matter where in the range the underlying asset price falls. Of course, there would be a similar loss were volatility to fall. The ratioed straddle thus responds almost entirely to changes in implied volatility and to little else.

If someone had the opposite view, that implied volatility might fall in the future, the opposite position could be adopted. A short straddle, obtained by selling puts and calls at the same exercise price, gives exactly the opposite profile to those illustrated previously. Figure 11.15 provides an explicit illustration of an unratioed short straddle, showing profit profiles over time and profit profiles with changes in volatility.

FIGURE 11.14
Volatility Profit Profile for Delta-Neutral Straddle

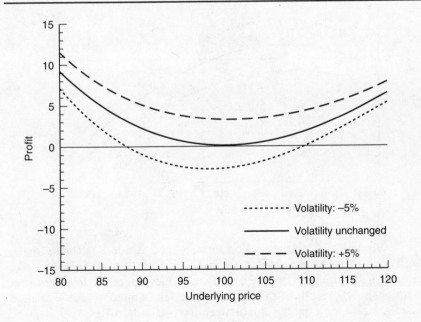

FIGURE 11.15
Short Straddle

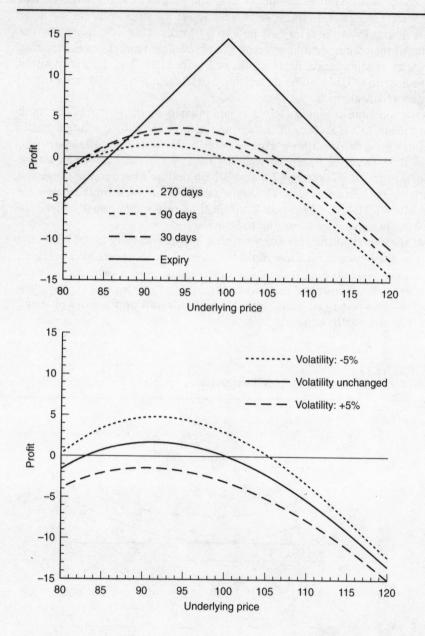

Strangles. A common alternative to the straddle is the *strangle*, which is constructed in a similar way but uses options with different strike prices. Usually, strangles employ out-of-the-money options to lower the premium cost. The resultant profile will look very similar to the V-shaped straddle, except for a flat bottom between the two strike prices:

Buying a put with lower strike	{-1,	0,	0}
Buying a call with higher strike	{ 0,	0,	+1}
Net result	{-1,	0,	+1}

Figure 11.16 pictures the time and volatility profit profiles for a long strangle built by buying equal amounts of 90 puts and 110 calls. As both these options are out-of-the-money, the premium in this case is considerably less than for the straddle, only 7.11 compared to 14.44.

If the strangle is held to maturity, two conflicting factors influence the break-even levels for the underlying asset price. On the one hand, the strangle premium is much lower, which tends to lessen the amount by which the asset price must move. On the other hand, the asset price must move a certain amount in either direction before one or other of the options becomes in-the-money. This "dead space" tends to increase the amount that the asset price must move before the strangle breaks even. The net effect is to make the gap between break-even points equal to twice the premiums paid plus the gap between the strike prices, and this gap will always be wider than that for the equivalent straddle.[2] In this example, the underlying asset must move below 82.89 or above 117.11, and this will only occur with a statistical probability of 35.8%. In fact, there is a 41.4% chance that the underlying asset will finish in between the strike prices, so that both options expire out-of-the-money.

Comparing a strangle with a straddle thus far, the strangle has the disadvantage that it is less likely to result in a profit if held to maturity and is quite likely to end up worthless. Counteracting this, the strangle has the advantage of being much cheaper than the straddle, minimising the initial outlay and the amount that can be lost if the asset price remains static.

However, compare the volatility profile of the strangle shown in the second part of Figure 11.16 with that for the straddle in Figure 11.13—they are virtually identical. This means that a strangle is almost as efficient at taking advantage of a change in implied volatility as a straddle, though it typically costs half as much. For an explanation of this, refer back to Figure 10.45 in the previous chapter, which showed, among other things, the vega of options with different maturities. For long-dated options, the vega is much the same for options slightly in-the-money or slightly out-of-the-money as it is for an at-the-money option. This means that the sensitivity of a strangle built with out-of-the-money options will be much the same as that for a straddle constructed from at-the-money options. In these examples, the vega for the straddle was 0.61 compared with 0.53 for the strangle—87% of the volatility sensitivity for just 49% of the premium.

---

[2] This is because the gap in premiums between two similar options having different strike prices is always less then the gap between the strike prices. This is evident by examining Figures 10.11 and 10.12.

FIGURE 11.16
Long Straddle

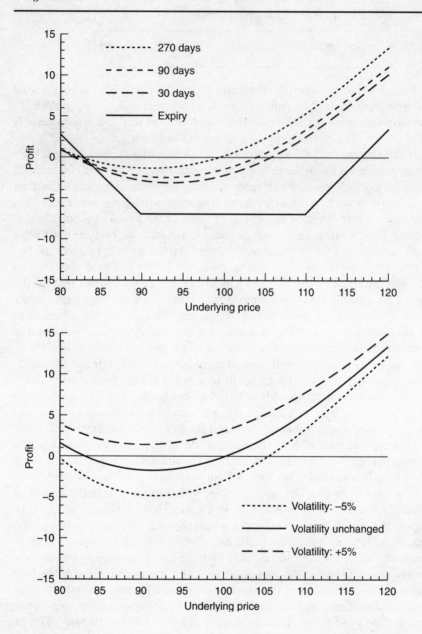

Butterflies. Another variation of the straddle is the *butterfly* spread. This is a little more complex than the previous spread, because it involves buying and selling options with three different strike prices, equidistant from one another. A long butterfly is built by buying one option at the lowest strike price, selling two options at the middle strike price, and buying one option at the highest strike price. If the options are fairly priced, the butterfly can be constructed either from puts or from calls, giving exactly the same result both in terms of premiums paid and final outcome.

The classic shape of a long butterfly, an inverted "V" with wings, can be predicted by combining the characteristics of its components, illustrated here with call options:

Buying a call with lower strike	{0,	+1,	+1,	+1}
Selling two calls with middle strike	{0,	0,	–2,	–2}
Buying a call with higher strike	{0,	0,	0,	+1}
Net result	{0,	+1,	–1,	0}

The profit and volatility profiles are illustrated in the example of Figure 11.17, which uses strike prices of 90, 100, and 110. Since the same number of options are being bought as sold, the net premium paid will be quite small, an outflow of just 1.98 in this case. Note from the diagram that the classic butterfly shape does not emerge until very close to maturity. At all other times, the butterfly spread is almost riskless, as the very flat curves on the left of Figure 11.17 demonstrate.

The maximum loss to the holder of a long butterfly occurs if all the options expire out-of-the-money or if they all expire in-the-money. This will occur if the underlying asset price finishes below the lowest strike price or above the highest strike price. In both cases, this maximum loss is limited to the net premium paid and is therefore quite small. On the other hand, a long butterfly makes money if the asset price remains fairly static, and maximum profits are earned if the asset price equals the middle strike price at expiry. Note that this is in the opposite sense to the behaviour of a long straddle or strangle, which loses money if the underlying asset remains static. Once again, this is because the long butterfly has an inverted V-shape, while a long straddle is V-shaped the right way up.

A corollary of the low net premium for the butterfly is that the break-even points are much closer together than those of the corresponding straddle. Here the gap is the difference between the lowest and highest strike prices less twice the premium paid. Compare the break-even points of 91.98 and 108.02 for the butterfly with 85.56 and 114.44 for the straddle reviewed earlier.

Another contrast with straddles or strangles is the almost complete lack of the butterfly's response to changes in implied volatility. This is evident from the completely flat characteristic of the volatility curves shown in the second part of Figure 11.17. Since vega for long-dated options is fairly flat over a wide range of underlying asset prices, the positive vega contributed by the options bought will be almost perfectly offset by the negative vega of the options sold. As maturity approaches, vega for all options declines, so the vega for the entire portfolio will remain small.

Those wishing to take advantage of perceived changes in implied volatility should use straddles or strangles rather than butterflies. Where butterfly

FIGURE 11.17
Long Butterfly

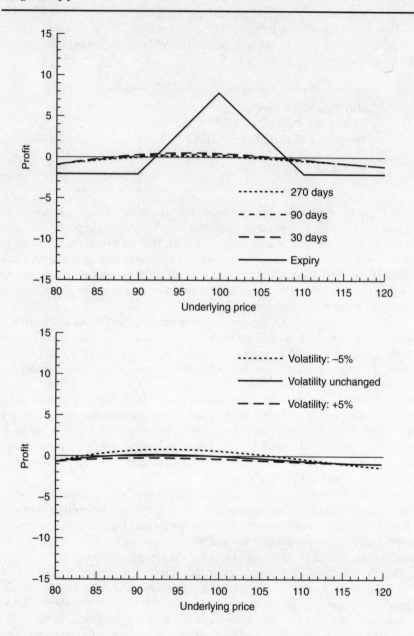

spreads are most commonly used is close to maturity, where they provide a low-cost and low-risk means of profiting either from a static market (by using a long butterfly) or from a market expected to shift up or down very soon (by using a short butterfly spread).

Condors. A condor is very similar to a butterfly spread, except that there are two middle strike prices rather than one. This is analogous to the relationship between a straddle and a strangle. Specifically, a long condor is assembled by buying an option at the lowest strike, selling an option at the next strike, selling another option at the next strike, and buying an option at the highest strike. As with the butterfly spread, there is no difference between using call options or put options all the way through. A condor incurs about the same net premium cost as the equivalent butterfly, so the maximum potential loss and the gap between break-even points is similar. The maximum potential profit is slightly less for the condor, as it has a flattened top, but this maximum profit is earned over the range of asset prices between the middle strikes rather than at a single point. Figure 11.18 illustrates the characteristics of the condor, from which it is evident that there is not much to choose between a condor and a butterfly spanning the same range of strike prices.

Ratio spreads and backspreads. There is a whole family of spreads involving buying one type of option and selling a multiple of the same type at a different strike price. The term *ratio spread* is reserved for portfolios in which more options are sold than bought, while *ratio backspreads* apply where more options are bought than sold. Whether there is a net premium inflow or outflow will depend upon the gap between strike prices and the ratio of contracts bought and sold. However, ratio spreads are normally designed to incur a net premium cost (by buying options which are more in-the-money than the options sold), while backspreads usually bring in net premium (by buying options more out-of-the-money than the options sold). Depending upon whether calls or puts are used, four different permutations are possible; these are illustrated in Figure 11.19.

As is evident from the diagram, ratio spreads have unlimited loss potential, because more options are sold than bought. Conversely, ratio backspreads have unlimited profit potential.

Ratio spreads and backspreads have both directional and volatility characteristics. To illustrate the generic behaviour of these ratio spread structures, the call ratio spread will be used as an example here, and the findings can then be generalised to cover the other three permutations. The simplest call ratio spread comprises buying one call at a lower strike price and selling two calls at a higher strike:

Buying a call with lower strike	{0,	+1,	+1}
Selling two calls with higher strike	{0,	0,	–2}
Net result	{0,	+1,	–1}

The {0, +1, –1} characteristic confirms the profile pictured at the top left

FIGURE 11.18
Long Condor

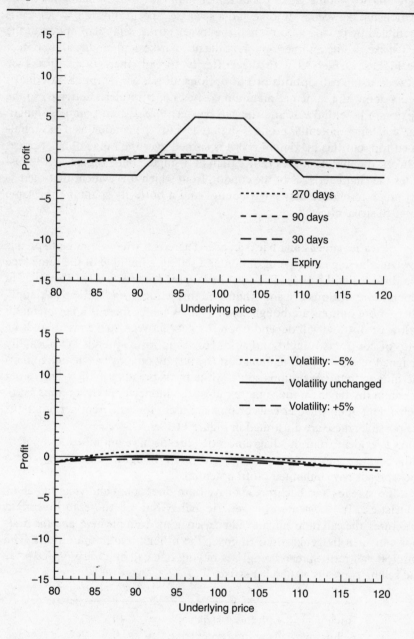

of Figure 11.19: a flat profile, a rising section, and finally a falling section. Figure 11.20 illustrates this with a specific example using options struck at 90 and 100. In this particular example, there is actually a net inflow of premium amounting to 3.87.

FIGURE 11.19
Ratio Spreads and Backspreads

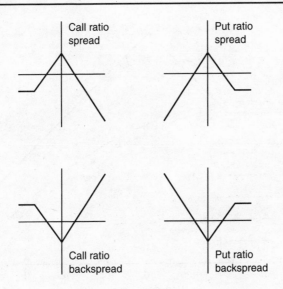

TABLE 11.2
Ratio Spread and Backspread Strategies

	Price More Likely to Fall	Price More Likely to Rise
Market expected to be stable	Call ratio spread	Put ratio spread
Market expected to be unstable	Put ratio backspread	Call ratio backspread

Until maturity is imminent, the behaviour of this call ratio spread is similar to that of a simple short call position, with limited profits if the market falls and mounting losses if the market rises. In the few weeks just prior to maturity, however, time decay becomes highly favourable to the holder if the asset price is close to the higher strike price, with maximum profits being achieved at the strike price itself. This latter feature is reminiscent of a short straddle position, and this can be seen from the volatility profile in the second part of Figure 11.20, which shows rising profits for a decline in implied volatility.

The call ratio spread is therefore of benefit to someone who feels that the market will either be stable or, if it moves, is likely to fall. The other ratio spreads and backspreads would be suitable, depending upon the combination of views as to market stability or instability and the likely direction of any move. Table 11.2 summarises the possible permutations.

FIGURE 11.20
Call Ratio Spread

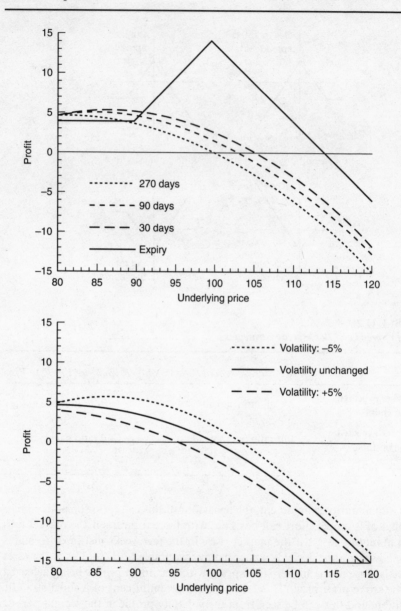

Generally, ratio backspreads are preferred when the market is expected to be unstable, so the holder can benefit either from the net premiums received if all options expire out-of-the-money or from the unlimited profit potential if the favoured directional move occurs. On the other hand, ratio spreads benefit either from price stability, so that the holder benefits from the beneficial time decay of the options sold, or, once again, from the expected directional move.

11.4 ARBITRAGE STRUCTURES

When the basic building blocks were introduced at the beginning of this chapter, some basic relationships were defined between calls, puts, and the underlying asset. These can be restated as follows:

Buying a call option	$\{\ 0,\ +1\}$
Selling a put option	$\{+1,\ \ 0\}$
Net result	$\{+1,\ +1\}$ (equivalent to buying the underlying asset)

and

Selling a call option	$\{\ 0,\ -1\}$
Buying a put option	$\{-1,\ \ 0\}$
Net result	$\{-1,\ -1\}$ (equivalent to selling the underlying asset)

These relationships are just another way of expressing the put-call parity theorem introduced in the previous chapter. Rearranging equation 10.22 gives a straightforward relationship between the price of calls and the price of puts on noninterest bearing assets:

$$C - P = S - Xe^{-rt} \tag{11.1}$$

where
  C is the call premium
  P is the put premium
  S is the underlying asset price
  X is the strike price
  r is the continuously compounded riskless rate of interest
  t is the time to maturity (expressed as a fraction of a year)

There are similar expressions for options on currencies:

$$C - P = Se^{-r_b t} - Xe^{-r_p t} \tag{11.2}$$

where
  S is the spot exchange rate
  r_b is the continuously compounded interest rate in the base currency
  r_p is the continuously compounded interest rate in the pricing currency

and other symbols are as defined before. For options on futures where premiums are paid up-front, the expression is

$$C - P = (F - X)e^{-rt} \tag{11.3}$$

where

F is the futures price

and other symbols are as defined before. If the premium payments are deferred, as with exchange-traded options on LIFFE, the relationship is even simpler:

$$C - P = F - X \tag{11.4}$$

If prices for calls, puts, and the underlying asset ever deviate from these relationships, a riskless arbitrage would be possible. The sequence of transactions that would profit from these mispricings are called conversions and reversals.

A *conversion* comprises the strategy of selling a call, buying a put with the same strike price and time to maturity, and buying the underlying asset. The characteristic is perfectly flat, because the combination of a short call and long put creates a synthetic short position in the underlying asset, which is then offset by the long position in the asset itself:

Selling a call option	$\{ 0, -1\}$
Buying a put option	$\{-1, 0\}$
Buying the underlying asset	$\{+1, +1\}$
Net result	$\{ 0, 0\}$

The *reversal* is the opposite strategy: buying a call, selling a put, and selling the underlying asset, and this will have the same flat characteristic.

For example, on March 16, 1993, the closing price for the CBOT T-bond June futures was $109^{22}/_{32}$. There was a range of options on these futures, and the June 112 calls closed at $^{49}/_{64}$, while the June 112 puts closed at $3^2/_{64}$. Expressing all these prices as decimal fractions, we have

June future	109.6875
June 112 call	0.765625
June 112 put	3.03125

The last trading date for these options was May 21, 1993, for a period lasting 66 days. Taking U.S. interest rates as 3%,[3] applying equation 11.3 gives the expected difference between call and put prices as

$$C - P = (109.6875 - 112)e^{-0.0296 \times (66/360)} = -2.3000$$

The actual difference in prices is –2.265625, close, but not exactly the same. The call price is too high in relation to the put price. A strategy of selling the call, buying the put, and buying the future—a conversion—would appear to be profitable. The cash flows upon executing the strategy are, in theory, a net payment of $2,265.63. For the sake of illustration, suppose that

---

[3] This converts to a continuously compounded rate of 2.96% .

the future settled at 110 at the end of the last trading day. The call would expire worthless, but the put would expire in-the-money, resulting in a short futures position marked-to-market with a profit of $(112–110) \times \$1,000 = \$2,000$. This short futures position would then be used to close out the original long position, which would by then be showing a profit of $(110–109.6875) \times \$1,000 = \$312.50$. The total profit would then be \$2,312.50, compared to an original investment of \$2,265.63. Allowing for interest of \$12.46 to finance the initial premium outflow, the net profit is \$34.41, equivalent to the arbitrage gap of –0.034375 between the actual and expected call-put differential.[4] This may not seem like a large profit, but executing the strategy with, say, 1000 contracts would net over \$34,000, in theory at least.

Unfortunately, there are three potential flaws in these calculations. First, margin requirements have been ignored. The CBOT requires option sellers to deposit the premium received plus a màrgin requirement with the exchange. There would also be a need to lodge initial margin against the long futures position and possibly to pay variation margin as well. Most of this could be done with interest-bearing securities, but some of the arbitrage profit could be eroded for any part of the margin that had to be financed in cash. Second, the arbitrage gap is roughly equal to just one tick on the futures price and two ticks on the options prices. Securing a guaranteed profit would require three separate trades to be executed, and there is therefore a possibility that one or more prices could slip before all the trades were completed. Third, no allowance for transaction costs or commissions has been made.

Nonetheless, the possibility of executing a conversion or reversal serves to ensure that the prices for calls, puts, and the underlying asset all trade within a very narrow range defined by equations 11.1 to 11.4.

Conversions and reversals may also be the end product of a sequence of trades, even though the original intention might have been otherwise.

For example, an investment manager holds shares currently priced at 100, financed by borrowing at 10%. He believes that the share price will remain static and decides to write some out-of-the-money European-style call options against those shares in the expectation that he can collect the premium income without the options being exercised against him. He sells nine-month calls struck at 110 to bring in premium income of 5.84. Table 11.3 shows the initial position, together with progressive valuations as time passes.

Unexpectedly, after three months the share price rallies to 120. The calls are now in-the-money and valued at 16.56. The profit for the investment manager at this point is the gain in the shares of 20, less the loss on the options of 10.72 and less financing costs of 2.35: a net profit of 6.93. The investment manager feels that the rally will be short-lived and the share price will eventually fall back. He therefore wishes to lock in the profits realised so far. One way to do

---

[4] The minute difference between \$34.375 and \$34.41 arises because equation 11.3 assumes a compound interest calculation, but in practice the market uses simple interest for periods up to one year.

TABLE 11.3
Illustration of Conversion

	Initial Position t = 0	Shares Rally t = 3 months	Buy Puts t = 3 months	Final Position t = 9 months
Shares	+100.00	+120.00	+120.00	}
Call option	−5.84	−16.56	−16.56	} +110.00
Put option			+1.44	}
Borrowing	−94.16	−94.16	−95.60	−95.60
Interest		−2.35	−2.35	−7.13
Net value	0.00	+6.93	+6.93	+7.27

this would be to buy back the calls, liquidate the shares, and repay the borrowing. The net proceeds of 6.93 could then be invested for six months, growing to 7.27. However, buying back the calls may be difficult if they were OTC options, and selling the shares might incur unnecessary transaction costs.

The other alternative is for the investment manager to buy puts with the same strike price and maturity as the calls originally sold, thereby creating a conversion. The puts are fairly valued at 1.44, and the cost of acquiring these will slightly increase the financing requirement.

With the conversion in place, it does not matter what the share price is when the options expire. If the share price is above the strike price, the call will be exercised against the investment manager, who can deliver the shares against the short call position to receive 110. If the share price is below the strike price, the investment manager will exercise the puts and deliver the shares, again receiving 110. This can be used to repay the borrowing plus interest, leaving a net balance of 7.27, exactly the same as if the portfolio had been liquidated at the three-month stage.The conversion, acquired in stages, has had the desired effect of neutralising the portfolio against any further developments in the price of the underlying asset.

A final variation on arbitrage structures is the *box*, which is a combination of a conversion at one exercise price and a reversal at another exercise price. Since each component is already riskless, the box is also a riskless structure, built entirely with options. Conventionally, a long box is a conversion at the higher strike coupled with a reversal at the lower strike. This can also be viewed as the combination of a bull call spread and a bear put spread.

As with conversions and reversals, it may occasionally happen that market prices move sufficiently out of line to permit an arbitrage profit. More often, boxes arise in a way similar to the conversion illustrated in the previous example, as a sequence of separate transactions. For example, someone originally having a bullish view of the market might have bought a bull call spread. Later, when the market was about to turn, he may have found that buying a bear put spread at a different strike price was slightly more profitable than reversing the original transactions but was equally effective at locking in the profit.

11.5 CAPS, FLOORS, AND COLLARS

Most of the option combinations we have considered so far have involved mixing options of different types or different strike prices, but usually with the same maturity date. This section discusses an important group of instruments used quite extensively to hedge interest rate risks: caps, floors, and collars. As we shall shortly see, caps and floors are groups of options of the same type, usually with the same strike price, but covering a series of nonoverlapping periods.

If a borrower requires finance for a single short period in the future and wishes to protect against a rise in interest rates, there are a number of choices available. One strategy would be to fix the interest rate now, either by borrowing directly at a fixed rate, by buying FRAs, or by selling futures. This has the benefit of avoiding risk, but the borrower then loses the opportunity to benefit if rates decline in the future. An alternative strategy would be to buy an option providing interest rate protection. A call on an FRA, sometimes called an *interest rate guarantee*, would provide the right, but not the obligation, to buy an FRA on the date when the borrowing rate was fixed. If rates had risen above the strike rate by then, the option would be exercised, and this would cap the borrowing rate at the strike level. A put option on an interest rate future would have a similar effect. On the other hand, if rates had fallen, the borrower would simply let the option expire and could take advantage of the lower borrowing rates.

If the borrower's need were longer term, finance would normally only be available on a floating-rate basis, and the term would be split into a number of periods, with the interest rate for each successive period fixed at the start of that period. A borrower wishing to obtain protection under these circumstances could fix the rate by buying a strip of FRAs or by selling a strip of futures. Each FRA or future would cover one interest period during the lifetime of the loan. Of course, there is a tailor-made product that provides the equivalent of a strip of FRAs, namely, the interest rate swap explained in Chapter Nine. Once again, while this solution provides certainty, it denies the borrower the opportunity to benefit from any decline in interest rates during the lifetime of the loan. The alternative is to buy a strip of call options on FRAs (or put options on interest rate futures) with the option expiry dates matching the fixing dates of the loan. At each fixing date, the borrower would compare the prevailing interest rate to the strike rate and would exercise the relevant option if it were in-the-money or let it expire otherwise.

Just as the swap is a tailor-made product equivalent to a strip of FRAs, an *interest rate cap* is a customised product equivalent to a strip of options. Table 11.4 summarises the relationship between FRAs, swaps, IRGs, and caps.

TABLE 11.4
Classification of Interest Rate Products

	Single Period	*Multiple Periods*
Guaranteed interest rate	FRA or future	Swap
Protection against higher rates plus ability to benefit from lower rates	IRG or futures option	Cap

FIGURE 11.21
Example of Protection Afforded by Interest Rate Cap

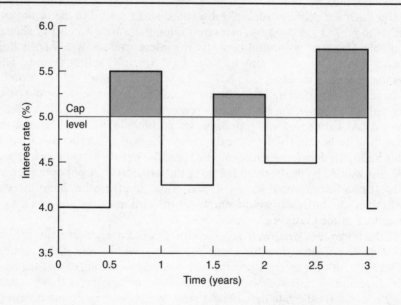

A borrower using an interest rate cap obtains protection against higher rates, but can enjoy the benefits if interest rates fall. Figure 11.21 illustrates the effect of a 5% three-year cap. At each reset date, if interest rates are below the cap rate, the borrower simply pays the prevailing market rates and takes advantage of these lower rates. On the other hand, if the interest rates on any reset date are higher than the cap rate, the cap will provide a payoff to offset the consequence of the higher rate, effectively limiting the borrowing rate to the cap level.

As with any option-based product, the borrower gains protection against the downside (higher interest rates) while benefiting from the upside (lower interest rates). With the particular sequence of rates pictured in Figure 11.21, the borrower would pay interest based on LIBORs of 4%, 5%

(capped), 4.25%, 5% (capped), 4.5%, and 5% (capped). The simple average of these rates is 4.625%, while the weighted average is almost the same at 4.616%. If the borrower had used a swap instead, he would pay a constant rate throughout and would not benefit in any period when the market rate fell below the swap rate.

If the market had been able to foretell the strange sequence of interest rates that occur in this illustration, the swap rate would have been 4.86%. On the face of it, the cap works out about 24bp cheaper, but then we have not yet considered what the cost of the cap would have been in this case.

Pricing a cap is actually done by working out the price of each of the individual options within the cap structure as a whole. Figure 11.22 provides a schematic representation of a three-year semi-annual cap, showing that it comprises five separate options or *caplets*.

It is not usual to include the first interest period for two reasons. First, if the borrowing starts immediately, the interest rate for the first period is already known, because the cap trading date and the first setting date are one and the same. An option covering the first period would have zero time to expiry and therefore zero time value. Second, the strike rate for most caps is set such that the first interest period is out-of-the-money. An option covering the first period would therefore have no intrinsic value.[5]

FIGURE 11.22
Schematic Representation of Three-Year Cap

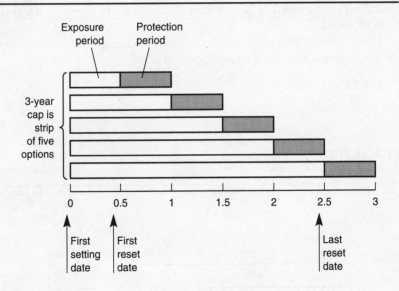

---

[5] If the strike rate was such that the first period was in-the-money, the additional cost of the cap can be calculated by using the same formula as is used to determine the settlement sum of an FRA (see equation 4.2).

Each caplet involves two periods of time, the exposure period and the protection period. The exposure period for a caplet starts when the cap is purchased and finishes on the interest reset date of one of the borrowing periods. The exposure periods therefore vary in length, the first one being one interest period long and the last one being equal to one interest period less than the cap's term. The protection period for a caplet corresponds to one of the interest periods of the underlying borrowing and is normally 3, 6, or 12 months long. The protection periods therefore are usually all of similar length, differing only because one period may be a few days longer or shorter than the next owing to calendar effects.

Figure 11.23 shows the exposure and protection periods in detail for a single caplet and assumes that the cap is arranged on the same day as the borrowing facility. The diagram shows four explicit dates:

A is the dealing date.
B is the value date when interest starts accruing on the borrowing facility.
C is the date interest starts accruing on the period protected by the caplet.
D is the date interest stops accruing on the period.

The exposure period of length t is the period between B and C, while the protection period of length T runs from C to D.

Most practitioners use a modified version of the standard Black-Scholes (B-S) model for valuing the caplets. Although the assumptions behind the B-S formula are not strictly upheld in this application, the speed and acceptability of the model compensate for any theoretical imperfections.

The B-S model was presented in the previous chapter, but for convenience we will reproduce the formula and symbols here:

$$C = SN(d_1) - Xe^{-rt}N(d_2) \qquad\qquad (11.5)$$

FIGURE 11.23
Detailed Diagram of Caplet

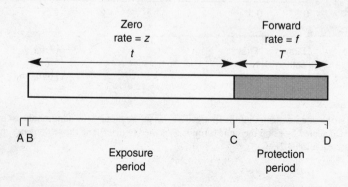

and

$$d_1 = \frac{\ln\left(\frac{S}{X}\right) + \left(r + \frac{\sigma^2}{2}\right)t}{\sigma\sqrt{t}} \text{ and } d_2 = d_1 - \sigma\sqrt{t} \tag{11.6}$$

where

C	is the value of a call option
S	is the current price of the underlying asset
X	is the strike price
r	is the continuously compounded riskless rate of interest
t	is the time to maturity
$N(.)$	is the cumulative normal distribution function
σ	is the volatility of the underlying asset returns

To use this formula, it is first necessary to replace S and X with values suitable for a caplet. If a caplet is exercised, the holder should receive a sum of money at the end of the protection period sufficient to compensate for the extra interest paid on the borrowing facility. We can write this sum as follows:

$$caplet\ payment = A \times (i - x) \times T \tag{11.7}$$

where

A is the principal amount
i is the interest rate at the reset date of the protection period
x is the cap rate
T is the length of the protection period

This is equivalent to the caplet holder paying out AxT and receiving AiT. Compare this to the exercise of an ordinary call option where the holder pays out the strike price and receives the underlying asset—there is a direct analogy. The quantity AxT is comparable to the strike price of an ordinary option, and AiT is similar to the underlying asset. While there are close parallels, we are not quite ready to substitute these expressions into equation 11.5.

The strike price of an ordinary option is paid over when the option expires, but the payment of AxT is deferred until the end of the protection period. It is therefore necessary to discount the caplet payment back to the beginning of the protection period. The appropriate rate to use is the forward rate for the protection period, which is the market's best guess of what i will eventually be and is also the rate at which a bank could secure a riskless hedge. We can therefore make the following substitution for X in equation 11.5:

$$X \equiv \frac{AxT}{(1 + fT)} \tag{11.8}$$

where
f is the forward rate over the protection period

In the B-S model, S is the current price for the underlying asset, but the expression AiT refers to the amount received at the very end of the protection period. To make the two equivalent, we must first substitute the forward rate f for the future interest rate i and then discount the expression back to the present time. This gives us the following substitution:

$$S \equiv \frac{AfTe^{-zt}}{(1 + fT)} \tag{11.9}$$

where

z is the continuously compounded zero coupon rate over the exposure period.

Making these substitutions into equations 11.5 and 11.6, we obtain the following expression for the caplet premium:

$$CAPLET = \frac{Te^{-zt}}{(1 + fT)} [fN(d_1) - xN(d_2)] \tag{11.10}$$

and

$$d_1 = \frac{\ln\left(\frac{f}{x}\right) + \left(\frac{\sigma^2}{2}\right)t}{\sigma\sqrt{t}} \text{ and } d_2 = d_1 - \sigma\sqrt{t} \tag{11.11}$$

where

$CAPLET$	is the caplet premium expressed as a percentage of the principal amount
T	is the length of the protection period
t	is the length of the exposure period
z	is the continuously compounded zero coupon rate over the exposure period
f	is the forward rate over the protection period
x	is the cap strike rate
s	is the volatility of the forward interest rate

Note that z is the appropriate rate to use as the riskless rate and has been substituted for r throughout. Also, A has disappeared because the caplet premium is normally quoted as a percentage of the principal rather than as an absolute amount.

Equations 11.10 and 11.11 therefore provide a means of pricing each individual caplet within a cap. The cap premium as a whole is simply the sum of the separate caplet premiums. Table 11.5 illustrates the pricing of a full interest rate cap with a strike rate set at 5%.

The table shows the zero coupon and forward rates for each caplet period and the swap rates for completeness. Using these rates and the implied volatility figures given, equations 11.10 and 11.11 have been used to calculate the caplet premiums for each period within the cap. Note that there is a term structure of volatilities just as there is a term structure of interest rates. The figures used here suggest that the market expects interest rates in the short term to be more volatile but to stabilise as rates eventually rise as predicted by the forward yield curve.

TABLE 11.5
Cap Pricing Example

Period	Time	Swap Rate (%)	Zero Rate (%)	Forward Rate (%)	Volatility (%)	Caplet Premium (%)
1	0.5	3.25	3.25			
2	1.0	3.50	3.53	3.75	15	0.00
3	1.5	3.69	3.73	4.07	14	0.01
4	2.0	3.88	3.92	4.46	14	0.06
5	2.5	4.02	4.08	4.64	13	0.09
6	3.0	4.17	4.23	4.95	13	0.17
7	3.5	4.31	4.39	5.26	12	0.24
8	4.0	4.46	4.55	5.59	12	0.34
9	4.5	4.60	4.71	5.91	12	0.45
10	5.0	4.75	4.87	6.25	12	0.55
Total						1.91

With a cap strike rate of 5%, the 6- to 12-month forward rate at 3.75% is so out-of-the-money that the first caplet premium covering the second interest period is negligible.[6] Thereafter, the caplet premiums in this example grow in size because the forward rates gradually rise through the strike rate and because the exposure periods become longer.

The total cap premium amounts to an up-front payment of 1.91% of the amount borrowed. This might seem a sizeable premium for a 5% cap when prevailing rates are just 3.25%, but there are two significant factors.

First, while the current interest rate is just 3.25%, the forward rates suggest that interest rates will have risen to 6.25% by the end of the cap period. Although the first few caplets are out-of-the-money compared with the forward rates for the periods concerned, the later ones are very much in-the-money. For this reason, the appropriate rate to compare with the strike rate is not the current short-term rate but the swap rate for the cap period. In this example, the five-year swap rate is 4.75%, so the cap is almost at-the-money.

Second, the 1.91% is an up-front premium covering the entire five-year period. This is a bit like saying that the interest on a five-year loan is 25% when it was really only 5% per annum. If the cap premium were amortised over the lifetime of the cap rather than being paid in one installment up-front, the premium paid semiannually in arrears would be just 0.43% (i.e., 0.215% of the principal paid each half-year). This may be a fairer way of assessing cap premiums.

---

[6] Assuming that interest rates are lognormally distributed, there is less than a 0.5% chance of the first caplet expiring in-the-money.

In practice, many users of interest rate caps seek to lower the cost of protection by selling a *floor* at a lower strike rate. If buying a cap is equivalent to buying a strip of call options on FRAs, selling a floor is like selling a strip of put options on FRAs. If interest rates fall through the floor level on any reset date, the relevant *floorlet* will be exercised against the seller, who must pay the difference between prevailing rates and the floor rate. The effect of selling a floor is to limit the benefit from a fall in interest rates once the floor level is reached.

Using the figures of the previous example, the borrower selling a floor at 3.75% would bring in up-front premium income of 0.45%, reducing the net cost of the cap from 1.91% to 1.46%, a saving of about one-quarter. However, with interest rates initially at 3.25%, the first interest period would already be in-the-money and require an immediate payment of 0.25% under the floor (the 0.50% in-the-money amount for six months). More than half the value of the floor in this example actually comes from the very first interest period. If the borrower wished to benefit from the low rates prevailing initially, the floor could be arranged solely to cover the later periods, but the floor premium would then drop to just 0.20%. Unfortunately for the borrower wishing to use a floor, the steepness of the yield curve used in this example makes caps relatively expensive and floors relatively valueless.

The combination of selling a floor at a lower strike rate and buying a cap at a higher strike rate is called a *collar*. Collars are popular tools for hedging interest rate risk over an extended period because they provide protection against a rise in rates and some benefit from a fall in rates. By setting the cap rate at or below the borrower's threshold of pain and the floor rate high enough to bring in sufficient premium income, the collar can be tailored to provide a reasonable compromise between interest rate protection and cost.

By juggling with the cap and floor rates, it is possible to create a zero-cost collar—one for which there is no net premium to pay. Using the set of rates shown in Table 11.5, a five-year zero-cost collar could be created with a cap at 6.00% and a floor at 4.01%. The borrower would pay nothing for the collar up-front nor over the life of the borrowing, but would be guaranteed a borrowing rate over the five years no higher than 6.00% and no lower than 4.01%. For many, this would be a more attractive solution than a fixed rate swap at 4.75%, particularly if they felt that rates were not going to rise as high as the forward curve predicted.

11.6 SWAPTIONS

An alternative form of long-term interest rate protection is the *swaption*. As the name suggests, a swaption is an option to enter into an interest-rate swap on some future date. A *payer's swaption* is the right to pay the fixed rate on the swap, while a *receiver's swaption* is the right to receive the fixed rate.[7]

Swaptions are very similar to other options, but instead of the underlying instrument being some tangible asset like a share or an amount of some foreign currency, the underlying instrument in a swaption is an interest rate swap. The expiry date in this case is the date upon which the swaption may be exercised into the underlying swap, while the strike price of the swaption is the fixed rate of the underlying swap. Swaption premiums, like those on caps and floors, are normally quoted as a percentage of the notional principal and are paid up-front.

European swaptions can be exercised into the underlying swap or cash settled solely on the expiry date of the swaption. American and semi-American (see Section 11.8) swaptions are also available, and these come in two varieties. In a *variable swaption*, the underlying swap has a fixed tenor, no matter when the swaption is exercised. In a *wasting swaption*, the underlying swap has a fixed maturity date, so the tenor of the underlying swap becomes shorter the later the swaption is exercised.

Swaptions provide another financial engineering tool for handling interest rate risk and are therefore often compared with swaps and caps. A good way to understand how swaptions relate to these other products is to consider an example. Suppose that a construction company knows that it will have to borrow floating-rate funds for four years, but starting in one year rather than immediately. It faces the risk that interest rates may fluctuate over the next five years, and some of the ways in which the company may meet this problem are

- Do nothing. This is the simplest strategy. If rates rise during the loan itself, it will be forced to pay the higher rate, though the company will benefit whenever rates fall.
- Enter into a deferred-start swap. The company could enter into a four-year swap deferred one year, whereby it pays the fixed rate and receives the floating rate. This will lock the company into a rate now. The company is completely protected against a rise in rates but cannot benefit from a fall in rates.
- Buy a deferred-start cap. Buying a four-year cap deferred one year will provide protection against any rise in rates during the life of the loan while also allowing the company to benefit if rates fall.
- Buy a swaption. The company could buy a one-year payers swaption into a four-year swap. In one year, the company would exercise the swaption if swap rates had risen above the strike rate or would allow the swaption to expire otherwise.

---

[7] A minority use the terms *call swaption* and *put swaption*, but these terms are ambiguous, and practitioners themselves differ on whether a call swaption is the right to pay the fixed rate or to receive the fixed rate.

Using the set of rates listed in Table 11.5, and assuming that swaption volatility was 12%, Tables 11.6 and 11.7 provide a comparison between these different alternatives.

Note from Table 11.6 the difference between, on the one hand, the regular swap rates for four- and five-year maturities and, on the other hand, the four-year swap deferred by one year. The deferred-start swap rate is considerably higher because of the steepness of the yield curve used. The cash flows under the deferred-start swap are similar to those of the regular five-year swap, except that the first two semiannual payments are omitted. Since these would involve substantial net payments by the fixed-rate payer, their omission has to be offset by higher fixed payments over the remaining periods.

Table 11.7 gives a comparison between the swaption and the deferred-start cap for two different strike rates. The strike at 5.10% was chosen to be at-the-money, while the 6.00% strike was set at a reasonable point out-of-the-money. The cap premium is substantially more expensive than that for the swaption, and this highlights two very important distinctions between these two products.

First, a swaption only provides protection against movements in interest rates during the initial exposure period. In the case of the one-year swaption into a four-year swap, the exposure period is just one year long. By contrast, the cap provides protection against interest rate movements right up to the expiry date of the last caplet. In the current example, this extends out to four-and-a-half years.

Second, a swaption can only be exercised once, whereas a cap has multiple exercise dates. This gives the holder a greater deal of protection. For example, consider what would happen if interest rates stayed low for the first two

TABLE 11.6
Example Swap Rates

4-year swap	4.46%
5-year swap	4.75%
4-year swap deferred 1 year	5.10%

TABLE 11.7
Example Cap and Swaption Premiums

	Swaption	Deferred-Start Cap
Strike = 5.10%	0.85%	1.76%
Strike = 6.00%	0.09%	0.80%

years and then rose sharply thereafter. The swaption would expire worthless after one year and so would the first two caplets. However, the remaining caplets would continue to provide protection and would limit the borrower's costs for the last three years of his commitment.

For these reasons, namely, a longer exposure period and multiple exercise dates, caps include more time value than the equivalent swaption. Neither product is superior. The cap costs more but offers the buyer more options, quite literally. The choice between a swaption and other products depends upon the objectives of the buyer, and this will be reviewed further in Chapter Fifteen (Sections 15.4 and 15.5).

Swaptions can be priced using a methodology similar to that used for pricing caplets.[8] If a payers swaption is exercised, the holder enters into the underlying swap paying the strike rate of the swaption and receiving the floating rate. If s is the current swap rate for a deferred swap matching the underlying swap, receiving the floating rate is equivalent to receiving s instead. Exercising the swaption is therefore equivalent to paying the strike rate and receiving s. The present value of paying the strike rate is

$$x \sum_{i=t_1}^{i=t_2} \frac{v_i}{F} \tag{11.12}$$

where

x is the strike rate for the swaption
v_i is the discount factor at the end of the ith period from now
t_1 is the period from now when the deferred swap would start
t_2 is the period from now when the deferred swap would end
F is the number of times per year that coupons are paid

In the above example of a one-year swaption into a four-year semiannual swap, $t_1 = 3$, $t_2 = 10$, and $F = 2$, so the discount factors v_3 to v_{10} would be used. The expression in equation 11.12 can therefore be substituted for the expression Xe^{-rt} in equation 11.5. Similarly, the present value of receiving s can be written as

$$s \sum_{i=t_1}^{i=t_2} \frac{v_i}{F} \tag{11.13}$$

where

s is the swap rate for the deferred swap matching the underlying swap

and this expression can be substituted for S in equation 11.5. This gives the full formula for a payers swaption as

---

[8] The methodology presented here is adequate for swaptions having an option period short in comparison with the maturity of the underlying swap. In other cases, a yield-curve model based on the binomial lattice should be used.

$$payers = [sN(d_1) - xN(d_2)] \sum_{i=t_1}^{i=t_2} \frac{v_i}{F} \qquad (11.14)$$

and a similar expression for the receivers swaption

$$receivers = [xN(-d_2) - sN(-d_1)] \sum_{i=t_1}^{i=t_2} \frac{v_i}{F} \qquad (11.15)$$

The formulae for d_1 and d_2 are as given in equation 11.11, except that s should be substituted where f appears.

11.7 COMPOUND OPTIONS

If it is possible to buy an option on a swap, then why not an option on a cap? There is no reason why not, and such a product is known, not surprisingly, as a *caption*. There are no prizes for guessing what *floortions* and *collartions* are. All of these are examples of options on an option, sometimes called a *compound option*.

Compound options come in four possible configurations: a call on a call, a call on a put, a put on a call, and a put on a put. The first two give the holder the right to buy the underlying option, while the second two confer the right to sell. The underlying option can itself, of course, be a call or a put. Most compound options are struck at-the-money, so that the strike price agreed at the outset is the same as the premium quoted for the underlying option.

There are two main reasons why compound options are bought: to provide protection in a contingency situation when protection may or may not be needed and as a form of risk insurance cheaper than buying options outright.

As an example of the first application, consider a German company tendering for a sizeable project for a U.S. client. The tender process will take two months. If the company is successful in winning the tender, the project will eventually result in payment of a fixed amount of U.S. dollars one year from now. The German company is concerned about the resultant currency risk, for if it wins the tender and if the dollar should fall thereafter, the revenues converted back into D-marks may prove insufficient to cover costs. The company cannot load the quotation with a margin to cover potential currency fluctuations, because this would almost certainly make its tender uncompetitive.

One solution would be for the company simply to buy a conventional put option on U.S. dollars expiring in one year. This may, however, prove too expensive. Using the following market rates:

$/DEM spot rate	1.7000	D-mark one-year interest rate	6%
Volatility	12%	Dollar one-year interest rate	3%

a one-year at-the-money put on the dollar would cost DEM 0.0567. Even for a $1million project, spending almost DEM 100,000 may be rather too much to commit merely at the tendering stage. Of course, if the company were unsuccessful in winning the tender, it could always sell the option back after two months. If the $/DEM exchange rate remained where it was, the action of time decay would reduce the value of the option to DEM 0.0537, a loss of just over 5% of the premium spent. If, however, the dollar appreciated to DEM 1.7500, something very possible, the option would fall to DEM 0.0370, a drop in value of more than one-third. The problem here is that a currency option is exposed to currency movements by its very nature. If there is an underlying currency position that the option is hedging, the currency exposure from the option and the underlying position should net to zero. If the underlying position fails to materialise, though, the exposure from the option can create rather than solve problems.

A compound option may prove to be just the tool in such circumstances. In this example, there are two conditional events necessary for the company to suffer a loss: if the company is successful in winning the tender and if the dollar should fall thereafter. A compound option mirrors this structure by offering two occasions when the holder can exercise a choice. The first occasion is the expiry date of the compound option. If the company were successful in winning the tender, it could exercise the compound option, pay over the strike price, and receive the underlying option.[9] The second occasion would arise if the company had been successful, had bought the underlying option, and found that the dollar had fallen below the strike price. Under these circumstances, the company could exercise the underlying option and sell its dollar proceeds for D-marks at the guaranteed rate.

Using the same market rates, the company could buy the requisite compound option having the specification set out in Table 11.8. The strike price for the compound option is set to the current premium of the underlying

TABLE 11.8
Compound Option Specification

	Compound Option	*Underlying Option*
Type	Call on Put	Put on U.S. Dollar
Maturity	60 days from now	360 days from now
Strike price	DEM 0.0567 per dollar	DEM 1.7000 per dollar
Premium	DEM 0.0128 per dollar	DEM 0.0567 per dollar

---

[9] Actually, the rational decision—whether or not to exercise the compound option—does not depend upon the result of the tender. If the tender were successful but option prices had fallen below the strike price of the compound option, it would be more sensible to buy the required option in the open market. Conversely, if the tender were unsuccessful but the compound option was in-the-money at expiry, it should be cash settled or exercised and the underlying option immediately sold.

option, making it at-the-money. This reflects normal market practice, though it is quite feasible to set the strike price at any reasonable level. Note that the premium for the compound option is just DEM 0.0128, less than one-quarter the price of the underlying option. Protection at the tendering stage can therefore be achieved at a fraction of the cost.

It is important to remember, however, that if the compound option is exercised, the strike price of DEM 0.0567 must be paid over in order to acquire the underlying option. A total of DEM 0.0695 will have been spent to acquire an option that would originally have cost only DEM 0.0567 to buy. This is not a special feature of compound options, though. Whenever an out-of-the-money or an at-the-money option is exercised, the total price paid to acquire the underlying asset will be more than the cost if the asset had been bought originally instead of the option. What an option provides in compensation is the opportunity to avoid losses if the underlying asset falls in price.

The second reason why compound options are bought—as a form of risk insurance cheaper than buying options outright—is considered in more detail in Chapter Thirteen (Section 13.12).

Pricing compound options is somewhat complex. Geske[10] offers an iterative solution to the problem for compound options in general, and Rubinstein[11] has extended this work to encompass compound currency options. The binomial and similar models may also be used.

11.8 EXOTIC OPTIONS

This chapter opened by drawing attention to the tremendous versatility offered by options. Nowhere is this more evident than in the profusion of "second generation" or exotic options, which vary one or more of the conditions or features of standard options. Many of these products service a genuine need and provide a valuable extension to the range of financial engineering tools available for managing risk. Others are novel and innovative but perhaps will prove to be short-lived. One or two are certainly interesting but are probably solutions for which a problem has yet to be found.

The diverse nature of some exotic options makes it difficult to categorise them. However, in discussing the various products, we will group them under three headings:

- *Variations on contract terms*—where some basic feature of the standard terms is varied to create a new product.

- *Path-dependent options*—covering any option where the final payoff depends upon the path taken by the underlying asset price over time, rather than solely on the price at maturity.

---

[10] See Geske, Robert, "The Valuation of Compound Options," *Journal of Financial Economics* 7 (1979), pp. 63–81.

[11] See Rubinstein, Mark, "Exotic Options," unpublished manuscript (University of California at Berkeley, 1990).

- *Multi-factor options*—where the final payoff depends upon the prices of two or more underlying assets.

Variations on Contract Terms

Semi-American or Bermudan options. A European-style option only allows exercise on the expiry date, while an American-style option allows exercise at any time. A Bermudan-style or semi-American option is halfway between an American and a European option, allowing exercise to take place only on specific dates during the option's life. An example of where such an option would be useful is when an issuer has arranged a swap to cover a bond puttable by investors on a number of specific dates. If the investors put the bond back to the issuer, the issuer may wish to cancel the swap. A Bermudan-style swaption, in which the underlying swap maturity decreases on every allowable exercise date, would provide one solution.

Digital or binary options. The payoff under a standard option depends upon the amount by which the option is in-the-money at expiry. A call, for example, will pay out max$(0, S–X)$, where S is the underlying price at expiry and X is the strike. A digital option pays out a predetermined fixed amount A if the option is in-the-money at expiry and zero otherwise. The extent to which the digital option is in-the-money is therefore not relevant. Figure 11.24 sketches the payoff from a standard option compared with that from a digital option. Digital options can come in two flavours: *all-or-nothing* and *one-touch*. An all-or-nothing digital option only pays out if it is in-the-money at expiry, while a one-touch digital option will pay out so long as the option was in-the-money at some stage during its life. In the latter case, the payout can either be paid immediately when the option goes in-the-money or be deferred until normal maturity. One-touch digital options are therefore path-dependent.

FIGURE 11.24
Payoffs from Standard and Digital Options

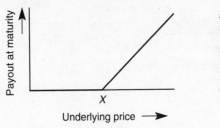

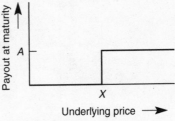

Pay-later or contingent options. These are options for which there is no premium payable unless the option is exercised. However, the option must be exercised if it is in-the-money at expiry, even if the intrinsic value is less than the premium. Figure 11.25 pictures the payout profile. The advantage to the option buyer is that no premium is ever payable if the option expires out-of-the-money. This is a little like a hypothetical car insurance policy where no premium would be payable if there was no claim in a given year. Buying a pay-later option is equivalent to buying a standard option and selling an all-or-nothing digital option in which the latter premium is set to match that of the standard option, and the digital payout is adjusted accordingly.

Delayed option. This confers the right for the holder to receive at some future time another option with the strike price set equal to the underlying price on that date. This is like a compound option with a zero strike price (i.e., nothing further to pay), but the strike price of the underlying option is not determined until the compound option is exercised.

Chooser option. This variation allows the holder to choose on some future date whether the option is a put or a call. This is similar to a straddle but cheaper, because after the choice is made the holder only has one type of option, whereas the holder of a straddle continues to have both a call and a put right up to maturity.

Path-Dependent Options

Average-rate, average-price, or Asian options. For a standard option, the payoff on maturity is the difference between the strike price and the underlying price on the expiry date. With an average-rate option, instead of using the underlying price solely on the expiry date, the average of the under-

FIGURE 11.25
Payout from Contingent Option

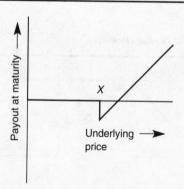

lying asset prices over a period of time is used. There are many permutations for the averaging process:

- The samples can be taken monthly, weekly, daily, or over any other pre-specified cycle.
- The averaging period can cover the entire life of the option or some sub-period.
- Either an arithmetic or a geometric average can be calculated.[12]

Which method is used will normally be determined by the user's underlying exposure. For example, consider a company buying fixed quantities of goods from a foreign supplier on the last day of each month over a six-month period. A six-month average-rate option, with monthly arithmetic averages being calculated using the spot rate prevailing at 11 AM on the last day of each month, would probably afford the most suitable protection. Average-rate options are cheaper than standard options because the average of the underlying asset price over a period of time is less volatile than the underlying price on a specific date, and this reduces the option's risk and hence its time value. Figure 11.26 illustrates an average-rate option involving averaging once a week over the last six weeks of the option's life.

FIGURE 11.26
Illustration of Average-Rate Option

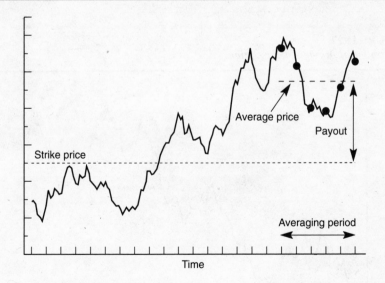

----

[12] The arithmetic average is the most popular, because it is easier to understand and calculate and is the method of averaging that most commonly reflects the underlying risk exposure. Unfortunately, valuing arithmetic average-rate options is much more difficult than valuing those using a geometric average.

Average-strike option. This is similar to the average-rate option in that the underlying price over a period of time is averaged. This time, however, the strike price of the option is set to the average price, and the payout is the difference between the strike and the asset price on the maturity date. Figure 11.27 illustrates the averaging process for an average-strike option, showing how the payout at maturity is calculated.

To clarify the difference between a standard option, an average-rate option, and an average-strike option, we can express the payout from a call option in each case as follows:

Standard option $\max(0, S_T - X)$
Average-rate option $\max(0, S_A - X)$
Average-strike option $\max(0, S_T - S_A)$

where S_T is the underlying price on the expiry date, S_A is the average of the underlying prices over the averaging period, and X is the strike price. The nature of the underlying risk exposure will define which of these payout schemes, and hence which type of average option, is most suitable. To illustrate this, consider three different German companies, each of which sells goods in the United States.

1. Company A makes occasional and irregular exports. The goods cost DEM 1.4 million to manufacture, and the company needs to make at least a 20% profit margin. Price competition fixes the selling price in the United States at $1 million. There is a six-month gap between

FIGURE 11.27
Illustration of Average-Strike Option

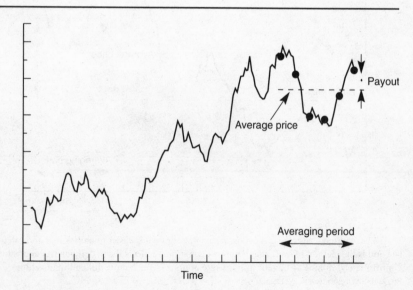

receiving the order and eventually receiving payment in dollars. Company A should buy a standard put option on the U.S. dollar (call option on D-marks) struck at $1 = DEM 1.6800.

2. Company B makes regular shipments to the U.S. and is paid in dollars on the last day of every month. These remittances are immediately exchanged into D-marks at the prevailing spot rate. It faces the same cost and pricing structure as Company A. Company B should therefore consider buying at the start of each year a 12-month average-rate put option on the U.S. dollar with a strike price of $1 = DEM 1.6800 and with the payout being determined by the average of the exchange rates at the end of each month.

3. Company C has its manufacturing facility in the United States. Each month the plant incurs expenses of $833,333, which are remitted by the parent company. The plant is engaged on a large project that will be completed at the end of the year, whereupon payment of $12 million will be received. These cash flows provide the requisite 20% return when measured in dollars, but the profit margin in D-marks is exposed to the exchange rate at the end of each month and most particularly at the end of the year. In this case, the company should consider buying a 12-month average-strike put option on the U.S. dollar.

In the cases of Companies A and B, their costs in D-marks are fixed at the outset, and this dictates the strike price of $1 = DEM 1.6800. The D-mark costs for Company C are not known until the end of the year, which is why the strike price for its option must be determined by the average of the exchange rates.

Lookback option. This is similar in some respects to the average-strike option in that the strike price for a lookback is also set when the option expires. However, rather than use the average of the underlying asset prices, the holder of a lookback option can look back and choose the best price achieved during the lifetime of the option. For a lookback call, the strike price will therefore be the minimum price seen during the option's life, while for a lookback put the maximum price is used.

Lookback options may seem to provide a significant advantage over American-style options because the holder never needs to worry that he might miss the best time to exercise the option. The lookback will always be exercised at the best possible price. Furthermore, the lookback option can never expire out-of-the-money. The worst that can ever happen is that the price on the expiry date is the lowest seen during the lifetime for a lookback call (or the highest price seen for a lookback put), and the lookback then expires at-the-money. Unfortunately, because the payoff for a lookback option will almost always be greater than that for a standard option, lookbacks are much more expensive and seldom worth the price in practice. Moreover, there are few situations in real life that create an underlying exposure matching the payoff from a lookback.

Cliquet or ratchet option.[13] This product was first developed for use on the French CAC 40 stock index but has since found applications elsewhere. The strike price for a cliquet is set initially but is then reset to match the prevailing asset price on a set of predetermined dates. Whenever the strike price is reset, any intrinsic value is locked in. For example, if the initial strike price were 100, and the price rose to 110 on the first reset date, the strike price would be reset to 110 and gains of 10 would be locked in. If the underlying price subsequently fell to 95 on the next reset date, the strike would again be reset, but no further gains would be locked in. A rise to 103 by the following reset date would lock in additional gains of 8. A cliquet option is therefore like a strip of short-term delayed options.

Ladder option. This works in the same way as a cliquet, but the strike price is reset when the underlying asset price reaches the next step in a set of predetermined levels, no matter when this occurs. Contrast this with the cliquet option, where the strike price is reset on a particular date, no matter what the level of the market is at the time. For example, if the initial strike price is 100, the rungs of a ladder call option could be set at 110, 120, 130, and so on. If the market reached 110, the strike price would be reset to 110 and the gain of 10 locked in. If the market reached 120 at a later stage, the strike price would be reset to 120 and a further gain of 10 locked in. A ladder option can be constructed from a strip of barrier options, to be discussed shortly.

Shout option. This is similar to both the cliquet and ladder options. With a cliquet option, the strike price is reset on predetermined dates, while the strike reset for a ladder option takes place at predetermined market levels. With a shout option, the point at which the strike price is reset is not determined in advance but is at the discretion of the buyer, who can "shout" whenever he believes it to be most advantageous. With an initial price of 100, if the buyer shouts at 114, the gain of 14 is locked in and the strike price is reset to 114. The buyer will then receive a minimum payout of 14 plus any intrinsic value present when the option expires.

Barrier or knock-out or kick-in options. In a barrier option there are two price levels established at the outset. One is the normal strike price, but the other is a specified barrier or trigger level. What happens if and when the underlying asset price touches or moves through the barrier level depends on the type of barrier option. An "out" option starts out like an ordinary option but is extinguished if the barrier level is breached. An "in" option, on the other hand, is activated if and when the barrier is touched. Barrier options occasionally give the buyer a prespecified rebate if the option is knocked out or if it fails to kick in.

---

[13] The author acknowledges Richard Cookson of *Risk* magazine for having drawn his attention to this type of option.

For a call barrier option, the barrier price is normally set below both the strike price and the current underlying price. This gives rise to *down-and-out* calls and *down-and-in* calls. For puts, the barrier is also set out-of-the-money and therefore at a higher price than both the strike price and the underlying asset price, hence *up-and-out* puts and *up-and-in* puts. Figure 11.28 illustrates some of the features of a down-and-out and a down-and-in call. In the example, the barrier is touched about one-quarter of the way through the lifetime of both options. This extinguishes the down-and-out call, which will provide no payoff and activates the down-and-in call. The underlying asset later rises above the strike level, and the down-and-in call eventually expires in-the-money.

For down-and-out calls and up-and-out puts, the possibility that the option could be extinguished makes these options cheaper than standard options. If the underlying price descends through the barrier level of a down-and-out call, the option immediately ceases to exist, even if the asset price subsequently rises. A standard option would continue until the expiry date, when it would deliver a payoff if it were then in-the-money.

Some users of barrier options are simply attracted by the lower premiums, but this can be a dangerous reason because an "out" option ceases to afford protection once the barrier is breached, while an "in" option may never be activated. A more suitable reason would be that the characteristics of the barrier option agree with the strategy of the user.

As an example, suppose that a British company is about to export goods to the United States and has fixed the selling price in U.S. dollars. The proceeds from the sale will be received in three months' time. The exchange rate

FIGURE 11.28
Illustration of Barrier Options

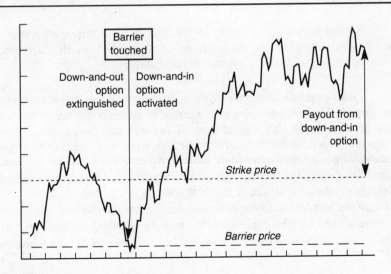

is £1=$1.5000 spot, and £1=$1.4890 three months forward. The company is adversely exposed to a rise in the British pound and would make insufficient profits if the pound rose above $1.6000. On the other hand, if the pound fell to $1.4500 at any time, the company would immediately wish to lock in its additional profit by selling its dollars forward. Under these circumstances, a down-and-out call on the pound with the barrier set at $1.4500 would prove ideal, because it would provide exactly the protection required at a lower cost than for a standard call option. If the pound never reached the barrier level, the call would behave just like a standard call, providing a payout if the pound was above $1.6000 at expiry. On the other hand, if the pound ever touched $1.4500, the option would be extinguished, but the company would execute the forward trade, thus rendering the option unnecessary thereafter.

Multi-Factor Options

Rainbow or outperformance options. The payoff from a rainbow call is determined by the highest price achieved by two or more underlying assets, while that from a rainbow put is calculated from the worst performer. Symbolically, the call payoff is max $(0, \max(S_1,S_2,...,S_n) - X)$, where S_1, S_2, etc., are the asset prices of the n assets on the expiry date and X is the strike price. For example, a rainbow call option might offer an investor a return equal to the maximum gain from either the FTSE 100, CAC 40, DAX, and S&P 500 stock indices.

Basket options. This could be considered a variation of a rainbow option, except that the payoff here is the weighted average of the prices within the basket of underlying assets. An example could be an OTC option to cover a specific basket of shares held by an investor. Options on stock-indices such as the FTSE 100 or the S&P 500 are, in effect, exchange-traded basket options.

Spread options. The payoff in this case is the difference between a pair of asset prices. As an example, an option could pay the difference between sterling and D-mark six-month interest rates.

Quanto options. In a quanto option, the payoff depends on one underlying price, but the size or value of the exposure depends upon another. The name "quanto" is an abbreviated form of *quantity-adjusting option*. Often, quanto products manifest themselves in options quoted in one currency upon an underlying asset denominated in another. An example would be an option on the Nikkei stock index with a payout in dollars so that the index expiring at 17,000 on a call option struck at 16,000 would pay out $1,000.

It may not be immediately apparent why an option on a foreign stock index should result in a variable exposure to the underlying asset—after all, an index is just a dimensionless number. The reason becomes clear, however, when one considers what the option writer must do to hedge such an option. For a Nikkei stock-index option, the underlying asset is a market-weighted basket of Japanese stocks. In order to hedge the call option sold, the option writer should therefore buy delta times the value of this underlying basket. However, the value of the underlying asset, and hence the size of the exposure, will depend upon the $/¥ exchange rate. If the basket were worth ¥17,000 in yen, at $1=¥100 the size of the underlying asset would be $170. With no change in the index, if the dollar weakens to $1=¥95, the size of the exposure increases to $178.95. The size of the underlying exposure therefore varies even though the underlying price, namely, the Nikkei index, has not changed.

11.9 PRICING EXOTIC OPTIONS

The pricing of exotic options is, unfortunately, much more complex than pricing standard options. There are three broad methods available.

Closed-form solutions. For most exotic options, there is a *closed-form* solution. In other words, a formula exists that expresses the fair option price as some function of the input variables. In a number of these cases, the formula is much more complex than the Black-Scholes equation. For example, the closed-form solutions for compound options require an iterative technique and use a bivariate normal distribution. In a few cases, such as arithmetic average-rate options, there is no known closed-form solution that provides an exact answer, although approximations do exist.

Binomial models. Any option can be valued using the binomial technique, but the problem becomes much more complex for path-dependent options, because every possible path through the binomial lattice must be evaluated individually. Suppose that at each step, the underlying asset price can either rise by a factor of 1.1000 or fall by a factor of 0.9091. Two possible paths after three steps are

   100, 110, 121, 110
and
   100, 110, 100, 110

In each case, there are two up-moves and one down-move, so the final price is the same for each path. A standard option would have the same value whichever path was chosen, because the terminal value of the option only depends upon the underlying price at expiry, not upon how the price got there. An average-rate option would have two different terminal values, however, because the average price over the first path is 110.25, but only 105 over the second path, even though the terminal values are the same.

Path-dependent options therefore have the unfortunate effect of exploding the size of the binomial lattice, as pictured in Figure 11.29. In general, for n steps, the standard lattice needs just $(n + 1)$ terminal valuations, while the path-dependent option needs 2^n. There are over a million different paths to evaluate when pricing a path-dependent option using a 20-step binomial model, and this makes the task quite time-consuming even with a powerful computer.

As an illustration of what is involved, Tables 11.9 and 11.10 show the calculations involved in pricing an average-rate option with the following characteristics:[14]

FIGURE 11.29
Binomial Lattices for Standard and Path-Dependent Options

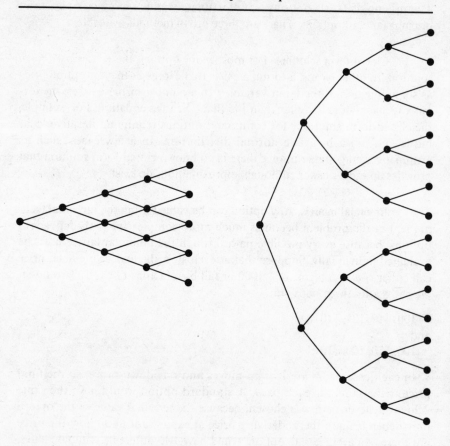

---

[14] See Chapter 10 for an explanation of the variables and methodology used.

TABLE 11.9
Binomial Pricing—Asset Values

TABLE 11.10
Binomial Pricing—Option Values

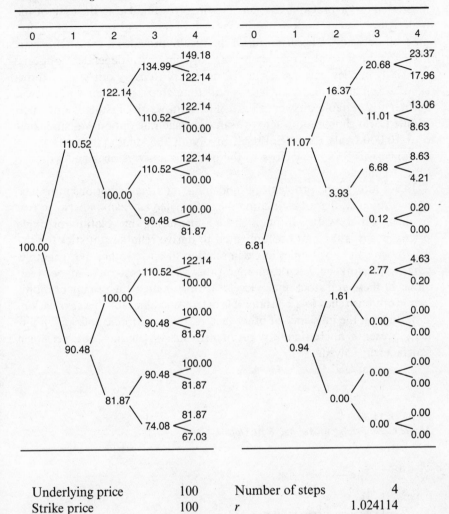

	Underlying price	100	Number of steps	4
	Strike price	100	r	1.024114
	Time to maturity	360 days	u	1.105171
	Volatility	20%	d	0.904837
	Interest rates	10%	p	0.595389

The rightmost column of Table 11.10 shows the terminal values of the average-rate option at expiry, using the arithmetic average of the five observed underlying asset prices. This is then folded back using the technique described in Section 10.8. The answer in this simple four-step binomial model is remarkably close to the answers of 6.88 and 6.94 obtained using two alternative analytical models, although a more complex binomial model would need to be used in practice.

Monte Carlo simulation. When all else fails, it is possible to value any option using a Monte Carlo simulation approach, like the examples illustrated in the previous chapter. This involves simulating the path of the underlying asset at random over thousands of trials and valuing the option on each occasion. The mean of all the results provides a reasonable estimate for the fair value of the option. For some path-dependent options, especially barrier options, it may be necessary to carry out tens of thousands of simulations, each with small time steps, in order to obtain a sufficiently reliable answer. Figure 11.30 shows the result of one such Monte Carlo simulation where the same average-rate option was simulated over 10,000 trials, each trial itself involving 365 steps. The mean value obtained was 6.79, very close to the previous answers obtained with the other techniques.

In addition to the problems of modelling, multifactor options introduce a new difficulty, that of estimating the anticipated *correlation* between two financial variables. It is difficult enough measuring the volatility of single prices, but it is far more complicated to derive reliable statistics for the way in which two variables move in relation to one another. For example, what is the link between exchange rates and interest rates or between either of these and stock-index levels? Unfortunately, the pricing of multifactor options relies to a considerable extent on values for this correlation. Filtering out the influence of other factors, both economic and sociopolitical, presents a challenging problem, one which has not yet been satisfactorily solved.

FIGURE 11.30
Monte Carlo Pricing of Average-Rate Option

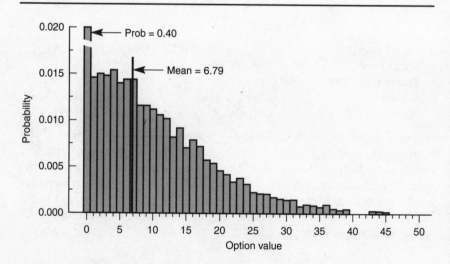

11.10 PRICE COMPARISONS BETWEEN EXOTIC OPTIONS

The vast range of choice between different kinds of exotic options, each one having several permutations, means that there is a wide range of option prices available. In order to allow some kind of comparison, Table 11.11 shows the premiums for 12 exotic currency options at three different levels of underlying price. Although currency options have been used to furnish this illustration, the findings apply equally well to most other underlying assets.

All the options shown have the same general specification:

Underlying	$/DEM exchange rate
Option type	Call on dollars/put on D-marks
Strike price	DEM 1.7000
Time to maturity	270 days
Dollar nine-month interest rate	3%
D-mark nine-month interest rate	6%
Volatility	12%

The table shows the option premiums in D-mark points for three levels of the underlying: 20pfg out-of-the-money, at-the-money, and 20pfg in-the-money.

TABLE 11.11
Comparison of Exotic Option Prices

		S = 1.5000 (OTM)	S = 1.7000 (ATM)	S = 1.9000 (ITM)
Standard call		134	873	2397
Average-rate	Averaging period: 270 days	10	486	2120
	Averaging period: 90 days	84	759	2301
Average-strike	Averaging period: 270 days	441	500	558
	Averaging period: 90 days	232	263	294
Down-and-out	Barrier: S −1000	130	753	1641
	Barrier: S −750	123	656	1342
	Barrier: S −500	105	507	972
Pay later		955	1624	2814
Compound	Call on call	50	205	346
(60-day maturity)	Put on call	49	197	322
Lookback		1330	1507	1684

Starting with the average-rate options, these show a considerable savings, with the at-the-money option being about half the price of the standard option premium. Premiums for two averaging periods are shown, one starting immediately and lasting throughout the life of the option, while the other covers just the last three months. As the averaging period becomes shorter, the average-rate option becomes more like a standard option, and the premiums rise accordingly.

The average-strike options have similar prices at all three levels of the underlying price, because the concept of being in- or out-of-the-money does not apply to an option in which the strike price is set later. In all three cases, the option premium is exactly 2.94% of the underlying asset price. This time the option premium declines as the averaging period becomes shorter because there is less opportunity for the final asset price to drift away from the average strike.

The down-and-out options show savings of between 14% and 42% for the at-the-money options, depending upon where the barrier is set. The table shows option prices for three barrier levels: 10pfg, 7.5pfg, and 5pfg below the current spot rate. Premiums are cheaper the closer the barrier is set to the current underlying price, but this increases the chance that this option will be extinguished.

Although prices for down-and-in options are not shown, it is easy to prove that

$$C_{std} = C_{do} + C_{di} \qquad\qquad (11.16)$$

where

$\quad C_{std}$ is the premium for a standard option
$\quad C_{do}$ is the premium for a down-and-out option
$\quad C_{di}$ is the premium for a down-and-in option

To see why, consider owning a portfolio of one down-and-out option and a similar down-and-in option. If the barrier is not touched, the "in" option is never activated, but the "out" option remains at expiry to behave just like a standard option. If the barrier is touched, the "out" option is extinguished, but the "in" option is activated to remain in existence until expiry. Either way, the owner ends up holding one standard option at maturity. The combination of the two barrier options therefore gives the same payout as a standard option at maturity and must therefore be equivalent in value at any time prior. Thus, knowing the price of any "out" option and that of the corresponding standard option means that the price of the "in" option can be readily calculated.

The premiums for pay-later options are all more expensive than their standard counterparts, the at-the-money pay-later option being approximately twice as expensive. In fact, it can be shown that the fair price for a pay-later option is approximately the premium for a standard option divided by its delta. This is why the out-of-the-money pay-later option is so outrageously expensive, being some seven times the price of its standard counterpart. This pricing provides proof, if proof were needed, of Milton Friedman's maxim that "there's no such thing as a free lunch."

Some of the cheapest options are the compound options illustrated, but it must be remembered that the premium shown does not buy the underlying option. If the underlying option is eventually required, the strike price must be paid when the compound option is exercised. For example, if the compound option were acquired when $/DEM was at 1.7000 and this option was later exercised to receive the underlying option, a total premium of 1078 points would have been paid instead of the 873 points to acquire the standard option at the outset.

Finally, the lookback options are some of the most expensive, having a premium of 8.9% of the underlying price. As with the average-strike options, there is no concept of being in- or out-of-the-money for these options either. A buyer would have to pay double to acquire the advantages of a lookback option as compared to the price of the equivalent at-the-money option, and few circumstances in real life would warrant such a premium.

As a further comparison of different exotic options, Figure 11.31 analyses six 270-day options with a strike price, where relevant, of 1.7000: a standard call, an average-rate call, an average-strike call, a lookback call, a down-and-out call with the barrier set at 1.6500, and a compound option with 60 days to expiry. The graphs show the fair premiums for underlying prices extending from 1.4000 to 2.0000. In addition to the points already made, notice how similar the profile of the 270-day down-and-out option is to that of an option near expiry. As the barrier approaches, so does the option's imminent demise, and so it is not surprising that the option behaves like one just about to expire.

FIGURE 11.31
Comparison of Exotic Option Premiums

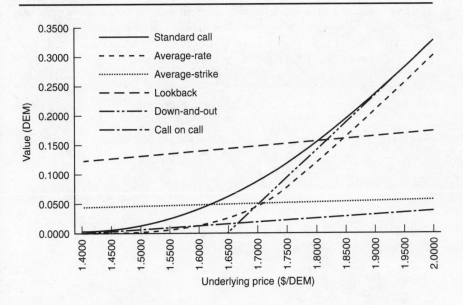

11.11 EMBEDDED OPTIONS

Many financial instruments include option-like properties. Here are some examples:

- A convertible bond confers the right to exchange the bond for a given number of common shares of the issuer.
- A mortgage-backed security securitises a portfolio of residential fixed-rate mortgages, each of which grants the mortgager the right to prepay the debt. Prepayments will accelerate when interest rates fall, because borrowers are able to refinance themselves at a lower cost.
- A callable bond allows the issuer to call back the bond on certain dates prior to the normal maturity. As with the mortgage-backed security, a borrower may opt to do this if interest rates fall sufficiently.
- A puttable bond is one that the investor can put back to the issuer, which may be attractive if interest rates have risen since the bond was issued.

The option feature is readily apparent in all these cases. However, there are other products which do not appear to have option-like qualities, but actually do. Consider these:

- A "guaranteed income" investment that offers 133% of the gain in the FTSE 100 stock index over five years or the investor's money back in full if the FTSE falls.
- A "participating forward" allows a UK company to buy U.S. dollars at a guaranteed exchange rate and to share in any savings if sterling should strengthen beyond the fixed rate.

In some cases, option technology has improved our understanding of how existing financial instruments should be priced. In other cases, developments have opened up new opportunities, allowing innovative financial engineering products to be created. The last two examples are cases in point. These, and many other tools, will be explained further in Part Two.

II

TECHNIQUES

Chapter Twelve

Applications for Financial Engineering

This chapter sets out the main applications in which financial engineering techniques may be profitably employed. One use in particular—hedging—is explored in greater depth, reviewing the sources of financial risk, setting hedging objectives, and measuring hedge efficiency.

12.1 APPLICATIONS OF FINANCIAL ENGINEERING

The applications for financial engineering can be summarised under four main headings: hedging, speculation, arbitrage, and structuring.

Hedging. An entity already exposed to risk can attempt to eliminate the exposure by adopting an opposing position in one or more hedging instruments. A simple example is the case of a borrower who buys an FRA to hedge against the effects of fluctuating interest rates. A perfect hedge is one in which the hedging instrument matches the original exposure perfectly in every detail. If such an instrument is available, risk can be eliminated completely, as illustrated in Figure 12.1.

In practice, such perfect correlation between the original exposure and the hedging instrument may not always be obtainable, and the hedge may prove to be less than perfect. Nonetheless, almost any properly designed hedge will

FIGURE 12.1
Illustration of a Perfect Hedge

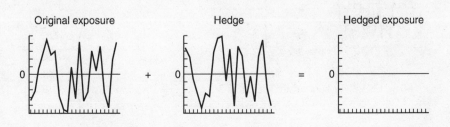

329

provide a much safer overall result than having no hedge at all. It would be a poor hedge indeed that created more risk than the original exposure.

The hedge illustrated in Figure 12.1 matched every fluctuation of the original exposure, hedging both adverse and beneficial movements in the underlying price; the end result was absolute certainty. Others exposed to risk may prefer a hedge that eliminates only the bad outcomes. Such a hedge is illustrated in Figure 12.2, where the hedge compensates against adverse swings in the original exposure beyond a certain level, but allows any beneficial swings to pass through unchanged. The end result is a capped exposure.

Speculation. Someone wishing to take advantage of a particular view of the market can speculate on anticipated changes, thus creating an exposure where none existed before. Speculation often takes the straightforward form of buying something whose price is expected to rise or selling something whose price is expected to fall. For example, a good deal of the $1,000 billion traded in the currency markets each day arises from the actions of short-term currency speculators, although few take positions as large as that of the renowned George Soros, who sold $10 billion worth of sterling prior to Britain's departure from the ERM in September 1992 and made $1 billion profit in the process.[1] It is not always necessary to use derivative instruments in order to speculate, but the tools of financial engineering can prove very advantageous for several reasons:

- *Gearing*. Most derivatives offer tremendous gearing, because they allow positions to be adopted with the minimum of capital outlay. For example, a speculator can bet on a rise in the British gilt market through buying long gilt futures contracts on LIFFE. A position in £1 million of gilts can be achieved for an outlay of just £20,000, and this initial margin could be deposited in interest-bearing securities

FIGURE 12.2
Illustration of a Hedge Producing a Capped Exposure

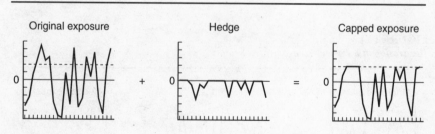

Original exposure   Hedge   Capped exposure

[1] Many articles have been written about this. See, for example, Anatole Kaletsky, "How Mr Soros Made a Billion by Betting against Sterling," *The Times* (October 26, 1992).

rather than cash.[2] This gearing of 50 times is by no means unusual with derivative instruments.

- *Ability to assemble complex strategies.* Using derivatives as basic building blocks, it is possible to create highly tailored exposures that would be difficult to achieve any other way. For example, a speculator could bet on a narrowing in the interest differential between D-marks and dollars or could position himself to take advantage of the market moving to within a specific range of prices.

- *Ability to create exposures impossible otherwise.* Some views are simply impossible to take advantage of without using derivatives. The speculator who believes that market volatility will decline has little choice but to use options.

Arbitrage. There is a profusion of inter-related financial products, and in many cases it is possible to synthesise one product from a combination of others. FRAs and interest rate futures are very similar to one another. Interest rate swaps are similar to a strip of FRAs. Caps and swaptions are tightly bound to their underlying instruments. Close mathematical relationships therefore exist linking the prices of comparable instruments.

Under normal circumstances, the actual prices of related products will follow these mathematical relationships almost exactly. As an illustration, consider the example cited in Chapter Seven (Section 7.2), in which the quoted prices for dollar and sterling FRAs exactly matched the respective futures prices for dollar and sterling interest rate contracts.

Occasionally, however, prices may slip out of line for a short while. This may happen in turbulent markets or when there is a large physical separation between markets as, for example, in the case of futures quoted in Chicago against FRAs quoted in London. When this happens, arbitrageurs will quickly intervene, buying in the market where the price is cheap and selling where the price is dear. They aim to profit from any difference in prices, but without assuming any risk. The action of arbitrageurs is actually beneficial on the whole because, in driving up underpriced instruments and driving down overpriced ones, it rapidly restores market prices to their natural equilibrium.

For all practical purposes, we can therefore assume that market prices of related instruments are exactly in line with one another. Users of the widely quoted financial engineering tools like FRAs, caps, swaps, and so on should therefore not spend too much time shopping around for mispriced instruments. Such bargains rarely exist. It is more fruitful to spend time instead on selecting the most appropriate financial strategy. Of course, for the unusual or exotic products that are individually priced, it does make sense to compare the quotations from two or three different market makers. Where there are price differences, it does not necessarily imply that arbitrage profits are

---

[2] This calculation uses the LIFFE margin schedule dated November 19, 1992.

possible. The spreads involved in creating a riskless arbitrage may eliminate any apparent arbitrage profits, as may the risk of executing several deals simultaneously before the prices have moved. Alternatively, one cheap quote may simply reflect the preferences or underlying position of one particular market maker.

Structuring. Financial engineering can be used to restructure the characteristics of a particular transaction or exposure. As a simple example, a bond issuer may use an interest rate swap to switch the stream of floating-rate obligations into fixed-rate payments. A more sophisticated borrower with a D-mark liability may use a diff swap to convert floating D-mark payments into D-mark-denominated payments priced at a particular margin above dollar interest rates. An investor with a view that six-month dollar interest rates will stay at around 3½% to 4% may convert a regular FRN into a reverse floating-rate note paying 11%—LIBOR to gain an immediate yield advantage of at least 3%. All these are examples of structured finance techniques that exploit the versatility of financial engineering tools to alter cash flows and financial exposures according to the needs of users.

Most of Part II of this book will be devoted to hedging, the first of the applications discussed here. Successive chapters will show how financial engineering can help to manage and hedge currency risk, interest rate risk, and equity risk. Speculation will not be covered as a separate topic, although some of the hedging examples will feature users having speculative leanings. Arbitrage will not be considered further, other than to assume that the activities of arbitrageurs help to ensure that prices of similar instruments are comparable. Finally, one chapter will be devoted entirely to structured finance and will demonstrate how financial engineering techniques can be used to better meet the preferences of investors, borrowers, and other participants in the financial marketplace.

12.2 SOURCES OF FINANCIAL RISK

Risk is all-pervasive, affecting individuals, companies, and governments in almost every area of their activities. Financial risk is the impact on the financial performance of any entity exposed to risk. It is difficult to draw up a foolproof classification, but the principal effects of financial risk can be categorised under the following major headings.

Currency risk. This arises from exposure to movements in exchange rates. Currency risk is often subdivided into transaction risk, in which currency fluctuations affect the proceeds from day-to-day transactions, and translation risk, which affects the value of assets and liabilities on the balance sheet. An example of transaction risk would be the purchase by a British manufacturer of machined components produced by a Swiss company and invoiced in Swiss francs. Translation risk would affect the published accounts of a Dutch-based industrial conglomerate with subsidiaries in the United States. Chapter Thirteen will examine how currency risk can be managed.

Interest rate risk. This arises from the impact of fluctuating interest rates and will directly affect any entity borrowing or investing funds. The most common exposure is simply to the level of interest rates, but some entities may be vulnerable to the shape of the yield curve. The management of interest rate risk is a large subject, and Chapters Fourteen and Fifteen are devoted to this topic.

Equity risk. This affects anyone holding a portfolio containing one or more shares that will rise and fall with the level of individual share prices in particular and with the level of the stock market in general. In addition, companies whose shares are publicly quoted may face difficulty in obtaining finance or in bidding for orders if their shares fall significantly in value. Equity risk will be discussed in greater detail in Chapter Sixteen.

Commodity risk. This risk arises from any change in commodity prices. Commodities include "soft" commodities such as foodstuffs and "hard" commodities such as metals. A coffee manufacturer such as General Foods will find that the price of processed coffee will depend to a large extent on the price of coffee beans. A collapse in supply, perhaps caused by a blighted crop, will push up prices and lead to a slump in demand. Commodity risk may have a wider impact than at first meets the eye. A firm such as Lucas Industries, which produces components for car manufacturers, would be hit badly by a rise in oil prices, because this might discourage people from driving and lead to a cut in car production. Also affected, though perhaps one step removed, would be the out-of-town shopping centre or drive-in cinema, both of which rely on people using their cars.

Liquidity risk. This is the potential risk arising when an entity cannot meet payments when they fall due. It may involve borrowing at an excessive rate of interest or facing penalty payments under contractual terms or selling assets at below-market prices (this is sometimes classified as *forced-sale* risk). Banks in particular are concerned about liquidity risk, because their successful operation depends absolutely upon trust and confidence, and failure to meet payments at the appointed time could destroy that confidence. A prime example of this is the case of Continental Illinois, which depended in large part on funding from interbank lines and CDs. Continental pursued an aggressive lending policy in the energy sector during the early 1980s, and subsequently experienced severe loan losses on this portfolio. However, it was not these bad debts that caused the failure of Continental in 1984, but the drying up of its access to the interbank and CD markets.

Counterparty risk. All transactions involve one or both parties in counterparty risk, the loss that could arise if one party were to default on its obligations. An alternative name for counterparty risk is credit risk. The magnitude of this risk depends upon the size of all outstanding positions with a particular counterparty, the size of transactions due for settlement on a particular day, and whether any netting arrangements are in force.

Practitioners often distinguish between *settlement risk*, which is the loss that can arise from the settlement of transactions on a given day, and *replacement risk*, which is the potential loss if a transaction has to be replaced prior to its maturity date. As an example, suppose that a customer executed a forward deal buying £10 million against dollars at a rate of £1 = $1.6000. With one month left to mature, the one-month forward price for sterling is £1 = $1.5000. If the customer were to declare bankruptcy, the replacement cost of the deal would be $1 million. On the other hand, if the customer were to declare bankruptcy on the settlement date after receiving the £10 million, but before paying the $16 million, the settlement risk would be the full $16 million.

Derivative transactions usually involve less risk than cash market transactions, because the principal amounts are not normally exchanged. Among derivatives, futures are the least risky because of the financial standing of the clearinghouse and the daily settlement of gains and losses through the margining mechanism.

Operating risk. This is the risk arising out of day-to-day operations and procedures. An obvious operating risk is that arising from fraud, and all institutions must undertake procedures to prevent or minimise this threat. However, operating risk can occur in other ways, and a potentially mounting problem stems from the increasing reliance on technology. Large-scale dealing operations depend upon computers, and a bank suddenly without its computer systems could find itself in a similar position to that of the well-publicised case when air traffic controllers suddenly faced blank radar screens following the loss of all their computer systems. At least in the case of the bank, lives would not be at stake. One well-known case arose in 1985, when the Bank of New York installed a new computer system and failed to test it adequately. The bank was unable to process the receipts arising from sales or transfers of U.S. Treasury bonds and was forced to borrow in excess of $20 billion overnight from the Federal Reserve until the fault could be rectified.

Other market risk. There are many residual market risks that come under this heading. Among these are *volatility* risk, which affects option traders, and *basis risk*, which has a far wider impact. In general, basis risk arises whenever one kind of risk exposure is hedged with an instrument that behaves in a similar, but not necessarily identical, way.

One example would be a company using three-month interest rate futures to hedge its commercial paper or euronote program. Although eurocurrency rates, to which futures prices respond, are well correlated with commercial paper rates, they do not invariably move in lockstep. If commercial paper rates moved up by 50bp but futures prices dropped by only 35bp, the 15bp gap would be the basis risk in this case.

Another example is the use of proxy currencies as hedging instruments. Liquidity in some currencies, for example the D-mark, is much greater than in some others, such as the Danish krone. Banks and companies often used derivatives denominated in D-marks to hedge a krone exposure, relying on their experience that the two currencies were highly correlated, especially as both were linked closely together inside the ERM and permitted to fluctuate only within a narrow 2½% band. When the ERM collapsed in August 1993, this relationship died with it and exposed hedging programs using proxy currencies to another form of basis risk.

Model risk. Some of the latest financial instruments are heavily dependent on complex mathematical models for pricing and hedging. If the model is incorrectly specified, is based on questionable assumptions, or does not accurately reflect the true behaviour of the market, banks offering these instruments could suffer extensive losses.

12.3 ACCOUNTING AND ECONOMIC RISK

When assessing risk exposure, it is vitally important to distinguish between *accounting risk* and *economic risk*.

Accounting risk is the risk that can be measured from an entity's financial accounts. Information about transactional cash flows, the location and denomination of assets and liabilities, and the maturity structure of the balance sheet enable an objective assessment of the magnitude of the risks that are faced. Accounting risk is therefore largely a backward-looking concept, looking at how cash flows, assets, and liabilities have been affected by risk in the past or how they may be affected by changes that take place right now.

Economic risk goes much further and is concerned with the broader impact of risk upon an entity's entire operations. As such, economic risk is often concerned with second- and third-order effects as the impact of risk ripples through the economic system.

As one example of the distinction between accounting and economic risk, consider what effect a rise in interest rates would have upon a typical manufacturing company.

The accounting risk will be relatively easy to quantify. Any floating-rate liabilities, bank borrowing facilities for example, will incur greater costs, while floating-rate assets, perhaps a deposit account, will earn more interest. If the company has used any financial engineering tools to hedge its exposure, these will show profits or losses, depending upon the nature of the hedge.

The economic risk, however, is wider but less obvious in its impact. Suppliers faced with higher interest costs will demand payment sooner, while customers may take extended credit and pay later. This will worsen the company's cash flow, leading to more borrowing and yet higher interest costs. Worse, higher interest rates may slow down economic activity, resulting in less demand for the company's goods. In addition, the higher rates may encourage overseas investors, leading to a temporary increase in the strength of the domestic currency. This will reduce the price of imported goods in terms of the domestic currency while at the same time increasing the price of exported goods in foreign currency terms. The net effect: a worsening of the company's competitive position and a further reduction in the company's fortunes.

A few far-thinking companies have taken steps to hedge not only against the accounting risks they face but also against their economic risk exposure. Starting in 1989, Union Carbide undertook a statistical analysis to determine what, if any, relationship existed between the level of interest rates in the economy and the company's financial performance. Multivariate regression was employed in order to isolate the effect of interest rate movements from those of other economic influences. Using data gathered over a 12-year period, Union Carbide found that its operating income actually declined as interest rates fell and undertook a hedging program to reduce this economic exposure. This was fortunate timing, because U.S. interest rates started to fall at the beginning of the 1990s. Union Carbide's results for 1991 showed a 45% reduction in operating income, but this was partially offset by savings from a 15% fall in interest costs.[3]

This illustration of economic risk has focused on interest-rate risk, but economic risk can be even more subtle when it comes to currency exposure. As another example, consider a mythical manufacturing company based in St. Louis, Missouri, having the following operating features:

• All raw materials purchased from local suppliers and paid for in U.S. dollars.

• All labour and other production costs incurred in U.S. dollars.

• All production machinery purchased from machine-tool manufacturers based in the United States and paid for in dollars.

• All finished goods sold in the U.S. Midwest and priced in U.S. dollars.

• All financing in dollar-denominated borrowings from local banks.

It seems fairly obvious that the one problem this company does not face is currency exposure. It operates in the very centre of the United States, far from any foreign shores. All its costs are based in U.S. dollars and all its revenues likewise.

Looking deeper, however, one important factor has been omitted from this analysis—competition. We operate in a world market, and even if our mythical company is not interested in exporting outside the United States, companies elsewhere may be very interested in importing their goods into

---

[3] See Elayne Sherian, "Smarter than the Average Payer," *Risk* 5, no. 11 (December 1992).

the States. If the dollar strengthens against other world currencies, the price of imported goods in the United States becomes cheaper, and this could well threaten the cosy existence of our mythical Midwest manufacturer.

Although we have illustrated the economic risk arising from currency exposure with an invented example, there are many real-life stories. One only has to consider the fate of the British motorcycle and consumer electronics industries to see economic risk on a grand scale.

12.4 DEFINING HEDGING OBJECTIVES

When hedging was defined earlier in this chapter, two different hedging examples were illustrated. In one, dubbed the "perfect" hedge, a hedging instrument was found that exactly mirrored the underlying risk. By combining the two, a completely flat and riskless result was obtained. In the second example, the hedge only came into effect when the underlying risk exceeded a predetermined threshold of pain. This had the effect of capping the risk, thereby limiting the adverse fluctuations, but allowing the benefits from benign fluctuations to pass through.

These two illustrations demonstrate that hedging can take on a number of forms, and one person's "perfect" hedge may be another's straitjacket. Before any hedging scheme can be designed, and certainly before any hedging decisions are implemented, it is vital to clarify what the scheme is meant to achieve. The answers to four key questions will help to define what a particular client's hedging objectives actually are.

Complete protection. Risk has already been defined as *any* variation in an outcome, so complete protection against *any* movements in price implies hedging against both adverse and benign outcomes. Nonetheless, for some clients, absolute certainty may be exactly what they want. If this is the case, the appropriate financial engineering tools to use are those with straight-line or symmetric characteristics[4] such as FRAs, SAFEs, forwards, futures, or swaps. When coupled with the underlying exposure, all of these tools attempt to guarantee a particular financial outcome, thus securing as complete protection as possible against market price risk.

Upside versus downside. Other clients may wish to have the best of both worlds—protection against the downside while enjoying the benefits of the upside. In these cases, options or option-based risk management solutions are likely to be the preferred choice, but the number of possible permutations is infinite. To narrow the choice, the client needs to indicate the balance between his dislike of downside losses and his liking for upside savings. For

---

[4] Refer back to Chapter Ten (Section 10.1) for a discussion of symmetric versus asymmetric characteristics.

many clients, the trade-off will not be symmetrical, because the desire to avoid losses for most companies is greater than the desire to realise savings.

Defining Hedging Objectives

- **Does the client simply wish to obtain complete protection against any movements in price?**

- **If a degree of risk is to be tolerated, how does the desire to obtain upside savings compare with the wish to avoid downside risk?**

- **How averse is the client to paying for risk protection?**

- **What is the client's view of the likely direction, magnitude, and timing of market movements?**

As an example, consider the following nonexclusive propositions:

- Paying a £200 insurance premium to avoid a 1-in-100 chance of losing £10,000.
- Paying £200 to buy a lottery ticket with a 1-in-100 chance of winning £10,000.

The situations are very similar, but most people would agree to paying the £200 premium to avoid the £10,000 loss, but would not buy the £200 lottery ticket giving them an equal chance to gain £10,000. Many financial engineering solutions reflect this reality by providing stronger protection against the downside than opportunities to benefit from the upside, but any structure can be tailored to suit the exact preferences of each client.

Paying for protection. Ironically, while individuals and companies are quite prepared to pay insurance premiums on risks like fire and theft, there is often a marked reluctance to pay for protection against financial risks. This can partly be explained by the fact that traditional insurance is a centuries-old business, and many people take for granted the need to buy insurance, while financial risk management techniques have only been developed since the 1980s and have yet to become as firmly established as insurance. Another reason is that some financial engineering tools, especially option-based ones, may appear expensive in relation to the perceived risk. The truth is that many individuals underestimate the true extent and impact of financial risk because it is less tangible than physical risk. They may therefore believe that a financial risk premium is excessive, when in reality it may be fairly priced in relation to the true level of risk.

Nonetheless, banks have responded to the aversion of clients who prefer to pay little, if anything, for hedging against financial risk and have devised a wide range of low-cost and zero-cost risk management solutions. For example, a bank can buy a portion of the client's profit opportunities in return for selling the requisite level of protection and by striking a balance between the two can arrive at a net cost of zero. The chapters that follow are replete with examples.

View of the market. Many clients have their own views of what may happen to market rates in the future. For example, they may believe it likely that the pound sterling will strengthen against the D-mark, or that interest rates in Japan will rise, or that dollar interest rates may rise, but more slowly than the implied forward rates predict. In all these circumstances, such views can and should be incorporated into the hedge design. A client who believes it most unlikely that interest rates will fall will be easily persuaded to sell a floor in order to finance the purchase of a cap. On the other hand, a client who thinks that the dollar will almost certainly rise will be reluctant to pay for protection against the dollar falling.

Once the client's attitudes, views, and preferences are known, one or more hedging schemes can be designed appropriate for his needs. After the scheme is implemented, the client will be concerned to see how well the hedge is performing, and the next section discusses how this can be assessed.

12.5 MEASURING HEDGE EFFICIENCY

Measuring hedge efficiency is not the same as measuring hedge profitability, although many users may equate the two.

Consider the scenario of a German car manufacturer that has started to export to the United States. Orders result in shipment three months later, and the goods are invoiced and paid for in U.S. dollars one month after shipment. The company therefore knows four months in advance what its sales proceeds in dollars will be and, being prudent, decides to hedge its currency exposure by selling the dollars four months forward. Suppose that the forward rate is $1 = DEM 1.6000, thus fixing the amount of D-marks received at DEM 1.6 million on a sale of $1 million. Four months later, out of curiosity, the company decides to check the spot exchange rate prevailing on the day the D-marks are actually received. It turns out that the D-mark has gained in strength, and the spot dollar was trading at $1 = DEM 1.5000. The manufacturer is well pleased that it had decided to hedge, because the forward deal resulted in proceeds DEM 100,000 greater than would have been received had the company simply sold its $1 million on the spot market—a DEM 100,000 "profit."

Following its successful experience with hedging, the manufacturer repeats the strategy on receiving the next order. By coincidence, the forward rate once again is $1 = DEM 1.6000. On this occasion, however, it is the dollar's turn to strengthen, and four months later the dollar is trading at $1 = DEM 1.7000. The manufacturer is now upset, because the hedge has now resulted in a "loss" of DEM 100,000.

Is the company justified in being upset? Did it first profit by DEM 100,000 and then lose DEM 100,000? How efficient was the hedge?

The answers to all these questions depend entirely upon the hedging objectives that the company established at the outset. If the company's original goal was to realise proceeds of DEM 1.6 million from the transaction, then the forward deal producing this cash flow is a perfect hedge and therefore 100% efficient. The company really is not justified in being upset if the spot rate later turns out to be more advantageous. In terms of achieving its objective of DEM 1.6 million, looking at the spot rate is irrelevant for the company. So too are the concepts of gaining or losing DEM 100,000 in this example.

Of course, it is an understandable human reaction to regret setting up a hedge if the market rate eventually goes in favour of the original exposure, but it is always easy to fault a decision with the benefit of hindsight.[5] What matters when judging the quality of a hedging decision are the original objectives and the information available at that time.

With this in mind, we can now define five alternative measures of hedge efficiency. The choice of the right one to use depends upon the hedging objectives.

1. **Objective: Achieve a target financial result; more is better, less is worse.**
This is typical of many hedging situations. The particular result may be a target investment rate or target financial proceeds from a business transaction. The hedge efficiency can be defined simply as

$$Hedge\ efficiency = \frac{T_{ACT}}{T_{TGT}} \tag{12.1}$$

where
T_{ACT} is the actual financial result
T_{TGT} is the target financial result

For example, if funds were actually invested at 7.82% and the target rate was 8.00%, the hedge efficiency would be 97.75%.

2. **Objective: Achieve a target financial result; less is better, more is worse.**
This is similar to the previous case, except that the exposure is in the opposite direction. Examples would include a target borrowing rate, or target project costs. In this case, the formula can be rearranged thus:

$$Hedge\ efficiency = \frac{T_{TGT}}{T_{ACT}} \tag{12.2}$$

As an illustration, if target project costs were FFR 6.8 million, but actual costs after hedging turned out to be FFR 7.1 million, the hedge efficiency would be 95.77%.

---

[5] Interestingly enough, the *break-forward* deal was created in the late 1980s to exploit just this feeling of regret. This deal, which allows the client to break the transaction if it becomes too unfavourable, is explained in Chapter Thirteen (Section 13.11).

3. **Objective: Achieve a target financial result subject to a minimum acceptable result.** This is also similar to the first case, except that there is a second threshold, which sets the minimum acceptable result. The hedge efficiency in this case can be calculated thus:

$$Hedge\ efficiency = \frac{T_{ACT} - T_{MIN}}{T_{TGT} - T_{MIN}} \qquad (12.3)$$

where

T_{MIN} is the minimum acceptable financial result

and the other symbols are as defined before.

Suppose that the target proceeds from a financial transaction are £5 million, and the break-even proceeds were £4 million, thereby setting the minimum acceptable result. If actual proceeds turn out to be £5.2 million, the hedge efficiency would be 120%.

4. **Objective: Achieve a target financial result subject to a maximum acceptable result.** This is like the previous example, except that the conditions are reversed once again with the imposition of a maximum acceptable result. The hedge efficiency here is

$$Hedge\ efficiency = \frac{T_{MAX} - T_{ACT}}{T_{MAX} - T_{TGT}} \qquad (12.4)$$

where

T_{MAX} is the maximum acceptable financial result

and the other symbols are as defined before.

A company's borrowing facility is due to be renewed shortly. The target borrowing rate is 8%, with a maximum permissible rate of 9%. After hedging, the company manages to borrow at 8.10%, giving rise to a hedge efficiency of 90%.

5. **Objective: Maintain the status quo.** This is different from the hedging objectives discussed so far. In this case, any deviation from the present situation is deemed undesirable. In the four previous situations there was always a directional preference, and this meant that hedge efficiencies greater than 100% could be recorded if the target was bettered.

Many banks run portfolios of financial instruments that they wish to hedge from any deviations in market rates. Perfection here is a hedged portfolio whose value is totally unaffected when market prices change. A portfolio that is imperfectly hedged leaves it exposed to possible gains or losses if market rates move. Although a movement of rates in one direction could lead to fortuitous profits from an imperfectly hedged portfolio, the bank would rightly argue that the market could just as easily have moved in the other direction.

The appropriate measure of hedge efficiency in this case is

$$Hedge\ efficiency = \min\left(1 - \frac{\Delta T}{\Delta U}, 1 + \frac{\Delta T}{\Delta U}\right) \tag{12.5}$$

where

ΔT is the change in the total value of the hedged portfolio
ΔU is the change in the total value of the unhedged portfolio.

For example, suppose a bank is hedging a portfolio of FRAs with interest rate futures. Following a shift in the yield curve, the value of the hedged portfolio increases by \$1,512, while the FRAs alone lose \$20,000. The hedge efficiency is 92.44% in this case.

Note that the definition of hedge efficiency given in equation 12.5 precludes efficiencies greater than 100%. The best result attainable is an efficiency of 100%, and this is achieved when $\Delta T = 0$, i.e., when the hedged portfolio does not change in value at all. For any deviation in portfolio value, whether positive or negative, $\Delta T \neq 0$, and the efficiency will decline from 100%. If the hedge is totally ineffective, $\Delta T = \Delta U$, and the hedge efficiency will be zero. It is possible for negative efficiencies to be recorded if the hedge actually exaggerates the effect of market rate fluctuations.

It is important to set proper hedging objectives and then to measure hedge efficiency correctly. Failure to do so may lead to the wrong decisions being taken, either before or after the event. As a particular illustration of this, consider the problem that beset the German national airline Lufthansa in the mid-1980s. It placed an order with the Boeing Corporation for delivery of jets approximately one year later, to be paid for in U.S. dollars. At the time, the dollar was uncharacteristically strong. Lufthansa believed that the most likely scenario was for the dollar to weaken over the following year. However, it was worried. If the market appeared to be acting irrationally in overpricing the dollar when the aeroplanes were ordered, what if the market were even more irrational when it came to paying for them? Lufthansa reviewed the alternatives:

1. Buy dollars forward.
2. Buy a currency option (call on dollars/put on D-marks).
3. Do nothing now, and buy dollars spot when the jets were due for delivery.

Since Lufthansa already thought that the dollar was overpriced when it placed the order, it was reluctant to buy dollars at what it considered was an inflated price. This ruled out the first alternative. Unfortunately, the currency option market was not as liquid as it is nowadays, and the cost of hedging would have been prohibitive for the size of the deal, eliminating the second possibility. Alternative (3) seemed attractive if Lufthansa's view held, but this strategy would be abhorrent for a conservative company. After all, failure to hedge a known currency exposure is tantamount to speculation.

In fact, Lufthansa executed a fourth strategy:

4. Buy half the required dollars forward.

The company reasoned as follows: If the dollar weakened, as it expected, Lufthansa would gain by 50% of any such move, since half the original exposure was left unhedged. If the dollar were to strengthen unexpectedly, any resultant costs would be halved, for similar reasons.

What happened? The dollar fell substantially, just as Lufthansa had believed. As it was able to buy half the required dollars in the spot market at a much lower price, the company saved a great deal compared to the cost of the jets one year earlier. One would think that the executives responsible should have been amply rewarded for their astuteness, but no. They lost their jobs amid what nearly became a national scandal. Why? The accounts that year reported separately (1) the purchase of jets and (2) the forward purchase of dollars. There was no recognition that the jets had been purchased some 25% cheaper as a result of the fall in the dollar, but the forward purchase of dollars was recorded as a currency loss of sizeable magnitude. Even though the combination of the hedge with the underlying exposure saved money for Lufthansa, the accounts did not couple the two results, nor did they reflect the rationale behind the hedging strategy.

If there is a moral to be learned, it is this: If a hedge is designed against a specific exposure, then the financial results of the two should be reported together, as one indivisible entity. The exposure and the hedge should be metaphorically placed together in a box, the lid slammed tightly shut, and the temptation to peek inside to see how each separate item is doing should be firmly resisted.

12.6 THE FINANCE DIVISION AS A PROFIT CENTRE

With increasing attention being focused on the financial performance of a company's operating divisions, the finance division in many companies is now considered as a profit centre. There is nothing wrong with this in principle, but it does raise some important questions of profit measurement.

How should the transfer prices be set? In any company where one division provides materials or services to another, the tricky issue of transfer pricing arises. Sometimes these can be determined fairly rationally, but in many instances transfer prices can be set quite arbitrarily. Suppose the finance division exchanges D-marks for sterling on behalf of a British-based operating division, or raises SwF5 million for five years at a fixed rate in order to finance a new factory near Zurich. Should it add a margin to whatever spot FX rate it receives from the bank? Should it charge a fixed fee? Should it charge interest in floating sterling, and treat any difference between floating sterling coupons and fixed SwF coupons as profit or loss? Unless the company can establish a clear policy in which these issues can be fairly resolved, the concept of the finance division as a profit centre becomes meaningless.

How does one measure the economic value of hedging? A simple strategy for a finance division would be to cover all known exposures using forward deals, thereby fixing costs. Against this would be the valid criticism that a number of opportunities to save on costs may be missed. For example, fixing the cost of a 5-year dollar loan at 6% when current 6-month rates are only 4% incurs an immediate cost of 2%. There is also the less tangible benefit from ironing out fluctuations in corporate earnings. For companies in some sectors, this can be pivotal. When the extent of computer company Wang's borrowing grew to the extent that a drop in earnings could put the company into liquidation, customers sought other suppliers. *The Wall Street Journal* quotes one potential buyer:[6]

> . . . before the really bad news, we were looking at Wang fairly seriously [but] their present financial condition means that I'd have a hard time convincing the vice-president in purchasing . . . At some point we'd have to ask 'How do we know that in three years you won't be in Chapter 11?'

Smithson cites the example of Wang, and goes on to present his case that hedging really does lead to tangible financial savings for companies.[7] The problem is in measuring these savings sufficiently reliably so that the true performance of the finance division can be determined.

The difficulties in answering these questions should not deter companies from creating a profit center out of their finance division, but it is extremely important that the pursuit of profits does not lead to disaster. When does deliberate under- or over-hedging cease to be "taking a prudent view of the markets" and become outright speculation? The case of Volkswagen's 1987 foreign exchange losses of DEM 473 million is well known, as is the more recent loss of £150 million by Allied Lyons in 1991. Foreign exchange losses of DKr 160 million (about $25 million) turned net financial income of DKr 54 million into a net loss of DKr 74 million for the Danish pharmaceuticals company Novo Nordisk during the first half of 1993.

In the case of Allied Lyons, a combination of aggressive profit seeking, inadequate internal systems and controls, and staff who were ignorant of the risks they were taking on led to an estimated exposure of about £1.5 billion against the dollar. A good deal of this arose from naked positions in currency options in which Allied Lyons had sold call options on the dollar. When the company attempted to reduce its exposure, which had originally been within internal limits of £500 million, it inadvertently increased the position but did not realise it until their bankers were called in to clean up

---

[6] "Tough Pitch: Marketing on the Defence," *Wall Street Journal.* (October 18, 1989).

[7] Charles Smithson, "Something or Nothing", *Risk* 5, no. 11 (December 1992).

the mess. The company chairman, Sir Derrick Holden-Brown, who later resigned over the matter, admitted[8] that their treasury team had been "dealing in foreign currency instruments which were inappropriate, and in which it lacked the requisite trading skills."

A sad epilogue to this story was the rush by other British companies to reassure their shareholders that they did not use options. While this was an understandable action in order to allay fears, it would be a great mistake for companies to deny themselves the undoubted advantages flowing from the correct use of options just because one company got it wrong. Like many powerful tools, options can deliver tremendous benefits when used properly but can prove dangerous if placed in the wrong hands. The next chapter shows how, used correctly, options can form the basis for the sound, prudent, and profitable management of currency risks.

---

[8] See "An Unenviable Record," *Financial Times*, May 4, 1991.

Chapter Thirteen

Managing Currency Risk

Chapter One has already portrayed the extent of currency volatility since the breakdown of fixed exchange rates in the early 1970s (see Section 1.3). Although some currency pairs still remain closely linked, such as the U.S. and Canadian dollars or the Dutch guilder and the D-mark, the major world trading currencies are free to float. FX transactions involving the U.S. dollar, the Japanese yen, the D-mark, and other major European currencies are all subject to currency risk. The most ambitious attempt by governments to reduce this risk, through the creation of the EMS and the ERM, has resulted in abject failure.

Under these circumstances, managing currency risk is vital for any organisation exposed to the influence of fluctuating exchange rates, and this is not limited solely to those executing FX transactions. Economic risk affects a much wider cross-section of companies, including the mythical manufacturing company discussed in the previous chapter, whose every transaction was denominated in U.S. dollars.

This chapter starts with a brief review of managing currency risk using "straight-line" products such as forwards and SAFEs. The bulk of the discussion, however, is devoted to option-based risk management strategies, which permit a rich assortment of objectives to be achieved.

13.1 FORWARDS, SAFEs, AND FUTURES SOLUTIONS

If the client's objective in managing currency risk is to eliminate the impact of any fluctuation in exchange rates, the answer is a forward exchange contract of some kind. Such an instrument will establish a firm price today for a foreign exchange deal to take place some time in the future. There is a range of choices available here, and these can be subdivided into three headings: cash instruments, SAFEs, and exchange-traded futures.

Cash instruments. Into this category fall all the traditional tools of the FX market. The simplest is the outright forward, which fixes the rate for the exchange of agreed amounts of each currency on a particular date in the future. A variation is the option-dated forward, which allows the client to execute the exchange on any date within a prespecified range. Long-term foreign exchange (LTFX) deals are one or more outright forward deals, but for dates further than one year into the future. Finally, the foreign exchange swap is the exchange of agreed amounts of each currency on one date and the reexchange on another date. Most commonly one date is spot and the other forward, but forward-forward deals are regularly done where both dates are forward.

The great advantage of these cash instruments is that they are all OTC products, and every aspect of the transaction can be tailored to meet the specific needs of each customer. Deals can be arranged of almost any size—whether round or odd amounts for almost any value date—whether standard or odd-dated and between almost any pair of currencies—whether major, minor, or "exotic."

A French-based customer due to pay $1.73 million dollars in 10 weeks can thus obtain a firm quotation for an outright forward deal fixing the amount of French francs to be paid in exchange for the dollars that he needs. If the exact timing is unknown, but will definitely fall in the range 8 to 12 weeks from now, the bank can quote for the option-dated forward. If the French company is contracted to pay $500,000 annually for the next five years, an LTFX deal will convert the dollar obligations into a fixed French franc liability on each date. Finally, if the company decides to make a short-term investment of $1 million repayable after eight months, a swap will fix the French franc amounts both at the outset and at the maturity of the deal.

SAFEs. These OTC derivatives were discussed at length in Chapter Five. They are off-balance-sheet, noncash alternatives to the forward-forward swap. Forward-forward swaps tie up a customer's lines of credit from the time the deal is arranged until the final reexchange of principal on the far leg of the deal. A SAFE allows a customer to fix the swap points on a forward-forward deal, but with a minimal usage of credit lines. The customer needing to execute a forward-forward deal could therefore use a SAFE instead, which may prove more attractive and less costly. When the time came for the first leg to be done, the customer would execute a regular swap. The settlement sum under the SAFE would then compensate the customer for any difference between the swap points prevailing, and the points originally agreed.

Exchange traded futures. Although currency futures were the very first kind of financial futures created, trading volumes have never approached those of other futures contracts, largely due to the depth and flexibility of the OTC market. Competition between banks and the wide and rapid dissemination of FX prices have ensured the narrowness of the spreads quoted. One of the prime advantages of futures markets, price transparency, is therefore equalled by the OTC market, while the need to manage daily futures margins—often considered an administrative burden by customers—has no parallel in the OTC market.

A recent innovation, the rolling spot contract launched by the CME in June 1993, seeks to remove one of the barriers against greater acceptance of currency futures. Although there is a fixed cycle of quarterly maturity dates, the rolling spot contract has an effective maturity of just two working days and therefore trades like a spot deal. The user can enter into a contract at any time and can maintain the position as long as he wishes, because the margining system includes an automatic feature that allows for the cost or benefit in rolling the position from one day to the next. Whenever the user wishes to convert the futures position into a real cash transaction, there is an *exchange for physicals* (EFP) provision, which does just that.

The key advantage of the rolling spot contract is that it avoids all the physical cash flows and attendant settlement risks associated with running a spot position and rolling it using short-term swaps to defer the cash flows. If there is a disadvantage, there is still the need to maintain a daily account, but this cannot be worse than managing the flows of principal from a series of short-term swaps.

The common feature of all these solutions is that they enable the user to fix the rate for an exchange of currencies to take place on some future date. This eliminates the uncertainty, and hence the risk, arising from the volatility of spot rates. However, fixing the rate removes not only the downside risk, but also the possibility to benefit from advantageous movements in the spot rate. To take advantage of these, while maintaining protection against adverse fluctuations, option-based techniques must be used.

13.2 OPTIONS ARE CHAMELEONS

The chameleon is a small lizard that has the interesting ability to change the colour of its skin to match its surroundings. If it rests on a leaf, it looks like a leaf. If it crawls on the ground, it looks like the ground. In other words, the chameleon can behave like different things.

Options have a similar feature. A deep in-the-money option behaves just like the underlying asset. If the underlying asset changes by one point, so will the option. A deep out-of-the-money option, on the other hand, behaves like nothing at all.[1] If the underlying asset price moves, the option just sits there and does nothing. As the strike price of an option moves from being totally out-of-the-money to being completely in-the-money, the nature of the option changes smoothly from complete inertness to complete emulation of the underlying. In fact, the delta of an option measures precisely how similar the option is to the underlying asset.

Figure 13.1 illustrates this property by showing the profit profiles at expiry for various call options on the U.S. dollar against D-marks. Each

---

[1] Well, perhaps it behaves like a dead chameleon.

FIGURE 13.1
The Chameleon-Like Behaviour of Options

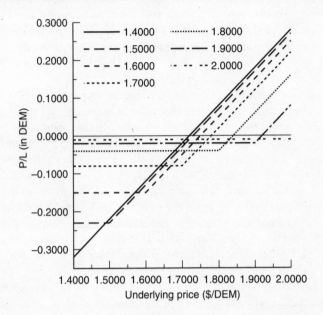

option is identical except for the strike price, which varies in 10pfg steps from 1.4000 to 2.0000. The options are all fairly priced with 270 days to maturity at a time when the spot dollar was trading at $1 = DEM 1.7000. For the purposes of this illustration, implied volatilities are all assumed to be the same. The graph shows the profits to one who buys an option on $1 and holds the option until maturity.

At one extreme is the option struck at 1.4000, deep in-the-money. The characteristic for this option is the diagonal line from bottom-left to top-right, with a break-even point a fraction above $1 = DEM 1.7000. The shape is identical to the profile of simply buying $1 rather than an option on $1. The only difference in the range displayed is the constant gap of 2.37pfg between the option strategy and the simple one of buying the underlying. This reflects the small time value of the deep in-the-money option and is the value to the option holder of being able *not* to exercise the option in the unlikely event that the dollar were to fall below DEM 1.4000.

At the other extreme is the out-of-the-money option struck at 2.0000, whose profile is the flat line just below the x-axis. The shape of this characteristic is identical with doing nothing, except for the constant gap this time of 0.75pfg between the option's result and zero. Once again, this is just the time value of the out-of-the-money option, which is the value to the holder of being able to buy dollars at DEM 2.0000 in the unlikely event that the dollar should rise above this level.

In between lie all the other option profiles, each one sharing some component of the diagonal characteristic from the underlying asset and some element of the flat characteristic from the "do-nothing" strategy. The at-the-money option struck at 1.7000, for example, displays equal amounts of each.

While Figure 13.1 shows the profile for seven specific strike prices, there is in fact a complete continuum of profiles ranging smoothly from deep out-of-the-money to deep in-the-money. Figure 13.2 illustrates this using a three-dimensional representation of the profit profiles.

On the left side of Figure 13.2 is a 3D graph with separate axes for original strike price (front to back), underlying price at maturity (left to right), and profit or loss (bottom to top). At the very back of the diagram is the horizontal line showing the completely flat profit profile of the deep out-of-the-money option. As one moves toward the front of the picture, the strike price moves lower and further into the money until one reaches the totally diagonal profile at the very front for the deep in-the-money option. An alternative view of this 3D graph is the contour diagram on the right side of Figure 13.2, which shows the view looking from directly above. The darkest shading is reserved for the outcomes producing the greatest losses, while the lightest regions show the biggest profits. Contour lines join areas of equal profit or loss and are spaced 5pfg apart, with the zero profit contour clearly marked.

One of the themes that will permeate this chapter is the way in which the nature of the hedge will change depending upon the degree of "moneyness" of the options used. With deep out-of-the-money options, the hedge will be almost nonexistent, and the full extent of the underlying exposure will come through. With deep-in-the-money options, all the techniques illustrated will behave in the same way as a simple forward contract, and the ability to bene-

FIGURE 13.2
Continuum of Profiles

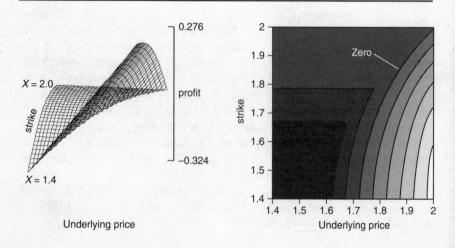

fit from benign movements in the market price will disappear. Only between these two extremes will the distinctive features of each technique be realised.

13.3 THE SCENARIO

To illustrate the various approaches to hedging currency risk, we will take the case of a German company that is due to pay $1 million in 270 days' time. As hedging objectives, the company wishes:

- To prevent excessive losses in case the dollar rises.
- To benefit, if at all possible, should the dollar weaken.
- To minimise the cost of providing protection against adverse movements in the dollar, while obtaining an adequate degree of protection.

The dollar is currently trading at $1 = DEM 1.6634 spot and at DEM 1.7000 nine-months forward. Nine-month interest rates are 6% and 3%, respectively, for the D-mark and dollar, while 20-day historic volatility is 12% annualised. The company has no particular view as to the direction of future market movements, but feels that it would be most unlikely for the dollar to stray outside the range DEM 1.4000 to DEM 2.1000 over this period.[2] This range will therefore form the horizon of possible exchange rate movements that the company will contemplate.

Table 13.1 summarises the premiums for European-style options at various strike levels, all quotations being in D-mark points per dollar. Notice

TABLE 13.1
Option Premium Quotations

Strike	Call on $ (put on D-mark)	Put on $ (call on D-mark)	Implied Volatility
1.4000	2,925	57	15%
1.5000	2,056	145	14
1.6000	1,285	332	13
1.7000	672	676	12
1.8000	367	1,328	13
1.9000	202	2,120	14
2.0000	115	2,991	15
2.1000	69	3,902	16

---

[2] Taking "most unlikely" to mean the range ±2 standard deviations, which captures 95.4% of possible outcomes under the assumption of normal returns, 12% annual volatility implies a range of prices from DEM 1.3732 to DEM 2.0810 after 270 days. See the discussion on volatility in Chapter Ten (Section 10.9) for an explanation of how this range can be calculated.

that the market maker has quoted premiums with a higher implied volatility for in- and out-of-the-money options, compared with the implied volatility used for at-the-money options. This is quite usual and compensates for the finding that market prices do not in practice follow the lognormal distribution but tend to follow a distribution with "fatter" tails.[3] This means that the probability of a large shift in market prices is, in real life, slightly greater than the lognormal distribution would predict. If this feature were ignored, a standard pricing model (which assumes lognormality) would underprice in- and out-of-the-money options. To avoid this unfortunate consequence, market makers increase the volatility figures used as inputs to the standard model when pricing options with strike prices away-from-the-money.

Using this set of quotations, we will now explore various ways for the German company to manage its currency risk, while bearing in mind the hedging objectives just defined. In nearly every case, we will assume that the company wishes to set up a hedge and then to leave it until maturity. For this reason, the graphs will show the results solely at maturity rather than beforehand. The final section of this chapter will, however, review dynamic hedging strategies.

13.4 COMPARING HEDGING STRATEGIES

The clearest way to compare different hedging strategies is to graph the resulting profiles, but there are several methods for doing this.

The first alternative is to think as a dealer would. The German company is obliged to pay dollars in nine months and so is effectively short the forward dollar. The profit-and-loss profile of this unhedged position is a diagonal line, with profits if the spot $/DEM in nine months is below 1.7000 and losses otherwise. This profile is graphed in Figure 13.3, which shows profits and losses against the eventual value of the $/DEM.

For example, if the spot $/DEM turns out to be $1 = DEM 1.4000 when the company needs to buy its dollars, the profit of DEM 300,000 represents the savings compared to the forward price prevailing at the outset. At the other end of the scale, if the spot $/DEM were to finish up at $1 = DEM 2.1000, the company would incur an extra DEM 400,000 in costs. The breakeven is at $1 = DEM 1.7000. If the spot rate at the end of the nine-month period matches the forward rate at the outset, the company neither gains nor loses through being unhedged.

To avoid this currency risk, the company could buy an at-the-money call option struck at DEM 1.7000, for a total cost of DEM 67,200. Figure 13.4 graphs the original exposure, the profit profile of the option at maturity, and the combined result. The diagonal line representing the original exposure is

---

[3] The statistical term for a distribution with a thinner peak and fatter tails is *leptokurtic*. The opposite, a distribution with a fatter, flatter peak and thinner tails is *platykurtic*.

FIGURE 13.3
Profit and Loss for Unhedged Company

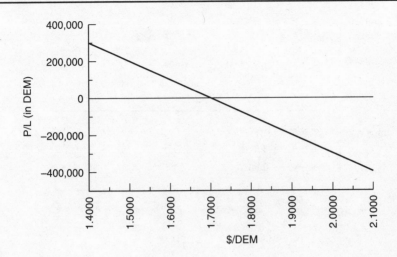

the same as in the previous figure, while the profile of the option has the familiar shape characteristic of a call. Finally, the solid line showing the total result is just the arithmetic sum of the two components.

To explain the shape of the total result, we will divide the graph into three regions. First, to the left of the strike price at DEM 1.7000 the call expires worthless, so the total result is the same as that of the original exposure less the DEM 67,200 option premium. Then, at the strike price itself, the underlying exposure shows neither profit nor loss, but the option still expires worthless, leaving a net loss of DEM 67,200 because of the premium paid. Finally, above DEM 1.7000 the option expires in-the-money with a payout that increases at exactly the same rate as the mounting losses from the original exposure. In this region, the rising profile from the option and the falling profile from the original exposure cancel out to leave a flat result, but one showing a constant DEM 67,200 loss reflecting once again the option premium paid.

The graphs of Figure 13.4 are therefore one way of presenting the company's profiles from the original exposure plus the option hedge. The financial outcome is measured in terms of "profits" and "losses" measured relative to the original forward rate, just as a dealer might measure the result from this strategy. The financial outcome can also be considered as being relative to the result that the company would have obtained had it hedged completely by buying its dollars through an outright forward deal. This is a perfectly valid way to measure the result, but there are other choices.

The second alternative is to look at the company's costs. How much will the purchase of dollars cost? How much does the option cost? The answers to these questions are shown graphically in Figure 13.5. This time, the diagonal line representing the original exposure goes the other way, rising from

FIGURE 13.4
Profit and Loss Using an At-the-Money Option Hedge

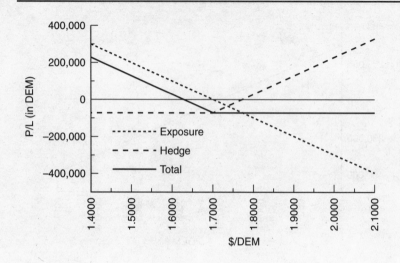

FIGURE 13.5
Alternative Representation of At-the-Money Hedge

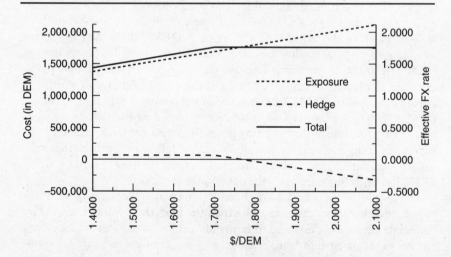

left to right. This is because, without a hedge, the company's cost in D-marks will be bigger the higher the exchange rate prevailing when the company buys its dollars. The option profile also appears upside down, with a positive cost to the left of DEM 1.7672, and a negative cost (i.e., net income) above this break-even exchange rate. Finally, the total result shows that the option hedge caps the company's aggregate cost at DEM 1,767,200 for any value of the dollar above DEM 1.7000, although aggregate costs are slightly higher than for the unhedged exposure for values of the $/DEM below the breakeven rate of DEM 1.7672.

Both portrayals are equivalent ways of looking at the same situation. One viewpoint is that of the dealer, who is concerned with profits and losses measured relative to the rates at the outset. The other viewpoint is that of the company, which concentrates on total costs in absolute terms.

There are some advantages with the first method. In the first place, the profile of a call looks call-shaped on the graphs, with the diagonal section sloping up to the right. A secondary benefit is that all the financial quantities are the same order of magnitude, so they can all be clearly displayed on the one graph. On the other hand, the second method draws attention to overall costs, and this is the emphasis that most corporate users of financial engineering tools focus upon, rather than thinking about the relative "profits" and "losses" from exposures and hedges. Another spin-off from the second method is that the effective exchange rate can be read directly from the diagram. This is shown clearly in Figure 13.5.

It is possible, however, to obtain the best of both worlds. By treating costs as *negative cashflows*, we can still maintain the corporate focus on costs, but it enables us to draw all the graphs the "right" way up, using the same convention as used in Figure 13.4. Now calls look call-shaped once again, and the total result for the company is drawn using the common-sense convention that a lower result is worse and a higher result is better. Figure 13.6 depicts the same at-the-money hedge using this third representation, and this is the scheme that will be used for the remainder of this chapter.

FIGURE 13.6
Final Representation of At-the-Money Hedge

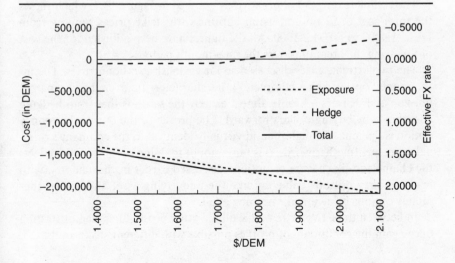

13.5 BASIC OPTION HEDGES

The German company in our scenario is obligated to pay dollars in nine months' time and is therefore adversely exposed to the risk that the dollar may strengthen when the time comes to buy the $1 million required. The simplest and most obvious option-based hedge is for the company to buy a nine-month call option on the U.S. dollar. The only issue that needs to be resolved is to select an appropriate strike price.

At one extreme is the most in-the-money option struck at DEM 1.4000 at a premium cost of DEM 0.2925 per dollar. At first sight, this option seems to guarantee that the German company could buy its dollars at a price no higher than DEM 1.6925 (the DEM 1.4000 strike price plus the DEM 0.2925 premium), with a total cost *less* than the prevailing forward rate of DEM 1.7000. However, this simple calculation does not take into account the timing of the cash flows involved. The option premium is paid up front, but the exercise price would only be paid at the expiry of the contract. With a straightforward forward contract, the cash flows all take place at maturity. To place everything on the same basis, we need to allow for the cost of financing the option premium over the nine-month time span. With rates at 6% per annum, the interest adds another DEM 0.0132 per dollar to the cost of the option hedge, bringing the maximum cost to DEM 1.7057. The extra DEM 0.0057 compared with the forward price of DEM 1.7000 is the value to the company of being able *not* to buy its dollars under the option contract in the unlikely event that the dollar falls below DEM 1.4000.

At the other extreme is the DEM 2.1000 strike option which costs very little, only DEM 0.0069 per dollar, or DEM 6900 in all, but which affords very little protection. The dollar would have to climb by DEM 0.4000 before the option even began to have any value at expiry. By this time, the company would have paid out an extra DEM 400,000 to purchase its $1 million.

The complete range of alternatives is graphed in Figure 13.7, which shows the total cost of $1 million using options with strike prices ranging from DEM 1.4000 to DEM 2.1000. All the figures have been adjusted for the cost of financing the premiums over the nine-month period.

The two extreme cases discussed so far establish two boundaries. The in-the-money option has a completely flat characteristic over the company's horizon and delivers a profile almost exactly the same as that from hedging completely by buying dollars forward. The profile of the out-of-the-money option is diagonal throughout and virtually identical to the company's original exposure. In other words, it is tantamount to doing nothing. This reflects the chameleon-like nature of options discussed earlier in this chapter, with in-the-money options behaving like the underlying asset and out-of-the-money options behaving like nothing at all.

In between these two extremes lie all the other possibilities, demonstrating once again the continuum of profiles possible with different strike levels.

FIGURE 13.7
Basic Option Hedges

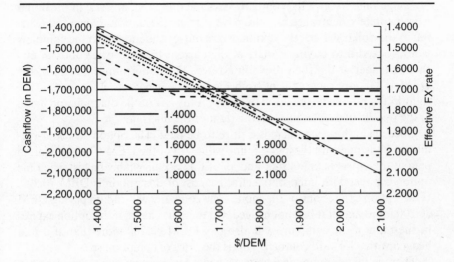

As the strike price decreases from DEM 2.1000, the options provide a greater degree of protection. The region where costs are capped becomes wider and, perhaps even more importantly, the level at which costs are capped becomes lower. Contrast, for example, the DEM 1.6000 strike with the DEM 1.8000 strike options. The first option limits exposure over the range DEM 1.6000 to DEM 2.1000 (and higher, of course) to a maximum cost of DEM 1,734,300. The second option only limits the exposure over a narrower range, starting at DEM 1.8000, and costs can rise as high as DEM 1,838,400. It therefore seems that options with lower strike prices are definitely better because they set a lower ceiling on costs over a wider range.

Unfortunately, nothing in this world comes free, and the additional protection from options that are more in-the-money carries with it a higher price tag. With a premium of DEM 0.1285 per dollar, the option struck at DEM 1.6000 costs more than 3½ times as much as the one struck at DEM 1.8000 whose premium is only DEM 0.0367. This has implications for the company's costs if the dollar should fall. Suppose that the dollar was trading at just DEM 1.5000 at the end of nine months. In that case, both these options would expire worthless. However, the company would incur additional costs of DEM 95,900 in premium and financing costs if it bought the DEM 1.6000 rather than the DEM 1.8000 option.

None of the options considered is superior to any other. The additional protection provided by options further in-the-money is desirable, but their additional cost is not. The cheapness of out-of-the-money options is attractive, but their relative ineffectiveness is not. If the dollar rises, the best options are the ones most in-the-money. If the dollar falls, the low-cost out-of-the-money options perform best.

Right in the middle is the option struck at-the-money forward, and this offers a real compromise. It caps costs at the present level of the forward exchange rate, so once the company pays the premium, any rise in the dollar is immediately neutralised by the payout from the option. Conversely, any fall in the dollar will see the option expire out-of-the-money, so the company is not locked into buying dollars at the current forward price but can buy them cheaper at the then-prevailing rates. The compromise nature of the DEM 1.7000 option is evident from Figure 13.7, where its characteristic lies right in the middle of the diagonal lines on the left of the diagram and again in the middle of the flat lines on the right of the diagram.

Once again, however, there is a price to be paid. The option struck at-the-money is the one with the highest time value. All of the DEM 67,200 premium paid at the outset is time value, and all of this will inevitably be lost when the option expires. With interest, the effective cost of this option is DEM 70,200. If the option expires out-of-the-money, the company will end up paying DEM 70,200 more than if it had not hedged. On the other hand, if the option expires in-the-money, the company will also pay DEM 70,200 more than if it had hedged with a forward contract. This is the price of compromise.

There is therefore no ideal choice when considering a basic option hedge. A balance must be sought between the degree of protection provided, and the cost of acquiring that protection. There are no right and wrong answers, and companies exposed to risk need to select the particular compromise that best satisfies the hedging objectives that they have set.

13.6 SELLING OPTIONS WITHIN A HEDGING PROGRAM

When marketing option-based solutions, one of the principal problems that banks experience is the cost of the products they are selling. Companies don't like paying up front for protection against currency fluctuations, and they don't like paying sizable premiums. For example, in the case of the German company, the up-front premium of DEM 67,200 for the at-the-money option is almost 4% of the amount at risk. Some companies, especially those working to tight margins, may find this excessive.

Suppose the company in our scenario is buying the goods from the United States at a cost of $1 million in order to sell them in Germany at a fixed price of DEM 1,900,000. If the company uses a forward contract to guarantee the exchange rate, it secures a DEM 200,000 profit, equivalent to 11.8%. If it hedges with the DEM 1.7000 option, the premium and financing costs of DEM 70,200 consume 35% of the company's profit margin. If it chooses the DEM 1.8000 option instead, while the hedging costs of DEM 38,400 are almost halved, the company faces increased currency exposure. Should the dollar rise to DEM 1.8000 or higher, the company's profits would decline to just DEM 61,600, wiping out 69% of the original DEM 200,000 profit margin.

From the company's viewpoint, this seems to present a dilemma. It cannot afford to buy option-based protection, because the option premium looks too high. On the other hand, it cannot afford to go unhedged, because of the consequences of a rise in the dollar. If it chooses the forward contract, the company secures a certain profit margin but gives up any opportunity to benefit from a decline in the dollar.

The answer to this problem is to tailor the option-based hedge so that it provides the benefits required, but no more. The trouble with the basic option hedge is that there is a single point at which the characteristic changes. Once the underlying asset price moves through the strike and makes the option in-the-money, the option provides unlimited protection against further adverse movements in the underlying asset, no matter how bad they become. On the other hand, once the underlying asset price moves the other way so that the option is out-of-the-money, the client can benefit to an unlimited extent from beneficial movements in the underlying asset, no matter how big these movements are. Figure 13.8 shows this graphically for the German company buying the at-the-money option. There is unlimited protection against increases in the dollar above DEM 1.7000, regardless of how high it goes, and there is unlimited potential for the company to benefit if the dollar falls below DEM 1.7000, regardless of the depths to which it might descend.

Such unlimited protection against a rise in the dollar and such unlimited potential to profit from a fall are not what the German company necessarily wants. In setting out its objectives, the company stated that it did not think the dollar would move outside the range DEM 1.4000 to DEM 2.1000. Why then pay for protection or opportunities outside this range?

FIGURE 13.8
Unlimited Protection and Potential from Basic Option Hedge

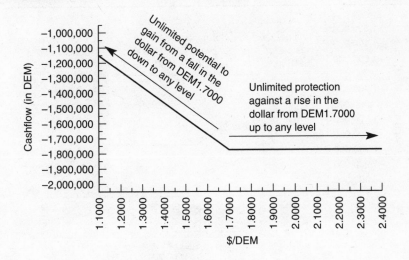

In fact, the bank can tailor a hedge to operate solely within this range and not outside. If the company buys protection against a rise in the dollar from DEM 1.7000 up to DEM 2.1000, but no higher, this will be less expensive than buying a protection that operates for all values of the dollar above DEM 1.7000. Similarly, if the company sells off its opportunity to profit from a fall in the dollar below DEM 1.4000, it can use the proceeds to lessen the cost of protection. The resulting profile could, in principal, look like the one pictured in Figure 13.9.

Using the nomenclature defined in Chapter Eleven (Section 11.1), we can characterise the shape of this profile as {0, –1, 0, –1}, while that of the basic option hedge of Figure 13.8 is {–1, –1, 0, 0}. Using the building block approach, the tailored hedge can be created using the following steps:

Underlying exposure	{–1,	–1,	–1,	–1}
Buy a call with intermediate strike	{ 0,	0,	+1,	+1}
Basic option hedge	{–1,	–1,	0,	0}
Sell a put with a low strike	{+1,	0,	0,	0}
Sell a call with a high strike	{ 0,	0,	0,	–1}
Net result	{ 0,	–1,	0,	–1}

FIGURE 13.9
Tailored Hedge

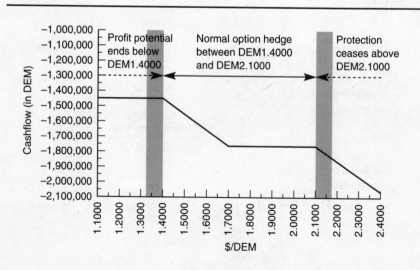

The basic hedge has unlimited profit potential as the underlying asset, the dollar in this case, goes lower and lower. The German company can sell off this potential by selling a put option at a lower strike price and use the premium income to offset the cost of the call being purchased. Through this call, the basic hedge also provides unlimited protection for an ever-higher dollar. This protection can therefore be stopped at a particular level by selling a call at a higher strike price. Again, the premium income from selling this call can be used to offset the expense of the call being purchased.

The essence of this technique is to tailor the protection profile to suit the particular needs of the client. Options are purchased to provide protection where it is needed. Options of the same type can then be sold in order to turn off the protection where it is not needed, and options of the opposite type can also be sold in order to sell off profit potential where it is not wanted.

Some companies have an almost pathological fear of selling options, perhaps after hearing horror stories of multimillion pound losses such as those realised by the unfortunate Allied-Lyons in 1991, as described in the previous chapter. However, there is the world of difference between a company's selling options as part of a tailored option-based hedge and selling options as a highly risky way of gaining premium income. As part of a well-designed hedge, option sales are balanced by option purchases elsewhere or by the underlying exposure. In the example of Figure 13.9, the calls sold are balanced by the calls purchased at a lower strike price, while the puts sold are balanced by the beneficial underlying exposure to a falling dollar. Nowhere in the resulting profile is the company's risk any greater after having sold options than it was from its original position.

To avoid the complexity of assembling option-based hedges and overcome any aversion among companies to buying or selling options, banks often construct a complete package and give it a proprietary name. The next few sections discuss some of the many permutations available, such as participations, ratio-forwards, and break-forwards. In many cases, these packages are carefully designed such that the premium income from the options sold is exactly equal to the premium expense of the options purchased, creating a zero-cost risk management solution. One of the best known among these is the zero-cost collar, and this is explained in the next section.

13.7 COLLARS, RANGE-FORWARDS, FORWARD-BANDS, AND CYLINDERS

Collars, range-forwards, forward-bands, and cylinders are different names for the same product, one which allows exposure over a defined range, but which collars the exposure outside this range.

A *collar* is usually constructed by buying an option of one type to limit the downside risk and selling an option of the opposite type to limit the upside potential. Both options are normally out-of-the-money, which leaves a range either side of the current price within which the hedge is inactive. Figure 13.10 illustrates three different collars suitable for the German company in our scenario. All have a cap set at DEM 1.8000 but floors ranging from DEM 1.4000 to DEM 1.6000. In each case, the collar is built by buying a call on $1 million struck at DEM 1.8000, and selling a put also on $1 million struck at the respective floor levels. Table 13.2 summarises the net premiums involved.

All the collars have the same broad shape: a diagonal section in the middle, and flat sections either side. The diagonal section corresponds to the original exposure, with lower costs if the dollar should fall and higher costs if the dollar rises. The only difference is the net premium paid. The 1.6000/1.8000

FIGURE 13.10
Example of Collars

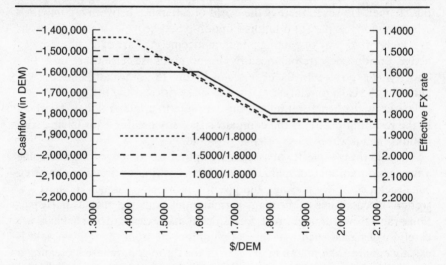

TABLE 13.2
Net Premiums for Collars

| | *Premiums Paid(+)/Received (−) in DEM* | | | |
| | | | | *Net with* |
Collar Range	*Call*	*Put*	*Net*	*Interest*[*]
1.4000/1.8000	+36,700	−5,700	+31,000	+32,400
1.5000/1.8000	+36,700	−14,500	+22,200	+23,200
1.6000/1.8000	+36,700	−33,200	+3,500	+3,700

[*] Rounded to the nearest DEM 100.

collar is interesting in this regard, because the premium from the put sold almost exactly matches the premium of the call purchased. At just DEM 3,700 after financing costs, the tiny net premium here means that the diagonal section of this collar differs from the underlying exposure by just DEM 3,700 in this central range. The other collars have somewhat greater net premiums, making their profile just a little more expensive, both in the diagonal section and in the capped parts. As compensation for their additional cost, the other caps allow the company to receive greater savings in case the dollar falls, because the floors are set at progressively lower strike levels.

There are three factors that a client can specify when requesting a quotation for a collar:

- The strike price for the cap.
- The strike price for the floor.
- The net premium to be paid.

These are interrelated and, for a given level of underlying price, interest rates, and volatility, specifying two of these items automatically determines the third. A company will typically choose to set the strike price for the cap and the net premium and then ask the bank to quote for the strike price of the floor. The cap strike level usually corresponds to the level of financial risk that the company finds acceptable, and the net premium is commonly specified to be zero in order to create a zero-cost hedge. Table 13.3 sets out the floor levels for various zero-cost collars, while Figure 13.11 graphs the resulting profiles including one for a nominal DEM 1.7000 cap.

Once again, the continuum of profiles is clearly evident from the diagram.

At one extreme, the DEM 1.7000 cap results in a completely flat profile equivalent to hedging by buying $1 million nine months forward. The reason for this is that a DEM 1.7000 cap is at-the-money forward, and so the floor level must also be struck at the same price in order to create a zero-cost collar. Buying a call and selling a put option at the same strike price creates a synthetic long position in the underlying asset, so the zero-cost collar in this special case is equivalent to a simple forward contract.

TABLE 13.3
Floor Levels for Zero-Cost Collars

Cap Level	Floor Level
1.8000	1.6133
1.9000	1.5382
2.0000	1.4738
2.1000	1.4193

FIGURE 13.11
Zero-Cost Collars

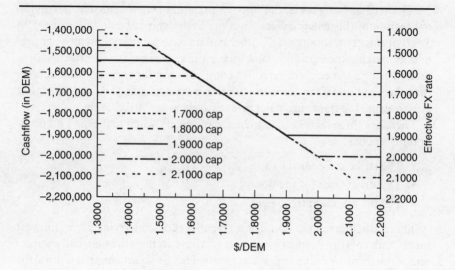

At the other extreme, the profile from the DEM 2.1000 cap is a diagonal line almost identical to the profile from the unhedged original exposure. Setting the cap level so high means that the floor level must be moved all the way down to DEM 1.4193 in order to establish a zero-cost collar. Unless the dollar breaks out of this range, both options will expire out-of-the-money, and so the option hedge will be nonexistent to all intents and purposes. This leaves the $1 million liability effectively unhedged.

In between, the other zero-cost collars allow a reasonable compromise between the maximum cost if the dollar should rise and the minimum cost if the dollar falls. For example, with the DEM 1.5382/1.9000 collar, the maximum cost to the German company to buy $1 million is DEM 1,900,000, while the minimum cost is DEM 1,538,200.

Zero-cost collars have proved to be a very attractive product to companies, for a number of significant reasons:

- They provide protection against an adverse move in FX rates beyond a certain point.
- They allow the company to benefit from beneficial currency movements, up to a certain point.
- They are free.

13.8 CORRIDORS

As we have just seen, the profile of a collar consists of a diagonal section in the centre and two flat sections either side. The *corridor* is just the opposite, with a flat central part and diagonal characteristics elsewhere. Whereas the idea of a collar is to permit exposure within a defined band but eliminate risk outside this range, the corridor creates certainty within the range but allows exposure outside. A collar was created by selling off unwanted profit opportunities in order to finance the protection needed. A corridor is created by buying options to obtain the protection required and then selling options of the same type, but more out-of-the-money, in order to sell off the protection where it is not needed.

To illustrate how corridors work, we will examine three corridors with different permutations of strike price and amounts of underlying asset. Table 13.4 summarises the components of each one and compares the structure with a simple at-the-money call.

It is not normally possible to create a zero-cost corridor, because the option sold is always more out-of-the-money than the option purchased. However, there are two ways to create a corridor having effectively a zero cost. One method is to set the strike price of the out-of-the-money option sold so that the premium matches the time value of the in-the-money option purchased. The net premium paid is then equal to the intrinsic value of the in-the-money option. If this option is eventually exercised, the total amount paid out will then be equal to the original forward price, thus making the effective cost of the option strategy zero. The first of the corridors in Table 13.4 has been designed with this objective in mind.[4] The second way to achieve a zero cost is for the option sold to be based on a multiple of the underlying asset. The problem with this alternative is that the resulting exposure will be greater in size than the original exposure, gearing up the potential for losses. This alternative must therefore be treated with caution.

TABLE 13.4
Net Premiums for Corridors

	Call Purchased	Call Sold	Net Premium	Net Premium with Interest
Corridor	1.6000	1.8184	95,700	100,000
Corridor	1.7000	1.9000	47,000	49,100
Ratio corridor	1.7000	2.0000*	47,000	49,100
Simple call	1.7000		67,200	70,300*

*Call sold on 1.75 times the underlying amount.

---

[4] For this to work properly, the net premium paid out should be made equal to the *present value* of the intrinsic value, rather than to the intrinsic value itself. The 1.6000/1.8184 corridor illustrated here does this.

Figure 13.12 shows the three corridors specified in Table 13.4, and compares them with the profile from the basic strategy of buying an at-the-money call struck at DEM 1.7000. To provide further references, the diagram also shows the diagonal profile of the original exposure, and the flat profile from the riskless hedge using a forward purchase of dollars at DEM 1.7000.

Each of the corridors illustrated has the shape described at the beginning of this section: a flat central section with diagonal profiles on either side. The flat section of the DEM 1.6000/1.8184 corridor provides the German company with $1 million at the fixed price of DEM 1.7000, provided that the dollar ends up somewhere in the range between the two strike prices. This is the same price as could be fixed with a forward contract. If the dollar drops below DEM 1.6000, the company begins to benefit and would save DEM 200,000 if the dollar fell to DEM 1.4000, a 30pfg fall from the forward price of DEM 1.7000. However, if the dollar ends up higher than DEM 1.8184, the corridor offers no further protection, and the company would begin to pay more and more for its dollars. However, the loss will always be less than if the company had not hedged, because the losses only begin to mount once the dollar exceeds the higher strike price of DEM 1.8184.

The second example illustrates a corridor using options that are less in-the-money. It offers a region without risk if the dollar ends up anywhere between DEM 1.7000 and DEM 1.9000, allowing the company to buy its dollars at an effective cost of DEM 1.7491, only slightly worse than the for-

FIGURE 13.12
Examples of Corridors

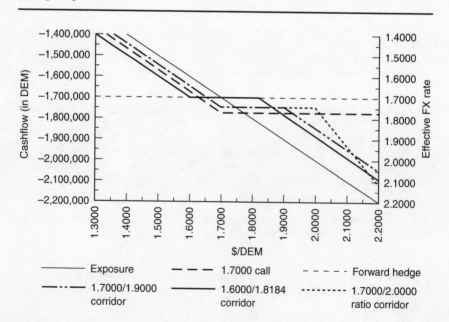

ward rate of DEM 1.7000. Compared with the first corridor, the DEM 1.7000/1.9000 strategy incurs an initial outlay of less than half the premium and outperforms the previous example for most outcomes of the dollar, apart from a central region between DEM 1.6500 and DEM 1.8700.

The final example is of a ratioed corridor using calls struck at DEM 1.7000 and DEM 2.0000. However, instead of both calls being based on an underlying asset size of $1 million, the calls sold are for a multiple of 1.75 times. This particular strategy has been designed so that the net premium outlay of DEM 47,000 is the same as for the previous example, even though the calls sold are cheaper. The advantage of this is to create a wider range over which the company's cost of dollars is constant. In this case, the company would pay the same fixed price of DEM 1.7491 as before, but over the wider range from DEM 1.7000 to DEM 2.0000. The penalty is that losses begin to grow faster once the dollar exceeds the higher strike level because of the ratio gearing. Nonetheless, the ratioed corridor only fares worse than the previous example if the dollar ventures beyond DEM 2.1350, and would only prove worse than the unhedged exposure for values of the dollar beyond DEM 2.3350, something that is most unlikely to happen.

13.9 PARTICIPATING FORWARDS

We have now examined a number of cases in which the purchase of one option has been financed by the selling of another. In all but one instance, the underlying amount of the option sold has matched that of the option purchased, which in turn was equal to the size of the original exposure. The variables until now have been the strike prices, and hence the net premium paid.

With a *participating forward*, the strike price of the option sold is made equal to the strike price of the option bought and is therefore fixed. The variable here is the underlying amount of the option sold, which is adjusted so as to create a zero-cost product. Of course, the options bought and sold must be of opposite types—one a call and the other a put—as there would be no sense in buying and selling the same type of option at the same strike price and maturity date.

A participating forward only works if the option purchased is out-of-the-money[5] so that the option sold will be in-the-money and therefore more expensive. This means that the underlying amount can thus be ratioed down in order to make the net premium zero.

One way to look at the participating forward is to regard it as an adaptation of the zero-cost collar discussed earlier. Let us start with the first collar itemised in Table 13.3, which had a cap struck at DEM 1.8000, and the floor level adjusted to DEM 1.6133 so that the net premium was zero. Now con-

[5] If the option bought is in-the-money, the product becomes a ratio forward, discussed in the next section.

sider what would happen if the cap level and zero net premium were kept the same, but the strike price of the floor was gradually raised. As the level of the floor increased, the value of the option sold would also rise, allowing the floor's underlying amount to be reduced in order to maintain a zero net premium. Table 13.5 shows the floor prices at various strike prices from DEM 1.6133 up to DEM 1.8000 and analyses the underlying amount necessary to cover the cost of the cap premium. As the figures show, the ratio of floor amount to cap amount is simply the ratio of cap to floor prices.

The effect of gradually reducing the size of the underlying floor amount is to reduce the proportion of profit opportunities sold off. Starting with the zero-cost collar, the cap:floor ratio of 1.00 means that 100% of the company's ability to profit from a weaker dollar is transferred away. As the floor is raised, the cap:floor ratio decreases. By the time this ratio declines to 0.28, only 28% of the profits are given away, allowing the company to participate in the remaining 72%. A 72% participating forward has thus been created. Figure 13.13 graphs this gradual transition.

A 100% participation in profits would be shown as a diagonal line with a 45° slope, assuming that the graph was drawn with both axes on the same scale. A 72% participating forward would therefore have a slope of $0.72 \times 45°$, or about 32°. Another way to measure the participation is to examine the company's savings if the dollar falls below the DEM 1.8000 level. With the dollar at DEM 1.4000, for example, the company would pay DEM 1,510,500 for its $1 million, making the effective FX rate DEM 1.5105. This is a DEM 0.2895 saving for a DEM 0.4000 fall in the FX rate, equivalent to a 72% profit participation.

This is just one example of a participating forward, which gives the company a 72% participation in any gains from the dollar finishing below DEM 1.8000. There are, of course, an infinite number of variations, just as with the zero-cost collar. The company can choose either the degree of participation or the strike level at which the participation starts. The closer the strike level to the prevailing forward rate, the lower will be the degree of participation. Table 13.6 illustrates this by setting out the strike levels for a selection of participation rates.

TABLE 13.5
Creating a Participating Forward from a Zero-Cost Collar

Cap Strike	Cap Price (DEM per $)	Cap Amount	Floor Strike	Floor Price (DEM per $)	Cap:Floor Price Ratio	Floor Amount
1.8000	0.0367	1,000,000	1.6133	0.0367	1.00	1,000,000
1.8000	0.0367	1,000,000	1.6500	0.0480	0.76	763,900
1.8000	0.0367	1,000,000	1.7000	0.0676	0.54	542,600
1.8000	0.0367	1,000,000	1.7500	0.0980	0.37	374,500
1.8000	0.0367	1,000,000	1.8000	0.1328	0.28	276,300

FIGURE 13.13
Creating a Participating Forward from a Zero-Cost Collar

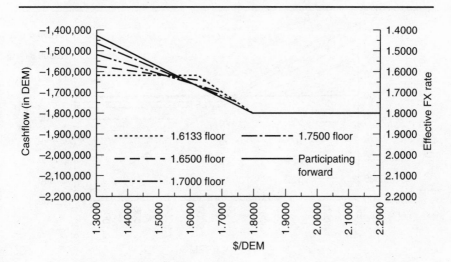

At the extreme, the strike level could be set equal to the forward rate, but the participation rate would be zero. This is because the forward rate is the equilibrium price at which potential gains and losses are exactly balanced, and a bank selling a participating forward struck at this rate could not therefore afford to give away any of its profits. As the strike level moves away from the forward rate, the company is dealing at a slightly disadvantageous rate, and so the bank can now afford to let the company share in the potential profits. For example, if the strike level is set at DEM 1.7512, which is only about 3% away from the forward rate, the company can obtain a 50% share of the bank's profits should the dollar fall below this strike rate.

The effect of having different strike prices and participation rates is more clearly seen in Figure 13.14, which graphs the resulting profiles for all the participations listed in Table 13.6.

The now familiar continuum is once again in evidence. At one extreme, the 0% participation at DEM 1.7000 is exactly the same as a simple forward deal and has the flat profile characteristic of a complete hedge. As the strike moves to the right, the company locks in protection, but at a progressively off-market rate. The flat part of successive profiles therefore sinks lower in the diagram, reflecting the extra cost of dealing at a higher exchange rate. For example, the 50% participation struck at DEM 1.7512 fixes the maximum cost at DEM 1,751,200. However, in return for paying a higher maximum price, the company can reap savings at a progressively greater rate when the dollar falls below the strike price. At the other extreme, the 99% participation in profits from a very off-market price of DEM 2.1839 has the diagonal profile characteristic of a nonexistent hedge, which is effectively what such a participation would be.

FIGURE 13.14
Various Participating Forwards

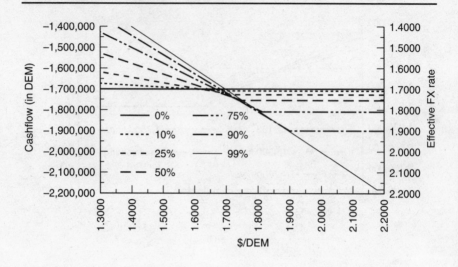

TABLE 13.6
Price Levels and Participation Rates

Participation Rate	Strike Level
0%	1.7000
10	1.7071
25	1.7203
50	1.7512
75	1.8087
90	1.8950
99	2.1839

Participating forwards thus provide another very attractive tool for currency hedging:

- They fix the company's maximum cost in case of adverse movements in FX rates.
- They allow the company to benefit from beneficial currency fluctuations, with no limitation on the savings that can be made.
- They are "free."

13.10 RATIO FORWARDS

Consider what would happen if one started with a participating forward, but moved the strike price to the other side of the forward rate. The option bought would now be in-the-money, and the option sold would be out-of-the-money. In order to construct a zero-cost product, options would have to be sold on a multiple of the original exposure. This is perfectly possible, and the resulting product is called a *ratio forward*.

The advantage of a ratio forward is that the buyer acquires an in-the-money option free, enabling him to buy the underlying asset at a price better than the current market price. The disadvantage is that the buyer has had to sell a multiple of the out-of-the-money options in order to finance the option purchased. If these options eventually expire in-the-money, the ratio forward buyer may have to pay out on a multiple of the underlying exposure, and this could cost a great deal.

As an illustration of what is possible, Table 13.7 lists the strike levels for various gearing ratios. For example, by selecting a gearing of 2:1, the German company in our example could buy dollars at the fixed rate of DEM 1.6496, which is five "big figures" better than the current market rate. The downside is that the company will begin to lose if the dollar drops below the strike level, because the 2:1 gearing effectively reverses the direction of the company's exposure to a falling dollar. As Figure 13.15 shows, if the dollar falls below DEM 1.6000, the company would pay DEM 1.7000 for its dollars, and a further fall of 10pfg to DEM 1.5000 sees the company's costs rise by 10pfg to DEM 1.8000 per dollar.

The situation becomes even worse with higher gearing ratios. First, while there is an attractive benefit from being able to obtain the underlying asset at a price better than the forward rate, this benefit diminishes very rapidly. Note how the flat sections of the profiles in Figure 13.15 become progressively closer. More importantly, the adverse gearing becomes more and more severe, leading to potentially catastrophic losses.

FIGURE 13.7
Price Levels and Gearing Ratios

Gearing Ratio	Strike Level
1:1	1.7000
1.5:1	1.6706
2:1	1.6496
3:1	1.6194
4:1	1.5976
5:1	1.5805

FIGURE 13.15
Various Ratio Forwards

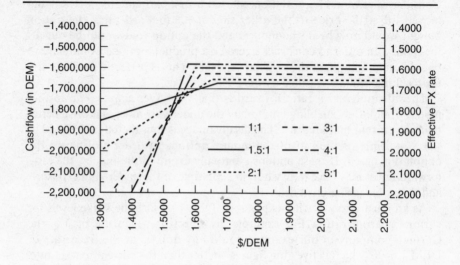

For this reason, the ratio forward is a product to be used with extreme caution owing to the limited upside and the unlimited downside. As with the ratioed corridor, the ratio forward is a product that can increase the buyer's risk. It should only be used if the company has a very firm view of the market's likely direction, if the gearing ratio is strictly limited, and if the company puts in place a stop-loss strategy to limit the downside if the market goes the wrong way.

13.11 BREAK-FORWARDS, FOXs, FORWARD-REVERSING OPTIONS

Break-forwards and the other terms are all alternative names for the same concept: a forward contract that can be broken, a forward contract with optional exit (FOX), a forward contract that can be reversed. The idea is to package with a forward deal the ability for the client to break out of the commitment should market rates go in favour of the original exposure and against the forward.

The spark for creating the concept probably arose out of the regret that many companies experienced at having hedged when the market eventually moved in their favour. "If only we hadn't hedged . . .," and, "If only we could get out of this wretched forward deal . . . ," no doubt are sentiments that have been voiced innumerable times. The proper establishment of hedging objectives and the correct measurement of hedge efficiency (both discussed in the previous chapter) should avoid these later pangs of regret. However, it is an understandable human reaction to exploit hindsight in criticising earlier decisions, and the break-forward provides an answer.

Building a break-forward is actually quite simple. The bank is selling the customer an option to reverse the forward deal but is not charging an explicit premium. The cost of the option plus any financing costs must therefore be loaded into an off-market forward rate.

To illustrate how this works, we can return to our example of the German company that needs $1 million. It can buy these dollars forward at the market price of DEM 1.7000 but now wants an option to sell them should the dollar fall below a certain price. Suppose it chooses DEM 1.6000 as the break price. The normal price of the put on dollars struck at this level is DEM 0.0332 per dollar. With financing costs, this rises to DEM 0.0347. Packaging these together and building the DEM 0.0347 premium into an off-market forward rate, we have the following:

- Company buys $1 million at DEM 1.7347.
- Company has the right to break the forward contract and buy its dollars on the spot market if the dollar falls below DEM 1.6000 in nine months' time.

Note that the company is always obligated to buy dollars at the contracted rate of DEM 1.7347. What the break-forward allows is for the company to break out of the commitment at the break price, but it effectively loses the ability to benefit from the decline in the dollar from DEM 1.7347 to DEM 1.6000. The latter is just an opportunity cost, because the company was presumably happy to pay the guaranteed price of DEM 1.7347 and the break-forward allows it to benefit once the dollar moves below the break price of DEM 1.6000. Nonetheless, one can still imagine the complaints of some companies when the exchange rate finishes anywhere below the off-market forward rate: "If only we hadn't hedged. . . bet!"

To illustrate something of the range of possibilities available, Table 13.8 lists combinations of break prices and off-market forward rates, while Figure 13.16 illustrates the resulting profiles.

TABLE 13.8
Break Prices and Forward Rates

Break Price	Forward Rate
1.7000	1.7707
1.6500	1.7502
1.6000	1.7347
1.5500	1.7233
1.5000	1.7152
2.0000	2.0125
1.0000	1.7000

FIGURE 13.16
Various Break-Forward Contracts

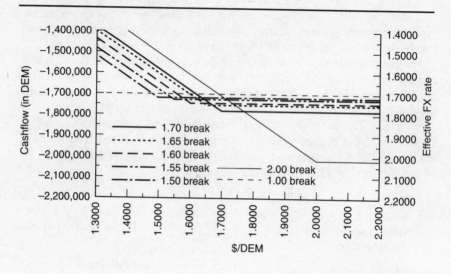

The higher the break price, the sooner the company can break out of the forward contract and profit from a lower dollar. This advantage is balanced by the company dealing at a forward rate further away from the current market price. For example, if the break price is set to the prevailing forward rate of DEM 1.7000, the off-market rate offered to the company rises to DEM 1.7707, more than 4% higher. As the break price is set lower, the opportunity to reverse the forward contract recedes, but the company is able to deal at a forward rate closer to the true market rate. A break price of DEM 1.5000 allows the company to execute the forward deal at DEM 1.7152, less than 1% higher than the actual forward rate.

The continuum of possibilities is once again in evidence and is made clearer in Figure 13.16 by the inclusion of break-forward contracts at the extreme prices of DEM 1.0000 and DEM 2.0000. With the break price set to DEM 1.0000, the chance of the contract being broken is infinitesimal, so the company deals at the true forward rate of DEM 1.7000, and the break-forward degenerates to the completely flat profile of a regular forward contract. At a high break price of DEM 2.0000 the contract will almost always be broken, so the company will almost inevitably deal at the prevailing spot rate. The off-market rate is then set very high, but very close to the break price. In the example shown, the off-market rate at DEM 2.0125 is just a fraction above the break price of DEM 2.0000. Since the forward contract is almost invariably broken, the hedge becomes virtually nonexistent, and the diagonal profile of the original exposure dominates.

If looking at Figure 13.16 gives some readers a strange feeling of *déjà vu*, then there is a perfectly valid explanation. The profiles illustrated here are virtually identical to those of Figure 13.7, which showed the profiles from hedging with a simple call. A moment's reflection will reveal that the combination of buying the underlying asset and buying a put creates a synthetic call. The only difference between the break-forward and hedging with a real call is the timing of the premium. In the case of the break-forward, the option premium is effectively paid in arrears and added to the price of the asset at maturity. The DEM 1.7000/1.7707 break-forward could therefore be replicated by letting the company buy a DEM 1.7000 call and lending the DEM 0.0672 premium for nine months.

13.12 USING EXOTIC OPTIONS

Chapter Eleven (Section 11.8) reviewed a variety of exotic options and gave some examples of their practical use. Of the wide range of exotics available, we will single out the three which are most commonly used.

Average-rate and average-strike options. These are suited for hedging applications in which the underlying exposure is not linked to a transaction taking place on a single date, but to a series of transactions that take place over a period of time. The more widespread of the two varieties is the average-rate option, and this would be the ideal hedging vehicle if a company was regularly paying or receiving funds denominated in another currency. Case 13.1 illustrates the position of a British wine importer in just this situation. Chapter Eleven (Section 11.8) has already provided some other short illustrations showing how both the average-rate and the more unusual average-strike options could be used in managing exposure to fluctuating exchange rates on multiple transactions.

In addition to handling transaction risk, average-rate options would also be appropriate for a company hedging its balance sheet against translation risk, so long as the company used average rather than year-end rates when drawing up its accounts. Another source of currency exposure, economic risk, is even better candidate for the use of average-rate options, because the factors that give rise to economic risk operate over an extended period of time and are sensitive to the average exchange rate over a period rather than on a single day.

Barrier options. These are attractive because they are cheaper than standard options, but a note of caution must be sounded here. Cost savings for knock-out options only become significant when the barrier is brought relatively close to the prevailing market rate, but this increases the chance that the option will be extinguished, and the protection conferred will disappear. Similarly, knock-in options are cheaper when the barrier is set relatively far from the present market rate, but then there is a strong likelihood that the option will never be activated.

Case Study 13–1
Using Average-Rate Options

American Wine Importers Ltd. (AWI) is a British-based company specialising in the importation of fine Californian wines into the United Kingdom. On May 31, 1992, the company is preparing its annual budget for shipments to take place between July 1992 and June 1993. The company is entering into a contract to import 5,000 crates of wine per month at the fixed price of $90 per crate, the amount to be paid on the last business day of each month.

The pound has risen steadily since the beginning of the year and is now trading at £1=$1.8260. AWI's finance director believes that, while the pound may continue to strengthen for a little while, it will more likely fall back to its five-year average level of around $1.7000. If so, the company's profitability would be threatened, since the minimum acceptable profit margin on the consignment would be breached if the pound fell to $1.7500 or below.

AWI considers two possible alternatives offered by its bank:

1. A strip of forward contracts, fixing the exchange rate at £1=$1.7560 for each monthly consignment.

2. An average-rate option, struck at $1=£0.5556 and priced at £0.0212 per $1.

AWI decides to go for the average-rate option, on the basis that the forward contract does not allow the company to benefit from the current strength of the pound.

The details of the average-rate option are as follows:

Type	Average-rate deferred start call on $/ put on £
Strike price	$1 = £0.5556
Premium	£0.0212 per $1
Underlying amount	$5,400,000
Total premium	£114,480
Expiry date	June 30, 1993
Averaging period	July 1, 1992 to June 30, 1993
Averaging method	Arithmetic average of closing spot rates on last business day each month (12 observations)
Payout	On July 2, 1993 based on difference between strike and average price

Over the 12-month period covered by the contract, the pound initially rose but then crashed dramatically during the ERM crisis in September 1992. Table 13.9 summarises the exchange rates and resulting cash flows. As can be seen, the strength of the pound at the beginning meant that the company was only paying around £230,000 per month, compared to the cost of £256, 264 under the forward strip. After September, however, payments increased markedly, rising to a peak of £315,700 in February 1993.

TABLE 13.9
Cash Flows for American Wine Importers Ltd.

Date	FX Rate (£/$)	Invoice Amounts ($)	Invoice Amounts (£)	FX Rate ($/£)
May 92	1.8260			
June	1.9010			
July	1.9192	$450,000.00	£234,472.70	0.5211
August	1.9834	450,000.00	226,883.13	0.5042
September	1.7740	450,000.00	253,664.04	0.5637
October	1.5660	450,000.00	287,356.32	0.6386
November	1.5042	450,000.00	299,162.35	0.6648
December	1.5140	450,000.00	297,225.89	0.6605
January 93	1.4865	450,000.00	302,724.52	0.6727
February	1.4254	450,000.00	315,700.86	0.7016
March	1.5030	450,000.00	299,401.20	0.6653
April	1.5727	450,000.00	286,132.13	0.6358
May	1.5585	450,000.00	288,739.17	0.6416
June	1.5103	450,000.00	297,954.05	0.6621
Total	1.6098	$5,400,000.00	£3,389,416.35	0.6277

The average exchange rate over the period was $1=£0.6277, leading to a payout of £389,340 when the option expired. The company's net outlay, including the option premium, was therefore £3,114,556.35, which corresponds to an effective exchange rate of $1.7338. While this turn out is marginally more expensive than the forward strip would have been, AWI could have benefited if the pound had remained strong—an opportunity that would have been denied to AWI if it had used the strip of forward deals.

The most appropriate applications for barrier options are those in which the user's hedging strategy includes a contingency plan setting out exactly what action would be taken if the barrier were hit. Case 13.2 illustrates just such a strategy as used by a British high-technology company.

Compound options. Chapter Eleven (Section 11.7) provided a detailed example of one application for compound options: to provide protection in a contingency situation when the need for protection was dependent upon success in winning a commercial bid. Here we explore another common application: a cheap form of risk insurance.

Case Study 13–2
Using Barrier Options

Videotech Ltd. is a British company producing state-of-the-art digital image processing equipment used in television studios. It has just won an order to deliver a $5 million system to a New York TV company. Delivery and invoicing (in U.S. dollars) will take place in six months' time. Right now, spot sterling is trading at $1 = $1.5000, and the six-month forward rate has been quoted as £1 = $1.4782.

Videotech is adversely exposed to a rise in the British pound. The company's treasurer believes that the British economy is about to stage a strong recovery, making a rise in the pound quite likely in his view. One easy solution would be for Videotech to sell its $5 million receivable at the forward rate, thereby receiving £3,382,492 in six months' time. This would provide the company with a satisfactory return.

However, the treasurer is tempted by the possibility to gain in case the pound should dip at any time over the next six months. With economic uncertainty, he believes that such a possibility is very likely. The obvious choice is for Videotech to buy a call on sterling, which would protect it against a rise in sterling but allow the company to profit from any fall. Unfortunately, the price of a six-month at-the-money spot option is considered too expensive at £0.0232 per dollar, because the proceeds net of premium costs would be only £3,217,333 if the option were exercised, and this is less than the company's benchmark of £3.25 million.

Videotech goes instead for a knock-out option, with a strike price at $1.5000 and a barrier at $1.4350. The premium quoted is £0.0164 per dollar, which is 29% cheaper than the standard option. At the same time, Videotech leaves instructions with its bank to sell forward dollars should the spot rate fall to $1.4350 at any time. This strategy ensures that Videotech covers its exposure in the event that the option is extinguished. There are now two possible scenarios:

1. Sterling never drops to $1.4350 and the option stays alive. In this case, the option behaves like a standard call option. If the pound is below the strike price at expiry, the option expires worthless, and Videotech executes a spot deal to buy pounds and sell dollars. If the pound is above $1.5000, Videotech exercises its option and receives £3,333,333 at maturity. When the option premium of £82,000 is deducted from this, Videotech is left with £3,251,333. This is the smallest possible sterling amount which the company can receive and is just above the benchmark proceeds of £3.25 million.

2. Sterling drops below $1.4350, the option is extinguished, and Videotech executes a forward deal to sell dollars and buy pounds. Suppose this happens after three months have elapsed, and the forward rate that Videotech receives is $1.4244. This leads to eventual sterling proceeds of £3,510,250, or £3,428,250 after the option premium is taken into account, almost £50,000 more than from the simple forward deal first considered by the company.

The description "cheap" has to be interpreted with care. It is certainly true that the initial premium for a compound option is cheaper than that for the underlying option. However, if the compound option is exercised to obtain the underlying option, the total premium paid will be more than if the underlying option had been acquired in the first place.

With this warning about the interpretation of "cheap" in mind, Case 13.3 examines one specific example where compound options can be used as a very cost-effective form of risk insurance.

13.13 SELLING OPTIONS OUTSIDE A HEDGING PROGRAM

In every case considered so far, whenever options were sold, the motivation was to generate funds in order to pay for other options being purchased. Selling options with no position in the underlying asset can be risky because of the unlimited potential for losses. However, a company with an existing exposure does have an underlying position. What if options were sold against that position?

The German company in our scenario has a need for dollars. Its position is short $1 million. If it sells a put option on $1 million there are two possible outcomes at maturity:

1. If the dollar is below the strike price, the option will be exercised against the company, which will end up buying dollars at the strike price. Normally an option seller loses out when an option is exercised, but in this case the company needs dollars anyway and so benefits in two ways if the option expires in-the-money. First, the company is able to buy the dollars it needs at a fixed price, and second, it has already received the option premium, which lowers the effective cost of the dollars.

2. If the dollar is above the strike price, the option expires worthless. The company gets to keep the premium received but has no protection against the rise in the dollar. The premium income therefore softens the blow by lowering the effective cost of the dollars purchased, but the option fails to compensate for a progressively stronger dollar.

As a specific example, suppose the company sells the dollar put struck at DEM 1.7000 for an initial consideration of DEM 0.0676 per dollar. This premium can be invested to earn interest over the nine-month period and will be worth DEM 0.0706 when the option expires. If the dollar ends up below DEM 1.7000, the company receives $1 million through the exercise of the option, but the premium received lowers the effective cost to DEM 1.6294, a saving in excess of 4%. If the dollar ends up higher then DEM 1.7000, the company must buy its dollars on the open market and must pay the going rate. The effective cost will then be the spot rate less DEM 0.0706.

Case Study 13–3
Using Compound Options

German Car Imports Inc. (GCI) is a U.S.-based company that imports and distributes Mercedes, BMW, and other prestige German cars. In six weeks' time, GCI is due to pay DEM 3,800,000 for the import of 30 cars. The dollar has recently risen to DEM 1.7000 but has met resistance at this level stemming from opinion about some important economic figures due out in Germany exactly a week from today. Unconfirmed market rumours suggest that these figures will be very favourable, and if these rumours are correct, the D-mark may recover to DEM 1.6500. On the other hand, if the figures are not so favourable, the dollar may break through the resistance level at DEM 1.7000 to reach DEM 1.7500.

GCI would suffer from a strengthening in the D-mark but does not want to cover at the current forward rate of DEM 1.7064 in case the D-mark weakens. A call on the D-mark struck at DEM 1.7000 is quoted at $0.0114 per DEM (equivalent to DEM 0.0328 per dollar). This is considered quite expensive, as volatility is high in anticipation of the forthcoming economic announcement. As an alternative, GCI seeks quotations for a number of short-term compound options with the following specification and obtains these figures:

Compound Option				
Type		Call on Put		
Strike price		$0.0114 per DEM	(DEM 0.0328 per $)	
Maturities (days)	7	10	14	
Premiums	0.0024	0.0028	0.0033	($ per DEM)
	0.0068	0.0080	0.0096	(DEM per $)

Underlying Option	
Type	Put on $/Call on DEM
Strike price	DEM 1.7000
Maturity	45 days
Premium	$0.0114 per DEM (DEM 0.0328 per $)

GCI decides to purchase a call on the dollar put, and chooses the 10-day maturity for the compound option, reasoning that the $/DEM exchange rate may not have settled sufficiently any sooner. The premium paid is therefore $0.0028 per DEM, a total of $10,640 in all. We will now consider three possible scenarios for the economic figures when they are announced:

1. The economic figures are good for Germany, and the D-mark strengthens to DEM 1.6500. With a strike price of DEM 1.7000, 35-day puts on the dollar are now trading at $0.0197 per DEM (equivalent to DEM 0.0537 per $). The compound option is well in-the-money, so GCI exercises it, paying a further $0.0114 per DEM, or $43,320. GCI has therefore spent a total of $53,960 to acquire the underlying option, which would now cost $74,860. Of course, had GCI bought the underlying option at the outset, it would have cost only $43,320.

2. The economic figures turn out bad, and the D-mark weakens to DEM 1.7500. The underlying option is now available at just $0.0023 per DEM (DEM 0.0071 per $) should GCI wish to purchase it. The compound option therefore expires worthless, so the original premium of $10,640 is lost. However, if GCI had bought the underlying option at the outset, the loss would have been $34,580—more than three times as much.

3. The economic figures are neutral, and the DEM remains at DEM 1.7000. The underlying option loses a little time value and is now trading at $0.0080 per DEM (equivalent to DEM 0.0230 per $). Once again, the compound option expires worthless, and GCI forgoes the premium of $10,640. However, the loss in time value for the underlying option is $12,920—an even greater amount.

We can now compare the strategy of buying the compound option with that of buying the underlying option at the outset under the three outcomes. If the D-mark strengthens, GCI is $10,640 worse off with the compound option strategy. If the D-mark remains the same, GCI actually gains $2,280 even though the compound option expires worthless. Finally, if the D-mark weakens, GCI is $23,940 better off with the compound option. GCI is therefore happy with its decision to go for the compound option.

FIGURE 13.17
Selling Options Outside a Hedging Program

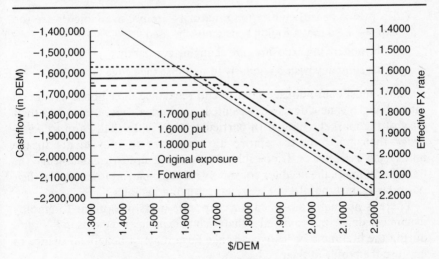

Figure 13.17 illustrates the profiles from a strategy of selling dollar puts using three different strike prices and compares these with the flat profile from buying dollars forward and the diagonal profile of the original exposure. The lower the strike price of the put sold the less likely it is to be

exercised, and so the profile approaches that of the original exposure. The higher the strike, the more likely the option is to expire in-the-money and the more the profile approaches that of the forward hedge.

It must be emphasised that selling options outside a hedging program does not provide any protection whatsoever, only a dilution of the risk. The German company might consider the strategy as a possible way to reduce costs, if it believed the market was most likely to remain static. However, the company would be well advised to buy an out-of-the-money call option as a kind of "disaster insurance" to provide protection in case the market were to move sharply against the original position. Interestingly enough, this amendment would create a collar, bringing us full circle in our review of strategies.

13.14 DYNAMIC HEDGING

Companies using options to hedge their currency exposure often employ a static hedging technique. This involves designing a hedging strategy, implementing it at the outset, and then leaving it alone. The options' maturity is designed to match the timing of particular transactions or exposures. When this particular time comes, in-the-money options are exercised or cash-settled, and the option payoff compensates for any adverse market movements that have occurred.

There are a number of circumstances when a dynamic hedging program is more beneficial

- If options of sufficiently long maturity are not available or are too expensive, so that a rolling hedge must be used.[6]
- If the underlying exposures are changing constantly.
- If the company wishes regularly to optimise the hedge.

Banks must continuously balance and rebalance their books as market rates change, as new deals are executed, as old deals mature, and as their view of the market changes. In particular, they will usually aim to *delta-hedge* their portfolio to remove any exposure to movements in the underlying asset prices. If possible, they will attempt to *gamma-hedge* the book to minimise the need for constantly rebalancing and to immunise their positions against the effect of step changes in market rates.

There is normally less need for corporate users of options to employ dynamic hedging, but companies that wish to exploit movements in FX rates during the lifetime of a hedge can take advantage of beneficial swings to improve the profile of their hedges.

---

[6] A rolling hedge comprises buying short-date options and then rolling them at or just before maturity into new short-date options. For example, to cover a two-year period start by buying a six-month option. When the first option matures six months later, buy another six-month option and repeat for the remaining periods.

A method frequently employed is to *roll up* or *roll down* the hedge when rates move in favour of the original exposure. It is easiest to illustrate this technique with a basic option hedge, but it can just as easily be applied to most of the other hedges illustrated in this chapter.

To illustrate rolling down a hedge, let us return to the German company introduced at the beginning of this chapter that had a $1 million payable in nine months. Assume that it starts with a basic option hedge and buys a call on the dollar struck at DEM 1.7000 for an up-front premium of DEM 0.0672 per dollar.

Three months later, the dollar falls so that the spot rate stands at DEM 1.5767, and the forward rate is now at DEM 1.6000. While the value of the call has declined to DEM 0.0188, a loss of DEM 0.0484, the underlying position makes the company 10pfg per dollar better off. At this point the company could roll the hedge down to a strike price of DEM 1.6000 by liquidating the existing DEM 1.7000 call and buying one struck at DEM 1.6000. The new premium payable would be DEM 0.0523, resulting in a net outlay of DEM 0.0335 per dollar.

Suppose that the dollar falls again, and three months later the spot dollar is trading at DEM 1.4889 and the forward dollar at DEM 1.5000. The company could repeat the process, and roll the hedge down from DEM 1.6000 to DEM 1.5000. This time, the option it is holding will have fallen to just DEM 0.0065, and the new option bought will cost DEM 0.0352, a net outlay of DEM 0.0287 per dollar. We can now summarise the transactions that have taken place.

At $t = 0$	Buy 9 month call struck at DEM 1.7000 @DEM 0.0672	−67,200
At $t = 3$ months	Sell 6 month call struck at DEM 1.7000 @DEM 0.0188	+18,800
	Buy 6 month call struck at DEM 1.6000 @DEM 0.0523	−52,300
		−33,500
At $t = 6$ months	Sell 3 month call struck at DEM 1.6000 @DEM 0.0065	+6,500
	Buy 3 month call struck at DEM 1.5000 @DEM 0.0352	−35,200
		−28,700

The company started with an at-the-money option struck at DEM 1.7000 for an outlay of DEM 0.0672. Ignoring the cost of financing the premium, the initial strategy therefore established the maximum rate for purchasing dollars as DEM 1.7672. After rolling down the hedge, the company ended up with an option struck at DEM 1.5000 for a total cost of DEM 0.1294, so that the most the company can now pay for its dollars is DEM 1.6294. The effect of this strategy is therefore to lock in gains from favourable movements in the underlying asset price, thereby establishing a new ceiling to the company's costs.

Figure 13.18 illustrates the strategy by showing the initial profile, the result after the first roll, and the final result after the second roll. As a reference, the diagram also shows the profiles from the forward hedge and the original exposure. It is interesting to note that after the first roll, the option strategy establishes a maximum cost comparable with that of the forward hedge. After the second roll, the company cannot pay more than DEM 1.633,900 when premium financing costs are taken into account, which is almost 4% cheaper than the original forward rate. Furthermore, the company stands to benefit from any decline in the dollar below DEM 1.5000.

Although the strategy of rolling a hedge has been illustrated with a basic option hedge, the principle works equally well with collars, corridors, participations, and other hedging structures. If the underlying asset price has moved in favour of the original exposure, options with strikes more in-the-money can be financed from the gains made, locking in savings and establishing a new ceiling for maximum costs. Although dynamic hedging may involve additional cash outflows prior to maturity, these will be more than offset by inflows at maturity. Alternatively, if the underlying asset price has moved against the original exposure, hedgers using structures like the corridor may prefer to buy back options sold as part of the hedge in order to avoid further losses if the market continues in the same direction.

FIGURE 13.18
Rolling Down a Hedge

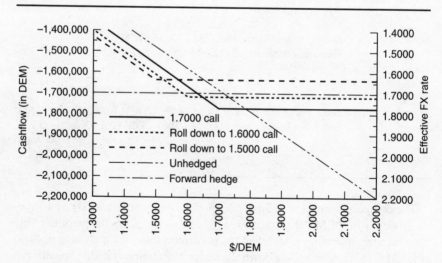

13.15 WHICH STRATEGY IS BEST?

This chapter has perhaps presented a bewildering array of financial engineering techniques to handle currency risk. The reader may be tempted to
ask, Which technique is best? Unfortunately, the answer to this question is
that no one technique is best for everyone. It depends upon the nature of
the exposure, the risk preferences of the user, and his view of the market.
Defining the user's hedging objectives carefully, as set out in Chapter
Twelve (Section 12.4), will narrow down the selection, and the summary
presented in Table 13.10 may help to clarify the choices available.

TABLE 13.10
Comparison of Hedging Structures

Strategy	Advantages	Disadvantages
Forward	No premium payable Provides guaranteed outcome	No ability to benefit from upside
Basic option hedge	Provides unlimited protection Unlimited ability to benefit from upside	Premium may be too expensive
Collar	Provides unlimited protection Limited ability to benefit from upside Smaller or zero-cost premium	Some losses if market moves adversely
Corridor	Price certainty over central range Unlimited ability to benefit from upside if market moves significantly	Protection ceases after a certain point
Participating Forward	Unlimited ability to benefit from upside	Forward component is at off-market rate
Ratio Forward	Ability to execute forward deal at better-than-market rate	Potential to suffer large losses from highly geared position
Break Forward	Ability to benefit if market moves significantly	Forward deal is at off- market rate

Chapter Fourteen

Managing Interest-Rate Risk Using FRAs, Futures, and Swaps

The term *interest-rate risk* implies an exposure to movements in interest rates, but this is a very general concept. As we saw in Chapter Nine, there are swap rates, zero-coupon rates, forward rates, and par yields, all of which are interest rates. Even after focusing upon just one type of rate, there is a range of different maturities from as short as one day to as long as forever. So in its widest sense, interest rate risk can encompass exposure to any type of interest rate at any point on the maturity spectrum. In practice, however, nearly all exposures fall into one of three much narrower categories.

First, there is exposure to a short-term rate of a specific maturity, but covering a single period in the future. A company treasurer who needs to borrow for three months, but starting in six months time, is a prime example. His exposure is to the three-month rate, but six months forward from now. This is exposure to a *short-term forward rate*.

The second exposure is also to a short-term rate of a specific maturity, but over a number of future periods. An investor who has just purchased a five-year FRN having coupons reset every six months is exposed to the six-month rate over the next 10 periods. The exposure here is to *a strip of short-term forward rates*.

Finally, there is exposure to an interest rate of one specific maturity. A pension fund that has purchased a 20-year fixed-income bond is exposed to movements in 20-year bond yields. A bank having executed a five-year swap is exposed to five-year swap rates. In both these illustrations, the exposure is to *spot yields*, namely, yields covering the period from now until a specified future date.

Forward rates and spot rates are closely linked, of course, and formulae for converting from one to the other were developed in Chapter Nine (Section 9.9). Nonetheless, in reviewing interest-rate risk we shall distinguish between different exposures according to which rate is the most prominent. For example, the investor with the five-year FRN will be thinking about the trend in future six-month rates and may consider entering into a swap to convert the floating receipts into a fixed stream. His focus will initially be on short-term forward rates. If the investor executes a five-year swap with his bank, the bank will subsequently focus on the five-year swap rate when managing the interest rate risk. Although the two risks are substantially the same, the viewpoints are different.

In dealing with interest-rate risk, this chapter will concentrate on techniques that seek to guarantee a particular result, thereby eliminating all uncertainty. The principal tools used here will be FRAs, futures, and swaps. The next chapter will then examine how option-based tools can be used to manage interest-rate risk more selectively, providing protection against the downside, together with the possibility to benefit from the upside.

14.1 USING FRAs

A full description of FRAs appeared in Chapter Four with a simple illustration of their use in hedging. FRAs cover a single specified period in the future and are therefore suitable for hedging exposures to short-term forward rates. In practice, FRAs are readily available in all major currencies, covering standard contract periods up to one year in length and up to one year into the future. In addition to all the standard contracts, such as 1×4 or 3×9, banks are normally prepared to quote for odd-dated periods such as a 3½-month contract period 4½ months in the future. In the case of nonstandard contracts, however, banks will usually quote a wider bid/offer spread to cover the extra cost of hedging.

If a user's interest-rate exposure is LIBOR-linked, and if the period covered exactly matches the dates of one of the standard contracts, an FRA can provide a perfect or near-perfect hedge. Case 14.1 studies a German industrial company using FRAs to lock in a particular rate. The FRA hedge proved perfect in practice, because the company was borrowing under a LIBOR-linked facility over a standard period. The company therefore achieved precisely the borrowing rate it expected when the hedge was set up. Note that hedging with FRAs guarantees a particular outcome, whether this is for better or worse. In the example illustrated, once the company has bought the FRA, its effective borrowing rate is inextricably linked to the FRA contract rate. If interest rates eventually fall below this rate, the company will not be able to benefit.

If there is any mismatch between the period of the risk exposure and the period covered by a standard FRA or between the interest rate bases used, the user has three broad choices.

The easiest route is for the user to exploit the flexibility of the OTC market and obtain a customised quotation from a bank. The advantage of this alternative is that the resulting contract can be tailored to fit the specification of the underlying risk exposure, once again resulting in a near-perfect hedge. Against this is the slightly higher cost of entering into a nonstandard FRA contract, which is usually reflected in a rate just a little removed from the theoretically fair market rate.

Case 14–1
Using FRAs to Lock in a Borrowing Rate

Kraftwerk GmbH is a medium-sized German industrial company producing high-quality machined components for other manufacturing companies. In November 1992, Kraftwerk's Director of Finance is planning the company's budget for 1993 and anticipates a seasonal borrowing requirement averaging DEM 5 million from May to November of the coming year.

Interest rates have been relatively high for Germany since the early 1990s, mainly as a result of the economic impact of reunification. From an average of around 5% in the years 1985–1989, interest rates have shot up to their current level of 9%. To obtain a more precise idea of the structure of interest rates, the Finance Director contacts his bank and obtains the following quotations for cash and FRA rates.

Euro-Currency Deposits		*FRAs*			
1mo.	$8^{11}/_{16}$– $8^{15}/_{16}$	1×4	8.75	1×7	8.37
2mo.	$8^{3}/_{4}$– 9	2×5	8.43	2×8	8.10
3mo.	$8^{11}/_{16}$ – $8^{15}/_{16}$	3×6	8.12	3×9	7.83
6mo.	$8^{7}/_{16}$– $8^{11}/_{16}$	4×7	7.82	4×10	7.57
9mo.	$8 – 8^{1}/_{4}$	5×8	7.61	5×11	7.40
12mo.	$7^{13}/_{16}$– $8^{1}/_{16}$	6×9	7.40	6×12	7.23
		9×12	6.93		

The downward-sloping yield curve in the cash market and declining prices in the FRA market both point to expectations of sharply lower interest rates in Germany over the next year. Kraftwerk's Finance Director is not so sure that rates will be lower and, if they are, whether they will be as low as the implied forward rates suggest. He therefore decides to lock in the six-month forward rate by buying an FRA with the following specification:

Notional principal	DEM 5,000,000	Fixing date	Tue, May 18, 1993
Dealing date	Wed, Nov 18, 1992	Settlement date	Thur, May 20, 1993
Spot date	Fri, Nov 20, 1992	Final maturity date	Mon, Nov 22,1993
Contract rate	7.23%	Contract period	186 days

On May 18, 1993, D-mark LIBOR fixes at 7.63%. While rates did decline from the $8^{11}/_{16}$% offer rate in November 1992, the Finance Director was correct in his supposition that rates would not fall to 7.23%. The settlement sum received on May 20, 1993 was DEM 9,941.43, calculated according to equation 4.3 thus:

$$\frac{(0.0763 - 0.0723) \times 5000000}{(360/186) + 0.0763} = 9,941.43$$

Kraftwerk was able to invest the settlement sum at 7.00% to earn an extra DEM 359.55 interest, bringing the total proceeds from the FRA to DEM 10,300.98 by the final maturity date. On May 18, Kraftwerk was able to borrow the DEM 5,000,000 it needed at the prevailing rate of 7.63% plus its normal borrowing margin of 30bp. This facility was drawn down on May 20 and repaid 186 days later on November 22. On this final maturity date, the cash flows were as follows:

	DEM
Total proceeds from FRA	10,300.98
Interest payable on DEM 5 million borrowed for 186 days at 7.93%	204,858.33
Net borrowing costs after deduction of FRA proceeds	194,557.35

The net borrowing cost of DEM 194,557.35 gives an effective borrowing rate of 7.53%, which is the FRA rate plus Kraftwerk's 30bp margin, exactly what was expected. The FRA has therefore enabled Kraftwerk to lock in the precise borrowing rate it anticipated when setting up the hedge.

The second alternative is to hedge with the closest available standard FRA contracts and accept the residual basis risk, namely, that the hedge will perform slightly differently from the underlying exposure. Depending upon the gap between the original exposure and a standard FRA, the basis risk will not be large and will almost invariably be just a fraction of the unhedged risk exposure.

The last alternative is to hedge with standard FRA contracts, but to manage the basis risk. Since users of futures contracts face exactly the same problems, methods have been developed within the futures market to minimise basis risk. These techniques are examined in detail in the next section and, to avoid repetition, will not be repeated here. FRA users who have nonstandard exposures, but wish to use standard FRAs, can apply the same techniques.

14.2 USING SHORT-TERM INTEREST-RATE FUTURES

One of the key differences between FRAs and futures is the flexibility of the former compared with the standardisation of the latter. It is possible, in theory at least, for a client to ask a bank to design an FRA tailored to match the exact features of a particular interest-rate exposure. With futures there is no such choice, and users have to accept the standard features of the contracts quoted. This means that there are a number of headings under which differences may arise between a risk exposure and the particular futures contract used to hedge. Table 14.1 summarises the potential problem areas.

Fortunately, for every problem area, there is a solution. Apart from the timing problem caused by a mismatch between the exposure date and the futures expiry date, all of the other difficulties itemised in Table 14.1 can be

TABLE 14.1
Potential Problem Areas Caused by Standardisation of Futures

Principal at risk	Contract size is fixed, e.g., $1million
Exposure period	Contract length is fixed, e.g., three months
Exposure date	Contracts mature on fixed dates, e.g., third Wednesday of March, June, September, and December
Exposure basis	Contract settlement linked to one market rate, e.g., LIBOR
Settlement sum	Futures tick value is constant, e.g., $25
Margining	Maintaining margin account leads to unpredictable cash flows through life of contract

solved by calculating the futures hedge ratio properly. Section 14.3 explains exactly how this should be done. In some circumstances, using a strip hedge can further reduce the basis risk arising from any mismatch in the exposure period, and Section 14.4 compares the use of the strip with the more common stack hedge. There is even a way of dealing with the one outstanding difficulty—the exposure date problem—and Section 14.6 presents a practical solution.

Methods therefore exist to circumvent the problems caused by standardisation of futures contracts. However, it should be pointed out that many of the techniques reviewed are merely refinements enabling the hedger to approach perfection ever more closely. Once the basic hedge ratio is calculated, and this depends solely on the amount of principal at risk and the length of the exposure period, a simple futures hedge will normally neutralise at least 80% of the risk exposure.

Whether a user needs to go to the trouble of applying some of the more sophisticated techniques depends upon how important it is to achieve 100% hedge efficiency. For many companies, the effort involved may simply not be worthwhile. In the case of very large risks run by other companies or the tiny profit margins that some banks operate within, the quest for the perfect futures hedge may be the *sine qua non* of success.

14.3 CALCULATING THE HEDGE RATIO

With a customised FRA hedge, the characteristics of the FRA can be adjusted to match the original risk exposure. Once this is done, the behaviour of the hedge should mirror that of the underlying risk. In particular, the change in market value of the hedge should offset exactly the change in value of the exposure. In other words, the tick values should be the same.

There is no such flexibility for the futures contract, whose tick value is always constant. If it is not possible to tailor an individual contract so that its tick value matches that of the underlying risk, the alternative is to adjust the number of standard contracts used. The essence of calculating the correct hedge ratio is then to determine how many futures contracts must be bought or sold such that the aggregate tick value of the hedge portfolio matches that of the underlying risk.

By taking the appropriate factors into account, the hedge ratio can adjust for

- Principal at risk   • Settlement sum
- Exposure period   • Margin flows
- Exposure basis

The first two factors are of paramount importance, and no futures hedge can be constructed without taking these into account. The remaining factors add further layers of sophistication and would only be necessary for large or rate-critical hedges. To reflect this, we will define the hedge ratio as having two major components:

$$HR = HR_{basic} \times HR_{advanced} \tag{14.1}$$

where

HR	is the final hedge ratio
HR_{basic}	is the component of the hedge ratio adjusting for principal at risk and exposure period
$HR_{advanced}$	is the component of the hedge ratio adjusting for exposure basis, settlement sum, and margin flows

Each of the hedge ratio's major components can in turn be broken into its constituents thus:

$$HR_{basic} = HR_{principal} \times HR_{period} \tag{14.2}$$

and

$$HR_{advanced} = HR_{expbasis} \times HR_{settlement} \times HR_{margin} \tag{14.3}$$

where

$HR_{principal}$	is the component of the basic hedge ratio adjusting for principal at risk
HR_{period}	is the component of the basic hedge ratio adjusting for the length of the exposure period
$HR_{expbasis}$	is the component of the advanced hedge ratio adjusting for the exposure basis
$HR_{settlement}$	is the component of the advanced hedge ratio adjusting for the settlement sum
HR_{margin}	is the component of the advanced hedge ratio adjusting for margin flows.

For noncritical applications, it is possible to set $HR_{advanced} = 1$ and use just the basic hedge ratio. Alternatively, if one or two of the components of $HR_{advanced}$ are important, they can be calculated properly and the remaining component(s) set to unity.

We will now show how each of these hedge ratio components can be calculated and then illustrate the construction of a futures hedge with a specific example.

Principal at risk. This is one of the easiest components to calculate; it is simply the ratio of principal at risk to the notional principal of the futures contract.

$$HR_{principal} = \frac{Principal\ of\ underlying\ risk\ exposure}{Notional\ principal\ of\ futures\ contract} \tag{14.4}$$

For example, if the underlying risk exposure was a $50 million borrowing, and this was being hedged with the three-month eurodollar contract, which has a notional principal of $1 million, $HR_{principal}$ would simply be 50.

Exposure period. This is also straightforward to calculate; it is the ratio of the length of time covered by the underlying risk to the length of time covered by the deposit underlying the futures contract.

$$HR_{period} = \frac{Period\ covered\ by\ underlying\ risk}{Period\ covered\ by\ deposit\ underlying\ futures\ contract} \tag{14.5}$$

Note that the denominator has nothing to do with the time from now until expiry of the futures; rather it is the fixed period specified as part of the contract definition. For example, if a one-year borrowing commitment was being hedged by the three-month eurodollar contract, the fixed period would of course be three months, and HR_{period} would be four.

Exposure basis. Nearly all futures contracts are based on three-month LIBOR, the most popular being the contracts on eurodollars, euroyen, euromark, and three-month sterling. There are very few exceptions, the most notable being the 30-day Federal-funds contracts at the CBOT and the one-month LIBOR contract at the CME. Trading volume in both these cases is unfortunately somewhat limited.

In nondollar currencies, the choice is therefore limited to the respective three-month contract, while the relative lack of liquidity in the very short-term dollar contracts may effectively rule them out.[1] This restriction may not present a problem if the underlying exposure is directly linked to the three-month LIBOR rate in one of the above-mentioned currencies, but there are many situations where the risk exposure may differ, for example:

---

[1] The Federal-funds contract is also unusual in having the settlement linked to the *average* of Fed funds rates during the contract month rather than to the rate prevailing on any one day.

- Borrowing linked to bank base or prime rate.
- Borrowing or investment linked to commercial paper rates.
- Borrowing denominated in a currency where no interest rate futures contract exists.

The solution in all these examples is to use a related futures contract and to adjust the hedge ratio according to the relationship between the eurocurrency rate underlying that contract and the interest rate underlying the risk.

As an example, consider the case of a U.S. company whose borrowing is linked to prime rate. Eurodollar rates and prime rate tend to move together, but if the company is to use eurodollar futures successfully as a hedge, the interrelationship between these rates must be defined more closely. Fortunately, there is a statistical technique that can determine the nature of this association. By performing a *regression analysis* on past observations of eurodollar rates and the prime rate, it is possible to obtain an equation of the form

$$PRIME = \alpha + \beta \times EURO \tag{14.6}$$

In relation to futures hedging, the most im. ortant aspect of this equation is the β coefficient, which defines the extent to which prime rate moves when the eurodollar rate changes. Another important by-product of the regression analysis is the correlation coefficient, normally given the symbol ρ, which measures the reliability of the relationship as defined by the equation.

To illustrate how regression analysis works, Figure 14.1 shows a scatter diagram of monthly observations on eurocurrency and prime rates over a three-year period.[2] The leftmost point, for instance, represents one particular month where eurodollar rates were 5.68% and prime rate was 7.90%. The line of best fit, defined by equation 14.6, is also shown in the diagram.

With the data used in this particular illustration, the regression analysis produces the following formula linking prime rate with eurodollar rates:

$$PRIME = 2.38 + 0.87 \times EURO$$

This formula means that, whenever eurodollar rates change by 100bp, the prime rate moves in the same direction by only 87bp. In addition to determining the values for the coefficients α and β, the regression analysis also calculated the value of the correlation coefficient as being 0.92. This indicates a very strong link between the two sets of observations in this case.

What we have been looking for is a suitable value for $HR_{expbasis}$—the factor that specifies how the hedge ratio should be amended to adjust for the exposure basis. In fact, $HR_{expbasis}$ is simply the β coefficient from the regression analysis. In other words:

---

[2] The figures used here are actual market rates, but users planning to hedge should carry out their own regression analysis using the most recent data available. Spreadsheet packages such as Microsoft® Excel and Lotus® 1-2-3® include regression facilities that make the task of performing this analysis quite straightforward.

$$HR_{expbasis} = \beta \qquad\qquad (14.7)$$

If the U.S. company is hedging a borrowing facility linked to the prime rate, the number of futures contracts required must be reduced by a factor of 0.87 to allow for the finding that prime rate tends to move less than the eurodollar rate. If the company does not make this adjustment, it will end up being overhedged.

Settlement sum. The settlement sum for an FRA[3] explicitly takes into account the number of days in the contract period and is discounted to allow for the sum being paid at the beginning of the contract period rather than on the final maturity date. If the settlement sum for interest rate futures contracts were calculated in the same way, the tick value could be as low as £11.25 for a sterling three-month contract, as discussed in Chapter Seven (Section 7.1). Tick values, however, are constant for any particular type of short-term interest rate futures contract, regardless of day counts or discounting conventions. The eurosterling contract on LIFFE, for example, always has a tick value of £12.50. This means that the settlement sum can be as much as 10% too large

FIGURE 14.1
Applying Regression Analysis

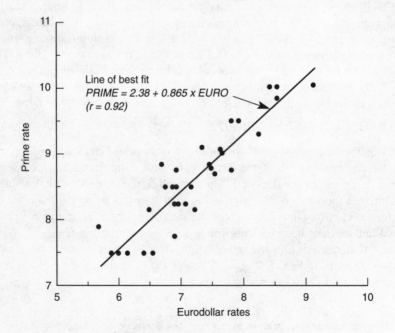

---

[3] See equation 4.2 in Chapter Four.

or 5% too small if this anomaly is not taken into account. To adjust for this feature, the hedge ratio can be modified by $HR_{settlement}$ defined thus:

$$HR_{settlement} = \frac{1}{t\left[\dfrac{BASIS}{DAYS} + 1 - \dfrac{FP}{100}\right]} \tag{14.8}$$

where

t is the nominal length of the futures contract (in years)

$BASIS$ is the day-count convention (e.g., 360 for dollars, 365 for sterling)

$DAYS$ is the actual number of days in the futures period (usually 91, but not always)

FP is the current futures price.

For example, if eurosterling futures were trading at 93.72 and the contract length was 91 days, $HR_{settlement}$ would be 0.9819.

Equation 14.8 provides the correct hedge ratio adjustment, assuming that the futures contract is held until maturity. If it is planned that the hedge will be liquidated prior to the maturity of the contract, a modified version of the formula must be used:

$$HR_{settlement} = \frac{1}{t\left[\dfrac{BASIS}{DAYS} + \left(1 - \dfrac{FP}{100}\right)\left(1 + \dfrac{T}{DAYS}\right)\right]} \tag{14.9}$$

where

T is the number of days prior to maturity that the futures position will be closed out.

Margin flows. Having to manage the daily mark-to-market process and the attendant flows of variation margin is a mixed blessing. Apart from the administration involved, paying or receiving variation margin prior to the liquidation or maturity of the futures position can distort the result of a futures hedge. It is not the flows of margin *per se* that causes this distortion, but the interest paid or earned on these flows. Whether the flows of margin are positive or negative, the effect of interest will increase the magnitude of the flows, and so the size of the futures hedge must be scaled down accordingly.

Suppose that a user has taken into account all preceding adjustments and has calculated that the number of contracts required is N. Ignoring the interest on variation margin, the sum that will eventually be received when the contracts mature or are liquidated is

$$VM_{total} = N \times (F_T - F_0) \times TV \tag{14.10}$$

where

VM_{total} is the total variation margin paid or received, ignoring interest

N is the number of futures contracts

F_0 is the futures price at inception
F_T is the futures price at maturity or liquidation
TV is the tick value of the contract

Let us make the assumption that the futures price moves in a linear fashion from F_0 to F_T so that the flow of variation margin on any day t will be given by

$$VM_t = \frac{N \times (F_T - F_0) \times TV}{D_H} \qquad (14.11)$$

where

VM_t is the variation margin on day t
D_H is the number of days in the hedging period

Let us now assume that the user can either borrow or invest at a rate of interest i. The variation margin flow on day t will now result in interest of $VM_t \times i \times [(D_H - t)/BASIS]$ on the remaining days until maturity. Summing this expression over the lifetime of the hedge, and simplifying, gives

$$VM_{total} = \sum_{t=1}^{D_H}\left[VM_t \left(1 + i\ \frac{(D_H - t)}{BASIS}\right)\right]$$

$$= N \times (F_T - F_0) \times TV \left[1 + \frac{i}{2}\ \frac{(D_H - 1)}{BASIS}\right] \qquad (14.12)$$

$$= VM_{total} \times \left[1 + \frac{i}{2}\ \frac{(D_H - 1)}{BASIS}\right]$$

where

i is the rate of interest for short-term lending or borrowing

In other words, the variation margin actually paid or received is increased by the factor on the extreme right of equation 14.12. To allow for this, the hedge ratio must therefore be decreased by this factor, giving

$$HR_{margin} = \frac{1}{\left[1 + \frac{i}{2}\ \frac{(D_H - 1)}{BASIS}\right]} \qquad (14.13)$$

Adjusting the hedge ratio in this way is known as *tailing the hedge*. Note that equation 14.13 does not include either F_0 or F_T because these variables cancel out. It is therefore not necessary to guess where the futures price may ultimately settle, nor even whether variation margin will be paid or received. The only information needed is the prevailing interest rate i and the length of the hedging period D_H. Although the rate of interest for lending and borrowing will differ in practice, this makes very little difference to the calculation of HR_{margin}.

To illustrate the construction of an adjusted futures hedge, Case 14.2 looks at the case of a London-based investment fund attempting to hedge its interest-rate exposure in the aftermath of the September 1992 sterling currency crisis.

Case 14–2
Using Futures with an Adjusted Hedge Ratio

Fund Management Company Ltd. (FMC) runs a number of investment funds, each one denominated in one of the world's major currencies. On October 5, 1992, FMC was reviewing strategy for its sterling-based fund. The £25 million proceeds from a maturing investment are due to be received on Monday, March 15, 1993, and FMC wishes to place this on short-term deposit for a six-month period. The company has an arrangement with a major bank whereby it will receive a rate for the entire period fixed at 25bp below the bank's base rate two working days prior to making the deposit.

The impact of recent developments on UK interest rates is, however, causing FMC some concern. Just two weeks ago sterling was driven out of the European ERM, and base rates have just been lowered by 1% from 10% to 9%. The futures market is already discounting another half-point fall by December and a further half-point by next March. However, FMC believes that with sterling outside the constraints of the ERM, interest rates in Britain will actually fall further and faster than the futures market expects.

FMC therefore decides to hedge with LIFFE eurosterling futures and proceeds to calculate the appropriate hedge ratios based upon the following details:

Today's date	Mon, Oct 5, 1992	Current base rate	9%
Fixing date for deposit	Thur, Mar 11, 1993	Current futures price (Mar 93)	92.05
Value date for deposit	Mon, Mar 15, 1993	Hedging period	157 days
Maturity date for deposit	Wed, Sep 15, 1993	Deposit period	184 days
Deposit size	£25,000,000	Maturity date for future	Wed, Mar 17, 1993
Contract size	£500,000	Futures period (Mar 93)	91 days

Regression equation $BASE = -0.05 + 0.9889 \times EURO$

Using the relationships defined in equations 14.4, 14.5, 14.7, 14.8, and 14.13, FMC was able to calculate the following hedge ratios:

$HR_{principal}$	50.0000	HR_{basic}	101.1000
HR_{period}	2.0220	$HR_{advanced}$	0.9509
$HR_{expbasis}$	0.9889		
$HR_{settlement}$	0.9779	HR	96.1360
HR_{margin}	0.9832		

FMC therefore buys 96 March 93 eurosterling contracts at a price of 92.05, depositing £120,000 in interest-bearing securities as the initial margin. (The margin requirement has since changed.) The futures price of 7.95% implies a base rate of 7.81%, and therefore an investment rate for FMC of 7.56%.

A few weeks later, base rates in Britain were lowered to 8%, and the price of March 93 futures stabilised at around 94, implying a drop in rates to 6% by that time. FMC therefore collected over £200,000 in variation margin almost immediately and was able to invest this to earn £4,463.02 in interest on the margin inflows before eventually liquidating the futures position.

On March 11, 1993, FMC sold its futures at 94.10 to realise £246,000 profit (205 ticks at £12.50 per tick). With interest, the total profit from the futures hedge was therefore £250,463.02. This sum, together with the principal of £25 million, was invested on March 15, 1993 for six months at 5.75%, 25bp below the then base rate of 6%.

> The interest earned over the six-month period was £731,917.53, making the final proceeds on September 15, 1993 amount to £25,982,380.55. This increase of almost £1 million on the original principal of £25 million is equivalent to receiving 7.79%. Using equation 12.1, the hedge efficiency was 103%, within 3% of perfection. The extra 23bp fortuitously realised in this case was mainly due to the lack of convergence between the futures and the underlying eurosterling rates.

14.4 STACK VERSUS STRIP HEDGES

The methodology discussed in the previous section defines *how many* futures contracts should be bought or sold. It does not, however, specify *which* contracts should be used. The answer depends upon two factors:

- The liquidity of the particular futures market.
- The period covered by the underlying risk exposure.

For some contracts on some futures exchanges, liquidity only exists in the nearest contract. In such cases, there is really only one choice: use the nearest contract regardless of the underlying risk exposure properties. Where liquidity exists across a range of futures maturity dates, and in particular where it extends beyond the final maturity date of the underlying risk, there are two strategies available—the stack hedge and the strip hedge.

To illustrate the difference between these two techniques, consider hedging a $10 million six-month borrowing that commences at the beginning of March. Using equations 14.2, 14.4, and 14.5, the basic hedge ratio is 20, implying that 20 futures contracts must be sold.

The *stack hedge*, as the name implies, involves using a stack of futures contracts all with the same maturity date. The contract selected should be the first one maturing *after* the rate is fixed on the underlying risk exposure. There is no point in buying a contract that matures earlier, because the position will need to be rolled into the later contract to preserve the hedge. In the case of the $10 million borrowing, this means selling 20 March contracts right now and then liquidating them in early March, the moment the rate is fixed on the loan.

The *strip hedge*, also self-evident from its name, involves using a strip of futures contracts that covers the underlying exposure as closely as possible. Once again, the first contract in the strip should mature after the rate is fixed on the underlying risk, while the period covered by the last contract in the strip will normally extend beyond the underlying exposure. To hedge the $10 million borrowing with a strip hedge will therefore entail selling 10 March and 10 June contracts.

A strip hedge is therefore only relevant for underlying exposures whose maturity is longer than the period covered by a single futures contract. In practice, this normally means an exposure having a maturity that is some multiple of the futures period. For shorter maturities, or in the case of illiquid futures markets, the stack hedge is the clear choice. Figure 14.2 illustrates both techniques and should help to make the distinction between them somewhat clearer.

The stack hedge is easier to implement, because it involves executing a trade in only one futures contract, whereas a strip hedge will involve trades in several. The drawback, however, is that the stack hedge introduces another *basis risk*. Hedging a six-month rate with three-month futures contracts relies on the implicit assumption that three-month and six-month rates move together. If this assumption is valid, then futures prices will track the three-month rate, which in turn will move in step with changes in the six-month rate. The three-month futures would then be a reasonable hedge for an exposure linked to the six-month rate. If, however, the assumption is not valid, the stack hedge will be less than perfect, and the strip hedge will prove more reliable.

FIGURE 14.2
Stack versus Strip Hedges

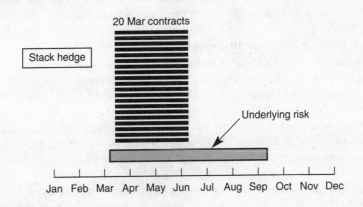

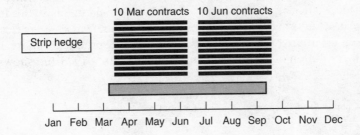

The reason why a strip hedge minimises this particular basis risk lies in the way that strips of futures combine to give a single forward rate. If $f_1, f_2, \ldots, f_n$ are the individual forward interest rates implied by a strip of n consecutive futures contracts, then the single forward rate f_{strip} implied by the entire strip is given by equation 14.14, where the period covered is less than or equal to one year:

$$(1 + ntf_{strip}) = (1 + tf_1) \times (1 + tf_2) \times \ldots \times (1 + tf_n) \qquad (14.14)$$

or by equation 14.15 for periods greater than a year:

$$(1 + f_{strip})^{nt} = (1 + tf_1) \times (1 + tf_2) \times \ldots \times (1 + tf_n) \qquad (14.15)$$

where

f_{strip} is the futures strip rate
f_n is the interest rate implied by the nth futures contract
n is the number of contracts in the strip
t is the nominal length of the futures contract (in years)

Given the efficiency of financial markets in general and of futures markets in particular, f_{strip} will closely follow the forward rate over the strip period. If this were not the case, an arbitrage opportunity would open up. For example, if the futures strip rate were lower than the market forward rate, arbitrageurs could sell futures and sell the equivalent FRAs and capture the profit from any gap between the prices.

In the case of the March–June strip illustrated in Figure 14.2, the strip of two three-month contracts will follow the six-month forward rate from mid-March to mid-September. Most important is what happens when the March contract finally matures. At that time, the relationship between three-month and six-month rates will not matter, because the strip rate will match the prevailing six-month rate. For example, if the yield curve is positive, so that six-month rates were higher than three-month rates, the forward rate implied by the June contract will lie above the March implied rate.[4] This will price the strip rate above the three-month rate, and arbitrage will ensure that it matches the six-month rate. The opposite would be true if the yield curve were negative: the six-month rate would lie below the three-month rate and be matched by the strip rate.

The implication is that hedgers using stack hedges will be exposed to a basis risk. If the slope of the yield curve changes between the time the hedge is established and the time when the hedge is liquidated, the stack hedge will not be 100% efficient. A strip hedge, if available, would minimise this basis risk, because the strip rate would follow the exposure rate much more closely.

To see whether this basis risk is significant in practice, Figure 14.3 plots the evolution of eurodollar rates from 1985 until 1993 and shows all

---

[4] See Chapter Seven (Sections 7.2 and 7.3) for a full explanation.

FIGURE 14.3
Eurodollar Rates, 1985–1993

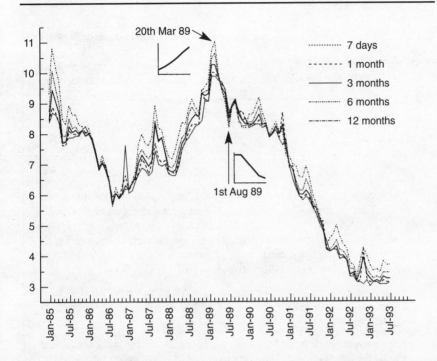

maturities ranging from seven days to one year. At first glance, the rates appear to move in unison, as a tightly-packed bunch. Indeed, a statistical analysis shows that the correlations between movements in rates with adjacent maturities, for example, three- and six-month rates, are all in excess of 0.99. Even the correlation between seven-day and one-year rates is as high as 0.96.

Despite this appearance, it is nonetheless possible for the basis to change very substantially. The two thumbnail sketches within Figure 14.3 illustrate this by showing the yield curves on two dates just four months apart. On March 20, 1989, the yield curve was upward-sloping with one-year rates more than 1% above short-term rates. By August 1, that year, the yield curve had inverted, and the one-year rate was now 56bp below short-term rates. This degree of twist in such a short time could have wreaked havoc with a stack hedge.

Even when the yield curve does not change direction so dramatically but just alters its slope, a stack will be less efficient than a strip hedge. Case 14.3 provides a concrete example of just such a situation, which arose after interest rates in Great Britain fell following sterling's exit from the ERM in September 1992.

Case 14–3
Stack versus Strip Hedge

FMC, the fund management company introduced in Case 14.2, needs to hedge against a fall in sterling interest rates between today—October 5, 1992—and March 15, 1993, when the company will receive £10 million that it plans to invest at LIBID for one year. Market rates on October 5, 1992, are as follows:

3 months	9%	Mar 93	92.25
6 months	8³/₄%	Jun	92.33
12 months	8⁷/₁₆%	Sep	92.27
		Dec	92.04

Using equation 14.14, the one-year forward rate implied by the futures strip is 8.01%. This is already 43bp down from the prevailing 12-month rate of 8⁷/₁₆%, but FMC believes that sterling rates will be much lower by March next year.

FMC first calculates the hedge ratio using the techniques previously described and finds that it needs to buy 75 futures contracts altogether. The company then considers two alternative strategies:

1. Implement a stack hedge by buying 75 MAR 93 contracts.
2. Implement a strip hedge by buying 19 MAR, 19 JUN, 19 SEP, and 18 DEC contracts.

After reviewing the potential basis risk inherent with the stack hedge, and encouraged by the depth and liquidity of the market in sterling futures, FMC decides to execute the strip hedge. Given a 12bp gap between LIBID and LIBOR, the company expects to earn 7.89% on its investment.

On March 11, 1993, FMC agrees to invest its £10 million for value on March 15 at the prevailing rate of 5¹/₂%. At the same time, the company liquidates the futures hedge at the following prices:

Mar 93	94.10	Sep	94.72
Jun	94.51	Dec	94.69

The futures hedge gained £213,525. With interest on the variation margin, not only during the five months while the contracts were held, but also over the 12 months of the investment period, the final proceeds are £229,101.25, equivalent to 229bp on a £10 million one-year investment. The effective yield was therefore 7.79%, just 10bp below the expected rate. Using equation 12.3, and setting T_{MIN} to 5.5%, the strip hedge proved to be 96% efficient.

Had FMC chosen the stack hedge instead, the effective investment rate would only have been 7.36%, and the hedge efficiency would therefore have dropped to 78%. In this example, the strip hedge therefore proved much more effective at hedging the interest rate risk.

To summarise: A strip hedge is the ideal choice when the length of the underlying exposure is a multiple of the futures period and if there is acceptable liquidity in the later futures contracts. If the exposure period is shorter, if the back contracts are illiquid, or if the application is not so critical that 100% hedge efficiency is the goal, then the stack hedge is an acceptable and simpler alternative.

14.5 DIFFERENT KINDS OF BASIS RISK

The term *basis risk* has been used a number of times already in this chapter in a number of different contexts. In general, basis risk arises when there is a difference between the behaviour of the underlying exposure and that of the hedging instrument. There are, however, a number of distinct causes of basis risk, and it is now appropriate to categorise them properly. Two of the following headings have already been discussed, while the third one will be analysed in the next section.

Exposure basis. This form of risk arises when the basis for determining the interest rate differs between the exposure and the hedge. A good example would be an investor hedging rate risk on a 90-day T-bill portfolio by using three-month futures contracts. Although both rates cover a similar duration, there will be discrepancies between fluctuations in Treasury bill yields and movements in eurocurrency rates. Section 14.3 showed how the hedge ratio can be adjusted to allow for this form of basis risk, but there is no way of eliminating this particular risk.

Period basis. As the name suggests, this risk occurs when the duration of the exposure and hedge differ. When the exposure is a multiple of the length of the hedging instrument, this basis can be minimised or even neutralised completely using a strip hedge, as explained in the previous section. If the exposure period is shorter than the hedging instrument, the hedge ratio can also be adjusted using equation 14.5, but this time a residual basis risk will remain.

Convergence basis. The price of a short-term interest rate derivative such as an FRA or a future will usually differ from the prevailing cash market rate, because the derivative reflects the forward interest rate, while the cash market reflects the spot interest rate. When the derivative is a futures contract, the gap between futures and cash prices is called the basis; this was defined in Chapter Seven (Section 7.3). Basis in this context is governed by the shape of the yield curve, for it is the slope of the yield curve that determines the relationship between spot and forward interest rates. As a derivative approaches maturity, the basis will gradually decline until it reaches zero on the maturity date itself. If the design of a hedge involves holding a derivative until maturity, there is no risk that the hedge result will differ from the market rate underlying the hedging instrument. If, however, the hedge design necessitates liquidating the hedge prior to its normal maturity, there will be a risk that basis will not have converged as expected. This would happen if the yield curve changes shape after the hedge is established.

All three types of basis risk thus relate to different aspects of the yield curve. Exposure basis arises when there are two different yield curves: one for the exposure and the other for the hedging instrument. Period basis and convergence basis are both caused by changes in the shape of a single yield curve, but at different points in the maturity spectrum. Period basis occurs when the yield curve changes shape between the tenor of the futures contract and the tenor of the exposure and is therefore affected by slightly longer-term rates. In contrast, convergence basis arises from the short-term yield curve bending. Section 14.4 explained how the period basis could be handled with a strip hedge; the next section analyses how convergence basis can be reduced using spreads.

14.6 MANAGING THE CONVERGENCE BASIS

To see how convergence basis can be managed, it is first necessary to understand exactly how it arises in the first place, and this is most easily done with a specific illustration. Suppose that time $t=0$ is mid-December, and the short-term yield curve is defined by the rates tabulated in Table 14.2.

TABLE 14.2
Example Yield Curve at $t=0$

Tenor (months)	Zero-Coupon Rate
1	8.53%
2	8.76
3	8.95
4	9.16
5	9.30
6	9.41
7	9.49
8	9.57
9	9.64
10	9.70
11	9.76
12	9.81

Using the techniques explained in Chapter Nine (Sections 9.8 and 9.9), it is possible to calculate a set of discount factors from any yield curve and then to derive a set of forward rates for any specific date in the future. Figure 14.4 shows the initial yield curve at $t=0$ and projected yield curves for the following three months.

The final yield curve in mid-March when $t=3$ is a stable rate structure such that all future projected yield curves will be the same. In particular, the three-month rate at $t=3$ is projected to be 9.65%, and all futures maturing in mid-March or thereafter will be priced at 90.35.

As the diagram shows, the yield curves are projected to rise steadily over the next three months, so that three-month rates starting at 8.95% will increase to 9.30%, 9.52%, and finally to 9.65%. With March futures at 90.35, the basis is therefore projected to be +70bp at $t = 0$, +35bp at $t = 1$, +13bp at $t = 2$, and zero at $t = 3$.

Suppose a company needs to borrow $30 million for three-months commencing in mid-February at $t = 2$. A basic hedge would involve selling 30 March contracts at 90.35, with a view to buying these back after two months when the loan was drawn down. The borrowing rate implied by this hedge is the futures implied rate of 9.65% less the expected basis of +13bp, or 9.52%, in other words, the three-month forward rate in two months.

If rates turn out just as expected, the company will borrow at the then prevailing rate of 9.52%. The futures can be bought back at 90.35, the same as the original price, and will therefore generate neither profit nor loss. The

FIGURE 14.4
Projected Yield Curves

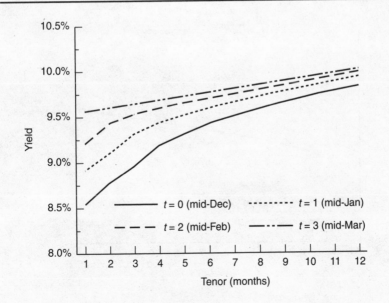

hedge would therefore be perfect, because the actual borrowing rate would precisely match the expected rate.

Now let us explore some less comfortable alternatives. What if there was a parallel shift in the yield curve? What if the yield curve were to change shape and twist? Figure 14.5 illustrates these two possibilities.

If all interest rates were to rise by a constant amount, say 50bp, all forward rates would also rise by about 50bp, and all futures prices would fall by a similar amount. Under these circumstances, the company would be forced to borrow at 10.02% instead of the 9.52% expected. Fortunately however, the futures price would have dropped to 89.86, enabling the company to make a 49bp profit on the hedge. The net borrowing rate would thus be 9.53%, within 1bp of the expected result. Depending upon whether equation 12.2 or 12.5 is used, the hedge efficiency can be expressed as 99.90% or 98%. Either way, the hedge has proved near-perfect despite a considerable jump in interest rates.

While the basic hedge can cope admirably with a parallel shift in the yield curve, it is not so successful if the yield curve changes shape. Suppose that the yield curve became steeper, pivoting about the three-month point, exactly as pictured in the last graph of Figure 14.5. The three-month interest rate would still be 9.52%, enabling the company to borrow at this rate, but all other rates would be different. In particular, the forward rates would be higher and futures prices lower. With the rate scenario illustrated, the company would find that it could buy back the futures at 90.15, making a

FIGURE 14.5
Parallel Shifts and Twists in the Yield Curve at t=2

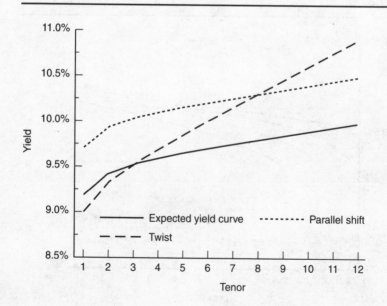

spurious profit of 20bp. This is all very well, but this profit could have been a loss if the yield curve had twisted the other way.

The risk arising from convergence basis has thus manifested itself following an unanticipated nonparallel change in the shape of the yield curve when the hedge was liquidated prior to its maturity. Note the qualifications: *unanticipated* and *nonparallel*. It is evident from Figure 14.4 that the yield curve was expected to change shape as time progressed. These anticipated changes in the yield curve do not cause problems, because the pricing of futures and other derivatives takes these changes into account. Furthermore, we have already shown that a parallel shift in the yield curve does not cause difficulties either. The problems arise from an unexpected steepening or levelling of the yield curve.

The answer to the problem lies in executing a spread strategy in addition to the basic futures hedge. As Chapter Seven (Section 7.8) has already demonstrated, a futures spread is exposed to the slope of the yield curve. By adding a suitable spread position, the slope risk of the basic hedge can be offset by the slope exposure of the spread. After some analysis it is possible to show that the number of contracts required to minimise the convergence basis risk is

$$N_{spread} = N_{basic} \times \frac{t_{prior}}{t_{contract}} \qquad (14.16)$$

where

N_{spread}	is the number of contracts in the spread hedge
N_{basic}	is the number of contracts in the basic futures hedge
t_{prior}	is the length of time between the hedge being liquidated and the futures maturity date
$t_{contract}$	is the length of time covered by the futures contract (usually 91 days)

Note that the sign of N_{spread} is the same as that of N_{basic}. In other words, if the basic hedge involves selling futures, the spread hedge will also involve selling spreads. The decision whether to buy or sell the spread there has nothing to do with the view of how interest rates may evolve.

In the example of the company planning to liquidate the basic hedge at $t = 2$, one month prior to the maturity date of the futures contracts, N_{spread} would be $-30 \times \frac{1}{3} = -10$ contracts. The full hedge would then comprise

1. Selling 30 March contracts at 90.35.
2. Selling 10 March–June spreads (i.e., sell 10 March and buy 10 June contracts) at par.

After the twist in the yield curve, the March contracts will fall to 90.15 and the June contracts to 89.58. The result of the complete hedging strategy would therefore be a

1. Profit of 20bp from the basic hedge: (90.35 – 90.15).

2. Loss of 19bp from the spread position: ⅓ × [(89.58 – 90.15) – (0)].

The net result would be a 1bp profit. The net borrowing cost would therefore be 9.51%, within 1bp of the expected result of 9.52%. Addition of the spread hedge has therefore returned the futures hedge to almost 100% efficiency, despite the unexpected twist in the shape of the yield curve.

The spread hedge will improve hedge efficiency under most circumstances when the yield curve changes shape, but it will not always produce as perfect a result as the one shown here. How efficient the spread hedge proves to be will depend upon the precise way in which the yield curve twists. If the yield curve remains rigid and pivots about the three-month rate, the spread hedge should be almost perfect. Close examination of Figure 14.5 will reveal that the scenario illustrated does satisfy this condition. This finding means that a combination of basic and spread hedges will perfectly hedge any change in rates brought about by a combination of a parallel shift in the yield curve plus a pivoting of rates around the three-month rate. There are other shape changes that will also result in 100% hedge efficiency, and even those that do not will generally be improved by the spread hedge. Whether it is worthwhile implementing this additional strategy will depend upon how critical the application is.

14.7 INTERPOLATED HEDGES

The final example in the previous section involved hedging a $30 million three-month risk commencing in mid-February with two structures:

1. Basic hedge selling 30 March futures.

2. Spread hedge selling 10 spreads in March and June futures.

If the hedge was initially established in late December, after the maturity date of the December contracts, there would have been no other choice. Had the hedge been set up earlier, however, there would have been an alternative, the *interpolated hedge*.

As the name suggests, an interpolated hedge is one in which the exposure period falls across or between two or more contract periods and can therefore be hedged with a mixture of the overlapping contracts. In the case of a three-month exposure starting in mid-February, there is a one-third overlap with the period covered by the December contract and a two-thirds overlap with the period covered by the March contract. This would suggest creating an interpolated hedge by selling 10 December and 20 March contracts. Interestingly enough, this combination can also be viewed as a

1. Basic hedge selling 30 March futures.

2. Spread hedge selling 10 spreads in December and March contracts.

The net position is exactly the same. This means that an interpolated hedge is no different in principle from the combination of a basic and spread hedge, except that the spread uses contracts one expiry date earlier.

Note that interpolated hedges have only a limited life. When the near contract expires, the hedge must be rolled into the next contract period, which will create the spread hedge discussed in the previous section. There is therefore little advantage in implementing the interpolated hedge if there is sufficient liquidity in the far contracts, because it will involve extra work in rolling the hedge. If there is sufficient depth in the longer-date futures, it is generally easier to set up the basic and spread hedge right at the outset and to leave it.

14.8 COMBINING THE TECHNIQUES

We have thus far presented a range of hedging techniques for managing exposure to short-term forward rates. The simplest method is to apply a basic hedge according to the length of the exposure period and the amount at risk. Where futures or standard FRAs are used, additional refinements can be added:

- Adjusting the hedge ratio to account for exposure basis, the settlement sum, and margin flows.
- Using a strip hedge where the exposure period is long.
- Using a spread or interpolated hedge where there is a gap between the exposure date and derivative dates.

The more refinements that are added, the closer the hedge will approach perfection. It is for the user to decide at what point the pursuit of perfection must surrender to the cost of designing and implementing the hedging scheme.

14.9 FRAs VERSUS FUTURES

Table 6.3 in Chapter Six has already presented a general comparison of futures and cash markets, while Chapter Seven (Section 7.7) included a detailed comparison of FRAs with short-term interest rate futures.

The single most important contrast is the flexibility of the FRA against the standardisation of the futures contract. Nevertheless, despite the rigidity and inflexibility of futures contracts, the techniques presented in this chapter allow a hedger to attain near perfection in the performance of an interest rate hedge. In favour of futures is their tremendous liquidity and the attendant ease with which positions can be reversed or adjusted if necessary. Also in favour of futures is the almost complete lack of credit risk, but against this must be weighed the administrative chore of running the margin account. Finally, contract sizes in interest rate futures tend to be quite large, and

FRAs might therefore be the only viable alternative for the medium-sized company with exposures less than $1 million or £500,000.

There is therefore no universally better choice between FRAs and futures, and both are used extensively for managing exposure to short-term forward rates. For most companies, however, the scales probably tip in favour of using FRAs, especially if there is little likelihood that a hedge will need to be reversed or liquidated prior to the normal maturity date. Companies should, however, check that they are obtaining a reasonable quotation with an acceptable spread if a two-way price is requested. Banks make use of both products, trading FRAs between themselves and making heavy use of futures in order to hedge their own interest rate exposures.

14.10 USING SWAPS

The discussion has so far concentrated on exposures to a single short-term forward rate. We can now turn our attention to risks influenced by a series of short-term forward rates. If FRAs and futures were the appropriate tools to handle exposure to a single forward rate, the multi-period equivalent of an FRA—the interest rate swap—is the obvious tool for managing exposure to multiple interest periods in the future.

Since swaps are invariably OTC instruments, they can be tailored to suit both the requirements of the user and the characteristics of the underlying exposure. There is often a greater need to customise a swap, because there are many more variables than for an FRA covering just a single interest period. Fortunately, the longer time period covered by a swap makes their inherent profitability that much greater, and banks do find it worthwhile to design nonstandard swaps to meet a specific application. Nonetheless, the majority of swap applications can be handled by the assortment of plain-vanilla swaps that are traded on the highly liquid swaps market.

Swap applications can be split into two main categories. Asset-linked swaps originate when a swap is bound with a particular asset in order to change the characteristics of the income stream for investors. Liability-linked swaps arise from the need to alter a borrower's cash flows. To some extent, this division is somewhat artificial, because a swapped debt instrument is both a liability to the issuer and an asset to the investor who holds the bonds. The distinction, if one exists, emphasises the party whose needs were the strongest driving force when the swap structure was created.

To illustrate some of the varied ways in which swaps can be applied, the following examples and case studies will demonstrate liability-linked, asset-linked, and nonstandard swaps in action. A final scenario will explore two ways in which an existing swap may be cancelled.

Liability-linked swap—floating-to-fixed. One of the most straightforward swap applications is converting a floating-rate borrowing facility into a fixed-rate one, thereby eliminating any further exposure to interest rate movements. As an example, consider a company currently borrowing floating-rate for three years at six-month LIBOR + 80bp. The corporate treasurer fears that interest rates may rise and therefore wishes to lock in the cost of funds at present levels. After receiving an acceptable quotation for three-year semiannual swaps at 7.40–46% against LIBOR flat, the company enters into a three-year semiannual swap as the fixed-rate payer. The cash flow streams are depicted in Figure 14.6, from which it is evident that the swap effectively converts the floating rate obligation of LIBOR + 80bp into a fixed-rate obligation of 8.26%. This will insulate the company against any rise in interest rates, although it will also prevent the company from benefiting should interest rates fall.

Liability-linked swap—fixed-to-floating. Somewhat less common is the switch from fixed-rate to floating-rate financing, but a swap can facilitate this conversion. An example would be the case of a company that issued seven-year fixed-rate debt two years ago paying an annual coupon of 9.75%. It chose to borrow fixed-rate mainly to avoid interest-rate risk, but also because it did not think that interest rates were likely to drop. Since then, its view has been proved wrong, and interest rates have fallen dramatically. The yield curve is currently very steeply upward-sloping, with 6-month LIBOR at 4.5%, 12-month LIBOR at 5%, two-year swaps at around 6%, and five-year swaps at roughly 7%. The finance director now wishes to take advantage of the lower rates currently available and obtains a quotation for five-year annual swaps at 6.95–7.05% against 12-month LIBOR flat. If the company enters into a five-year annual swap receiving the fixed-rate at 6.95%, the liability will be converted into a floating-rate obligation at LIBOR + 280bp, as shown in Figure 14.7. With 12-month LIBOR at 5%, the cost of borrowing would therefore fall from 9.75% to just 7.80%, a very substantial saving.

A problem with this strategy is that the company now becomes exposed to rising interest rates. The steep upward-sloping yield curve implies that 12-month rates in five years time would be around 9.5%. Borrowing at LIBOR+280bp would push the effective rate to 12.3% under these circumstances, considerably higher than the original fixed rate of 9.75%. The swap

FIGURE 14.6
Liability-Linked Floating-to-Fixed Swap

FIGURE 14.7
Liability-Linked Fixed-to-Floating Swap

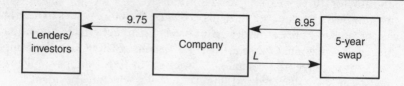

therefore provides an immediate saving of 1.95%, but could give rise to future costs of a similar order or even more should rates rise as the forward yield curve predicts. If the company decides to enter into this particular liability-linked swap, this is tantamount to taking the view that rates will not rise as much or as fast as the yield curve suggests.

Liability-linked swap—fixed-to-floating-to-fixed. Once a liability has been swapped, there is nothing preventing the corporate treasurer from entering into additional swaps at a later date. This might be motivated by a shift in the borrower's requirements, a change in outlook, or to take advantage of a beneficial movement in market rates. As an example of this kind of dynamic hedging, consider the case of a company that two years ago borrowed for an original tenor of five years at a fixed rate of 8.65%, and entered at the same time into a swap receiving fixed at 8.26% against paying six-month LIBOR flat. After swapping, the company's liability is effectively floating-rate at LIBOR + 39bp. Suppose that swap rates have now fallen, so that three-year semiannual swaps are now quoted at 5.80–85%. The company can now switch back to fixed-rate to take advantage of the lower rates now available. If the company enters into a second swap paying the fixed-rate at 5.85% for three years against receiving six-month LIBOR flat, the net cost of the entire structure is a fixed-rate liability of 6.24%, as Figure 14.8 shows. The saving of 2.41% compared to the original fixed borrowing cost of 8.65% is just the difference between the two swap rates.

Liability-linked swap—cross-currency floating-to-floating. Large companies, especially multinationals, are able to tap the capital markets in several countries and in a number of currencies. This opens up several alternative sources of finance, and the availability of interest rate and cross-currency swaps means that finance can be obtained from the cheapest market and swapped into the currency and format desired. As an example, a multinational chemicals company based in the UK that is planning a new debt issue finds that it can issue sterling-denominated 10-year debt at 8.20% fixed, or dollar-denominated floating-rate debt for a similar maturity at dollar six-month LIBOR+12bp. Ten-year sterling interest rate swaps are 8.02–07% against six-month LIBOR, dollar interest rate swaps are quoted at

FIGURE 14.8
Liability-Linked Fixed-to-Floating-to-Fixed Swap

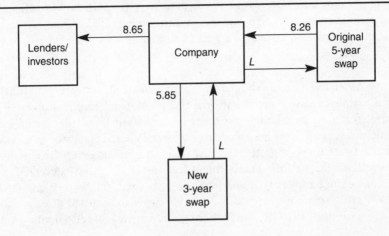

7.55–65%, also against six-month LIBOR, and the sterling-dollar cross-currency basis swap is quoted at sterling six-month LIBOR–5bp/LIBOR–1bp against dollar six-month LIBOR flat. The company's existing exposure creates a preference for floating-rate sterling finance, leaving two choices:

- Borrow fixed-rate sterling at 8.20% and swap into floating using the sterling interest rate swap.
- Borrow floating-rate dollars and switch into floating-rate sterling using the cross-currency basis swap.

The first alternative creates floating-rate sterling finance at LIBOR + 18bp. The second alternative, using a cross-currency swap is just a little more complex, but is justified in this case by the savings made possible. Rather than use a plain-vanilla basis swap, the company can enter into a nonstandard cross-currency swap paying sterling LIBOR + 11bp and receiving dollar LIBOR + 12bp.[5] This structure exactly matches the floating-rate dollar financing and therefore ensures that all dollar cash flows net to zero. The remaining liability comprises just the payments of sterling at LIBOR + 11bp, resulting in a saving of 7bp over the first alternative. The two alternatives are illustrated in Figure 14.9.

Asset-linked swap—floating-to-fixed. Many borrowers issue floating-rate notes, but many investors require a fixed-income security. A swap can

---

[5] The standard swap would involve the company receiving dollar LIBOR flat against paying sterling LIBOR–1bp. This is less neat, because it leaves the company with a small residual cash flow in dollars of 12bp. Adding this 12bp margin to the dollar flows means adding about 12bp to the sterling flows, creating the nonstandard basis swap actually used.

easily effect this transition. For example, the portfolio manager of a pension fund may have purchased a prime quality seven-year floating-rate note paying six-month LIBOR+43bp, but wish to swap the cash flows to create a fixed-income stream. If swaps for this maturity are quoted at 7.55–60%, the resulting structure will generate a fixed return of 7.98%, as Figure 14.10 makes clear.

Asset-linked swap—fixed-to-floating-to-fixed. For every liability-linked swap structure there is a mirror-image asset-linked one. Figure 14.8 illustrated the dynamic hedging strategy of a company that had issued fixed-rate debt, swapped this into a floating-rate liability, and then swapped back into fixed-rate financing after interest rates had fallen. Investors can also employ dynamic portfolio management techniques. Take the example of an investor holding a five-year bond paying 6.55% fixed, but who believes that interest rates are about to rise. If five-year swaps are quoted at 6.22–28% against six-month LIBOR, the investor can create a synthetic floating-rate

FIGURE 14.9
Liability-Linked Cross-Currency Floating-to-Floating Basis Swap

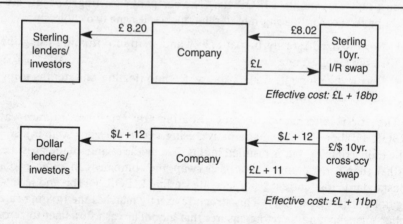

FIGURE 14.10
Asset-Linked Floating-to-Fixed Swap

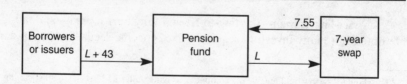

note paying LIBOR + 27bp. Two years later interest rates have indeed risen, and three-year swaps are now quoted at 7.85–92% against six-month LIBOR. By entering into the reverse swap, the investor can create a new synthetic fixed-rate bond paying 8.12%. The 1.57% yield pick-up is the difference between the fixed rates for the two swaps. The final structure is pictured in Figure 14.11.

Nonstandard swap. The possibilities to tailor swaps are almost unlimited, and almost any feature of a swap's characteristics can be amended to match the specific requirements of the swap counterpart. Chapter Nine (Section 9.4) reviewed most of the nonstandard swap structures commonly found. Case 14.4 reviews the circumstances surrounding one particular company's needs and the way in which these were met through the creation of a hybrid swap structure in which one leg featured both fixed-rate and floating-rate payments.

Cancelling a swap. In most cases, companies using swaps to hedge long-term interest-rate exposures will enter into a swap that matches their existing obligations and then maintain the swap until maturity. On occasions, however, the company's position or viewpoint may change, and the swap may no longer be needed. In such circumstances there are three broad choices.

FIGURE 14.11
Asset-Linked Fixed-to Floating-to-Fixed Swap

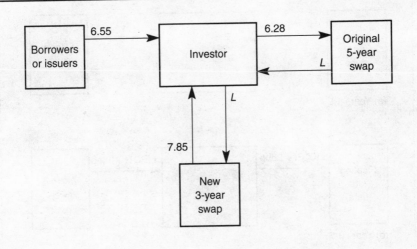

Case 14–4
Using a Nonstandard Swap

Associated Manufacturing Industries Inc. (AMI) is currently servicing $50 million of 12.25% fixed-rate debt with an original maturity of five years. Since obtaining the borrowing facility three years ago, interest rates have fallen by between 2% and 3%. Unfortunately, AMI's competitors are now able to borrow five-year funds at around 10%, and the additional interest burden—in excess of $1 million per year—is placing AMI at a significant disadvantage. Moreover, when the existing facility matures, AMI will need to refinance its present facility for a further three years, but the company fears that interest rates will have risen by then.

AMI has therefore asked its bankers to structure a nonstandard swap, which must simultaneously achieve two objectives:

- Borrowing costs under the existing facility must be reduced to below 11% for the remaining two years.

- Interest costs under a new three-year floating-rate borrowing facility at LIBOR + 25bp, to commence in two years, must also be limited to a maximum of 11%.

The left side of Figure 14.12 depicts the cash flow streams arising from AMI's debt obligations, while the right side illustrates what the swap must achieve. For the first two years, AMI pays a fixed-rate of F% into the swap,

FIGURE 14.12
Nonstandard Swap Structure for AMI Inc.

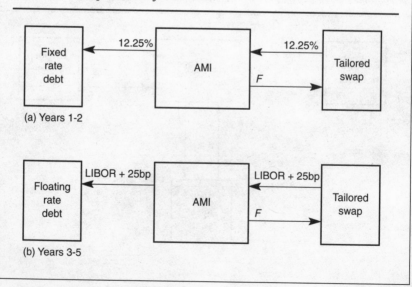

and receives 12.25% fixed. So long as F is less than 11%, this structure will achieve the first objective. In the remaining three years, AMI again pays F% into the swap, but this time receives LIBOR + 25bp, thus achieving the second objective. The swap effectively replaces the fixed-rate debt obligations of the first two years and the floating-rate obligations of the last three years with a fixed-rate cash flow at F%. This makes the swap distinctly nonstandard, having one fixed leg and one hybrid fixed-floating leg.

Using the set of rates for standard swaps shown in the adjoining table, AMI's bank was able to structure and price the requisite nonstandard swap with F set at 10.91%. AMI is therefore able to save 1.34% from its present funding costs and lock into a fixed sub-11% cost now for floating-rate funding due to commence in two years' time. These are the two goals that AMI established.

Quoted Rates for Standard
Annual/360 Swaps

Tenor	Swap Rate
1 year	10.12%
2 year	10.00
3 year	9.90
4 year	9.82
5 year	9.75

Perhaps the simplest option is for the company to enter into a second swap whose purpose is to negate the first. This has the advantage that the existing swap need not be touched but the disadvantage that there will be small residual cash flows if the two swaps do not exactly cancel each other out. For example, suppose a company originally entered into a seven-year swap paying 7.46% annually against receiving LIBOR flat. Two years later the company decides that it no longer needs the original swap and attempts to reverse it by entering into another swap, this time receiving the fixed-rate for five years against paying LIBOR flat. The two floating-rate streams will match exactly, so long as the second swap is taken out on the anniversary of the first. However, unless the two swap rates are identical, which is most unlikely, the two fixed-rate streams will not net to zero. For example, if the second swap was concluded at 6.75%, the company would end up paying the difference of 71bp per annum for the next five years.

The problem of using an offsetting swap is potentially worse if the company tries to offset the original swap on a day other than one of the fixing dates. Either the company will have to tolerate a timing mismatch for the two swaps, which could be months apart, or seek a quotation for a nonstandard swap, which will normally be more expensive.

The second choice is to approach the swap counterparty, normally a bank, and ask for a quotation to cancel the swap. As an example, the company currently paying 7.46% fixed under a swap with five years remaining until maturity might be quoted a cancellation fee of 298bp if prevailing swap rates had dropped to 6.75%. The calculation here is relatively straightforward and involves the bank evaluating the net present value of the future cash flow streams under the swap. Table 14.3 shows how this calculation would be done, and the technique can easily be extended to value swaps on days other than a fixing date. Using the zero-coupon valuation method, as explained in Chapter Nine (section 9.7), there is no need to take into account accrued interest between payment dates. Each future cash flow, fixed or floating, is present-valued using the calculated or interpolated discount factor for that date, and the net present value of all these flows gives the fair price for cancelling the swap.

If the cancellation fee were set to 298bp on a swap with a nominal principal of £10 million, the company would therefore make a single payment of £298,000 in order to extinguish all future obligations under the swap. This payment is designed to compensate the swap counterparty for losing the benefit of receiving a 7.46% coupon when interest rates had fallen below that level. Of course, if interest rates had risen, the fixed-rate payer would expect to receive rather than pay the fee if the swap were cancelled.

The third possible way to cancel a swap is to assign the obligations under the swap to a willing third party. If the swap has a non-zero net present value, however, a fee must be paid by one of the parties to the other. This fee will be similar or identical to the cancellation fee just discussed and provides compensation for the party taking on an off-market swap. Assignment is often the least favoured alternative because of the credit risk implications.

TABLE 14.3
Cancelling a Swap

Year	Swap Rates	Discount Function	Original Fixed Payments	Current Fixed Payments	Difference	PV of Difference
1	5.00%	0.952381	746,000	675,000	71,000	67,619.05
2	5.50	0.898217	746,000	675,000	71,000	63,773.41
3	6.00	0.838645	746,000	675,000	71,000	59,543.82
4	6.38	0.778906	746,000	675,000	71,000	55,302.29
5	6.75	0.717471	746,000	675,000	71,000	50,940.42
NPV						297,178.99

14.11 HEDGING BOND AND SWAP PORTFOLIOS

The last form of interest-rate risk manifests itself as exposure to a single long-term interest rate or spot yield. This is in contrast to the risks discussed earlier in this chapter, for which the exposure was to one or more forward rates. The two most common situations in which this long-term interest rate risk arises is when institutions hold portfolios of bonds or swaps.

Most banks running a large book of swaps use an integrated risk management technique. Rather than attempt to hedge the swaps portfolio separately, the exposures arising from swaps, FRAs, interest rate futures, bond futures, bonds, and any other interest-rate instrument are all combined and just the net exposure is managed. This avoids the suboptimal and more costly approach whereby each book is separately hedged.

There are two major steps involved in implementing this method. For each instrument within the portfolio

1. Identify the specific point(s) on the yield curve where exposure exists.
2. Evaluate the present value of a basis point (PVBP) at each such point.

The PVBP provides a precise figure defining how much the instrument will change in present value given a 1bp movement in the yield curve at that point. As an example, the five-year swap analysed in Tables 9.7 and 9.8 is only sensitive to the five-year swap rate, and the five-year PVBP is $4,026.17. If the five-year swap rate were to rise by 1bp, the swap would be worth $4,026.17 more to the fixed-rate payer. Immediately after the rate for the first floating leg is fixed, however, this particular swap would also have an exposure to the 12-month rate and a 12-month PVBP of −$934.49. A rise in the twelve-month rate of 1bp would make the swap worth $934.49 *less* to the fixed-rate payer.

Once all the PVBPs are known, the exposures at each point in the yield curve can be aggregated, and the combined risk at that point hedged with the appropriate instrument. For points in the yield curve up to about two years, a combination of FRAs and interest rate futures can be used. From this point until 10-year maturities, swaps provide a liquid and efficient hedging instrument, but bonds can also be used. Beyond 10 years, bonds and bond futures currently provide the only effective hedging tools.

To continue the example just discussed, let us assume that a bank was the fixed-rate payer on the above-mentioned swap, and the interest rate for the first floating leg has just been determined. The resulting exposure could be hedged in two parts. Selling a strip of 37 eurodollar futures contracts covering the period up to one year into the future would hedge the exposure to 12-month rates, while buying $12,839,304 face value of a five-year zero-coupon bond would hedge the exposure to five-year rates. This particular hedge has been designed so that the PVBP of the hedging instruments closely matches the PVBP of the swap, but many other permutations of hedging instruments could have been chosen with the same end result.

14.12 HEDGING BOND PORTFOLIOS WITH BOND FUTURES

Although hedging a bond portfolio can be viewed as a subset of the wider task of hedging interest-rate risk, a particularly common activity is the hedging of bond portfolios using just bond futures. This section will therefore explain how this particular task can be accomplished.

Chapter Eight (Section 8.3) explained how bond futures were priced and noted how bond futures tend to track movements in the cheapest-to-deliver bond. This enabled us to design a simple but effective technique for hedging a portfolio containing just the cheapest-to-deliver bond, whereby futures contracts are sold with a nominal value equal to the conversion factor times the face value of the bonds to be hedged. In the example given in that chapter, a portfolio containing $10 million of the cheapest-to-deliver bond with a conversion factor of 1.1298 was successfully hedged by selling 113 futures contracts.

In practice, however, investors will hold bond portfolios that are much more widely diversified. Such portfolios can also be successfully hedged with bond futures, but the hedge design must now be executed in two stages:

1. Determine the relative volatility of the bonds to be hedged compared with the cheapest-to-deliver bond.
2. Determine the relative volatility of the cheapest-to-deliver bond compared with the bond futures contract.

The number of futures contracts required to hedge the holding of any target bond is then

$$N = \frac{NOM_{TGT}}{NOM_{FUT}} \times RV_{TGT \to CTD} \times RV_{CTD \to FUT} \qquad (14.17)$$

where

NOM_{TGT}	is the nominal value of the target bond
NOM_{FUT}	is the nominal value of the futures contract
$RV_{TGT \to CTD}$	is the relative volatility of the bond to be hedged compared with the cheapest-to-deliver bond
$RV_{CTD \to FUT}$	is the relative volatility of the cheapest-to-deliver bond compared with the futures contract

This formula is quite logical. If, hypothetically, the price of the target bond tends to move twice as much as that of the cheapest-to-deliver bond, and the price of the cheapest-to-deliver bond tends to move twice as much as that of the futures contract, it is sensible that futures contracts amounting to four times the nominal value of the target bond need to be held to effect a satisfactory hedge.

The method for determining the relative volatility of the target bond with respect to the cheapest-to-deliver bond depends upon the similarity between them. If both are government bonds, their respective yields will tend to move together. In this case, relative volatility can be measured mathematically using bond duration, and this technique will be explained very shortly. If the target bond is different, for example a eurobond or a corporate bond, then there is a distinct possibility that the yield spread between the target bond and the cheapest-to-deliver bond may change when yield levels change. In that case, relative volatility should be measured using regression analysis.

Assuming that the target and cheapest-to-deliver bonds are both priced from the same yield curve and that this yield curve tends to exhibit parallel rather than nonparallel shifts, the relative volatility between the two bonds can be determined using the modified duration of the two bonds. From the basic definition of modified duration[6] the change in the price of any bond caused by a small change in interest rates is given by

$$\Delta P = -MD \times P \times \Delta i \tag{14.18}$$

where

ΔP is the change in the price of a bond
MD is the modified duration
P is the price of the bond
Δi is the change in interest rates

It follows directly from equation 14.18 that the relative volatility of the target bond can be calculated as

$$RV_{TGT \to CTD} = \frac{\Delta P_{TGT}}{\Delta P_{CTD}} = \frac{MD_{TGT}\, P_{TGT}}{MD_{CTD}\, P_{CTD}} \tag{14.19}$$

where

MD_{TGT} is the modified duration of the target bond
MD_{CTD} is the modified duration of the cheapest-to-deliver bond
P_{TGT} is the price of the target bond
P_{CTD} is the price of the cheapest-to-deliver bond

Some textbooks and practitioners advocate using the ratio of the conversion factors of the two bonds as a surrogate for relative volatility. This is totally wrong. Conversion factors are principally influenced by the coupon of a bond, whereas price volatility is largely a function of a bond's maturity. One is not a substitute for the other. If the target bond was a long-dated low-coupon bond and the cheapest-to-deliver bond was a short-dated high-coupon bond, the relative volatility calculated properly using modified duration would be much greater than one, but the relative volatility calculated from conversion factors would be much less than one. The resulting hedge could easily be out by a factor of two or more times. Using conversion factors to measure relative volatility therefore has no foundation either in theory or in practice.

---

[6] See any textbook on bond mathematics for an explanation of this point, such as Frank J. Fabozzi, *Fixed Income Mathematics* (Chicago: Probus, 1993).

If the target and cheapest-to-deliver bonds are priced from different yield curves, it may be better to rely on a regression analysis using recent historical data. The daily price movements between the two bonds of interest can be analysed to determine the slope of the regression line, as illustrated in Figure 14.1 and discussed earlier in this chapter. Proprietary information services such as the Bloomberg system make this kind of analysis very straightforward.

These techniques therefore provide an answer to the first stage in designing an appropriate hedge. The answer to the second stage is much easier and has already been encountered in Chapter Eight (Section 8.6). Rearranging equation 8.12 slightly, we obtain

$$RV_{CTD \to FUT} = \frac{\Delta P_{CTD}}{\Delta FP} \approx CF_{CTD} \tag{14.20}$$

where

ΔP_{CTD} is the change in the price of the cheapest-to-deliver bond
ΔFP is the change in the price of the bond futures contract
CF_{CTD} is the conversion factor of the cheapest-to-deliver bond

We now have everything we need in order to design a reasonable futures hedge designed to insulate a bond or portfolio against movements in interest rates.

To illustrate this technique, Table 14.4 itemises the contents of a portfolio of six different U.S. T-bonds on October 5, 1992. The market value of the portfolio in October 1992 was a shade over $120 million for bonds having a face value of exactly $100 million. Of the six bonds in the portfolio, only two

TABLE 14.4
Hedging a Bond Portfolio with Bond Futures Contracts

		October 5, 1992		February 22, 1993				
Bond	Nominal Amount ($m)	Price	Yield (%)	Price	Yield (%)	Modified Duration	Relative Volatility	Number of Contracts
6⅜ Jul 99	12	103-12	5.76	103-29	5.63	5.40	0.4382	59.4
13⅛ May 01	16	146-03	6.13	145-16	6.01	5.61	0.6435	116.3
6⅜ Aug 02	22	101-02	6.22	101-21	6.13	7.20	0.5709	141.9
9⅜ Feb 06	8	122-26	6.74	125-08	6.46	8.08	0.7789	70.4
11¼ Feb 15	24	143-07	7.30	147-26	6.96	10.03	1.1274	305.7
7¼ Aug 22	18	98-28	7.34	102-25	7.02	11.94	0.9271	188.5
TOTAL	100							882

would be deliverable under the T-bond futures contract, and neither of these was the cheapest-to-deliver bond. The cheapest-to-deliver bond was, in fact, the 9¼% February 2016, which was priced at exactly 121-00 on October 5, 1992, to yield 7.35% and had a conversion factor of 1.1298 and a modified duration of 10.52 years.

Suppose that the portfolio manager was satisfied with the gains achieved thus far and wished to secure the value of the portfolio against any further developments in market prices over the next few months. The table shows the results of using equations 14.17, 14.19, and 14.20 in order to calculate the appropriate bond futures hedge.

For example, the number of futures contracts required to hedge the first bond in the portfolio is given by

$$\frac{12,000,000}{100,000} \times \frac{5.40 \times 103.375}{10.52 \times 121.00} \times 1.1298 = 59.4$$

Note that it is the conversion factor of the cheapest-to-deliver bond that is used in every case, not that of the target bond.

Since most of the bonds have shorter maturities and larger coupons than the cheapest-to-deliver bond, the relative volatilities are, with one exception, less than one. The total number of futures contracts needed turns out to be 882, rather less than the 1,000 that might be suggested by a naive estimate based on nominal values alone. The portfolio manager therefore needed to sell 882 futures contracts and selected the March 93 contract, then trading at 104–13.

In late February 1993, the portfolio manager decided to lift the hedge, before liquidity in the March contract started to dry up. The 882 futures contracts were sold at a price of 110–10 to realise a loss of

882 contracts × 189 ticks × $31.25 = –$5,209,312.50

At the same time, the general fall in bond yields had lifted the value of the portfolio from $120,008,750.00 to $122,108,750.00, a gain of exactly $2,100,000. At the same time, the coupon income accrued over the 140-day period was $3,445,087.19. Ignoring any interest earned on the coupons received[7] the net gain in the value of the portfolio was $335,774.69 after the loss on the futures is taken into account. Using equation 12.5, this result implies a hedge efficiency of almost 94%.

To be absolutely correct, however, one should measure the hedge efficiency by comparing the behaviour of the hedged portfolio with the outcome if the bond portfolio had been completely liquidated and the proceeds invested to earn interest. If the bond portfolio had been sold off, the value of the investment would have grown from $120,008,750.00 to $121,292,176.91, assuming that short-term interest rates were 2.75%. When this is taken into account, the hedge efficiency falls to 78%.

---

[7] This is a reasonable assumption in this case, since almost 70% of this coupon income was received just one week before the hedge was lifted.

Either way, this is still a fairly impressive result, but the hedge was not perfect for a number of reasons:

1. The futures price did not exactly track the price of the cheapest-to-deliver over the period.
2. The yield curve did not move in a parallel shift. Five-year bond yields moved down by around 12bp, while 30-year yields dropped by about 33bp.
3. The bond future selected was not ideal for all of the bonds in the portfolio. In particular, one of the bonds was a short-dated high-coupon bond whose price actually fell despite the fall in bond yields.[8]

To achieve even greater efficiency, a more sophisticated hedge could have been constructed by using some of the shorter-term bond futures contracts now available or by using a combination of swaps and futures. This would have brought the maturity profile of the hedging instruments closer to that of the bonds being hedged, thereby removing some of the basis risk that arose in this illustration.

As with all hedge design, the end user must balance the advantage of simplicity against the cost of residual risk emanating from an inefficient hedge and structure the scheme accordingly.

---

[8] The fall in price of the 13⅛ of May 2001 was due to the steep amortisation of the substantial bond premium.

Chapter Fifteen

Managing Interest-Rate Risk—Using Options and Option-Based Instruments

The common feature of all the techniques discussed in the previous chapter is that they guarantee a certain outcome. Whether the original exposure arose from a single short-term forward rate, a series of short-term forward rates, or a single long-term spot rate, the requisite solution attempted to eliminate risk completely. For some exposed to interest-rate risk, this remedy might be just what they wanted. However, as the introduction to Chapter Ten has pointed out, risk includes both adverse and benign outcomes. The complete eradication of risk means the avoidance of beneficial outcomes as well as bad ones, and others exposed to risk may not want this. The alternative solution is to use those financial engineering tools that provide protection against the downside, while preserving the opportunity to benefit from the upside—options and option-based instruments.

This chapter starts by showing how interest rate options can be used to hedge against exposure to a single short-term forward rate. This will illustrate the basic principles of using option-based products in managing interest rate risk. More commonly, however, interest-rate risk manifests itself over an extended period of time, and multiperiod products such as caps, floors, and collars are the appropriate tools to use. A substantial part of this chapter is therefore devoted to discussing how these popular products can be applied. As various approaches to managing interest-rate risk are reviewed, the parallels with currency risk management will become very evident. A later section will highlight these links by illustrating how ideas originally developed in the currency markets have been successfully transferred to the interest rate market. Finally, the chapter ends with a detailed comparison of the wide and sometimes confusing range of interest rate products discussed in this chapter and the previous one and provides some important criteria to guide users toward the most appropriate technique to use in a given situation.

15.1 INTEREST RATE GUARANTEES

An FRA guarantees a specific interest rate for a nominated time period in the future. An option on an FRA, often called an *interest rate guarantee* (IRG), grants the holder the right to choose between:

1. A specific interest rate.

2. The interest rate prevailing at the time.

A borrower could buy a call option on an FRA struck at a particular interest rate. If rates eventually turned out higher than the strike rate, the borrower would exercise the option and use the underlying FRA to cap the borrowing cost. If rates turned out lower, the borrower would allow the option to expire and simply borrow at market rates. Similarly, an investor could use a put option to guarantee a minimum investment rate.

To give a specific example, a company may need to borrow for a six-month period starting in six months' time. One alternative is for the company to buy a 6×12 FRA, which might be quoted at 8%. Whichever way rates turn out six months later makes no difference to the company once it has bought the FRA. It will borrow based on a six-month LIBOR of 8%. The other alternative is for the company to buy a call option struck at 8% on the same FRA. After paying the premium, which might amount to 16bp of the nominal principal, the company waits to see how rates evolve over the next six months. If interest rates end up higher than 8%, the company exercises the option and buys the FRA, which is immediately cash-settled to ensure borrowing based on a LIBOR of 8%. If rates end up lower than 8%, the company allows the option to expire, and borrows at whatever rate prevails. The effect of the IRG is that the company can borrow at the prevailing rate or at 8%, whichever is better.

Table 15.1 lists typical quotations for IRGs at a time when the prevailing six-month rate and the 6×12 FRA are both quoted at exactly 8.00%. Each instrument guarantees the six-month rate in six-months' time, the call options guaranteeing a maximum borrowing rate, while the put options guarantee a minimum investment rate. The table shows actual and annualised premiums for five different strike rates ranging from 7% to 9%. For example, the premium for the 7.5% call option is an up-front payment of 32bp of the nominal principal. As the period covered by the guarantee lasts exactly six months, this 32bp premium is equivalent to 64bp on an annualised basis.

TABLE 15.1
Illustrative Premiums for Interest Rate Guarantees

Strike Rates	Calls (borrower's guarantee)		Puts (investor's guarantee)	
	Actual	*Annualised*	*Actual*	*Annualised*
7.0	51	102	4¼	9
7.5	32	64	8½	17
8.0	16	32	16	32
8.5	9½	19	33	65
9.0	6½	13	53	106

Note: All premiums are in basis points.

Since the strike rates are quoted on an annualised basis, it is a little easier to interpret these premiums if we look at the annualised figures. The call struck at 7.0% is very much in-the-money, and virtually the entire 102bp is intrinsic value. At first glance, one might expect that the intrinsic value should be 100bp for a call option struck at 7.00% when the forward rate is 8.00%. In fact, the intrinsic value is just 92½bp, because the option premium is paid at the outset, and the eventual option payout under an IRG is normally discounted in the same way as the settlement sum with an FRA. In the case of the call struck at 7.00%, the nominal 100bp intrinsic value must therefore be discounted at the 8% forward rate for the six-month period covered by the guarantee and then at the 8% cash-market rate for the six-month period until the option matures. This gives the 92½bp intrinsic value mentioned above and therefore a time value of 9½bp. The remaining call premiums decline as the strike rate is raised, although the time value component reaches a maximum when the guarantee is struck at-the-money. The put options reveal a similar pattern, although the prices run in the opposite direction, increasing as the strike rate is raised. This makes sense, of course, because the put options grant the right to invest at the strike price, and this advantage becomes greater the higher the strike rate.

The profile of an IRG is no different from that of any other basic option-based product. Figure 15.1 illustrates the effective borrowing cost against the interest rate eventually prevailing and shows the profiles for guarantees struck at five different rates. In each case, the effective borrowing cost has been adjusted to account for the fact that the premiums are paid in advance. This means, for example, that using the option struck at 7.00% with a premium of 102bp will lead to a maximum borrowing cost of 8.10% rather than the 8.02% that might be expected from a casual inspection of the figures. To provide a comparison, the diagram also shows the flat profile for an FRA hedge with the contract rate set to 8.00% and the diagonal profile for the original exposure without any hedging.

At one extreme, the borrower could achieve complete immunity from the effects of changing interest rates by buying the FRA, which fixes the eventual borrowing rate under all eventualities. The resulting profile is the horizontal straight line at 8.00%. The most in-the-money IRG has a similar characteristic for all interest rates above the strike rate of 7.00% but allows the borrower to benefit should rates eventually fall below this level.

At the other extreme, the borrower who chooses not to hedge will suffer from the full effects of any movement in interest rates. If rates are low, the borrowing cost will also be low. If interest rates are high, the effective cost will grow in line. This gives rise to the diagonal profile in Figure 15.1 for the "no hedge" strategy. This time, it is the most out-of-the-money guarantee, the one struck at 9.00%, that exhibits a similar characteristic. This instrument is cheap but offers no protection against a rise in interest rates until the strike rate of 9.00% is reached. Only then does it cap the borrower's costs.

In between, the other IRGs offer various compromises between premium cost, degree of protection against higher rates, and ability to profit from

FIGURE 15.1
Profiles for Interest Rate Guarantees

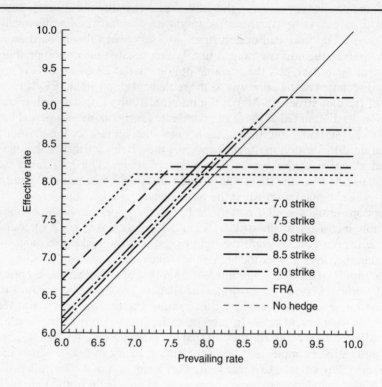

lower rates. This is exactly the same behaviour as that exhibited by the currency option solutions presented in Chapter Thirteen, where the chameleon-like nature of options was first discussed. Hedging with deep in-the-money options gives a profile almost the same as using the corresponding forward contract, here the FRA. Deep out-of-the-money options cost little but offer little in the way of protection, so the resulting profile looks just like that of the underlying exposure. Only between these two extremes do IRGs provide a true balance between protection and beneficial exposure.

15.2 USING CAPS AND FLOORS

Caps and floors were first introduced in Chapter Eleven (Section 11.5), which also explained how they were priced. Using the term structure of interest rates and volatilities shown in Table 15.2, we can calculate a representative set of cap and floor prices at different strike levels. Table 15.3 summarises the results of these calculations for caps and floors on six-month LIBOR with maturities ranging from two to seven years. Each price is quoted both as an up-front premium and as an amortised rate. For example, the five-year cap struck at 5% could either be paid as an up-front premium of 1.91% of the nominal principal or as a regular payment at the rate of 0.43% per annum paid six-monthly in arrears (i.e., 0.215% paid twice a year).

When evaluating cap premiums, it is important to compare the strike price with the swap rate, not the prevailing short-term rate. To do otherwise may give

TABLE 15.2
Term Structure of Interest Rates and Volatilities

Time (years)	Swap Rate (%)	Zero Rate (%)	Forward Rate (%)	Volatility (%)
0.5	3.25	3.25		
1.0	3.50	3.53	3.75	15
1.5	3.69	3.73	4.07	14
2.0	3.88	3.92	4.46	14
2.5	4.02	4.08	4.64	13
3.0	4.17	4.23	4.95	13
3.5	4.31	4.39	5.26	12
4.0	4.46	4.55	5.59	12
4.5	4.60	4.71	5.91	12
5.0	4.75	4.87	6.25	12

TABLE 15.3
Examples of Cap and Floor Premiums

		Cap Strike Rates				Floor Strike Rates		
		4%	5%	6%	7%	4%	4.5%	5%
	2 year	43	7	–	–	66	137	222
Up-front	3 year	121	33	7	–	74	158	266
premiums	5 year	413	191	80	31	79	174	303
	7 year	892	535	310	175	80	178	314
	2 year	22	3	–	–	35	72	116
Amortised	3 year	43	12	2	–	26	56	95
premiums	5 year	93	43	18	7	18	39	68
	7 year	151	91	53	30	14	30	53

Note: All quotations are in basis points.

a misleading impression. With the term structure used here, short-term rates are 3.25%, so the five-year cap struck at 5% may seem well out-of-the-money and therefore expensive at 1.91%. Table 15.2 reveals, however, that the five-year swap rate is 4.75%, so the 5% cap is virtually at-the-money. With the yield curve sloping steeply upwards, short-term rates may start low at 3.25%, but they are forecast to rise above 6% by the end of the five-year period covered by this particular cap. Early interest periods are likely to be out-of-the-money, but later cap periods are likely to be very much in-the-money.

As with all options, caps and floor premiums can be divided into two components: intrinsic value and time value. This is easier to appreciate if we study the amortised premiums rather than the up-front quotations. The five-year cap struck at 4% is quoted at 93bp. Since the five-year swap rate is 4.75%, this premium can be split into 75bp of intrinsic value and 18bp of time value. A few moments inspecting the figures in Table 15.3 will reveal that the time-value component is greatest for caps struck at-the-money, as was explained in Chapter Ten (Section 10.10). This feature makes the long-dated at-the-money caps the most expensive.[1]

Evaluating the performance of a cap is a little more complex than evaluating IRGs because of the multiperiod nature of these products. In Figure 15.1 it was possible to show the complete cost/benefit relationship for an IRG by graphing the effective borrowing rate against the rate prevailing in the single period covered by the IRG. Two variables give rise to a two-dimensional graph that can be perfectly represented on paper. To achieve the same completeness with a 10-period cap, the effective borrowing rate over the life of the cap would need to be evaluated simultaneously against the interest rates prevailing during each of the 10 periods. A computer could produce the figures, but drawing the result would require 11-dimensional graph paper, something that no stationer seems to stock.

Thus, to evaluate cap performance and to enable comparisons to be drawn between caps at different strike levels, we must restrict ourselves to a subset of possible rate scenarios. Figure 15.2 graphs the set of future six-month interest rates implied by the forward rates of Table 15.2 and shows two further paths: one in which rates rise at 50bp per year slower than the implied forward rates and another in which rates rise 50bp per year faster. For example, the six-month rate in 4½ years could either be 6.25% as the forward rate implies, 225bp lower at 4.00%, or 225bp higher at 8.50%. These two paths—corresponding to rates drifting by ±50bp per year from the implied forward rates—will be used as the extremes of feasible interest rate movements for the following analysis, and all intermediate paths will be

---

[1] The word *expensive* should be interpreted carefully here. In-the-money options cost more than at-the-money ones, but the buyer obtains intrinsic value that will be preserved if the underlying price does not change. Paying for something that is durable is not expensive. Time value, on the other hand, will always decay to zero at maturity. Paying for something that will eventually become worthless is expensive.

FIGURE 15.2
Alternative Rate Scenarios

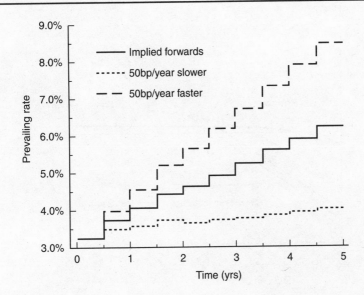

examined. This subset does not, by any means, encompass every conceivable path that interest rates could take, but it does cover the more probable outcomes. Later in this chapter we shall analyse a wider set of possible interest-rate scenarios using Monte Carlo simulation.

Consider a company about to borrow for five years under a facility in which the interest rate is reset every six months based on the prevailing LIBOR rate. Using the set of interest-rate scenarios developed in Figure 15.2, we can assess the resultant exposure using different hedging strategies. Figure 15.3 shows the company's effective borrowing rate over the five-year period for caps struck at 4%, 5%, 6%, and 7%, the premiums for which were tabulated in Table 15.3. As a comparison, the diagram also shows the straight-line profiles that result from using a straight interest rate swap or from the decision not to hedge at all.

The most in-the-money cap—the one struck at 4%—exhibits a virtually flat characteristic almost identical with that of the swap. While it limits the maximum borrowing cost over a wide range, it is not so effective in allowing the borrower to benefit if rates stay low. Although this cap demands the biggest premium, equivalent to 93bp per annum, the major part of this is intrinsic value, and most of the caplets will expire in-the-money under most of the scenarios examined. The effective cost of the cap is therefore quite small, and the maximum effective borrowing cost can never exceed 4.84%.

This maximum cost can easily be deduced by applying the following reasoning. The worst possible scenario is for rates to rise above 4% after the

FIGURE 15.3
Effective Borrowing Rate Using Different Caps

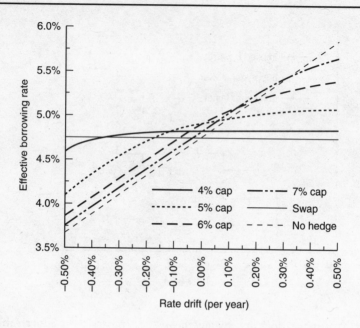

first period; each caplet would then expire in-the-money, thereby capping the effective cost at 4.93%, the 4% strike rate plus the 93bp amortised cost of the cap premium. The rate for the very first period is already fixed at 3.25%, however; this 75bp saving spread over the 10 periods of the loan is equivalent to 9bp. The net maximum cost is therefore 4.93%−0.09% = 4.84%.

In contrast, the most out-of-the-money cap behaves much like the no-hedge strategy. The up-front premium is very small, equivalent to just 7bp per annum, but the 7% cap offers little in the way of protection. Only if rates drift up by at least 17bp per annum do any of the caplets expire in-the-money. Even if rates drift up by the full 50bp annum considered here, this cap only provides a payoff in the last three interest periods.

In between these two extremes lie the other two caps, which offer a compromise performance. The 6% cap requires an up-front premium of 80bp, equivalent to just 18bp and provides "disaster insurance" to limit the company's costs should interest rates rise this much. As is evident from Figure 15.2, however, only in the later periods of some of the upward-drifting rate scenarios is this likely to happen, so the protective nature of this cap is only visible to the right of Figure 15.3.

This range of behaviour, from the almost complete protection afforded by the 4% cap to the almost nonexistent cover offered by the 7% cap, follows the same continuum of possibilities first seen with the currency option-based hedges discussed in Chapter Thirteen. The only difference is that the cap graphs in Figure 15.3 are curved, while the currency option profiles comprise straight lines. The reason for this arises from the multiperiod nature of caps.

With a single-period currency option there are just two discrete possibilities at maturity: the option will expire either out-of-the-money or in-the-money. If the former, the option will not provide protection, and the diagonal profile of the underlying risk profile will be revealed. If the latter, the option will offset the underlying risk, and the result will be the horizontal profile characteristic of a hedged risk. There will be a sharp transition from one profile to the other at the strike price of the option. With a multi-period cap, some of the caplets will expire in-the-money while some will not. As the drift parameter is increased, a greater proportion of the caplets will expire in-the-money, but there is no single point at which all the caplets suddenly switch from expiring out-of-the-money to expiring in-the-money. This means that the transition in behaviour from the diagonal out-of-the-money characteristic to the horizontal in-the-money profile is a gradual one.

15.3 COLLARS, PARTICIPATING CAPS, CORRIDORS, AND OTHER VARIATIONS

We have just seen the broad similarity between the behaviour of interest rate caps and that of the currency option products reviewed in Chapter Thirteen. Indeed, it can be said that all option-based products behave in a similar way. Furthermore, techniques developed in one market can usually be applied in another. This section will explore some of the products that have started life as a tool for managing one kind of market risk but have easily and successfully been applied to the management of interest-rate risk.

One of the most common forms of interest-rate protection nowadays is the collar, a concept first introduced in Chapter Eleven (Section 11.5) and then studied in greater depth in Chapter Thirteen (Section 13.7) within the context of currency risk. Table 15.4 shows a variety of quotations for interest rate collars, and is split into two parts. The first part lists a set of collars where both the cap level and the floor level have been prespecified, and the table shows the net premiums that must be paid. The second part illustrates a set of zero-cost collars where both the cap level and zero premium have been preset, leaving the floor level as the remaining variable to be determined.

Starting with the figures in the first part of Table 15.4, it is evident that most of the collars illustrated involve the payment of a net premium. For example, the five-year 4–5% collar requires a net payment up front amounting to 113bp of the nominal principal, but this represents a saving of 40% when compared with the cost of the 5% cap alone. In return for this saving, the collar buyer is obliged to borrow at a rate no less than the floor level, which in most of the cases illustrated has been set higher than present six-month rates. For example, any of the collars embodying a 4% floor will compel the buyer to borrow at 4% for the initial six-month period, even though the six-month rate prevailing at the outset is only 3.25%.

TABLE 15.4
Quotations for Collars

	Net Premiums Paid for Specified Collars (bp)			
	3.5% floor 5% cap	4% floor 5% cap	4% floor 6% cap	4.5% floor 6% cap
2 years	−11	−60	−66	−136
3 years	+13	−41	−67	−151
5 years	+171	+113	+1	−94
7 years	+514	+455	+230	+131

	Floor Levels for Zero-Cost Collars		
	5% cap	6% cap	7% cap
2 years	3.33%	3.12%	2.79%
3 years	3.65	3.32	3.15
5 years	4.58	4.01	3.62
7 years	–	4.99	4.48

Some of the collar combinations illustrated actually have a negative net premium. This means that the collar buyer would actually receive the up-front payment from the bank, not the other way round. Although this might seem attractive, this situation can only arise if the protection purchased by the cap component is minimal, while the savings opportunity sold under the floor component is substantial. For example, if interest rates followed the implied forward rates, the buyer of a 4.5–6% collar would end up paying out under the collar for the first two years of the five-year period and would only receive a payment from the collar in the very last six-month period. Against this would be the certain benefit of an up-front receipt of 136bp, equivalent to 31bp per year.

In many cases, companies using collars prefer not to have to balance an up-front premium against future cash flows from the collar, but elect instead to purchase a zero-cost collar. The second part of Table 15.4 therefore shows a set of zero-cost collars in which the floor level has been adjusted so that the premium income from the floor sold exactly matches the premium cost of the cap purchased. For example, a three-year zero-cost collar incorporating a cap at 5% would involve selling a floor at 3.65%. Naturally, the more the cap is in-the-money, the higher the floor level will need to be in order to bring in sufficient premium income, thereby making the floor more in-the-money as well.

To illustrate the behaviour of these zero-cost collars, we can use the same set of rate scenarios that were used to produce Figure 15.3. The three five-year zero-cost collars listed in Table 15.4 were analysed to produce the set of graphs shown in Figure 15.4. Clearly visible is the characteristic of a collar

FIGURE 15.4
Effective Borrowing Rate Using Different Zero-Cost Collars

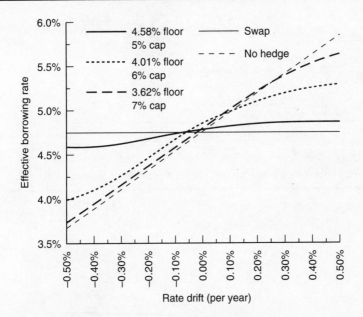

whereby both maximum and minimum costs are limited. Once again, there is the by-now familiar continuum of possibilities with the profile of the out-of-the-money 3.62–7% collar looking very much like the diagonal no-hedge profile at one extreme and the in-the-money 4.58–5% collar very much resembling the horizontal swap profile at the other.

Another idea transferred from the currency markets is the idea of a participating cap. This idea was explained in Chapter Thirteen (Section 13.9) under the heading *participating forward*, which is the name given to the equivalent FX product. A full description of how this product works can be found in that section, but, briefly, it can be built by buying a cap and selling a floor at the same strike rate, with the nominal principal of the floor adjusted to create a zero-cost combination. Table 15.5 gives some examples of participating caps with different strike levels and participation rates.

As an example, the first participating cap shown will cap the borrower's costs if LIBOR rises above 5% and will allow him to enjoy 37% of the savings in any period if interest rates fall below that level. Moreover, the participating cap will cost the borrower nothing in the way of premium. If six-month LIBOR was 6% in one period, the borrower would pay interest based on a LIBOR of just 5%. If LIBOR was 4%, the borrower would pay 4.63%, receiving 37% of the 100bp reduction below the strike rate.

Figure 15.5 illustrates the performance of these participating caps. At first glance, the picture looks very similar to the previous diagram. Participations

TABLE 15.5
Participating Cap Quotations

Cap/Floor Strike Rate	Cap Price	Floor Price	Cap Amount	Floor Amount	Cap/Floor Price Ratio	Participation Rate
5%	191	303	1,000,000	630,363	0.63	37%
5.5	125	459	1,000,000	272,331	0.27	73
6	80	637	1,000,000	125,589	0.13	87
7	31	1034	1,000,000	29,981	0.03	97

FIGURE 15.5
Effective Borrowing Rate Using Different Participating Caps

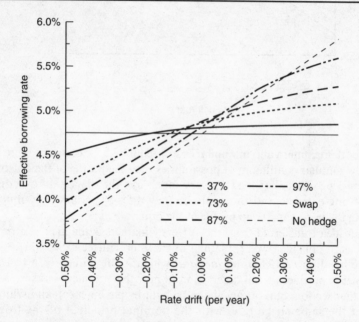

exhibit the same kind of transition from the swaplike nature of the 37% participating cap to the 97% participation that is almost identical to the no-hedge profile. There is a difference in shape however. A zero-cost collar limits the effective borrowing cost both on the upside and the downside but allows the borrower to benefit fully from any drop in interest rates between the two strike prices. A participating cap limits the effective borrowing costs only on the upside, allowing unlimited ability to benefit from a fall in interest rates, but offering the borrower only a portion of these savings.

Many other combinations are possible, and the possibilities using option-based products like caps and floors are almost limitless. The next few paragraphs provide some ideas.

A *corridor* could be constructed by buying a cap at one strike and selling a cap at a higher strike. For example, buying a 5% five-year cap and selling a 6% five-year cap would result in a net up-front premium of 111bp, a 42% saving over the basic cost of the 5% cap. Only if rates rose substantially would the borrower be forced to pay out on the 6% cap, and even then the receipt under the 5% cap would reduce the effective borrowing cost in that period by 1%.

A corridor is a vertical option spread. An alternative strategy for the borrower is to use a horizontal spread, buying a cap for one maturity and selling a cap with the same strike rate but for a different maturity. For example, suppose a borrower believed that interest rates would follow the path predicted by the implied forward rates shown in Table 15.2 and therefore thought that six-month rates will eventually rise above 5%, but only after three years. Buying a five-year cap struck at 5% would cost 191bp up-front but simultaneously selling a three-year cap at the same strike rate would bring in 33bp, thereby lowering the net premium to 158bp and achieving a saving of 17%. If rates follow the path predicted, neither cap will involve any payouts for the first three years, so the borrower would not suffer any cash outflows during the lifetime of the shorter-date cap but will gain from the initial premium inflow.

Another way to look at this combination is to consider it as a *deferred-start cap*, for that is exactly what it is. For the first three years, the long and short cap positions cancel exactly, leaving a two-year cap deferred by three years. This is one example of using financial engineering techniques to construct a hedge that better matches a borrower's needs.

Another example of fine tuning can be witnessed in the form of a *step-up cap* or a *step-up floor* in which the strike rates increase during the lifetime of the instrument. A borrower may be better able to afford a higher borrowing rate in the future but still require protection against a very substantial hike in interest rates. With the set of rates shown in Table 15.2, a standard five-year 5% cap would cost 191bp. However, if the strike rate were allowed to increase by 50bp each year during the lifetime of the cap, culminating at 7% in the final year, the cap premium would in this case fall to just 44bp, a saving of 77%. Of course, the buyer of a step-up cap does not get something for nothing. The lower premium buys a lesser degree of protection, and none of the caplets would expire in-the-money if rates followed the implied forwards. In the case of a downward sloping yield curve, *step-down caps* and *step-down floors* would be alternative possibilities.

In Chapter Thirteen (Section 13.10) we saw that a ratio forward was an extension of the participating forward using strike prices the other side of the prevailing market rate. The same idea can be extended to caps and floors. Table 15.5 tabulated participation rates for participating caps with strike rates all being above the five-year swap rate used in the example of 4.75%. If a ratio forward struck at 4.5% were created, the gearing ratio would be 1.6 times, but this would secure a better-than-market borrowing rate of 4.67%, assuming interest rates followed the implied forward curve. With the strike rate reduced to 3.5%, the effective rate would drop even more, to 4.24%, which is an impressive 51bp below the prevailing swap rate. Unfortunately, the gearing ratio would have risen to an alarming 27.9 times, something that neither the borrower nor his bankers would wisely accept.

Other variations are possible, including the potential to use exotic options like those described in Chapter Eleven (Section 11.8). Although some of the more unusual inventions have not yet been marketed as interest-risk management solutions, this is probably just a matter of time; a number of exotic option-based products have already appeared.

An *average rate cap* compensates borrowers using a floating rate facility under which the rate can be altered at any time, not just on reset dates. A perfect example would be a customer borrowing using a loan facility linked to the bank's base or prime rate. The average rate cap, sometimes known as a *base rate cap*, will provide compensation for any periods when the bank's base rate exceeds the predetermined strike rate, in return for an up-front premium payment.

Barrier caps that incorporate a trigger rate have also been developed. In an upward-sloping yield curve environment, an up-and-in barrier cap features a trigger rate set higher than the cap rate. This type of cap is not triggered unless interest rates rise through the trigger rate, at which point the product operates as a normal cap. Another variation is the down-and-out cap, which is extinguished if rates reach a trigger level set below current rates. Both forms of barrier option result in premium savings and operate on the principle that interest rates often tend to trend rather than to fluctuate at a given level. Thus, if an up-and-in barrier cap is triggered, the protection is most likely to be needed thereafter, while the protection provided by a down-and-out barrier cap is probably no longer required after being extinguished if rates fall.

Pay-later or *self-funding caps* also exist and have the advantage that they cost nothing up front. The premium for such caps is always quoted on an amortised basis and is only paid in those periods when the cap is in-the-money. If the protection was not needed, the pay-later cap therefore comes free and no premium need have been wasted for protection that turned out to be unnecessary. However, as we saw in Chapter Eleven (Section 11.8), the premium for a pay-later option is much greater than for a standard option, something like double the price for an at-the-money option. A borrower should therefore only consider a pay-later cap if he believes that rates will rise substantially above the cap rate and not merely hover around that level.

15.4 USING CAPTIONS AND SWAPTIONS

Caps and swaps provide two different styles of interest-rate protection; options on these products add yet another dimension. Captions and swaptions can be used in a variety of situations, but they are particularly relevant for:

- Contingent situations.

- Providing cheaper rate protection.
- Handling embedded debt options.
- Extending or curtailing swaps.
- Speculation.

We will discuss each of these applications in turn.

Contingent situations. There are many instances when a company's need for interest-rate protection is contingent on some external factor beyond its control. One common example is when a company is tendering for some project in which the success or failure of the tender will dictate whether finance will be raised and, hence, whether rate protection is required. Another example arises in takeover situations, when financing of the proposed acquisition and the accompanying hedging program will both be dependent on the success of the bid.

Under these circumstances, entering into a deferred-start swap or buying a deferred-start cap may not be ideal. The swap would bind the company into a series of contractual payments, which would be totally unnecessary if the bid or tender fails. While there is no compulsion to exercise a cap, the up-front premium would be a substantial and wasted expense if the contingency did not arise.

Buying a swap option, or an option into a cap, may well provide the company with the contingent protection that it needs at a substantially reduced price. Table 15.6 compares prices for three comparable products: a six-month swaption into a four-year swap, a four-year cap deferred six months, and a six-month caption into a four-year cap. All of these would be suitable choices for a company with a contingent borrowing requirement of four years commencing in six months' time. The products have been priced using the rates presented in Table 15.2, and two representative strike levels have been used. The first is 4.79%, which is the price for a four-year swap deferred six months, and is therefore at-the-money for all the products. The second is set to 5.50%, just a little out-of-the-money.

If the company entered into a deferred swap contract, this would obligate it to make fixed payments at 4.79% over the four-year period. Not only are

TABLE 15.6
Comparison of Swaption, Deferred Cap, and Caption Premiums

	Strike Rate = 4.79%	Strike Rate = 5.50%
Swaption	82bp	14bp
Deferred cap	165bp	84bp
Caption	˙38bp	23bp

these higher than the prevailing six-month rates, the company may not even require the floating-rate finance if the particular contingency did not arise. An at-the-money swaption gives the company the right to enter into the deferred swap, but not the obligation. After six months, the company could exercise the swaption if the underlying borrowing requirement did arise, and if swap rates were higher than the 4.79% strike rate at the time. The up-front payment of just 82bp is probably an acceptable price to pay for this type of interest-rate protection.

Buying the deferred cap meets with the same objection as the swap contract, in that the protection may not be needed if the contingency does not transpire. The 165bp up-front premium may also be daunting as an up-front expense, particularly if the protection turned out not to be needed. Against this is the possibility that the company could sell the cap after six months if it proved surplus to requirements.

The cheapest form of rate protection is the caption, at least in terms of up-front expense. At just 38bp it is less than half the price of the swaption and less than one-quarter the price of the deferred cap. It gives the company the opportunity to buy a cap at 165bp, should the need arise, or to take advantage of lower cap prices if interest rates or volatility levels fall over the initial six-month period. The underlying cap is also an effective risk management tool, providing protection against the possibility of higher rates while allowing the company to benefit from lower borrowing costs if interest rates stay low. The only drawback is that the total cost of the cap would be 203bp if the caption is exercised, which is 23% more than the cost of buying the deferred cap initially.

Providing cheap rate protection. Some borrowers may look to swaptions and captions as a low-cost means of securing protection against higher interest rates. Paradoxically, this view is valid only if the borrower believes that the protection will *not* be needed. Buying an underlying instrument through exercising an option is always more expensive than buying that instrument at the outset. This is because all option premiums comprise time value as well as intrinsic value, and the time value component is never recovered if the option is exercised or held to maturity. So if a borrower believes there is a good chance that a swaption or caption will be exercised, it is usually better to buy the underlying instrument to begin with. In the example just cited, the swaption buyer pays an 82bp up-front premium for the right to enter into the swap, yet there would be no cost at all if the borrower entered into the deferred swap instead. The same principle is true with the caption, where the caption premium of 38bp is over and above the 165bp cost of the underlying cap, which must be paid if the cap is eventually bought.

Suppose a borrower believes that interest rates, though they may rise, will not rise as fast as predicted by the implied forward rates. Entering into a swap would be expensive because the swap is priced as the weighted average of the forward rates, which the borrower believes are too high. Better to use a swaption or a caption, which can be exercised if the borrower's view proves wrong but can be discarded otherwise and advantage taken of the lower market rates.

To give a specific example, consider a company borrowing for five years when market rates are as shown in Table 15.2. Suppose the company believes that forward rates will climb gradually to 5%, not the 6.25% implied by the forward yield curve. Now compare the strategy of entering into a five-year swap at 4.75% with buying a one-year swaption into a four-year swap struck at the same rate. The swaption premium would be 157bp in this case. The swap would lock the borrower into an effective rate of 4.75% regardless of interest rates over the next five years. The swaption would allow the borrower to take advantage of the much lower rates prevailing initially and then to exercise the swaption only if rates did not turn out as planned.

With the swaption, if the borrower's view was correct, the effective borrowing cost would average out to 4.50% after taking the swaption premium into account. This represents a saving of 25bp compared with the swap strategy. Even if the company's view proves incorrect and the swaption is then exercised, the effective borrowing cost rises to 4.83%, just 8bp over the original swap rate. The only danger with the swaption strategy would be if rates stayed low initially, so that the swaption was not exercised, and then rose later when the company would have no rate protection in place.

Handling embedded debt options. Corporate bonds frequently incorporate a call provision allowing the issuer to repay the debt prematurely if interest rates fall. This is particularly true when interest rates are high. A typical bond issue might have a maturity of 10 years, but be callable on any coupon date after the first three years. In effect, the bond investors have sold the bond issuer a call option on the debt, and this is embedded into the bond. The issuer can use a swaption to monetise this option, thus releasing its value.

Suppose a large company has just issued a seven-year fixed-rate bond callable after two years. The company can now sell a two-year receiver's swaption exercisable into a five-year swap with a strike rate equal to the bond coupon. If interest rates have fallen below the coupon rate in two years' time, the company will call the bond and refinance by issuing an FRN at the lower rates then available. At the same time, the swaption will be exercised against the company so that it becomes the fixed-rate payer under the swap. The net result is that the company ends up paying fixed coupons at the same rate as before but has retained the up-front swaption premium. If rates stay high, the bond is not called and the swaption expires worthless. Either way, the company will continue to pay fixed coupons at the original rate but receives an up-front premium equivalent to the value of the embedded option.

Extending or curtailing swaps. Borrowers may sometimes require an option to extend or curtail the maturity of an existing swap. This can easily be achieved with a swaption. Suppose a borrower is currently the fixed-rate payer on a swap with three years until maturity, but he needs the option to extend this for a further two years. Buying a three-year payer's swaption into a two-year swap with a strike rate equal to the fixed-rate on the existing swap will exactly fulfill the borrower's requirement. Another borrower paying the fixed-rate on a five-year swap, but needing the ability to shorten the maturity to three years, can buy a three-year receiver's swaption into a two-year swap with a strike rate equal to that of the original swap. If the swap needs to be curtailed, the borrower exercises the swaption and enters into a new swap whose cash flows cancel those of the original one.

A variation of this is the *collapsible swap*, which is analogous to the break-forward contract examined in Chapter Thirteen (Section 13.11). A company planning to borrow in the future may wish to protect against a rise in interest rates but may also want to benefit in case rates fall. One solution would simply be to buy a payer's swaption, but this involves an up-front premium. An alternative is to enter into a deferred-start swap as the fixed-rate payer and simultaneously buy a receiver's swaption having the effect of cancelling this swap. To finance the receiver's swaption, the deferred-start swap is executed at an off-market rate. If rates rise, the company continues with the swap agreement, allowing the swaption to expire worthless. If rates fall, the company executes the swaption to cancel the swap and enters into a new swap at the lower market rates. Note that a swap cancellation fee will nevertheless be chargeable, as the swaption strike rate was set to the market rate of the deferred-start swap, but the actual swap was done at an off-market rate.

As an example, using the Table 15.2 rates, a four-year swap deferred by one year would be priced at 5.10%, while a one-year receiver's swaption into this swap would normally command a premium of 85bp. Instead, the swaption premium could be amortised and absorbed by an off-market rate of 5.34% for the swap. If the swap is cancelled through the exercise of the swaption, the cancellation fee would be about 87bp.

Speculation. While this book is not primarily concerned with the use of financial engineering tools as vehicles for speculation, derivative instruments are often attractive in view of the gearing they offer. Buying option-based products can be particularly effective because of their limited cost, limited downside risk, and unlimited upside potential, and swaptions are no exception. A speculator believing that interest rates will rise could buy a payer's swaption. For instance, a one-year payer's swaption into a four-year swap struck at 5.10% might cost 85bp in up-front premium. If four-year swap rates rise to 6% after one year, the swaption could be cash-settled for 324bp, a profit of more than 280%. If rates stay steady or fall, the most that the speculator could lose would be the swaption premium.

15.5 COMPARISON OF INTEREST RISK MANAGMENT TOOLS

The availability of FRAs, futures, swaps, IRGs, caps, floors, collars, captions, and swaptions, to name just the standard products now available, provides a bewildering choice of risk management tools for those exposed to interest-rate risk. As an initial guide through this maze, Table 15.7 provides a summary of the major characteristics for each of these products. Most of the table is self-explanatory, except perhaps for the terms used to describe the type of protection. The expression *fixed* means that the rate effective obtained is absolutely certain, regardless of the way in which interest rates evolve. *Selective* means that the borrower or investor will receive protection against the downside, while retaining the ability to benefit from the upside.

Which is the best tool to use in any given situation depends very much on the user's hedging objectives, as set out in Chapter Twelve (Section 12.4) under four specific headings:

- Wish to obtain complete protection against all rate movements.
- Relative preference for upside savings compared with desire to avoid downside risk.
- Aversion to paying for risk protection.
- Client's view of market developments.

We will review each of these in turn to determine how they influence a user's choice.

Complete protection. If complete certainty is required, the choice is straightforward: use FRAs and futures to cover short-term exposures or swaps for longer-term ones. It is as simple as that.

TABLE 15.7
Comparison of Interest-Rate Risk Management Tools

	Periods Covered	Number of Exercise Opportunities	Maturities Available	Type of Protection
FRAs	Single	-	Up to 2 years	Fixed
Futures	Single	-	Up to 4 years	Fixed
Swaps	Multiple	-	Up to 10 years	Fixed
IRGs	Single	1	Up to 2 years	Selective
Caps, floors, and collars	Multiple	Many	Up to 10 years	Selective
Swaptions	Single/multiple*	1	Up to 10 years	Selective
Captions	Single/multiple*	1/many*	Up to 10 years	Selective

* The second term applies if and when the option is exercised.

Upside versus downside. The moment that a user wishes to obtain protection against the downside risk while preserving some upside opportunities, an option-based solution is dictated. If the risk is short-term, selecting an IRG with the strike rate chosen to balance protection, benefits, and premium cost should provide an acceptable solution. Alternatively, a combination of IRGs to create a collar, corridor, participation, or some other variation may deliver a more attractive package of benefits for the user. For longer-dated risks, similar considerations apply, but using the multiperiod versions of these products. Thus, a cap, collar, corridor, or participating cap will deliver the same kind of trade-offs.

Paying for protection. If the desired form of risk management solution is considered too expensive, there are various choices. A reduced-cost or zero-cost product such as a collar or participation may deliver the required level of protection and be financed by the sale of some of the profit opportunities. If the preferred choice was to buy a cap, then a caption may provide a cheaper route, at least initially. Similarly, a swaption is a low-cost alternative to the swap. Note the warning given earlier: if a caption or swaption is eventually exercised, the total cost will be more expensive than if the underlying instrument had been bought at the outset.

View of the market. With interest-rate risk, particularly one that extends over several years, the user's view of the market is actually quite crucial in designing the optimal hedge. The key is to compare the user's opinion on how interest rates will develop over the exposure period with the view of the market, namely, the implied forward rates. Note that it is the set of implied forward rates that sets the benchmark for all floating-rate finance and investment, not the swap rates nor the current short-term rate. We will analyse the three different possibilities that could occur:

- User believes that rates will rise faster than the implied forward curve.
- User believes that rates will rise, but more slowly than the implied forward curve.
- User believes that rates will follow the path of the implied forward curve, more or less.

Figure 15.6 illustrates these scenarios using an upward-sloping yield curve, and the detailed discussion will concentrate on the strategies that a borrower might be expected to follow. However, Tables 15.8 to 15.10 summarise the conclusions of the analysis for investors as well as borrowers, and the findings can be generalised for the less common environments in which the yield curve slopes down.

View: Rates will rise faster than implied forwards. In this case, a borrower will certainly need protection against higher interest rates, and a swap

FIGURE 15.6
Alternative Views of Market Rates

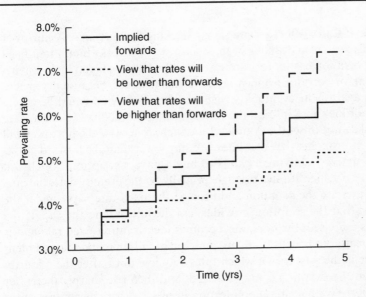

will be preferable to a cap for two reasons. First, the swap is priced as the weighted average of the implied forward rates and will therefore seem cheap when compared to the forward rates envisaged by the borrower. Second, the time value of a cap gives the borrower the right to exercise each caplet or, indeed, the right not to. If the borrower believes that rates will rise faster than the market, he is fairly certain to exercise a substantial majority of the caplets. Paying for the right not to exercise them is therefore of little value and a waste of premium expense.

As an adjunct to entering into a swap as the fixed-rate payer, the borrower could also sell a floor and use the premium income to lower the effective borrowing cost. This would be done in the expectation that most of the floorlets would not be exercised. With a rising yield curve, however, the floor level would have to be set fairly high in order to bring in sufficient up-front premium to make this worthwhile. Note that such a strategy actually reverses the direction of the borrower's exposure, resulting in a higher effective borrowing cost when rates are lower. This is perhaps most easily understood if one thinks of a swap as being equivalent to buying a cap and selling a floor at the same strike rate. The floor component of the swap neutralises the benefit of lower interest rates on the borrower's original exposure. Selling another floor turns the benefit of lower rates into a cost. This strategy is therefore only to be advised if the borrower has a strong view that rates will move up quickly and sharply.

A third possibility is to buy a zero-cost participating cap with a low strike rate, and therefore a low participation rate. Given the view that rates will rise faster than the implied forwards, the low participation rate is no disadvantage, and the low strike rate will provide protection at a rate close to the prevailing swap rate.

View: Rates will rise more slowly than implied forwards. A borrower holding this view would find a swap expensive, for it locks him into a fixed rate based on a forecast of forward rates that he believes is too high. Buying a cap, collar, or corridor is much better in this instance, because it provides protection against the eventuality that the borrower's view could be wrong but does not lock him into an unattractive rate. If a collar is chosen, care must be taken not to set the floor level too high; otherwise the borrower will fail to benefit from his view that rates will stay lower than the forward curve.

An alternative to buying a cap is to buy a payers swaption, which will invariably be cheaper. If rates rise unexpectedly by the exercise date, the borrower can exercise the swaption and become the fixed-rate payer under the swap. Note that the swaption provides less flexibility than the cap. If the swaption is exercised, the borrower becomes locked into a fixed rate and is unable thereafter to benefit from any subsequent falls in market rates. Potentially worse is the scenario in which rates stay low until after the maturity date, so that the swaption is not exercised, and then rise sharply thereafter when the borrower has no rate protection in place. A cap, by contrast, provides flexible rate protection throughout the period exposed to risk.

Similar in some ways to the swaption is the strategy of buying a caption, and this presents a third possibility. Being less expensive than the swaption, this choice is potentially the best, provided that rates do stay low and the caption is not exercised. However, the caption strategy is vulnerable to the same pitfall as the swaption strategy if rates stay low on the exercise date and then rise thereafter, leaving the borrower without protection.

View: Rates will follow the implied forward curve. This heading would also include the borrower who professes to have no view about the future evolution of interest rates. In this case, the broad choice is between a swap and zero-cost solutions like the zero-cost collar or participating cap. All of these will provide similar outcomes if rates do in fact follow the path suggested by the set of implied forward rates. Neither captions nor swaptions would be recommended here; buying either of these other than an at-the-money would provide too little protection to be worthwhile, and buying them at-the-money will be expensive if rates stay "static," i.e., if they simply follow the track of the forward rates.

Table 15.8 summarises these recommendations, not only from the borrower's viewpoint as discussed so far, but also from the viewpoint of the investor or lender. As is apparent, there is a symmetry between the optimal strategies: where the borrower would buy a cap, the investor would buy a floor, and so on.

TABLE 15.8
Recommended Strategies for Hedging Interest-Rate Risk

View	Borrower Strategy	Investor Strategy
Rates will be lower than implied forward curve	Buy cap Buy collar Buy cap corridor Buy payers swaption Buy caption	Swap (fixed-rate receiver) Swap and sell cap Buy participating floor
Rates will follow implied forward curve	Swap (fixed-rate payer) Buy zero-cost collar Buy participating cap	Swap (fixed-rate receiver) Sell zero-cost collar Buy participating floor
Rates will be higher than implied forward curve	Swap (fixed-rate payer) Swap and sell floor Buy participating cap	Buy floor Sell collar Buy floor corridor Buy receivers swaption Buy floortion

To provide a numerical basis for objective comparison, it is helpful to carry out a *scenario analysis* in which the performance of different hedging strategies are compared against a number of possible rate scenarios. Using the three scenarios pictured in Figure 15.6, Table 15.9 shows the effective borrowing cost under 10 different hedging schemes, while Table 15.10 shows the equivalent strategies and resultant returns for an investor. In every case, the figures apply to a five-year exposure using the initial set of rates shown in Table 15.2. Recommended strategies are shown in bold, and confirm the suggestions made in Table 15.8.

These scenario analyses enable a user to compare different hedging strategies under identical conditions. They have the great advantage that the analyses are relatively easy to carry out and that the sequences of rates selected can reflect the set of particular outcomes considered most likely or most feared by the user. However, they cannot give the complete picture, because they concentrate on a very small number of possibilities.

A more comprehensive analysis can be undertaken using Monte Carlo analysis in conjunction with a yield curve model, which will generate sequences of interest rates for evaluating alternative hedging schemes. It would be practically impossible to consider every conceivable scenario, not only because there are an infinite number of possibilities, but also because the precise probabilities for every rate sequence are unknown. However, a well-constructed Monte Carlo analysis can provide the user with an idea of the distribution of outcomes going far beyond those obtainable from particular scenario analyses.

Such an analysis was undertaken to evaluate the performance of four distinct hedging schemes: a 4.75% swap, a 5% cap, a 4–6% zero-cost collar, and

TABLE 15.9

Scenario Analysis Showing Effective Borrowing Costs Using Different Hedging Strategies

	Amortised Net Premium	Low-Rate Scenario	Neutral Scenario	High-Rate Scenario
Do nothing	-	4.22	4.75	5.28
Swap (fixed-rate payer)	-	4.75	**4.75**	**4.75**
Swap and sell 4.5% floor	(39bp)	4.76	4.63	**4.59**
Buy 5% cap	43bp	4.63	4.90	5.02
Buy 6% cap	18bp	**4.40**	4.91	5.21
Buy 4% to 6% collar	0bp	**4.36**	**4.84**	5.13
Buy participating cap at 5% (37% share)	0bp	4.71	**4.81**	**4.85**
Corridor: buy 5% cap and sell 6% cap	25bp	**4.45**	4.75	5.09
Buy 1yr payers swaption → 4yr 5% swap	23bp	**4.45***	4.90	4.92
Buy 1yr caption → 4yr 5% cap	13bp	**4.35***	5.03	5.15

* Not exercised.

TABLE 15.10

Scenario Analysis Showing Effective Investment Returns Using Different Hedging Strategies

	Amortised Net Premium	Low-Rate Scenario	Neutral Scenario	High-Rate Scenario
Do nothing	-	4.22	4.75	5.28
Swap (fixed-rate receiver)	-	**4.75**	**4.75**	4.75
Swap and sell 4.5% cap	(43bp)	**5.17**	4.91	4.50
Buy 4.5% floor	39bp	4.23	4.63	5.11
Buy 5% floor	18bp	4.18	4.68	**5.20**
Sell 4% to 6% collar	0bp	4.36	**4.84**	**5.13**
Buy participating floor at 4.5% (39% share)	0bp	**4.55**	**4.70**	4.89
Corridor: buy 5% floor and sell 4% floor	50bp	4.37	4.66	5.08
Buy 1yr receivers swaption → 4yr 5% swap	15bp	4.51	**4.60***	5.13*
Buy 1yr floortion → 4yr 5% floor	11bp	4.59	4.64*	5.17*

* Not exercised.

a participating cap at 5%. Five thousand rate sequences were generated at random, all starting with six-month rates at 3% and an expectation of rising interest rates over the next five years. The six-month rates in the final period were normally distributed with a mean of 6.46% and a standard deviation of 1.63%, but intermediate rates could be higher or lower. Figure 15.7 illustrates three typical rate sequences.

FIGURE 15.7
Illustrative Sequences for Six-Month Interest Rates

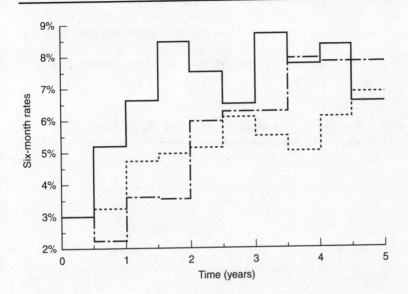

The effective borrowing cost under each scheme was recorded for every rate sequence and the outcomes analysed to produce the set of results summarised in Table 15.11, and illustrated in Figure 15.8. We can interpret these figures in the following way:

1. The narrowest range of outcomes is generated by the swap, of course, which fixes the borrower's costs at 4.75% regardless of the interest-rate environment.

2. The widest range arises under the cap, where the effect of the cap premium sets the maximum effective borrowing cost to 5.21%. This extreme outcome occurs if rates rise above the cap rate of 5% after the first interest period and stay above this level for the remainder of the borrowing. If rates fall, the cap allows the borrower to benefit without any penalty other than the cost of the cap premium.

3. The collar has the advantage of being a zero-cost product, but the higher cap level selected means that the maximum borrowing rate is somewhat higher than for the 5% cap. The mean rate is also higher, reflecting the upward bias used in the rate scenarios generated. If rates fall, the collar allows savings until the floor is reached at 4%, denying the borrower any further benefit beyond that point.

4. Finally, in this example the participating cap appears to outperform the collar. As the participating cap rate was set at 5%, the maximum borrowing rate is much lower than that of the 4%–6% collar. The worst

case, as with the straight cap, is when rates rise immediately after the first period. However, the participating cap outperforms the straight cap under those circumstances because of the zero net premium. The participating cap is only inferior to its plain-vanilla cousin under low-rate scenarios in which the straight cap is unencumbered by the need to share savings with the cap counterparty. Note, however, that the spread of possible outcomes is the narrowest other than for the swap itself.

TABLE 15.11
Performance Summary under Monte Carlo Analysis for Four Hedging Strategies

	Swap	*Cap*	*Collar*	*Participating Cap*
Minimum rate	4.75%	2.42%	4.00%	3.88%
Maximum rate	4.75	5.21	5.78	4.92
Mean rate	4.75	4.76	5.02	4.75
Standard deviation	0.00	0.42	0.43	0.15

FIGURE 15.8
Probability Distribution for Different Hedging Strategies

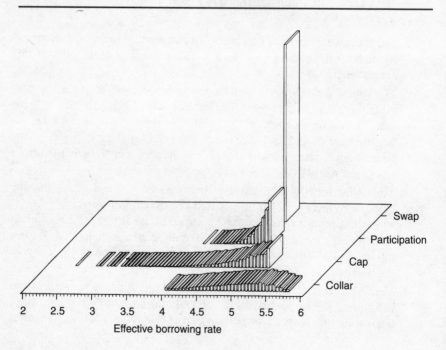

The full set of distributions is shown in Figure 15.8, which makes it much easier to make a visual comparison between the various alternatives. The shape of these probability profiles and the relative degree of uncertainty associated with each strategy may help borrowers and investors choose from among the different hedging schemes. This is one of the advantages of the Monte Carlo technique.

Chapter Sixteen

Managing Equity Risk

Equity risk manifests itself as variation in the value of individual shares or that of an equity portfolio. This is essentially a price risk, as indeed is currency risk. The methods used to manage equity risk therefore have much in common with those discussed in Chapter Thirteen for handling currency risk. As we proceed though the various risk management techniques in this chapter, the close parallels will be readily apparent.

We will start by presenting methods for taking advantage of anticipated movements in share prices, but without resorting to the purchase of the shares themselves. The next sections will discuss ways of handling the risk arising from holdings of individual shares, demonstrating both aggressive and conservative strategies. All the examples describe a mythically named company called Amzo, but all the option prices are based on the quoted prices of a real company whose shares were trading at 100p at the time.

Later sections will progress to equity portfolios and explain how index derivatives and option replication strategies may be used. Option-based techniques will feature prominently throughout because of the relatively wide availability of stock and stock index options and the great flexibility that these tools confer.

16.1 BULL AND BEAR STRATEGIES

The simplest strategy for an investor who is bullish about the prospects for a particular company's shares is to buy the shares outright. However, if options on these shares are available, a range of other possibilities are opened up, including:

- Buying call options.
- Buying a bull spread.
- A "90:10" strategy.

Similarly, the bearish investor can buy put options or a bear spread. In none of these cases is it necessary to buy or sell the underlying shares; the positions are all created through the purchase and sale of stock options. We will examine each of the bull strategies in turn; the bear strategies do not warrant individual attention because they are simply the mirror images of the corresponding bull strategy.

Buying call options. Buying a call option will enable the purchaser to benefit from a rise in the underlying share price but to be protected from a fall. The broad choice is between options that are out-, at-, or in-the-money, and this is probably best seen graphically. Suppose that Amzo's shares are currently trading at 100p, two-month at-the-money call options are priced at 4½p, and out-of-the-money calls struck at 110p are priced at 1p for a similar maturity. Figure 16.1 compares the strategy of buying the shares outright, buying the calls struck at 100p, and buying the 110p calls. In each case, the quantity of shares under consideration is 1,000, and the underlying price moves shortly after the strategy is put in place.

In straight money terms, buying the shares outright outperforms either of the option strategies. This may seem surprising at first sight, because options are normally thought of as highly geared instruments. However, Figure 16.1 compares the financial performance of the shares with that of options on the same *number* of shares, not the same *value* of shares. Apart from options that are completely in-the-money, the value of an option will always change by less than the value of the underlying shares, this sensitivity being described by the option's delta. For a rise in share price of 10p, the two options illustrated here will rise by 7½p and 4p, respectively. Similarly, if the share price falls by 10p, the two options will fall by 3½p and 1p. These figures give rise to the monetary gains and losses illustrated in Figure 16.1, remembering that the diagram graphs the performance based on a portfolio of 1000 shares.

The gearing becomes more obvious if we graph the percentage gain and loss of the three strategies; this is shown in Figure 16.2. For a ±10% increase in the share price, the at-the-money option shows a swing from a 78% loss to a 167% gain, while the out-of-the-money option goes from a 100% loss to an

FIGURE 16.1
Comparison of Call Option Strategies: Absolute Gains and Losses

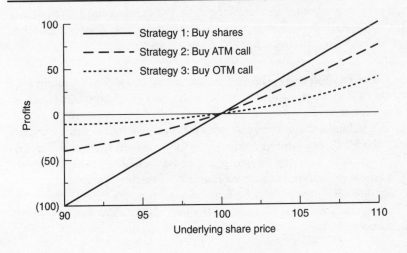

FIGURE 16.2
Comparison of Call Option Strategies: Percentage Gains and Losses

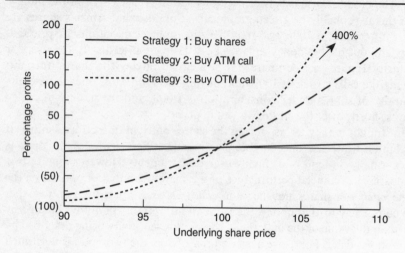

impressive 400% gain. Investors tempted by the last strategy should remember that although huge gains are indeed possible, the most likely outcome when buying an out-of-the-money option is that it will expire worthless, giving rise to a 100% loss.

Buying a bull spread. The bull spread has been examined in some depth in Chapter Eleven (Section 11.2). The main advantages over a straight call option are that the bull spread is cheaper, and suffers far less from the effect of time decay. However, the buyer of a bull spread gives up the opportunity to continue to gain once the underlying share price rises above the higher strike price. Figure 16.3 compares the performance of a 90p–110p bull spread after one month with that of the underlying shares and a straight call. Note that the bull spread incurs no losses if the underlying price is unchanged in one month's time, whereas the straight call loses one-third of its value.

The 90:10 strategy. The idea behind the so-called 90:10 strategy is to guarantee a minimum return by investing the bulk of the funds available in riskless interest-bearing deposits but to obtain a limited exposure to risk by using the balance of funds to buy options on a particular share or stock index. The 90:10 description comes from the usual split between deposits and options, although any desired split can be used. The strategy is essentially a conservative one, because the majority of the funds are committed to risk-free deposits, thus preserving most of the investor's capital even if the options expire worthless. However, if the underlying shares rally substantially, the 90:10 strategy can actually outperform the share-only strategy

FIGURE 16.3
The Bull Spread

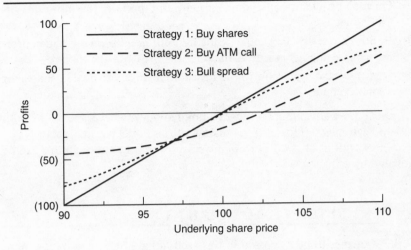

FIGURE 16.4
The 90:10 Strategy

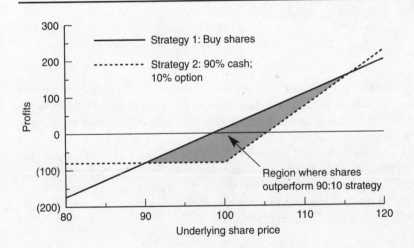

because of the gearing available from the options. The performance of the 90:10 strategy is illustrated in Figure 16.4, which demonstrates that it provides a better result for the investor either if there is a substantial rise in the underlying share price or if there is a substantial fall.

The three option strategies reviewed so far, as well as the corresponding bear strategies, all share some important advantages over more simple tactics involving just buying or selling the underlying shares:

- Options have limited downside risk if the market moves against the investor's view.
- Options provide high leverage potential, especially the more out-of-the-money they are.
- Positive curvature or gamma leads to *profit acceleration* in which profits increase at a faster rate as the option moves into-the-money.
- Options make it possible for an investor effectively to deal in shares for a forward date.

Against these advantages it must be pointed out that leverage works both ways and can magnify losses if the market moves in the wrong direction. At-the-money options also suffer from adverse time decay, although this can be mitigated by using spread strategies.

16.2 RETURN ENHANCEMENT

All the strategies to be discussed in this section have one thing in common: they provide a means of enhancing the return from an existing or anticipated holding of shares. Specifically, we will look at

- Selling covered calls.
- Ratioed selling covered calls.
- Selling naked puts.
- Ratioed selling puts.

Selling covered calls. A common strategy among investors holding shares is to sell call options on those shares. Since the investor already holds the shares that would need to be delivered if the option expires in-the-money, this strategy is also known as *covered call writing*. As an example, suppose a particular investor holds 10,000 shares in Amzo that are currently trading at 100p. The investor believes that Amzo shares will not rise over the next few months but will probably stay static. He therefore writes two-month call options on these shares struck at-the-money for a premium income of 5p per share. There are now three outcomes at expiry:

1. Amzo shares stay static at 100p, as expected. The options expire worthless, and the investor pockets the 5p premium to boost the return from the shares.
2. Amzo shares rise, and the options expire in-the-money. The investor delivers his holding of Amzo shares at the exercise price of 100p, but the premium income of 5p means that he has effectively sold his shares at 105p.
3. Amzo shares fall, and the options expire worthless. The investor still holds on to his shares, which have not been protected from the fall in

market price, but the premium income cushions the effect of the fall by boosting the effective value by 5p a share.

Figure 16.5 shows the investor's profit profiles at expiry, not only using the at-the-money option discussed above, but also using in- and out-of-the-money options. Selling calls creates a guaranteed price for profit-taking if the share price rises and enhanced portfolio value equal to the premium received if the price remains static or falls. The lower the strike price of the option sold, the lower is the price ceiling established, but this ceiling is effective over a wider range of share prices, including situations where the share price falls. In the example illustrated, if the investor sells a 90p call for a premium received of 12p, a price ceiling is established at 102p, even if the underlying share price drops to 90p. A higher strike establishes a higher price ceiling but brings in less premium.

Note once again that covered call writing provides no protection to the investor at all. On the contrary, it actually sets an upper limit to the value of the shares, but it does increase the value of the holding if the share price stays static or falls.

Ratioed selling covered calls. A variation of the previous strategy is to sell call options on a portion of the shares held. This brings in less premium income but allows the investor to benefit from the part of the portfolio left uncovered if the share price rises above the strike price. Figure 16.6 illustrates the profit profile from the strategy of selling at-the-money options on 50% of the shares held. When compared to the corresponding profile shown in Figure 16.5, the price enhancement is half, but there is a 50% participation in profits above the strike price of 100p.

FIGURE 16.5
Covered Call Writing

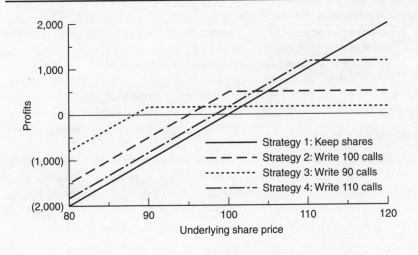

FIGURE 16.6
Ratioed Covered Call Writing

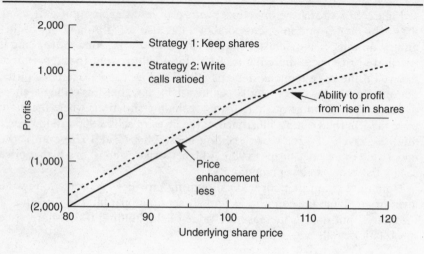

Selling naked puts. This strategy differs somewhat from the others presented in this section, for it starts with the investor holding no shares at all but having a neutral to bullish view on the prospects for a particular company. If the shares are bought outright, the investor would suffer the financing cost, something that would be unattractive if the share price stays static. An alternative is for him to sell naked puts instead. This is not a risky strategy, provided that the investor is already inclined to buy the underlying shares and therefore does not mind if the put is exercised against him. Suppose the investor sells two-month at-the-money puts on 10,000 Amzo shares, the number of shares that he would be quite willing to buy. Amzo is currently trading at 100p, and the puts are priced at 3½p per share. There are three possible outcomes at expiry:

1. Amzo's share price stays static. The puts expire worthless, and the investor can simply keep the £350 premium income or use it to lower the effective cost of buying Amzo shares to 96½p.

2. Amzo's share price rises, for example, to 110p. Again, the puts expire out-of-the-money, giving the investor the option of either keeping the £350 premium income or using it to subsidise buying the shares at 106½p. Of course, had the investor bought Amzo shares originally, the profit would have been £1,000.

3. Amzo shares fall, and the option is exercised against the investor. This means that the investor ends up buying Amzo shares at an effective price of 96½p, which is cheaper than the original market price. He has also had the opportunity to earn interest on his funds over the two-month option period.

The complete profile is graphed in Figure 16.7. Note that this is virtually identical to Figure 16.5, because combining a long position in the underlying asset with a short position in call options creates a synthetic short put position. This is part of the building block approach explained in Chapter Eleven (Section 11.1).

Ratioed selling puts. There is an alternative and almost equivalent strategy to the ratioed selling of calls. An investor who believes that the value of his shares will most likely stay static, but may increase, can sell a portion of his portfolio and also sell puts equal to the portion sold. For example, if the investor currently holds 10,000 Amzo shares and sells half, he would sell put options on the 5,000 shares just sold. If Amzo shares stay static or rise, the puts expire worthless allowing the investor to benefit from both the premium income received and also any profits on the proportion of shares still held. If Amzo shares fall, against the investor's expectations, the puts are exercised against him, and he ends up holding the same number of shares as were held originally, but with the benefit of the premium income received at the outset. The profile of this strategy is the same as that already pictured in Figure 16.6.

16.3 VALUE PROTECTION STRATEGIES

The strategies in the previous section were concerned with enhancing the return from an existing share portfolio whose value was expected to remain static. All the strategies involved selling options in order to provide premium income, but this established a ceiling on the value of the portfolio. By con-

FIGURE 16.7
Selling Naked Puts

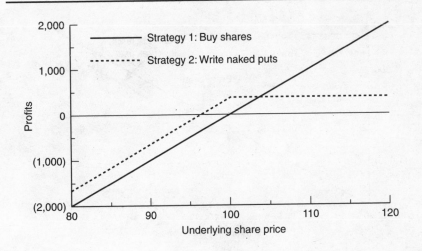

trast, the value protection strategies discussed here have the opposite objective. They seek to create a floor below which the value of a share portfolio cannot fall but allow the investor to continue to benefit if share prices rise. Not surprisingly, these strategies all involve buying options to provide the degree of protection sought. We will examine three possible schemes:

- Buying puts.
- Liquidating the shares and buying calls.
- Buying a collar.

Buying puts. This is the simplest and classic way to protect the value of a share portfolio. Buying puts at- or slightly out-of-the-money establishes a price floor. If the share price drops below this level, the puts can be exercised and the shares sold at the price guaranteed by the strike price. If the share price rises, the puts expire worthless and the investor continues to benefit from the increased value of the shares held. The only drawback of this strategy is the cost of the premium income, which lowers the effective level of the price floor and depresses any benefit from a rise in the underlying share price. In fact, the share price must rise by the amount of the premium income for the strategy to break even, as illustrated in Figure 16.8.

Liquidating the shares and buying calls. Buying puts while holding the underlying asset creates a synthetic long call position. Thus an alternative strategy to the one just discussed would be for the investor to liquidate the share holding, invest the proceeds to earn interest, but buy call options in order to continue to participate in any further rises in the underlying share

FIGURE 16.8
Buying Puts

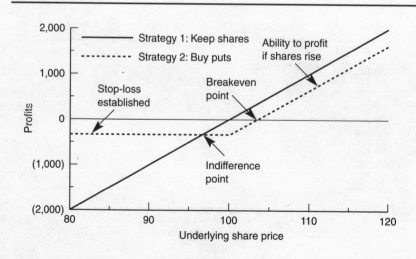

price. The fact that calls rather than the underlying shares are now held means that the investor is protected against a sharp drop in the share price. The shape of the profile is identical to that illustrated in Figure 16.8.

Buying a collar. The tactic of tailoring option-based risk management solutions to meet users' needs has already been extensively explored in Chapters Thirteen and Fifteen. In particular, financing the purchase of protective options with the sale of others is the basis for collars, corridors, participations, and other structures. The simplest of these structures, the collar, involves selling out-of-the-money calls in order to finance the purchase of puts. If done for the same number of shares as are actually held within the portfolio, the puts purchased establish a floor price while the calls sold establish a price ceiling. Juggling the two strike levels will vary the amount of protection acquired, the extent of profit opportunities sold off, and the net premium paid.

Figure 16.9 illustrates a two-month collar with an at-the-money floor at 100p and a ceiling at 105p acquired for a net premium of just 1p. The worst outcome is for the share price to remain static or to fall, but in such cases the investor would lose just 1p per share in value. If the share price rises during the two-month period, the investor will gain for the first 5p increase, until the ceiling of 105p is reached, but would gain no more from any further price appreciation. If the ceiling is reached, the effective value per share is 104p (the 105p ceiling less the 1p net premium paid). For a small up-front premium, this collar therefore guarantees a minimum effective share price of 99p and the opportunity to benefit fully until the effective ceiling at 104p is reached.

FIGURE 16.9
A Collar Strategy

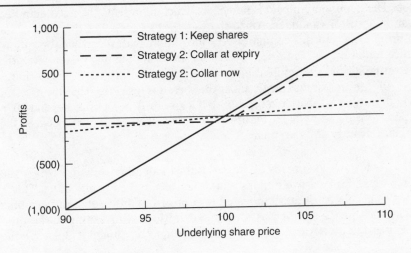

16.4 VERTICAL, HORIZONTAL, AND DIAGONAL SPREADS

Chapter Eleven (Section 11.2) introduced the concept of option spreads, and these can readily be applied in the context of equity derivatives.

Vertical spreads. A vertical spread, the buying and selling of options that differ only in their exercise price, has already been discussed in Section 16.1 with an illustration of the bull call spread. However, bull and bear spreads can arise as the end result of a dynamic hedging strategy executed over a period of time, even though the scheme may not have been planned at the outset. When this happens, it is sometimes known as *rolling up into a spread* or *rolling down into a spread*. This has been illustrated in Chapter Thirteen (Section 13.14) in the context of currency hedging and works just as well in the management of equity risk.

Suppose that a speculator believes that Amzo shares, currently at 100p, are about to rise. Rather than incur the financing cost of investing in the shares directly, he buys a four-month out-of-the-money call struck at 110p for a premium cost of 3p. One month later, Amzo shares have risen, as expected, and are now trading at 110p. The investor now sells a three-month option also struck 10p out-of-the-money at 120p and also for a premium of 3p. The investor's net premium is now zero, having bought and sold calls at 3p each, but he is now the holder of a 110p–120p bull call spread. After rolling up into this spread, the investor can gain a maximum of 10p if Amzo's shares keep on rising or break even if they stay static or fall, but he cannot lose.

The opposite strategy, rolling down into a spread, can occur if an investor's original strategy goes wrong. Suppose an investor buys a four-month at-the-money call on Amzo struck at 100p for a premium of 7p. Unfortunately, Amzo's shares fall to 90p after one month, so that the call is now worth just 2p. The investor could roll down into a 90p–100p spread by selling two of the 100p calls at 2p and buying a 90p at-the-money call for 5½p. The net premium paid is now 8½p, which represents the maximum loss that the investor can make. Amzo shares need to rise to 98½ for the investor to break even, but this compares very favourably with the original position, which had a break-even price of 107p. By lowering the break-even level, the investor sacrifices the potential to make unlimited profits if Amzo shares take off—the maximum profit under the spread is just 1½p—but the investor may think this is a better compromise if a rise in Amzo's price beyond 107p is now considered unlikely. Figure 16.10 shows the comparison between the original strategy and the spread.

Horizontal spreads. A horizontal or calendar spread involves the purchase and sale of two options that differ only in their expiry dates. This is often a speculative strategy intended to profit from differential rates of time decay on short-dated versus long-dated options. For example, the one-month at-the-money call on Amzo's shares might be quoted at 3p, while the

FIGURE 16.10
Rolling Down into a Spread

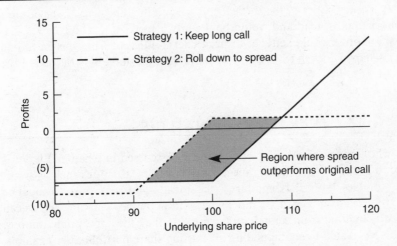

FIGURE 16.11
Calendar Spread

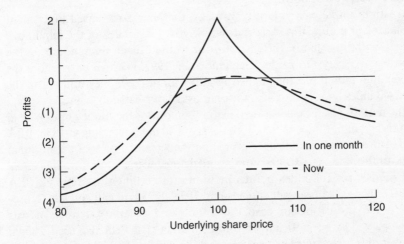

four-month call at the same strike might command a premium of 7p. Selling the one-month and buying the four-month option would therefore incur a net premium cost of 4p. If Amzo's share price was unchanged after a month, the short-dated option would expire worthless, while the premium of the now three-month option might have decayed to 6p. The net value of the calendar spread would therefore have increased from 4p to 6p, an increase of 50% over one month. Figure 16.11 sketches the profit profile from this strategy showing the peak profit at 100p, and break-even levels at 96p and 107p.

Diagonal spreads. Combining the concept of a horizontal and vertical spread gives a diagonal spread, where options are bought and sold at two different strike prices and maturity dates. Such a spread mixes the directional characteristics of the vertical spread with the time decay behaviour of the horizontal spread and would be used by a speculator who believes that the share price would settle at a specific level different from the prevailing price. Chapter Eleven (Section 11.2) provides some good illustrations of the resulting profiles.

16.5 OTHER OPTION STRATEGIES

The whole range of other option strategies discussed in Chapter Eleven is open to the equity investor or speculator. Volatility structures such as straddles, strangles, butterflies, condors, ratio spreads, and backspreads can all be used to take advantage of an anticipated shift in implied volatility. These can either be built up from scratch by buying or selling the appropriate options, or can be created by manipulating an existing share portfolio. For example, an investor long in shares can create a straddle by buying put options on twice the number of shares held. This will yield profits either if implied volatility increases or if there is a substantial shift in the underlying share price, whether up or down.

As an example of a volatility strategy, the New York-based investment management group BEA Associates took good advantage of the temporary hike in volatility that occurred just prior to the French referendum on the Maastricht Treaty. On Friday, September 18, 1992, just two days before the referendum took place, the implied volatility for at-the-money options on the CAC-40 index had risen to 47% for options that were due to expire at the end of the month, just 12 days away. Volatility on out-of-the-money options had also risen, but not by as much. With the CAC-40 index standing at 1850, BEA sold at-the-money straddles for a premium income of 7.35% of the notional value of the index. (CAC-40 contracts are defined with a unit of trading equal to FFR 200 per full index point.) In addition to selling the straddles, BEA bought 1650–1725 bear put spreads and 1975–2025 bull call spreads to provide some protection in case the anticipated volatility reduction was accompanied by a significant shift in the market. The firm also used a small number of futures contracts to ensure that the strategy was delta-neutral at the close of business that day. The net premium received was thus reduced to 5.88% after the 1.47% cost of the two spreads was taken into account.

Figure 16.12 graphs the resulting maturity profile, based on the fact that BEA traded 200 index option contracts at each strike price.[1] Note the two zero-risk corridors created by the purchase of the bear and bull spreads.

---

[1] See Lillian Chew, "No Mean Feat," *Risk* 6, no. 2 (February 1993).

FIGURE 16.12
Volatility Trade on CAC-40 Index

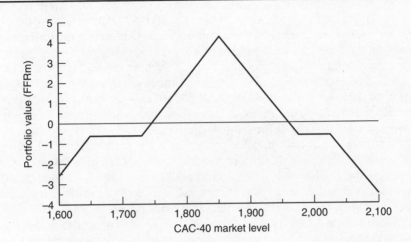

With this structure, BEA was short volatility, but well-protected against a shift in the market of up to ±10%.

On the Monday immediately following the referendum, there was fortunately little change in the level of the market, but option volatility fell back to 25% just as expected. All positions were closed out for a total cost of 4.36%, resulting in a net profit amounting to 1.52% of the FFR 74 million nominal exposure, a little over FFR 1.1 million in absolute terms.

In addition to volatility strategies, arbitrage structures such as conversions, reversals, or boxes can also be exploited using equity derivatives. Occasionally prices in the market move out of line, opening up an opportunity for an arbitrageur to extract a riskless profit, but such opportunities are relatively few and far between. More often, a conversion or reversal is created when an investor or speculator wishes to close out an existing position and insulate it against further developments in market prices. Comprehensive examples of all these strategies have already been presented in Chapter Eleven (Section 11.4).

16.6 USING STOCK INDEX FUTURES AND OPTIONS

The examples so far have all referred to hedging or speculation involving the shares of a single company. At the other end of the spectrum are problems arising from well-diversified portfolios of shares. Fortunately, the availability of stock index futures and options makes the task of managing portfolio risk much easier. Chapter Eight has already explored how stock index futures work and has shown how these instruments can be used to transmute share portfolios into interest-earning deposits, and vice versa. In this section we shall concentrate on stock index options.

Stock index options work just like ordinary stock options, except that the underlying asset is a stock index such as the S&P 500 rather than the price of an individual share. They come in two varieties. Options on the index itself, such as the S&P 100 stock index option, provide solely for cash settlement on expiry, while options on index futures, such as the FTSE 100 contract, can also be exercised into the underlying futures contract. Where both types of options co-exist—as with the S&P 500 index—the premiums for European-style index and index futures options tend not to differ, but American-style index futures options normally have call prices exceeding those of the index option, while put prices are usually cheaper. The divergence of American-style option prices arises from the possibility of early exercise and the fact that index futures tend to trade at a premium over the spot index price, making index futures call options more in-the-money than the equivalent index option with the same strike price.

Index options or index futures options can be used in much the same way as stock options and with the same variety of hedging structures or speculative positions. A speculator wishing to profit from a rise in the level of shares generally, but to limit losses in case the market should fall, can buy a call option or a bull call spread to achieve this objective. Alternatively, a portfolio manager holding a well-diversified share portfolio can use index options or index futures options to create a cap, floor, collar, or any of the other structures examined earlier in this chapter.

As an example of the first of these uses, consider an speculator who is bullish about the prospects for the U.S. stock market. It is February 22, 1993, and the S&P 500 index stands at 435.25. The speculator believes that the market will rally by 5% to 10% over the next two months but will then fall back. He does not wish to pick individual shares nor incur the transaction costs in building up a portfolio that he plans to hold only over a short time. Finally, he does not wish to be exposed to downside risk in case his view proves wrong; this rules out the use of index futures. The speculator decides to buy a bull call spread in April S&P 500 index options (the so-called SPX contracts) and enters into the following transactions:

Buy 50 April 440 SPX calls at 5½ ⎫ Net premium paid 4¼
Sell 50 April 455 SPX calls at 1¼ ⎭

At $100 per full index point, the net premium is therefore 4¼ × 50 × $100 = $21,250.

On March 16, 1993, just three weeks later, the market has risen to 451.37. The speculator decides to close out the position and take profits a little earlier than expected, especially as the market has fallen back a little over the past few days. The position is unwound with the following deals:

Sell 50 April 440 SPX calls at 15   ⎫ Net premium received 10¼
Buy 50 April 455 SPX calls at 4¾ ⎭

The proceeds bring in 10¼ × 50 × $100 = $51,250, leaving the speculator with a net profit of exactly $30,000 on the original investment of $21,250—a 141% gain in three weeks. The maximum potential profit of $53,750 (equivalent to a 253% gain) would have been achieved if the speculator had held on to the spread until the option maturity date and if the market had risen above 455 at that time. The worst outcome would have been for the market to stay below 440 before the expiry date in April, whereupon the speculator would have lost the entire $21,250 premium invested. These extremes illustrate the highly geared nature of option performance.

As an alternative to liquidating the position in mid-March, the speculator in this example could have used the tactic of rolling up into a spread at a higher level. Instead of liquidating the position as illustrated above, he could have executed the following transactions:

Sell 50 April 440 SPX calls at 15 ⎫
Buy 100 April 455 SPX calls at 4¾ ⎬ Net premium received 8⅝
Sell 50 April 460 SPX calls at 3⅛ ⎭

Although this reduces the immediate proceeds to $43,125 and the profits to $21,875, the speculator now has a "free" 455–460 bull spread that allows him to participate in a further increase in the market up to 460. Many other permutations are possible.

Stock index options can also be used by the portfolio manager having a broad holding of shares. The success of any strategy based on these options will depend upon how closely the portfolio tracks the market index. A well-diversified portfolio will present few unexpected problems if it tends to track the market index very closely. The number of index options required in this case can be calculated using a similar technique to that demonstrated in Chapter Eight with stock index futures (see Section 8.12). For example, suppose that a portfolio comprised shares currently valued at £26,000,000 and these are to be hedged using FTSE 100 options, which are defined as having a value of £10 per full index point. If the FTSE 100 index was currently at 3,045, the number of contracts required would be

£26,000,000/(£10 × 3045) = 854 contracts

For other portfolios there will be a residual basis risk, part of which can be handled by adjusting the number of option contracts used. The first step is to conduct a regression analysis just like the ones described in Chapter Fourteen (Section 14.3). In that context, a scattergraph like the one illustrated in Figure 14.1 was used to examine the relationship between prime rate and eurodollar rates. Here we need to do the same thing by determining the relationship between the value of the portfolio and the level of the market index. Specifically, the portfolio manager must use regression analysis to estimate the parameters of equation 16.1:

$$P_t = \alpha + \beta I_t + \varepsilon \tag{16.1}$$

where
- P_t is the value of the portfolio at time t
- I_t is the value of index at time t
- α is the intercept parameter
- β is the slope parameter
- ε is an error term that accounts for unpredictable portfolio movements not correlated with the index

Assuming that the correlation coefficient (a by-product from the regression analysis) shows a strong and reliable relationship between the portfolio value and the market index, the most important parameter is β. The beta coefficient expresses numerically by how much the portfolio value will move when the index changes. For example, if $\beta = 2$ for a particular share portfolio, it means that the portfolio value will increase by twice as much as that of the index when the market rises and decrease twice as fast as the index when the market falls.

Once the beta for a particular portfolio is known, the number of option contracts required is simply multiplied by beta to obtain the correct number for an options hedge. If the £26 million portfolio to be hedged had a β of 1.24, the number of options would need to be increased from 854 to 1,059. Being more volatile than the market, a greater number of option contracts would be necessary to hedge the risk. This number then forms the basis for any of the option strategies discussed earlier. For example, to construct a collar the portfolio manager would buy 1,059 put options at a lower strike price and sell 1,059 calls at a higher strike.

The remaining basis risk arises out of the error term ε in equation 16.1, which accounts for the unpredictable fluctuations in portfolio value that are independent of the index. If the correlation coefficient is high, then this error term will be small, and hedges based on index options will prove efficient. If the portfolio is poorly correlated with the index, the portfolio manager would either have to accept a high degree of basis risk or use a basket option, as described in Section 16.10.

16.7 PORTFOLIO INSURANCE

Portfolio insurance is a technique that was developed in the early 1980s and was highly popular until the stock market crash in October 1987, although the technique continues to be used, albeit on a much reduced scale. Portfolio insurance is sometimes confused with program trading and asset allocation because they all have certain similarities.

Program trading. This generally refers to computerised systems capable of suggesting or initiating trades that are intended to exploit risk-free arbitrage opportunities in the market. Schemes specifically associated with the equity markets usually try to identify and exploit any gaps appearing between the price of index futures and the prices of the constituent shares.

Asset allocation. This often refers to the practice of using stock index futures or bond futures as a cheap and flexible means of adjusting the mix of an investment portfolio. Chapter Eight (Section 8.12) has already illustrated how an interest-bearing deposit can be completely converted into a synthetic share portfolio using stock index futures and also how the reverse process can be achieved. By buying and selling variable amounts of stock index and bond futures, a portfolio currently containing an arbitrary mix of cash, bonds, and equities can be converted into one having any other desired mix. This is usually much cheaper than liquidating unwanted holdings and purchasing the desired assets.

Portfolio insurance. This term was coined by two academics, Leland and Rubinstein,[2] to describe a strategy whereby an equity portfolio can be made to behave like a call option, with limited downside and unlimited upside potential. It was first developed for pension fund investors, whose actuarial liabilities require the fund to earn an absolute minimum return but who prefer to earn a higher return if possible. The call-like profile can be achieved in several ways:

- Buy shares or bonds and buy a protective put option on these assets to establish a floor price.
- Invest in risk-free interest-bearing deposits and buy call options on a market index to obtain the upside potential.
- Use a dynamic asset allocation strategy.

The first two possibilities are equivalent and are obvious choices. After all, if the desired profile has the characteristic shape of an option, why not just use an option? The problem is a practical one: most stock and stock index options are available only with a limited maturity, typically just a few months in the future. Long-term equity options are generally only available in the form of warrants on particular shares or have extremely limited liquidity.

The third possibility involves dynamically allocating a fund between different types of assets according to market conditions. When the stock market is rising, a greater proportion of the fund should be committed to equities. Beyond a certain high point, the fund would be completely invested in equities, benefiting fully from any further rise in the stock market. Conversely, when the market is falling, the portion in equities should be cut back

---

[2] See Rubinstein, M. and H. Leland, "Republicating options with positions in stock and cash," *Financial Analysis Journal* 43, no. 5 (1987), pp. 25–32. The two authors teamed up with a third partner to create LOR Associates, a U.S.-based consultancy advising on the application of portfolio insurance concepts.

and the resources switched into interest bearing deposits or possibly bonds, thereby cushioning the value of the portfolio against further losses. By the time the market has reached a certain low threshold, the fund would be completely invested in deposits, and its value would no longer fall if the stock market dropped further. A floor level for the fund is thus established. In between, the fund would contain a portion of deposits and equities, and its response to movements in the stock market would be diluted accordingly. The net result of this dynamic asset allocation strategy is sketched in Figure 16.13, where the option-like characteristic is very evident.

In fact, this idea is equivalent to the method used in Chapter Ten (Section 10.8) as the basis for pricing options, namely, that a short position in call options can be completely hedged by borrowing money and investing it in a proportion of the underlying asset. In other words, the combination of some of the underlying asset with some borrowing is equivalent to a long position in a call option. Exactly the same combination is being used with dynamic asset allocation. In effect, part of a 100% investment in interest bearing deposits is "borrowed" and used to buy shares. As the portion of the fund invested in equities varies with different levels of the market, the full option-like behaviour of the resulting strategy emerges.

The only drawback with the dynamic asset allocation strategy so far described is the extensive transaction costs that would be involved as shares were bought and sold in order to ensure that the correct portion of funds was committed to equities at all times. This could be mitigated to some extent by having fewer trigger levels at which the portion of equities needed to be rebalanced. Figure 16.13 shows 10 such points, and this could be reduced to four, say, but the option-like performance would become much cruder.

What made portfolio insurance a successful strategy was the use of futures to achieve the dynamic asset allocation. Instead of actually buying or

FIGURE 16.13
Dynamic Asset Allocation

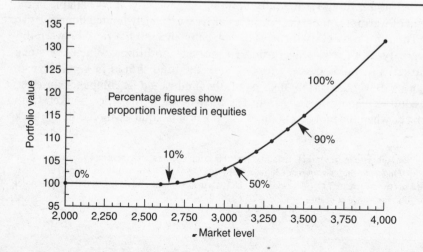

selling shares, stock index futures are bought or sold to accomplish the required mix between shares and riskless deposits. Transaction costs for futures are far less than the corresponding commissions on share deals, and the desired effect could therefore be realised much more effectively.

Portfolio insurance was, and still is, a very worthwhile strategy. Unfortunately, the scheme fell from favour in the aftermath of the 1987 stock market crash. The problem was that a significant number of share portfolios were being controlled by portfolio insurance schemes following a sustained rise in the level of the market. This meant that most portfolios were fully invested in equities, either through physical holdings of shares or synthetically through long positions in index futures. The initial fall in the stock market triggered a wave of selling orders for the futures contracts as the portfolio insurance schemes sought to rebalance the portfolios with a smaller proportion of equities. The flow of orders came so thick and fast that the index futures began to trade at a significant discount to the value of the underlying shares. This had the unfortunate effect of triggering program trading systems set up to exploit this kind of arbitrage. The program trades immediately started to sell shares, which in turn drove the index even lower. A chain reaction was in progress with the eventual consequences that are now well known.

This does not mean that portfolio insurance as a strategy is doomed. The ideas are still valid, especially the use of futures as a means of effecting dynamic asset allocation. However, portfolio managers need to be aware that these schemes cannot absolutely guarantee that a floor level will be effective if the market drops sharply and suddenly, as it did in 1987. In addition, the systems, the investor's portfolio, and the market itself must all be protected against the lemming like behaviour of unthinking computer programs in the event that markets behave in an odd and unanticipated way.

16.8 GUARANTEED EQUITY FUNDS

A variation on the concept of portfolio insurance is the idea of the *guaranteed equity fund*, a retail product marketed under a number of different proprietary names. This promises the small investor a return equal to a specified multiple of the growth of a particular market index over a period or the investor's money back if the index should fall. As an example of the genre, many UK building societies since 1992 have offered a package with the following typical specification:

Return	133% of the percentage rise of the FTSE 100 index over the specified period.
Period	June 1, 1993, to June 1, 1998.
Settlement price	Average of daily closing prices over final six months.
Guarantee	100% return of investment returned if FTSE 100 falls over period.
Management fees	Nil.
Early withdrawals	Subject to certain restrictions and penalties.
Amounts	£500 to £250,000 can be invested.

For many investors, this provides a very attractive package indeed. If they were interested in an equity-linked return, there were few simple choices other than to invest in shares directly. This would have involved sizable transaction costs, and it would be uneconomic to build a well-diversified portfolio with such a small investment. Even if the larger investor bought a reasonable spread of shares similar in composition to the index, they would only provide a return comparable with the index, not a third more as promised by the guaranteed equity fund. A shareholder would benefit from dividends received, but these would be unlikely to amount to 33% over five years, even taking reinvestment interest into account. Finally, the package provides a cast-iron guarantee—the return of 100% of the investor's money in the event that the market falls over the period.

The institutions offering this product structured the package in one of two ways:

1. Purchase a five-year zero-coupon bond with a nominal value equal to the amount invested, plus a five-year at-the-money call option on 1.3333 times the amount invested.
2. Invest in a well-diversified portfolio of shares, plus a five-year at-the-money put option, plus a five-year at-the-money call option on 0.3333 times the amount originally invested, the options purchased being financed from the stream of dividends on the shares.

These are equivalent structures, and the choice largely depends on the investment preferences of the institution concerned. For example, fund managers already hold well-diversified share portfolios and may naturally lean toward the second alternative.

As an example of the pricing of these products using the first hedging structure, suppose that long-term yields are 8.25%, and that a five-year at-the-money index option can be bought for an up-front premium of 20%. For every £100 invested, the distribution is

Purchase zero-coupon bond with a nominal value of £100	£67.28
Purchase call option on £133.33	£26.67
Total cost	£93.95

This leaves £6.05 out of every £100 invested to cover marketing, transactions costs, management fees, and so on.

The pricing of guaranteed equity funds is subject to the level of interest rates, owing to the high price sensitivity of the zero-coupon bond. As interest rates fall, the bond becomes more expensive, reducing the profit margin or forcing a lower index profit participation rate. This is only partially mitigated by the reduction in cost for the call option. For example, if interest rates drop by 1%, the bond increases in value by £3.19, but the option cost reduces by £2.36. This takes 83p from the margin, a reduction of 14%. In Britain, participation rates offered by institutions have dropped from the 133⅓% shown in the illustration above, to 110% more recently, as sterling interest rates fell following the sterling crisis in September 1992 and the subsequent withdrawal from the ERM.

16.9 WARRANTS AND CONVERTIBLES

Although there is insufficient space to discuss these products in depth—they each deserve a book to themselves—this chapter would not be complete without a brief review of warrants and convertibles.

A *warrant* is like a long-term option on a particular company's shares. There is one significant difference other than the tenor: the exercise of a warrant usually involves the issue of new shares by the company, whereas an option is nondilutive. In addition, warrants are not normally available for the range of maturity dates and strike prices available with ordinary equity options; a given warrant issue will have one specific strike price and will expire on one particular date. There is one piece of jargon that can cause confusion: the premium. With regular options, the premium is the price paid for the option. The equivalent term with warrants is just the *price*. The *warrant premium* is normally understood to mean the amount by which the warrant price plus the strike price exceeds the prevailing share price. For example, a warrant priced at 20p with an exercise price of 150p would have a 70% premium if the issuer's current share price was 100p.

Warrants are frequently used in conjunction with a new bond issue, to act as a "sweetener," and are particularly prevalent in the Japanese equity markets. If the company performs well, the investor can eventually exercise the warrant and buy the company's equity at a price fixed at the outset. In the meantime, the investor has the security of holding the company's fixed-income debt, which also acts as a fallback position in case the company's prospects decline. After issue, warrants can usually be detached from the accompanying bond and traded independently.

A few companies actively use warrants as a means of promoting shareholder value and of obtaining a steady stream of new investment. Each year since 1988 the British conglomerate BTR has issued bonus warrants free to its shareholders, with an exercise price set just out-of-the-money.

From the investor's viewpoint, warrants can be used in the same way as equities, to provide a way of investing in the shares of a specific company, but with a relatively low capital outlay at the start. Another strategy allows an investor already holding shares to liquidate them but to maintain an equity stake. This tactic is called *cash extraction* and is straightforward in concept. The investor sells the shares, uses part of the money to buy warrants on the same number of shares, and invests the remainder to earn interest. It should be remembered, however, that out-of-the-money warrants do not move one-for-one with the share price prior to maturity. Once the investor has switched from shares to warrants, a rise in the share price of 100 might be followed by a rise of just 40 in the warrants. Some immediate profit potential may therefore be forgone, as is the opportunity to receive dividend income.

A *convertible* bond is one that can be converted into a fixed number of shares on or after a given date in the future. The attractions for investors are similar to those arising from warrants: the immediate safety of relatively secure debt plus the ability to switch into equity if the company's share price rises sufficiently. There are several differences between warrants and convertibles, however. A convertible provides the investor with a stream of income and a floor price through which the convertible cannot fall, except in default; a warrant provides no income and can expire worthless. Moreover, the exercise of a warrant requires a further investment of cash, whereas the conversion of a convertible does not.

Convertibles are often used by medium-sized companies with strong growth prospects. The possibility of conversion can tempt investors to accept a lower rate of interest than the company would otherwise be forced to pay. This benefits the issuer, as does the ability to raise cash now by the issue of deferred equity at a higher price than that currently prevailing, lessening the dilutive impact of the new capital raised.

In addition to the option embedded within the convertible, namely, the investor's option to switch from debt into equity, convertibles are often issued with other explicit options. One type is a call provision, which gives the issuer the right to call back the issue on or after a particular date in the future, either at par or some premium. This effectively gives the issuer a means to force conversion or the opportunity to refinance at a lower cost if rates have dropped. Another type is a put option, which allows the investor the right to put the convertible back to the issuer, sometimes at a premium. This provides a safety feature for the investor, who can liquidate the bond if the issuer's share price fails to grow according to expectations. Although this enables the issuer to float the convertible at a slightly lower coupon rate, the idea has fallen into disfavour following the recent bad experience of some British companies whose shares had suffered disastrously from the recession in the early 1990s. Companies such as Saatchi & Saatchi, Next, and Ratners were all forced to redeem their bonds at premiums of around 130% when the put options were exercised against them, at a time when their financial positions were already precarious.[3]

16.10 EXOTIC EQUITY DERIVATIVES

Chapter Eleven (Section 11.8) introduced a wide range of so-called exotic options, a number of which have now appeared as specialised equity derivative

---

[3] See Graham Cooper, "No Puts Please, We're British," *Risk* 6, no. 7 (July 1993).

products. Here we provide some examples of the most significant offerings that have emerged, but the scope is almost endless, being limited only by the imaginations of the financial engineers designing and pricing the various packages.

Basket options. Some hedging applications may involve situations in which the exposure is broader than exposure to a single share price but narrower than exposure to the entire market. For example, a fund manager may want to hedge a portfolio comprising shares in a single industry sector such as chemicals or motors. In such cases, an index option would be too broad, or may even be useless, if the financial performance of the particular portfolio was poorly correlated with that of the market as a whole. Buying options on each of the individual shares would provide a hedge, but this would prove very expensive because the investor would receive no allowance for the reduction in portfolio risk that occurs when individual risks are pooled. A *basket option*, tailored for the particular application, would normally provide a much better solution.

A basket option, as the name implies, is an option on a basket of securities. The payout at maturity is based on a weighted average of the prices of the component securities rather than on the price of a single instrument. An investor or a portfolio manager would approach a bank with details of the portfolio to be hedged, and the option specification would be designed to match the particular securities, strike value, and maturity required. Although this will require a specialised quotation, the cost of an option on a portfolio will always be less than the cost of a portfolio of options. The user could buy a put basket option to establish a floor level below which the portfolio value could not fall or could sell a call basket option to bring in premium income by establishing a price ceiling for the portfolio.

Rainbow or outperformance options. These offer the buyer a payoff based on the maximum (or minimum) price achieved by several underlying prices. An example would be a rainbow call on the German DAX, the British FTSE 100, and the French CAC-40 stock indexes. The call buyer would receive a payoff based on whichever index showed the greatest appreciation over the option period. Such an option would solve the dilemma faced by fund managers as to which market they should invest in or how they should allocate capital between markets, since the rainbow option would always guarantee the best possible performance.

Outperformance options have been marketed by a number of banks as *relative performance options* (RPOs). For example, in August 1992 the Swiss Bank Corporation issued put warrants on the spread between the DAX and the Swiss Market Index (SMI) expiring in March 1993. In the United States, RPOs have been created on various combinations of individual stocks, industry groupings, or market indices and are sometimes used by fund managers who have already outperformed a particular benchmark and wish to protect their position.

Quanto options. These provide investors with a means of participating in the performance of a foreign stock market, but without the associated currency risk. Suppose a U.S. investor believes that the British stock market will rise by 15% over the next few months, whereas the U.S. market will rise by only 10%. If he buys a call option on the shares of a single British company or a stock index call option on the FTSE 100 as a whole, he will benefit if the particular company goes up or if the market as a whole should rise as expected. However, the payout in both cases would normally be in sterling and would need to be exchanged back into dollars. If the pound fell 10% against the dollar over the lifetime of the option, this would wipe out the advantage of having invested in Britain.

Quantos eliminate this problem, because the option payout is denominated in the investor's domestic currency at a predetermined exchange rate. For example, a quanto call on the FTSE 100 index struck at 3,000 might pay out $10 for each full index point. If the index reached 3,100 at expiry, the investor would receive $1,000 regardless of the sterling/dollar exchange rate at the time.

Compared with a standard equity option, the pricing of quanto options depends upon a number of additional factors, including the interest rate differential between the two currencies involved, the volatility of the exchange rate, and, most particularly, the correlation between the underlying asset and the exchange rate. Handling the problems arising from this correlation effect is one of the current challenges facing market makers dealing in these kinds of option products.

To provide an illustration of how these factors interrelate, Figure 16.14 shows the fair prices for dollar-denominated at-the-money quanto options on the FTSE 100 having a maturity of one year. The graphs trace out the prices both for calls and puts under the two different interest-rate scenarios set out in Table 16.1. Also marked on the diagram are the option prices for standard sterling-denominated options on the FTSE 100.

As might be expected, the standard and quanto calls are both more expensive within the higher sterling interest-rate environment of Scenario 2 than under the lower sterling rates prevailing in Scenario 1.[4] The same cost-of-carry considerations make the puts more expensive under the first scenario. Not so

TABLE 16.1
Interest Rate Scenarios for Quanto Illustration

	Scenario 1	Scenario 2
Sterling interest rates	4.0%	6.0%
Dollar interest rates	7.0	3.5

---

[4] See Chapter Ten for an explanation of this.

FIGURE 16.14
Illustration of Quanto Option Prices

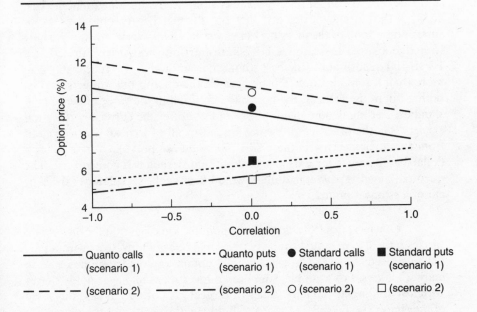

obvious is the fact that this would also be true for the quanto options even if the sterling rates were identical within the two environments. This is because the foreign currency component of quanto options responds to forward exchange rates, which are influenced by the interest-rate differential between the two currencies; standard equity options respond only to the domestic interest rate. Scenario 2 features lower dollar interest rates, which makes the forward pound cheaper in relation to the spot rate. The quanto call option, which embodies the right to sell pounds and receive dollars at a fixed rate, therefore becomes more valuable if the forward pound is weaker.

The effect of correlation is also significant and in this example serves to reduce the value of calls and to increase the value of puts as the correlation coefficient becomes larger. A positive correlation here implies a positive association between the level of the FTSE 100 index and the value of the pound; as the pound rises, so does the FTSE 100, which is very plausible. Note that the existence of correlation does not imply causality, just association.

Consider how the holder of a quanto call option paid in dollars fares as the index/currency correlation increases. A rise in the FTSE 100 will lead to a larger dollar-denominated payout, but the value of this payout will be diminished as the dollar falls against the pound. The benefit from a higher FTSE 100 is therefore partially offset by a reduction in the value of the dollar, so the price of a quanto call will be less than that of a standard index call option paid out in sterling. A similar argument explains why the puts become more expensive as correlation increases.

Investors thinking of buying quanto options should not, however, be tempted by any apparent cost advantage over standard options, nor should they rule out a quanto if it happens to cost more. Quantos are often the best choice if the currency hedge that they provide matches the objectives, exposure, and outlook of the investor. For example, a U.S.-based investor wishing to hedge against losses on a UK share portfolio might well find that a FTSE 100 quanto put is the best solution, even though it will probably cost more than a standard put. This is because the quanto put protects against both a fall in the value of the portfolio and a fall in the value of sterling. A standard sterling-denominated put would not offer the currency protection element. On the other hand, buying a quanto call as a cheap way to benefit from an anticipated rise in the FTSE 100 might not prove so attractive for a dollar-based speculator if he also thought that sterling was going to rise. The quanto, fixing the payout in dollars, would deprive the speculator of the benefit of a stronger pound.

Other exotics. Knockouts, compounds, lookbacks, and other exotic species have also migrated to the equities markets, and investors with a particular objective or exposure can usually obtain a quote from one or more market makers. For example, suppose an investment manager holds shares currently trading at 100 and wishes to protect his position in case the value of the shares should fall, but plans to liquidate the position if the shares rise to 105. The ideal choice would be a knockout put with a strike price of 100 and a barrier at 105. Such an option would provide exactly the protection required and would be cheaper than a standard put option.

Occasionally, issuers will incorporate knockout features as part of a structured financing. In April 1993, for example, the Swiss pharmaceuticals company Roche issued $1 billion of seven-year bonds. Attached to each $10,000 bond were 46 European-style knockout warrants convertible into the company's *Genussschein* nonvoting stock in May 1996, 60 warrants being required to obtain one Genussschein. At the time of issue, the Genussschein was trading at SFR 4,100. The warrants, which were effectively call options with a zero strike price, had two additional features that modified the payout profile. First, there was an embedded short call struck at SFR 6,000 that capped the value of the warrant at this level. However, since the cap was set some 50% above the prevailing stock price, it was not seen as a disadvantage. Second, the warrants incorporated a knockout put struck at SFR 4,500 with a barrier at SFR 5,000. This established a floor at SFR 4,500, unless the put was extinguished by the Genussschein reaching the barrier during the lifetime of the warrant. With the performance of the company's stock prior to the issue, most investors thought that if the Genussschein reached the SFR 5,000 level, it was unlikely to fall back thereafter. The knockout feature allowed the embedded put to be priced more cheaply.

The warrants were initially priced at SFR 65.3, effectively 4% below the value of the underlying stock. If the stock failed to rise, the existence of the floor at SFR 4,500 guaranteed a minimum effective return of 4.57% over the three-year period, similar to the yields then available on Swiss Government bonds. On the upside, if the Genussschein rose above SFR 6,000, the effective return on the warrants was 14.74%. This provides an attractive combination, but the yields would have been lower but for the knockout feature.

Chapter Seventeen

Commodity Risk

We have so far concentrated exclusively on two principal sources of financial risk: currency risk and interest rate risk. Many organisations, however, are exposed to a third source: commodity risk. In this chapter, we will discuss the nature of commodity risk and review some of the methods by which it may be handled. Fortunately, we will not need to break much new ground here, because all the tools and techniques used to manage commodity risk have exact parallels with those employed in the management of interest-rate and currency risk. We will therefore be able to avoid repetition by referring back to concepts and methods explained earlier.

17.1 COMMODITY RISK

Commodity risk arises in any situation where an organisation is affected by fluctuations in the price of some commodity. There is a very wide range of physical assets that can nowadays be treated as commodities. The list includes

- Metals, such as copper, gold, and platinum.
- Agricultural products, such as wheat, lumber, soy beans, and pork bellies.
- Energy products, such as crude oil, gas, and natural and refined petroleum products.
- Property and real estate.

Any organisation that either produces or consumes significant amounts of these items is therefore exposed to commodity risk. Obvious candidates would include oil companies, airlines, car manufacturers, and food processors. However, commodity risk can also have indirect effects that are less apparent but can be equally devastating in their impact. Although they neither produce nor consume oil directly, tour operators and travel companies are extremely vulnerable to the cost of oil, because a significant component of the price of an overseas holiday package is the cost of the airline flight, which in turn depends on the cost of aviation fuel. A rise in the price of oil will ultimately raise the price of an overseas holiday and may eliminate a significant proportion of a travel company's business if holiday makers decide to stay at home.

Commodity risk is in many ways more pervasive than currency or interest rate risk, and this probably explains why commodity derivatives have been around far longer than financial derivatives. The first derivatives to be traded on the Chicago Board of Trade, established in 1848, were commodity futures. It was not until 1972 that the first financial futures contract was created, but these relative newcomers now overwhelmingly dominate the exchange-traded derivatives market. In 1992, only 2 out of the world's top 20 exchange-traded contracts were commodity derivatives—the crude oil contract at NYMEX and the corn contract at the CBOT—and these were well down the pecking order in 5th and 19th place, respectively.[1]

Many companies exposed to commodity risk probably feel that such exposure is a necessary and unavoidable feature of their business. For example, a company operating in the coffee business may feel that it has to accept the ups and downs in demand caused by fluctuations in world coffee prices. To some extent this may be true, but proper use of commodity derivatives can help to smooth out and cushion some of the worst effects of commodity price instability.

Until the late 1980s, the only commodity risk management tools available were exchange-traded futures and options. These have a limited range of maturities, seldom extending more than one year into the future. While these provide protection against price fluctuations in the short term, they are unable to provide guaranteed protection for extended periods. While a company could resort to the tactic of using a rolling futures hedge, this is only capable of fixing a series of different prices over a succession of shorter periods; this is not the same as fixing a single price over the longer term. The lack of long-term commodity price protection may be one reason why commodity futures and options have not been used as extensively as they might have been.

Recent developments have heralded an upsurge of interest in financial engineering solutions for managing commodity risk, and a spate of new products has now emerged. Inspired by the success of interest rate tools such as swaps, caps, collars, and swaptions, similar products have been developed for the commodities market. Use of commodity swaps is now growing steadily, and commodity caps, collars, and even options on commodity swaps are now available. In the remaining sections of this chapter we will review how these new products have been created and how they can be used.

17.2 CREATING COMMODITY DERIVATIVES

The starting point for building most commodity derivatives is the commodity futures market. In order to create and market any derivative financial product, it is necessary to find a way of hedging it; otherwise the market maker would be burdened with an unmanageable risk. It would, of course, be possible to hedge a commodity derivative with the underlying commodity, but in

---

[1] See "Directory and Review 1993," *Futures and Options World* (1993), p. 9.

most cases this would be highly undesirable. No financial institution really wants to count acres of corn or herds of cattle among its assets. Commodity futures provide a clean, liquid, and low-cost way of hedging exposure to the underlying commodity.

The price of many commodity futures is related to the spot price of the underlying commodity through the same cash-and-carry pricing mechanism explained in Chapter Eight (Section 8.3). Table 17.1 illustrates the set of futures prices at the close of business on October 5, 1993, and we can use these figures to investigate the relationships between cash and futures prices. As an example, someone selling the August 94 gold futures contract could hedge the price risk by buying gold and holding it for the 10-month period until the futures expired. Unlike bond futures and stock index futures contracts, however, with gold there is no flow of coupon or dividend income to offset the pure cost of financing the hedge. With U.S. interest rates at around 3%, we would therefore expect the gold futures contracts to be priced at a 3% per annum premium above the cash price, and the gold prices in Table 17.1 do just that.

Gold is somewhat special in that storage costs are relatively low, wastage and deterioration do not occur, and there is no seasonal pattern to the sequence of prices throughout the year. These conditions do not always

TABLE 17.1
Commodity Futures Closing Prices on October 5, 1993

	Crude Oil[a]	Heating Oil[b]	Live Hogs[c]	Corn[d]	Gold[e]
Cash price	18.40	54.70	50.00	2.34½	353.00
Nov 93	18.39	55.43			353.80
Dec	18.58	56.26	50.80	2.36½	354.80
Jan 94	18.71	56.64			
Feb	18.83	56.54	50.27		356.50
Mar	18.93	55.49		2.44¾	
Apr	19.01	54.24	47.95		358.20
May	19.09	53.14		2.50¼	
Jun	19.16	52.59	52.12		359.90
Jul		52.71	50.92	2.53¼	
Aug			49.45		361.60
Sep				2.50	

[a] Light sweet crude oil contract on NYMEX ($ per barrel).
[b] Heating oil no.2 contract on NYMEX ($ per barrel).
[c] Live hogs contract on CME (¢ per pound).
[d] Corn contract on CBOT ($ per bushel).
[e] Gold contract on COMEX ($ per troy ounce).

apply for other commodities, however. The storage costs for oil are higher than for gold, and the asset is less attractive as collateral for a secured loan. The crude oil futures prices in Table 17.1 therefore appreciate at a faster rate than the gold contracts, rising at over 6% per annum. Heating oil, which is a by-product of crude oil, exhibits a strongly seasonal pattern, with prices peaking in the winter months around January and then falling away with the summer months. Agricultural products, like the live hogs and corn contracts illustrated, also show strong seasonality linked to rearing and harvest cycles. Products such as these are also perishable and subject to deterioration, which may cause the cash price to stand at a premium over the futures market when shortages occur.

The relationship between commodity futures prices and cash market prices is therefore much more susceptible to the laws of supply and demand than that for financial futures. When demand for the commodity rises, as with heating oil in the winter, the futures price will be higher than the cash-and-carry arbitrage pricing would suggest. When supply outstrips demand, as with live hogs in the spring or heating oil in the summer, the futures price will be lower and may even fall below the cash market price. This last condition, when the futures price falls below the cash market price, is known as *backwardation*, to distinguish it from the more usual *contango* market, where futures prices are at a premium.

Although the relationship between the commodity futures and cash prices is therefore not as straightforward as for financial futures, the two markets do move in unison. If prices in the cash markets rise, then so do commodity futures, and by a similar amount. As an example, Table 17.2 compares prices for the corn contracts on two separate dates, showing that the change in the cash price was exactly mirrored by changes in the near-dated futures contracts. This means that commodity futures, especially the highly liquid near-dated contracts, can be used as an effective proxy for the underlying commodity when hedging other commodity derivatives. Although the longer-dated contracts do not move so much, this is only to be expected. A short-term fluctuation in cash prices does not necessarily imply a permanent change in prices, so the short-term contracts respond but the long-term ones do not. If, however, there was a structural change in the market affecting long-term expectations for commodity prices, then the longer-dated contracts would shift accordingly.

Now that we have established the viability of using commodity futures as a proxy for the underlying commodity, the creation of other commodity derivatives is relatively straightforward.

Commodity options may be priced using the standard Black-Scholes or binomial models and dynamically hedged by buying or selling commodity futures contracts for an amount equal to delta times the amount underlying the option contract. To price commodity caps, floors, and collars, the premiums from the strip of component options are aggregated, as explained in Chapter Eleven (Section 11.5). In this regard these commodity derivatives are directly analogous to their interest-rate counterparts.

TABLE 17.2
Changes in Corn Cash and CBOT Corn Futures Prices

	Price on Oct 5, 1993	Price on Oct 8, 1993	Change in price	Open Interest on Oct 8, 1993
Cash price	2.34½	2.39½	+0.05	
Dec 93	2.36½	2.41½	+0.05	160,342
Mar 94	2.44¾	2.49½	+0.04¾	49,473
May	2.50¼	2.54	+0.03¾	17,526
Jul	2.53¼	2.56¾	+0.03½	13,394
Sep	2.50	2.51½	+0.01½	1,698
Dec	2.45½	2.45½	–	8,660
Mar 95	2.52	2.52	–	10

Short-term commodity swaps may be priced and hedged using a strip of futures contracts.[2] Just as with an interest rate swap, the commodity swap rate is the weighted average of the forward commodity prices, using the set of zero-coupon discount factors as the weights. To price longer-dated swaps, where suitable futures contracts may not be available, the market maker must extrapolate the commodity forward price curve in order to estimate what the likely commodity futures prices would be if they existed. A stack hedge can then be used to hedge a longer-dated swap, utilising the technique explained in Chapter Fourteen (Section 14.4).

When compared to financial futures, commodity futures markets exhibit less liquidity and wider spreads. Hedging commodity derivatives is therefore costlier and involves a greater degree of basis risk. For example, a market maker could use a stack of short-dated commodity futures contracts to hedge a five-year oil swap and continue to roll the futures hedge at every expiry date. However, if the basis between cash and futures should eventually differ from the original estimate made when the swap was priced, the market maker would suffer a basis risk.

Basis risk can also occur when a market maker uses futures to cross-hedge a commodity swap. For example, an aviation fuel swap can be hedged with crude oil futures, since there are no aviation fuel futures contracts available. Crude oil and aviation fuel prices tend to move closely, but as the relationship is not perfect, the basis risk remains.

The price of a commodity swap must therefore take account of the difficulties caused by spreads, basis risk, and financing the variation margin, as well as some of the other problems reviewed in Chapter Fourteen (e.g., non-coincidence of futures and exposure dates). Nonetheless, commodity swaps

---

[2] See Satyajit Das, "Oil and Commodity Swaps," *Journal of International Securities Markets* 4 (1990), pp. 227–50.

can be priced at a sufficiently attractive level to offer cost-effective risk management solutions for those exposed to commodity risk. The next section provides some examples from this burgeoning market.

17.3 USING COMMODITY DERIVATIVES

Commodity futures and options can be used in exactly the same way as interest rate and currency futures and options. The techniques have been thoroughly documented in the previous four chapters.

Prices for single commodity transactions taking place up to a year in the future can be fixed using commodity futures, and the various methods presented in Chapter Fourteen may be employed equally well here to improve hedge efficiency. For example, adjusting the hedge ratio to account for exposure basis, the timing of the settlement sum, and margin flows will help to improve the effectiveness of a commodity futures hedge, as will the use of spread and interpolated hedges when the exposure and futures maturity dates do not coincide.

If a hedger wishes to obtain protection from adverse movements in commodity prices but to continue to benefit from favourable moves, exchange-traded or OTC commodity options provide the answer. As an example, Figure 17.1 illustrates the effective price paid on October 5, 1993, to pur-

FIGURE 17.1
Hedging Using Commodity Options

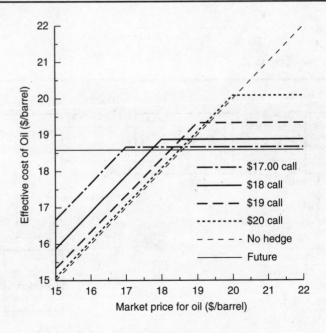

chase December oil using four different NYMEX call options. Also shown are the cost profiles obtained by using the December futures contract and the result for the buyer if no hedge was in place.

These profiles offer no surprises and share the same characteristics as those of currency and interest rate options that we have seen in earlier chapters. The $17 in-the-money call exhibits a price characteristic close to that of the futures hedge—a fixed cost over most of the price range illustrated, but with a small possibility to save money if oil drops below $17 a barrel. At the other end of the scale, the out-of-the-money option struck at $20 has a profile resembling the no-hedge alternative, allowing considerable savings if the oil price is low but only offering protection once oil rises through $20 a barrel. As usual, the options struck near-the-money provide a compromise performance in between these two extremes.

Chapters Thirteen, Fifteen, and Sixteen have already provided a wealth of more advanced option-based solutions for managing currency, interest rate, and equity risk. In addition to the basic option hedge illustrated in Figure 17.1, collars, corridors, participations, and other option structures, all work equally well in managing commodity risk, and there is therefore no need to provide duplicate examples here.

Commodity swaps are also little different from their interest-rate cousins and allow a counterparty to lock in a fixed commodity price on a series of dates in the future. A typical structure is illustrated in Figure 17.2, which shows how commodity swaps can benefit both producer and consumer alike.

In the illustration, the oil producer enters into a commodity swap as the fixed price receiver, agreeing to receive periodic payments at a fixed price of $19.20 per barrel on a nominal quantity of oil against paying the market

FIGURE 17.2
Example of a Commodity Swap

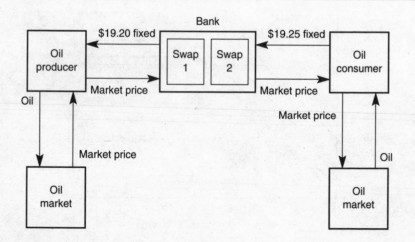

price. When the producer actually sells oil into the market, he delivers oil and receives the prevailing market price. The producer's cash flows linked to market prices therefore net out, and the effect of the swap is therefore to fix the price at which the producer sells his oil.

In a similar way, the oil consumer enters into another commodity swap with the bank, this time paying the fixed price of $19.25 per barrel and receiving the market price. The consumer in turn then pays the market price when he buys oil in the spot market. Once again, the market-related cash flows cancel each other out, and the oil consumer ends up paying a fixed price for oil, regardless of the market rate.

Both producer and consumer have eliminated their exposure to fluctuating oil prices, and the swap thus ensures price certainty for both parties. Assuming the bank can match the timings and nominal sizes of both swaps, it profits from the margin between the fixed prices on the two swaps. Alternatively, the bank could hedge each swap separately in the futures market.

It is important to note that no exchange of the physical commodity ever takes place. The commodity swap is based on a nominal quantity of the underlying commodity, for example, a million barrels of oil per month, but this nominal quantity is only used as the basis for calculating the swap payments. If the spot oil price was $19.00 on one fixing date, the oil producer would receive $200,000 net on a nominal quantity of 1 million barrels, while the oil consumer would pay $250,000 net. As with interest rate swaps, the periodic payments are normally settled by a single net payment from the debit counterparty to the credit counterparty.

Commodity swaps have been transacted in oil, orange juice, coffee, cocoa, maize, cotton, sugar, and wheat.[3] One variation on the standard swap structure is a swap under which the floating price is based on an average of daily market prices over a period rather than on the spot commodity price on a given day. This would suit users buying and selling the commodity on a continual basis rather than periodically. Another variation involves the fixed-price payer granting a receiver's swaption in return for a lower swap price. This might be attractive in contango markets where the futures stand at a considerable premium to the spot price.

The commodity swap/swaption combination works thus: Without the swaption, the commodity consumer would be faced with a fixed swap rate considerably higher than the prevailing commodity price. By selling the swaption on a nominal commodity amount equal to that underlying the swap, the commodity consumer can use the premium to lower the swap price and fix costs at a lower level. If commodity prices should rise, the swaption expires worthless and the consumer keeps the premium. If prices fall, the receiver's swaption is exercised against the consumer, who ends up paying the fixed price on double the original nominal amount. In the latter instance, although the consumer is paying above-market prices on a larger quantity of

---

[3] See William Falloon, "Golden Horizons," *Risk* 6, no. 2 (July 1993), pp. 24–25.

the commodity, we must presume the price must still be an attractive one; otherwise the consumer would not have entered into the swap in the first place. Since the consumer ends up swapping double the original quantity of the commodity if the swaption is exercised, this structure is sometimes called a *double-up commodity swap*.

The most recent developments in commodity swaps have produced property and real estate swaps, and inflation-index swaps. There has also been some progress in the design and marketing of swaps and other derivatives on distressed loans, credit quality, insurance, tax, and even antipollution credits.[4]

The first real estate swap was transacted in January 1993 with Morgan Stanley acting as principal to two counterparties. The first, a large U.S. pension fund, agreed to make payments linked to a property index (the so-called Frank Russell-NCREIF index) in return for receiving dollar LIBOR, while the second counterparty, a medium-sized life insurance company, paid LIBOR in return for receiving the property-linked payments. The pension fund's motive was to effect an asset allocation switch from property to equity, but without selling or buying the underlying assets. The real estate swap allowed the fund to convert from property to LIBOR, and a second LIBOR-for-equity swap, also transacted with Morgan Stanley, completed the property-to-equity switch. Such a transaction marks a very early stage in the development of a real estate swap market, and this particular deal was only feasible because the bank managed to find two suitable counterparties for which to arrange a back-to-back deal. The potential difficulties caused by the lack of a liquid market in property and subjectivity in carrying out property valuations may hinder further development, at least for the time being.

Inflation-index swaps are somewhat more esoteric and have initially been proposed in the United Kingdom, where a small market in index-linked government bonds exists that could provide a possible hedge and where the recently privatised utility companies may be potential users. Constrained by legislation to limit their price rises to the prevailing rate of inflation, these utilities may prove to be natural payers of the index in return for receiving a fixed stream of income. Inflation-indexed caps may be another possibility, but the market in all these inflation derivatives is currently at a nascent stage.

An example of a distressed loan derivative is a put option on a loan portfolio struck at, say, 60% of the loans' face value. If the loan portfolio proves to be less creditworthy than the strike price, the holder of the put option would receive a payment equal to the difference between the portfolio realisation and the strike price. Alternatively, a swap could be structured where the floating side is linked to the performance of the loan portfolio. Other structures have been postulated.

The desire by general insurers to offset their risks is long established and has hitherto been satisfied by the reinsurance market. The creation of insurance

---

[4] See Rosemary Bennett, "Rocket Scientists Produce a Fresh Wave of Solutions," *Euromoney* (March 1993) pp. 46–54.

futures and options at the CBOT, with prices linked to loss ratios in the United States, has provided an alternative solution, albeit one that has yet to take off.

The list of potential new applications for commodity derivatives is endless. As the examples mentioned here have shown, it is in theory possible to design a derivative product for any situation where risk manifests itself. Some products, such as the oil swap, have already shown considerable growth, while others have yet to achieve a critical mass. There are many practical difficulties, not least in finding indices that are generally accepted and then in being able to hedge the derivative. Nevertheless, if banks find a demand for a particular design, few problems are insurmountable.

17.4 HYBRID COMMODITY DERIVATIVES

Almost all the commodity derivatives reviewed so far have involved some kind of exchange between a commodity index and money. However, once it is possible to offer an option or a swap from one commodity index to money, the fixed financial payments become a common denominator, and it is therefore possible to structure a derivative between any two commodity indices. Alternatively, a standard financial instrument such as a bond can be structured to include commodity-linked payoffs. Such products are called *hybrid commodity derivatives*. Examples include

- Oil-indexed notes, such as those issued by Standard Oil of Ohio in 1986. The bond issue included a regular coupon bond plus a commodity-linked zero-coupon bond. The payoff at maturity from the latter component comprised a stated face value plus an additional sum equal to 170 times the amount by which the prevailing oil price exceeded $25, but subject to a cap at $40. For example, if oil was trading at $30 a barrel, the bonus payment would equal $850 per bond. This structure enabled the issuer to raise finance at a cost lower than otherwise possible and provided the investor with a low-cost means to speculate on the oil price. If the oil price rose, Standard Oil could meet the additional obligations through increased revenues received.

- Principal-indexed gold bond, in which the bond repays a principal of $1,000 plus 2.5 times the excess of the gold price above $400 per ounce.

- Oil- and currency-linked bond, in which the principal and coupon payments are linked to the price of oil denominated in a nondollar currency. The export prospects for a Japanese car maker would be cut if either the oil price increased or the yen strengthened, resulting in a reduction in the company's income. With such exposure, the company might prefer to obtain finance whereby the repayment of coupon and principal was inversely linked to the price of oil and the strength of the yen. A suitable formula for the index might be $(50 - P) \times S/3333$, where P was the price of oil in dollars and S was the spot dollar-yen exchange rate.

For such products to succeed, there must be an incentive for issuers to create the hybrid in the first place, and investors must be motivated to buy them. The first condition will be satisfied if the instrument is structured in such a way as to reduce the issuer's cost and/or risk. Investors are often encouraged by an unusual market opportunity, the ability to participate or speculate in a market they may not normally have access to, and the prospect of an above-market return. The second requirement can therefore often be met by skilful distribution, effective marketing, and keen pricing.

Chapter Eighteen

Structured Finance

Thus far, each of the chapters has concentrated on a single topic, whether it be a tool such as swaps or options, or a technique, such as managing interest-rate risk. This final chapter explores how financial engineering tools and techniques can be assembled in various ways to create novel, and sometimes unusual, financial structures.

With the huge variety of permutations possible, it would be impossible to illustrate every product that has ever been offered. Instead, the chapter presents examples illustrating each of the principal concepts, and demonstrates how these ideas can be combined to satisfy the ever-changing preferences of investors and borrowers.

It is difficult to organise all the solutions into watertight categories, so we shall first deal with the simpler liability-linked and asset-linked structures before proceeding to such ideas as quanto structures, leveraged floaters, and cross-currency issues.

18.1 LIABILITY-LINKED STRUCTURES

Supply and demand conditions within the capital markets can sometimes lead to differences between issuer and investor preferences, differences caused by diverging needs, by opposing views as to the likely direction of market rates, or by other factors. An issuer may want or need one kind of liability, while investors may require another. Derivative structures are ideal in this situation for altering the nature of a debt issue so that the needs of all parties may be satisfied.

The most basic conversion is between fixed and floating rates, and the interest rate swap provides the standard solution to this need. An issuer who prefers fixed-rate financing, but who can obtain a preferential rate by issuing floating-rate debt, can enter into a swap as the fixed-rate payer to effect this switch.

More complex conversions involve callable and puttable bonds. An issuer may wish to obtain fixed-rate finance, but with the flexibility to call the bond and reissue at a lower rate if interest rates fall. An alternative to a callable bond is for the company to issue a noncallable fixed-rate bond and buy a receivers swaption. If rates stay high, the company lets the swaption expire worthless. If rates do fall, the company can exercise the swaption and enter into the underlying swap that will convert the fixed-rate bond into a synthetic floating-rate liability at the lower prevailing rates. The company could remain floating if it thought rates would go lower or could swap back into fixed at a swap rate lower than the coupon on the original bond. The premium on the swaption might prove to be lower than the additional cost of a callable compared with a noncallable debt issue.

Alternatively, the issuer may prefer the lower cost of a puttable bond, which gives the investor the right to put the bond back to the issuer if rates rise. If the company has already issued a callable bond at a higher coupon, it can sell both a payers swaption and a receivers swaption to effect the change. The up-front swaption premiums can be used to lower the effective cost of the present liability. If rates subsequently rise, the payers swaption will be exercised against the company, forcing the company to pay a higher effective coupon on its debt. This is equivalent to the investors putting the bond. On the other hand, if rates fall, the company can call the debt and refinance at a lower rate, but the benefit of this will be cancelled by the receivers swaption being exercised against the company. The combined effect of the two swaptions is to negate the call feature embedded within the original bond issue and to replace it with the desired put feature in return for an immediate reduction in the effective borrowing cost.

There are many other permutations along the same lines, and Table 18.1 summarises the various switches that are possible between fixed-rate, floating-rate, callable, and puttable issues. Each row in the table refers to the form of finance planned or in place, while each column shows how the desired form of financing can be obtained. For example, to convert an FRN to callable fixed-rate debt, the issuer would pay the fixed on a standard swap and buy a receivers swaption (or simply pay the fixed on a cancellable swap, which amounts to the same thing).

In addition to changing the callability or puttability of an issue, a borrower can use swaps, caps, and floors to alter the interest rate exposure. Chapters Fourteen and Fifteen have already reviewed the more usual application of these tools to switch between floating and fixed liabilities or to establish ceilings on floating rate obligations. The same tools can be used in less conventional ways to create more unusual structures such as the reverse or leveraged floaters explained later in this chapter. Here we will present ways to take advantage of situations where the shape of the yield curve creates a wide spread between short-term and long-term rates.

When the yield curve is steeply positive, as in the case of dollar rates in the early 1990s, borrowers may wish to take advantage of the historically low long-term rates by issuing long-term debt, but without giving up the opportunity to benefit from even lower short-term rates. The corporate treasurer may face a dilemma in choosing between issuing 10-year fixed rate debt at 6.75%, which is attractive when compared with rates of 9% and 10% in the not-too-distant past, and issuing a 10-year floating-rate note with a current LIBOR of 3.25%. One obvious answer is for the borrower to issue the fixed-

TABLE 18.1
Reengineering Debt Structures

		Debt required			
		Fixed-Rate	*Floating Rate*	*Callable Fixed-Rate*	*Puttable Fixed-Rate*
Debt Issued	*Fixed-Rate*	—	Receive fixed on standard swap	Buy receivers swaption	Sell payers swaption
	Floating-Rate	Pay fixed on standard swap	—	Pay fixed on swap and buy receivers swaption	Pay fixed on swap and sell payers swaption
	Callable Fixed-Rate	Sell receivers swaption	Receive fixed on swap and sell receivers swaption	—	Sell payers swaption and sell receivers swaption
	Puttable Fixed-Rate	Buy payers swaption	Receive fixed on swap and buy payers swaption	Buy payers swaption and buy receivers swaption	—

rate debt and then to enter into a 10-year swap paying LIBOR against receiving, say, 6.25% fixed. This creates floating-rate financing at an effective cost of LIBOR + 50bp. While this realises the benefit of low short-term rates, it provides no protection against rates rising in the future.

Another solution to this dilemma is to divide the total financing period into several portions and to adopt a different strategy for each segment. An example is illustrated in Figure 18.1, where the 10-year period is split into two parts. Entering into a four-year swap paying LIBOR against receiving 4.46% gives floating-rate financing at LIBOR + 229bp over the first four years. Although the LIBOR margin is quite high, the very low level of short-term rates means that the first coupon is only 5.54%, 121bp cheaper than the rate of interest on the fixed-rate debt. Buying a deferred floor covering the remaining six years would cost 62bp per annum over that period for a floor struck at 6.75%. The combination of a fixed-rate liability together with a purchased floor creates a synthetic capped FRN, in this case resulting in a liability of LIBOR + 62bp capped at 7.37%. For the borrower who believed that interest rates were more likely to stay low in the first few years, but was unsure about later years, this combination of strategies may provide the best compromise between low financing cost and safety.

18.2 ASSET-LINKED STRUCTURES

After security, one of the most important features of any asset is the return offered, and one of the goals of structured assets is to find ways in which this yield may be enhanced. One answer is to offer a security in which the return

FIGURE 18.1
Segmenting Risk Management Strategies

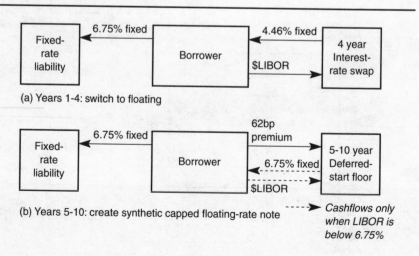

(a) Years 1-4: switch to floating

(b) Years 5-10: create synthetic capped floating-rate note

is linked to some index whose performance reflects the views of certain investors. In return for accepting a specified risk, the investors receive an above-market return. Currency-linked assets are discussed in Section 18.5, near the end of this chapter. Here we explore issues in which the coupon, redemption price, or both are linked to an interest-rate index of one kind or another.

Spread notes. A spread note is an instrument structured so that the return is linked to the spread between two LIBOR rates. An example was a note arranged by Credit Suisse First Boston (CSFB) in May 1993 for an investor who thought that the yield spread between one-year French franc LIBOR and one-year D-mark LIBOR would narrow, not merely from the 225bp spread then prevailing, but to below the 100bp spread implied by the two yield curves at the time. A one-year zero-coupon note with a redemption price equal to $100\% + (10 \times (1.72\% - S))$, where S was the spread between the two one-year LIBORs at redemption. If the spread had narrowed to the 100bp margin expected by the market, the note would have provided a return of 7.2%, while the return would rise to 10% if the spread narrowed to 72bp. The same effect could have been achieved with a coupon-bearing note in which the coupon was linked to the spread using a similar formula.

Swap-linked notes. In a falling yield environment, bond prices will rise. The greater the duration of a bond, the more the bond price will rise for a given change in yield. This makes long-maturity bonds more attractive, because these have a greater duration. Unfortunately for the investor, long-term bond yields tend to move less than short-term yields, so this makes shorter-maturity bonds more attractive, since these will exhibit a greater yield volatility. Investors must normally seek a compromise between these two effects. To provide one answer to this problem, short-term notes can be structured with a redemption value linked to medium-term swap rates. This linking involves a multiplier, thus making the bond simulate the price sensitivity of a bond with a much longer duration. In one example, a two-year D-mark note paid either a 6.30% annual coupon or a single 13.00% coupon on the maturity date (these alternatives are financially equivalent), but had a redemption price equal to $100\% + (15 \times (6.39\% - S))$, where S was the five-year swap rate at maturity. For every fall in five-year swap rates of 1%, this formula increases the redemption value by 15%, thereby making the note similar to a bond with a modified duration of 15 years, but responding to five-year rates.

Deleveraged floating-rate notes. When short-term rates are low, investors have a number of ways of enhancing current yield without having to lock into higher fixed-rate returns. Reverse and collared floaters, discussed later in this chapter, offer two solutions linked to short-term rates. At the other end of the maturity spectrum, investors have been offered floating-rate notes with coupons linked to long-term yields. One possibility is a note in which the coupon on each fixing date is the yield on an index of 10-year U.S. Treasury notes, the constant maturity treasury (CMT) yield, less a fixed margin whose size depends on the initial slope of the yield curve. A variation on this, introduced in 1993, is the *deleveraged floating-rate note*, in which the coupon is a fraction of the CMT yield plus a margin. An example would be a note paying 50% of the CMT yield plus 150bp. This will pay an initial coupon higher than the prevailing short-term rate, though the yield advantage will decline if the slope of the yield curve narrows.

Index amortisation swaps. One of the most prominent sections of the U.S. securities industry is the mortgage-backed securities market. These instruments are fixed-income products, but with the added feature that mortgagers can prepay their loan if interest rates fall. These prepayments are passed through to the holders of these instruments. One of the most difficult tasks in pricing mortgage-backed securities is to anticipate and model the prepayment behaviour of borrowers under different interest-rate scenarios. Moreover, hedging these securities is difficult, because they feature negative convexity over certain ranges of interest rates. With a mortgage-backed security, falling interest rates will trigger mortgage repayments at par, which counteracts the normal tendency for bond prices to continue rising as interest rates fall. The *index amortisation swap* is designed as a hedge against mortgage-backed securities, because the principal is amortised according to a preset formula linked to prevailing interest rates. For example, the percentage amortised at each fixing date might be $25 \times (7 - i\%)$, where i is the prevailing three-month LIBOR, subject to a minimum amortisation of 0% and a maximum of 100%. Under this formula, amortisation would start when interest rates fell below 7%, and would be complete if they dropped to 3% or lower.

18.3 QUANTO STRUCTURES

One significant financial innovation developed in the early 1990s is the *differential swap*, also known as a *currency-protected swap* (CUPS) or a *cross-index basis swap* (CRIB). In essence, a diff swap is a special variation of a basis swap. In a regular basis swap, one floating rate is exchanged for another floating rate, for example, three-month U.S. LIBOR against 30-day U.S. commercial paper. Although the bases may be different, the currency underlying both rates is the same. In a differential swap, however, one of the floating rates is indexed to the LIBOR of a foreign currency, but all payments are made in a single currency. An example would be an investor who would pay six-month dollar LIBOR and receive six-month D-mark LIBOR less a specific margin, but with the D-mark indexed payments being made in U.S. dollars.

The impetus for creating diff swaps arose at a time when short-term interest rates in the U.S. were extremely low, but with a steeply positive yield curve, while D-mark short-term rates were high, but with a negative yield curve. Table 18.2 illustrates a scenario typical of interest rates at the time.

Dollar-based investors were keen to obtain a higher yield than available from dollar-denominated securities. However, the normal alternative of switching into D-mark or other overseas investments meant taking a currency risk. If the dollar appreciated by more than a few percentage points against the other currency, the additional return would be eliminated. Worse still, a significant strengthening of the dollar could even result in a negative return being earned.

The differential swap completely solved the currency exposure problem. Although the floating rate was indexed to the foreign currency interest rate, the payments were all denominated in U.S. dollars. An investor entering into a three-year semiannual diff swap might pay six-month U.S. LIBOR against receiving six-month D-mark LIBOR less 196bp, but paid in dollars. Note that this does not mean a conversion of the D-mark indexed coupons into dollars at some exchange rate, but a straight payment in dollars at whatever rate is implied by the index. For example, if D-mark LIBOR was 8.50%, the investor would receive a 6.81% coupon (8.50%–1.69%) paid in dollars. If the notional principal under the swap was $100 million, this would mean a $6.81 million coupon.

The attractiveness of the deal is obvious. By using the diff swap in conjunction with existing dollar-denominated floating-rate securities, the investor can swap the low dollar yield for a much higher return linked to D-mark interest rates without suffering any currency exposure or the inconvenience of working with foreign currencies. Instead of receiving 3.88% on dollar-denominated investments, the investor would start by receiving 6.73% (8.69%–1.96%), an immediate pick-up of 285bp. Figure 18.2 illustrates the advantage of entering into the diff swap.

This virtual doubling of dollar yields is not without some risk to the investor. With the yield curves being steeply positive for the dollar and nega-

TABLE 18.2
Example of Forward Rate Scenario

Period	Dollar	D-Mark
1–6 months	3.88%	8.69%
7–12 months	4.30	8.40
13–18 months	5.49	7.90
19–24 months	6.27	7.58
25–30 months	6.59	7.38
31–36 months	7.28	7.02

FIGURE 18.2
Asset Return Enhancement with Differential Swap

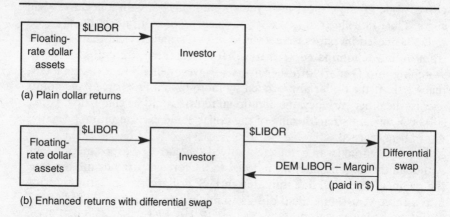

(a) Plain dollar returns

(b) Enhanced returns with differential swap

tive for the D-mark, the market was predicting a rise in dollar interest rates and a fall in D-mark rates. If future interest rates followed the implied forward curve, the investor using a diff swap would see his return fall from 6.73% to 5.06%, while dollar LIBOR would have risen to 7.28%, an opportunity loss of 222bp.

Nevertheless, diff swaps have enjoyed considerable success, because many investors did not believe that dollar rates would rise as high as the positive yield curve would suggest, nor that D-marks rates would fall as much as that implied by the negative yield curve. Although investors were prepared to see some erosion of the advantage conferred by the diff swap, they believed that any reduction would not be sufficient to wipe out the large benefit assured by the first and possibly subsequent fixings.

In the above example, the investor receiving D-mark LIBOR less 196bp against paying dollar LIBOR will gain in any period when D-mark LIBOR is more than 196bp higher than dollar LIBOR. However, the yield pickup in the very first period has the effect of moving the break-even point very much in favour of the investor. If the initial 285bp up-front saving is amortised over the remaining five semiannual periods, it is equivalent to a 52bp saving per period, lowering the break-even point from 196bp to 144bp. Now D-mark six-month LIBOR only has to remain at least 144bp above dollar LIBOR for the diff swap to prove profitable over its lifetime.

Diff swaps can also be used with success by borrowers. For companies based in countries where short-term interest rates are relatively high, such as Germany or Britain in the early 1990s, it can be advantageous to use a diff swap to switch from high domestic short-term rates to lower overseas interest rates. For example, a German company could issue a normal D-mark denominated note linked to D-mark LIBOR and then enter into a diff swap receiving D-mark LIBOR against paying dollar LIBOR plus 212bp, but paid in D-marks. This structure is illustrated in Figure 18.3. With dollar

FIGURE 18.3
Liability Cost Reduction with Differential Swap

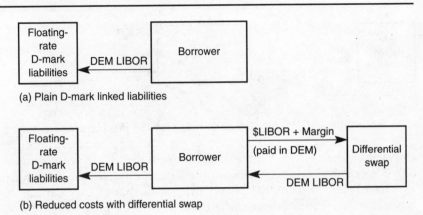

(a) Plain D-mark linked liabilities

(b) Reduced costs with differential swap

LIBOR initially at 3.88%, this would offer an initial saving of 250bp when compared with the D-mark LIBOR of 8.50%, and the company would continue to save, provided that the spread between the LIBOR rates remained above 212bp.

Going further, a borrower can actually issue debt that incorporates an embedded diff swap, giving investors direct access to the level of interest rates in another country. For example, a U.S. corporation could issue dollar-denominated debt paying a coupon of D-mark LIBOR less 220bp, but paid in dollars. If investors thought that D-mark interest rates would stay high, but the company thought that D-mark rates would decline, both sides would be happy with the deal.

Alternatively, the company could issue the debt and then enter into another diff swap with a bank at a finer margin, to achieve sub-LIBOR financing. This last idea is pictured in Figure 18.4, where the company receives under a second diff swap DEM LIBOR less 196bp, but denominated in dollars, against paying dollar LIBOR flat. This eliminates the company's exposure to D-mark interest rate levels and secures funding at dollar LIBOR less 24bp, a very attractive rate.

Although relatively simple in concept to understand, diff swaps are difficult for banks to hedge. While investors and borrowers are protected against currency risk—this feature is one of the key attractions of the diff swap over conventional currency swaps—it is the banks who must shoulder the resulting currency risk instead. The problem for banks trying to hedge diff swaps is that the size of the currency exposure depends on the way that interest rates move. Standard currency options are therefore of limited usefulness, and quanto options must be used. This in turn requires banks to estimate the correlation between the exchange rate and interest-rate differential, a notoriously difficult quantity to measure or model.

FIGURE 18.4
Debt Issue with Embedded Differential Swap

In addition to diff swaps, a range of other related products have emerged.
Diff caps and *diff floors*, also known as cross-currency caps and floors, offer
an upper or lower limit on the difference between the LIBORs of two currencies. For example, a diff cap may provide a payout if dollar LIBOR exceeds
D-mark LIBOR by more than 50bp. This is analogous to a regular cap that
becomes in-the-money when a single LIBOR exceeds a predetermined strike
rate. Here, the diff cap goes in-the-money when the expression ($ LIBOR-
DEM LIBOR) exceeds the strike margin of 50bp. Diff caps and diff floors
became necessary when leveraged diff instruments were created, because the
investor would otherwise run the risk of receiving a negative coupon under certain circumstances. These leveraged products are discussed in the next section.

An extension of the diff cap is the *spread rate cap*, which also limits the
differential between two LIBORs, but where the payout is denominated in a
third currency. An example would be a cap on the spread between D-mark
and French franc LIBORs, paid in dollars. *Spread rate floors* exist as well.

Currency-protected absolute rate caps and floors are like ordinary caps and
floors, except the payout is denominated in another currency. For example, a
U.S.-based investor receiving a dollar-denominated coupon of D-mark
LIBOR less 220bp might want to floor his net return at 3.50%, thus requiring a floor struck at a D-mark LIBOR of 5.70%. However, the payouts
under a regular D-mark floor would be denominated in D-marks, exposing
the investor to a currency risk. A suitable currency-protected floor struck at
a D-mark LIBOR of 5.70% would pay out in dollars, removing the currency
exposure problem.

18.4 DELAYED-RESET, REVERSE, CAPPED, COLLARED, AND LEVERAGED FLOATERS

A conventional floating-rate note pays a coupon reflecting the prevailing
short-term rates in the currency concerned. Compared to some of the structures explained in this section, such simplicity will seem positively tame.

Delayed-reset floaters. Conventional floating-rate notes fix LIBOR
at the start of each coupon accrual period and pay interest at the end. In a

delayed-reset floater, the interest in each period is set just one or two days prior to the payment itself. If investors believe that interest rates will rise throughout the life of the note, the delay in setting LIBOR each time will allow investors to capture the higher rates anticipated. This structure is also available as a variation on the normal interest rate swap, where it is known as a *delayed-reset swap* or a *LIBOR-in-arrears swap*. In a rising yield curve environment, such a swap will command a higher fixed rate than a conventional swap, because the floating leg is being valued using the delayed, and therefore higher, forward rates. An investor who believed that floating rates would rise more slowly than that implied by the forward yield curve might choose to buy a conventional FRN and pay the regular floating coupons into such a swap to receive a higher fixed rate than otherwise available.

Reverse floating-rate notes. In a conventional floating-rate note, the investor receives a coupon that rises and falls in step with the interest rate index, usually LIBOR. Investors who believe that LIBOR will fall have two broad alternatives. One is to invest in a fixed-rate security whose return will not fall if LIBOR goes down. Another possibility is to invest in a *reverse floating-rate note* whose coupon is designed to rise when LIBOR falls. A specific example would be a D-mark-denominated bond with a coupon equal to 15% less D-mark LIBOR. With D-mark LIBOR at 8.50%, the initial coupon would be a below-market 6.5% return, but this would rise as LIBOR fell, increasing to 9% if LIBOR dropped to 6%.

An issuer can engineer a reverse floater very easily using the structure pictured in Figure 18.5. Under the note, the borrower pays out 15% but effectively receives D-mark LIBOR. By entering into a standard interest rate swap, the borrower can pay LIBOR and receive 7.40%, switching the reverse floating liability into a fixed liability of 7.60%. If the borrower preferred floating-rate finance, he could enter into the swap for double the nominal principal instead, resulting in a net liability of LIBOR + 20bp.

Capped floaters. These are FRNs incorporating a cap that limits the floating coupon once LIBOR reaches a certain level. For example, with current LIBOR at 3.75%, such a note might pay LIBOR + 15bp, subject to a maximum coupon of 6%. Effectively, the investor has sold the issuer a cap,

FIGURE 18.5
Reverse Floating-Rate Notes

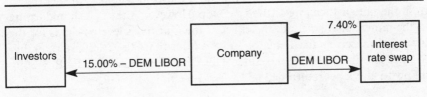

which has both a benefit and a cost. The benefit is the cap premium, which provides the investor with an above-market return. The cost is the opportunity cost of losing the possibility to benefit from ever-higher coupons should interest rates rise above the cap level. Investors who believe that interest rates will remain below the cap level will naturally prefer the enhanced return offered by the capped floater, because they believe that the additional benefit conferred will be earned without an offsetting cost.

Collared floaters. These are merely extensions of the capped floaters just outlined. In addition to establishing a ceiling for the floating payments, a collared floater also features a minimum coupon rate. For example, a collared floater might pay LIBOR subject to a floor at 4.75% and a ceiling at 6.50%. Such a product can be engineered by taking an FRN, selling a cap to create a capped floater, and then buying a floor to obtain the collared floater. With an upward-sloping yield curve, a collared floater can offer a much-enhanced return in comparison to current short-term rates, because both the floor and the cap are priced from the strip of steeply rising forward rates. Under this environment, caps will be relatively expensive, while floors will be relatively cheap. In the example cited here, the investor can effectively sell an out-of-the-money cap struck at 6.50%, use the premium received to buy an out-of-the-money floor struck at 4.75%, and find that the floor level is more than 100bp above prevailing short-term interest rates.

Leveraged capped floaters. These are more aggressive versions of the capped floaters previously discussed. Instead of incorporating a cap whose notional principal matches that of the note, a leveraged capped floater embeds a cap on a multiple of the note's principal. On the plus side, the additional premium earned provides the investor with a return even higher than that of the capped floater. On the minus side, instead of the coupon being capped at a certain level, the return will actually decline as LIBOR increases. For example, if the note included a cap on four times the principal struck at a LIBOR of 7%, the investor might receive an enhanced premium of LIBOR + 30bp. This is double the premium over LIBOR compared with the unleveraged capped floater in the previous example, and that was struck at a lower rate. However, if LIBOR rises through the cap level of 7%, the leveraged nature of this product will cause the investor to start losing income quite rapidly.

To make the structure easier to visualise, Figure 18.6 shows the individual cash flows arising from each component of the instrument. The note pays LIBOR, while the total premium from the leveraged out-of-the-money cap is 30bp per year. In any period when the cap is out-of-the-money, the net return from the note is therefore LIBOR + 30bp. However, if the cap should expire in-the-money in any period, the effect of the four times levered cap is for the investor to receive a fixed coupon of 28% (four times the 7% strike rate), but to pay four times LIBOR in return. This combines with the LIBOR + 30bp inflow to give a net return of 28.30% less three times LIBOR.

FIGURE 18.6
Leveraged Capped Floater

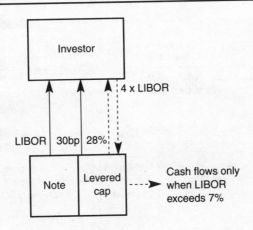

We can summarise this by saying that the note pays a coupon equal to min (28.30 – 3 × LIBOR, LIBOR + 0.30). This peaks at 7.30% when LIBOR is at 7%, dropping thereafter to 4.30% if LIBOR is at 8%, and the coupon falls further to only 1.30% if LIBOR rises to 9%. In theory, the coupon could be negative if LIBOR rose above 9.43%, but in practice such notes would normally embed a levered collar rather than a levered cap to avoid this happening. As with any geared instrument, the investor would need to balance the relatively small yield enhancement if rates stayed low with the possibility of earning a low or even zero return if rates rose too high.

Leveraged diff floater. Figure 18.4 showed how a borrower could issue dollar-denominated debt containing an embedded diff swap and then use another diff swap to eliminate the D-mark linked cash flows and obtain sub-LIBOR funding. Combining this idea with the concept of a leveraged floater gives a leveraged diff floater, which offers the investor a return equal to a multiple of the spread between two interest rates plus or minus some margin.

In the example pictured in Figure 18.7, the investor would receive twice the difference between D-mark and dollar LIBORs, plus an additional 84bp, but paid in dollars. If D-mark LIBOR was at 8.50% and dollar LIBOR at 3.88%, the investor would receive a coupon of 10.08% in dollars, an impressive 620bp above the normal dollar rate. Of course, if D-mark rates fell to more than 42bp below dollar rates, the investor's coupon would, in theory, become negative. To prevent this, the leveraged diff floater would normally incorporate a leveraged diff floor that becomes in-the-money if the differential between D-mark and dollar rates falls to below -42bp.

Figure 18.7 illustrates how such a leveraged diff floater could be engineered. The company hedges the leveraged diff component of its liability to

FIGURE 18.7
Leveraged Differential Floater

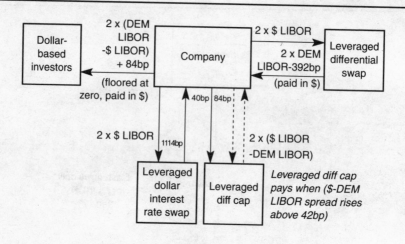

investors by entering into another leveraged diff swap on twice the notional principal. The company's net exposure is now simply a constant outpayment of 4.76% (the 392bp margin on the diff swap plus the extra 84bp paid to the investors). The premium on the leveraged diff floor[1] might be 40bp, bringing the total obligation to 5.16%.

If the company wanted to achieve a fixed rate, this is already attractive, being about 40bp below the prevailing swap rate for the dollar. Alternatively, this liability could be swapped into floating using a single interest rate swap at 5.57% to achieve sub-LIBOR financing of LIBOR–41bp or using a levered swap on double the principal to obtain a liability of twice LIBOR–598bp. It is this last possibility that is shown in the diagram. With dollar LIBOR initially at 3.88%, the company can borrow at just 1.78%, 210bp below LIBOR rate.

The leveraged diff floater therefore benefits investor and borrower alike. The investor can obtain an initial return of 10.08%, while the company can borrow at 1.78%. Both are extremely favourable rates when compared with dollar LIBOR of 3.88%. The 830bp benefit shared by the two parties comes from the various swap counterparties. The leveraged diff swap initially pays 532bp (2 × 8.50 – 3.92 – 2 × 3.88), while the leveraged interest rate swap pays 338bp net (11.14 – 2 × 3.88), a total of 870bp. The missing 40bp is the option premium.

Both sides are vulnerable to an increase in dollar interest rates, while the investor is also exposed to a reduction in D-mark rates. This structure would

---

[1] Note that the diff floor is actually represented as a diff cap in the diagram. This is because a diff floor limited (DEM–$) rates from falling below –42bp is equivalent to a diff cap limiting ($–DEM) rates from rising above 42bp, and it is easier to conceptualise caps or floors with positive strike rates.

therefore be favourable only to those parties who thought that the margin between these currencies would stay high.

Reverse diff floater. This time, combining the concept of a reverse FRN with a diff floater gives the *reverse diff floater*, a security paying a fixed rate less some floating-rate margin, but denominated in another currency. The illustration in Figure 18.8 shows an investment paying 12.80% less D-mark LIBOR, but paid in dollars. Even with D-mark LIBOR starting at 8.50%, this pays an above-market coupon of 4.30% to investors, which compares favourably with the 3.88% return available from the dollar. If D-mark rates fall, the coupon will rise accordingly. Such an investment would be beneficial to a dollar-based investor who thought that D-mark rates will fall faster than dollar rates.

The reverse diff floater can be engineered and hedged by using the combination of a diff swap and a regular interest rate swap, as pictured in Figure 18.8. The cash flows from the swaps combine and net with the obligation to the investors to give a fixed-rate dollar liability of 5.27%. As with the reverse floater already discussed, the company could double up the nominal principal on the ordinary interest rate swap to achieve sub-LIBOR floating-rate financing at dollar LIBOR – 30bp.

18.5 DUAL CURRENCY AND CROSS-CURRENCY STRUCTURES

While some investors shun currency risk, others may wish to take advantage of possible exchange rate movements or to speculate on a particular view.

FIGURE 18.8
Reverse Diff Floater

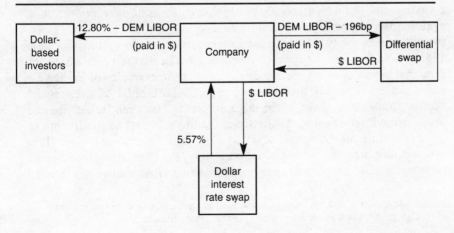

While this could be achieved by taking an explicit position using conventional foreign exchange instruments, there may be institutional restrictions or procedures preventing this. An alternative is to use an instrument that embodies the desired currency exposure.

Dual currency notes. An investor with a neutral to bullish view on a particular currency, but unwilling to risk principal if this view proved false, can buy a *dual currency note*. These instruments repay principal in the investor's domestic currency, but pay coupons in a foreign currency. For example, a yen-denominated bond could pay an above-market coupon in Italian lire. This structure is simpler than a quanto structure, because both the index and the payments are in the same foreign currency. The investor enjoys a higher coupon, Italian lire rates being higher than yen rates, but does not have the currency protection afforded by a diff swap or currency protected structure.

Cross-currency convertible. This offers the investor the option to convert from a bond denominated in one currency to one denominated in another. For example, a French borrower may issue a FFR 500million 9.45% seven-year note convertible in two years into a $100 million 8.25% note with the same final maturity date. If the dollar had strengthened since the issue date or the spread between French franc and dollar yields had widened, conversion would be advantageous. Such an issue would certainly be attractive to an investor who shared this view, offering the opportunity to benefit if the dollar strengthened or yields widened as expected but offering protection by allowing him to remain in French francs if the market were to move otherwise. In this example, the issuer may elect to buy a cross-currency swaption to hedge the conversion risk.

Currency-indexed medium-term note. A number of instruments have been structured in which the principal on maturity was linked to a currency exchange rate, but with an embedded option component offering protection against adverse currency swings, unlike a dual currency note. An early example of this was the ICON (Indexed Currency Option Note), introduced in 1985. More recently, medium-term notes have been offered in which the principal is linked to two exchange rates, as in the example[2] of a one-year note structured to match the views of one particular U.S.-based investor who wanted to take advantage of the large differential between Italian lire and Swiss franc interest rates. At the time, the lire was part of the European Exchange Rate Mechanism (ERM), and the investor did not believe there was much chance of a lire devaluation against the D-mark. Moreover, the investor thought that inflationary problems in Switzerland would weaken

---

[2]See Banu Qureshi, and Jim Durrant, "A Structured Deal", in *A Guide to International MTNs*, supplement to *Corporate Finance*, September 1992, pp. 23–26.

the Swiss franc against the D-mark. The proposed structure was denominated entirely in U.S. dollars with an 8.27% coupon, 125bp above prevailing rates, and a redemption price given by the following formula:

$$100\% \times \left[0.95 + \max\left(1.05 \times \frac{ITL/\$_{spot}}{ITL/\$_{mat}} - \frac{SFR/\$_{spot}}{SFR/\$_{mat}}, 0\right)\right]$$

If exchange rates remained absolutely stable, the MTN would be redeemed at par. If either the lire strengthened or the Swiss franc weakened, the redemption value would increase accordingly. For example, with a 5% appreciation of the lire against the franc, the note would provide an annual return of 13.52%, while the existence of the currency option established a floor at a return of 3.27%. This was just as well, following the abrupt departure of the lire from the ERM in September 1992.

18.6 FINALÉ

In this chapter, we have only been able to provide a few examples of how financial engineering techniques can be applied to better meet the needs of investors and borrowers. Just like Lego® bricks, basic components like swaps and options can be assembled in many different ways to create novel and elegant financial structures. Almost anything is possible nowadays: if a company needs to swap the floating oil price against the FTSE 100 index, it can be, and probably has been, done.

The progress achieved since 1980, both in terms of product innovation and market size, has been phenomenal. In those days, neither FRAs nor swaps had been invented, while trading in option-based products was negligible. Now the market appears to know no bounds, and new products and structures are announced regularly. All that is required is imagination to conceive a new product and at least one counterparty with a need to fulfil. Although few things in this world are without cost, fierce competition between financial institutions has ensured that spreads are kept to a minimum, and the price that a user must pay to restructure exposures and to manage risk is generally a very fair one.

Newcomers to derivatives are sometimes rather wary of the possible dangers they think these instruments might involve. On the contrary, properly understood and used in the correct way, they offer a marvelously effective way to minimise financial risk. In this book, we have attempted to present a compendium of the products available and a handbook of methods for their successful use. We hope that it provides insight, ideas, and inspiration in helping the reader gain a clearer understanding of financial engineering tools and techniques.

Index